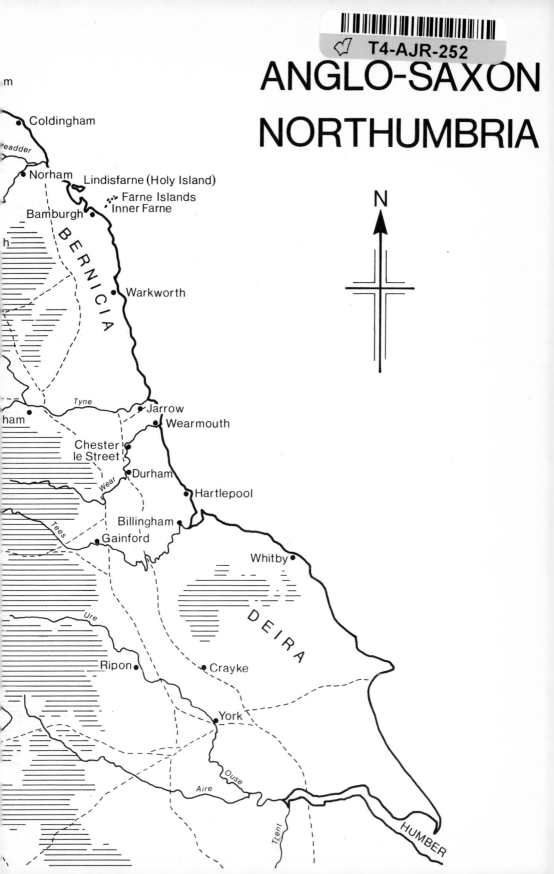

ANGLO-SAXON
NORTHUMBRIA

N

m

Coldingham

Leadder

Norham Lindisfarne (Holy Island)
          Farne Islands
          Inner Farne

Bamburgh

B E R N I C I A

h

Warkworth

Tyne

ham

Jarrow

Wearmouth

Chester
le Street

Wear

Durham

Hartlepool

Billingham

Gainford

Tees

Whitby

D E I R A

Ure

Ripon   Crayke

York

Ouse

Aire

Trent

HUMBER

ST CUTHBERT,
HIS CULT AND HIS COMMUNITY
TO AD 1200

Frontispiece. The Lindisfarne Gospels lying upon St Cuthbert's tomb, 3 September 1987.

ST CUTHBERT,
HIS CULT AND HIS COMMUNITY
TO AD 1200

edited by
Gerald Bonner
David Rollason
Clare Stancliffe

THE BOYDELL PRESS

© Contributors 1989

First published 1989 by The Boydell Press
an imprint of Boydell & Brewer Ltd
PO Box 9, Woodbridge, Suffolk IP12 3DF
and of Boydell & Brewer Inc.
Wolfeboro, New Hampshire 03894-2069, USA

ISBN 0 85115 510 3

British Library Cataloguing in Publication Data
St. Cuthbert, his cult and his community to AD 1200.
1. Christian church. Cuthbert of Saint, Bishop of
Lindisfarne, ca 635 – 687
I. Bonner, Gerald, II. Rollason, D.W. (David W.) III.
Stancliffe, Clare
270.2′092′4
ISBN 0-85115-510-3

Library of Congress Cataloging-in-Publication Data
St. Cuthbert, his cult and his community to AD 1200 /
edited by Gerald Bonner, David Rollason, Clare
Stancliffe.
        p. cm.
    Includes index.
    ISBN 0-85115-510-3 (alk. paper)
    1. Cuthbert, Saint, Bishop of Lindisfarne, ca. 635-
687 — Congresses. 2. Chester-le-Street (England) —
Church history — Congresses. 3. Durham (England)
— Church history — Congresses. 4. Lindisfarne
Gospels — Congresses. I. Bonner, Gerald. II.
Rollason, D. W. (David W.) III. Stancliffe, Clare.
BX4700.C8S7 1989
274.28′6 — dc 19   88-16805
                                               CIP

⊙ The paper used in this publication meets the minimum
requirements of American National Standard for Information
Sciences — Permanence of Paper for Printed Library Materials,
ANSI Z39.48-1884.

Printed in Great Britain by The Camelot Press PLC, Southampton

TO THE MEMORY OF THREE GREAT SCHOLARS

WILHELM LEVISON
(1876 – 1947)
Professor of History in the University of Bonn
Honorary Fellow of the University of Durham

BERTRAM COLGRAVE
(1888 – 1968)
Reader in English in the University of Durham

JULIAN BROWN
(1923 – 1987)
Professor of Palaeography at King's College, London

Acknowledgements

We are grateful to the following for permission to reproduce illustrations in this volume: to the British Library for plates 11, 13, 14, 15, 22, 32, 37, and 42; to the Dean and Chapter of Durham for plates 10, 12, 19, 20, 23, 31, 34, 35, 36, 38, 44, 49, 50, 51, 52, 54, 55, and 57 and figures 19 and 21; to Harvey Miller Publishers for plate 21 (Alexander, illustration 84); to the Trustees of the British Museum for plate 53; to the University of East Anglia for plates 58, 59, and 60; to the Bibliothèque Municipale, Besançon for plate 5; to the Bibliothèque Nationale, Paris, for plates 9, 16, 18, 24, and 26a and c; to Trinity College, Dublin, for plates 17 and 26b; and to the Biblioteca Apostolica Vaticana for plates 6 and 7.

Figure 22 was drawn by Yvonne Beadnell.

The publisher and editors of this book are grateful to the Twenty-Seven Foundation for a grant towards the cost of the plates.

Contents

Preface

This book is based on papers read to a conference held in Durham on 14 – 18 July 1987 to mark the 1300th anniversary of the death of St Cuthbert. The conference excited very considerable interest, not only in the Durham area but also much further afield. Over 250 people attended the main sessions and an even larger number heard the evening lectures associated with the conference. Scholars came from all over Britain and, indeed, the world; but so too did large numbers of local people and others with a more general interest in the subject. It was altogether a heartening demonstration of the strength of interest which can still be aroused by a figure from the remote past.

The conference itself and this publication owed much to the support and assistance of the University of Durham History Department and St John's College, where the conference was held. We should like to extend our thanks to these as well as to Messrs Boydell and Brewer, who were willing to take on the publication of this volume at an early stage. Above all we should like to thank the contributors for their efforts at the conference and after it, and for their patience with the editors. It need hardly be said that without them there would have been neither conference nor volume. We have attempted to standardize spellings and the system of references, but we should like to emphasize that no attempt has been made to reconcile the views expressed here. Readers will find different opinions and approaches, and it is hoped that this will prove one of the volume's attractions.

One of the greatest scholars associated with these studies is not represented here. Professor Julian Brown was to have given a paper at the conference, but his untimely death earlier in the year left both it and the world of scholarship much the poorer. He was nevertheless very much in the minds of those who were here in Durham, and the formative character of his scholarship is apparent in the palaeographical papers in this volume.

Gerald Bonner
D. W. Rollason
Clare Stancliffe
Durham, February 1988

List of Plates

List of Figures

Abbreviations

Alexander   J. J. G. Alexander, *Insular Manuscripts, 6th to the 9th Century* (A Survey of Manscripts illuminated in the British Isles, vol. I; London, 1978)

ASC   *Anglo-Saxon Chronicle*, cited *sub anno* and, where necessary, by the conventional manuscript sigla, A-G; ed. J. Earle and C. Plummer, *Two of the Saxon Chronicles Parallel* (2 vols.; Oxford, 1892-9); trans. D. Whitelock *et al.*, *The Anglo-Saxon Chronicle* (London, 1961), and in *EHD*, pp. 145 – 61

ASE   *Anglo-Saxon England* (Cambridge, 1972 –)

BCS   W. de Gray Birch, *Cartularium Saxonicum: A Collection of Charters Relating to Anglo-Saxon History* (3 vols. and index; London, 1885 – 99), cited by charter number

BL   British Library, London

BM   British Museum, London

CCSL   Corpus christianorum, series latina (Turnhout, 1953 –)

CHE   *The Church Historians of England*, vol. III, part ii, *containing the Historical Works of Symeon of Durham*, trans. J. Stevenson (London, 1855)

CLA   E. A. Lowe, *Codices Latini Antiquiores: A Palaeographical Guide to Latin Manuscripts Prior to the Ninth Century* (11 vols. and supplement; Oxford, 1934 – 71)

Cod. Lind.   *Evangeliorum quattuor Codex Lindisfarnensis, Musei Britannici Codex Cottonianus Nero D. IV*, ed. T. D. Kendrick *et al.* (2 vols.; Oltun and Lausanne, 1956 – 60).

Corpus   *Corpus of Anglo-Saxon Stone Sculpture in England* (British Academy; Oxford, in progress 1984 –): vol. I, R. Cramp, *County Durham and Northumberland* (in 2 parts; Oxford, 1984); vol. II, R. N. Bailey and R. Cramp, *Cumberland and Westmorland and Lancashire North of the Sands* (Oxford, 1988).

CSEL   Corpus scriptorum ecclesiasticorum latinorum (Vienna, 1866 –)

DCM   R. A. B. Mynors, *Durham Cathedral Manuscripts to the End of the Twelfth Century* (Oxford, 1939).

De miraculis   *Capitula de miraculis et translationibus sancti Cuthberti, Chapters concerning the Miracles and Translations of St Cuthbert*, cited by chapter; ed. *Sym. Op.* I, 229 – 61. Page references, where necessary, are to this edition.

EEMF	Early English Manuscripts in Facsimile
EHD	*English Historical Documents c.500 – 1042*, ed. D. Whitelock (2nd edn.; London, 1979)
EHR	*English Historical Review*
HDE	*Historia Dunelmensis ecclesiae, the History of the Church of Durham* attributed to Symeon of Durham, cited by book and chapter; ed. *Sym. Op.* I, 3 – 169; trans. *CHE*, pp. 621 – 711. Page references, where necessary, are to *Sym. Op.* I.
HE	*Baedae Historia ecclesiastica gentis Anglorum*, Bede's *Ecclesiastical History of the English People*, cited by book and chapter; ed. and trans. *HE* (C and M); ed. *HE* (Plummer)
HE (C and M)	*Bede's Ecclesiastical History of the English People*, ed. and trans. B. Colgrave and R. A. B. Mynors (Oxford Medieval Texts; Oxford, 1969)
HE (Plummer)	*Venerabilis Baedae Opera historica*, ed. C. Plummer (2 vols.; Oxford, 1896)
HR	*Historia regum, the History of the Kings*, cited *sub anno* or by chapter; ed. *Sym. Op.* II, 3 – 283; trans. *CHE*, pp. 425 – 617. Page references, where necessary, are to *Sym. Op.* II
HSC	*Historia de sancto Cuthberto, the History of St Cuthbert*, cited by section; ed. *Sym. Op.* I, 196 – 214. Page references, where necessary, are to this edition
JEH	*Journal of Ecclesiastical History*
JTS	*Journal of Theological Studies*
Libellus	Reginald of Durham's *'Little Book' about the Wonderful Miracles of Blessed Cuthbert which were Performed in Recent Times*, cited by chapter; ed. J. Raine, *Reginaldi monachi Dunelmensis Libellus de admirandis beati Cuthberti virtutibus quae novellis patratae sunt temporibus* (SS 1; Durham, 1835). Page references, where necessary, are to this edition
MGH	Monumenta Germaniae Historica
PL	Patrologiae cursus completus, series latina, ed. J.-P. Migne (221 vols.; Paris, 1844 – 64)
Plummer	See *HE* (Plummer)
RS	Rolls Series (Rerum Britannicarum Medii Aevi Scriptores or Chronicles and Memorials of Great Britain and Ireland during the Middle Ages)
Relics	*The Relics of Saint Cuthbert*, ed. C. F. Battiscombe (Oxford, 1956)
SC	Sources chrétiennes
SS	Surtees Society (Durham)
St Cuthbert	J. Raine, *St Cuthbert, with an Account of the State in which his Remains were found upon the Opening of his Tomb in Durham Cathedral, in the year 1827* (Durham, 1828)

Sym. Op.	*Symeonis monachi Opera omnia*, ed. T. Arnold, RS (2 vols.; London, 1882 – 5)
Two Lives	*Two Lives of Saint Cuthbert*, ed. and trans. B. Colgrave (Cambridge, 1940; reprinted 1985)
VCA	*Vita sancti Cuthberti auctore anonymo*, the anonymous *Life of St Cuthbert*, cited by chapter; ed. and trans. *Two Lives*, pp. 59 – 139 and notes, pp. 310 – 40
VCM	Bede's metrical *Life of St Cuthbert*, cited by chapter; ed. W. Jaager, *Bedas metrische Vita sancti Cuthberti* (Palaestra 198; Leipzig, 1935)
VCP	*Vita sancti Cuthberti auctore Beda*, Bede's prose *Life of St Cuthbert*, cited by book and chapter; ed. and trans. *Two Lives*, pp. 141 – 307 and notes, pp. 341 – 59
VW	*Vita sancti Wilfrithi Deo digni episcopi*, the *Life of St Wilfrid* by Stephanus, cited by chapter; ed. and trans. B. Colgrave, *The Life of Bishop Wilfrid by Eddius Stephanus* (Cambridge, 1927; reprinted 1985)

Introduction

Cuthbert is one of the best-known figures of early Northumbria. His life, c.635 – 87, spans the transitional period from paganism to Christianity in the north-east, and still catches people's imagination and their interest: the paradox of the young man who rode armed to the monastery of Melrose, having resolved to leave all to become a monk; of the Anglo-Saxon who was schooled in the traditions of Irish Christianity, but rose to prominence within the church after the prohibition of certain Irish traditions, when influences from Rome and Gaul were making themselves felt; and, the greatest paradox of all, that of the out-going pastor who was also irresistibly drawn to the solitary life. For it was one and the same Cuthbert who took such trouble over the needs of others while prior of Melrose and then Lindisfarne, and, ultimately, as bishop; but who in the mean time withdrew for many years to live as a hermit on the remote island of Farne. Indeed, although Cuthbert was appointed bishop of Lindisfarne in 685, he retired to his island hermitage for the last few months of his life, dying there on 20 March 687.

He was buried in the monastic church on Lindisfarne but his tomb was opened in 698 and his body, which was found to be undecayed, was translated to a coffin placed above the floor of the church — a procedure which at that period constituted effective canonization. A further translation may have taken place from Lindisfarne to Norham on the River Tweed in the early ninth century; and Cuthbert's body was certainly taken by the Lindisfarne community when it began a period of wandering around northern England, probably in 875. For over a century (883 – 995) that community settled in Chester-le-Street before making its final move to Durham in 995. Cuthbert's body and his cult seem to have remained the focus of the community at Durham as in its earlier homes. In 1083 the Norman bishop William of St Carilef replaced the Anglo-Saxon community of St Cuthbert with Benedictine monks from Monkwearmouth and Jarrow, but veneration for the saint did not slacken. In 1104 his body was examined to confirm that it was still incorrupt and then translated into a shrine in the new Norman cathedral which stands in Durham to this day. Cuthbert remained one of the most important English saints throughout the middle ages. Even at the Reformation his body still seems to have been to some extent undecayed and this may explain why the pectoral cross, portable altar, stole and braids, and the precious fabrics in which the body was wrapped were not carried off by Henry VIII's commissioners, but were all reburied in the remains of the original wooden coffin — to be found in the nineteenth century and preserved in Durham to this day.

Perhaps surprisingly for a figure of such importance, no full study has been devoted to Cuthbert since the publication in 1956 of *The Relics of Saint Cuthbert*, edited by C. F. Battiscombe. The present volume aims to bring up to date the scholarship presented then, but also to widen the field of debate and to offer a wide-ranging interdisciplinary approach to a complex subject. It uses, for example, new insights gained from the considerable advances made since 1956 in the study of saints' lives and cults in the middle ages. The book is in four parts. In the first, contributors address the problems of Cuthbert's career itself, the genesis of the early lives of the saint, and the beginnings of his cult. Much here is new and controversial: the extent to which Cuthbert's career is to be seen against an Irish background and how this was handled by his early hagiographers; the functions of miracle stories in the early lives and their capacity, in Bede's hands at least, to transmit spiritual images of great sophistication; the reasons why such a relatively large number of early lives was written and above all why Bede chose to write a prose life when a very similar life had already been written at Lindisfarne; and the problems of the development and significance of Bede's hitherto rather neglected metrical life of the saint. It is sobering to see how much progress these papers make in understanding a supposedly well-known figure. Even the accepted chronology of his life has been shown to require revision.

The immediate background for the later, perhaps most important, years of Cuthbert's life was the great island monastery of Lindisfarne, and Part Two seeks to explore the cultural environment it offered in the seventh to eighth centuries, particularly through a study of manuscripts and archaeology. The papers in this part reflect a vigorous debate on the extent of the Lindisfarne scriptorium's production and influence. Here too there is much that is illuminating — even in the explorations of a manuscript as well known as the Lindisfarne Gospels. The final paper examines the question of how far artistic traditions accompanied St Cuthbert's community after its departure from Lindisfarne in 875.

In 1827, and again in 1899, the tomb of St Cuthbert in Durham Cathedral was opened and a series of treasures recovered from it. The sectarian background to the 1827 opening in particular is interpreted in the first paper of Part Three, that of Richard Bailey, as an aspect of the then continuing controversy surrounding Catholic emancipation. Bailey's paper shows how less-than-scholarly motives lay behind the 1827 opening and how fragments of the treasures were subsequently dispersed, and he provides for the first time a handlist to such scattered fragments as have been identified. The remaining papers in this part are devoted to aspects of these treasures themselves. They show how much progress has been made since 1956 in understanding the metalwork, the development of iconography, and the decoration and construction of the seventh-century coffin; and also in understanding the textiles, especially the silks which stand out in these papers as a collection of the first importance.

The final part is devoted to St Cuthbert's community at Chester-le-Street and Durham. Its history at the former is relatively little understood, yet it may be of considerable significance. The papers here bring to bear the evidence of manuscripts, archaeology, sculpture, and topography to throw new light on the character both of Chester-le-Street itself and the community there. Close studies of texts have permitted a re-assessment of the relationship between the community and the West Saxon kings, and of the development of the right of sanctuary at Cuthbert's body, symbolized even now by the great Sanctuary Knocker at Durham Cathedral. Finally two studies take the history of Cuthbert's cult into the twelfth century, discussing and re-assessing the work of two neglected Durham historians of that age, Symeon and Reginald.

The papers here are a remarkable testimony to the manifold interest of the life, cult, and community of St Cuthbert. They owe much to the vigour and range of modern scholarship; but the richness of their subject matter also bears witness to the sheer creative force of the image of a person who died over 1300 years ago. Why that person should have assumed such importance and why he retained it for so many centuries after his death is perhaps the central question which this volume seeks to address.

PART ONE

St Cuthbert,
the Lives and the Early Cult

Elements in the Background to the Life of St Cuthbert and his Early Cult

J. CAMPBELL

21 May, 685, was a memorable day in Cuthbert's life. He spent it with Queen Iurminburh, her husband, Ecgfrith, king of the Northumbrians, being at that time on campaign against the Picts. Their party was being shown round the sights of Carlisle by its *prefectus* when, suddenly, the saint stood still. First he leaned on his staff and looked at the ground. Then he lifted his eyes heavenwards, sighed; and spoke. 'Oh! Oh! Oh!, I think that the war is over and that judgement has been given against our people in battle.' So indeed it proved, for on that very day Ecgfrith was defeated and killed at Nechtansmere, and most of his army died with him.[1] Cuthbert was a prophet in more senses than one. He had, Bede says, warned the king not to go on that expedition.[2] His advice proved sound. Bede makes it clear that the defeat at Nechtansmere marked a turning point in the history of Northumbrian rule in the north. Until then Northumbrian kings had enjoyed some kind of authority over most or all of north Britain. From then on the great days of Northumbrian power were done (even though Ecgfrith's successor Aldfrith seems to have stabilized the position in southern Scotland and later kings sometimes won victories further north).[3] Similarly in the south: after Ecgfrith's defeat by the Mercians in 679 no Northumbrian king had authority anywhere south of the Humber.

Thus Cuthbert's lifetime coincided with the apogee of Northumbrian power. He was born not far from the end of the reign of Edwin, who, Bede says, had *imperium* over the whole island of Britain, Kent apart; as did Oswald (634 – 42) and Oswiu (642 – 70), though neither can have enjoyed such power for more than part of his reign.[4] The power of Ecgfrith may not have equalled that of his father Oswiu, but it exceeded that of all his successors. The

---

[1] *VCA* IV, 8, *Two Lives*, pp. 123 – 4; cf. pp. 243 – 4 (*VCP* 27).
[2] *HE* IV, 24 (26) (Plummer I, p. 266).
[3] F. M. Stenton, *Anglo-Saxon England* (3rd edn., Oxford, 1971), pp. 88 – 92.
[4] *HE* II, 5 (Plummer I, p. 89).

3

anonymous biographer reveals, as Bede does not, that the young Cuthbert had been directly involved in at least one Northumbrian campaign; probably one of Oswiu's.[5]

The rise of these kings' power brought two things which much affected the church in Cuthbert's Northumbria: involvement with Ireland, and wealth. The seventh-century Irish-Northumbrian nexus was even more complex than Bede tells us. For example, we now know that there had been important English exiles in Ireland even before the reign of Aethelfrith.[6] Or again, it has been shown that Oswiu's Irish wife or mistress was the daughter of the northern Uí Néill king Colmán Rímid, so that there is a serious possibility that she was the sister or half-sister of Finan, bishop of Northumbria; a circumstance that could have much to do with the events of 664.[7] Bede's words on the consequences of the battle of Nechtansmere strongly suggest the reality of Northumbrian authority in the north before 685: 'Nam et Picti terram possessionis suae, quam tenuerunt Angli; et Scotti, qui erant in Brittania, Brettonum quoque pars nonnulla libertatem receperunt'.[8] For most of Cuthbert's lifetime Northumbria may well in an important sense have extended to the Western Isles. There were elements in Northumbrian monasticism which may make most sense if we think of Northumbria not so much as simply 'influenced' by Ireland but rather as being part of a continuum with it, in which an important element was the exercise of Northumbrian authority over Irish Scotland.[9]

Northumbrian kings plundered in the north and levied tribute there. Bede says of Aethelfrith that those people whom he did not exterminate he made tributary.[10] When he describes Iona as *quasi familiarum quinque*, this may not be simply a topographical observation but rather an extract from a Northumbrian tribute-list.[11] One may be tempted to think of early Scotland as likely to have been rather barren in pickings for dark age predators. The reverse could have been the case. The Picts may have retained the benefits of many generations of successful parasitism upon Roman Britain. When such a king as Ecgfrith ravaged their lands (*depopulans . . . vastabat; atroci et feroci sevicia devastaret*[12]) these may have been well worth the ravaging. Suggestive of this

---

[5] *VCA* I, 7: 'in castris contra hostem in exercitu sedens'.
[6] H. Moisl, 'The Bernician Royal Dynasty and the Irish in the Seventh Century', *Peritia* 2 (1983), pp. 103 – 26.
[7] F. J. Byrne, *Irish Kings and High-Kings* (London, 1973), pp. 104, 111.
[8] *HE* IV, 24 (26) (Plummer I, p. 267).
[9] J. Campbell, 'The Debt of the Early English Church to Ireland', in *Irland und die Christenheit. Bibelstudien und Mission*, ed. P. Ní Chatháin and M. Richter (Stuttgart, 1987), pp. 336 – 7.
[10] *HE* I, 34 (Plummer I, p. 71).
[11] C. Hart, 'The Tribal Hidage', *Transactions of the Royal Historical Society* 21 (1971), pp. 336 – 7. The *quasi* somewhat weakens this suggestion.
[12] *VCA* IV, 8; *VCP* 27.

possibility are the silver chains found in Scotland.[13] Successful war brought
not only tribute, but also slaves, who could be sold abroad.[14] When Bede
sought an image for souls being led to the mouth of hell, what he found was
that of slaves being led off into captivity to the jeers of a crowd.[15]

Such scenes have lain behind the development of the Northumbrian church;
for there was much about it that was extremely expensive. Substantial areas of
land were given to churches and to bishops. Perhaps even more important, so
too were substantial amounts of bullion. In a brilliant book Professor Dodwell
has brought out the importance of the golden element in the life of the Anglo-
Saxons and of their churches.[16] He shows how numerous their golden
treasures were, how important gold was to them as more than just a store of
value. Here, as often, Bede is the odd man out. He tells us something about
treasures; but he is not enthused by them and his imagery is not shot through
with gold as Aldhelm's is. A stronger impression of the treasures of
Northumbria is given by Alcuin in his poem on the bishops and churches of
York. Oswald, he says, arrayed altars with silver, gold and jewels, and hung
the hallowed walls with silks.[17] Wilfrid II (718 – 32) covered the altar and
crosses with gilded silver.[18] Ecgberht (732 – 66) decorated the church of York
with silver, gold and gems and hung up silk hangings with exotic figures.[19]
Archbishop Aelberht (*c.* 767 – 80) raised a great altar covered with gold, silver
and jewels with an altar cross weighing many pounds of silver and erected
another altar covered with pure metals and precious stones,[20] and so on. In all
descriptions of Northumbrian churches by others than Bede, stress is laid on
gold and silver, jewels and silk: this is true of Ripon, Hexham and the cell of
Lindisfarne described by Aethelwulf, as of the churches of York. They are a
reminder that behind the achievements of the Northumbrian church lay great
wealth; and that the 'Northumbrian renaissance', like the 'Carolingian
renaissance', may have depended largely on the fruits of conquest.

---

[13] R. B. K. Stevenson, 'Pictish Art', in *The Problem of the Picts*, ed. F. T. Wainwright (Edinburgh, 1955), p.111: 'massive silver chains' over eighteen inches long. The ninth-century St Ninian's Island treasure also reveals something of the wealth of the north: A. Small, *et al.*, *St Ninian's Isle and its Treasure* (2 vols., Oxford, 1973). For the 'relatively rare' (but then, as site finds they would be) objects of quality from the Pictish area, L. Alcock, 'A Survey of Pictish Archaeology', in *Pictish Studies. Settlement, Burial and Art in Dark Age Northern Britain*, ed. J. G. P. Friell and W. G. Watson (Oxford, 1984), p. 27. If the *Gododdin* is accepted as evidence for the wealth of the north *c.*600 then its numerous references to gold are significant: K. H. Jackson, *The Gododdin* (Edinburgh, 1969), pp. 115, 117, 122, 123, 125, 130, 133, 142.

[14] D. Pelteret, 'Slave Raiding and Slave Trading in early England', *ASE* 9 (1981), pp. 99 – 114, esp. pp. 99 – 103.

[15] *HE* V, 12 (Plummer I, p. 306).

[16] C. R. Dodwell, *Anglo-Saxon Art, a New Perspective* (Manchester, 1982).

[17] Alcuin, *The Bishops, Kings, and Saints of York*, ed. P. Godman (Oxford, 1982), lines 275 – 83.

[18] Ibid., lines 1222 – 7.

[19] Ibid., lines 1266 – 88.

[20] Ibid., lines 1488 – 1507. Alcuin's poem provides the only evidence for these gifts and for the very existence at York of the great church of the Holy Wisdom; see Godman's comments, p. lx.

It is true that in the eighth century Northumbrian kings ceased to conquer; but here it is worth noticing that if they did not conquer, neither were they conquered and made tributary by other kings. One might have expected the great kings of eighth-century Mercia to have profited by the apparent weakness of Northumbria, but there is little sign of this. The *Anglo-Saxon Chronicle* says that Aethelbald of Mercia ravaged Northumbria in 737.[21] The annals in continuation of Bede state, *s.a.* 740, that Aethelbald attacked Northumbria while Eadberht was away fighting the Picts.[22] Even if the *Chronicle* has the date right, so that there were two invasions rather than one, this is the last Mercian invasion of Northumbria recorded in the eighth century. We hear no more of warfare between these kingdoms until 801 when, according to the *Historia regum* annals, Eardwulf led an army against Cenwulf of Mercia. Cenwulf had the aid of *aliarum . . . auxilia provinciarum plurima* but nevertheless the war lasted long. Ultimately peace was made between these kings by the bishops and *principes* of the English.[23] It is hard to know what to make of such cryptic telegrams from the past, not least when they have been edited in the tenth century. But it certainly does not sound as if Cenwulf had the walkover which some modern estimates of Northumbrian and of Mercian power might have led one to expect.

Although the overlordship of seventh-century Northumbrian kings extended south of the Humber, that of eighth-century Mercian kings did not extend north of the Humber. The independence of Northumbrian kings was connected with that of the Northumbrian church, which derived from the re-establishment of the archbishopric of York in 735. Theodore's quickness in riding to the north soon after his arrival in England in 669 indicates how anxious an archbishop of Canterbury could be to exert authority in Northumbria.[24] The exclusion of such authority after 735 paralleled the exclusion of that of Southumbrian kings.

The period after the death of Aldfrith in 705 saw the beginnings of a period of instability in kingship in Northumbria.[25] In 716 the throne went for the first time in over a century to someone not descended from Aethelfrith and this inaugurated a period in which representatives of what seem to be four lineages came in and out of power. These were exciting times. In the period 732 – 806 there were ten kings and eleven reigns. Of these kings, three died by violence, one of them 'wickedly killed by his own household', five were driven into exile, one resigned the throne, apparently not willingly, one apparently willingly. There was a great deal of violence in eighth-century Northumbria,

---

[21] *ASC s.a.* 737.

[22] *HE* (C and M), pp. 572 – 4. Plummer I, p. 362 shows that this event probably took place in 741.

[23] *HR s.a.* 801.

[24] *HE* IV, 1 (Plummer I, pp. 204 – 6).

[25] D. P. Kirby, 'Northumbria in the Time of Wilfrid', in *Saint Wilfrid at Hexham*, ed. D. P. Kirby (Newcastle upon Tyne, 1974), pp. 1 – 34 is the best account of Northumbrian politics in this period.

and the state of affairs by the end of the century is reflected in Alcuin's angry letters about his native land: for example, that to Eardwulf, king of Northumbria in 797, warning him that avarice, fraud, injustice, perjury and adultery had led his predecessors to lose life and kingdom. In the next year Alcuin seems to have detected no improvement: 'our kingdom has almost perished from intestine dissensions and false oaths', etc., etc.[26]

We should exercise a certain restraint before going all the way with such views. A general point: bloody and unstable struggles for power at the top of a state do not necessarily indicate chaos throughout society; a brief study of many periods in the history, for example, of ancient Rome will confirm this. The greatest intellectual and artistic achievements of the Northumbrians belong, after all, to the eighth century. Because Bede writes so much more fully of the seventh century than the eighth (largely because he sets the earlier period up as a model for his own time) one can almost forget that his major work belongs to the eighth century: and that the *Ecclesiastical History* was dedicated to Ceolwulf, who had a very troubled reign and was almost a usurper.[27] The great days of the school of York were those of the mid eighth century. Not all the reigns of the kings of Northumbria were short and inglorious: witness that of Eadberht, 737 – 58. The apparently sorry tale of the annals may conceal, may even perhaps to an extent represent, a fairly successful system of government. They tell us nothing about the machinery of government: though we have sufficient evidence to suggest that in large parts of the kingdom the system of administration on the small shire basis which we find in Domesday and in later evidence goes back to, and probably indeed beyond, the period with which we are concerned.[28] There are some indications of something like a hierarchy of officers; the suggestion of Dr Thacker that the *patricii* who appear at certain periods in later eighth-century Northumbria were in fact mayors of the palace raises many interesting possibilities.[29] Possible parallels with Merovingian Gaul are of particular interest because of the way in which recent work on the Merovingian regime has suggested how the violent and unstable surface of events may in fact conceal a system for the repeated establishment and maintenance of consensus among a ruling class.[30] This reminds one of an older view, which saw the numerous depositions of Northumbrian rulers in the eighth century as evidence for formal, in a sense constitutional, action.[31] And although one cannot set much store by the actual

[26] Ep. nos. 108, 122, ed. E. Dümmler, *Epistolae Karolini aevi* II (MGH, Epistolae 4; 1895).

[27] Kirby, as at n. 25 above, p. 20.

[28] G. W. S. Barrow, 'Northern English Society in the Early Middle Ages', *Northern History* 4 (1969), pp. 1 – 28 is one of the most important accounts.

[29] A. T. Thacker, 'Some Terms for Noblemen in Anglo-Saxon England *c.*650 – 900', *Anglo-Saxon Studies in Archaeology and History*, ed. S.C. Hawkes, D. Brown and J. Campbell, 2 (1981; = British Archaeological Reports, British series 92), pp. 201 – 36, esp. 215 – 17.

[30] P. J. Fouracre, 'Merovingians, Mayors of the Palace, and the Notion of a "Low-Born" Ebroin', *Bulletin of the Institute of Historical Research* 57 (1984), pp. 1 – 14.

[31] F. Liebermann, *The National Assembly in the Anglo-Saxon Period* (Halle, 1913), pp. 54 – 8.

words used in our main source, the annals called those of Symeon of Durham, since the actual choice of words is in large measure that of Byrhtferth of Ramsey writing in the later tenth century,[32] other authorities whose phrasing is contemporary use language suggestive of the importance of assemblies. These include, of course, Bede's famous account of Edwin's council debating the possibility of accepting Christianity.[33] If this is not near-contemporary evidence, that of Eddius is such, when he tells how judgement was given against Wilfrid on his return from Rome in 680;[34] so too is that of the annals in continuation of Bede when they refer to Aethelwold 'a sua plebe electus'.[35] It is worth recalling that one reason why so much stress is laid on the violence of Northumbrian coups and none on the possibility of there having been something like a constitutional system, is that in recent decades dark age historians have been far fonder of feuds than of constitutions, impelled in this choice perhaps by excessive apprehension of anachronism. What was that, as it were, segment of an amphitheatre doing at Yeavering, if it were not for formal meetings of some importance?[36]

The violence, the wealth and the civilization of Cuthbert's Northumbria were alike produced by the Northumbrian nobility. Let me sum up a few commonplaces about the nobility of early Anglo-Saxon England in general and of Northumbria in particular, most of them established by Chadwick nearly seventy years ago, so far as they can be established from our texts.[37] A few noblemen appear as of very grand status, such as the apparent dynasty with names alliterating in B in who may have had a kind of marcher responsibility in the late seventh and early eighth centuries,[38] but most noblemen in the works of Bede and his contemporaries generally appear as *ministri* or as *comites*. The former are in the immediate service of the king or some other lord, the latter are generally older and have been settled on a landed estate, though remaining liable to royal service. Young noblemen expected to spend their early years of manhood in the service of a king, frequently as warriors, and would take service, if need be, outside their own kingdom. Bede said that the shortage of land in Northumbria caused by the

[32] C. Hart, 'Byrhtferth's Northumbrian Chronicle', *EHR* 97 (1982), pp. 558 – 82; M. Lapidge, 'Byrhtferth of Ramsey and the Early Sections of the *Historia Regum* attributed to Simeon of Durham', *ASE* 10 (1982), pp. 97 – 102. For the sources for Northumbrian history in this period, D. N. Dumville, 'Textual Archaeology and Northumbrian History Subsequent to Bede', in *Coinage in Ninth Century Northumbria*, ed. D. M. Metcalf (Oxford, 1987), pp. 43 – 56.
[33] *HE* II, 13 (Plummer I, pp. 111 – 12).
[34] *VW* 34.
[35] *S.a.* 758 (Plummer I, p. 363).
[36] B. Hope-Taylor, *Yeavering, an Anglo-British Centre of Early Northumbria* (London, 1977), pp. 119 – 22. The name of an apparent royal vill (*VCA* IV 6, *HR s.a.* 758), *Methel Wongtune*, is suggestive in this context if Plummer (*ASC* II, p. 119) is right in suggesting that it means 'town of the field of discussion'.
[37] H. M. Chadwick, *Studies on Anglo-Saxon Institutions* (Cambridge, 1905), pp. 308 – 48. Cf. Thacker, 'Some Terms for Noblemen', as at n. 29 above.
[38] Thacker, art. cit., pp. 215 – 16.

excessive granting of estates for monastic and pseudo-monastic purposes was driving young noblemen to take service *overseas*.[39] How far the nature of noble land-tenure was changing in this period; whether for example hereditary tenure was becoming of altogether new importance is too complicated a subject to consider here, not least since Mr Wormald's important contribution.[40] One can be sure that, early or late in the period, much noble conduct was determined by an ethic, key and related elements in which were the obligations of lordship and of feud. A lord was supposed to provide for his men; they were supposed to stand by him if need be till death. Society was riven and held together by feud: much of book III of Bede's *History* is devoted to the long feud between the royal lines of Bernicia and Deira. Heavy indeed was the obligation on a man to revenge the death of his lord.

One can hazard a few more generalizations about the grandees of seventh-century England. One is that dress and personal ornament were intensely important to them. Here archaeology assists us very directly by showing with what magnificence the ruling class was fitted out and decorated. If the treasures of Sutton Hoo are hardly matched elsewhere, nevertheless much that is magnificent has come from other graves. In such magnificence textiles were important. The scraps and impressions of these which survive in secular graves are unimpressive to see; but they are sufficient to show how many kinds of textile were used and how elaborately woven they were. (At least twenty-seven such different varieties of weave were represented at Sutton Hoo.[41]) The concentration and display of wealth in personal ornament, still sometimes seen in women, was something which for much of the past was just as important for men. In Anglo-Saxon, as in late medieval times, a nobleman might wear on his person the value of a considerable estate.[42] There was something of the Elizabeth Taylor about dark age potentates.

As important as jewels and clothes were feasting and drinking. The great significance of communal self indulgence for Germanic noblemen is brought out in *Beowulf* as it is by Tacitus. If the one is too late, as the other is too early to be directly relevant for our purposes, we have enough contemporary evidence to link the two; and to indicate large elements in noble life which were both communal and alcoholic. All kings were frequently to be found, as

[39] *Ep. ad Ecgberhtum* 11 (Plummer I, p. 415).
[40] P. Wormald, *Bede and the Conversion of England: The Charter Evidence* (Jarrow Lecture, 1984), esp. pp. 20 – 2.
[41] E. Crowfoot, 'The Textiles', in R. Bruce-Mitford, *The Sutton Hoo Ship-Burial* III, pt. i, ed. Angela Lane Evans (London, 1983), pp. 416 – 17. Further indications of the sophistication of the textiles available come in such descriptions of ecclesiastical gifts as in a letter of Boniface in which he describes a cloak he is sending to Daniel, bishop of Wessex, 'not made of pure silk but mixed with goats' wool', *S. Bonifatii et Lulli Epistolae*, ed. M. Tangl (MGH, Epistolae selectae 1: 1916), no. 63, p. 131. The significance attached to dress appears for example when we are told that when Wilfrid left home, he and his *pueri* were given 'arma et equos *et vestimenta*' (my emphasis) such that they might stand before a king (*VW* 2).
[42] K. B. McFarlane, *The Nobility of Later Medieval England* (Oxford, 1973), pp. 96 – 8. Aldfrith gave three hides of land for two silk cloaks: Bede, *Historia abbatum* 9 (Plummer I, p. 373).

Ceolred of Mercia was (when he went mad), 'apud comites suos splendide epulante'.[43] Some indication of the nature of such splendour is given by the table-ware and, not least, drinking vessels from Sutton Hoo and Taplow.[44]

Life could also be exceedingly violent. A recurrent note in the annals of Northumbria is that of the death of noblemen, not in their beds. For example: '779 the high reeves of Northumbria burnt Beorn the ealdorman on 25 December'.[45] What we probably have is an episode of the kind which recurs in Norse sagas (e.g. that of Burnt Njal) in which a noble was trapped, with his men, in his hall and it and they were burnt.[46] The advantages of dealing with an enemy in this way are obvious: the possibility of effective resistance is much reduced and the number of relations and followers left alive to prosecute an ensuing feud is helpfully diminished. That Beorn perished on 25 December suggests that he was nabbed at his Yule feast.

The moral obligations of feud and of lordship could create much stress. This has been well brought out by Colin Chase in his consideration of Bede's account of the death of Oswine, king of Deira.[47] Professor Chase uses the (admittedly much later) *Vita Oswini* to show the kind of feeling which such a description as Bede's could arouse. Bede says that when Oswine saw that his enemy Oswiu had larger forces, he thought it better not to fight, but rather, to wait for better times. So, he sent his own men home; and hid. The later author dramatizes this into a dialogue in which Oswine says that he would rather go into exile than have his retinue die for him. The retinue protest and say: 'it is better that we should die in battle than that we should become a byword for cowardice in the songs of the people'.[48] Men in positions such as those of Oswine or of his men faced horrible dilemmas in which exile or death were often the only ways out. No wonder they drank so much.

An inkling of the likely relations between a great ecclesiastic and secular rulers can be gained from an episode, a regrettable episode, in the *Life* of Cuthbert's younger contemporary, Guthlac.[49] One of Guthlac's followers proposed to murder him, in order to occupy his *domus* and, I quote, 'to enjoy the greatest veneration of kings and princes', i.e. to usurp his role as a holy man. A holy man could have very exalted contacts: it went with the status, and much of what is known of the high nobility comes from the hagiographical record of such contacts. Prominent among those of Cuthbert were the royal

---

[43] *S. Bonifatii . . . Epistolae*, ed. Tangl, no. 73, p. 153.

[44] See the account by R. Bruce-Mitford and K. East, in Bruce-Mitford, *The Sutton Hoo Ship-Burial* III, i, pp. 316 – 406.

[45] *ASC s.a.* 779; *HR s.a.* 780. *ASC s.a.* 687 and *HR s.a.* 769 could refer to similar episodes.

[46] *Njal's Saga*, trans. M. Magnusson and H. Pálsson (Harmondsworth, 1960), pp. 263 – 73.

[47] C. Chase, 'Beowulf, Bede and St Oswine, the Hero's Pride in Old English Hagiography', in *The Anglo-Saxons, Synthesis and Achievement*, ed. J. D. Woods and D. A. E. Pelteret (Waterloo, 1985), pp. 37 – 48.

[48] Ibid., p. 44.

[49] *Felix's Life of Guthlac* 35; ed. B. Colgrave (Cambridge, 1956), p. 112.

abbesses: Aebbe (coyly described by the anonymous *Life* as 'a widow', more helpfully by Bede as Oswiu's *soror uterina*), *sanctissima, sapientissima*;[50] another friend was Aelfflaed, King Ecgfrith's sister, with whom we find him feasting: they were *simul in convivio sedentes*.[51] One should not regard such ladies as atypical of their class. This was a period in which great royal ladies if widowed or unmarried became abbesses. It was not for nothing that the ninth-century *Liber vitae* of Lindisfarne classed queens and abbesses together: *nomina reginarum et abbatissarum*, the categories were hardly distinguishable;[52] that this is so is a reminder of how difficult, indeed how futile, it can be to seek to distinguish the ecclesiastical from the secular in this period. The presence of these princesses and their rich houses was, as Professor Cramp has reminded us, one of the great distinctions between the generation of Cuthbert and that of Aidan.[53] Aidan would probably have been hardly, if at all, remembered were it not for Bede.[54] If one asks why it was that the cult of Cuthbert far exceeded, indeed swamped, that of Aidan, Bede's stress on how far Aidan sought to limit his social relationships with kings and nobles, may provide us with a clue.[55] Aidan was a foreigner, and difficult; Cuthbert a fellow countryman, perhaps congenial.

It was not just royal abbesses whom Cuthbert visited: his *vitae* find him also in the houses of two *comites* and a *prefectus*.[56] We may suppose that when he was not in his monastery (perhaps to an extent when he was) his time was spent with the Northumbrian nobility, to which he almost certainly belonged. Bede records twenty-four miracles performed by, or in association with Cuthbert between his entering the monastery of Melrose and his death. Of these ten show him in royal or noble company.[57] Monasteries were becoming very important to that nobility and were to be more important still. The relationship between aristocracy and monasticism was crucial to the nature of Cuthbert's work and cult: and it can easily be somewhat misunderstood if we regard it simply in the light of the demands of St Benedict or St Columbanus, or in that of the judgements of Bede or the late David Knowles. Modern historians judging eighth-century monasteries are often the denizens of

---

[50] *VCA* II, 3; *VCP* 10; *Two Lives*, pp. 80, 188.

[51] *VCA* IV, 10; *Two Lives*, p. 126. (This phrase is that of the anonymous; Bede has 'dum hora refectionis ad mensam consedissent': *VCP* 34, p. 262.)

[52] *Liber vitae ecclesiae Dunelmensis*, ed. A. H. Thompson, vol. I (SS 136; 1923), folio 13ʳ.

[53] R. Cramp, 'Northumbria and Ireland', in *Sources of Anglo-Saxon Culture*, ed. P. E. Szarmach and V. D. Oggins (Kalamazoo, 1986), pp. 185 – 201, at pp. 192 – 3. Michael Roper's argument that monasteries in Cuthbert's generation (including his own) were much more generously endowed than had previously been the case is important: 'Wilfrid's Landholdings in Northumbria', in *Saint Wilfrid at Hexham* (as n. 25 above), p. 64.

[54] J. Campbell, 'The Debt of the Early English Church to Ireland', as at n. 9 above, p. 337. Cf. Kirby, 'Northumbria in the time of Wilfrid', in *St Wilfrid*, p. 14.

[55] J. Campbell, *Essays in Anglo-Saxon History* (London, 1986), pp. 17 – 18.

[56] *VCP* 25, 29, 31 (possibly the *comites* of 25 and 31 were the same man).

[57] They are those recorded in *VCP* 10, 15, 23, 24, 25, 27, 29, 31, 34, 35.

Barchester applying the standards of Monte Cassino to establishments which resembled the former more than they did the latter.

A late seventh or an eighth-century monastery often had many of the aspects of a special kind of nobleman's club. The correspondence and the conciliar documents of the period tell us, time and time again, what many of the members were most interested in: conviviality and clothes.[58] Even at Lindisfarne the brethren feasted at Christmas in a manner which alarmed Cuthbert.[59] Even at Jarrow Abbot Ceolfrith had to leave for a time because of the nobles there who would not abide his discipline.[60] Some idea of the reality of monastic life can be found in, for example, Theodore's *Penitential*, and, in particular, what it lays down about drink. A monk who got drunk to the point of vomiting was to do forty days penance; but the passage concluded by laying down that 'if it is for gladness at Christmas or Easter or for any festival of a saint, and he then has imbibed no more than is commanded by his seniors, no offence is committed'.[61] In such a context one should recall how unpopular St Guthlac made himself as a member of the monastic community at Repton when he would not drink alcohol.[62] Conviviality mattered even in the best-conducted monasteries. Put beside the provision of the council of Clovesho (747) that monasteries are not to harbour poets, harpists, etc.,[63] a contemporary letter from Cuthbert, abbot of Wearmouth/Jarrow, to Lul, asking for a harpist. He has a *cithara*, he says, but no one to play it.[64] It seems not unlikely that the harpist was required for purposes of entertainment rather than of religion; and it is striking that they should have been willing to bring a harpist all the way from Germany. As Mr Wormald has powerfully pointed out, it is in the context of monastic entertainment that one should seek for the origins of much Anglo-Saxon poetry, certainly not only the religious poetry.[65]

[58] Cf. pp. 13 – 14 below.

[59] *VCP* 27.

[60] Anonymous *Life of Ceolfrith* 8 (Plummer I, p. 390).

[61] I, 1; ed. A. H. Haddan and W. Stubbs, *Councils and Ecclesiastical Documents relating to Great Britain and Ireland* (3 vols., Oxford, 1869 – 71) III, p. 177. The translation is that of J. T. McNeill and H. M. Gamer, *Medieval Handbooks of Penance* (New York, 1938), p. 184. A penitential attributed to Bede (for which see A. J. Frantzen, 'The Penitentials attributed to Bede', *Speculum* 58 (1983), pp. 573 – 95) in repeating this provision tones it down rather, retaining a penalty but saying it should be 'much lighter' than 40 days penance: Haddan and Stubbs, *Councils* III, p.331.

[62] 'Hac igitur ex causa omnibus fratribus illic cohabitantibus aspero odio habetatur', *Felix's Life of Guthlac* 21, p. 84.

[63] Can. 20; Haddan and Stubbs, *Councils* III, p. 369. Bishops to see to it that monasteries are not to be 'ludicrarum artium receptacula, hoc est, poetarum, citharistarum, musicorum, scurrorum'.

[64] *S. Bonifatii . . . Epistolae*, ed. Tangl, no. 116, p. 251. Cf. D.K. Fry, 'Anglo-Saxon Lyre Tuning Pegs from Whitby, N. Yorks', *Medieval Archaeology* 20 (1976), pp. 137 – 9.

[65] P. Wormald, 'Bede, ''Beowulf'' and the Conversion of the Anglo-Saxon Aristocracy', in *Bede and Anglo-Saxon England*, ed. R. T. Farrell (British Archaeological Reports, Brit. series 46; Oxford, 1978), pp. 32 – 95.

If the *mores* of the beer hall found an ecclesiastical home, so too did the ethic of the *comitatus*. Alcuin's acceptance of its values is often remarked upon: the best evidence is his letter to Charlemagne in which he commends Torhtmund, a follower of the late King Aethelred, who had avenged the blood of his lord.[66] The distinction between a secular and an ecclesiastical following was an imprecise one. Not only did great churchmen have lay retinues, but clerical, like lay followers were described as *ministri*.[67] Boniface's anxiety that his men should be looked after after his death resembles the attitude of a lay lord: those near the pagan frontier could get bread, but not clothing unless they had help.[68] His *plurimi domestici* indeed died with him at Dokkum, as Ecgfrith's had at Nechtansmere.[69] The idea of a clerical community as a unit of lordship appears in Alcuin's use of the expression 'of the *Bealdhunings*' to mean 'of the community of which Bealdhun is head'.[70] The same idea appears in the provision by the council of Clovesho (747) that 'nemo suscipiat majorem congregationem quam sustenare possit'. The canon adds that if anyone has incautiously done so already, he is not violently to exact *opera* from them 'antequam illis victum ac vestimentum juxta habitum professionis suae possit concedere'.[71] This reference to food and clothing taken with that in the letter of Boniface's just cited indicates that an abbot or a bishop's following could be regarded as men who served him and for whom he had to provide. The fate of such a clerical retinue could be as hard as that of a secular one when their lord was in trouble; witness, for example, King Eadwulf's threat: 'I swear by my salvation that, unless he [Wilfrid] has left my kingdom within six days, any of his companions whom I shall find shall perish'.[72]

Some, probably very many, monks and clerks drank and thought like noblemen, owned slaves and treasures and probably lived in halls like noblemen. It was a particular source of distress to their critics that they also dressed like noblemen. When Cuthbert's sober garb is stressed,[73] it is because other clerics were less restrained. Nothing is more conspicuous about objurgatory writing on the early English church than the repeated emphasis

---

[66] Ep. 231, ed. Dümmler.

[67] *Felix's Life of Guthlac* 43, 46; pp.132, 142: in both passages *ministri* probably means something more than 'servants'.

[68] *S. Bonifatii . . . Epistolae*, ed. Tangl, no. 93, pp. 213 – 4.

[69] Cuthbert, archbishop of Canterbury to Lul, *S. Bonifatii . . . Epistolae*, ed. Tangl, no. 111, p. 235.

[70] Ep. 7, ed. Dümmler. This usage suggests that some place-names in *ingas* could indicate monastic sites.

[71] Can. 28; Haddan and Stubbs, *Councils* III, p. 374.

[72] *VW* 59: 'de sodalibus eius quoscumque invenero, morte peribunt'.

[73] *VCA* IV, 1: Cuthbert maintained *vilitas* in his dress, though nevertheless supporting *episcopi dignitatem*. Bede (*VCP* 16) has a slightly different emphasis: Cuthbert kept to a middle way in dress; and his example is followed at Lindisfarne 'so that no one has a garment of varied or costly colouring'.

on dress.[74] English noblemen liked rich, loud clothes,[75] and their tastes did not change on entering the church. Boniface's complaint about clerics wearing clothes with dragons on them is indeed about the best evidence we have for the actual wearing of Byzantine or oriental silks in early England.

In seeking to understand the monastic mode of life it is important to bear in mind some of the circumstances which could lead to a man becoming a monk. Some monks entered monasteries as children as Bede did.[76] Some may have become monks because they were ill, like the nobleman, one of the companions of the king, whom Wilfrid had to serve when first he entered the community at Lindisfarne.[77] Others fled or were driven from the threats and miseries of their violent world. For example, in the annals we meet Alric, once *dux*, now *clericus*; Edwin, once *dux*, later *abbas*.[78] Alcuin was insistent that Osbald, who had made a brief and unsuccessful attempt to make himself king of Northumbria, should become a monk, putting this into a penitential context by emphasizing the bloodshed in which Osbald had been involved.[79]

A different emphasis appears in another account of the connection between violence and monasteries, of special importance to us because it deals with the foundation of a cell of Lindisfarne within a generation of the death of Cuthbert. It is in the poem *De abbatibus*, by Aethelwulf, written in the very early ninth century and describing the history of a quasi-dependency of

---

[74] Council of Clovesho 747, can. 19: monks and nuns not to be clad *pompaticis . . . indumentis* (Haddan and Stubbs, *Councils* III, p. 369); can. 28: the clergy not to imitate the laity 'in vestitu crurum per fasciolas nec per coculas in circumdatione capitis modo pallii laicorum' (ibid., p. 374). Similarly, nuns are not to wear fine clothes: council of 786: *canonici*, *monachi* and *monachae* 'illo habitu vivant quo orientales monachi degunt . . . et non tinctis Indiae coloribus aut veste preciosa' (ibid., p. 450). In 747 it was laid down that *domicilia sanctimonialium* ought not to be homes of drunkenness, luxury, etc., and in them attention ought to be given to sober living, psalmody, etc., rather than 'texendis et plectendis vario colore inanis gloriae vestibus studeant operam dare' (Clovesho can. 20; ibid. p.369). This reference to the actual production of rich clothes in nunneries is a reminder that noble, even royal, women might weave and embroider, cf. Einhard, *Vita Karoli magni imperatoris* 19 (ed. L. Halphen, *Éginhard, Vie de Charlemagne* (4th edn. Paris, 1967), p. 58). For Aldhelm on the sartorial indulgences and temptations of nuns, and for an important discussion of the very rich clothes of great ladies of the day, see E. Crowfoot and S. C. Hawkes, 'Early Anglo-Saxon Gold Braids', *Medieval Archaeology* 11 (1967), pp. 42 – 86. Alcuin warned Higbald, bishop of Lindisfarne, against 'vanity in raiment', ed. Dümmler, no.20. More striking is his objurgation to Eardwulf, king of Northumbria, to observe 'moderation in life and dress'. Why should 'apparel' loom so large as to come in tandem with life? Alcuin's letter to another king of Northumbria, Aethelred, Dümmler no.16, alludes to the sack of Lindisfarne, associating it with divine punishment, which has been attracted by sin. In this connection he mentions first fornication, next immoderate clothing. After some observations on the cutting of hair and trimming of beards, he goes on: 'The princes' superfluity is poverty for the people'. It is a reminder that rich dress (above all if personal ornaments are included with it) may have been a major source of expenditure for the great and so, perhaps, a real burden on the people.

[75] Crowfoot, 'The Textiles', as at n. 41 above for the prominence of checks and stripes.

[76] *HE* V, 24 (Plummer I, p. 357).

[77] *VW* 2: 'nobilis ex sodalibus regis'.

[78] *HR s.a.* 796, 801; cf. ibid. *s.a.* 799, Osbald, 'quondam dux et patricius et ad tempus rex, tunc vero abbas'.

[79] Ep. 109, ed. Dümmler.

Lindisfarne, very possibly, as Dr Howlett has suggested, at Bywell.[80] Its founder was a *dux* called Eanmund and Aethelwulf is explicit on his motives: he was fleeing from the persecution of the tyrannical king of Northumbria, Osred.[81] One very conspicuous example of political failure being contained (in two senses) in a monastery — again of Lindisfarne — is the retreat there twice, in 731 and 737, of Ceolwulf, the king to whom Bede dedicated his *Ecclesiastical History*.[82] It is of some interest that the, probably much later, Lindisfarne story was that the presence of the ex-king in the community was associated with the introduction of wine and beer there.[83]

Aethelwulf's description of the monastery in *De abbatibus* contains much of value besides the account of its foundation. The poem itself, a most intricate performance, is the best evidence we have for the long continuance of Latin learning in Northumbria. It brings out the magnificence of the treasures of the monastery.[84] It shows in various ways the importance of relationships with Ireland.[85] One passage suggests, though it does not prove, that one of the monks was married; perhaps many of them were.[86] If so here is another resemblance to Irish monasteries. We ought to bear in mind the possibility that some of the institutions which Bede denounced in his *Letter to Ecgberht* were nothing other than monasteries such as many monasteries in Ireland were, institutions which provided not so much retreats from the world as special ways of organizing parts of it.[87] To actually get away from the world, even in the seventh century, you needed, as Cuthbert found, to become a hermit.

But Cuthbert in the end ceased to be a hermit and became a bishop. It is interesting to consider the tone in which his *vitae* speak of episcopacy. We are told that in referring to Boisil's prophecy that he would become a bishop, Cuthbert used to say 'Even if I could hide myself in a tiny dwelling on a rock . . . even then I should fear lest the love of wealth should tempt me'.[88] Similarly it was on wealth that the abbess Aelfflaed mused when she considered the possibility of Cuthbert's becoming a bishop.[89] Undoubtedly some or many bishops of this period were conspicuous in wealth and power.

---

[80] Aethelwulf, *De abbatibus*, ed. A. Campbell (Oxford, 1967); D. R. Howlett, 'The Provenance, Date and Structure of *De Abbatibus*', *Archaeologia Aeliana* 5th ser. 3 (1975), pp. 121 – 30.

[81] *De abbatibus* 2 – 4 (pp. 4 – 9).

[82] For important comments on this see Kirby, as at n. 25, pp. 20 – 21.

[83] *Vita S. Oswaldi* 21 (*Sym. Op.* I, p. 361); cf. *Chronica . . . Rogeri de Houedene*, ed. W. Stubbs (RS 51, 4 vols., 1868 – 71) I, p. 8.

[84] Lines 448 – 50, 649 – 51; cf. the visionary treasures described in lines 760 – 95.

[85] Campbell, 'The Debt of the Early English Church to Ireland' (as at n. 9 above), p. 345. I was wrong in admitting with Kenney that the monastery to which the poem relates might have actually been in Ireland. Lines 140 – 2 make it clear that this was not so.

[86] Ibid., pp. 344 and n. 82.

[87] E.g. Kathleen Hughes, *Church and Society in Ireland, A.D. 400 – 1200*, ed. D. Dumville (Variorum reprints; London, 1987), VIII and IX.

[88] *VCP* 8.

[89] *VCP* 24.

Wilfrid may have been a very special case, and his career was certainly not an ordinary one; but it is most unlikely that he was unique in his wealth and his armed retinue.

Bede in his letter to Ecgberht laments how bishops levy *tributa* from villages which they had never so much as visited.[90] Bishop John of Hexham, like Wilfrid, rode around with a retinue including laymen.[91] Alcuin's observations to and on Eanbald II, archbishop of York (796 – *c*.808), are pertinent: he suggests that the archbishop is receiving the king's enemies and protecting their possessions. He complains about the size of the archbishop's retinue. 'What', he says, 'does he need with so many *milites*?': all or many of whom he indicates to have had followers of their own in turn.[92] There can be no doubt that bishops could have significant power and play significant parts in struggles for power. That is probably why it was that Acca, bishop of Hexham, was driven from his see at the same time as, and as Dr Kirby has suggested, probably in association with, the first deposition of King Ceolwulf in 731.[93]

There may have been something special about the power of archbishops in this period. It is interesting that in the record of the legatine council of 786 the archbishops, and only the archbishops, witness before their respective kings.[94] In the eighth century in Northumbria, archbishops were the only people, other than kings, in whose names coin was struck.[95] Liebermann imaginatively, but quite unprovably, suggested that the archbishops of Northumbria may have had a special status inherited from pagan high-priests, suggesting that the high-priest Coifi as speaking first in Edwin's conciliar debate as described by Bede may be indicative of such status.[96] Be that as it may, it is worth observing that in relation to the remarkable period when the archbishop of York and the king of the Northumbrians were brothers, Ecgberht became archbishop before Eadberht became king, not the other way round.[97]

On one of his visits to the Abbess Verca Cuthbert was offered a drink, with a choice of beer or wine. 'Aquam inquit date mihi', 'Give me water', the saint

---

[90] *Ep. ad Ecgb.* 7 (Plummer I, p. 410). Campbell, *Essays*, pp. 49 – 50.

[91] *HE* V, 6 (Plummer I, p. 289).

[92] Ep. 209, ed. Dümmler. Alcuin indicates that Eanbald was not original in having such a retinue, rather was his more numerous than those of his predecessors. Eanbald is, he says, striving after the possessions of others and protecting the king's enemies. In letter no. 232 (801) he refers to the secular power of Eanbald in suggesting that he may have helped to bring his troubles on himself by receiving the king's enemies or protecting their possessions.

[93] 'Northumbria in the Time of Wilfrid', in *St Wilfrid*, pp. 20 – 1.

[94] Ep. 3, ed. Dümmler. (In the inferior text printed by Haddan and Stubbs, *Councils* III, pp. 459 – 61, the archbishop of Canterbury precedes Offa but he of York does not precede Aelfwold.)

[95] G. C. Brooke, *English Coins* (3rd edn., London, 1950), pp. 9 – 12.

[96] Liebermann, *The National Assembly*, p. 3.

[97] Ecgberht became bishop of York in 732, archbishop in 735; Eadberht became king in 737.

of course replied.[98] But the offer of wine is interesting. Set it beside another episode in the relationship between Verca and Cuthbert. We are told that when Cuthbert was preparing for his death, he mentioned a *sindonis* which she had given him and which his body was to be wrapped in.[99] It is not quite clear what *sindonis* means. Cuthbert said that he would not wear it while he was alive: this suggests that it was valuable and such as a less ascetic man might have worn. *Sindon* is sometimes translated 'muslin', but I wonder whether this may not be a reference to silk of the kind in which Cuthbert's body was wrapped, though the actual silks found in the coffin seem to be later.

These offers of wine and rich fabrics remind us, again, of the links between the life-style of the great men and women of the church and that of their counterparts in the world. They remind us also of the importance, for both groups, of imports. For example, among the luxuries which were in a sense necessities for the very great in south-eastern England in the early part of the seventh century were imports from the eastern Mediterranean: bronze vessels, silverware, ivory and amethysts.[100] Later in the century Bede saw Benedict Biscop as a kind of merchant travelling to the Mediterranean for rich goods: he was, he says, *religiosus emptor* of *spiritalium mercium*.[101] The key to much of the success and nature of Monkwearmouth/Jarrow is that its founder was rich enough to make extensive purchases, above all of books, overseas. In his most moving account of the death of Bede, a fellow monk describes how, when Bede knew he had not long to live, he sent for the priests of the monastery to give them *munuscula*, from the contents of his *capsella*: *piperum, oraria et incensa*.[102] Wilfrid's activities give a similar impression of involvement in circumstances in which distant connections, ships, the sea and the potentiality of trade, matter. If the ship in which he was wrecked on the coast of Sussex really did, as his biographer says, have 120 men in it, then it was of at least twice the capacity of the Sutton Hoo ship, which is, at over ninety feet long, the largest of the period known.[103] A great deal of what we see in Cuthbert's Northumbria has to be put into a context of sea traffic and of trade. As Professor Hill pointed out, it is striking how many of the major monasteries lie

---

[98] *VCP* 35; wine was warmed to give Cuthbert when he was near death, *VCP* 37 (p. 274). These references are among the earliest — I believe they are in fact the earliest — to the consumption of wine for non-sacramental purposes among the Anglo-Saxons.

[99] *VCP* 37.

[100] R. Bruce-Mitford and S. M. Youngs, 'Silver' and R. Bruce-Mitford, 'The Coptic Bowl' in *The Sutton Hoo Ship-Burial* III, i (as at n. 41 above), pp. 1 – 191, 732 – 87. B. Green, 'Ivory Rings', in J. N. L. Myres and B. Green, *The Anglo-Saxon Cemeteries of Caistor-by-Norwich and Markshall, Norfolk* (Reports of the Research Committee of the Society of Antiquaries of London, 30; London, 1973), pp. 100 – 3. The information on amethysts I owe to Mrs S. C. Hawkes.

[101] *Historia abbatum* 5, 6 (Plummer I, pp. 368, 369). Benedict Biscop is the father of the English import trade. In this sense: that he is the first Englishman of whom we can be sure that he purchased goods abroad for import into this country.

[102] Cuthbert, *De obitu Baedae* (Plummer I, p. clxiii): 'Pepper, vestments and incense'.

[103] *VW* 13. That Eddius actually points out that 120 was the number of years of Moses' age to some extent allays the suspicions which this coincidence of number may raise.

beside harbours;[104] and to take one example of the influence of the sea, a meeting at Whitby is much more likely to have been arranged there for the convenience of those who travelled by water than that of those who travelled by land. Northumbrian missionary activity in Frisia and the Rhineland may have to be put into a context of Northumbrian commercial contact with those areas; a contact in which Frisian slave merchants may have been very important; for, as is suggested earlier in this lecture, the export of slaves may have been crucial in the exploitation of Northumbrian conquests.[105]

The title of this lecture implies that the political and social circumstances of a church or a saint can be treated as something called background: as it were, the stage setting for religious drama. The unifying complexities of any society must ensure that in the last resort this is a fallacy: in an important sense there can be no such thing as ecclesiastical history, separating a church from its world. This view is not shared by the authors of our sources; and this makes the seventh and eighth centuries difficult indeed to apprehend. Even Bede at his, from our point of view, informative best, is by no means concerned to tell us most of what we want to know about politics or society. And in the last two books of the *Ecclesiastical History*, those which most concern the student of Cuthbert, he is by no means at his best. The nearer he gets to his own time, the less he tells us about real events; he disliked much which was happening in his own day and found it easier to idealize the past than to dwell on the present. His work becomes increasingly visionary, in a strict sense: the second book of his *Ecclesiastical History* contains two visions, book III one, book IV fourteen (excluding those to do with Cuthbert), book V, five, including the longest chapter in the book. His habitual discretion leads him to give us, for example, an idealized version of Wilfrid, very different from the powerful ruler who appears in Eddius.[106] It can come extremely close to humbug. Thus in the *Vita Cuthberti* he twice says that Aldfrith the future king was in exile in Ireland for the sake of study.[107] That Aldfrith did study in Ireland we can be reasonably sure; we can be almost equally sure that his principal reason for being there was fear of his half-brother Ecgfrith, who would have killed him if he could have caught him. It is amazing what an eighth-century author will fail to tell one and what he will dare to do. For example, Alcuin, in his poem on York, contrives to avoid mentioning Northumbria, Bernicia or Deira by

---

[104] R. Hill, 'Christianity and Geography in Early Northumbria', *Studies in Church History* 3 (1966), ed. G. J. Cuming, p. 131. Professor Cramp, 'Northumbria and Ireland' (as at n. 53 above), p. 192, points out the importance of Irish monasteries as centres of trade and the relationship of some English monasteries to harbours. Cf. S. E. Rigold, 'The Sutton Hoo Coins in the Light of the Contemporary Background of Coinage in England', in R. Bruce-Mitford, *The Sutton Hoo Ship Burial* I (London, 1975), p. 662, for the numismatic evidence which he argues shows that Reculver 'far from being a monastery established *in deserto* was clearly a major port throughout the seventh and early eighth centuries'.
[105] See p. 5 above.
[106] Campbell, *Essays* (as at n. 55), pp. 16 – 22.
[107] *VCP* 24, *Two Lives*, pp. 236, 238.

names and displays a marked capacity for distortion. Thus, when he relates the famous Bedan episode of the temporary rejection of King Oswald's alleged body by the monks of Bardney: though he almost certainly had no other account than Bede's to go by, he nevertheless transmutes it. The community of a royal monastery become *saevi coloni*, yokels.[108] In short, we cannot expect more than a very committed and selective and almost certainly distorted account of such a saint as Cuthbert from his *vitae*: it is their function to provide such an account. Our other sources are largely visionary and have a view of the nature of truth which most of us do not share. It is not easy to establish a context in which the moving, if probably deceptive, simplicities of the *vitae* of Cuthbert can be related to the grandeur of his grave goods. The real Cuthbert is hard to find and far to seek.

---

[108] Ed. Godman, as at n. 17 above, lines 367 – 9.

Cuthbert and the Polarity between Pastor and Solitary

CLARE STANCLIFFE

I THE LITERARY SOURCES

Cuthbert was born around 635, the year in which King Oswald summoned
Aidan from Iona to come and convert his people, and thus inaugurated the
Irish-dominated phase of Northumbrian Christianity. At this time not only
were the missionaries Irish, but Iona took responsibility for appointing
bishops of Northumbria.[1] The synod of Whitby in 664 changed this. Of
course, King Oswiu's decision to follow Roman, not Irish practices, did not
end the close links between Northumbria and Ireland. It did, however, end
Iona's authority over the Northumbrian church; hereafter the Northumbrian
kings and Archbishop Theodore (for his episcopate) took responsibility for
appointing Northumbrian bishops.[2] Further, Whitby ushered in a half
century during which at least some English churchmen regarded Christians of
the Iona tradition as schismatics, or even heretics. The validity of their orders,
and hence of their sacraments, was questioned or rejected outright.[3] We
should bear in mind that Cuthbert's prominence as a Northumbrian
churchman fell in this unhappy period, as do the first phase of his cult and the
writing of the earliest lives. Indeed, although Iona conformed to the Roman
Easter in 716 and tonsure in 718, Bede may still have been unaware of this
when writing his second, prose, *Life of Cuthbert*.[4]

By the time he wrote his *Ecclesiastical History c.*730, Bede not only knew that
Iona had conformed, he even structured his *History* around a contrast between
the good-for-nothing British, who had neglected to preach to their neighbours
and were therefore justly punished, and the charitable Irish, who deserved to

---

[1] *HE* III, 25, 26; IV, 4. Cf. III, 4.
[2] *HE* III, 28; IV, 2, 12, 27 (25); cf. *VCP* 24; *VCA* III, 6 and IV, 1.
[3] *HE* III, 25 and 28; IV, 2; *VW* 12, 14 – 15; Theodore, *Penitential* I, 9, and perhaps cf. I, 5; ed. A.
H. Haddan and W. Stubbs, *Councils and Ecclesiastical Documents relating to Great Britain and Ireland* (3
vols., Oxford, 1869 – 71), III, pp. 197, 180 – 2.
[4] A. A. M. Duncan, 'Bede, Iona, and the Picts', in *The Writing of History in the Middle Ages*, ed. R.
H. C. Davis and J. M. Wallace-Hadrill (Oxford, 1981), pp. 35, 40. Below, n.19.

be enlightened about the correct dating of Easter because they had evangelized the English.[5] As we tend to view the first century of Northumbrian Christianity through the lens of Bede's *History*, where the Irish mission to Northumbria is given generous treatment, we can easily forget that between 664 and 716 many saw things differently. This probably explains why Aidan from Iona, albeit the founder of Lindisfarne and Bernician Christianity, was relegated to obscurity, whereas Cuthbert rapidly became honoured as an important saint. Their lives had much in common, but Cuthbert's adherence to the Whitby decision allowed him to be viewed as paradigmatic in a way that Aidan, with his Iona origins and loyalties, could not.[6]

The same background lies behind the early lives of Cuthbert. At much the same time as a monk of Lindisfarne was penning the first life of Cuthbert (699 × 705), Adomnan, abbot of Iona, was writing the life of its founder, Columba (689 × 704, probably 697 × 704). Now the *Vita Columbae* has been seen as aimed at gaining support for the Columban connection in Northumbria as well as in Ireland.[7] Nor was this a vain hope, for the Northumbrian king, Aldfrith, was half Irish, being related to the Uí Néill which had such close links with Iona; he had previously lived in Iona, and he probably owed his throne to the Irish/Pictish alliance that had defeated and slain his predecessor, Ecgfrith, at Nechtansmere.[8] Adomnan enjoyed friendly relations with him, twice visiting him in Northumbria. Aldfrith had originally reinstated Wilfrid as bishop, but *c.*691 he drove him into renewed exile. His reign, lasting from 685 – 705, saw rival church groupings vying with each other for pre-eminence: within Northumbria, Wilfrid's party and the Lindisfarne community, certainly;[9] but beyond it, we should not forget Iona. For there are indications that the lives of Cuthbert and Columba originate in the same milieu. Besides belonging to a common hagiographical tradition that

---

[5] Ibid. pp. 41 – 2; T. M. Charles-Edwards, 'Bede, the Irish and the Britons', *Celtica* 15 (1983), pp. 42 – 52. H. E. J. Cowdrey, 'Bede and the "English People" ', *Journal of Religious History* 11 (1981), pp. 501 – 23.

[6] Alcuin barely mentions Aidan, when celebrating Northumbria's Christian past from a very Romanist viewpoint: Alcuin, *The Bishops, Kings and Saints of York*, ed. and trans. P. Godman (Oxford, 1982), lines 291 – 300, and introduction, pp. xlix – li. See Thacker, below, p. 113 and n.78.

[7] J. M. Picard, 'The Purpose of Adomnan's *Vita Columbae*', *Peritia* 1 (1982), pp. 160 – 77, esp. 172 – 7. Note Adomnan's emphasis on Columba's procuring victory for Oswald — something which Cuthbert was unable to do for Ecgfrith: *Vita Columbae* I,1, ed. A. O. and M. O. Anderson (London etc. 1961), pp. 198 – 202. By the tenth century, Cuthbert had acquired this ability (perhaps from Columba?), which he used on behalf of Alfred: *HSC* 16, and cf. *V.Col.* loc. cit. Both cite Joshua 1: 6, and assure the king of divine election as *rex* or *imperator* 'totius Britanniae'. Cf. Simpson, below.

[8] H. Moisl, 'The Bernician Royal Dynasty and the Irish in the Seventh Century', *Peritia* 2 (1985), pp. 103 – 26 at pp. 120 – 4.

[9] See Thacker, below.

drew upon the same sources, they share some unusual vocabulary;[10] they also share several types of story which are not part of their common hagiographical inheritance.[11] Perhaps, then, just as the *Vita Columbae* was written in part with an eye to Northumbria, so the anonymous *Vita Cuthberti* was written in part with an eye to Iona: it was proof for King Aldfrith that a homegrown Northumbrian saint could tread in the same paths of holiness as Iona's own founding saint. Cuthbert now became to Northumbria what Columba was for the Irish monasteries that looked to Iona.[12]

But Iona was only part of the wider background against which the anonymous *Vita Cuthberti* was written. More pressing, because nearer home, were the views of those, like Wilfrid's party, who saw adherents of Irish practices in tonsure and the dating of Easter as schismatics, with whom no communion was possible.[13] It is significant that around 700 the early 'Ionan' phase of Cuthbert's life was seemingly still too compromising for the author of the anonymous *Life*: for he insists that Cuthbert was first tonsured at Ripon (not, as was actually the case, at the Iona-tradition monastery of Melrose); and that he was given the Petrine (rather than the Irish) tonsure.[14] He surely knew that this was a rewriting of history;[15] but his determination to give Cuthbert an impeccable Roman ancestry within the church shows how important such matters seemed in Lindisfarne *c.* 700.[16] What appears to have happened, probably during Eadberht's episcopate, is a drawing together of Lindisfarne and Wilfrid's own foundation of Ripon. The latter clearly valued many of the traits we associate with Irish Christianity, such as the significance

[10] D. Bullough, 'Columba, Adomnan and the Achievement of Iona', *Scottish Historical Review* 43 (1964), pp. 125–30; vol. 44 (1965), pp. 17–21, 26–8. Gregory the Great's *Dialogues* are a further common source: G. Brüning, 'Adamnans Vita Columbae und ihre Ableitungen', *Zeitschrift für celtische Philologie* 11 (1917), at pp. 249–52, and cf. below.

[11] See appendix, and p. 25 below. So also does Jonas's *Vita Columbani*: see Thacker, below, pp. 112, 114. No verbal parallels have been noted between *V. Col* and *VCA*, which tells against one *Life* being directly known by the author of the other. But Lindisfarne could have had a copy of the (lost) life of Columba by Cummian the White.

[12] Alternatively the anonymous author may have been so steeped in the same ideals of sanctity as Adomnan that his portrayal of Cuthbert *ipso facto* resembles Adomnan's Columba.

[13] *VW* 12; above, n. 3.

[14] *VCA* II, 2; cf. Bede *VCP* 6. We must prefer Bede's account because of the first-hand testimony of Sigfrith; because Bede's account is inherently convincing, the anonymous's unconvincing (Leader Water, above which Cuthbert had been keeping sheep, is near Melrose, whereas Ripon is over 100 miles away; and a raw recruit to monasticism would not immediately have been made guestmaster); and, most conclusively, because Ripon was a gift from the subking, Alhfrith, shortly before the 664 synod of Whitby (*HE* III, 25), whereas in 651, when Cuthbert first became a monk, Alhfrith was almost certainly not yet a king (see Plummer II, 120, 189).

[15] Trustworthy witnesses of Cuthbert's Ripon miracle were still alive and known to the anonymous: *VCA* II, 2.

[16] Wilfrid's year as bishop of Lindisfarne, 687–8, appears to have been traumatic for the community there (*VCP* 40, *Two Lives*, pp. 286, 357), and Wilfrid still had his supporters: see Thacker and Higgitt, below.

of the eremetical life;[17] but this must not compromise absolute adherence to Roman traditions on matters of church order.

It was out of this complex background that the cult and early lives of Cuthbert emerged. By 730, when Bede was writing his *History*, the dust had settled: 'The debt . . . to the legacy of Lindisfarne and Iona could be fully acknowledged, and in the crucial place he gave to Cuthbert at the climax of his fourth book Bede did acknowledge it.'[18] In 700 the debt could not be so acknowledged. Even then, however, Cuthbert was being portrayed as the product of Celtic and Roman traditions; the groundwork was laid for the role of Cuthbert the unifier.

All this may seem a far cry from the subject of my paper; but we cannot consider Cuthbert's life divorced from the problems of interpreting our sources for it. Fortunately we have lives of Cuthbert from two rather different people: the anonymous monk of Lindisfarne, writing *c.* 700; and Bede, who wrote a verse life soon after 705 which he later revised, and a prose life *c.* 710 × 720,[19] while his *Ecclesiastical History* also contains much of relevance. Once we know enough to allow for their bias, these early lives can tell us much.

The earliest life was written by an unnamed monk of Lindisfarne at the prompting of Bishop Eadfrith and the whole community between 699 and 705.[20] Probably commissioned in the wake of the translation of Cuthbert's body in 698, it documented Cuthbert's holiness through miracles, providing a basis for — and encouragement of — the incipient cult. Its audience would have been, first, the monks of Lindisfarne[21] and visitors to Cuthbert's shrine; beyond that the church — and king — of Northumbria, and probably Christian circles further afield in England, at Iona, and on the continent.[22] Being written only twelve to eighteen years after Cuthbert's death, several named eyewitnesses of the events recounted were still alive. The *Life* is structured into four books, one for each phase of Cuthbert's life: before he became a monk, as a monk, as a hermit, and as a bishop — this last including his death, translation, and three subsequent miracles. The author's basic concern was to tell miracle stories[23] and stories showing prophecies come true.

[17] *HE* V, 1; *VCP* 46; *VW* 64.

[18] R. A. Markus, *Bede and the Tradition of Ecclesiastical Historiography*, Jarrow Lecture 1975, p. 12.

[19] The *terminus ad quem* for *VCP* is Eadfrith's death in 721, while in 725 Bede spoke of it as written 'nuper': Plummer I, p. cxlviii. But we cannot properly interpret this to mean *c.*720, as Plummer did: cf. Lapidge below p. 85 and notes 29 – 30.

[20] *VCA* I, 1; *Two Lives*, pp. 60, 13.

[21] NB 'videte fratres', *VCA* I, 3.

[22] For the early cult in Northumbria, see A. T. Thacker, 'The Social and Continental Background to Early Anglo-Saxon Hagiography' (unpublished D.Phil. thesis, University of Oxford, 1976), pp. 80 – 2. The continental MS tradition of *VCA* (*Two Lives*, pp. 17 – 20, 43 – 5) suggests that it reached the continent soon, before being overtaken by Bede's *VCP*: probably through Willibrord's mission, cf. *VCA* IV, 16 and Netzer, below.

[23] 'Virtutum tramitem enodabo', II, 1; and cf. such phrases as 'Unum adhuc miraculum . . . non omitto' (I, 6).

Ascetic-type miracles (e.g. the heavenly provision of food, and animal miracles) dominate in books II and III, healing miracles, which seemed particularly appropriate to Cuthbert's episcopate, in book IV.[24] The beginning or end of books often contain connecting passages or chapters characterizing Cuthbert's life in that phase, often emphasizing Cuthbert's saintly characteristics by describing them in words borrowed from the Bible or earlier saints' lives, above all Athanasius's *Vita Antonii* and Sulpicius Severus's *Vita Martini*.

The anonymous author strongly emphasizes that Cuthbert was predestined by God as one of the elect, right from childhood. In the opening chapters a child already addresses the eight-year-old Cuthbert prophetically as 'holy bishop and priest' and angels aid him, while as a young man still living a secular life Cuthbert sees a type of vision normally experienced only by contemplatives.[25] Bound up with this portrayal of Cuthbert as predestined from childhood is the fact that, despite the *vita*'s division into four books, the author sees no sequential development in Cuthbert's life. Instead he gives a flat block of stories on, say, Cuthbert the monk; or portrays him on Lindisfarne already 'contemplativam vitam in actuali agens'.[26] There is no attempt to chart Cuthbert's progress towards a more solitary and contemplative life — which is the more remarkable as Cuthbert's life *did* develop like that, and the *Vita Antonii* provides a model for such a sequential development. This, the anonymous ignored — probably because he stood in the tradition of Irish hagiography, where the idea of predestination and the concomitant static portrayal of a saint are the norm;[27] there may also be direct influence from the *Vita Martini*.[28] One other odd feature is that although the life was written by a Lindisfarne monk, only one story (set on the mainland!) and half another chapter deal with Cuthbert's period as prior of Lindisfarne. Perhaps there were virtually no miracles from this period;[29] or perhaps the terrible visitation of the plague around the early 680s broke the continuity of Lindisfarne traditions.[30]

For the historian, this early life has considerable merit, not least because the principles guiding the author's selection and presentation of material are not identical with Bede's, and are relatively straightforward. When the author quotes from other sources, he generally does so verbatim, and obviously; and

---

[24] See *VCA* IV, 2.

[25] *VCA* I, 3 – 5. M. Schütt, 'Ein Beda-Problem', *Anglia* 72 (1954), pp. 1 – 20, esp. pp. 12 – 14.

[26] *VCA* III, 1.

[27] E.g. Adomnan *V.Col.* III, 1, and cf. J. M. Picard, 'Structural Patterns in Early Irish Hagiography', *Peritia* 4 (1985), pp. 78 – 9. I would see these traits as owing more to the influence of Irish traditional tales than to Augustinianism (*contra* Schütt, art. cit.).

[28] Cf. C. Stancliffe, *St. Martin and his Hagiographer* (Oxford, 1983), pp. 94, 149 – 51.

[29] Possibly because this period was relatively brief (see below), or because the dissensions caused by Cuthbert's attempts to teach the monastic rule (*VCP* 16, p. 210) did not provide a suitable ambience in which happenings would be perceived as miracles wrought by Cuthbert.

[30] *VCP* 27 (pp. 246 – 8).

he normally does so only to describe Cuthbert's behaviour in general terms, not a specific incident. Nor will all parallels with other saints' lives necessarily be unhistorical; for Cuthbert sought to follow Christ, the pattern for all Christians, and probably also modelled himself on those very saints whose *vitae* influenced his biographer, seeing that they both came from Lindisfarne, and that Cuthbert taught by citing *patrum praecedentium gesta*, and resolved to live by the labour of his hands on Farne *iuxta exempla patrum* — probably thinking of St Antony.[31] In any case, the anonymous has not taken another saint's life as his model to such an extent that he stylizes all he says of Cuthbert to fit that model. Cuthbert may be described in words from the *Vita Antonii*, but the words are adapted to make them applicable to Cuthbert (who, for instance, was always cheerful);[32] and, while some of his miracles may be of the same type as those recorded of Antony,[33] the author wholly ignores the developmental aspect of the *Vita Antonii*. Again, at least four stories recall those told of St Benedict by Gregory the Great;[34] but the anonymous remains untouched by Gregory's didacticism, and by the frequency with which devils appear in his *Dialogues*, while many traits of Benedict find no answering echo in the anonymous's account of Cuthbert. The same reservations apply to the anonymous's use of Sulpicius Severus's *Vita Martini*: he borrows its wording to describe Cuthbert's attempt to unite the episcopal and monastic lives, and individual miracles or ways of introducing them may recall some passages of Sulpicius; but the parallels are limited,[35] and the anonymous does not *show* Cuthbert uniting his episcopal and monastic callings:[36] he simply gives us individual miracles performed by Cuthbert during his episcopate.

---

[31] *VCP* 7; *VCP* 19, and cf. Athanasius, *Vita Antonii* 25 (PL 73, col. 149. NB I cite *V.Ant.* according to the chapters in Evagrius's Latin translation.) Cf. G. Bonner, 'Saint Cuthbert — Soul Friend', in *Cuthbert, Saint and Patron*, ed. D. W. Rollason (Durham, 1987), pp. 28 – 30.

[32] See *VCA* III, 7, and cf. *V.Ant.* 13 and 40 (cols. 134, 156). Cf. Bonner, art. cit. pp. 26 – 7. See also below, n. 70.

[33] See appendix.

[34] See appendix. Direct knowledge of Gregory's *Dialogues* is confirmed by the verbal parallel describing the *corvus* who, *expansis alis . . . crocitare cepit*: *VCA* II, 5; Gregory, *Dialogi* II, 8, 3 (ed. A. de Vogüé, SC 260, p. 162).

[35] *VCA* II, 7 and *V. Mart.* 14, 1 – 2 (ed. J. Fontaine, SC 133, p. 282) is the only obvious one. I agree with Thacker (below) that books II and IV of *VCA* have a Martinian atmosphere; but the actual kind of miracles Cuthbert wrought in book II are, with the exception just noted, different. In book IV, healing miracles are too common in hagiography to be significant; the use of consecrated oil (*VCA* IV, 4 and *V. Mart.* 16) was normal; while the hallowed drink in *VCA* IV, 3 and 7 has no Martinian precedent. Further, although both saints were healed by angels, the incidents are very differently told (*VCA* I, 4 and *V. Mart.* 19, 4).

[36] Contrast Sulpicius emphasizing Martin's habitual use of ascetic practices for miracles (*V. Mart.* 14, 4; *Dialogi* II, 5, 6 (ed. C. Halm, CSEL 1, p. 186)); his continued humility (*V. Mart.* 16, 5; 25, 2 – 3; 26, 5; *Dial.* II, 1, 3 – 4; II, 3; III, 15); and his continuance in prayer, despite the demands made on him as bishop (*V. Mart.* 26, 2 – 4; *Dial.* II, 1, 2; II, 13, 8). Note too that while Martin's mature monks remained free for continual prayer, Cuthbert tried to support himself on Farne (*VCA* III, 5).

In other words, the anonymous enunciates the general characteristics of Cuthbert's life as a monk, hermit, or bishop in specific chapters which consist largely of quotations from other works[37] — and then appears to leave these general principles on one side while he gets on with the next batch of miracle stories. In these stories, the miraculous element and the parallels with incidents in other saints' lives may well be heightened; but most of them can be understood quite plausibly as being based on real events, which were perceived as miracles, while none of them is of the wholly impossible, magical type. Further, the miracles are told straightforwardly, within living memory of the events — and of the eyewitnesses cited —, and with accurate-sounding details.[38] It is the details and the incidental information which the anonymous lets fall which can best be relied upon, and from them we can glean much about Cuthbert's life: his custom of praying in solitude at night time, often by the shore; the normality of his preaching and teaching visits into the border country around Melrose when he was prior there; his perception and compassion, shown in his handling of Hildmer; his journeys far afield as a bishop, teaching, confirming, dedicating churches, blessing the sick, and visiting scattered communities.[39] The anonymous author is certainly wrong once, in depicting Cuthbert receiving the Petrine tonsure in Ripon. But we know why he doctors the story here, and at least it is obvious, and can be corrected by Bede. Probably Bede would have put the record straight if he had been wrong on other matters of substance.

Bede's prose *Life of Cuthbert* is in some ways the antithesis of the anonymous's.[40] He is excellent in portraying the sequence of events in Cuthbert's life. Gone are the predestinarianism, the flat blocks of material and division into four books; instead he gives a sequential account[41] which shows the development of Cuthbert's calling from boyhood to the monastery to the relative seclusion of St Cuthbert's Island, and finally to the full-blown seclusion of the Inner Farne, followed by his shouldering of the burden of pastoral care. Bede was also too careful a scholar to rewrite history blatantly,[42] and so he corrects the anonymous about Cuthbert's tonsuring. Further, Bede interviewed people himself and did not rely wholly on the earlier *Life*, thus introducing important new material, e.g. on the development of Cuthbert's life as a solitary, and on Boisil's and Cuthbert's deaths.[43] But Bede was a more

---

[37] *VCA* II, 1; III, 7; IV, 1.

[38] Cf. Berschin, below; and note the frequency with which individuals and places are named.

[39] II, 3 and 4; II, 5 – 7; II, 8; IV, 3 – 10.

[40] For *VCM*, see Lapidge and Thacker below. I shall concentrate largely on *VCP* because it includes more of the detailed information which is grist to a historian's mill.

[41] Cf. C. F. Altman, 'Two Types of Opposition and the Structure of Latin Saints' Lives', *Medievalia et Humanistica* n.s. 6 (1975), pp. 1 – 11; and Schütt, art. cit. pp. 14 – 20.

[42] Cf. *HE* III, 1. Bede may distort or give a false impression; but probably by omissions, rather than outright false statements, or by his imputing worthy but erroneous motives. See J. Campbell, 'Bede', in *Latin Historians*, ed. T. A. Dorey (London, 1966), at pp. 176 – 84.

[43] *VCP* 17 – 18; 8; 37 – 40. For Bede's concern for accuracy and his methods, see his preface (*Two Lives*, pp. 142 – 4). For information not in the *VCA*, he normally gives his source.

subtle writer than the anonymous; and so, for instance, he includes an elaborate death-bed speech of Cuthbert's which stresses the themes of unity and peace so near to Bede's own heart,[44] and which includes the warning to take his bones with them rather than that the monks should ever 'consent to iniquity and put your necks under the yoke of schismatics.' Presumably this is looking forward to a possible future when Lindisfarne might fall under domination by Christians who had not conformed to 'Roman' practices (the Picts?). But it is in the highest degree unlikely that Cuthbert, who appears to have enjoyed friendly relations with the Ionan Pictish church, would have thought like this. Is this Bede's own discreet way of expressing Cuthbert's commitment to the Roman cause, his equivalent of the anonymous's Petrine tonsure?[45]

Above all, Bede's subtlety and skill show in his shaping of the material to portray Cuthbert as an exemplary figure who at every stage of his life was concerned to help and teach others, while never relinquishing the contemplative ideal.[46] As Alan Thacker has shown, Bede here stylizes Cuthbert according to the monk-pastor ideal that he imbibed from Gregory the Great, explicitly pointing up Gregorian parallels to Cuthbert's miracles.[47] We thus need to handle Bede's account with care. He was a better historian in terms of weaving material into a sequential whole, he did additional research, and he wrote more on Cuthbert's contemplative life than the anonymous, and for all these reasons his prose *Life of Cuthbert* is valuable; but Bede's didactic concerns did lead him to portray Cuthbert in an essentially Gregorian mould, and this occasionally led him to alter the anonymous's account in the interests of didacticism, rather than truth.[48] We are thus fortunate in being able to set one *Vita Cuthberti* alongside the other, so having some control on each one's reliability.

One further source, the so-called *Annales Lindisfarnenses et Dunelmenses*, has been used since Plummer's time for its chronology of Cuthbert's monastic life. Plummer was doubtless misled by its first editor's belief that these annals, written into the margin of a twelfth-century copy of Easter tables, had at their core genuine Lindisfarne and Northumbrian entries from an early date.[49] However, the annals have since been re-edited and discussed by Wilhelm Levison, who has shown that the entries before 1066 were not being regularly

---

[44] E.g. his characterization of Adomnan as 'vir unitatis ac pacis studiosissimus' (*HE* V, 15).

[45] *VCP* 39; *Two Lives*, pp. 282 – 5, and cf. pp. 356 – 7. See Berschin's appendix below for this speech being in Bede's style, not Herefrith's. A biographer was allowed considerable license with the speeches placed in his protagonists' mouths. See D. P. Kirby, 'Bede and the Pictish Church', *Innes Review* 24 (1973), pp. 6 – 25 at pp. 10 – 13 for Cuthbert and the Picts, and for a possible context for Bede's remarks; cf. below, p. 31.

[46] *VCP* 9, 16, 22, 26.

[47] Thacker, 'Bede's Ideal of Reform', in *Ideal and Reality in Frankish and Anglo-Saxon Society*, ed. P. Wormald (Oxford, 1983), pp. 130 – 53 at pp. 138 – 42.

[48] See further below, pp. 31 – 3.

[49] Ed. G. H. Pertz, MGH, Scriptores 19 (1866), pp. 502 – 8. Cf. Plummer II, 266 – 7.

written up as events happened, but are a compilation put together at Durham in the twelfth century. It shares some features with Symeon of Durham's *Historia Dunelmensis ecclesiae*, and is based principally on Bede's *Ecclesiastical History*, the *Anglo-Saxon Chronicle*, and the Chronicle and Easter Cycles of Marianus Scotus (died 1082/3).[50] Some genuinely early jottings from the margins of Easter tables may have been incorporated;[51] but it should be regarded with extreme diffidence as a source for seventh-century Northumbria.

II   AN OUTLINE OF CUTHBERT'S LIFE[52]

Unusually for saints' lives, none of the lives of Cuthbert give any information on his birth or family background. We may deduce that Cuthbert was born *c*.635,[53] and that his family probably belonged to the lesser nobility or were perhaps well-to-do members of the freeman class of Bernicia.[54] Cuthbert grew to manhood in ordinary secular society; but two experiences when he was eight prompted him to take Christianity seriously,[55] and his readiness to pray for monks in imminent danger of drowning, even when it meant standing out from a jeering crowd, is striking.[56] It was as he was praying one night while shepherding in the Lammermuir hills that he saw the vision of Aidan's soul being carried up to heaven, which finally decided him to become a monk.[57] He thereupon entered the nearby monastery of Melrose, attracted by the reputation of its prior, Boisil.[58] The reference to Aidan's death dates this to 651.[59]

---

[50] 'Die "Annales Lindisfarnenses et Dunelmenses" kritisch untersucht und neu herausgegeben', *Deutsches Archiv für Erforschung des Mittelalters* 17 (1961), pp. 447 – 506.

[51] P. Hunter Blair, 'The Northumbrians and their Southern Frontier', *Archaeologia Aeliana* 4th ser. 26 (1948), pp. 106 – 12 (reprinted in Blair's *Anglo-Saxon Northumbria* (Variorum reprints; London, 1984)) argues pro such incipient annals; but see now Duncan (as n. 4) pp. 15 – 19.

[52] I make no pretence at giving a rounded account of Cuthbert; I seek only to establish the basic chronological outline of his life — itself a task more complex than is usually assumed, thanks to divergences between our sources.

[53] Calculated backwards from his becoming a monk *ab ineunte adulescentia* in 651: *VCP* 1; *HE* IV, 27(25). Bede was probably accurate over the onset of *adulescentia*, as he was (in *VCP* 1) over that of *pueritia* (in the fifteenth and eighth years repectively: Isidore, *Etymologiae* XI, ii, 3 – 4). This seems preferable to Colgrave's arguments, *Two Lives*, pp. 322 – 3.

[54] Total silence over his background and relatives perhaps tells against Cuthbert's belonging to the upper ranks of the nobility, as does his working as the shepherd of a lord (*VCA* I, 5). However, his journeying on horseback (*VCA* I, 6) and arrival at Melrose with horse, spear, and servant (*VCP* 6) is not the behaviour of a peasant; and his being fostered (*VCA* II, 7) may also point to noble birth. Cf. *Beowulf* lines 2428 – 31; ed. F. Klaeber (3rd edn. Boston, 1950), p. 91.

[55] *VCA* I, 3 – 4; *VCP* 1 – 2.

[56] *VCM* 3; *VCP* 3.

[57] *VCP* 4; *VCA* I, 5. Only Bede sees this vision as determining Cuthbert to become a monk.

[58] *VCP* 6; above, n. 14.

[59] *HE* III, 14; V, 24.

After some years at Melrose, Cuthbert accompanied his abbot, Eata, south to establish a new monastery at Ripon on a site given by King Alhfrith. Cuthbert was made guestmaster, a responsible office. Soon, however, Alhfrith came under the influence of Wilfrid, who converted him to Roman practices; and, on Eata's refusal to conform, he and his monks were ordered out of Ripon, and returned to Melrose. We cannot date this Ripon phase precisely, but its dénouement is all part of the increasing tension which necessitated the calling of the synod of Whitby, and it clearly had not lasted long. It must, then, have been late 650s/early 660s.[60]

Shortly after Eata and his monks had returned to Melrose, the synod of Whitby (664) pronounced in favour of accepting the Roman Easter and tonsure throughout Northumbria. Those who still adhered to Irish customs, including Colman, bishop of Northumbria, had to leave for Iona or Ireland. Tuda replaced Colman as bishop, while Eata became abbot of Lindisfarne.[61] It is usually stated that Eata then made Cuthbert (by now, it is thought, prior of Melrose) prior of Lindisfarne under him.[62] The authority for this is the *Annales Lindisfarnenses, s.a.* 664: 'Committitur interim ecclesia Lindisfarnensis Eatano abbati, ubi sanctus Cuthbertus constituitur prior.'[63] But the use of the word *prior* should make us wary. It is first attested in this sense in the early ninth century,[64] the normal seventh/eighth-century term being *praepositus*. In any case, the rest of the annal about Wilfrid and Chad carries the story up to 669, showing that the entry is a later composition summarizing all that followed from the synod of Whitby. We should therefore discard the twelfth-century *Annales* and look more closely at our early sources.

Bede begins chapter eight of his prose *Life of Cuthbert* with the monks' expulsion from Ripon, and then describes how Cuthbert and Boisil were both struck down by 'the plague which at that time carried off very many throughout the length and breadth of Britain.' Boisil died, but Cuthbert recovered and succeeded him as prior of Melrose, an office he held for some years before going to Lindisfarne. As prior of Melrose, one of Cuthbert's tasks was preaching to those who had lapsed into paganism because of the plague.[65] Now this plague is surely identical with the terrible plague of 664, which, according to Bede's *Ecclesiastical History*, followed soon after the synod of Whitby, carrying off Bishop Tuda and many others. In both sources the plague affected all Britain, and caused apostasy. Note too the *History*'s wording, *subita pestilentiae lues*, which tells against Plummer's theory that there must have been another plague (viz., that of the *Life of Cuthbert*) to carry off Boisil only a

---

[60] *HE* III, 25 and V, 18 (C and M pp. 296 – 7, 520 – 2); *VCP* 7 – 8. *VW* 7 – 8. Plummer II, 193 gives 661 as the year that Alhfrith transferred Ripon to Wilfrid.

[61] *HE* III, 26.

[62] Kirby, *Innes Review* 24, p. 10, is a shining exception.

[63] Ed. Levison, p. 480.

[64] Synod of Clovesho, 825; on the continent, the monastic decrees of 816/817. see Plummer I, p. xxviii, n. 5, and p. 370. I would like to thank R. Sharpe for these references.

[65] *VCP* 8 – 9. Bede's source was excellent: Herefrith.

year or so before 664.[66] Finally, note that Eata and Cuthbert only returned to Melrose shortly before the synod of Whitby, which does not leave Cuthbert sufficient time to be prior of Melrose *per aliquot annos*[67] if he transferred to Lindisfarne as early as 664.

Thus our early sources show that Cuthbert became prior of Melrose in 664 on Boisil's death, and remained there some years. Cuthbert's formation clearly owed much to Boisil, who had attracted him to Melrose in the first place, nurtured him there as a young man, teaching by word and example and foretelling the course of his life, and finally spent the last week of his life reading with him through John's Gospel.[68] When Cuthbert succeeded Boisil as prior, he followed Boisil's example in his extensive pastoral work among the country folk in remote areas, staying away to teach them for a week or more.[69] But at the same time, solitary vigils and prayers through the night — besides the customary communal office — were normal for him, as we see from his vigil by the shore, even in the sea, at Coldingham.[70] Perhaps the most interesting episode from these Melrose years is Cuthbert's journey to the Picts.[71] He sailed with two monks the day after Christmas, but they became stormbound in the *Niuduera regio*, with nothing to eat. Miraculously provided with food for Epiphany, the monks were later able to continue their journey. As Kirby has pointed out, to set sail for the Picts at that festive and wintry season — and with little or no food — implies that they planned to spend Epiphany with the Picts. This is particularly interesting as it shows Cuthbert on friendly terms with Pictish Christians *after* he had adopted the Roman tonsure and Easter in 664, but before the Picts had done so *c.* 715/717.[72]

For the way this Melrose period ended, we turn first to the anonymous *Life*, III, 1: Cuthbert served the Lord well at Melrose, performing many miracles, 'postremo tamen secularem gloriam fugiens clam et occulte abscedens enavigavit. Deinde a venerabili et sancto episcopo Eata invitatus, et coacte ad hanc insulam nostram que dicitur Lindisfarnae cum adiutorio Dei voluntatis advenit . . .' Here Cuthbert is portrayed as fleeing worldly glory (presumably resulting from his miracles) and sailing off. Was this a first attempt to seek an island hermitage? Perhaps; but as the Tweed is just about navigable as far upstream as Old Melrose, may be Cuthbert just left by boat. In any case, the picture corresponds with the anachoresis of a St Antony or St Hilarion: the

---

[66] *HE* III, 27 and 30; Plummer II, 195, only arguing so because he accepted the *Ann. Lindis.* 664 date for Cuthbert's transference to Lindisfarne: II, 267.

[67] *VCP* 9. Bede attributes the stories of Cuthbert's preaching and his visit to Coldingham to his time as prior: *VCP* 9 – 10, 12 – 14.

[68] *VCP* 6; 8; 22. See Ward below.

[69] *VCP* 9.

[70] *VCA* II, 3; *VCP* 10: *more solito*, as similarly in *VCP* 11 and 16, so confirming *VCA* II, 1, 'Pernoctabat in oratione sepissime'.

[71] *VCA* II, 4 (cf. *VCP* 11, and P. H. Blair, 'The Bernicians and their Northern Frontier', pp. 165 – 7, reprinted in *A – S Northumbria*).

[72] *Innes Review* 24, pp. 10 – 11.

hermit's withdrawal from everyday life — and especially, head-turning admiration — to somewhere where he can be alone for God.[73] This is surely how the anonymous intended the passage to be read: it marks the beginning of his third book, devoted to Cuthbert's life as a hermit, and the chapter is headed 'How, living according to the Scriptures, he finally took to a solitary life on an island . . .' The chapter duly allots just one sentence to Cuthbert's period as prior of Lindisfarne before bringing him to Farne as a hermit.

Bede's metrical *Life* also portrays Cuthbert's departure from Melrose as anachoresis, even heading the relevant chapter: 'qualiter anachoresim meditatus apud Lindisfarnenses monachos vixerit.'[74] Here, too, Cuthbert wishes to avoid human praise, and 'prefers to wander over the secret tracts of a solitary place, where, with God as witness, he may be free, guarded from the fame of human praise.' But then, at his bishop's command, he becomes a monk at Lindisfarne and his settling on Farne is postponed to the next chapter. Bede's wording is, however, more guarded than the anonymous's: Cuthbert *preferred* solitude, but there are no specific verbs to match the anonymous's *fugiens, abscedens, enavigavit.* What Cuthbert actually does is left studiously vague.

In his prose *Life,* Bede is even more diplomatic: the whole initiative now rests with Eata. When Cuthbert had been many years at Melrose and shown his spiritual powers, 'transtulit eum reverentissimus abbas ipsius Eata in monasterium . . . ut ibi quoque regulam monachicae perfectionis . . . doceret et . . . ostenderet.'[75] Here Eata deliberately transfers Cuthbert *so that* he can teach the Lindisfarne brothers. This is subtly different from the anonymous's account where Cuthbert's departure from Melrose was his own decision, occasioned by his desire to flee praise.

Which account comes closest to historical reality? That, I suggest, of the anonymous monk. For, writing within eighteen years of Cuthbert's death, while men like Herefrith were still alive, he probably knew what had happened; and why should he have portrayed the prior of Melrose, a man with great responsibilities, 'secretly and privately making off', unless that is what Cuthbert actually did? After all, it gave him problems with the structure of his *Life*; for it was probably his desire to get Cuthbert to Farne Island as soon as possible after his first move in that direction which explains why he placed the only story he tells of Cuthbert's time as prior of Lindisfarne out of sequence, at the end of book II. And, although the general picture of Cuthbert's anachoresis resembles the behaviour of eastern monks, I am not aware of the anonymous modelling this passage on any source. We can, however, understand why Bede should have wished to modify this passage. Bede was far more didactic than the anonymous, and was inclined to pass over

---

[73] *Vita Antonii* 24. *Vita Hilarionis* 34 (PL 23, col. 48B); also chs. 30, 33, 37 and 43. Cassian, *Conlationes* XX, 1 (CSEL 13, pp. 554 – 6). Cf. P. Rousseau in *JTS* n.s. 22 (1971), p. 391.
[74] *VCM* 14.
[75] *VCP* 16.

such doings of churchmen as set unfortunate examples.[76] From this viewpoint it would not do to show the prior of Melrose, who was probably in charge of that monastery on a day-to-day basis,[77] slipping away in pursuit of the eremetical life. In a closely comparable case, Bede discreetly omits Ceolfrith's exodus from Monkwearmouth where he was acting as prior, while Benedict Biscop was abroad.[78] Conversely, Bede emphasizes the goodwill of the abbot and monks of Lindisfarne when Cuthbert does eventually leave to become a hermit.[79]

When Cuthbert arrived at Lindisfarne, how long he spent there, and when he left for Farne, we cannot know with any precision. Bede says he was prior of Melrose 'per aliquot annos' (some years, a few years, or several years); and elsewhere, that he was at Melrose for 'many years'.[80] Both authors assign him 'many years' on Lindisfarne and Farne.[81] The anonymous and Bede's metrical life both say that Cuthbert was recalled after his departure from Melrose by *Bishop* Eata, who assigned him to Lindisfarne. This should mean 678 or later; however, Bede's prose life calls Eata 'abbot', which makes me chary of putting much weight on this point.[82] Despite the 'many years' assigned to Cuthbert's stay on Lindisfarne by both biographers, this phase may have been shorter than that spent at Melrose or Farne: this might partially explain their puzzling dearth of stories about Cuthbert at Lindisfarne.[83] Finally, the *Annales Lindisfarnenses* give 676 for Cuthbert's departure for Farne, assigning him nine years there, as does the tenth-century *Historia de sancto Cuthberto*.[84] This might derive from a jotting in the margin of an early Easter table, but we have no means of telling.

For Cuthbert's priorate at Lindisfarne, we depend almost wholly on Bede.[85] Clearly Cuthbert did not have an easy time. Within the monastery he had to persuade the brothers to accept a monastic rule rather than their traditional customs, and this aroused bitterness. Meanwhile he continued, as at Melrose, to visit and teach the neighbouring population. Bede also shows us Cuthbert continuing to spend whole nights in vigils, prayer, and psalmody, sometimes working or walking round the island. This is one indication of his continued desire for solitary prayer, which was taken further when Cuthbert retired to the tiny island south-west of the main monastery on Lindisfarne, now known

---

[76] Campbell, 'Bede', pp. 176–9.

[77] *VCP* 16 suggests that Eata was simultaneously abbot of Lindisfarne and Melrose.

[78] Cf. Bede, *Historia abbatum* 7 and the anonymous *Vita Ceolfridi* (or '*Historia abbatum*') 8: Plummer I, 370, 390–1.

[79] *VCP* 17; cf. also 22.

[80] *VCA* III, 1 and 7; *VCP* 17. *HE* IV, 37 (C and M, p. 430).

[81] *VCA* III, 1 and 7; *VCP* 17. *HE* IV, 37 (C and M, p. 430).

[82] *VCA* III, 1; *VCM*, lines 377–9; *VCP* 16. Eata bishop in 678: *HE* IV, 12; V, 24; though cf. *HE* III, 26.

[83] Cf. above, p. 25.

[84] Ed. Levison, p. 481. *HSC* 3.

[85] Cuthbert prior: *VCA* II, 8. See *VCP* 16 for what follows.

as St Cuthbert's Island.[86] Again, Bede is our only source. Cuthbert lived here
relatively secluded, '[fighting] with the invisible enemy, by prayer and
fasting'. He then won the abbot's and brothers' permission to go and settle on
Farne Island, remote and uninhabited (though formerly used by Aidan for
retreats).[87] Here Cuthbert built himself an oratory and a cell, surrounding
both by a wall so high that it shut out all save the heavens above.[88]

His life as a hermit now began in earnest, and we hear of his warfare with
the demons, the hermit's traditional enemies.[89] At first Cuthbert used to go
out from his cell to greet his visitors, but Bede portrays his gradual seclusion,
till he came to resemble a medieval anchorite within his enclosure:

> Then, when his zeal for perfection grew, he shut himself up in his hermitage,
> and, remote from the gaze of men, he learned to live a solitary life of fasting,
> prayers and vigils, rarely having conversation from within his cell with visitors
> and that only through a window. At first he opened this and rejoiced to see and
> be seen by the brethren with whom he spoke; but, as time went on, he shut even
> that, and opened it only for the sake of giving his blessing or for some other
> definite necessity.[90]

The underlying purpose of this anchoritic existence is explained by Bede: 'for
the sake of the sweetness of divine contemplation, [Cuthbert rejoiced] to be
silent and to hear no human speech.' For by such men '*will the God of Gods be
seen*'.[91]

But Cuthbert's direct involvement with other people did not die away;
perhaps it was intensified. For Bede shows us people still seeking him out,
even from the more distant parts of Britain, drawn by the reputation of his
spiritual powers.[92] They came to him as a spiritual guide, with their sins and
their worries, and he was able to put all into its proper perspective under God.
Here we see the paradox of the solitary, who, just because he has distanced
himself from the everyday bustle and come to terms with the noise inside
himself, has the insight to help others.[93]

Amongst Cuthbert's admirers were members of the royal family. In 684
Aelfflaed, the king's sister and abbess of Whitby, adjured Cuthbert to tell her

---

[86] *VCP* 17; identifiable from *VCP* 42.
[87] *VCP* 17; *HE* III, 16. it is 1½ miles offshore from the nearest part of the mainland, and nearly 7
miles south-east from Lindisfarne.
[88] *VCP* 17.
[89] *VCP* 17; 22. Brother Harold, SSF, a contemporary hermit living in Northumberland, has
spoken of his way of life as a battlefield, learning not to turn away from God; and of using silence
to come to terms with all the noise inside oneself, replacing it with the word of God. (BBC Radio
programme on St Cuthbert, broadcast 7 July 1987.) Maybe this 'noise' is the medieval hermit's
'demons'?
[90] *VCP* 18, trans. Colgrave, *Two Lives*, pp. 218 – 21.
[91] *VCP* 1; 17, citing Ps. 83:8.
[92] *VCP* 22. *VCM* 20. Cf. *VCA* III, 7.
[93] Cf. Cassian, *Con.* XXIV, 19.

what would become of her brother, King Ecgfrith, and who would succeed him; she also let slip that Ecgfrith wanted to make Cuthbert a bishop.[94] All turned out as Cuthbert prophesied: Cuthbert was elected to replace Bishop Tunberht of Hexham, and was most reluctantly compelled to submit.[95] His consecration was postponed till Easter 685, it being meanwhile arranged that he should go to the see of Lindisfarne, while Eata went to Hexham.

The anonymous author, quoting from Sulpicius's *Vita Martini*, claimed that Cuthbert the bishop still remained a monk — and anchorite — at heart and in his dress and bearing: he did not *'propositum monachi* et anachoritae *virtutem desereret.'*[96] Is this pure hagiographer's license? How could Cuthbert, with a diocese reaching from the Borders to Carlisle,[97] retain anything of his former solitary life? Surely a bishop was bound to get enmeshed in secular society; and are not its values implied by the richness of the pectoral cross he was buried with, and by his involvement in gift-exchange, even on Farne?[98] And what of his close relationship with Ecgfrith's family? These questions are valid, for Cuthbert as bishop was inevitably involved in secular society, as when looking after the queen while Ecgfrith was fighting the Picts.[99] But involvement does not necessarily lead to subservience: Cuthbert gave Ecgfrith advice which he did not like and refused to follow.[100] Cuthbert was not simply court chaplain, but preached and confirmed in remote areas and in villages stricken by the plague.[101] His 'retinue' comprised priests or devout Christians who would approach the house of a noble singing psalms or hymns, somewhat as in Aidan's days, while even when eating or talking with others, he remained open to spiritual revelations of a telepathic nature; and when offered wine or beer, he asked for water.[102] There are, however, signs of accommodation in his willingness to drink wine when ill, ride a horse when necessary, and keep a precious gift out of respect for its donor's feelings.[103] Perhaps it was just because of the difficulty of remaining wholly free from worldly concerns that Cuthbert needed the remoteness of Farne. For the most telling evidence of Cuthbert's remaining a monk and anchorite at heart was his decision to resign his bishopric within two years, when he felt death approaching, and to return to his hermitage on Farne. Again, the anonymous's wording is interesting: 'episcopatus sui secularem honorem sponte deserens'. He resigns willingly (*sponte*) what he had undertaken only on compulsion (*invitus et coactus*),

[94] *VCA* III, 6; *VCP* 24.
[95] *HE* IV, 28 (26); *VCP* 24; *VCA* IV, 1 'invitus et coactus lacrimans et flens, abstractus est'.
[96] *VCA* IV, 1, quoting (in italics) *V. Mart.* 10, 1 – 2.
[97] *VCP* 37, 38.
[98] Pl. 35. *VCP* 33, 37; cf. Ceolfrith's concern, *V. Ceolfridi* 22.
[99] *VCP* 27.
[100] *HE* IV, 26 (24) (C and M, p. 428).
[101] *VCA* IV, 5 – 6; *VCP* 32 – 3.
[102] *VCA* IV, 7 (and cf. IV, 5 – 6); cf. *HE* III, 5. *VCA* IV, 8, 10; *VCP* 27; 34. *VCP* 35.
[103] *VCP* 37. *VCA* II, 8 (cf. *VCP* 9). *VCP* 37.

abandoning (*deserens*) the 'worldly honour' of his bishopric, where previously he had accepted the episcopate without abandoning (*desereret*) his commitment as a monk. Bede understandably avoids such words, with their negative connotations for episcopacy.[104]

Cuthbert spent Christmas 686 with the brothers at Lindisfarne, and then withdrew to Farne.[105] It was an astonishing decision: to lay down the episcopal burden and remain in the Lindisfarne community when he sensed death approaching would have been understandable. But to sail off alone to an island hermitage which is frequently cut off for a week or more in rough weather, and from which all inhabited land is often blotted out by mist; to go there, alone, in winter, when death was approaching — that naked fact speaks volumes for Cuthbert's trust in God, and for what he saw as essential: 'that, freed from outside anxieties, he might await the day of his death, or rather his entrance into heavenly life, in the undisturbed practice of prayers and psalm-singing.'[106]

Cuthbert died on 20 March 687; and, had his wish been granted, he would have been buried in his cell on Farne, and not shipped back for honourable burial on Holy Island.[107]

III   PASTOR AND SOLITARY[108]

Cuthbert's life reveals two patterns: a progression towards the solitary life which begins in his teens with his night vigils and finds its ultimate fulfilment on Farne; secondly, and concurrently, a pastoral involvement which runs throughout, whether as guestmaster, prior, soulfriend, or bishop. Other themes could, time permitting, be profitably explored; but the pastor/solitary one appears as the leitmotif of Cuthbert's life, and is distinctive and intriguing. It is worth delving to the root of it.

For the background to western attempts to balance the calling to be a solitary focused continuously on God in prayer, and a Christlike outgoing love and availability for others, we should turn back to the fourth and fifth centuries. First, there is the Egyptian anchoritic model, transmitted to the west through Athanasius's *Vita Antonii* and writings of Jerome and Cassian. Antony's life comprised a series of progressive withdrawals further and further from society; but conversely once he had outfaced the demons in the desert and learnt to live in solitude, people flocked to him for help and counsel. Antony often refused to come out to the crowd, lamented his lost solitude, and

---

[104] *VCA* IV, 11; cf. *VCP* 34; 36.
[105] *VCP* 37.
[106] *VCP* 34.
[107] *VCP* 37 – 9. Cf. Herity, below.
[108] Lack of space allows only a compressed summary here; I hope to publish a fuller account elsewhere.

feared lest the miracles he wrought amongst them would puff him up with pride, and so he fled to the inner desert. After this, though often compelled to emerge to talk to people, he did so reluctantly, and never stayed long; for he likened a monk lingering in society to a fish out of water.[109] The rationale for such a life was provided for westerners by John Cassian. The monk's immediate object was purity of heart, which would enable him to contemplate God in accordance with the beatitude, 'Blessed are the pure in heart, for they shall see God.'[110] This goal could be attained only by one who stripped off all that bound him to the outside world, leaving behind even charitable works which were at most considered appropriate for the 'active' as opposed to the 'contemplative' life. Indeed, all that disturbed inner peace and purity must be shunned, hence the maxim: ' " a monk ought to flee women and bishops entirely." For neither allows him . . . to concentrate on the silence of his cell any further, nor to cleave to the divine vision through the contemplation of holy things with most pure eyes.'[111] Thus the eastern ideal of the contemplative life seemed inimical to the calling to be simultaneously a pastor and a contemplative.

The west, however, did not take over this ideal in its starkest form, but adapted it somewhat; it also learnt of eastern cenobitism. Further, the west experimented with ways of combining monasticism and pastoral care. The most strikingly original development is that of Augustine of Hippo, who created a true synthesis between the monastic and clerical lives.[112] Already living in a community before being pushed forward for ordination in 391, he responded by founding a monastery within the church precincts, and, when he was bishop, he obliged all his clergy to adopt a communal monastic life in the bishop's house. Of course, he wished that his episcopal duties left him more time within the monastery, but it is no longer a question of two callings apparently pulling in opposite directions. His ideal of the Christian life was of a *social*, not a solitary life; he looked back to the communal life of the apostles in Acts 4:32 – 7, not to Elijah and Elisha; and even a mystical vision of the kind normally associated with solitary contemplation could be a shared experience for Augustine.[113] He thus broke down the barriers between contemplatives and other Christians. Whereas Cassian had seen the contemplative and active lives in terms of a Mary/Martha contrast, Augustine saw the real contrast as lying between everyone in this world on the one hand; and, on the other, our blessed state in heaven. On earth we must all of us have something of Martha about us, and no one can attain more than the most fleeting glimpse of God. Further, the true contemplative life must flow over into love for man, especially in bringing others to the love of God. Thus for

[109] *V.Ant.* esp. chs. 24, 53.
[110] *Con.* I, 4 and 10.
[111] Cassian, *De institutis coenobiorum* XI, 18 (CSEL 17, p. 203).
[112] G. B. Ladner, *The Idea of Reform* (Cambridge, Mass., 1959), pp. 190 – 6, 334 – 40, 353 – 65.
G. Lawless, *Augustine of Hippo and his Monastic Rule* (Oxford, 1987), passim.
[113] *Confessiones* IX, 10.

Augustine, the two lives should be held in balance: 'none must be in leisure in such a way that in that leisure he does not ponder what is useful for his neighbor or be so active that he does not seek out the contemplation of God.'[114] The combination of helping others and practising contemplation becomes the ideal, though it must be added that Augustine's idea of contemplation, now something that we all should aim at, was different from Cassian's, and the actual vision of God somewhat receded from being the goal of this life to becoming attainable only in heaven.

Augustine's insistence on the interconnections between the active and contemplative lives bore fruit above all in his influence on Gregory the Great; for Gregory took over Augustine's teaching and developed it in his own influential writings.[115] Above all, he expanded upon how the claims of the two lives might be reconciled, preaching the superiority of the 'mixed' contemplative-cum-active life over that of the more purely contemplative. He portrays Jesus as the paradigm of the mixed life, and urges preachers to practise both; for the broader that each soul becomes in loving its neighbours, the higher it reaches in the knowledge of God. And as no one can cleave for long to contemplation, so when one sinks back it is helpful to engage in the good works of the active life which may in their turn act as a springboard towards divine contemplation. Gregory particularly emphasizes the role of preachers who bring others to God: this renders them superior to the pure contemplatives.

Meanwhile, a very different attempt at combining the monastic and episcopal callings had been made by St Martin, who, after various eremetical experiments, founded a monastery near Poitiers in 360, and continued to live as a monk even after his election as bishop of Tours *c.*371, founding a new monastery at Marmoutier, just the other side of the Loire from his episcopal city.[116] In Martin's life we can discern the tensions between his monastic yearnings, and the duties falling to a late Roman bishop; between Martin, and the cathedral clergy of Tours and his fellow bishops. Martin sought to delegate as much business as possible to his clergy, who appear not to have been monks, while he sat apart in an inner sanctum, his mind always focused in prayer.[117] Martin lived in his monastery, where all mature monks spent their time in prayer; he journeyed accompanied by monks, not clerics; and he wrought fewer miracles as a monk-bishop than as a simple monk.[118] Sulpicius's presentation of Martin as a perfect monk and perfect bishop is a literary *tour de force*, but it was not easy in real life. Nor was it easy to imitate in

---

[114] *De civitate Dei* XIX, 19, trans. Ladner, op. cit. pp. 337 – 8.

[115] C. Butler, *Western Mysticism* (London etc. 1922), pp. 195 – 241, 268 – 9, usefully collects the texts and illustrates the debt to Augustine. Gregory did not, however, take over Augustine's fusion of the clerical and monastic lives.

[116] *V.Mart.* 6, 4 – 7, 1; 9 – 10.

[117] Sulpicius Severus, *Dial.* II, 1, esp. §2; *V. Mart.* 10, 3; 26, 3 – 4. Stancliffe, *St. Martin*, pp. 346 – 8, 354 – 9. Cf. Ladner, op. cit. p. 351.

[118] *V.Mart.* 10, 6; *Dial.* II, 4, 1.

the full sense of combining true contemplation with episcopal office — at least as the latter developed on the continent.

In Ireland, however, the relationship between bishops and monks, and church leadership, responsibility, and pastoral care, all worked out rather differently — largely because the bishop's role developed along different lines there. In Ireland, each petty kingdom (*tuath*) had its own bishop, making for very small dioceses, and there was no political vacuum for bishops to fill, as in former provinces of the Roman Empire. Thus even a *tuath* bishop had nothing like the responsibilities and power that fell to bishops elsewhere. Further, confederations of monasteries grew up, each headed by its abbot, significantly termed *princeps*. The Columban confederation, headed by the abbot of Iona, is one example.[119] The abbot controlled the monastery's life and wealth; and large monasteries contained monks in episcopal orders who were responsible for all liturgical functions requiring bishops but still subject to their own abbot, the latter being the effective head of his church. All this meant that the governmental, administrative, and judicial concerns which weighed so heavy on continental bishops were light or non-existent for Irish bishops (and conversely, that monasticism and anchoritism could develop there without the bishop's restraining hand); and this explains why the Irish looked for a different kind of candidate for the episcopate: 'its qualification was saintliness of life, not administrative ability.'[120] So, for instance, Brigit is portrayed seeking out a solitary when she requires a bishop.[121] And just as anchorites with their ideal of contemplation were considered suitable as bishops, so emphasis is placed on monastic virtues for bishops: alongside the Antonian model, that of St Martin was influential in Ireland, and a man was considered competent to exercise pastoral care 'when he is competent to answer for his own soul first.'[122]

Amongst the Irish we often see a genuine pastoral concern going hand in hand with a deep yearning for the hermit's life of contemplation; as Columbanus put it: 'You know that I love the salvation of many, and seclusion for myself: the one for the progress of the Lord, that is, of His church; the other for my own desire.'[123] His life bears out these twin concerns. He preached among the heathen Swabians, planned to preach to the Wends, and of course spent much time organizing his monastic foundations in Burgundy where recruits streamed in, and where his efforts did much to respiritualize areas whose Christianity was only nominal. And yet he used to withdraw to a cave for solitary prayer to prepare for feast days. Often he withdrew for long periods at a stretch, sometimes being fifty days or more

[119] *HE* III, 4. R. Sharpe, 'Some problems concerning the organization of the church in early medieval Ireland', *Peritia* 3 (1984), pp. 230 – 70.
[120] A. H. Thompson in *Bede: His Life, Times and Writings*, ed. Thompson (Oxford, 1935), p. 62.
[121] Cogitosus, *Vita S. Brigidae*, preface (PL 72, cols. 777 – 8).
[122] 'Apgitir Chrábaid: The Alphabet of Piety' §18, ed. and trans. V. Hull, *Celtica* 8 (1968), pp. 68 – 9.
[123] *Epist.* 4, 4; ed. and trans. G. S. M. Walker, *Sancti Columbani opera* (Dublin, 1957), pp. 28 – 9.

away.[124] Another Irish *peregrinus*, Fursey, similarly pursued both pastoral and contemplative callings, but successively. While ill, Fursey had his famous vision, and this sent him out to preach throughout Ireland. After ten years, 'unable to stand the crowds overwhelming him', Fursey retreated with a few brothers to an island, and soon after left for East Anglia. Here Fursey again preached and founded a monastery, but then 'desiring to separate himself from every care of the world and of his own monastery', he entrusted the latter to others and withdrew to live the contemplative life; and then, when interrupted by the king's needs and heathen invaders, he finally withdrew to Gaul.[125] Here, the pattern is of lengthy successive periods of pastoral work, followed by seclusion, repeated two or three times over.

Seventh-century Northumbria was heir to all these ways of balancing the contemplative and the pastoral ideals; and, speaking very, very generally, the Cuthbert hagiography divides into the two main traditions discussed. On the one hand the anonymous *Life*, with its account of Cuthbert's attempted anachoresis when prior and the contemplative's somewhat negative attitude towards episcopacy, belongs in the Egyptian, Martinian, and Irish traditions.[126] On the other hand stands Bede, for whom the two most influential authors were Gregory and Augustine, whom he quotes about the active and contemplative lives. His Cuthbert exactly embodies his own teaching on how one rises from active perfection to the contemplative life, and on how the great apostles Peter and John were not simply a flawless active and flawless contemplative respectively, but both achieved perfection in both spheres.[127] Not surprisingly Bede omits Cuthbert's anachoresis and all negative phraseology about pastoral care and episcopacy, emphasizing instead Cuthbert's obedience to his abbot, that the solitary life was not necessarily superior to the cenobitic, and that Cuthbert, even as an enclosed contemplative, never ceased teaching other people.[128] He portrays Lindisfarne's Irish-derived constitution, where the bishop and his clergy formed part of the monastic community under the abbot, as being simply what Gregory had recommended to Augustine (of Canterbury) following the Acts 4:32 model.[129] His description of Cuthbert's clothing as neither showy not shabby is reminiscent of Possidius on Augustine's clothing,[130] and he explicitly compares Cuthbert's miracles to those of Antony, Benedict, *and Augustine.*[131]

---

[124] Jonas, *Vita Columbani*, esp. chs. 27; 8 – 12 (MGH, Scriptores Rerum Merovingicarum 4, pp. 102 – 4, 74 – 8).

[125] *Vita S. Fursei*, chs. 21, 24 – 9; ed. W. W. Heist, *Vitae Sanctorum Hiberniae* (Brussels, 1965), pp. 47 – 9.

[126] Gregory's Benedict, of course, leaves monasteries — but for strictly *pastoral*, not eremitic, reasons: *Dial.* II, 3 and 8,5.

[127] *Homelia* I, 9 (CCSL 122, pp. 64 – 5). M. L. W. Laistner, 'The Library of the Venerable Bede', in *Bede*, ed. Thompson, pp. 248 – 51. Thacker, 'Bede's Ideal', pp. 132 – 4, 138 – 45.

[128] *VCP* 22.

[129] *VCP* 16.

[130] *VCP* 16; *Vita Augustini* 22, 1, ed. A. A. R. Bastiaensen (Vite dei santi 3; 1975), p. 184.

[131] *VCP* 19 – 20; 38. Cf. Berschin, below, appendix.

Are we reduced, then, to saying no more than that the anonymous stylizes Cuthbert in one way, Bede in another? I do not think we need be so pessimistic about placing Cuthbert himself within the various traditions; for, as we saw in I above, there are limits to the *Lives'* stylization of Cuthbert. To begin with, it is clear that Cuthbert did not in reality belong to the Augustinian tradition with its emphasis on the social, not solitary nature of the ideal Christian life, with its insistence that the would-be contemplative should always put the church's needs before his own call to solitary contemplation, and with its premise that it was possible to live both the active and contemplative lives simultaneously. What Cuthbert actually did belies this ideal. What of the other hagiographic models? The Antonian model fits only for Cuthbert's eremetical side; but Cuthbert was a priest and bishop, and he was far more pastoral than Antony was: at Melrose he would journey out to preach to people — he did not simply respond to those who came to him. In many ways the Martinian model fits Cuthbert well: certainly it allows for both pastoral concerns and for a desire for a life of continuous prayer. However, even here the fit is not perfect; for Martin did not seek absolute solitude, and he remained at his post as a bishop to the bitter end, despite premonitions of his death.[132]

If we judge Cuthbert by what he did, rather than the way in which his hagiographers strive to present him, then clearly he fits convincingly into an Irish mould — which was in its turn influenced by Antonian and Martinian ideals, while not being identical with either. The idea of laying aside office and retiring to live the religious life may well owe something to the Irish.[133] Irish are such ascetic features as praying waist-deep in cold water, and Cuthbert's concern with penitence;[134] but beyond that, the whole practice of retreating to island hermitages is very Irish,[135] as also is the combination of genuine pastoral concern combined or alternating with a deep desire to cut loose from all ties and make off alone, for contemplation's sake. As far as the polarity between the pastoral and solitary callings is concerned, Fursey provides a closer analogy than either Antony or Martin — and it is all the more telling in that there are no obvious traces of the *Vita Fursei*'s wording in the *Lives* of Cuthbert.

In a sense, of course, this is only what we would expect in a country recently envangelized by the Irish, which on other evidence was deeply influenced by Irish ascetic spirituality.[136] But it is interesting because the Lindisfarne diocese was many times bigger than any Irish diocese, and Anglo-Saxon bishops had

---

[132] Stancliffe, *St. Martin*, p. 24. Sulpicius Severus, *ep.* 3, §§6 and 9 – 13 (SC 133, pp. 336 – 40).
[133] Ceollach, the Irish bishop of Mercia, felt free to leave it for Iona: *HE* III, 21, 24. Cf. also *V. Ceolf.* 2, 21, and C. Stancliffe, 'Kings who Opted Out', in *Ideal and Reality*, ed. Wormald, pp. 154 – 76.
[134] *VCA* II, 3; *VCP* 16.
[135] See Herity, below.
[136] Stancliffe, art. cit., esp. p. 168.

judicial duties more reminiscent of those of continental bishops.[137] Aidan, Eadberht (Cuthbert's episcopal successor), and other Irish-tradition bishops sought to retain the balance of solitary prayer and episcopal duties by periodically retreating to secluded places after Columbanus's pattern: in Bishop Eadberht's case, to St Cuthbert's Island for all of every Advent and Lent.[138] While we rightly marvel at the wealth implied by St Cuthbert's pectoral cross and the superb products of the Lindisfarne scriptorium, Eadberht's example should prevent us from being too cynical about the genuineness of the God-ward commitment of late seventh-century Lindisfarne bishops, and about the picture, which emerges from the *Lives*, of Cuthbert as a man who was determined to put the claims of God first. It is salutary to recall that Bishop Eadberht was not present at the translation of Cuthbert's body on 20 March 698 because, it being Lent, he was on his customary retreat on St Cuthbert's Island. And what is so impressive is that even when the excited monks came running to tell him of the incorruption of Cuthbert's body, Eadberht contented himself with giving them instructions, while he stayed put.[139] Would Cuthbert, in comparable circumstances, have acted any differently?

---

[137] Theodore, *Penitential* II, 2, 4; ed. Haddan and Stubbs, *Councils* III, 191.
[138] *VCP* 42. *HE* III, 16; IV, 3; V, 2.
[139] *VCP* 42.

APPENDIX

SELECT PARALLEL MIRACLES IN SAINTS' LIVES

(Note: I have excluded all Cuthbert's healing miracles as parallels there are so plentiful.)

A. Nature Miracles

Miracles wrought by/for saint

	(Cuthbert) VCA	VCP	VCM	Athanasius, V.Ant.	Sulpicius, V.Mart., ep., Dial.	Gregory I, Dial. II	Adomnan, V.Col.
Birds/animals serve him	II, 3, 5; cf. III, 5	10, 12, cf. 20	8, 10 cf. 18	—	—	II, 8	—
Divine provision of bread	I, 6; II, 2	5, 7	6, 7	—	(cf. D I, 11)	—	—
of other food	II, 4 & 5	11, 12	9, 10	—	—	II, 21	—
Makes water taste like wine	—	35	28	—	—	—	II, 1 turns it into wine
Prays, and a spring breaks out	III, 3	18	16	27	—	II, 5	II, 10
Late-sown barley thrives	—	19	—	—	—	—	II, 3
Moves impossibly heavy stone to build hermitage	III, 2	17	—	—	—	II, 9	—
Prayers change wind, help monks/sailors	—	3; cf. 36	3 (also cf. 5)	—	cf. D III, 14, 1-2	(cf. II, 33)	II, 12, 13 15, 45
Deflects flames from house by prayer	II, 7	14	12	—	VM 14, 1-2	(cf. I, 6)	—

B. Prophecies, Visions, Telepathy

	(C u t h b e r t)			Athanasius, V.Ant.	Sulpicius, V.Mart., ep., Dial.	Gregory I, Dial. II	Adomnan, V.Col.
	VCA	VCP	VCM				
Prophecies							
Saint prophesies concerning:							
king's death	III, 6	24	21	—	VM 20, 8-9	II, 15	I, 12-15
royal succession	III, 6	24	21	—	—	—	I, 9-11
own future office	III, 6	24	21	—	—	—	—
own death	IV, 9, 11	28, 36	30	56	ep. 3, 6	II, 37	III, 22-3
other	—	—	—	51, cf. 34	—	cf. II, 11, 16-17, 21	I, passim
Visions							
Visions of souls borne to heaven by angels	I, 5, 7 IV, 10	4, 34	4, 31	32	(cf. *ep.* 2, 3-5)	II, 35; cf. 34	III, 6-7, 9-12
Powers of perception, telepathy							
sees through devil's illusory fire	II, 6	13	11			II, 10	
aware of:							
fortunes of distant battle	IV, 8	27	29	—	—	—	I, 7-8, 43
man falling from height	IV, 10 man killed, angels carry off soul	34 angels carry off soul	31	—	—	—	III, 15 angels save man
something else terrible happening/ threatening	—	27 (plague)	—	31 (cf. 51)	cf. *D* III, 14, 7-9	II, 11, 17	I, 22, 28; II, 4 & III, 8 (disease)

Early Irish Hermitages in the Light of the Lives of Cuthbert

MICHAEL HERITY

The *Lives* of St Cuthbert provide much interesting detail on insular hermits' lives, some of which is reflected in the archaeology of Irish hermitages. The anonymous *Life*, for instance, recalls how, having dug through very hard and stony rock, Cuthbert made a place in which to dwell on the Inner Farne. This he enclosed with a rampart of stones compacted with earth and in it he made some little dwelling-places.[1] This *Life* also speaks of his digging a well, of his constructing a privy (*necessarium*) close to the sea; and it implies that the roof of the shelter built near the landing-place was thatched. It also relates that he spent some time 'digging and trenching the land' of the island.[2] The details of his burial and of the translation of his remains are also given.[3]

Bede's *Life*, written perhaps twenty years later, provides further detail, describing his hermitage as if it were still extant, the two buildings standing there, 'an oratory and another habitation suitable for common uses', and the larger guest-house close to the landing-place. The story of the birds is made more meaningful in Bede's version, which describes Cuthbert working the land and sowing wheat in order to provide his own bread.[4] On the authority of monks of Lindisfarne still alive, Bede describes Cuthbert's instructions for where and how he was to be buried.[5] Bede's *Life* also mentions his frequent genuflections and prayer.[6]

This paper aims to provide a description of the buildings and layout of some of the several early Christian hermitages, mainly on islands off the Atlantic coast of Ireland, together with their cross-slabs, their *leachta* (open-air altars), and other recurring features like lakes and mills. It is hoped that this material, much of which relates to the period from the beginnings of Christianity before

---

[1] *VCA* III, 1. Throughout this article, the *Journal of the Royal Society of Antiquaries of Ireland* is abbreviated as *JRSAI*.
[2] *VCA* III, 3, 4, 5.
[3] *VCA* IV, 13, 14.
[4] *VCP* 17, 19.
[5] *VCP* 37 (*Two Lives*, pp. 272–3).
[6] *VCP* 18.

St Patrick to the time of the translation of Cuthbert's relics in 698, will help to provide an understanding of the kind of features available within the Irish early Christian tradition by Cuthbert's time. This material finds echoes in the *paruchia* of Iona and may thus be quite closely relevant in reconstructing the appearance of Northumbrian hermitages and monasteries — including Hereberht's on Derwentwater — in the period before the introduction of the Rule of St Benedict. The writer of the anonymous *Life*, a member of the Lindisfarne community, credits Cuthbert with arranging 'our rule of life', composed then for the first time and observed 'even to this day' with the Rule of Benedict.[7]

Early Irish island foundations include Rathlin O'Birne, probably founded by Assicus of Elphin, perhaps about 500;[8] Inismurray and Aran, traditionally founded by Molaise and Enda in the early sixth century;[9] Inishglora, one of many foundations ascribed to Brendan the Navigator, who died *c*.577; Ardoileán (or High Island), ascribed to Fechín of Fore;[10] and Inishbofin, founded by Colman of Lindisfarne *c*.668.[11] The strong local tradition attributes the foundation of Caher Island, off the Mayo coast near Croagh Patrick, to St Patrick. (See fig. 1).

BUILDINGS AND LAYOUT

A small enclosure (pl. 1) close to the south shore of Inishark, a mile west of Inishbofin off the coast of county Galway, on which Colman of Lindisfarne founded his monastery some years after 664, is attributed to St Leo by local tradition. The enclosure is ovoid in shape, its longer east-west axis measuring about 18m internally, bounded by a curvilinear wall in which there is an entrance in the north-east; within, at the west end, stands a small clochán, now unroofed, with rectilinear interior and curvilinear exterior some 4.5m in diameter; its doorway is exceptionally placed towards the south-east corner. There are some confused grass-grown remains at the east end of the enclosure, not sufficient to allow one to reconstruct a building of stone. Analogy with several sites like Kildreelig and Illaunloghan in Kerry would suggest that a small oratory stood here. St Leo's penitential cell is pointed out as a small cave

---

[7] *VCA* III, 1.
[8] Tírechán, *Collectanea de S. Patricio* 22, 2; ed. and trans. L. Bieler, *The Patrician Texts in the Book of Armagh* (Dublin, 1979), pp. 140 – 1.
[9] Inismurray: *Félire Oengusso Céli Dé, The Martyrology of Oengus the Culdee*, under 12 August; ed. W. Stokes (Henry Bradshaw Society 29; London, 1905), p. 176; *Martyrology of Tallaght*, under 12 August; ed. R. I. Best and H. J. Lawlor (Henry Br. Soc. 68; London, 1931); A. Gwynn and R. N. Hadcock, *Medieval Religious Houses, Ireland* (London, 1970), p. 387. Aran: *Vita S. Endei* 13; ed. C. Plummer, *Vitae sanctorum Hiberniae* (2 vols; Oxford, 1910, repr. 1968), II, 66.
[10] For Brendan and Fechín's obits, see *The Annals of Ulster, sub annis* 577 and 665; ed. and trans. S. Mac Airt and G. Mac Niocaill, vol. I (Dublin, 1983), pp. 88 – 9, 136 – 7.
[11] *Annals of Ulster, sub anno* 668; *HE* IV, 4.

1. Map of Ireland showing sites referred to in the text.

in an inlet of the sea some metres east of the enclosure; a decorated slab, *Leac Leo*, apparently of early Christian type, existed on the island until some years ago.[12]

On the tiny island of Illaunloghan in the Portmagee channel between Valencia Island and the mainland of county Kerry stand the remains of a hermitage, probably the dwelling-place of a lone hermit (fig. 2, 4, after Henry (as n. 13), fig. 16). Here are a stone-built oratory close to the east end of the island and, 18m away, a stone-built clochán, its doorway in its east side facing the oratory across an open space. The third element here is an A-roofed slab-tomb typical of the area, 10m north of the west facade of the oratory and enclosed within a tiny burial area.[13] These foundations are examples of the simplest true hermitages, the dwellings of single hermits on islands off the west coast. Another is the little-known foundation clinging precariously to shelves around the pinnacle of the Skellig rock, high above the main monastery, at the north end of which are the remains of a *necessarium* constructed in the same manner as Cuthbert's on Farne.[14]

The focal buildings at Killabuonia (fig. 2,3) are sited on two adjacent walled terraces running roughly east and west about 500 feet up on a steep south-facing slope with a view west to Skellig Michael, over nine miles away to sea. On the upper terrace is a ruined oratory of Gallarus type, about 4.2 by 2.4m internally; beside it to the south near the line of the west facade are an upright cross-slab and the Priest's Grave, a low stone reliquary with A-roof and a circular hole in its west gable.[15] Françoise Henry noted how closely this layout corresponded to that described by Cuthbert in outlining the arrangements concerning his burial.[16] On the west side of the open space fronting this facade, 7.5m away, is a fine beehive hut or clochán, its doorway opening onto the lower terrace below the retaining wall of the upper one; a stone stair is conveniently placed to provide access from below to the open space above. The general layout of the site is oblong, governed in part, at least, by the terraces; the size of the nuclear pair of terraces is 69m east-west by 36m north-south. There are now few signs of an enclosing wall.

Other foundations which probably began as the dwellings of single hermits appear to have been enlarged subsequently to take a small community. One such, where the buildings of the original foundation can be differentiated from the later structures, is on Rathlin O'Birne Island off the coast of Donegal (fig. 2,1). Here is a tiny oratory within which, on the north wall, is a dry-walled *leaba* (literally, bed) resembling the tomb of a founder saint covered with rounded pebbles of white quartz and with a cross-inscribed slab at its east and

[12] G. H. Kinahan, 'Proceedings', *JRSAI* 11 (1870-71), pp. 203 – 4.
[13] F. Henry, 'Early Monasteries, Beehive Huts, and Dry-stone Houses in the Neighbourhood of Caherciveen and Waterville (Co. Kerry)', *Proceedings of the Royal Irish Academy* 58C (1957), pp. 45 – 166, at pp. 96 – 8 and fig. 16.
[14] Henry, art. cit., pp. 127 – 9; cf. *VCA* III, 4.
[15] Henry, art. cit., pp. 101 – 6, fig. 18.
[16] Ibid., pp. 155 – 6; *VCP* 37 (*Two Lives*, pp. 272 – 3).

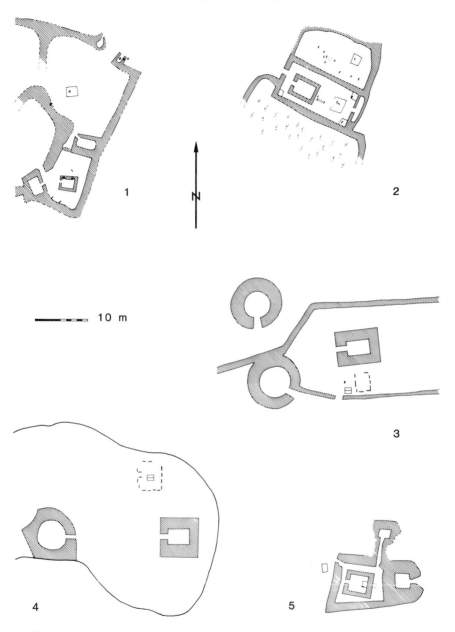

2. Simple plans of layout of hermitages: 1) Rathlin O'Birne; 2) Caher Island; 3) Killabuonia
(after Henry 1957); 4) Illaunloghan (after Henry 1957); 5) Ardoileán.

west ends.[17] This stands within a small dry-walled enclosure measuring 9.75 by 6m, the outline of which is roughly rectilinear. Within this stand a number of small erect slabs of mica-schist which may mark the graves of the early hermits. Opposite the west door of the oratory, at the south-west corner of the enclosure, are the remains of a rectilinear dry-stone building with east doorway, its north-west wall set obliquely to the two longer walls adjoining it. This appears to be the hermit's cell. A second building, possibly a guesthouse, stands at the north edge of the oratory enclosure. Its doorway appears to be in the north-west corner looking out into a larger walled enclosure north of the first which incorporates two well-houses in its north wall and has two *leachta* within it. These *leachta* and some cross-inscribed slabs are discussed below in the section on pilgrimage rounds.

The nucleus of the hermitage at Caher Island (fig. 2,2) is a rectangular area 6.5 by 13.8m, enclosed by a dry-stone wall with the entrance in the west end. The wall at the east end is broader, up to 2.05m, to incorporate a wall-chamber 5m long by 1m wide and 50cm high. Inside the enclosure are the remains of a church built in late medieval style but of unusually small size, 5 by 3.95m externally. Immediately east of this is a line of upright grave-slabs, two of them decorated, the most southerly of which has a recumbent decorated slab overlying a grave to the east of it which is called Leaba Phádraig (Patrick's Bed). It appears that the presence of these graves limited the space available for the building of the medieval church. In the open space east of here is a free-standing *leacht* or open-air altar, about 2.5m square and standing up to 95cm in height, built of slab-shaped stones.

At Ardoileán the oratory is placed within a much smaller enclosure of roughly rhomboid shape, about 8m east-west by 7m north-south, its entrance at the north-west corner (fig. 2,5).[18] The oratory is an early Christian building 5.25 by 4.60m externally, built in dry-walling of the highest quality. Its west doorway is battered in the normal early Christian fashion and the oratory was refurbished in late medieval times from the level of the lintel of this doorway upwards. Outside its east end a decorated stone slab-shrine, probably a reliquary of the founder saint, Fechín, stood in 1820, when it was described by George Petrie.[19] A tiny clochán or beehive stone hut with rectilinear interior about 2 by 1.70m stands on the north side outside the enclosure; it is attached to the focal enclosure around the oratory by the remains of a covered passageway which enters the enclosure through an archway. This may have been the abbot's cell but the arrangement whereby access to it could only be gained through the oratory enclosure suggests that in some way its occupant had the character of an *inclusus*. A second, larger clochán, apparently for communal

[17] P. Walsh, 'The Monastic Settlement on Rathlin O'Birne Island, County Donegal', *JRSAI* 113 (1983), pp. 53–66.

[18] M. Herity, 'The High Island Hermitage', *Irish University Review* 7 (Spring 1977), pp. 52–69.

[19] M. Herity, 'The ornamented tomb of the saint at Ardoileán, Co. Galway', in *Ireland and Insular Art, A.D. 500–1200*, ed. M. Ryan (Dublin, 1985), pp. 141–3.

use, abutted the east end of this focal area, its entrance facing east into the main body of the hermitage. Immediately outside the entrance to the oratory enclosure are the remains of a dry-walled *leacht*. Wakeman's drawing,[20] made for the Ordnance Survey in 1839, shows one cross-slab standing upright in the north-east corner of the oratory enclosure in a manner resembling the slabs in the focal area at Caher Island. This slab is now lost.

At all of the sites described, except at Caher Island, we may speak of two focal buildings, the oratory and the hermit's cell. One classic arrangement is that found at Inishark, Killabuonia and Illaunloghan, where the doorway of the oratory opens onto an open space beyond which is a clochán with its doorway facing east onto the same open space. The lives of the saints commonly use the word *platea* or *plateola* for this open space.[21] At Rathlin O'Birne and at Ardoileán the nuclear cell is intimately connected with a small rectilinear open space which surrounds the oratory. The focal enclosure at Caher Island follows a norm which is quite distinct: the oratory is placed at the west end of the enclosure, with the reliquary of the founder saint, other burials and a *leacht* standing in the open space to the east. Here there is no hermit's cell, unless the penitential chamber within the thickness of the east wall of the enclosure is to be regarded as such. At all of these sites except Inishark a reliquary of the founder saint appears to have been present; at many, decorated cross-slabs stood within, or at the perimeter of, the enclosure.

LAKES, MILLS, AND THE CUSTOM OF IMMERSIONS

Colman sited his monastery on Inishbofin beside a small lake, as did Fechín at Ardoileán, the south wall of the enclosure being built straight along the edge of the larger of two lakes at the west end of the island.[22] At Rathlin O'Birne Assicus chose to build his hermitage on the east side of a low knoll close to the landing-place on the north side of the island. At the west side of this knoll is a small area of standing water, now draining into the sea through a deep channel. This tiny lake, the size of which varies with the seasons, is incorporated within the crescent-shaped outer enclosure and surrounded on all four sides by walls, enclosing an area roughly 45 by 50 metres. A tiny pond 15 by 24 metres stands on the south side of the focal enclosure at Caher Island. Fed by a well which springs from its north-west corner, it is delimited by the south wall of the enclosure and the steep outcrop opposite as well as by walls at its east and west ends. It is now filled with mud which supports a growth of yellow iris; the mud is up to 50cm deep, suggesting an original maximum depth of up to 90cm for the pond. (Pl. 2.)

---

[20] Royal Irish Academy MS 12 T9.
[21] M. Herity, 'The layout of Irish early Christian monasteries', in *Irland und Europa, die Kirche im Frühmittelalter*, ed. P. Ní Chatháin and M. Richter (Stuttgart, 1984), pp. 105–116, at pp. 108–9.
[22] Herity, 'High Island', p. 52.

One plausible explanation for the occurrence of these small lakes might be that they were reservoirs to provide the motive power for water-mills; indeed at Ardoileán a stone platform which probably formed the foundations of a mill-house within which a horizontal mill was worked stands at the end of a mill-race which issues from the south-west side of the larger lake beside the monastery. The presence of a water-mill suggests the existence of a community rather than a single hermit, however, and there is no evidence for a similar mill at either Caher or Rathlin O'Birne. At Iona the place-name *Sruth a' Mhuilinn* (the mill stream) on the north side of the main enclosure suggests the ancient presence of a water-mill on the stream which runs from there to the east shore of the island.[23] As the Rathlin O'Birne and Iona foundations are similar in extent, layout and orientation, perhaps Rathlin O'Birne also had a water-mill?

The anonymous *Life* describes how Cuthbert dug and trenched the land of his island, while Bede's *Life* describes him working the land and sowing, first wheat and afterwards, when it failed, barley.[24] Though some land divisions are visible on Ardoileán, the only potential evidence of ancient cultivation remaining exists in a small enclosure on the south side of the smaller lake.[25] The anonymous *Life* implies, however, that after a lapse of two or three years Cuthbert shut himself in and ceased digging and sowing. This further implies that his food was supplied from the mainland. The evidence of any ancient cultivation will have been obliterated by extensive later ridging at both Caher and Rathlin O'Birne. Small field systems surrounding many small monastic sites on both mainland and islands may attest the growing of cereals and herbs as a regular practice at sites such as Rathlin O'Birne in Donegal, Skellig Michael in Kerry, and Inishglora, off the coast of Mayo. There is evidence of an extensive set of terraced gardens around the tiny foundation on Inishvickillane, one of the Blasket Islands off the coast of Kerry, and the remains of similar terraced fields can still be discerned around Kildreelig, Killabuonia and Loher, and around Teampall Geal on the Dingle peninsula. Imported pottery of Thomas's Class B meanwhile gives evidence of the importation of wine to the south-west,[26] along with bread a necessity for the celebration of the eucharist.

Another explanation can be offered, either as an alternative for, or in addition to the one put forward above. It appears that it was the custom for many of the Irish saints to mortify themselves by immersing themselves in cold

---

[23] The Royal Commission on the Ancient and Historical Monuments of Scotland, *Argyll: An Inventory of the Monuments*, vol. IV: *Iona* (Edinburgh, 1982), p. 32.

[24] *VCA* III, 5; *VCP* 19.

[25] Herity, 'High Island', p. 61.

[26] C. Thomas, 'Imported Pottery in Dark-Age Western Britain', *Medieval Archaeology* 3 (1959), pp. 89–111, at p. 91. T. Fanning, 'Excavation of an Early Christian cemetery and settlement at Reask, County Kerry', *Proceedings of the Royal Irish Academy*, 81C (1981), pp. 67–172.

water.[27] A hymn in Irish attributed to Fíacc, for instance, mentions that Patrick stood 'all night in ponds', even in the cold season; this practice is also recorded by his seventh-century biographer, Muirchú. Immersion is also recorded for Ciarán of Saighir, Comgall of Bangor, Kevin of Glendalough and, in a very late *Life*, for Colmcille of Iona. The practice is also ascribed to St Kentigern who, like Colmcille, is said to have recited the whole psalter while immersed in water. The custom is related of Welsh saints too: Illtud, Gildas, Cyngar, Gwynllyw, and of the Breton saints Gurthiern and Brynach. It is said of Guenaël of Landevennec that while the brethren were asleep he recited the seven penitential psalms immersed up to his shoulders in the watercourse that ran around the monastery. It appears also that Dryhthelm of Melrose, Wilfrid, and Aldhelm of Malmesbury adopted this practice of ascetic immersions, and the Frankish monk Wandrille (d.667) is also said to have immersed himself nightly while reciting the psalms.

Both the anonymous *Life of Cuthbert* and Bede's *Life* recount, on the authority of Plecgils and others, an incident which happened at Coldingham. It appears that Cuthbert, on a short visit there, continued his habit of singing the psalms as he kept vigil during the night and going into the waves 'up to his loincloth'. After this as he prayed on his knees on the sandy part of the shore two otters came out of the sea, warmed his feet with their breath and tried to dry him with their fur.[28] Gougaud quotes one piece of evidence relating that Evagrius stood naked in a well in winter during a sojourn in the desert of the Cells in Nitria, Lower Egypt, about 382.[29] It may well be that the widespread practice of immersions by early saints in Ireland, often apparently at night and often while reciting the psalms, is evidence of the existence of such a practice in the early western church. It may be too that the many examples of the custom in the Northumbrian church are due to influence from Ireland and Iona.

THE *TURAS* OR PILGRIMAGE ROUND

The anonymous *Life* records a miracle which happened at Lindisfarne in the year in which that *Life* was written. A paralytic youth, given up by the 'skilled physicians of our monastery' as incurable, asked the abbot for the shoes which were on the feet of the incorrupt body of Cuthbert at the translation of his relics. That night he put the shoes on his feet and slept. In the morning he arose, quite cured. And on the next day 'he went round the places of the sacred martyrs (*circuibat loca sanctorum martyrum*), giving thanks to the Lord'. Bede's version of the story is essentially the same, with somewhat more detail;

---

[27] L. Gougaud, *Devotional and Ascetic Practices in the Middle Ages* (London, 1927), pp. 160–3, q.v. for what follows.
[28] *VCA* II, 3; *VCP* 10.
[29] Gougaud, op., cit., p. 159.

it ends 'when morning came he went to the church and, with everyone watching and congratulating him, he went round the holy places (*circuiuit loca sancta*) praying and offering the sacrifice of praise to his Saviour'.[30]

What are the *loca sanctorum martyrum* of the anonymous *Life*, the *loca sancta* of Bede's? It appears that they were close to the church, within the bounds of the monastery and within sight of the community. It may be that the past imperfect tense of *circuibat* in the anonymous *Life* suggests that the paralytic made his rounds of them continuously. Could it be that what is described is the *turas* (literally, a journey) or pilgrimage round commonly associated with Irish foundations?

At Inismurray, off the coast of Sligo, the *turas* begins at the shrine over the saint's burial-place, Teach Molaise, the pilgrim saying set prayers. The pilgrim then goes from station to station within the monastic enclosure and around the periphery of the island, circling each station sun-wise (*deiseal*), arriving back at Teach Molaise for the sixteenth and final station. The stations are marked by *leachta*, dry-built platforms of stone, on most of which are placed decorated cross-slabs. Five of the stations are dedicated to the great Trinity (*Trionóid Mhór*), the little Trinity (*Trionóid Bheag*), St Patrick, the Virgin Mary and Colmcille; a sixth is called Reilig Odhráin, as at Iona.[31]

At Caher Island the stations of the pilgrimage-round are placed within the east end of the focal enclosure of the monastery and to the north and south of it.[32] The focal point is the tomb of the founder saint called Leaba Phádraig. Most stations at Caher Island are marked by a *leacht* like those of Inismurray and an upright pillar-stone or slab decorated on its west or east face; exceptionally, three or four slabs are unornamented; one of these stands on the south side of Portatemple, the landing-place immediately below the hermitage, and appears to be the equivalent of the decorated landing-place slabs on other islands.

At Rathlin O'Birne we encounter the simplest arrangement of all. Here, within the focal oratory, is what appears to be a shrine of the saint marked at its head and foot by simple cross-slabs of mica-schist. Two *leachta* in the outer enclosure have tiny slabs with simple incised crosses placed upon them. The well-house at the entrance to the outer enclosure has three cross-decorated slabs associated with it, a slab with cross pattée now lying among the roof-stones, a tiny slab with simple crosses like those on the *leachta* standing upright on the roof and, at its north-east corner, the most elaborate of the cross-slabs on the island. It is decorated on both main faces; on its north-east face is inscribed a wreathed *Chi-Rho*, on its south-west face an equal-armed cross-in-circle (fig. 3, left).

[30] *VCA* IV, 17; *VCP* 45.
[31] W. F. Wakeman, *A survey of the antiquarian remains on the island of Inismurray* (Dublin, 1893), pp. 127, 139 – 50. RCAHMS, *Iona*, pp. 32, 250.
[32] F. Henry, 'The Antiquities of Caher Island (Co. Mayo)', *JRSAI* 77 (1947), pp. 23 – 38, esp. pp. 28 – 9, fig. 2.

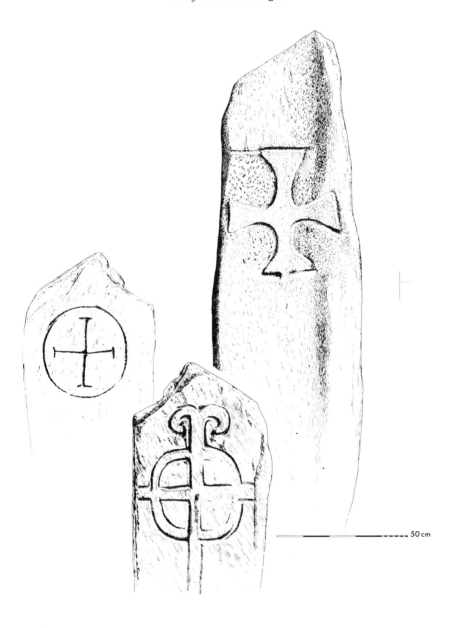

50 cm

20 cm

3. Cross-slabs: left and centre, that above landing-place, Rathlin O'Birne; right, Tallavbaun, county Mayo.

The *turas* at Glencolumbkille on the Donegal mainland opposite Rathlin O'Birne follows a circuit about three miles long around the valley floor and along its northern side.[33] It begins and ends in the churchyard, which probably marks the site of an early monastery; most of the fifteen stations are marked by *leachta* or small enclosures with cross-slabs, six of them tall cross-ornamented pillars. The *turas* is normally performed on the feast-day of Colmcille, 9 June, and the only personal name now associated with any of the stations is that of Colmcille.

At Rathlin O'Birne the inscribed crosses are simple and primitive. The wreathed Chi-Rho however is an accomplished work of early date. All of the Caher slabs are most accomplished and can conservatively be assigned to a range of dates in the sixth and seventh centuries. There are a number of points of overlap between the art of the slabs at Caher and those of the *turas* at Inismurray; though the Latin cross is prominent at Inismurray it appears that the slabs of its *turas* can also be dated to the sixth and seventh centuries. Apart from a small number of primitive designs, the main series at Glencolumbkille appears to be homogeneous and to date to the second half of the seventh century.

The *leachta* often associated either with cross-ornamented slabs or primitive crosses are found at many sites in the west of Ireland, on offshore islands and on the mainland. These appear to be evidence of the ancient custom of the *turas*. This custom may be related to the ancient stational observance followed at Rome during Lent. On the appropriate days, the Christian community of the city assembled in a designated church, the *ecclesia collecta*, and then with the Pope passed in procession to another church, the station church (*statio*, literally a watch), where the liturgy of the eucharist was celebrated at the grave of the saint.[34]

It appears that if we are to locate the stations of a *turas* at Lindisfarne we should seek the positions of open-air altars or small enclosures, ideally with cross-slabs or free-standing crosses. One such may be the socketed stone, probably a base to hold a cross-slab or cross, in an enclosure known as the Cockpit on the Heugh, which appears not to have been interpreted hitherto in this way.

THE CROSS-SLABS

A survey of the islands off the west coast of Ireland and some foundations on the mainland opposite reveals a sizeable corpus of art in stone. The relatively few free-standing crosses are greatly outnumbered by the series of decorated

[33] L. Price, 'Glencolumbkille, Co. Donegal, and its Early Christian cross slabs', *JRSAI* 71 (1941), pp. 71 – 88.
[34] P. Parsch, *The Church's Year of Grace* (Minnesota, 1964), pp. 71 – 2. G. G. Willis, *Further Essays in Early Roman Liturgy* (London, 1968), ch. 1, esp. pp. 9 – 16.

cross-slabs, most of which were documented by Crawford and Henry.[35] It appears that these slabs function as grave-markers, upright or recumbent, as pillar-stones set up at landing-places or on the stations of pilgrimage rounds, and in one case as parts of a decorated slab-shrine.[36] They were also placed in prominent positions close to the perimeter of focal monastic enclosures at Caher Island and Ardoileán. A brief examination is conducted here of a small sample from the earliest foundations to indicate their nature and context.

Three important slabs were set up above landing-places on Rathlin O'Birne, Oileán MacDara, and Ardoileán. The Rathlin O'Birne slab (fig. 3, left) is gable-shaped. On its south-west face is an encircled equal-armed cross with simple bar terminals, similar in form to one at Teampall Geal, Ballymorereagh, in county Kerry.[37] On its north-east face is an incised design unique in Ireland, a Chi-Rho of monogram form, not unlike that at Drumaqueran, county Antrim, published by Hamlin and dated by her to the range sixth to possibly eighth century.[38] At Rathlin O'Birne, however, the Rho element is of a more elaborate form with a back-serif, more in the style to be expected in a manuscript, perhaps, than any known in Irish or British stone sculpture. Here also the cross is wreathed, a concept borrowed from the world of late antiquity and not commonly presented in this fashion in Ireland. It seems probable that this Chi-Rho slab is an early representation of the form in Ireland. The foundation at Rathlin O'Birne is ascribed to the Gaul Assicus, St Patrick's disciple and metal-worker, who spent the seven years before his death as a hermit here. It is not improbable that this slab is the work of Assicus himself, a noted artist whose patens were seen by Tírechán towards the end of the seventh century at Armagh, Elphin, and Seól.[39]

The cross-slab standing above the landing-place on Oileán MacDara (fig. 4) is decorated on both the east and west faces with designs in contrasting styles. On the east face is a Latin cross outlined by a single broad ribbon with expanded terminals at head and arms; the foot of the cross is formed by the folding of either end of the ribbon into a rectilinear maze pattern. The slab is shaped to allow the arms of this cross to break through its sides. Bosses are placed at the crossing of arms and shaft and in the upper quadrants between the arms. In the lower quadrants there appear to be pairs of bosses with central depressions set one above the other. The manner in which the foot is formed resembles one element of the decoration on the east face of the Carndonagh marigold slab where a somewhat more elaborate key pattern issues from the

---

[35] H. F. Crawford, 'A Descriptive List of Early cross-slabs and Pillars', *JRSAI* 42 (1912), pp. 217 – 44; 43 (1913), pp. 151 – 69, 261 – 5, 326 – 34. F. Henry, 'Early Christian slabs and Pillar Stones in the West of Ireland', *JRSAI* 67 (1937), pp. 265 – 79.

[36] Herity, 'The ornamented tomb' (as above, n. 19).

[37] J. Cuppage, *Archaeological Survey of the Dingle Peninsula* (Oidhreacht Chorca Dhuibhne; Ballyferriter, 1986), p. 269 and fig. 151 (f).

[38] A. Hamlin, 'A Chi-Rho carved stone at Drumaqueran, Co. Antrim', *Ulster Journal of Archaeology* 35 (1972), pp. 22 – 8, at p. 24.

[39] Tírechán *Collectanea* 22, 1 – 2; ed. Bieler, pp. 140 – 1.

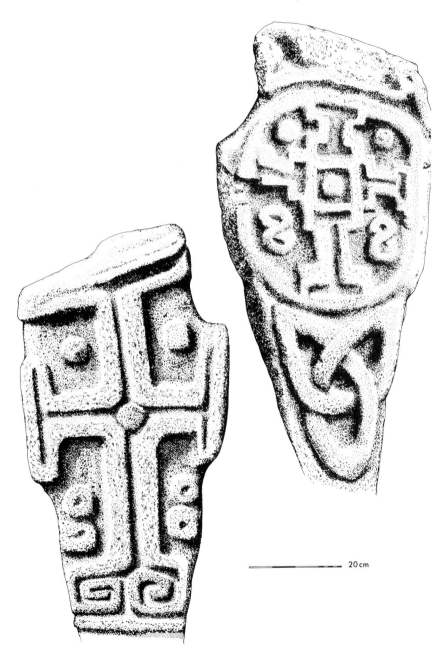

20 cm

4. *Landing-place cross-slab at Oileán MacDara, county Galway, left, east face, right, west face.*

foot of a simple cross formed with a twist pattern.[40] The design on the west face of the Oileán MacDara slab is in two parts: above a large and somewhat awkward triquetra knot is a cross within a circle. A bossed square at the centre supports arms, head, and shaft which have expansions at the extremities and at the attachments to the central square. In the upper quadrants are two circular bosses, in the lower a pair of matched S-shaped or figure-of-eight motifs. The design of the encircled cross is strongly reminiscent of metalwork, resembling the openwork ornaments on chatelaines found with Merovingian burials of the sixth and seventh centuries, some of which are on display in the National Museum at St Germain-en-Laye, Paris. This comparison is strengthened by the S-shaped ornaments in the lower quadrants, described by Bigger as serpents,[41] which may also be paralleled on Merovingian metalwork of similar date.[42]

The cross-slab above the south landing-place at Ardoileán (pl. 3) has a deeply cut Latin cross in relief with expanded triangular terminals on its principal face, the arms of the cross protruding through the sides of the slab. Within the frame of the cross is a second, formed with a single, loosely twisted ribbon, expanding to create a lozenge-shaped void at the centre of the cross and triangular spaces in the terminals. Within the triangular expansion at the head there is a triquetra knot; there may have been others in the arms and foot. The less-weathered side of the head of the slab expands slightly to accommodate a spiral joined to the upper terminal. Simple incised crosses ornament the other broad face of the slab and the end of the west arm. Françoise Henry has analysed the occurrence of simple twists on Irish early Christian carvings at Templeneiry, Fahan Mura, Carndonagh, Inismurray and Inishkea, noting their Coptic affiliations and assigning them to the seventh century;[43] on this assessment the slab at the Ardoileán landing-place can be assigned to the same period as that on Oileán MacDara.

The fourteen decorated slabs on Caher Island are a varied group disposed within the focal enclosure and on stations of the pilgrimage round close to it. Probably the most interesting is Henry's Slab A,[44] a revised drawing of which is presented here (fig. 5). It stands on the *leacht* at the east end of the church. The slab, of grey coarsish grit, is cut from a stone broadly triangular in shape, narrowing towards the butt. Its west face is ornamented with a Greek cross-in-circle above a pair of affronted dolphins, below which a small trapezoidal area has been dressed to a flat surface. At the head of the slab the edges have been worked in a curve to follow the outline of the circle enclosing the cross,

---

[40] H. F. Crawford, *Irish Carved Ornament* (Dublin, 1926), plates xxiii/iv, 29.

[41] F. W. Bigger, 'Cruach MacDara off the Coast of Connemara: With a Notice of its Churches, Crosses and Antiquities', *JRSAI* 26 (1896), pp. 101–12 at p. 110.

[42] Cf. É. Salin, *La civilisation mérovingienne d'après les sépultures, les textes et le laboratoire* (4 vols.; Paris 1949–59), vol. I, fig. 140; B. Arrhenius, *Merovingian Garnet Jewellery* (Stockholm, 1985), figs. 209, 234.

[43] 'New Monuments from Inishkea North, Co. Mayo', *JRSAI* 81 (1951), pp. 65–9 at pp. 68–9.

[44] Henry, *JRSAI* 77, pp. 23–38; see her fig. 4 for Slab A.

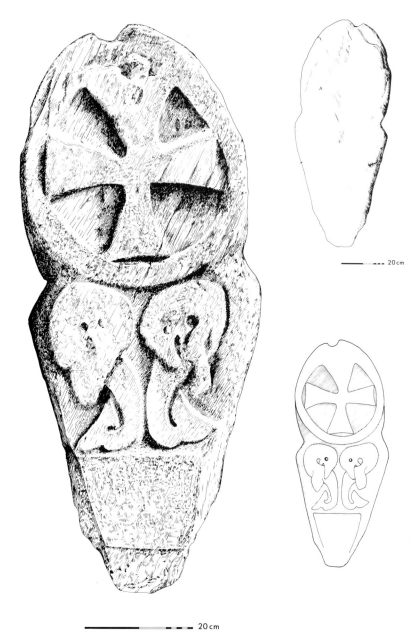

5. Cross-slab with dolphins from central leacht *in focal enclosure, Caher Island.*

producing a shouldered effect on the long sides. The dolphins stand about 30cm high, their bodies twisted in an S-shape. The tails curve outwards and upwards towards the edges of the slab; the upper bodies curve inwards above the dorsal fins so that the upper backs support the encircled cross. The heads turn inwards, the beaks biting back on to the bellies; the eyes are marked by drilled circles. The composition is unitary, the affronted dolphins supporting the encircled cross.

Henry has pointed out that the iconography is one which can be broadly paralleled in the early Christian world and has drawn attention to the parallel of the hanging bowl escutcheon from Faversham where a Latin cross with expanded terminals is supported between the bodies of two dolphins.[45] Haseloff gives other useful comparanda for the association of dolphins with crosses.[46] The attitude of the dolphins on the Caher slab, biting back on their own bodies, sets them within a second set of contexts, those of the Germanic and Merovingian worlds. The animal biting on its own body or on that of another is a common motif introduced from the Germanic world into Insular ornament as in the Book of Durrow.[47] The S-curve of the dolphins' bodies is also reminiscent of S-shaped animals depicted in Merovingian jewellery.[48] It appears therefore that at Caher Island this classical motif may well be under influences from the European continent which can be dated to the sixth century or the early part of the seventh.

The cross-slab in the south-east corner of the focal enclosure has a simple cross outlined with a broad band incurving at the crossing of arms and shaft (fig. 6, left). There is a large flat circular boss at the centre of the head with four smaller ones placed within the terminals. The outline of the upper part of the slab is cut to emphasize the shape of the cross, while the lower part of the slab is left undressed. A very similar cross with better proportions (fig. 6, right) is outlined on a slab at Kill, near Streamstown, on the mainland of county Galway, discovered recently by Michael Gibbons and Jim Higgins; here the upper part of the slab is worked into a frame containing all but the arms of the cross, which is itself outlined by a broad band standing in relief. There are tiny projections on either side of the slab near the head.

The slab on the penitential station to the north of the focal enclosure at Caher[49] is a Latin cross made with broad incisions (pl. 4). A circular boss with central depression is outlined at the centre of the head. The upper and lower terminals of the cross expand into wide curliques. Two similar crosses are known on slabs at Inismurray; interestingly, both have simple twist ornament resembling that of the landing-place cross at Ardoileán and its

---

[45] Ibid., p. 37.
[46] G. Haseloff, 'Insular animal styles with special reference to Irish art in the early medieval period', in *Ireland and Insular Art*, ed. Ryan (as n. 19 above), pp. 44 – 55, at pp. 44 – 5.
[47] U. Roth, 'Early insular manuscripts: ornament and archaeology, with special reference to the Book of Durrow', in *Ireland and Insular Art*, ed. Ryan, pp. 23 – 9.
[48] Cf. P. Lasko, *The Kingdom of the Franks* (London, 1971), fig. 33.
[49] Henry, *JRSAI* 77, fig. 2L, fig. 7D.

20 cm

6. Cross-slabs: left, at Caher Island, SE corner of focal enclosure; right, Kill, near Streamstown, county Galway.

milieu.[50] An incised cross on a slab at Inishkea North has a similar design and stands on a stalk like those mentioned below.[51] A similar date seems appropriate.

At Tallavbaun on the mainland opposite Caher Island is a tall pillar which is published here for the first time (fig. 3, right). It appears to have stood within a small ecclesiastical foundation, now ruined, with a view towards Caher Island. On its west face near the top is an equal-armed cross in relief; in form it is similar to the encircled cross on the dolphin slab at Caher, the arms expanding in gently curved lines, and it has been left quite plain. The cross stands on a projection issuing from the foot. This is one of a type of cross known in both manuscripts and carvings in Ireland. The closest comparison is with the encircled cross on the Arraglen ogham stone on the slopes of Mount Brandon in Kerry;[52] other comparanda in Kerry are to be found at Reask, Knockane, Maumanorig, and Kilvickadownig; further examples are known at Inishcealtra in Clare and at Inishkea North and Inismurray. Similar crosses standing on stems with expanded terminals are represented in the Cathach, the Book of Durrow, and the Echternach Gospels.[53] The Tallavbaun cross seems thus to date to the seventh century, probably its first half.

This is a sample of the extensive evidence to be derived from a detailed survey of monastic foundations in the west of Ireland. Interesting reconstructions relating to the earliest period continue to issue from the combination of the archaeological and historical records, foremost among them the *Lives* of Cuthbert.

---

[50] Wakeman, *Survey*, figs. 46, 47.
[51] F. Henry, 'Remains of the Early Christian Period on Inishkea North, Co. Mayo', *JRSAI* 75 (1945), pp. 127 – 55, plate xxviii, Slab 5.
[52] Cuppage, *Archaeological Survey*, fig. 137 and plate 11 (pp. 249 – 50).
[53] Henry, *JRSAI* 81, p. 69.

The Spirituality of St Cuthbert

BENEDICTA WARD, SLG

Forty-seven years ago, Bertram Colgrave wrote in his preface to the *Two Lives of St Cuthbert*, 'These Lives of St Cuthbert throw considerable light on the secular history of the golden age of Northumbria. They also illustrate one of the most important periods of the English Church'.[1] Rarely has an historian been so prophetic. Since then, scholarship has continued to illustrate the truth of that comment, showing each year how the *Lives* of St Cuthbert, combined with the study of art, archaeology, and artifacts as well as charters and laws, do indeed throw light upon many facets of life in Northumbria in the seventh century. Moreover, it has been equally clear that the cult of St Cuthbert, like so many saints' cults, throws even more light upon many and varied facets of later medieval life, whether in the times of the Danish invasions, the monastic revival, or the Norman conquest. There is much profit in exploring the *Lives* in this way; but how it would have surprised Bede, let alone Cuthbert. For Bede did not write his *Life of St Cuthbert* to provide later historians with interesting information about 'the secular history of the golden age of Northumbria', nor was he intending to give later readers a biography in the style of Boswell, of 'Cuthbert in His Times'. It is right to look carefully at the form of the work and examine its sources and antecedents, to see it as a reflection of its cultural setting, to look at the audience for which such work was intended; but it seems only fair to try also to see what Bede himself wanted to convey in his picture of Cuthbert.

The 'horizontal' approach to Cuthbert as a man related to other men needs to be complemented by the 'vertical' approach to Cuthbert as he related to God, for in the *Life of St Cuthbert*, both in verse and in prose, Bede, like the anonymous writer before him, was writing the life of a saint; the form of their texts and the content of them were both part of the tradition of Christian hagiography. Their aim was to show that Cuthbert was holy, that is, that he showed in his life the marks of Christ crucified and that God had shown his love for that life of discipleship by signs and wonders, before and after death, just as he had done in the case of other holy ones in earlier times and other places. Moreover, their aim was to write in such a way that Cuthbert's

[1] *Two Lives*, p. vii.

65

holiness should continue to have meaning in the lives of others. A hagiography is above all pragmatic, practical: it shows one of that great cloud of witnesses in the detail of his life on earth as he walked in the footsteps of the Man of Galilee; and it poses the invitation of the angels at the tomb: 'Come and see; he is not here, he is risen.' The accounts of Cuthbert are not only a window onto the dead past; they are a stream of living water where he who is alive in Christ shows the race that is set before those who come after. They are not rather poor biographies; they are first-rate hagiographies.

I intend therefore to speak about the 'spirituality' of Cuthbert, as about something alive and immediate. But at once there are problems in even getting beyond the first word. What is 'spirituality'? It is not a word Cuthbert would have recognized, nor indeed a medieval word at all. Its earlier use was in the plural, 'spiritualities', referring to spiritual jurisdiction as opposed to temporal jurisdiction, the 'lords spiritual' as opposed (and how often literally opposed) to the 'lords temporal'. 'Spiritualité' has of course undergone a later transformation and in its French form there is a very good chance that 'un spirituel' will be someone who is witty, lively, or even mad. These are not the uses of the word Dr Stancliffe had in mind, I think, when she asked me to talk about the 'spirituality of St Cuthbert'. There is another use of the word 'spirituality' nowadays, which I regard with caution, since it seems vaguely gnostic, in which it means the non-material aspect of things, as in 'the spirituality of the motor bike', 'the spirituality of progress', 'the spirituality of electronics': a passive use of the phrase, referring, I hope, to human reaction to these objects. A more active use of the phrase is current in 'the spirituality of Islamic culture', and this is closer to the use I want to make of the term. To see the desires and religious aspirations of men within their cultural context can be extremely illuminating, especially in connection with non-literate societies, and is perhaps partly what has been done in many discussions this week. But as far as Cuthbert is concerned it has its limits, partly because much of the information about his society comes in fact from the *Life* itself, but also because this is still an approach which differs from that of the writers of the earliest *Lives*. I prefer, therefore, to take a middle way, and combine this modern use of the word 'spirituality' (which is perhaps closer to 'mentality') with another meaning given to it in the nineteenth century when it was coined. It was used then to describe a field of study earlier called ascetic theology, and/or mystical prayer. By 'spirituality', then, I mean what Cuthbert himself thought and said and did and prayed in the light of the Gospel of Christ. It seems to me that both Bede and Cuthbert would recognize this approach.

But this at once poses another problem, for what can be known about this inner kingdom? The way to know the heart of a man of the past is usually through his writings, and nothing survives directly from Cuthbert himself. He is seen only through the lens of observers, and moreover neither of his earliest biographers ever met him. That is surely a perilous way to see anyone, especially when I am proposing to look at what Thomas Merton described as a point of pure truth [at the centre of our being], a point or spark which belongs entirely to God, which is never at our disposal, from which God disposes of our lives, which is inaccessible to the fantasies of our mind or the brutalities of our own will.[2]

It is rare to reach any awareness of that kind of 'spirituality' in oneself — how much less in others — ; but it is such a centre that illuminates and governs thought, word, and action, and by looking wisely at the external moments, some apprehension of the centre can be touched. I want to suggest that the early *Lives* of St Cuthbert give us that wise view; but before examining them in order to come near the inner life of Cuthbert as he faced towards Christ, there is one obvious method of narrowing the scope of the inquiry. That is by saying at once what his life of prayer was not: it was not, for instance, the rosary, it was not the Stations of the Cross, it was not matins and evensong, it was not the piety of fourth-century Egypt or eleventh-century Canterbury, or sixteenth-century Spain. Cuthbert was not a monk of Jarrow in the days of Bede, nor was he a monk of Durham either in the time of Symeon, or in the time of Reginald, nor was he a Benedictine in any sense whatever; and he was not a Sister of the Love of God, either.

That is rather a negative comment; but perhaps it has at least been a warning signal not to shape Cuthbert in our own image. He was a man of his own time and place, and much about him ought to be alien, strange, perhaps at times entirely opaque. But while bearing that essential element of otherness in mind, I want to suggest that there is a more positive approach possible to Cuthbert. After all, there is a minimum of fact about Cuthbert which is agreed upon even by the severest historians: he actually lived. No one has ever suggested, as they have with both St Antony of Egypt and St Benedict of Nursia, that he was made up; and he lived in Northumbria in the mid seventh century. He chose to be a monk and hermit and he was also a bishop. I suggest that it can safely be inferred also that Cuthbert, noble or poor, was a man for whom his Christian life was a serious matter; and that his friends and colleagues were also men of integrity and not hypocrites. Cuthbert was known to them as a man of prayer, like them concerned primarily with what Jeremy Taylor called 'Following after the most holy Jesus, which is truest religion and most solemn adoration'.[3] It was two such men, Cuthbert's near contemporaries, following a way of life very like his own, who wrote about him fairly soon after his death, while there were still people alive who had known him well. They also were neither fools not liars but men of excellent intelligence and literary competence, one of them the first in the great tradition of English historians. The question these men asked about Cuthbert may not be ours, but it is a valid one; they were not interested in his noble connections, his love of gold, beer, or small animals, not even in whether he was clever, brave, or

---

[2] Thomas Merton, *Conjectures of a Guilty Bystander* (London, 1965), p. 142.
[3] Jeremy Taylor, *The Life of our Blessed Lord and Saviour, Jesus Christ, the Great Exemplar of Sanctity and Holy Life*, in *Complete Works*, ed. R. Heber, revised J. Eden (6 vols; London, 1847), II, 47 – 8.

great; they only wanted to know how this frail human being had put on the Lord Jesus Christ through life and into death. There are always those who do and those who write and the life of Cuthbert was made articulate by those who wrote about him. They chose small pictures from his life, and presented them with a wealth of interpretation directed to elucidating this central theme.

With this agreed minimum of fact in mind and accepting the innate honesty of the writers in terms of their own concerns, I suggest that there is one way in which these, and indeed other, hagiographies, can shed light upon their subject. Recently in the cathedral church of Durham, the manuscript of the Lindisfarne Gospels was placed on the grave of Cuthbert; I suggest that this is what both the anonymous monk of Lindisfarne and Bede did in their *Lives* of St Cuthbert: they placed over Cuthbert's life the Bible. With that overwhelmingly beautiful book, the Lindisfarne Gospels, the most beautiful thing about it is not its decoration but its content, the Gospel, the Good News, of Jesus Christ; just so the most important part of the *Lives* of St Cuthbert are not in the beauty of detail but those parts that link Cuthbert with the biblical tradition of sanctity, which is done most of all by the quotations the writers give from the Scriptures. In a first glance through a hagiography or any ancient text, the modern eye tends to skip the biblical quotations as mere pious trimming. I believe this to be an error of method. The illuminations of the Lindisfarne Gospel take on a world of new meaning if seen in connection with the text; the inner meaning of the *Lives* of St Cuthbert is made clearer, not more obscure, by examining the parts of the Scriptures that are placed over that life.

The best text for this examination is the prose *Life* by Bede, pre-eminently a man of the Bible, whom Boniface called 'that keen investigator of the Holy Scriptures;[4] and for Bede, the text of the Bible was not read alone. The fathers of the church had read the sacred page and commented on its various layers of meaning, in the conviction that the Holy Spirit was continually revealing the full truth of the written word, and it is just these interpretations that Bede collected and extended in his commentaries on the Bible. It seems to me useful therefore to examine the biblical quotations used by Bede, and to some extent by the anonymous writer, in connection with the standard patristic interpretations of those passages, which were familiar to those reading the *Lives* as they no longer are to most of us. Such study is particularly illuminating in this case since very often Bede himself gave the common interpretation of the texts is his commentaries on the Scriptures. The texts can be used as a lens held over the life of Cuthbert to show more distinctly the intimacies of a life lived in the light of the sacred page. It is possible that what will emerge most of all will be the spirituality of Bede, but I think this is not altogether the case. Bede looked deeply into the *Life* already written at Lindisfarne, and in his metrical *Life* he had already pointed out the interior

---

[4] *Letters of St Boniface*, trans. E. Emerton (Columbia, 1940), Letter to Ecgberht, no. 75, p. 168 (= ep. no. 91 in Tangl edition, cit. Lapidge, below p. 78, n. 7).

meaning of many episodes, using the *Life* as he used the Scriptures.[5] With the information about Cuthbert before him, supplemented by other sources, he set about presenting the inner significance of the text. This was the common approach to a text in the ancient world, where the surface meaning was seen as a thin layer, beyond which lay riches for the taking, and this was pre-eminently true of the text of the Bible as both Bede and Cuthbert used it. Such meditation of the text was to them common ground, not a different way of looking at things. While Cuthbert had never seen the Lindisfarne Gospels, he knew the Scriptures so well that he staked his life on the message they contain. In writing his account of Cuthbert, Bede is using the Scriptures as a lens, but it need not be a distorting lens. It is necessary to be alert in case what is revealed is the spirituality of the observers, for one sees what one is able to see, what one expects to be there; and, indeed, there is no objective observer of saints. Some of what the anonymous monk and Bede wrote is coloured by their own prejudice and more is coloured by a standard tradition of hagiography; yet the early lives are the nearest documents to Cuthbert in time, they come from men with similar preoccupations, they are directly concerned with Cuthbert's 'spirituality', and they are especially sensitive to the words of the Scriptures which formed the basis of his life. It seems to me therefore at least instructive not to try to sift factual detail from hagiographical *topos* in the *Lives* but rather to examine certain biblical texts that Bede (and to some extent the anonymous writer also) used to convey their understanding of the inner life of Cuthbert. Since it would be a very lengthy task to look at all the quotations from the Bible in the *Lives*, I want to look at the use of three biblical quotations which are used at key points in the *Life of St Cuthbert* and see what they convey about the inner truth of the stories they illustrate.

The first text I want to examine is the account which only Bede gives of the monastic education of Cuthbert at Melrose, which he says he heard from Herefrith of Lindisfarne, who knew it from Cuthbert himself. Cuthbert was received at Melrose by Boisil, and after his sojourn at Ripon returned there, where 'most diligently he paid heed both to the words and the deeds of the blessed Boisil as he had been accustomed to do before.'[6] Boisil died of a plague which had affected Cuthbert also. Herefrith, a priest of Lindisfarne and later abbot there, who was in the monastery at the time, told Bede how, in the last week of his life, Boisil proposed to spend his time teaching his disciple:

> Cuthbert . . . answered, 'And what, I ask you, is it best for me to read, which I can yet finish in one week?' He replied: 'The evangelist John. I have a book consisting of seven gatherings of which we can get through one every day, with the Lord's help, reading it and discussing it between ourselves so far as it is necessary.'[7]

[5] Cf. Michael Lapidge, below pp. 86 – 93.
[6] *VCP* 8, pp. 180 – 1.
[7] Ibid. pp. 182 – 3.

Fifty years later, perhaps these words were remembered at another death-
bed and with another Cuthbert: ' ''There is still one sentence not completed,
dear master.'' ''Then write it quickly.'' ''Now it is done.'' '[8] Bede's last
anxious gift to the Anglo-Saxon Christians was a translation of St John;
perhaps it was the story told him by Herefrith that so moved Bede that he
chose to communicate St John to others at his own death. There are three
points I want to make about this passage. First, why did two teachers offer St
John to their Anglo-Saxon converts? How did they understand him? St John's
is called 'the eagle gospel' by St Jerome, in his Preface which was as well
known as the text, because it is 'about the divinity of Christ . . . the rest of
contemplation . . . the mysteries of God.'[9] It is this fact of the divinity of
Christ that Boisil conveys to his disciple in those last days as the fundamental
basis of faith. Secondly, not only the content but the fact that they spent seven
days in reading were significant for Bede. In his commentary on Genesis,[10]
Bede devotes some time to the mystical meaning of six and eight, relating such
measurements of time to the whole work of creation and recreation, in which
the eighth day is the everlasting day of the great Easter of heaven. So it was not
lightly said that they read the Gospel together for seven days, for the eighth
was the entry of Boisil into heaven, into the rest of the day that is forever.
Thirdly, and for Bede this was the most important aspect of the story, he saw
significance in the way in which they read the Scriptures: 'They dealt', he
says, 'with the simple things of ''the faith that works by love'' ' (Gal. 5:6).[11] A
later commentary expressed exactly Bede's understanding of this verse from
Galatians as being about faith which finds its expression in love:

> Without love faith is useless; faith with love is Christian. Otherwise it is
> demonic. The devils also believe and tremble (James 2:19). Those who do not
> believe are lower and worse than the demons. But there is a great difference
> whether one believes Him to be Christ or believes in Christ. Even the devils
> believe Him to be Christ; he who believes in Christ, however, is he who hopes in
> Christ and loves him.[12]

In this seven days of reading, Boisil 'declared all Cuthbert's future to
him,'[13] but this was no special and secret revelation or prophecy; Boisil's
insight into Cuthbert's future came *because* they were reading the Scriptures,
not apart from it. This reading became in itself the fundamental basis for the
whole of Cuthbert's life as a servant of God. This light from the sacred page
was to lead Cuthbert to Farne; but even more, as Boisil saw, it was to bring

---

[8] *De Obitu Baedae*, ed. Plummer, *Op. hist.* I, pp. clxiii – clxiv.
[9] Jerome, 'Preface to the Gospels': *Biblia Sacra juxta Vulgatem Versionem*, ed. B. Fisher *et al.* (2 vols.;
Stuttgart, 1983) II, p. 1516.
[10] Bede, *Libri quattuor in principium Genesis usque ad nativitatem Isaac et eiectionam Ismahelis
adnotationum*, ed. C. W. Jones, CCSL 118A, p. 103.
[11] *VCP* 8, p. 182.
[12] Walafrid Strabo, *Glossa Ordinaria*, 'Epistola ad Galatas', PL 114, cols. 582 – 3.
[13] *VCP* 8, p. 182.

him back to the service of 'the faith that works by love' as bishop. On the island, Cuthbert was alone, sealed into prayer, grounded more and more into faith; as monk and especially as bishop he did not stay in a cell or even in a monastery; he was always away, preaching, weeping with the penitent, in the faith that finds its issue in love. The biblical context of the quotation underlines the training Boisil gave through St John's Gospel: 'for in Christ Jesus there is neither circumcision nor uncircumcision but the faith that works by love' (Gal. 5:6). As bishop, Cuthbert was not a monk's monk, nor did he confine himself to a select group; his teaching was for the poor and needy, and his companions were lay men and even women. The close walk with God that he knew on Farne came from the light of the Scriptures as he read them with Boisil, and that love of God issued in the service of love for all. He was not a divided man torn by two vocations, the one to solitude, the other to service, but someone who from the basis of faith did the works of love whatever the circumstances. In his *Ecclesiastical History of the English Nation*, Bede's final summary of Cuthbert's life is that he 'received from [Boisil] a knowledge of the Scriptures and the example of a life of good works.'[14] *Verbo et exemplo docere*: his was a faith exercised both in solitude and in preaching to the poor.

My second example is perhaps the most familar section of the *Life of Cuthbert*. Cuthbert, as a monk of Melrose, was invited to visit Aebbe, the abbess of Coldingham, and sister of King Oswiu. Coldingham was a monastery which, it seems from Bede's *Ecclesiastical History*, may have needed all the instruction, both in word and example, that its royal abbess could get for it. When the Irish ascetic, Adomnan, saw the abbey some years later, he wept and told the abbess that the behaviour of her community was a scandal:

> All of them, men and women alike, are sunk in slothful slumbers or else they . remain awake for the purposes of sin. And the cells that were built for praying and reading have become haunts of feasting, drinking, gossip, and other delights; even the virgins who are dedicated to God put aside all respect for their profession and, whenever they have leisure, spend their time weaving elaborate garments with which to adorn themselves as if they were brides, so imperilling their virginity, or else to make friends with strange men.[15]

The frivolity of the gay young nuns of Coldingham raises a smile now, but no one smiled at the time; to assume the life of a monk or nun was a serious matter even for royalty and decadence was not accepted as either normal or nice. Such a relaxed state of affairs was dangerous and it could hardly be the work of a few years. Perhaps when Cuthbert went there, it was this atmosphere of scarcely subdued eroticism which troubled him when he followed his custom of praying at night and which sent him to the beach to stand praying in the icy waters of the sea, that old monastic remedy for lust. What followed when he returned to the sand is another theme altogether:

[14] *HE* IV, 27 (25) (C and M, pp. 432 – 3).
[15] Ibid. IV, 25, pp. 424 – 7.

There followed in his footsteps two little sea animals, humbly prostrating
themselves on the earth; and, licking his feet, they rolled upon them, wiping
them with their skins and warming them with their breath.[16]

A walk on the beach at night, so often fruitful for the English. A man alone by
the sea, singing to himself and taking a dip, with small furry animals rubbing
round his ankles. How attractive; is this perhaps, and how consoling it would
be, the spirituality of Cuthbert? But this most private, intimate moment of the
prayer of Cuthbert is not so superficial for either the anonymous writer or
Bede when they place over it the lens of the Scriptures. For the anonymous,
Cuthbert is Daniel, thrown into danger of lust, as Daniel was thrown into the
den of lions, and Cuthbert, like Daniel, is ministered to by the animals.[17] For
the fathers of the church, Daniel was never just the eunuch of King
Nebuchadnezzar; he was Christ, who 'thought it not robbery to be equal with
God but emptied himself' (Philippians 2:7) and came down, a new Daniel,
into this animal den of the world. For Bede the emphasis is different though
equally scriptural; he uses the words of the Gospel spoken by Jesus to his
disciples after the Transfiguration, 'Tell the vision to no man until the Son of
Man be risen again from the dead.' (Matth. 17:19) In his commentary on the
Transfiguration Bede restated the patristic understanding of this moment of
vision as the second epiphany of Christ, parallel to the baptism of Christ in the
Jordan, the two revelations of the Christ as the Son of God.[18] The 'vision' seen
on the shore of the North Sea centuries later was for Bede the same epiphany
of God, by water and by light. It was a moment of such awe and terror that the
observer, like the disciples, 'was stricken with . . . deadly fear'.[19] He had not
been watching a man on a beach with his pets; he had seen the face of Christ in
a man so transfigured in prayer that the right order of creation was in him
restored. For Bede, Cuthbert with the animals was an even more awesome
sight than for the anonymous writer: he was the new Adam, once more at
peace with all creation, naming the animals, who were the first servant and the
first friend. And as in the story of Cuthbert and Boisil, this is also a scene
which leads towards entry into the kingdom through the gateway that is called
death. There are two other points Bede is making here: one is that Cuthbert,
renewed and purged by prayer, goes back to '[sing] the canonical hymns with
the brethren':[20] the common life of charity and praise, however lax, is still the
place for the exercise of the faith that works by love. And secondly there is a
third otter. Bede describes the two otters as 'prostrate before him on the
sand';[21] and when he describes the cleric of Coldingham, lying trembling
before the feet of Cuthbert, he describes him in the same attitude: 'he

---

[16] *VCA* II, 3, pp. 80 – 1; cf. *VCP* 10.
[17] *VCA* II, 3, pp. 82 – 3.
[18] Bede, *In Lucae evangelium expositio*; ed. D. Hurst, CCSL 120, p. 205.
[19] *VCP* 10, pp. 190 – 1.
[20] *VCP* 10.
[21] *VCP* 10, pp. 190 – 1.

approached Cuthbert and, stretching himself on the ground, tearfully entreated his pardon'.[22] The relationship of man with the animals is transfigured easily and naturally in the love and worship of the first two otters, and while the third otter is also taken into that same transfiguration, it is by tears of repentance and through the gate and grave of death.

For my third passage I have chosen the moment when that death was fulfilled, and again Bede's source was Herefrith. When the anonymous author describes the death of Cuthbert, he presents a picture of peace and order:

> Being attracted by the love of his former solitary life he returned to the island . . . He remained alone, satisfied with the converse and ministry of angels, full of hope and putting his trust wholly in God.[23]

It is a bland enough description; but there is a discreet hint of something more harsh in his choice of a phrase from Mark 1:13, where angels ministered to Christ, but after the forty days of temptation in the wilderness. Bede dares to go closer to the last days of Cuthbert through what he heard from Herefrith who was with him, and he makes of it a revelation of the ultimate truth of the life of the saint. Herefrith had described how Cuthbert was left alone on Farne before his death, suffering in the darkness of a storm for five days.[24] Bad weather had prevented Herefrith's return to the sick man, and Cuthbert had also been subject to a tempest both external and interior. He had dragged himself to the hut on the shore, out of a great courtesy towards the brothers who would come back, and Herefrith found him there, without food or drink, his face marked by disease and pain. It was not a quiet and interesting illness that he was suffering but a disgusting sore that suppurated. And he had endured also that ultimate terror, about which Herefrith says he did not dare to inquire. It was surely the dereliction which is at the heart of the Gospel, when God was forsaken by God. This last darkness of the saints in their union with Christ is the most fundamental part of Christian sanctity and perhaps the most difficult to approach. It is not, I think, something interesting to endure nor a particularly spiritual condition. Often it consists in disgusting disease, long pain, loneliness, sometimes the anguish of doubt and despair, helplessness mental as well as physical. And it is not confined to those officially called saints. Perhaps it is not inappropriate to draw a parallel with the last years of a very great medieval historian and contemporary, Helen Waddell:

> Helen Waddell's life seemingly ceased in the 1950s with the total eclipse of her dazzling gifts of intellect, winning charm, balance and humour, her ripe scholarship and deep spirituality. Mute, unheeding, unfeeling, blind to all beauty, a stranger to the family she had so loved, she sat day after day before a picture of Christ crucified . . .[25]

---

[22] Loc. cit.
[23] *VCA* IV, 11, pp. 128 – 9.
[24] *VCP* 37.
[25] Felicitas Corrigan, *Helen Waddell: a Biography* (London, 1986), pp. 355 – 6.

For Helen, the darkness lasted for fifteen years, for Cuthbert, for five days; but time, I think, is not here measured by the clock. It had never been the beauty of scenery that had drawn Cuthbert to Farne — indeed he seems to have taken great pains not to see it at all. For him it was the desert, the place of the cross. There was nothing there for Cuthbert but the stars and water among the rocks; and no one had really understood. Whenever the brothers came they got it wrong, right up to their demands for his body after his death. Even Herefrith could not speak clearly about the real significance of the island and the anonymous writer made no attempt. It was Bede, with his intuitive sympathy for the hermit and the ascetic, who perceived the truth, and it was Bede who provided a clear lens to see both those last mysterious days and the whole meaning of Cuthbert's life on the island. He does so not at the end but at the very beginning of the *Life of St Cuthbert*:

> The prophet Jeremiah consecrates for us the beginning of our account of the life and miracles of the blessed father, Cuthbert, when, praising the hermit's state of perfection, he says: 'It is good for a man to have borne the yoke in his youth; he sitteth alone and keepeth silence because he hath borne it upon him.'[26]

This is no random phrase from the Old Testament, nor a pious cliché about solitude. The commentary which gives this passage from Lamentations its solemnity is from the liturgy rather than the patristic texts and it is from the readings at night office for the last days of Holy Week in the Office of Tenebrae. The reading of Lamentations at Tenebrae belongs to one of the oldest layers of Christian liturgy,[27] and it seems certain that Bede knew the lessons in this form. When John the Chanter revised the liturgy at Wearmouth/Jarrow,[28] it is more than possible that he introduced there the readings for the last days of Holy Week that were already common in Rome.[29] These included the reading of the Lamentations of Jeremiah at Tenebrae, where they are set among responses about the passion and death of Christ. In one of the most beautiful pieces of liturgy ever written, these verses from Lamentations become the cry of the crucified: 'He sitteth alone and keepeth silence because he hath borne it upon him', with the respond, 'He was led as a lamb to the slaughter and while he was evil entreated he opened not his mouth; he was delivered unto death that he might give life unto his people.'[30] It may well have been with this interpretation in mind that Bede used this phrase of Cuthbert, seeing him in his life, and especially in that mysterious

---

[26] *VCP* 1, p. 154, and using the Authorised Version of Lam. 3:28, quoted there.

[27] *Dictionnaire d'archéologie chrétienne et de liturgie*, ed. F. Cabrol and H. Leclercq (15 vols.; Paris, 1903 – 53), XV, i, under 'Semaine sainte', cols. 1165 – 9.

[28] Bede, *Lives of the Abbots* 6; ed. Plummer, *Op. hist.* I, 369; trans. D. H. Farmer, in *The Age of Bede*, ed. Farmer (London, 1965/1985), p. 190.

[29] Cf. Cabrol and Leclercq, *DACL* XV, i, col. 1166, and XII, ii, cols. 2436 – 7 (under 'Ordines romani').

[30] Office of Tenebrae, Holy Saturday, 1st Nocturn.

darkness before his death, identified with Christ on the cross through the faith that worked continually by love.

Surely this is the real point about the early lives of Cuthbert. Some actual, physical details about his earthly life are there, but the writers are not directly concerned with them. There is no 'spirituality' there, if by that is meant the personal mental activities of Cuthbert when he prayed or when he taught. What the *Lives* do contain is a series of pictures of real events presented for their significance in relation to God. There is no way of stripping these stories of their piety in the hopes of finding a familiar and accessible figure at the centre. The anonymous and Bede do not write in that way. They use passages of the Scriptures that Cuthbert himself knew and by which he lived to illuminate the whole man. What they show, like all Christian hagiography, is that the words and deeds of this human being were gradually entirely filled, transfigured, with the presence of God in Christ reconciling the world to himself. A Christian saint is not remembered as wise or great or righteous but as a humble and sinful human being who learned, through who knows what agonies and darknesses, so to walk in faith in Christ through his daily life that at the point of death he revealed to others, if not to himself, that underneath are the everlasting arms. The hagiographer is one who shows this life of discipleship to readers for their encouragement and imitation. In the three passages examined from the *Life of St Cuthbert*, I do not at all suggest that the events did not take place, but that in each case the meaning of them is revealed by the use of Scripture: at Melrose, it is not Cuthbert's education linked to miraculous prophecy that is presented, but the whole basis of his life is shown to have been set by an acceptance of the faith that does the works of love; by the North Sea at Coldingham, Cuthbert was no animal-lover out for a walk, but the new Adam in whom the right ordering of creation was restored; and on Farne, the writers do not give a picture of a busy bishop longing to get away from it all to a lovely island with nature and scenery: they bring the reader into the presence of a man crucified with Christ, alone and keeping silence as he accepts death.

Such was the force of this love in this human being that after death his flesh continued to shine with wholeness and his living presence on the other side of Christ continued to be a refuge, the shadow of a mighty rock within a weary land. At the place where his body lay, in the sure and certain hope of a glorious resurrection, the poor and needy and terrified continued to find peace. It seemed ominously appropriate to Bede that when Cuthbert died the monks of Lindisfarne were singing psalm 60: 'O God, thou hast cast us out and scattered us abroad', and he tells the reader to note how the whole of that psalm was fulfilled afterwards.[31] But when he ended his prose *Life of St Cuthbert* he used a different psalm, a psalm not of judgement but of mercy and blessing, and that is surely the final message of Cuthbert, who did not leave his humble successor on Farne, Felgild, to endure deformity and pain, but cured him so

[31] *VCP* 40, pp. 286 – 7 (Anglican ps. 60 is Vulgate ps. 59).

that 'his face had always been free from this affliction, through the grace of Almighty God, who in this present age is wont to heal many, and, in time to come, will heal our diseases of mind and body; for he satisfies our desire with good things and crowns us forever ''with loving kindness and tender mercies''.' (Ps. 103 (102): 4)[32]

---

[32] *VCP* 46, pp. 304 – 7.

Bede's Metrical Vita S. Cuthberti

MICHAEL LAPIDGE

Bede's metrical *Vita S. Cuthberti* is a substantial poem of nearly 1000 hexameters[1] and is the metrical counterpart of the anonymous prose *Vita S. Cuthberti*, which on the whole it follows closely in outline. On twelve occasions, however, it departs from its model in order to recount miracles not contained in the anonymous *vita* and which had probably come to Bede's notice by way of oral report.[2] For this reason alone the metrical *vita* might have been valued as an independent source for the history of Cuthbert and his cult, were it not for the fact that the diction of the poem is difficult and oblique, and that most (though not all) of the twelve additional miracles were subsequently recorded by Bede in plainer language in his prose *Vita S. Cuthberti*.[3] I suspect, therefore, that Charles Jones spoke for most historians when, in discussing Bede's hagiography, he wrote that 'I have disregarded [Bede's] metrical *Life of Cuthbert* and shall continue to do so.'[4] In my view the metrical *vita* has been unfairly disregarded through failure to understand its literary form and to appreciate the nature of its diction. Properly understood, it provides fresh evidence for the development of Bede's poetic technique and for his conception of the cult of St Cuthbert.

From the brief prose epistle which serves as its dedication, we learn that Bede dedicated the poem to a friend and colleague named John who was about

---

[1] For *VCM* I use Jaager's critical edition of 1935. J. Stevenson's earlier edition, *Venerabilis Bedae Opera Historica Minora* (London, 1841), pp. 1 – 43, is based on three manuscripts of the English family, on which see below.

[2] The following chapters in *VCM* have no correlate in *VCA*: 3, 5, 17, 20, 25, 33, 34, 39, 42, 44, 45, and 46.

[3] Two chapters in *VCM* (5 and 42) were *not* treated in *VCP*. However, the content of ch. 5 is related in *HE* III,15, so only for ch. 42 is *VCM* the unique witness.

[4] C. W. Jones, *Saints' Lives and Chronicles in Early England* (Ithaca, NY, 1947), p. 217.

to set out on a journey to Rome; the poem was intended by Bede to console John during the travails of his long journey. Of John we are told only that he was a priest; regrettably we cannot identify him.[5] Greater certainty is attainable with respect to the date of the poem, for at one point (lines 546 – 55) Bede refers to the succession of Kings Ecgfrith and Aldfrith and, on Aldfrith's death in 705, the accession of his young son Osred, then aged eight years. Bede refers respectfully to Osred as Aldfrith's 'venerable offspring' (*uenerabile pignus*) and describes him as a 'new Josiah' who is mature 'more in spirit than in years.'[6] Bede's respectful reference to Osred is a useful pointer to the date of the poem for, with the procession of his youthful years, Osred turned from a young Josiah into a wicked Ahab, defiling nuns and murdering noblemen, with the result that he was assassinated, while still a teenager, in 716.[7] That Bede should refer to this young monster as *uenerabile* suggests that his poem was written very soon indeed after Osred's accession, before he had turned to sin and wickedness: in other words, within a year (or two at most) of 705.[8]

If this dating is correct, the metrical *Vita S. Cuthberti* is a relatively early work, written while Bede was in his early thirties. Further light can be thrown on its genesis and composition by consideration of its manuscript transmission. Broadly speaking, the work is preserved in some twenty manuscripts, which fall into two families, one of which circulated on the continent, the other in England.[9] In addition to these, however, there is a single manuscript of exceptional interest whose text stands outside these two families and which has never been properly investigated: namely, Besançon, Bibliothèque municipale 186, probably written somewhere in western Germany in the mid ninth century and containing, in addition to the metrical *Vita S. Cuthberti*, various works by Bede (*De natura rerum, De temporum ratione,* the *Chronica maiora*) and a

---

[5] The name *Iohannes* is surprisingly rare in sources of this period, being borne by two men only, both well known: John of Beverley and John the Archchanter from St Peter's, Rome. John of Beverley is ruled out as a possible recipient of Bede's poem because he had been bishop since 687, and a bishop is unlikely to have been addressed as *presbyter*; while John the Archchanter, who came to England with Benedict Biscop, seems to have returned to Rome soon after the council of Hatfield in 680 (see *HE* IV,18 (16)).

[6] Osred was presumably compared to Josiah because, like Josiah, he began to reign at the age of eight (IV Kings (Anglican II Kings) 22:1).

[7] Osred's wickedness is referred to at length in the famous letter sent *c.*746/7 by Boniface and various continental bishops to King Aethelbald of Mercia: 'Osredum quoque spiritus luxoriae fornicantem et per monasteria nonnarum sacratas uirigines stuprantem et furentem agitauit . . .' (ed. M. Tangl, *S. Bonifatii et Lullii Epistolae,* MGH, Epist. sel. 1 (Berlin, 1916), p. 153); cf. also Aethelwulf, *De abbatibus,* lines 37 – 51 (ed. A. Campbell (Oxford, 1967), pp. 5 – 7), and below, n. 29.

[8] The poem was erroneously dated to before 705 by Plummer, who mistook the reference to Osred as referring to Aldfrith: Plummer I, p. cxlvi.

[9] See Jaager, *VCM,* pp. 33 – 6.

collection of computistical materials that was demonstrably used by Bede.[10] The version of Bede's poem in Besançon 186 is so different from that of the two families that it cannot be considered a scribal variant, and is best treated as a separate redaction.[11] Uniquely among manuscripts of the poem, this Besançon redaction lacks the dedicatory epistle to Bede's friend John. For many of the miracles it has chapter headings which are entirely different from those in (what I shall henceforth call) the vulgate recension, that is, the one preserved in the twenty manuscripts and printed by Werner Jaager.[12] Most important, it has at more than 100 places a text substantially different from that of the vulgate recension.[13] Two examples will make clear the nature of the difference. The first occurs in chapter six, where Cuthbert seeks shelter from a rainstorm in a shippon. He ties his horse to the wall and sets about praying; and the horse, biting into the thatched roof, dislodges a warm loaf of bread miraculously hidden there. The Besançon version is as follows:

> Expectansque udos Dominum conponere flatus
> Parieti conectit equum, solitisque retentus
> Carminibus, cernit auido decerpere morsu
> Tecta casae . . .[14]

In the vulgate recension, however, the passage reads as follows:

> Parieti et adnectit quo uenerat ipse caballum,

---

[10] See pl. 5. I am grateful to Bernhard Bischoff for advice on the date and origin of the manuscript; he also observes that it is 'auf Kalbpergament geschrieben, was in Frankreich eine grosse Ausnahme ist'. The contents of the manuscript are described by A. Castan, *Catalogue général des manuscrits des bibliothèques publiques des départements* XXXII (1897), pp. 127 – 8; the metrical *V. Cuth.* is on ff. 1r – 24r. On the computistical materials, see C. W. Jones, *Bedae Opera de temporibus* (Cambridge, Mass., 1943), pp. 332, 352, 371, 372 and 376. On the (interpolated) version of the *Chronica maiora*, see below, n. 26.

[11] Jaager, *VCM*, pp. 36 – 42. It will be clear from what follows that I disagree fundamentally with Jaager on the nature and significance of the Besançon redaction.

[12] E.g., in ch. 26, where the vulgate recension has 'Oblatum in itinere iuuenem moriturum oratione reuocauit ad uitam', the Besançon recension has 'Morientem iuuenem orando reducit ad uitam'; or in ch. 31, where the vulgate has 'animam cuiusdam qui de arbore cadendo mortuus est ad caelum ferri conspexit', the Besançon recension has 'Quomodo animam cuiusdam de arbore cadentis ad caelum ferri conspexerit'. There are many differences of this sort, usually involving changes in the tense and mood of the verbs.

[13] Jaager lists most of the variant readings in the Besançon manuscript (with the sigil B) in his apparatus criticus. However, it should be noted that a later scribe of Besançon 186 worked systematically through the text of *VCM*, erasing original readings and replacing them with readings found in the vulgate recension, or recording vulgate readings in the margins with the note *al* (= *aliter*): see pl. 5. It is difficult to determine precisely the date of this later corrector (s. x?), but the vulgate text against which he was correcting the Besançon version probably survives as St Gallen, Stiftsbibl. 263 (s. x); see Jaager, *VCM*, p. 40.

[14] 'And waiting for the Lord to calm the rainy blasts, he ties his horse to the wall and, while occupied with his customary incantations/poems (*carminibus*) he sees it [? — we have to supply *illum* or some such word] snatch the roof of the hut with a greedy bite . . .'

> Expectansque udos Dominum conponere flatus.
> Diuinis horam dum sacrat laudibus almus
> Cernit equum subito ipsius decerpere morsu
> Tecta casae . . .[15]
>
>   (169 – 73)

In the vulgate recension, the potential ambiguity of the *solitis carminibus* (literally 'incantations' or 'poems') is replaced with the unambiguous *diuinis . . . laudibus* ('heavenly praise'). The object of *cernit*, which is not immediately clear in the Besançon version, is made explicit in the vulgate recension: *cernit equum*. Note also that the metrical technique of the vulgate recension is more proficient, as may be seen from the elisions in *pariet(i) et*[16] and *subit(o) ipsius*, and the fact that the *productio ob caesuram* in Besançon's *cernīt ăuĭdŏ* is not found in the vulgate.

My second example is more telling. In describing Cuthbert's building programme on Farne Island, the vulgate recension relates a miracle designed to demonstrate how even the sea was subservient to Cuthbert (in this case by casting up a piece of driftwood for his house). The Besançon version also describes the sea's subservience to Cuthbert, but prefaces its description with an allusion to a miracle — regrettably not told in full — in which some pregnant seals were apparently unwilling to undergo childbirth and drop their pups until they had received Cuthbert's blessing:

> Quid referam uitulas foetus sub fasce grauatas
> Non ausas illic uteri deponere pondus
> Ni prius ipse sacra dextra permitteret illis?
> Quarum illi patrium seruit cum fluctibus aequor.
> Namque basem domui fratres, qui uisere crebro
> Consuerant illum, puppi sibi ferre rogabat.[17]

The charming story of the seals finds no mention in the vulgate version, where instead we only hear at greater length of the sea's subservience to saintly men such as Cuthbert:

> Quid referam aequoreas iusto famularier undas,
> Obsequiumque illis elementa impendere, qui se

---

[15] 'And he ties the horse to the wall where he arrived, waiting for the Lord to calm the rainy blasts. And while the holy man hallows the hour in heavenly praise, he suddenly sees the horse snatch at the roof of the hut with a bite . . .'

[16] Indeed Besançon's scansion of *parieti* — whether *părĭĕtĭ* (by synizesis, as in Virgil, *Georgics* IV,297 and *Aeneid* II,442 and V,589) or *părīĕtĭ* — is metrically unsatisfactory; the vulgate *părĭĕt(i) ĕt* eases the problem. I am very grateful to Giovanni Orlandi and Neil Wright for advice on these metrical matters.

[17] 'What shall I say of the seals, weighed down with the burden of pregnancy, who did not dare to drop the offspring of their womb unless the saint had blessed them beforehand with his holy right hand? The seals' watery homeland also served the saint with its waves. For he asked the monks, who were in the habit of visiting him fairly often, to bring him by boat a foundation for his house.'

> Imperiis subdunt deuota mente supernis?
> Namque suis casulam structurus ibi usibus aptam
> Quam bases a ponti fulciret parte, rogabat
> Conueniens operi fratres adducere lignum.[18] (451 – 6)

The particular — and somewhat homely[19] — example of the Besançon version is replaced with more general reflection on how the elements serve those who serve divine commands. As in the previous example, the vulgate version shows greater metrical proficiency in its handling of elision (four examples compared to one in the corresponding passage in the Besançon version) and in its confident use of two monosyllabic words (*qui se*) to fill the sixth foot of a hexameter and create a sophisticated enjambement with pause after the fifth foot.

It is not possible here to analyse each of the hundred or so occasions where the Besançon (or B-) recension differs from the vulgate; however, several unmistakeable tendencies emerge from a close comparison of the two versions. For example, there are various places where a minor slip in scansion in the B-recension has been corrected in the vulgate:

> B: nec orbis contenta sinu trans aequora lampas
> vulg: nec i(am) orbis contenta sinu trans aequora lampas (25)

(Here *nec* has been wrongly scanned as a naturally long syllable in B; in the vulgate recension it has been made into a closed (hence long) syllable by the following *iam*, which in turn elides before the initial vowel of *orbis*.)

> B: quippe matutina qui uenerit algidus aura
> vulg: qui matutinis aduenerit algidus auris (193)

(In B the first syllable of *mātutinum* has wrongly been taken as short; the identical error is made in lines 234 and 887 of Besançon. In all three cases the slip has been corrected in the vulgate recension by altering the position of the word within the metrical foot so that it is correctly scanned as long.)

> B: femineis subito rogitat sic inbuta curis
> vulg: femineis subito rogitat sic anxia curis (501)

(Although the second syllable of *imbŭo* is indeed short, that of the past participle (*imbūtus*) is long; this oversight in B was evidently recognized and corrected by the substitution of the metrically acceptable synonym *anxia*.)

Metrical corrections such as these show the concern of a painstaking and proficient poet. So too does the elimination of *productio ob caesuram* which we

---

[18] 'What shall I say of the watery waves' subservience to the just man, and of how the elements serve those who subject themselves with devout application to heavenly commands? For Cuthbert, setting out to construct there a little house suitable for his needs which a foundation facing the sea would support, asked the monks to bring some wood appropriate for the purpose.'

[19] As far as I am aware, this miracle of the pregnant seals does not occur elsewhere in the hagiography of St Cuthbert. A miracle involving pregnant seals is related in Adomnan's *Vita S. Columbae* I, 41: see P. Boglioni, 'Il santo e gli animali nell' alto medioevo', *Settimane di Studio del Centro Italiano di Studi sull' Alto Medioevo* 31 (1985), pp. 935 – 93, at 943.

have seen in an earlier example. The same is true of the greatly increased number of elisions found in the vulgate recension. Elision was one aspect of Latin verse technique which proved particularly difficult for Anglo-Latin poets: compare its rarity in Aldhelm's poetry.[20] Notice, therefore, two places where the vulgate contains lines which have apparently been altered for no reason other than the incorporation of an elision:[21]

> B: nos ualet hac etiam genitor satiare ministra.
> vulg: nos ualet hac eti(am) omnipotens satiare ministra (301)

> B: dum premeret, sancti sumens oraria uatis
> vulg: dum premeret, sanct(i) accipiens oraria uatis (873).

In each case the change (*genitor/omnipotens*, *sumens/accipiens*) has no lexical significance and could only have been made for metrical reasons.

Another tendency which distinguishes the two versions is the vulgate's freer handling of lines taken over from earlier poets. Sometimes a hexameter in the B-recension is indebted to a late Latin poet, whereas in the vulgate version the immediacy of the debt is less clear because the line has been reshaped to fit more smoothly into its new surroundings. For example, a line in the B-recension is based unmistakeably on Arator:

> B: mentibus instet amor, sermonibus aestuet ardor
> Arator: mentibus instat amor, sermonibus aestuat ardor (I,147)

In the vulgate recension, however, the debt to Arator is slightly less obvious because the line has been reworked so as to incorporate an alliterating symmetry between the two halves of the hexameter (the change in meaning is insignificant):

> sensibus instet amor, sermonibus aestuet ardor (7)

The B-recension is closer to Arator; the vulgate version is perhaps closer to poetry.

There are often striking differences in factual detail between the two versions. For example, the B-recension, in describing the miracle of the woman (Hildmer's wife) possessed by a devil, asserts that Cuthbert was prior of Melrose at the time:

> namque Mailrosae fuerat iam tempore in illo
> praepositus cellae . . .

---

[20] See M. Lapidge, 'Aldhelm's Latin Poetry and Old English Verse', *Comparative Literature* 31 (1979), pp. 209–31, at 216–17.
[21] Other examples of hexameters recast so as to incorporate elision occur at lines 300, 676, 685, 688, 882, and 951.

That Cuthbert *was* prior of Melrose is a reasonable inference from the text of the anonymous *Vita S. Cuthberti*, for in the next chapter (*VCA* III,1) we are told explicitly that Cuthbert, then prior of Melrose, came at Eata's invitation to Lindisfarne. However, a closer reading of the anonymous prose *Life* (*VCA* II,8) establishes that Cuthbert *must already* have been prior of Lindisfarne at the time of the miraculous cure of Hildmer's wife, for the text says *illo tempore aecclesiae nostrae praepositus erat*, where 'our church' is unambiguously Lindisfarne. The vulgate recension of the metrical *vita* has Cuthbert correctly as prior of Lindisfarne at this point:

> tempore namque fuit Lindisfarnensis in illo
> praepositus cellae . . .   (347 – 8)

The natural — but erroneous — inference in the B-recension concerning Cuthbert's priorate at Melrose has been corrected to Lindisfarne, apparently as a result of closer attention to the text of the anonymous *Life*.

The Besançon redaction is a version of the poem which in many ways is less expert than the vulgate version: capable of a few peccadilloes of scansion, less confident in handling elision, more tenaciously dependent on poetic models such as Arator, occasionally capable of minor slips in comprehension of the anonymous prose *Life*. In my view it is inconceivable that a later redactor of the poem could have taken Bede's vulgate version and worked through it systematically suppressing most of its elisions, restoring verbatim reminiscences of poetic models at the expense of fluent diction, introducing errors of scansion and understanding of the prose source: for what would be the point of such an exercise?[22] It seems to me much more likely that the Besançon manuscript preserves an earlier and somewhat less competent draft of Bede's poem, and that this draft was subsequently revised by Bede himself. Certainly the diction of the Besançon redaction is thoroughly and recognizably Bedan: several of its unique lines embody phrases found elsewhere in Bede's poetry,[23] and even its occasional spelling peculiarities reproduce Bede's own orthography as we know it from the Moore and Leningrad manuscripts of the

---

[22] Jaager (*VCM*, pp. 36 – 42) assumes tacitly — without ever stating as much, and without questioning his assumption — that the Besançon version is a later reworking of the vulgate text, in which the redactor removed elisions ('hinzu kommt, dass ihn die . . . Elisionen . . . gestört haben werden'), omitted verses necessary for sense ('bisweilen sind ganze Verse fortgefallen, die aber notwendig sind'), misunderstood the text in, for example, altering the reference to Lindisfarne in lines 347 – 8 ('der Urheber des B-Textes, der sonst Kenntnis der Prosa zeigt, hat das [that is, the fact that Cuthbert was already prior at Lindisfarne] nicht beachtet') and in general reworked the text ('wie ist der Bearbeiter zu der Veränderung gekommen?').

[23] E.g., the phrase *peruigil en* beginning a line of the B-recension ('peruigil en iuuenis studuit dinoscere gressus') which corresponds to line 222 of the vulgate version ('illius incertos studuit dinoscere gressus'), recurs elsewhere in the vulgate version at line 127: 'peruigil en modico magnalia tempore creui'.

Historia ecclesiastica.[24] I take it, then, that the Besançon redaction is a hitherto unnoticed earlier draft, by Bede himself, of the metrical *Vita S. Cuthberti.*

The Besançon manuscript, as I have said, is of mid-ninth-century date, probably of West German origin. That it was copied from an earlier exemplar in some informal grade of Anglo-Saxon minuscule script is clear from the scribe's confusion of insular abbreviations: thus he mistakes *c̄* for *con-* rather than *cum* (hence the erroneous reading *secon* in line 442) and *ꝑ* (= *per*) for *post* in lines 846 and 853. The other contents of Besançon 186 corroborate the suspicion of an earlier Anglo-Saxon exemplar. The recension of *De temporum ratione* which it contains, for example, is related to copies from the area of the Anglo-Saxon mission centred in Fulda.[25] On the other hand, its version of the *Chronica maiora* contains interpolated entries pertaining to Merovingian affairs, the latest of which is the death of Charles Martel in 741.[26] Taken in combination, this evidence suggests that Besançon 186 was copied from a (lost) exemplar in Anglo-Saxon minuscule originating from the area of the Anglo-Saxon mission and dating from the second half of the eighth century.[27] It thus takes us back to the earliest continental phase of the transmission of Bede's writings to the continent, to the period of Lul's request to the abbot of Wearmouth/Jarrow for *libellos de uiro Dei Cudbercto metro et prosa conpositos.*[28]

Let me sum up my speculations thus far. Basing himself on the anonymous prose *Life of Cuthbert*, Bede produced while still a young man a metrical life of

[24] E.g., the spellings *promtim* and *sumto* in lines 151 and 152 of the Besançon version. Such spellings, without the intrusive -*p*-, are characteristic of Bede and are found consistently in both the Leningrad and Moore manuscripts of the *HE*: for *promtus*, see *HE* IV,2 and V,11, and for *sumtus*, *HE* I,12. The analogous spelling *consumtus* is found at *HE* I,19, IV,25 and 30, and V,23, as well as in the Budapest fragment of *VCM* (on which see below, n. 27), which is the earliest surviving manuscript of that work.

[25] See C. W. Jones, *Bedae Venerabilis Opera Pars VI: Opera Didascalica* (CCSL 123B), pp. 241 and 244.

[26] The *Chronica maiora* are interpolated with materials related to the so-called *Chronicon Moissiacense* (MGH, Scriptores 1, pp. 280 – 313) up to the death of Charles Martel in 741: see L. Delisle, 'Note sur un manuscrit interpolé de la Chronique de Bède conservé à Besançon', *Bibliothèque de l'Ecole des Chartes* 56 (1895), pp. 528 – 36, who does not, however, discuss the date or origin of the manuscript.

[27] The earliest known manuscript of *VCM* (a manuscript unknown to Jaager) survives as *membra disiecta* in Budapest and Tübingen: *CLA*, XI, no. 1589; on the Budapest fragment now in the National Szécheny Library, Cod. Lat. 441, see P. Lehmann, 'Mitteilungen aus Handschriften, V', *Sitzungsberichte der Bayerischen Akademie der Wissenschaften* 1938, no. 4, pp. 4 – 6; on the Tübingen fragment, formerly in Berlin, see H. Hornung, 'Ein Fragment der metrischen St. Cuthbert-Vita des Beda im Nachlass der Brüder Grimm', *Scriptorium* 14 (1960), pp. 344 – 6. The script of this manuscript is Anglo-Saxon set minuscule of s. viii², and has been compared by Bernhard Bischoff (*apud* Hornung, p. 344, n. 2) to that of a contemporary manuscript probably written at Fulda, *CLA*, IX, no. 1381. This manuscript shows that *VCM* was known probably at Fulda by s. viii² (see below, n. 28), and it will need to be collated by any future editor of *VCM*. The collations printed by Lehmann and Hornung clearly show that its text is of the vulgate recension.

[28] *S. Bonifatii et Lullii Epistolae*, ed. Tangl, p. 251 (a letter from Abbot Cuthbert of Wearmouth/Jarrow to Lul, dated 764, replying to his request for copies of Bede). On the export of manuscripts of Bede's writings to the continent at this time, see M. B. Parkes, *The Scriptorium of Wearmouth-Jarrow* (Jarrow Lecture, 1982).

that saint, probably by 705 or shortly thereafter. This early work reflects Bede's relative inexperience as a poet and it survives in but a single manuscript, now Besançon 186. Some years later, having acquired a more perfect grasp of metre and quantity, Bede thoroughly revised this earlier draft: and on that occasion he dedicated his revised poem to his friend John, then about to depart for Rome (this would explain why the Besançon manuscript lacks the dedicatory epistle).[29] It is not clear when the work of revision was done; but it is reasonable to think that when — in the light of Cuthbert's growing cult — Bede was at work on his prose *Life of Cuthbert*, his fresh consultation of the anonymous *Life* caused him to look again at his earlier poem: and he found it wanting in various respects. In other words, the work of revision which produced the vulgate version took place probably in the second decade of the eighth century, and was followed shortly afterwards by the completion of his prose *Life* not later than 721.[30] It is the later, revised version of the poem which enjoyed the widest circulation (hence I have called it the vulgate version), though there is some evidence to suggest that the earlier (Besançon) version was known to both Alcuin[31] and Aethelwulf.[32] In any event the Besançon version deserves to be printed and studied in its own right, for comparison of this early draft with Bede's more mature production can give us fresh insight into his poetic technique.

[29] In the dedicatory epistle to Iohannes, Bede explains that he had composed the metrical *Life* *nuper* ('beati Cuthberti episcopi, quae nuper uersibus edidi, gesta obtuli'), but it is not clear how great a lapse of time is implied by the word *nuper*: it could mean 'recently', but also 'formerly', 'once'. Nor is there any chronological implication in the fact that, when revising the Besançon version, Bede did not alter his remarks about Osred who, by the time Bede made his revision — on my interpretation, some time in the second decade of the eighth century — could no longer have been considered a *uenerabile pignus*. In mentioning Osred's reign in the *HE*, Bede passed over Osred's crimes in silence (*HE* V,22 and 24).

[30] Note that in the dedicatory epistle to *VCM* Bede apparently refers to the prose *vita* as imminent ('spero me in alio opere nonnulla ex his, quae praetermiseram, memoriae redditurum') — which is odd if ten or more years elapsed between the verse and prose *vitae*, but natural if he was revising the one and composing the other at roughly the same time. In the preface to the prose *vita* he refers to the metrical *vita*, which he claims was written 'some time ago' ('heroicis dudum uersibus edidi'); but as in the case of *nuper* (above, n. 29), it is impossible to determine how great a lapse of time is implied.

[31] See Jaager, *VCM*, p. 41, who notes that Alcuin erroneously stated that Bede composed his metrical *Life of Cuthbert after* the prose *Life* (*Versus de . . . sanctis Euboricensis ecclesiae*, lines 686 – 7: 'prosaico primum scripsit sermone magister / et post heroico cecinit miracula uersu'), an error which would be more easily explicable if Alcuin had had before him the Besançon version of *VCM*, which lacks the dedicatory epistle with its clear statement about the priority of the verse *Life*. Furthermore, one line of Alcuin's poem (line 712: 'ut mare cum beluis sancto seruire solebat') seems to refer in the words *cum beluis* to the miracle of Cuthbert and the pregnant seals which, as we have seen, occurs only in the Besançon version of *VCM*.

[32] One line of Aethelwulf's *De abbatibus* (299: 'se precibus cupiunt domino mandare profusis') seems to be modelled nearly verbatim on a line in the Besançon version: 'se precibus poscit domino mandare profusis'; the corresponding verse in the vulgate version is rather different (239: 'se poscit domino prece commendare profusa').

Before turning to his poetic technique, however, it is necessary to consider briefly the literary form of the metrical *Life.* We are now relatively well informed about the relationship of prose to verse as it was conceived by Anglo-Latin writers and applied in such *opera geminata* as Aldhelm's massive *De virginitate.*[33] The relationship of Bede's metrical *Life of Cuthbert* to its prose counterpart, the anonymous *Vita S. Cuthberti,* must be understood within this wider context. The technique of converting a prose text into hexameters was a pedagogic device practised in the schools of antiquity: we know, for example, that the prose of Plato and Xenophon was turned into Greek hexameters as a school exercise in Alexandrian schools.[34] In the first century AD Quintilian recommended such paraphrase as a grammarian's means of sharpening the wits of the young: his point being that such practice inculcated in students the difference between the vocabulary and means of expression characteristic of prose from that characteristic of verse.[35] With the burgeoning of Christian Latin literature from the fourth century onwards, we find that biblical prose — and especially the Gospels — becomes the subject of metrical paraphrase by poets seeking to supply a wider Christian reading public with literature of sophistication suitable to the tastes acquired studying Virgil and other Latin poets in classical schools.[36] From the point of view of the later middle ages, the biblical paraphrases which exerted the greatest influence were those of Juvencus, Caelius Sedulius, and Arator. Juvencus's *Euangelia,* completed in the early fourth century, is a synoptic account of Christ's life and passion in four substantial books which follow very closely, almost literally, the biblical account.[37] About a century later Caelius Sedulius produced in his *Carmen paschale* a hexameter paraphrase of the passion story; but his account is much freer than that of Juvencus, in that it frequently departs from the narrative in order to reflect on the typological significance of New Testament events: how they were prefigured in the Old Testament, their moral, soteriological and eschatological meaning.[38] The tendency away from literal paraphrase and towards allegorical exposition of the significance of New Testament events reaches its apogee in the sixth-century poet Arator, whose lengthy hexametrical paraphrase of the Acts of the Apostles was completed in 544 and read aloud

---

[33] See P. Godman, 'The Anglo-Latin *opus geminatum*: from Aldhelm to Alcuin', *Medium Aevum* 50 (1981), pp. 215 – 29, and G. Wieland, '*Geminus stilus*: Studies in Anglo-Latin Hagiography', in *Insular Latin Studies,* ed. M. W. Herren (Toronto, 1981), pp. 113 – 33.

[34] See K. Thraede, 'Epos', in *Reallexikon für Antike und Christentum* 5 (Stuttgart, 1962), cols. 983 – 1042, at 991 – 3.

[35] *Inst. orat.* I,ix,2 – 3 and X,v,9; see discussion by M. Roberts, *Biblical Epic and Rhetorical Paraphrase in Late Antiquity* (Liverpool, 1985), pp. 13 – 18.

[36] See Roberts, *Biblical Epic,* pp. 61 – 106.

[37] *Euangeliorum libri quattuor,* ed. J. Huemer (CSEL 24). See C. Marold, 'Über das Evangelienbuch des Juvencus in seinem Verhältnisse zum Bibeltext', *Zeitschrift für wissenschaftliche Theologie* 33 (1890), pp. 329 – 41, and Roberts, *Biblical Epic,* pp. 75, 135 – 7 and 162 – 4. Cf. Jerome: '[Juvencus] quattuor euangelia hexametris uersibus *paene ad uerbum* transferens' (*De uiris illustribus,* ch. 84; my italics).

[38] *Opera,* ed. J. Huemer (CSEL 10), pp. 1 – 154; see Roberts, *Biblical Epic,* pp. 165 – 71.

(in four sittings) before Pope Vigilius at the church of S. Pietro in Vincoli in Rome.[39] It is cast in two books of about one thousand lines each, the first dealing with Peter and the second with Paul. Arator's poem is more than a mere paraphrase of Acts: it might rather be described as a poetic commentary on them, in which the poet attempts to elucidate the inner meaning of each event by reference to Old Testament typology and Christian symbolism.[40] Each event is made to point to a general moral or spiritual truth. The literary form of Arator's poem is that, for each biblical event, he first gives a very brief prose summary (to remind the reader of the event in question) and then follows this with (usually) fifty to a hundred or more lines of exegesis on the figural significance of the event. His procedure will be clear from an example. In Acts 12:1 – 9, the biblical narrative describes the persecution of Herod, his murder of James and his capture of Peter (the day of capture is specified as Azymes or the Days of Unleavened Bread); Peter is to be guarded in prison by two soldiers until the feast of the Passover, but is miraculously released by an angel. The episode is treated as follows by Arator:

DE EO VBI BEATVS PETRVS CVM CVSTODIRETVR IN CARCERE, NOCTE ANGELVS EST INGRESSVS ET REFVLSIT HABITACVLVM PVLSATOQVE LATERE EIVS SECVM DVXIT VBI SE FERREA PORTA QVAE AD HIEROSOLYMAM MITTIT APERVIT; ET IBI VERITATEM LIBERATIONIS AGNOSCENS DEO GRATIAS EGIT.

> Clauditur obscuro, sed non sine lumine, Petrus,
> Carcere, nec possunt tenebrae caligine furua
> Ecclesiae celare diem; commune per omnes
> Supplicium timor ille facit; custodia Petri
> Publica poena fuit; proprium sed pastor ouile
> Seruato custode regit, quem ditat honore
> Ter Dominum confessus amor; de nomine petrae
> Nomen Petrus habens aeterna uocabula portat,
> Fundamenta gerens numquam passura ruinam.
> Exspectate tuis cunctoque in tempore carus
> Et nobis iam, Petre, ueni! Simul omnibus exi
> Quos stimulat nunc cura prior! Iam nocte profunda
> Angelus astra ferens ergastula candidus intrat
> Se comitante die; caeli ueniente ministro
> Carceris umbra fugit; pulsae periere tenebrae
> Lucifero radiante nouo; color exsulat ater,
> Et mutata uident nocturna crepuscula solem.
> Custodum uallante manu inter uincula Petro
> Corpore somnus erat; sed cum uigilaret in illo
> Quae nescit dormire fides, hoc Cantica clamant:

[39] *Aratoris subdiaconi de actibus apostolorum*, ed. A.P. McKinlay (CSEL 72).
[40] See Roberts, *Biblical Epic*, pp. 172 – 9.

'Dormio corde uigil.' Laeti documenta figurae
Discite, qui liquido meruistis fonte renasci,
Et quae forma manet sacrato in corpore Petri
Cernite corde pio . . .[41]

(I,1007 – 30)

There are several points to notice here. Although the episode is potentially of great interest as narrative, Arator is apparently not interested in it *as story*. The details of the biblical narrative (Herod's persecution, the murder of James, the dates of the events, the numbers of guards, and so on) have all been eliminated. Even the event itself (Peter released by the angel) is subsumed in various patterns of Christian imagery: daylight/darkness, Peter as the bedrock foundation of the church, Christ as shepherd, sleep/watchfulness. The tendency throughout is away from the expression of the particular to general and abstract terms: Peter is conceived not as a human apostle but as a symbol of the church. This tendency is evident in the non-particularized nature of the diction: thus we are not told simply that Peter was asleep when the angel arrived, but that 'there was slumber in the body of Peter' (*Petro / corpore somnus erat*). Arator is only interested in the figural significance of the event, not in the event itself: *documenta figurae / discite*. It is this concern which explains the oblique and abstract nature of Arator's poem.

An understanding of Arator's literary intentions can help to explain what Bede was attempting in his metrical *vita* of Cuthbert. There is no doubt that Bede was deeply steeped in Arator at the time he was working on the poem. In his own (first) commentary on Acts, the *Expositio Actuum Apostolorum* (composed at roughly the same time as the poem) Bede very frequently resorts simply to quoting Arator by way of commenting on a biblical passage; as he

---

[41] 'CONCERNING HOW WHEN ST PETER WAS CONFINED IN PRISON, AN ANGEL ENTERED AT NIGHT AND ILLUMINATED HIS CELL; AND HAVING STRUCK HIS SIDE LED HIM TO WHERE THE IRON GATE OPENED WHICH LEADS TO THE CITY OF JERUSALEM; AND REALIZING THERE THE TRUTH OF HIS FREEDOM, PETER GAVE THANKS TO GOD. Peter is enclosed in a dark cell, but not altogether without light: for shadows with their murky darkness cannot conceal the daylight of the church. This fear creates a torment shared by all the populace; the arrest of Peter was a public punishment. But the Shepherd rules His own sheepfold, having preserved His custodian, whom love, having confessed the Lord on three occasions, enriches with distinction. Peter, having his name from the name of a rock (*petra*), bears an eternal appellation, in supporting a foundation which shall never suffer collapse. Longed for by your followers and dear through all time, Peter, come to us now! Come forth together with all those who now are prompted by divine love! In the depth of night a shining angel, bearing the stars with him, enters the prison, daylight accompanying him; the darkness of the prison-cell disperses with the arrival of Heaven's agent; the shadows perish, driven out by this shining new dawn; blackness is put to flight and the nocturnal gloom, transformed, sees the light of day. There was slumber in the body of Peter, with a troop of guards keeping him in chains; but since that faith which knows not how to sleep was awake in him, the Song of Songs sings out: 'I sleep but my heart waketh' [Cant. 5:2]. Learn, happy people, the significance of this *figura*, you who have deserved rebirth in the clear fountain [of baptism], and observe in your religious hearts the symbol (*forma*) which abides in the holy body of Peter . . .'

says in the preface to that work, although he drew on other Christian Fathers, 'Arator was the greatest help of all'.[42] Furthermore, Bede's metrical *vita* is permeated with verbal reminiscences of Arator from beginning to end.[43] I should wish to go further, and suggest that the very form of Bede's poem is modelled on Arator. In producing a metrical paraphrase, Bede could — for the sake of argument — have followed the example of Juvencus and produced a closely literal version. But Bede's version is not literal. Like Arator, Bede prefaces each episode of his poem with a prose *capitulum* summarizing the event and alluding to its more detailed exposition in the anonymous prose *Life*; then follows a poetic exegesis of the event, usually of twenty to fifty lines' duration. For purposes of illustration I select the shortest verse-chapter of the poem (ch. 12). In the corresponding chapter of the anonymous prose *Life* (*VCA* II,7), we are told that Cuthbert came one day to *Hruringaham* (an unidentified village near Melrose) in order to visit Coenswith, his foster-mother; while visiting her, a fire in a house on the eastern edge of the village, fanned by a strong wind, threatened to destroy the entire village, but through his prayers Cuthbert averted the disaster. In Bede's poem a prose *capitulum* serves to remind us of the event as narrated in the anonymous *Life*, and then follows the poetic exegesis:

> QVOMODO FLAMMAS DOMVS CVIVSDAM ARDENTIS ORATIONE
> RESTINXERIT.
> Quin etiam ueri flammis crepitantibus ignes
> Arida deriperent tecti dum culmina quondam,
> Incubuit precibus, uentosque laresque retorquens
> Voce pericla fugat, iuuenum quae dextra nequibat.
> Nec mirum uati fragilem cessisse caminum,
> Igniferis satanae qui spicula torta pharetris
> Aetherio suerat umbone relidere Christi.[44]   (333 – 9)

Here once again the details (the names of the village and of the woman, the fact that she was Cuthbert's foster-mother and that he visited her often, and so on) have been eliminated; as in Arator, the focus here is on the figural meaning of the event, not the event itself: the fire in the village is seen as a

[42] M. L. W. Laistner, *Bedae Venerabilis Expositio Actuum Apostolorum et Retractatio* (Cambridge, Mass., 1939), p. 3.

[43] See M. Manitius, 'Zu Aldhelm und Baeda', *Sitzungsberichte der philosophisch-historischen Classe der kaiserlichen Akademie der Wissenschaften* 112 (1886), pp. 535 – 634, at 623 – 4, together with Jaager's *apparatus fontium*.

[44] 'HOW THROUGH PRAYER HE EXTINGUISHED THE FLAMES OF A CERTAIN BURNING HOUSE. What is more, when real fire with crackling flames would once have seized the dry thatches of a roof, he fell to prayer and, turning back the fire and wind, he puts the danger to flight with his word — something which the strong arms of the young men could not accomplish. Nor is it any wonder that a mere fire should give way to a saint, who was accustomed to repel the arrows cast from Satan's fiery quiver with the heavenly shield of Christ.'

figura of the fiery arrows of Satan's temptations. The episode is couched in general terms: a fire would have burned a roof. We are not told where the house (to which the roof belonged) was located, because such details are irrelevant to Bede's purpose — that of illustrating the timeless struggle between good and evil. I thus dissent from the opinion of Wilhelm Levison, who in remarking the 'vaguer outlines' of the metrical *vita*, noted that 'many proper names are omitted to suit the exigencies of the verses.'[45] It was not metrical exigency, but rather fidelity to the model of Arator, which caused Bede to excise details and to focus on the figural significance of event.

Understood on these terms, Bede's metrical *Vita S. Cuthberti* is a remarkable poem — remarkable above all for the abstract and figural nature of its language, and for the extreme compression and allusiveness of its diction. Something of these qualities can be seen from a close look at an extended passage of the poem. For convenience we may look at what is probably the best known of all the miracles, namely the story of Cuthbert and the sea otters (ch. 8).

> Interea iuuenis solitos nocturnus ad hymnos
> Digreditur, lento quidam quem calle secutus
> Illius incertos studuit dinoscere gressus.
> Ad mare deueniunt; collo tenus inditus undis
> Marmoreo, Cuthbertus agit sub carmine noctem.
> Egreditur ponto genibusque in litore fixis
> Expandit geminas supplex ad sidera palmas.
> Tum maris ecce duo ueniunt animalia fundo
> Vatis et ante pedes fulua sternuntur harena;
> Hinc gelidas uillo flatuque fouentia plantas
> Aequoreum tergunt sancto de corpore frigus.
> Supplice tum nutu sese benedicier orant.
> Qui parens uotis uerbo dextraque ministris
> Impendit grates patriasque remittit ad undas
> Ac matutino tectis se tempore reddit.
>   Haec comes ut uidit perculsus corda pauore,
> Semianimem curuo flatum trahit abditus antro.
> At reuoluta dies noctis cum pelleret umbras,
> Aeger adest uati, supplex genibusque uolutus
> Se poscit Domino prece commendare profusa,
> Inciderit maestam subito quod pondere noctem.
> 'Num nostrum e speculis', dixit, 'temptando latenter
> Lustrabas itiner? Sed nunc donabitur error
> Iam tibi poscenti, retices si uisa, quousque
> Decedam mundo.' Summique exempla magistri
> Exsequitur, misso renouans qui lumine caecos

[45] *Bede, his Life, Times, and Writings*, ed. A. H. Thompson (Oxford, 1935), p. 127.

Praecipit auctorem reducis celare salutis.
Tum prece languorem pellit culpamque relaxat.
Inque dies meritis crescenti summa tonantis
Gratia testis adest, pandunt miracula mentem.
Iamque prophetalis stellanti e culmine uirtus
Candida praerutilo irradiat praecordia flatu.[46]   (220 – 51)

Although this miracle makes an excellent story *as* story — told from the point
of view of the cleric who illicitly followed Cuthbert and was astonished to see
the otters perform their obeisance to the saint — Bede was simply not
interested in the narrative potential of the story. *Interea iuuenis*: although we
know from the anonymous prose *Life* (*VCA* II,3) that the miracle took place at
Coldingham at a time when Cuthbert, then prior at Melrose, was visiting at
the invitation of the abbess Aebbe, here in the poem we are given no
geographical orientation whatsoever, and the only temporal indication is that
the miracle took place when Cuthbert was a young man (*iuuenis*). It is part of
Bede's purpose to remove the episodes of Cuthbert's life from the temporal
and the local and to situate them in a timeless, placeless framework. We also
know from the prose source that it was Cuthbert's habit to spend every night
walking about on the seashore chanting hymns. Here in the poem the epithet
properly pertinent to the hymns, *nocturnus*, is transferred (by a device called
hypallage) to Cuthbert himself, so that he becomes, by a somewhat startling
and concise metaphor, a 'nocturnal youth'. As he sets out, 'someone' (*quidam*)
follows him — note that this follower is not specified in any way — slowly, or
rather, by means of 'a slow path' (here the epithet *lentus* is tranferred from the

---

[46] 'Meanwhile the nocturnal young man sets off for his usual hymn singing; someone, following
him by a slow path, sought to trace his unknown steps. They arrive at the sea; submerged in the
waves as far as his marble-white neck, Cuthbert spends the night chanting. He emerges from the
sea and, fixing his knees on the sea shore, he extends his two hands to the heavens in supplication.
Then two animals come from the depths of the sea and prostrate themselves on the golden sand at
the saint's feet. Then, warming his frozen feet with their fur and breath they wipe the watery cold
from the holy body. Then they beg in earnest supplication to be given a blessing. He, consenting
to their wishes, gives thanks to his attendants by his word and his right hand, and sends them back
to their native waters; and takes himself back to the dwellings in the early morning light.
   As the companion watches these things, he is struck to the heart with fear and, hidden in his
curved cave, he draws half-dying breath. But when the returning day had driven away the
shadows of night, he stands, sick, before the saint; and throwing himself on his knees in
supplication, he asks Cuthbert in profuse prayer to commend him to the Lord, because he had
stumbled upon a sad night with a sudden burden. "Did you observe my journey", he said,
"testing me secretly from your cave? But your error shall now be forgiven at your request, if you
remain silent about the things you have seen until I depart from this world." Cuthbert followed
the example of the great Teacher Who, after restoring the sight of the blind men, ordered them to
conceal the source of their recovered health. Then with prayer he expelled the illness and forgave
the sin. The highest grace of God is present as a witness to Cuthbert, growing in merit day by day:
his miracles reveal his spiritual state. And now a prophetic power, derived from the starry summit
of heaven, illuminates his shining heart with its brilliant radiance.'

unspecified follower to the path itself, creating another compressed metaphor). When they get to the sea, Cuthbert submerges himself up to the neck (*collo tenus . . . marmoreo*). In the prose *Life*, he goes in no farther than his loin-cloth; the submersion as far as his 'marble-white neck' owes more to Virgil (*Georgics* IV,523) than to reality, for it cannot have been easy to chant hymns while standing up to the neck in water. When he comes out he prays with his hands raised to the stars (another Virgilian reminiscence: *Aeneid* II,153), and it is then that the sea otters arrive. In the poem, however, they are only described abstractly as *animalia*;[47] the inexplicable nature of their advent is further suggested by their origin 'from the depths', *fundo* (it is not clear whether the genitive *maris* qualifies the 'depths' or the 'animals': an intentional ambiguity in Bede's language). They set to work to wipe the 'watery cold' (*aequoreum . . . frigus*) from the holy body. Bede's striving for abstract, generalized expression is here seen clearly through comparison with the diction of his earlier (Besançon) version. There the animals had wiped *aequoreas . . . sordes* from the saint's body — where the poet seems to have had in mind something concrete like sea weed (*sordes* means literally 'filth'); but in the revised, vulgate version any trace of concreteness has been replaced by the suggestively abstract expression 'watery cold'.

Attention shifts back to Cuthbert's follower, who is now described tersely as *comes*: he has become Cuthbert's 'companion', in effect because he has been watching him in secrecy. The potential narrative of the follower's action is immobilized and frozen into the single noun *comes*. When he sees Cuthbert bless the animals, he is struck to the heart with fear and can scarcely draw breath while hidden in his curved cave. Here the compression of Bede's poetic diction is seen at its best. We have not been told that, while Cuthbert went into the sea, the companion hid himself to watch, nor that the sea shore was bounded by cliffs, nor that these cliffs contained a curved recess which could serve as the 'companion's' hiding place. All this is concisely conveyed by the words *curuo . . . abditus antro*. Then when daylight comes, *aeger adest uati*: 'sick, the man stands before the saint'. Again, we have not been told what we know from the anonymous *Life*, namely that the cleric lay in fear and trembling among the rocks all night so that by morning he was sick to the point of death: the night of anxiety, the progress of the illness, all this is compressed into the word *aeger*. Bede exploits beautifully a peculiarity of Latin, which does not require defining articles for its nouns: not *ille aeger*, but simply *aeger*. Cuthbert forgives the man on condition he tell no one, and in this, Bede points out, Cuthbert followed the example of Christ who told the two blind men not to reveal who had healed them (Matth. 9:27 – 30). With this reference the chapter turns from particular miracle to figural significance, and ends with the general reflection that a prophetic power, derived from the starry summit of heaven, illuminates Cuthbert's shining heart with its brilliant radiance.

---

[47] They are also *animalia* in *VCA* (II,3); it is only in *VCP* (ch. 10) that they are specified as otters.

This poetry of Bede can never have been easy to understand. Even with the anonymous *Life* as a guide, each line of verse often requires several readings before its meaning becomes clear. I cannot agree with George Brown, who in his recent book on Bede observes that 'for anyone familiar with early medieval poetry the poem offers no great difficulty'.[48] On the contrary, because of its allusiveness and compression it is often extremely difficult, and was clearly intended to be so. We do wrong to regard such a poem as light bed-time reading. A better index of its intention is offered by Alcuin in the preface to his *Vita S. Willibrordi* where, commenting on the distinctive functions of the prose and verse parts of the work, he suggests that the verse 'should be meditated on in the privacy of one's room'.[49] As Arator's poem was intended as a meditation on the meaning of the acts of Peter and Paul, so Bede's poem was intended as a meditation on the life and significance of Cuthbert. Such meditation ideally involves deep concentration, and it is clear from the ways in which Bede revised his metrical *Life* that he was attempting to tighten its diction and thereby to sharpen the focus of the reader's meditation. In any event, it is wrong to look to this poem for narrative history of any sort; but properly understood is has much to tell us about how Bede conceived and practised the art of poetry.

---

[48] G. H. Brown, *Bede the Venerable* (Boston, 1987), p. 70.

[49] *Monumenta Alcuiniana*, ed. P. Jaffé (Berlin, 1873), p. 39: '. . . duos digessi libellos, unum prosaico sermone gradientem, qui puplice fratribus in ecclesia . . . legi potuisset; alterum Pierio pede currentem, qui in secreto cubili inter scolasticos tuos tantummodo ruminari debuisset.' On *ruminari* and meditation, see J. Leclercq, *The Love of Learning and the Desire for God*, trans. C. Misrahi (New York, 1961), pp. 78 – 9.

Opus deliberatum ac perfectum:
Why Did the Venerable Bede Write a Second Prose Life of St Cuthbert?[1]

WALTER BERSCHIN

When St Cuthbert died on 20 March, thirteen hundred years ago, he was immediately considered as a great saint, among the first of the Angles and Saxons in Britain. No less than three lives of St Cuthbert were written during the thirty or forty years following his death:

1) An anonymous monk of Lindisfarne wrote a monumental prose life in four books soon after 698. The work was commissioned by Bishop Eadfrith of Lindisfarne, whom we know as the begetter of the Lindisfarne Gospels.

2) Some years later the young Bede wrote a metrical *Vita S. Cuthberti* in forty-six chapters.

3) Finally, around 720 the same Bede wrote a second prose life of St Cuthbert, arranging it, like the metrical life, in forty-six chapters. He dedicated his work to the same Eadfrith of Lindisfarne to whom the first prose life of St Cuthbert had been dedicated.[2]

For the history of literature there is no problem about the first life of St Cuthbert. The Irish had a flourishing biographical literature — in Latin of course — throughout the second half of the seventh century. With Aldhelm of Malmesbury, the Angles and Saxons of the British Isles began to have good authors of Latin texts. An anonymous monk of Whitby had just published a life of Gregory the Great when the anonymous monk of Lindisfarne wrote the first life of an Anglo-Saxon saint. Anglo-Saxon England was taking over the leadership in insular Latin biography from the Irish and kept it until around 750. This is the particular significance of the first life of St Cuthbert for the history of Latin literature.

The metrical life added by the young Bede underlined both the importance of St Cuthbert as well as the quality of Anglo-Latin biography. The

---

[1] This article is a résumé of parts of my book, *Biographie und Epochenstil im lateinischen Mittelalter* (Stuttgart, 1988), vol. II, where I tried to present the literary history of early Irish-Latin and Anglo-Latin biography.

[2] The first prose life: *VCA*. Bede's metrical life: *VCM*. The second prose life (by Bede): *VCP*.

importance of St Cuthbert: who was the saint whose life the Latin public was accustomed to read in prose and in verse? It was St Martin of Tours. The quality of English biographical tradition: who were the authors who were willing and able to honour the saints by writing their metrical lives? Their names are Prudentius, Paulinus of Nola, Paulinus of Périgueux, Venantius Fortunatus. With his metrical *Life of St Cuthbert* Bede joins this illustrious circle. It is astonishing to see how rapidly the English gained competence in the use of Latin. We admire Bede's skill and courage and I do not think we have any problems in understanding why he wrote like this.

But there are problems connected with our third *Life of St Cuthbert*, the second prose life with which the Venerable Bede tried to replace the first prose life by the anonymous monk of Lindisfarne. Bishop Eadfrith requested a preface to this book and it is here that Bede informs us of the following: he has rigorously investigated the facts, making notes with the help of those who had known St Cuthbert. When this was done, he showed it to his principal witness, the priest Herefrith. He then put down on parchment the results of his rigorous investigation of the truth and expressed them in simple language quite free from all obscurities. For two days the work was read to the elders and teachers and carefully examined in every detail under Bishop Eadfrith's supervision. But not a word had to be changed. Everything was pronounced to be worthy of being read and being given to those whose pious zeal moved them to copy it. Many other facts concerning the life and virtues of the blessed man were brought forward, no less important than those which Bede had written down, 'which well deserved to be mentioned if it had not seemed scarcely fitting and proper to insert new matter or add to a work which was planned and complete': 'quae prorsus memoria digna videbantur, si non deliberato ac perfecto operi nova interserere, vel supradicere minus congruum atque indecorum esse constaret.'[3]

No word about the first prose life of St Cuthbert. If it was not for some continental manuscripts in which the first life of St Cuthbert is handed down to us, we would have no idea that such a work ever existed. In the preface to his *Historia ecclesiastica* the Venerable Bede, it is true, refers to some material about St Cuthbert. However, he does it in such a way that nobody would think of it being a monumental *Vita S. Cuthberti*, written before Bede, which it is. If we consider the fact that Bede usually mentioned the names of his witnesses and not seldom quoted them verbatim, we get the impression that Bede deliberately failed to mention the first *Life of St Cuthbert*. In his eyes this life was nothing but a quarry, where he found the material for his own building. Since we are in possession of his *opus deliberatum ac perfectum*, we should not bother ourselves with the first version; that is the reason why he mentions the decision of the elders and teachers that *his* life should be read and copied.

Why did he do so? Why did he ignore the older *Vita S. Cuthberti*?

We know of this replacing of older biographies by modern ones from 800 on.[4] In 800 exactly, Alcuin wrote a new life of St Richarius when the court of Charlemagne celebrated Easter at Centula/St. Riquier. Alcuin informs us that his intention was to improve the latinity of the text. He transformed Merovingian into Carolingian Latin and so did dozens of biographers after him. Had this been the intention of the Venerable Bede? Was he displeased with the latinity of the anonymous monk of Lindisfarne? In order to find an answer to that question I undertook a 'microscopic' test, as it were. I compared the prose of the anonymous monk of Lindisfarne with that of Bede in some selected chapters, above all a chapter in which the eight-year-old Cuthbert is shown as a leader among the sporting youth of the Angles.[5] It must suffice here to give some results that are of stylistic interest.

Bede's prose is far longer than that of the anonymous monk of Lindisfarne. It integrates didactic material, e.g. the names of the different ages of man in the above-mentioned chapter: *infantia, pueritia* . . . The biblical background is intensified. Details of Anglo-Saxon life are omitted: for example the fact that the young Angles were playing naked — as was customary among the Germanic peoples in the days of Tacitus (*Germania* 24,1). Other motifs of Mediterranean origin are introduced or emphasized. For example, among these boys sporting on the meadows of Northumbria Bede describes a child 'hardly three years old' who begins 'to exhort [Cuthbert] with the gravity of an old man not to indulge in idle games but rather steadfastly to control both mind and limbs.' This child is already present in the life by the anonymous monk of Lindisfarne, but there he is not yet the boy with the heart of an old man, the *puer senex* that Bede changed him into.[6]

Stylistically Bede is, of course, better than the anonymous monk of Lindisfarne — if 'better' means more classical, grammatical, antiquarian. Let me explain what I mean with just one example. Late Latin expanded the use of participles. In late antiquity you can use the present participle as a verbum finitum: our author from Lindisfarne writes, 'Interea quidam infans erat . . . qui incipiebat . . . ad eum dicere . . . et . . . plorans et lacrimans.' The predicate at the end of the subordinate clause is not a verbum finitum, *et ploravit et lacrimavit*, but a verbum infinitum, *et plorans et lacrimans*. Thus the enduring moment of the action is emphasized. The child was a weeping one. The Lindisfarne author very consciously made use of this new possibility of late Latin — which of course has its models in the language of the Latin Bible.

Bede knows that the 'better' authors, even in late Latin, did not use the present participle in this way, and thus eliminates it. He changes it into a participium coniunctum: 'luget ille corruens in terram, et faciem lacrimis

---

[4] The decisive Latin text is Alcuin's preface to the *Vita S. Richarii* (MGH, Scriptores rerum Merovingicarum 4, p. 389).

[5] *VCA* I, 3; *VCP* 1 (*Two Lives*, pp. 64 – 6, 154 – 8).

[6] E. R. Curtius, *Europäische Literatur und lateinisches Mittelalter* (Bern, 1954[2]), p. 108. C. Gnilka, *Aetas spiritalis: Die Überwindung der natürlichen Altersstufen als Ideal frühchristlichen Lebens* (Bonn, 1972).

rigans.' That is standard syntax. Bede's vocabulary is richer and more sophisticated than that of the Lindisfarne author. Let me mention just one word: *plorare*. It is the common word in late antiquity; the Romance words (French *pleurer*, Spanish *llorar*) derive from it. The 'better' word is *flere* and is chosen by Bede who writes *fletus*. Thus the motives for the stylistic change between *Vita* I and II are sometimes apparent. Very often, however, Bede says the same as his predecessor, just using other words. When he writes *quasi victor laetabundus* instead of *quasi in stadio triumphans*, *verbum vitae* instead of *verbum domini*, *delphininae carnis* instead of *delphini carnis* 'he seems to take delight in altering the language for the mere sake of alteration' (Plummer).[7] He had some sensitivity for stylistics, he knew his Latin grammar better than his predecessor, but at the same time he was still receptive to the biblical *sermo humilis* and the current Latin of his time, which was of course below his own stylistic level. Full of respect for his main witness, Herefrith, Bede puts Herefrith's report on Cuthbert's death into his life as Herefrith wrote it (and Herefrith's Latin was by no means better than that of our anonymous monk of Lindisfarne).[8] Stylistics are of some importance, but they are not the main reason why the Venerable Bede wanted to replace the prose life of St Cuthbert. Microscopic stylistic research could only partly answer our question as to why the Venerable Bede wrote a second prose life of St Cuthbert.

Let us see whether a 'macroscopic' view can help us. This time not single words, syntax, and motifs will be considered, but the structure of the *Vita* as a whole. Now not only prose lives I and II (Bede) are to be compared, but also the metrical life. *Vita* I by the anonymous monk of Lindisfarne has a form which I have called monumental. Its author arranges his *Life of St Cuthbert* into four books: the first book deals with the childhood and youth of St Cuthbert, the second book with life as God's servant; in the third Cuthbert is a hermit on Farne Island, and in the fourth bishop of Lindisfarne. The caesurae are appropriate, the composition is well done. Nonetheless, it meant almost a revolution in Latin biography. Why? Because a Christian Latin prose life had never before been arranged into four books. Venantius Fortunatus wrote many prose lives of saints, each in one book except that of the great Hilary of Poitiers, to whom two were devoted. Jonas of Bobbio wrote the *Life of St Columbanus and his Disciples* in two books. Adomnan of Iona arranged the *Vita S. Columbae* into three books. The only works in biographical Latin literature written in four books which are really comparable are the metrical *Life of St Martin* by Venantius Fortunatus, the *De virtutibus S. Martini* by Gregory of Tours, and the *Dialogi* by Gregory the Great. Our anonymous monk of Lindisfarne was, as we said before, the first to arrange a prose life of one saint into four books. He thus demonstrated that for him and his people St Cuthbert was comparable to the greatest saints of the west, to St Martin and St Benedict.

---

[7] Plummer I, p. xlvi.
[8] See appendix.

This monumental form was completely abandoned by Bede when he wrote the *vita metrica*. He arranged the content into a simple series of forty-six chapters. Ten or fifteen years later when he wrote the prose life, he changed several chapters, but altogether there was again a series of forty-six chapters. Obviously the Venerable Bede tried to achieve a parallelism between the metrical life and prose life. Since the metrical life had forty-six chapters, the prose life should not have forty-seven or fifty. Thus we can at least partly understand what Bede means with his remark (in his preface to the prose life): 'many other facts concerning the life and virtues of the blessed man [were brought forward,] no less important than those which we have written down, which well deserved to be mentioned if it had not seemed scarcely fitting and proper to insert new matter or add to a work which was planned and complete.' Any supplementary chapter would have disturbed the balance between metrical and prose lives, which had to have exactly the same proportions like the two tablets of a diptych.

But is that all? Bede considers his bipartite life an *opus deliberatum ac perfectum*. Is it 'planned and complete' only because the number of chapters of the new prose life is identical to that of the metrical life, or is there more to it as far as philological exegesis is concerned? Does *deliberatum ac perfectum* mean the very number forty-six, for example? In general, I am very sceptical about any speculation on hidden meanings of numbers. I was, and I still am, inclined to restrict the undeniable fact of number symbolism to a few works where this is obvious: Dante's *Divina Commedia* with its 100 cantos, for example. Does the number forty-six belong to these obvious cases? I first came across this number when I wrote my book on Greek in the Latin middle ages. I had to examine the role of St Augustine, who as a young man had hated Greek lessons when he had had to read Homer, but later as a bishop was forced to study Greek and sometimes gave short Greek lessons himself when he was preaching. His favourite Greek lesson (he gave it no less than three times in different forms) was the explanation of the name of our common father ADAM.

> Who does not know that all peoples originate in him and that in the four letters of his name, the four quarters of the earth are signified by the Greek names? For when east, west, north and south are said in Greek, as the Holy Scriptures mention in many places, in the initial letters you find ADAM; for the aforementioned four quarters of the earth are called *Anatolē, Dysis, Arctos, Mesēmbria*. If you write these four names one beneath the other, as in verse, in their initial letters you read ADAM.[9]

In the following homily, Augustine again returned to the topic, this time with a variation. The subject was the forty-six years needed to build the temple in Jerusalem:

[9] *In Iohannis evangelium tractatus* IX, 14 (CCSL 36, p. 98). The same explanation is found in Augustine, *Enarrationes in psalmos* XCV, 15 (CCSL 39, pp. 1352 – 3). See W. Berschin, *Griechisch-lateinisches Mittelalter: von Hieronymus zu Nikolaus von Kues* (Bern and Munich, 1980), pp. 69ff.

What does the number forty-six signify? You heard yesterday, in the four Greek letters of the four Greek words, that Adam is [present] throughout the whole world . . . How do we find the number forty-six even here? Because Christ's flesh was of Adam. For the Greeks count with letters. Where we have the letter A, they have alpha, and alpha is one. When they write beta, which is their B, as a number, numerically it is two. When they write gamma, numerically it is three. Where they write delta, it is numerically four; and thus they have numbers through the entire alphabet. What we call M, they call mu, and it signifies forty; for they say mu *tessaraconta*. Consider what number those letters produce, and there you will find the temple, built in forty-six years. For ADAM contains A which is one, D which is four, so you have five; again A which is one; that makes six; it also contains M which is forty; that is forty-six.[10]

The idea was so dear to St Augustine that he tried to prove the providential character of this number by physiological argumentation: every human being is formed in 276 days, that is in six times forty-six days.[11] Also in *De trinitate* he speaks of the symbolic meaning of the beloved number forty-six, which according to Augustine is the number of the *aedificatio* or *perfectio dominici corporis*.[12]

When Eugippius of Lucullanum wrote his *Excerpta ex operibus S. Augustini* in order to provide his contemporaries with the essence of Augustinian thought in one volume, he included no less than three of these five instances of Augustinian number symbolism concerning forty-six. This proves that during the sixth century St Augustine's readers were also pleased by that idea. And when the same Eugippius wrote his famous *Life of St Severin* he arranged it into a series of forty-six chapters.[13]

What did the Venerable Bede know of all this? He certainly came across the idea through Augustine or another church father like Pseudo-Cyprian. But did he believe in it, did he make use of it? In his book *De templo* there is a chapter *Quot annis templum sit aedificatum*: here, the Venerable Bede contents himself with the numbers given by the Old Testament, where forty-six does not appear in this context.[14] The basic text for the symbolism of forty-six is the Gospel of John 2: 19 – 22, where the Lord is irritating the Jews by his words, 'Destroy this temple, and in three days I will raise it up.' They answer, 'It has taken forty-six years to build this temple, and will you raise it up in three days?' St John explains, 'But he spoke of the temple of his body.' This passage

[10] *In Iohan. tr.* X, 12 (p. 108).
[11] *De diversis quaestionibus octoginta tribus* ch. 56 (CCSL 44A, pp. 95 – 6).
[12] *De trinitate* IV, 5, 9 (CCSL 50, pp. 172 – 3).
[13] Eugippius, *Excerpta ex operibus S. Augustini* ch. 276, sections 301, 301ᵃ, 301ᵇ (CSEL 9, i, pp. 879 – 82). On the number forty-six in Eugippius's *Commemoratorium vitae S. Severini*: Berschin, *Biographie und Epochenstil* I, 182.
[14] *De templo*, CCSL 119A, pp. 196 – 7.

was the Gospel for one of the Sundays in Lent, and Bede comments on it in one of his homilies (II, 1). There he rehearses Augustine's ideas on the importance of forty-six in the formation of the human body. For the first six days after conception the human being is like milk, during the next nine days he is changed into blood, in twelve further days he is consolidated, and on exactly the forty-sixth day all the limbs are perfectly shaped. Not only the body of man, but also his soul is formed in forty-six days (*corpus animamque designabat*).[15] In his commentary on Ezra and Nehemiah he repeated this idea,[16] and so I conclude that Bede was convinced that he had found in the number symbolism of forty-six something essential for Christian life.

Perfectio dominici corporis — that is how the Venerable Bede describes this number, following St Augustine. Was this not a very suitable concept for the description of a perfect man? If an author reflects on how to describe a saint who achieved perfection through following the Lord, how better could he symbolize the temple of this corporal and spiritual life than by referring to the number of 'perfection of the body of our Lord'? I do not know whether Bede was aware that he was not the first Christian biographer to do so. But I do not think that it is accidental that the number of chapters of both lives of St Cuthbert by Bede is of symbolic significance. Even when he wrote the metrical life of St Cuthbert, Bede tried to bring some theology and Christian anthropology into biography. Compared with the first life of St Cuthbert, the architecture of the *Vita metrica* seems to have become much simpler at first glance. But on closer examination the new structure was a great achievement. Biography gained a spiritual background; it could be read on several levels, as was customary in late antiquity and the middle ages. After the first step the second had to be taken. The *Life* of the anonymous monk of Lindisfarne and the *Vita metrica* of Bede did not match. The concept which Bede developed in the *Vita metrica* of a holy man as a perfect temple of God demanded a corresponding *opus deliberatum ac perfectum* in prose. That is not the only, but I think the main, reason why the Venerable Bede wrote a second prose life of St Cuthbert.

---

[15] *Homilia* II, 1: 'Qui etiam numerus . . . perfectioni dominici corporis aptissime congruit. Tradunt etenim naturalium scriptores rerum formam corporis humani tot dierum spatio perfici, quia videlicet primis sex a conceptione diebus lactis habeat similitudinem, sequentibus novem convertatur in sanguinem, deinde duodecim solidetur, reliquis decem et octo formetur usque ad perfecta liniamenta omnium membrorum . . . Sex autem et novem et duodecim et decem et octo quadraginta quinque faciunt; quibus si unum adiecerimus, id est ipsum diem, quo discretum per membra corpus crementum sumere incipit, tot nimirum dies in aedificationem corporis domini quot in fabrica templi annos invenimus.' In the next sentence he says that this symbolical number of *perfectio (aedificatio) dominici corporis* is true for any Christian man: *uniuscuiusque fidelium corpus animamque designabat.* (CCSL 122, p. 189.) Bede's words depend largely on Augustine's *De div. quaest.*, loc. cit.

[16] *In Ezram et Neemiam* II, 'Videbimus quia recte in aedificatione templi quadraginta et sex annorum potuerit summa computari . . . Templum . . . multiplicem habet figuram. Nam et unamquamque animam designat electam quae propter inhabitantem in se spiritum Christi domus ac templum eius recte vocatur . . . (CCSL 119A, p. 300).

APPENDIX

HEREFRITH'S REPORT ON CUTHBERT'S DEATH

(Bede's prose *Life of Cuthbert*, chapters 37 to 39)

At the beginning of chapter 37 Bede says that he wanted to describe the death of St Cuthbert in the words of the witness Herefrith: 'Cuius obitum libet *verbis illius*, cuius relatione didici, describere.' The next sentence is marked as a quotation: 'Tribus, *inquit* [videlicet Herefridus], ebdomadibus continuis infirmitate decoctus . . .' The following description exhibits a stylistic level that is below the standard of Bede's Latin: short paratactic sentences often beginning with the predicate and *et* or *at* and redundance of the possessive pronoun. I think that from the beginning of the quotation (*Tribus ebdomadibus*: *Two lives*, p. 272, line 3) throughout the whole of chapter 37 Bede reproduced Herefrith's report without alterations or with only slight corrections. The beginning of chapter 38 also shows some constructions which seem to be alien to Bede's Latin. I cannot imagine that Bede could have written: 'Qui cum ad nonam usque horam *intus* cum illo maneret, *sic* egrediens vocavit me: Episcopus, *inquiens*, te iussit *ad se* intrare. Possum *autem* tibi rem referre novam *permirabilem*, quia . . .' (redundant words are italicized). Immediately following this passage, with the quotation from Possidius, *Vita S. Augustini* (*In qua profecto*: *Two Lives*, p. 280, line 29), these alien elements in Bede's *Vita Cuthberti* disappear. The forementioned example which concludes chapter 38 was put into Herefrith's report by Bede.

At the beginning of Chapter 39 Bede returns to Herefrith's report by using *inquit* again: 'Intravi autem, *inquit* [scilicet Herefridus], ad eum . . .' The syntax becomes more complicated and seems no longer to cause the author any difficulties. How is this improvement in Herefrith's style to be explained? Perhaps when quoting the *ultima verba* of St Cuthbert Bede could no longer resist the temptation to correct Herefrith's Latin — as he had done with the Latin of the anonymous monk of Lindisfarne? All this needs further investigation. My first impression is that we have Herefrith's original text in Bede, *Vita S. Cuthberti* chapters 37 – 38 (*Two Lives*, p. 272 line 3 — p. 280 line 29).

Lindisfarne and the
Origins of the Cult of St Cuthbert[1]

ALAN THACKER

Few cults enjoyed the early and prolonged success of St Cuthbert at Lindisfarne. To achieve those heights a saint needed considerable promotion, the active manipulation of those who had something to give. Cuthbert's posthumous success depended on his community, who preserved the memory of his life and wonders, tended the sacred tomb, and staged elaborate ceremonies in his honour, especially on the anniversary of his death. This paper seeks to examine the aspirations of that community and the way in which it shaped the traditions relating to its most famous saint. There will be sections on the character of, and the models for, the cult itself and the literature which it produced, and a concluding discussion of the circumstances which inspired all this activity. Attention will be paid above all to the earliest, anonymous, life of the saint, and to the material from Lindisfarne recorded by Bede, since Bede's own attitudes have been discussed elsewhere.[2]

I

Lindisfarne was an important monastery. Besides being the chief house of a monastic confederation,[3] it also served as the pastoral centre of the royal estate on which it was founded and with which it was endowed.[4] Bede in his prose *Life* emphasizes the prior of Lindisfarne's role in preaching and administering

---

[1] I should like to record my grateful thanks to the British Academy for a research grant which made possible the completion of this paper, and to Clare Stancliffe and Richard Sharpe for much helpful advice.
[2] A. T. Thacker, 'Bede's Ideal of Reform', in *Ideal and Reality in Frankish and Anglo-Saxon Society*, ed. P. Wormald (Oxford, 1983), pp. 136 – 42, 148 – 50.
[3] E. Craster, 'The Patrimony of St. Cuthbert', *EHR* 69 (1954), pp. 179 – 80. That Lindisfarne had daughter houses is clear from Aethelwulf, *De abbatibus*, ed. A. Campbell (Oxford, 1967), 5, 23 (pp. 11, 59).
[4] I hope to discuss this aspect of early Anglo-Saxon monasticism more fully in a forthcoming book.

the sacraments to the surrounding *vulgus*, and the later parish of Islandshire indicates the focus of these activities.[5] Such pastoral involvement was by no means unusual. Though contemporary evidence is lacking, similar arrangements probably gave rise to the vast parishes attached to the minsters which succeeded most if not all the great Northumbrian communities.[6] There were also parallels in Gaul[7] and probably in Ireland.[8] On the continent, this combination of monastic and pastoral activity was often reinforced by a popular cult, whose guardians might make considerable efforts to render accessible the tomb and other relics associated with the saint.[9] Though the developments at Lindisfarne clearly fit into this context, they seem to have been exceptional. Bede at least considered them so, and in his prose *Vita Cuthbert* is made to offer advice on how to control 'the influx of fugitives and guilty men of every sort' whom he expected to resort to his tomb because 'unworthy as I am reports about me as a servant of God have gone forth.'[10] The monks of Lindisfarne were host to a highly public cult, which would compel them to have frequent dealings with secular authority. This, of course, must be linked to a further aspect of the Lindisfarne community: the fact that, following a unique insular usage, it was the seat of a bishop. The precise arrangements remain uncertain. In the earliest days Bishop Aidan had controlled the diocese while the abbot (whom he had chosen) ruled the monastery.[11] When Eata became bishop of Lindisfarne in 678 or 681 the abbacy and bishopric were perhaps combined, but under Cuthbert they were again probably separated; certainly Herefrith rather than Cuthbert was ruling the community when the saint returned to Farne.[12] Throughout, however,

---

[5] *VCP* 16; J. Raine, *The History and Antiquities of North Durham* (London, 1852), pp. 2 – 3, 50, 146. The finding of grave markers inscribed with feminine as well as masculine names may indicate an early parochial cemetery: *Corpus* I, i, pp. 202 – 7. Cf. Hartlepool: ibid., pp. 97 – 101; below, plate 39 d, e.

[6] E.g. Ripon, Hexham, Wearmouth, Jarrow: *Victoria Hist. of Yorks.* III, pp. 367 – 72; *A History of Northumberland* (15 vols.; Newcastle upon Tyne, 1893 – 1940), vol. III, by A. B. Hinds, p. 159; Richard of Hexham, *History of the Church of Hexham*, ed. J. Raine, *The Priory of Hexham* (2 vols., SS 44, 46), I, 23; R. Surtees, *The History and Antiquities of the Co. Palatine of Durham* (4 vols.; London, 1816 – 40), I, 224; II, 1, 66; E. Cambridge, 'The Early Church in Co. Durham', *Jnl. of the British Archaeological Association* 137 (1984), p. 75; D. J. Hall, 'The Community of St. Cuthbert: its Properties, Rights, and Claims from the Ninth Century to the Twelfth' (unpublished D.Phil. thesis, University of Oxford, 1984), p. 80.

[7] E.g. Jouarre, Faremoutiers, Luxeuil, Chelles: J. Guerout in *L'abbaye royale Notre-Dame de Jouarre* (Paris, 1961), pp. 34, 46 – 7; *Dictionnaire d'histoire et de géographie ecclésiastique* 16 (1967), col. 534 – 7; Jonas, *Vita S. Columbani* II, 8 (MGH, Scriptores Rerum Merovingicarum (= SRM) 4, pp. 122 – 3); *Vita S. Bertilae* 6 (MGH, SRM 6, pp. 106 – 7).

[8] R. Sharpe, 'Some Problems Concerning the Organization of the Church in Early Medieval Ireland', *Peritia* 3 (1984), pp. 251 – 63.

[9] E.g. St Gertrude at Nivelles: *De virt. S. Geretrudis* 4, 10; *Continuatio* 1 (MGH, SRM 2, pp. 466, 469, 472); Marquise de Maillé de la Tour-Landry, *Les cryptes de Jouarre* (Paris, 1971), pp. 36 – 41.

[10] *VCP* 37.

[11] *VCP* 16; *HE* IV, 27 (25).

[12] *HE* III, 26; *VCP* 37. The separation continued in the eighth century; during the episcopacy of Acthelwold, Guthfrith was abbot *c.*720 × 31: *HE* V, 1; Plummer II, pp. 272 – 3.

there can be no doubt that the bishop was always regarded as the principal figure, and it will be argued that his presence had a considerable effect on the nature of the cult at Lindisfarne, which can be shown to have had affinities with the great episcopal cults of Gaul.

The enshrinement was remarkably opulent. Whatever we make of Cuthbert's asceticism in life, in death he was honoured like an emperor. In 687 the saint himself ordered that his body was to be wrapped in a cloth given him by Abbess Verca, which he had refused to wear while alive, presumably because it was too precious. He wished to be interred in a stone sarcophagus given by another high ecclesiastic, Abbot Cudda.[13] The body itself was magnificently clothed. Its vestments included a white dalmatic comparable to those in which contemporary archbishops of Ravenna were buried,[14] a chasuble of the treasured silk *purpura*,[15] and an alb embroidered with gold thread.[16] A golden fillet adorned the brow of the saint and at his breast hung the famous gold and garnet cross.[17] The wooden coffin provided in 698 to house all this splendour, nothwithstanding the barbaric power of the figures carved upon it, might well seem an unworthy casing; but it was probably covered by a rich fabric — that at least was how such tombs were envisaged at the Lindisfarne dependency described in Aethelwulf's *De abbatibus*, where Cuthbert was undoubtedly venerated.[18]

All this suggests a wealthy community and a powerful cult. That Lindisfarne was rich is indicated by the production of the Lindisfarne Gospels, themselves associated with the cult of St Cuthbert, and an object which could only have been produced by a house with outstanding resources.[19] In life Cuthbert had been associated with the very great,[20] and in death the community made as much of him as they could. Besides the shrine stood the precious chasuble and the new shoes with which the body had been clothed at its burial, removed at the translation and exhibited separately as wonder-working relics.[21] The pit or trench, where water used to wash the holy corpse had been poured away, was also credited with miraculous properties and still

[13] *VCA* IV, 1; *VCP* 37. In 698 the body was wrapped in a fresh cloth, presumably another splendid fabric, though not the great Byzantine Nature Goddess silk: Higgins, below.

[14] Granger-Taylor, below.

[15] C. R. Dodwell, *Anglo-Saxon Art* (Manchester, 1982), pp. 145 – 50.

[16] Cf. the mantle in which the Frankish abbess Theudechildis was buried at Jouarre: Maillé, *Cryptes*, p. 77.

[17] C. F. Battiscombe, 'Introduction', in *Relics*, pp. 63, 99 – 114; R. L. S. Bruce-Mitford, 'Pectoral Cross', ibid., pp. 308 – 25.

[18] Aethelwulf, *De abb.* 22 (p. 58, lines 738 – 41). Cf. Gaul, where to place coverings (*palla*) over the shrine was one of the first duties of the faithful: M. Vieillard-Troiekouroff, *Les monuments religieux de la Gaule d'après les oeuvres de Grégoire de Tours* (Lille, 1977), pp. 318, 410 – 11.

[19] H. Mayr-Harting, *The Coming of Christianity to Anglo-Saxon England* (London, 1972), pp. 160 – 1; *Cod. Lind.* II, 5, 12.

[20] *VCA* I, 7; II, 3, 8; III, 6; IV, 3, 7 – 8, 10; *VCP* 10, 15, 23 – 5, 27, 29, 34.

[21] *VCP* 45; *VCA* IV, 14; *HE* IV, 31 (29). Battiscombe, in *Relics*, pp. 23 – 4. Presumably the chasuble was the *orarium* which restored the sight of a blind man: *VCM* 42.

shown to visitors in Bede's day.[22] So too was the hermitage on Farne, fragments of whose oratory, restored *a fundamentis* by Bishop Eadfrith, were distributed as relics by Cuthbert's second successor, Felgild, in the early eighth century.[23]

Two aspects of this activity require comment. First, there is the emphasis on the saint's corporeal remains: wonders were accomplished in the presence of the body itself, or by objects which had been in close physical contact with it. Secondly, there is the discovery at the translation of 698 that after eleven years of interment the saint's body had not corrupted — proof that Cuthbert's immaculate life had found favour with God, and undoubtedly a potent factor in the rapid growth of his prestige. Though such phenomena have come to be regarded as standard features of an early cult, it is nevertheless worth pondering how common they were in the England of Cuthbert's day. In fact, though the *Historia ecclesiastica* is studded with holy figures, few can be shown to have been the objects of cults before the late seventh century. In particular, few English bishops were venerated at their own sees. At Canterbury, for example, the cults of early archbishops remained shadowy affairs,[24] and even at Lindisfarne itself, where before 664 Aidan had been translated to the church of St Peter, no tomb miracles were recorded, though the saint performed wonders at other sites.[25] At Lichfield, St Chad's shrine was the focus of miracles, probably before 700, but even there the cult lacked the prestige supplied by incorruption.[26] In many ways, the most potent English parallel to events at Lindisfarne was not episcopal but monastic: the near contemporary enshrinement of Aethelthryth, abbess of Ely. Aethelthryth, unlike Cuthbert, was orignally buried humbly in a wooden coffin in the nun's cemetery. Sixteen years later in 695 she was transferred to a stone sarcophagus within the abbatial church. The splendid ceremonies, which included the re-vesting of the corpse (like Cuthbert's uncorrupted) anticipated those at Lindisfarne three years later.[27] Interestingly their origins lie in Gaul. The prime mover was Aethelthryth's successor, the Abbess Seaxburh, whose sister Aethelburh had been abbess of the Gaulish house of Faremoutiers. Like Aethelthryth, Aethelburh had been discovered uncorrupted at her translation seven years after her death in 664, and the ceremonies at this event clearly provided the model for those at Ely.[28]

In some ways the Lindisfarne cult seems to have looked directly to Gaul. The carved coffin, for example, though of wood, is of a shape which recalls

---

[22] *VCA* IV, 15; *VCP* 41.

[23] *VCP* 46.

[24] *HE* II, 3.

[25] *HE* III, 17; below.

[26] For the date of Chad's enshrinement see H. Wharton, *Anglia Sacra* (2 vols.; London, 1691), I, 427 – 8; R. Studd, 'Pre-Conquest Lichfield', *Trans. South Staffs. Archaeol. and Hist. Soc.* 22 (1980 – 1), pp. 28 – 30.

[27] *HE* IV, 19 (17).

[28] *HE* III, 8.

Merovingian stone sarcophagi,[29] and the saints and archangels carved upon it bear a distinct resemblance to those carved on a slab in Abbot Mellebaudis's funerary chapel at Poitiers;[30] significantly, in both cases apocryphal arch-angels, shortly to be deleted from the canon, were included.[31] This *theca* of Cuthbert's forms a notable contrast to that of his near contemporary and fellow countryman Chad, whose 'little wooden house', as Charles Thomas pointed out, must have been much closer in shape to the early open-air slab-shrines found in County Kerry.[32] Cuthbert's first burial in a stone sarcophagus also echoes Gaulish practice. In particular, one thinks of Jouarre. There in the late seventh century the holy abbess, Theudechildis, was interred in a stone sarcophagus later heightened by a purely ornamental second storey. The two-tiered arrangement recalls the enshrinement at Lindisfarne, where Cuthbert's wooden *theca* was raised over the original sarcophagus in which Eadberht was later to be buried.[33]

Where episcopal cults are concerned once again the nearest parallels come mostly from Gaul. The paradigm is obviously St Martin, whose remains were translated to a new basilica by Bishop Perpetuus in the late fifth century and enshrined in the eastern apse of the new basilica.[34] Though on a smaller scale, the Cuthbertine cult had many affinities with the great cult of Tours, with its focus on the tomb itself and its complement of dependent holy sites, including (as at Lindisfarne) the body's original resting place and various retreats once used by the saint.[35] But Martin was not the only exemplar. Perpetuus's activities were the prelude to a whole succession of episcopal cults in sixth- and seventh-century Gaul. Almost contemporary with events at Lindisfarne, for example, were the translations of Leodegar of Autun (d. 678), Audoenus of Rouen (d. 684), and Bonitus of Clermont (d. 709), all within a few years of their deaths, all accompanied by elaborate ceremonies and wonders, and all issuing in richly adorned monuments.[36] Gaul also offered several early instances of sanctified incorruption, including an episcopal one, Gregory of Langres, going back to the mid sixth century.[37] There too, as at Lindisfarne, the original sepulchre and the place where the body was prepared for burial were generally revered, and miracles were accomplished by drink infused with

---

[29] C. Thomas, *The Early Christian Archaeology of North Britain* (London, 1971), p. 147. Though Merovingian saints were often enshrined in stone sarcophagi, some 6th-century examples were made of wood: E. Kitzinger, 'The Coffin-Reliquary', in *Relics*, pp. 220 – 1; Vieillard-Troiekouroff, *Monuments*, pp. 407 – 9.

[30] E. Salin, *La civilisation mérovingienne* (4 vòls.; Paris, 1949 – 59), II, p. 47.

[31] Kitzinger, in *Relics*, pp. 273 – 7.

[32] Thomas, op. cit. pp. 141 – 7.

[33] Maillé, *Cryptes*, pp. 201 – 15, 221 – 38; *VCP* 42 – 3.

[34] Gregory of Tours, *Historia Francorum* X, 31 (MGH, SRM 1, i (1951 edn), p. 529).

[35] *Vita S. Eligii* I, 32 (MGH, SRM 4, p. 688); Troiekouroff, *Monuments*, pp. 155 – 7, 304 – 29.

[36] *Passio S. Leodegarii* I, 34 – 44; II, 20 – 32 (MGH, SRM 5, pp. 315 – 22, 342 – 56); *V. Audoeni* I, 17 – 18; II, 43 (MGH, SRM 5, pp. 565 – 7); *Vita S. Boniti* 30 – 44 (MGH, SRM 6, pp. 133 – 9).

[37] Gregory of Tours, *Vita patrum* VII (MGH, SRM 1, ii (1969 edn), pp. 236 – 40).

the dust which could be gathered from such sites.[38] These activities were all aspects of a strong emphasis on the saint's corporeal remains, evident, for example, in Eligius of Noyon's removal of hair and teeth from the uncorrupted head of St Quentin in 641, an event which strikingly anticipates the action of the monks at Lindisfarne in taking clippings from the hair of St Cuthbert in 698.[39]

It is necessary to lay stress on these parallels because it has been conventional to regard such phenomena as the norm for all western European saints' cults. But in fact in an insular context the Lindisfarne cult is remarkable: for if there were few English analogues before the late seventh century, in the contemporary Irish-speaking world they were rarer still.[40] It seems that in Ireland, though it was important to have possession of the body, as is apparent from Muirchú's account of the struggle for the relics of St Patrick,[41] the grave was esteemed less as a *locus* of miracles than as the site of the saint's *resurrectio* and hence the seat of his authority and power.[42] The only description of an early shrine occurs in the famous passage in Cogitosus's *Life of St Brigit*, which tells of the tombs of Brigit and her bishop Conlaeth in the church of Kildare, lying to the left and right of the altar, adorned with jewels, and with golden votive crowns suspended above them. Even there, however, a convincing catalogue of tomb miracles is lacking.[43]

The Irish church most likely to provide an exemplar for the cult of St Cuthbert was of course Columba's monastery at Iona. Here was a community which not only had the body of an indisputably historical holy man but was also the mother church of Lindisfarne. And indeed (as we shall see) Columban traditions undoubtedly left their mark on the piety both of Lindisfarne and Cuthbert. For the moment, however, it is necessary to stress that Iona's treatment of its saint's remains was very different from Lindisfarne's. Though clearly the community valued its status as the resting place of Columba's bones, and though other sites such as the hill where Columba conversed with angels were known and revered, there was no attempt to establish a tomb cult.[44] There was no translation for well over a century, and indeed Adomnan refers to the grave in terms which suggest that in his day it was not readily

---

[38] Ibid. VI, 7 (pp. 235 – 6); Gregory of Tours, *De Virtutibus S. Martini* II, 1 (MGH, SRM 1, ii).

[39] *HE* IV, 32 (30); *V. Eligii* II, 6 (pp. 697 – 9).

[40] For the only plausible record of a translation see Tírechán, *Collectanea de S. Patricio* 16, 8 – 10; ed. L. Bieler, *The Patrician Texts in the Book of Armagh* (Dublin, 1979), p. 136; cf. C. Doherty, 'The Use of Relics in Early Ireland', in *Irland und Europa: die Kirche im Frühmittelalter*, ed. P. Ní Chatháin and M. Richter (Stuttgart, 1984), p. 94.

[41] Muirchú, *Vita S. Patricii* II, 11 – 14; ed. Bieler, *Patrician Texts*, pp. 120 – 2.

[42] R. Sharpe, 'St Patrick and the See of Armagh', *Cambridge Medieval Celtic Studies* 4 (1982), pp. 40 – 3.

[43] Cogitosus, *Vita S. Brigidae*, 37 – 9 (*Acta Sanctorum* (in progress, Antwerp 1643 –) Feb. 1).

[44] Adomnan, *Life of Columba*, ed. A. O. and M. O. Anderson (London, 1961), II, 43 – 6; III, 23.

accessible to the faithful.[45] The most potent relics were the saint's tunic and the books 'in his own handwriting', portable objects which were carried to various parts of the island as the occasion demanded. There is no record of observances at the tomb.[46] In all this, as in so much else, Iona was conservative. The community was looking back to the tradition of the desert fathers, above all to St Antony, whose burial place was believed to have been concealed and whose biographer lays stress on the garments which the saint distributed on his death-bed.[47] Clearly, in their rapid and well-publicized translation the Lindisfarne community looked more to the traditions of the great Gaulish episcopal cults than to Iona.

II

One important duty of communities acting as guardians of these cults was the production of some written testimony of the saint, a *vita* or a book of miracles. Obviously such compositions might act as a form of advertisement or supply texts which could be read at the communal offices or in the refectory.[48] They were probably also used during the patronal festival, when they perhaps provided readings during the Vigil, or formed the basis of the preface, of one of the lessons, or of the sermon, at the mass itself.[49] The seven volumes of *Scriptores Rerum Merovingicarum* in the Monumenta series bear witness to the number of these writings produced in pre-Carolingian Gaul. There, however, *vitae* composed in Latin were assured of an audience;[50] in England such texts must have been much less accessible, comprehensible perhaps only to the educated clergy and a few unusually learned princes and nobles.[51] Did they therefore have a role at the patronal festival of a popular cult such as that of St Cuthbert? Obviously they could have formed the basis of a panegyric preached by the local bishop in the vernacular;[52] or they could have been read and simultaneously translated. Even so they must have had a more restricted appeal to ordinary pilgrims in England than to their counterparts in Gaul. And, of course, far fewer were produced: even allowing for known losses,[53] the handful which survives from pre-Viking England must represent a difference

---

[45] *The Life of St Columba by Adamnan*, ed. W. Reeves (Dublin, 1857), pp. 312–17; A. D. S. Macdonald, 'Aspects of the Monastery and Monastic Life in Adomnán's Life of Columba', *Peritia* 3 (1984), p. 284.

[46] Adomnan, *V. Col.* II, 44. Cf. ibid. II, 45.

[47] *Vita S. Antonii* 58–9 (PL 73).

[48] B. de Gaiffier, 'L'hagiographe et son public au XIe siècle', in *Miscellanea historica in honorem Leonis van der Essen* (Brussels, 1947), pp. 135–66.

[49] See my forthcoming book on the cult of the saints in early Anglo-Saxon England.

[50] See R. Collins, 'Observations on the Form, Language and Public of the Prose Biographies of Venantius Fortunatus' in *Columbanus and Merovingian Monasticism*, ed. H. B. Clarke and M. Brennan (British Archaeologial Reports, Internat. series 113; Oxford, 1981), at pp. 106–9.

[51] C. P. Wormald, 'The Uses of Literacy in Anglo-Saxon England and its Neighbours', *Transactions of the Royal Hist. Soc.* 5th series, 27 (1977), pp. 95–114, esp. 102–5.

[52] Collins, art. cit., p. 107.

[53] E.g. the Barking *libellus*: *HE* IV, 7, 10.

in kind from the production levels in contemporary Gaul.[54] It looks, then, as if the deeds of English saints, often in quite important communities, remained without written record. Clearly a formal *vita*, though extremely useful, was not essential to a cult's survival. So what purpose did it serve? I shall argue in the case of the Cuthbertine lives that though undoubtedly the usual liturgical and advertising functions were important, there were also other less obvious preoccupations prompting their authors to write as they did. The abundance of the Cuthbertine hagiography stems from the fact that the cult was being used as a vehicle for ideas to some extent extraneous to its survival and propagation. The anonymous author and, more especially, Bede were writing, so to speak, 'tracts for the times'.

Hagiography is commonly regarded, with some justice, as a very conventional genre. In Bolton's succinct phrase, its authors were more often interested in 'the similarity of events rather than their uniqueness'.[55] Certainly the Lindisfarne *Life* was much influenced by the great classic exemplars, works such as the writings of Sulpicius Severus about St Martin of Tours, Evagrius's translation of Athanasius's life of the Egyptian hermit Antony, and the *Dialogues* of Gregory the Great.[56] That is not to say that Cuthbert's saintliness was simply the literary creation of his hagiographers. There seems to have been no shortage of material showing him as an authentic ascetic and wonder-worker, and it is possible, indeed probable, that he was himself influenced by the ideals of the Sulpician Martin or the Athanasian Antony. Nevertheless, it is with the intentions of the Lindisfarne author rather than the saint himself that this paper is primarily concerned. The borrowings have generally been taken to suggest that the Lindisfarne *Life* was one of the most conventional of early English *vitae*. But the Lindisfarne author was no mere copyist. His work is a remarkably substantial one, distinctly innovatory in structure. Unlike any other western prose *vita*, it is divided into four books,[57] the first devoted to Cuthbert's early career, the second to his time as an active prior and pastor, the third to his life as a hermit on Inner Farne, and the fourth to his episcopate and posthumous cult. These groupings are both chronological and thematic; the only point at which chronology is disrupted is at the end of book II, where a miracle dating from Cuthbert's time as prior and active pastor at Lindisfarne is inserted after similar material from Melrose, thereby preceding the formal notice of Cuthbert's arrival at Lindisfarne which opens book III. Such a chronological/thematic treatment is unusual, and indicates intelligence and independence of mind. I would also argue that the anonymous's treatment of the classic models was purposeful and deliberate. In particular, it

[54] B. Colgrave, 'The Earliest Saints' Lives Written in England', *Proceedings of the British Academy* 44 (1959), pp. 35–60.
[55] W. Bolton, 'The Supra-Historical Sense in the Dialogues of Gregory the Great', *Aevum* 33 (1959), p. 209.
[56] Colgrave, *PBA* 44, pp. 37–40.
[57] The only parallels are the four *Dialogues* of Gregory the Great, a work of hagiography though not strictly a *vita*, and two works on St Martin: see Berschin, above.

is necessary to consider the use made of Sulpicius's writings on St Martin, which besides providing two verbatim extracts of considerable length,[58] coloured the Lindisfarne author's account of St Cuthbert's missionary journeys and pastoral activities as prior and bishop.[59] Cuthbert's techniques in performing miracles, his conquest of devilish illusions, his converse with angels, his dislike of spectators all have their counterpart in the Martinian prototype.[60] Like Martin, Cuthbert remained humble in heart and mean in vesture, maintaining his monastic ideals without neglecting his episcopal office.[61] Like Martin too he had to be compelled to accept episcopal consecration and ever afterwards retained a yearning for contemplative seclusion: there is an obvious resemblance between Martin's attachment to his desert-like retreat at Marmoutiers and Cuthbert's love of Farne.[62]

Other evidence that the anonymous had Martin especially in mind when writing the *Vita Cuthberti* is provided by the structure of the work which seems to owe something to Sulpicius's combination in the *Vita Martini* of a thematic arrangement of Martin's miracles with a chronological treatment of his early life.[63] Even the division into four books perhaps harks back to Martinian exempla, since both Fortunatus's metrical life of the saint and Gregory of Tours' account of his posthumous miracles have a similar four-fold arrangement. Of course, other models were also important, above all Evagrius's translation of the *Vita Antonii* in book III,[64] but even there Sulpicius's writings left their mark.[65] All this suggests that the anonymous thought of Cuthbert as primarily, like Martin, a holy monk-bishop, a view confirmed by the inclusion almost at the beginning of his work of a miraculous prophecy of the saint's episcopal destiny.[66] In this he was no doubt reflecting a preoccupation of the community as a whole: Bede, for example, cites a Lindisfarne source for a similar prophecy made by Boisil, prior of Melrose.[67]

---

[58] *VCA* I, 2; IV, 1. Cf. I, 5.

[59] *VCA* II, 4 – 7; IV, 3 – 7. Cf. the Sulpician Martin's zeal in visiting the remote villages of his and neighbouring dioceses and converting their pagan inhabitants: Sulpicius Severus, *Vita Martini* 11 – 17; *Ep.* 1, 10; 3, 6; all ed. J. Fontaine, SC 133; *Dialogi* II, 3 – 4, 9, ed. C. Halm, CSEL 1.

[60] Note especially the resemblances between Cuthbert's cure of a boy dying of plague and one of Martin's resurrection miracles: *VCA* IV, 6; Sulpicius, *Dial.* II, 4. For other parallels see: *VCA* II, 6 and Sulpicius, *V. Mart.* 22 (diabolic *inlusiones*); *VCA* IV, 5 and *V. Mart.* 7 – 8 (dislike of spectators); *VCA* II, 7 and *V. Mart.* 14 (power over fire); *VCA* I, 4, IV, 11 and *V. Mart.* 21, *Dial.* I, 25, II, 13 (converse with angels).

[61] *VCA* IV, 1; *V. Mart.* 10.

[62] *VCA* IV, 1, 9, 11; *V. Mart.* 10.

[63] C. Stancliffe, *St. Martin and his Hagiographer* (Oxford, 1983), pp. 86 – 95. I am grateful to Clare Stancliffe for this point. See now J-M. Picard, 'Structural Patterns in Early Hiberno-Latin Hagiograhy', *Peritia* 4 (1987, for 1985), pp. 67 – 82. I became aware of this paper too late to take account of its arguments.

[64] Stancliffe, above.

[65] *VCA* III, 5; *V. Ant.* 25; Sulpicius, *Dial.* I, 14; *Two Lives*, p. 328. Cf. *VCP* 19.

[66] *VCA* I, 3.

[67] *VCP* 8.

The guardians of Cuthbert's cult were anxious to present their saint as an appropriate patron for an episcopal see.

One area where Martinian ideals left their imprint was Ireland, and clearly in the late seventh century Lindisfarne was still marked by its Irish origins.[68] It has long been observed that Cuthbert's own mode of life had an Irish flavour. In particular, the markedly eremitic strain in his piety has a strongly Irish background; the structures on Farne — the round dwelling, oratory made of stone and turf, and the accompanying cross — sound very like Irish island hermitages, and the saint's early instructions about his burial accord with the position of the founders' tombs located at many such sites.[69] Such being the case, it is scarcely surprising that the anonymous *Life* exhibits especially close links with Adomnan's *Life of Columba*, a work written perhaps contemporaneously. Besides certain resemblances between the vocabulary of Adomnan and the anonymous,[70] there are also a number of themes common to both works. Both Columba and Cuthbert, for example, are imbued with a miraculous sensitivity to the fortunes of kings, especially when they were at risk in battle.[71] Columba was linked to his branch of the Uí Néill with the same close, almost magical bonds that tied Cuthbert to the house of Ecgfrith.[72] Both saints see visions of holy souls being borne to heaven.[73] There is one especially striking parallel: both authors relate a story in which their hero is spied upon by a suspicious monk while engaged in solitary prayer. In both versions the monk becomes thereby the witness to a miraculous demonstration of the saint's holiness, and is subsequently brought to admit his wilful intrusion and pardoned and bound to silence by the saint. Although there are no connexions between the wording of the two accounts, it is clear that they were shaped by the same hagiographical conventions.[74] The link is perhaps supplied by Melrose, a monastery which seems to have been especially closely connected with Lindisfarne and over which Eata retained the abbacy when he removed to the mother-house. Melrose, which preserved numerous Cuthbertine traditions with a distinctly Columban flavour,[75] may have possessed an early life of Columba. Some connexion with Iona is certainly indicated by Bede's story of the former brother of Melrose who was told by Boisil in a vision to instruct his master Ecgberht to convert Iona to the catholic Easter.[76]

---

[68] D. A. Bullough, 'Columba, Adomnan, and the Achievement of Iona', *Scottish Historical Review* 43 (1964), pp. 110 – 30; 44 (1965), pp. 17 – 33.

[69] *VCP* 17, 37; Thomas, *Early Christ. Archaeol.*, p. 85; Herity, above.

[70] Bullough, *Scot. Hist. Rev.* 43, pp. 129 – 30.

[71] *VCA* IV, 8; Adomnan, *V. Col.* I, 8.

[72] E.g. Adomnan, *V. Col.* I, 7, 10 – 14, 49; III, 5.

[73] *VCA* I, 5; IV, 10; Adomnan, *V. Col.* III, 6, 9, 11 – 14. *VCA* I, 5 is, however, closer to Gregory the Great, *Dialogues* II, 35 (ed. A. de Vogüé, SC 260) than to Adomnan.

[74] *VCA* II, 3; Adomnan, *V. Col.* III, 16.

[75] *VCA* II, 4 – 5. Cf. *HE* V, 12.

[76] *HE* V, 9.

Despite these links it cannot be denied that there are important differences between the works of Adomnan and the anonymous, in addition to the absence of tomb miracles already noted. Reference to pastoral activity and healing prominent in the Lindisfarne *Life* where they are heavily influenced by the Martinian prototype, are noticeably absent from the *Life of Columba*. Adomnan is much more prolix and his work more loosely structured, with chronology almost abandoned in favour of thematically grouped miracles. Above all, the *Life of Columba* contains some of the strongly fantastic and magical elements common to all early Irish *vitae*. These are virtually absent from the anonymous *Life*. Unlike Columba, Cuthbert does not behave like a Christian druid, engaging the heathen in magical contests and cursing and pronouncing doom upon those who oppose him.[77]

The ambiguous relationship between the *Vita Columbae* and the *Vita Cuthberti* reflects the complexity of Iona's relations with Northumbria in the late seventh century. However close the contacts between Iona and Lindisfarne before Whitby, afterwards they were clearly ruptured. One illustration of this is the complete eclipse of the cult of St Aidan. Even Willibrord, despite his long sojourn in Ireland, neglected him; though Cuthbert and Aethilwald of Farne appear in his calendar along with Patrick, Brigit, and Columba in the original hand, Aidan is only commemorated by a later addition.[78] After the defeat of Ecgfrith, however, and with the advent of the half-Irish Aldfrith, Iona looked set once again to become a force in Northumbrian affairs, and, as Clare Stancliffe suggests, Lindisfarne may have promoted the cult of Cuthbert in conscious rivalry to that of Columba.[79] Yet that cannot be the whole story. Ultimately Iona seems to have been more concerned about its position in Ireland and Dál Riada than in Northumbria,[80] and, as will be argued below, the monks of Lindisfarne developed cult and *vita* along lines rather different from their Columban counterparts, mainly in response to an internal threat.

Here another analogy is of great importance: the cults and hagiography characteristic of certain Gaulish monastic circles influenced by Irish *peregrini*. The monasteries associated with Fursey and his brother Foillan, for example, were the homes of important cults. Fursey himself had been enshrined since 654 in a structure 'like a little house' at the mayor Erchinoald's foundation at Péronne, his body an early example of incorruption.[81] The Pippinid sanctuary

---

[77] Adomnan, *V. Col.* II, 17, 20 – 3, 25, 33 – 4. Cf. Muirchú, *V. Pat.* I, 15 – 20, 25 – 26, 29; ed. Bieler, *Patrician Texts*, pp. 84 – 96, 100, 106, 112.

[78] *The Calendar of St Willibrord*, ed. H. A. Wilson (Henry Bradshaw Society 55; London, 1918), fols. 35ʳ, 35ᵛ, 37ʳ, 38ʳ, pp. 4 – 5, 8, 10, 21, 24, 32, 38; D. Ó Cróinín, 'Rath Melsigi, Willibrord, and the Earliest Echternach MSS', *Peritia* 3 (1984), pp. 17 – 42.

[79] Stancliffe, above.

[80] Adomnan constantly depicts the saint as present in spirit, through vision and prophecy, among his own kinsmen, the Cenél Conaill, and among his Irish monks and followers. On Dál Riada see M. J. Enright, 'Royal Succession and Abbatial Prerogative in Adomnán's *Vita Columbae*', *Peritia* 4 (1987 for 1985), pp. 83 – 103.

[81] *Vita S. Fursei* 10 (MGH, SRM 4, pp. 439 – 40); *HE* III, 19.

of Nivelles, where Foillan was a frequent visitor, housed the great cult of St Gertrude.[82] Though visionary and ascetic qualities were generally deemed appropriate to Gaulish saints, even bishops whose careers had been patently worldly,[83] such attributes were perhaps particularly noticeable in those figures who had links with Gallo-Irish communities. An especially striking example is the missionary bishop Amandus, who assisted at the foundation of Nivelles and had connexions with several of the *monasteria Scottorum*.[84] The author of his early *vita* was influenced by the same hagiographical models as Adomnan and the anonymous,[85] and his hero's career resembled Cuthbert's in several ways: he was a great traveller and evangelist; he was a notable ascetic, who for a while had lived in a cell by Bourges cathedral; he was a reluctant bishop who renounced his see before his death.[86]

Another instructive parallel is Jonas's *Life of Columbanus*, the Irish founder of Luxeuil and Bobbio. That work, which was written in 640,[87] well before the earliest insular life, was the product of an intellectual milieu linked with Iona and Lindisfarne. Jonas, unsurprisingly, was well acquainted with both the *Vita Antonii* and Sulpicius's writings on St Martin; indeed he emphasized Columbanus's personal devotion to the saint of Tours, whose deeds were evoked in his own dramatic wonders.[88] He and the Lindisfarne author adapted certain Sulpician themes and stories in similar ways, and in one instance quoted the same extracts from the psalms.[89] Like Cuthbert and Columba, Columbanus was much concerned with kings, though his attitude towards them is less friendly that theirs. All three saints were much visited by visions of every kind, and in particular received visions of momentous battles on which turned the fate of kings.[90] Other themes were common only to Iona and Luxeuil;[91] an especially telling instance is Jonas's omission, like Adomnan but unlike the Lindisfarne author, of all reference to a postumous cult at the tombs

---

[82] *Additamentum Nivalense de Foillano* (MGH, SRM 4, pp. 449 – 51).

[83] E.g. *Passio Praiecti* 5 (pp. 228 – 9); *Vita S. Apollinaris* 13 (MGH, SRM 3, p. 202); *V. Audoeni* I, 3 – 6, 8 (pp. 555 – 9).

[84] F. Prinz, *Frühes Mönchtum im Frankenreich* (Munich, 1965), pp. 165 – 6.

[85] The author quotes passages from the *Actus Silvestri*, including a list of virtues similar to, but not identical with, that used by Adomnan and the Lindisfarne monk: *V. Amandi* I, 8, (MHG, SRM 5, pp. 434 – 5). He also quotes from the *Vita Martini*: *V. Amandi* I, prol., 6, 9 – 10, 13, 15, 22 (pp. 429, 433, 435, 437, 439, 445).

[86] *V. Amandi* I, 5, 8, 13, 16, 18 – 20, 22, 26 (pp. 433 – 4, 436, 439 – 40, 442 – 5, 449).

[87] MGH, SRM 4, p. 31.

[88] Jonas, *V. Columbani* I, 1, 7, 20, 22, 25, 27 (MGH, SRM 4, pp. 66, 74, 92 – 3, 99, 101 – 4).

[89] Ibid. I, 7 – 8, 15, 17, 22, 27; *VCA* I, 6; II, 3, 5; III, 5; Sulpicius, *Dial.* I, 13 – 14; II, 9; Psalm 36:25; Bullough, *Scot. Hist. Rev.* 43, pp. 129 – 30; A. T. Thacker, 'The Social and Continental Background to Early Anglo-Saxon Hagiography' (unpublished D.Phil. thesis, University of Oxford, 1976), pp. 102 – 3.

[90] Jonas, *V. Columbani* I, 18 – 22, 24, 27 – 9; II, 5 – 6, 11 – 23, 25; *VCA* I, 4 – 5; II, 2; IV, 8, 10.

[91] E.g. Jonas, *V. Columbani* I, 11, 17; Adomnan, *V. Col.* II, 19; III, 22.

of the saint and of his immediate followers, though he included numerous death-bed scenes accompanied by signs and wonders.[92]

Clearly *vitae* from Gallo-Irish milieus resembled the works of both Adomnan and the Lindisfarne anonymous in important ways. But, like the anonymous and unlike Adomnan, they generally contained few markedly fantastic anecdotes. It seems that, even though there was considerable interchange between all three milieus, Lindisfarne's hagiographical traditions may owe as much to the followers of Fursey and Columbanus as to those of Columba. Hiberno-Northumbrian missionary activity in the Low Countries provides one possible point of contact. Lindisfarne certainly had links with Willibrord, and Willibrord had connexions with Amandus, whose church at Antwerp he had been given, and who appears together with Cuthbert and Aethilwald, Cuthbert's successor on Farne, among the original entries in his calendar.[93] Almost certainly there were other contacts.

III

What were the circumstances in which the Lindisfarne *Life of Cuthbert* was written? I have argued elsewhere that from an early date Cuthbert was promoted as the *Reichsheiliger* of the Northumbrian kingdom in conscious imitation of the cult of St Martin in Gaul.[94] This paper, however, will approach the development of the cult from a different, albeit complementary, angle.[95] The anonymous *Life* was composed shortly after the translation of 698 and before the death of King Aldfrith in 705, at a time when, after two or three troubled decades, the community at Lindisfarne seems to have been enjoying a period of enhanced prestige.[96] For the years after Whitby had not been easy. Whether or not, as Plummer conjectured, the death of Tuda in 664 forestalled plans to establish a Bernician see at Lindisfarne,[97] the fact remains that no bishop resided there from 664 to 678, while there was a single diocese based at York. It is not clear whether after the first division of the Northumbrian see in 678 Eata was installed at Lindisfarne or at Hexham, and it is only after the further division of 681 that Lindisfarne is once again certainly the seat of a bishop.[98] Indeed it is really the elevation of Cuthbert (after the false start of his appointment to Hexham) that ushers in a revival. Though doubt has been

---

[92] E.g. Jonas, *V. Columbani* II, 6, 10 – 14, 16 – 18, 20. I. Wood, 'The *Vita Columbani* and Merovingian Hagiography', *Peritia* 1 (1982), p. 67.

[93] *VCA* IV, 16; *Cal. of St Willibrord*, fols. 35ʳ – 36ʳ, pp. 4 – 6, 21, 24, 27; W. Levison, *England and the Continent in the Eighth Century* (Oxford, 1946), p. 48.

[94] Thacker in *Ideal and Reality*, pp. 148 – 50; 'Social and Continental Background', pp. 124 – 7.

[95] What follows owes much to the ideas of Professor W. Goffart, as expressed in his paper to the ISAS conference at Cambridge, 1985 and in personal discussion.

[96] *Two Lives*, p. 13.

[97] Plummer II, p. 323.

[98] *HE* IV, 12, 28 (26); Plummer II, p. 224; M. Roper, 'Wilfrid's Landholdings in Northumbria', in *Saint Wilfrid at Hexham*, ed. D. P. Kirby (Newcastle upon Tyne, 1974), pp. 74 – 5.

cast on them, there seems no good reason to dismiss the grants which the *Historia de sancto Cuthberto* records that King Ecgfrith made to Cuthbert. These included a substantial portion of the city of York itself, the nearby estate of Crayke, and in the far north-west lands around Carlisle and Cartmel. The latter, as David Hall has suggested, may represent a grant of ecclesiastical jurisdiction — perhaps indeed an extension of the diocese — as part of the integration of a former British kingdom into Northumbria.[99] The early lives do in fact make a point of associating Cuthbert with Carlisle, and Bede refers to a miracle performed among the mountains while the saint was on his way there from Hexham in terms which suggest that that area was then within his diocese.[100] Certainly that was the opinion of an early twelfth-century Durham writer, who cited among his sources a *liber antiquissimus* referring to a certain successor of Cuthbert whose see included *inter alia* Carlisle.[101] Ecgfrith's grants have their counterpart in his earlier gifts to Wilfrid in the 670s, and suggest that in the aftermath of Wilfrid's expulsion and, perhaps, of further trouble at Hexham, where Tunberht had been deposed in 684, Lindisfarne was regaining something of its old pre-eminence.[102] If so, that renaissance probably owes much to the personality of Cuthbert himself and his intimate relations with the royal house.

The death of Ecgfrith in 685 and the subsequent return of Wilfrid plunged all this in doubt.[103] The deaths of Eata and Cuthbert in 686 and 687 apparently paved the way for the temporary restoration of Wilfrid to something resembling his old position as bishop of the whole of Northumbria.[104] Certainly Wilfrid administered the see of Lindisfarne for a year after Cuthbert's death, an episode which left very bitter memories.[105] Though new bishops had been installed at Lindisfarne and Hexham before the end of 688, and Wilfrid himself had again been expelled from Northumbria by 691, the situation presumably remained unstable, since Wilfrid retained numerous supporters in the many churches and monasteries of his great *regnum ecclesiarum*.[106] Any prospect of his return must have been viewed with alarm at Lindisfarne and elsewhere.

That this was still a major issue is shown by Aldfrith's need in 703 to summon a fresh council at Austerfield, which ended acrimoniously with the

---

[99] Hall, 'Community of St Cuthbert', pp. 50 – 5; *HSC* 5 – 6.

[100] *VCA* IV, 5; *VCP* 32.

[101] Text edited by R. Sharpe, forthcoming in *Northern History*.

[102] *VW* 17; *HE* IV, 28 (26); Roper, 'Wilfrid's Landholdings', pp. 61 – 3.

[103] Possibly Cuthbert's own resignation was hastened by this event, which took place in the second year of Aldfrith's reign (May 686 × 687): *HE* V, 19; *VW* 44; Plummer II, 319.

[104] *VW* 43 – 4; *HE* V, 19; D. H. Farmer, 'Saint Wilfrid', in *St Wilfrid at Hexham*, ed. Kirby, p. 51.

[105] *VCP* 40; *HE* IV, 29 (27); and see below.

[106] *VW* 21, 45; *HE* IV, 29 (27); V, 2; *VCP* 40; Plummer II, pp. 273 – 4. Wilfrid's followers are discussed in Thacker, 'Social and Continental Background', pp. 236 – 41.

excommunication of Wilfrid and his followers.[107] The translation of Cuthbert's remains, and all the associated activities enhancing the cult, have to be seen against this background of uncertainty. For the monks of Lindisfarne, and perhaps for many others, Cuthbert must have seemed the patron of the new order. The reluctant bishop, forced from his hermitage, the friend of Ecgfrith and the seer who fortold the return of Aldfrith, he represented a notable contrast to Wilfrid who had so consistently and strenuously defended his own in the face of violent royal opposition. In the anonymous *Life* Cuthbert is carefully linked with many of the leading figures of the Northumbrian political and ecclesiastical establishment. Above all, he was the friend of the royal abbess Aelfflaed, clearly a crucial figure who had much to do with Wilfrid's return in 686 and again in 705.[108]

Such indeed was the success of the anonymous's work that when the time came (within a few years) to write the life of Wilfrid himself, the *Vita Cuthberti* provided an important model. Though Wilfrid's career stood in such contrast to Cuthbert's and was much more difficult to accommodate to the classic exemplars, the author of the *Vita Wilfridi* did his best. By his use of the anonymous *Life*, he was making a bid to take over the most potent (probably the only) native model and asserting that his hero was every whit as true a saint as Cuthbert.[109]

The re-writing of the Cuthbert legend so soon after it had been recorded by the anonymous of Lindisfarne has always seemed a puzzling affair. It might be supposed that his simple and straightforward *Vita* rapidly came to seem old-fashioned; but that is hardly convincing when one considers the considerable length and scope of the work itself (far more ambitious than most contemporary Gaulish lives), and the fact that in possessing such a production the community was probably very much better off than any other English cult centre of the time. The explanation needs to be sought not in the inadequacy of the Lindisfarne *Life* but in the continuing tensions within the Northumbrian ecclesiastical establishment and in Bede's preoccupation with reform.

The earlier of the two Bedan lives was the *Vita metrica*. Works such as this were obviously destined for a very restricted and élite audience. They were written to provide a commentary or meditation on an existing composition in prose — hence their elevated, reflective, and unspecific tone.[110] Nevertheless, a subsidiary intention seems to have been to up-date the corpus of miracle stories. The work contains several new episodes, in particular, the story of the monks threatened with shipwreck; an enlarged account of Cuthbert's life on

---

[107] *VW* 46 – 9.

[108] *VCA* III, 6; IV, 10; *VCP* 23 – 4, 34; *VW* 43, 60; D. P. Kirby, 'Northumbria in the Time of Wilfrid', in *St Wilfrid at Hexham*, pp. 19 – 24.

[109] For the influence of *VCA* on *VW* see Thacker, 'Social and Continental Background', pp. 264 – 5.

[110] De Gaiffier, *Miscellanea*, p. 135; P. Godman, ed., Alcuin: *The Bishops, Kings, and Saints of York* (Oxford, 1982), p. lxxxvi.

Farne and of his last days and death; and some extra material about the posthumous cult and the hermits who succeeded Cuthbert on Farne.[111] Bede wrote the poem in the reign of Osred, Aldfrith's son and successor, whom he lauds as a young Josiah,[112] and it has been suggested that from the start he planned it as part of a twinned composition, an *opus geminatum*.[113] Certainly the dedicatory epistle refers to another work on the saint which Bede intended to write, and the generally close relations between the chapter headings of the *Vita metrica* and the *Vita prosaica* point to their being seen as twin works. Nevertheless, it is likely that originally the *Vita metrica* was intended to be paired with the Lindisfarne *Life*. The preface was only added some ten years later when Bede was making the final revisions to his poem, and hence need not imply that he had it in mind to write his prose work *ab initio*.[114] Moreover, the *Vita metrica* follows the arrangement of the Lindisfarne *Life* very closely, whereas the prose *Life*, which finally came into being *c.*720,[115] somewhat alters the order of the chapters and adds much new material.[116] Probably, then, despite the coupling with the *Vita metrica* in its preface, the prose *Life* was not envisaged as part of the original scheme.[117]

One important model for thus proceeding from prose *vita* to metrical commentary is provided by the literature of the Martinian cult. In the late fifth and sixth centuries two verse lives of Martin were composed as counterparts to Sulpicius Severus's prose work. The earlier poem, by Paulinus of Périgueux, is more faithful to the Sulpician model, though it also includes posthumous material from an *indiculum* compiled by Bishop Perpetuus;[118] the later, by Venantius Fortunatus, is closer to the abstract reflective ideal pursued by Aldhelm and Bede.[119] Though, very curiously, Bede never shows knowledge of the Sulpician life, he had undoubtedly read both poems, from which he quoted on several occasions.[120] Their influence upon his work is further evidence for an attempt to model Cuthbert's cult on that of Tours in the early eighth century.

Bede's prose *Life*, though it is clearly linked with the *Vita metrica* and indeed formed the occasion of the despatch of the revised version of the poem to Lindisfarne, is in many ways set apart from the two earlier works. It includes much new material, mostly, it seems, the result of conversations with

---

[111] *VCM* 3, 17, 20, 33 – 4, 37, 39, 44 – 6.

[112] *VCM* 21 (lines 582 – 5); Jaager, *VCM*, p. 4; *VW* 59; Lapidge, above.

[113] Godman, op. cit., pp. lxxviii – lxxxviii; P. Godman, 'Anglo-Latin *Opus Geminatum* from Aldhelm to Alcuin', *Medium Aevum* 50 (1982), pp. 215 – 29.

[114] Lapidge, above.

[115] Plummer I, p. cxlviii.

[116] Jaager, *VCM* pp. 2 – 3, 5. New material is to be found in *VCP* 6, 8 – 9, 16, 23, 35, 37.

[117] *VCP* prol.

[118] Paulinus of Périgueux, *De Vita S. Martini*, CSEL 16, pp. 17 – 159; Gregory of Tours, *Virt. Martini* I, 2 (pp. 136 – 9).

[119] Fortunatus, *Vita S. Martini* (MGH, Auctores Antiquissimi 4, i, pp. 293 – 370).

[120] Thacker, 'Social and Continental Background', p. 112.

Herefrith, abbot of Lindisfarne at the time of Cuthbert's death in 687;[121] yet it does not supersede the earlier prose life, but rather takes its continued existence for granted. The tendency to abstraction which has been noted in the metrical *Life* also appears in a more limited form in the prose *Life*, with the omission of many names of places and witnesses included by the Lindisfarne author.[122] Interestingly, however, new episodes are fully documented with a full complement of place-names and personal names wherever possible.[123] It looks therefore as if Bede wrote his prose *Vita* partly to update the Lindisfarne *Life* and partly to harness the Cuthbertine cult to new concerns. Those concerns, as I have argued elsewhere, were Bede's attempted reform of the spiritual life of his people by means of a rejuvenated church.[124] They linked up with the ambitions of the Lindisfarne community and with the anxieties of a large section of the Northumbrian ecclesiastical establishment.

The Bedan *vitae* reflect a period when the cult of St Cuthbert was being vigorously promoted; in his dedicatory epistle to the *Vita metrica* Bede speaks of news of fresh wonders coming in daily to Jarrow.[125] This activity was taking place at a time of important political changes in Northumbria. After the death of Aldfrith Wilfrid had scored a notable triumph: he had secured the support of Abbess Aelfflaed and had been recognized as the adoptive father of the new king, Osred. Despite the opposition of the existing Northumbrian bishops (including presumably Eadfrith of Lindisfarne) he returned to Northumbria in 705, in control of his two principal monasteries and the bishopric of Hexham.[126] When he died in 709/10 he himself became the object of a cult and the subject of a *vita*.[127] Yet it is clear that hostility to the Wilfridians persisted. Wilfrid's famous arrangements for the disposal of his treasure, which included provision for buying the favour of kings and bishops, do not suggest confidence in the settlement;[128] nor does the author of the *Vita Wilfridi*, who expressly states that Wilfrid's abbots and followers everywhere feared the snares of their old enemies. His work is, in fact, overwhelmingly defensive, its tone well caught in the concluding miracle at the annual gathering on Wilfrid's feast day at Ripon, in which the saint's followers are surrounded by an arc of light, interpreted as 'a wall of divine help', and the bolts of their enemies turned back upon themselves.[129] These tensions probably continued unresolved throughout the early decades of the eighth century and perhaps found expression in the unexplained expulsion in 731 of Acca, Wilfrid's devoted follower and successor as bishop of Hexham — just as Bede was

---

[121] *VCP* 8, 23, 38 – 40.
[122] Plummer I, p. xlvi; *Two Lives*, p. 15; Jaager, *VCM*, p. 3.
[123] E.g. *VCP* 3, 6, 8, 35 – 7, 46.
[124] Thacker, in *Ideal and Reality*, pp. 130 – 53.
[125] *VCM* pref.
[126] *VW* 59 – 60; Farmer in *St Wilfrid at Hexham*, pp. 54 – 5.
[127] For the cult miracles see *VW* 66 – 8.
[128] *VW* 63.
[129] *VW* 68.

finishing the *Ecclesiastical History* and perhaps just before the revisions which, it has been suggested, produced the final version of the *Vita Wilfridi*.[130]

In the light of all this Bede's additions to the Cuthbertine corpus are very interesting. Clearly he had been assembling fresh material, especially from his own community at Jarrow and from Lindisfarne itself. The most significant and extensive additions are those which were made in the prose *Life* as a result of the conversations with Herefrith. It is not known whether Bede had discussed Cuthbert with Herefrith at the time he was composing his poem, in which he is never mentioned and from which several of his stories are omitted.[131] Nevertheless, Bede must by then have been in touch with some Lindisfarne source, since he already included in the earlier work a version of that enlarged account of Cuthbert's last days and death, which was to be given in an even more elaborate form in the prose *Life* where it is ascribed to Herefrith. That account is especially significant. In both versions it includes an attempt to make the figure of Cuthbert the rallying point of the opposition to the régime installed at Lindisfarne after his death, which was said to have brought a great storm of trouble on the community and the dispersal of many of the brethren.[132] Now, as has often been observed, though the exact nature of these troubles has never been specified, they coincide with the year in which Wilfrid ruled the church of Lindisfarne. Bede clearly identified the two events, since he alludes in the *Ecclesiastical History* to Wilfrid's year of rule at a precisely comparable point to that in the prose *Life* where he mentions the great blast of trouble.[133] The cult of Cuthbert is presented as strengthening the morale of the community at this time. Though his death ushered in misfortune, fortified by his protection, the community had emerged triumphant. It is surely significant that this theme first appeared in the Cuthbertine corpus just as Wilfrid was being restored to influence in Northumbria a second time.

Other material gathered by Bede suggests a further reinforcing of the posthumous cult. A much more prominent role is awarded to Bishop Eadberht, who rescued Lindisfarne from Wilfrid and was still ruling there at the time of the translation. In both metrical and prose lives Bede recounts Eadberht's praise of the miracle of Cuthbert's incorruption and alludes to his own (lost) attempt to put this into verse.[134] Clearly a cult of Eadberht was developing. His close association with the saint in death shows the esteem in which he was held, and in the *Ecclesiastical History* Bede states that the miracles done at the shrine testified to the merits of both men.[135] Lindisfarne's attitude to Eadberht is reflected in a story preserved by Alcuin, which tells of Eadberht

---

[130] Plummer I, p. 361; D. P. Kirby, 'Bede, Eddius Stephanus, and the Life of Wilfrid', *EHR* 98 (1983), pp. 107–8.
[131] E.g. *VCP* 8, 23.
[132] *VCM* 37; *VCP* 40.
[133] *HE* IV, 29 (27); *VCP* 40.
[134] *VCP* 42; *VCM* 38.
[135] *HE* IV, 30 (28).

miraculously protecting his flock from violently destructive winds.[136] All this perhaps represents a further emphasizing of the native episcopal traditions of the community; by the early eighth century Lindisfarne seems actively to have commemorated not only Cuthbert but his successors Eadberht and Eadfrith and, perhaps, Aidan — a more impressive galaxy of holy bishops than any other English see.[137]

Bede, in both the prose and metrical lives and in the *Ecclesiastical History*, testifies to the continuing vitality of the Cuthbertine cult in the early eighth century.[138] He drew strongly on the tradition of the community at Lindisfarne, who willingly collaborated with the foremost scholar of the day to show how through Cuthbert they had triumphed over their troubles. It is tempting to conclude that the desire for an updated version of the Lindisfarne *Life* in Osred's reign owes something to Wilfrid's return, and even perhaps that the publication of the *Vita prosaica* was intended as a riposte to the newly-written *Vita Wilfridi*.[139] Bede's own attitude is more difficult to determine. His presentation of Cuthbert reflects above all his desire to link Northumbria's leading saint with the reforming ideals formulated in his biblical commentaries.[140] Wilfrid's reaction to the division of his see and his fight to preserve his monasteries stood in the way of this. Though clearly Bede did not wish to cast scandal on one who had played such an important role in the establishment of catholic Christianity in Northumbria and elsewhere, it is not easy to believe that he wholeheartedly approved of Wilfrid.[141] At the very least he disliked the contentiousness which helped to bring divisions upon the church and sought to be as reticent about those divisions as he could. It is also perhaps worth remembering that the *Vita metrica* was written at a time when Bede believed that members of Wilfrid's household had accused him of heresy. His bitter and indignant reply to that accusation is notorious and comes close to accusing Wilfrid's immediate circle of being drunken boors.[142] Though Bede's affection for Acca seems to have been genuine and profound,[143] it was still perhaps in its infancy when the *Vita metrica* was written and the *Vita prosaica* first conceived. At that time the attitude of both Bede and Lindisfarne may have been harsher towards the Wilfridians; the threat may have seemed more acute than it proved in the event.

---

[136] *Poetry of the Carolingian Renaissance*, ed. P. Godman (London, 1985), p. 134 (lines 165 – 82).

[137] Relics of all these bishops accompanied the community when they left Lindisfarne in the 9th century: Battiscombe, in *Relics*, pp. 27 – 8.

[138] *HE* includes two new miracles which must represent some of the material deliberately omitted from *VCP*: *HE* IV, 31 – 2 (29 – 30).

[139] Kirby, *EHR* 98, pp. 101 – 14.

[140] Thacker, in *Ideal and Reality*, pp. 130 – 53.

[141] I cannot agree with G. Isenberg's view that Wilfrid is with Gregory the Great one of the two principal heroes of *HE*: *Die Würdigung Wilfrieds von York in der Historia Ecclesiastica Gentis Anglorum Bedas und der Vita Wilfridi des Eddius* (Münster, 1978), esp. pp. 18 – 58.

[142] C. W. Jones, *Bedae Opera de temporibus* (Cambridge, Massachusetts, 1943), pp. 132 – 5, 315.

[143] Plummer II, 315, 329 – 30.

It would seem, then, that Cuthbert's cult developed at a time of great strife within the Northumbrian ecclesiastical establishment and that this helps to explain both the quality and abundance of Cuthbertine hagiography. It was a contribution to a debate which had something of the quality of a pamphlet war. Cuthbert came to be seen as the patron of an important party within Northumbria, that of the king and the existing bishops (and by extension the patron of Northumbria itself). Hence the vigorous propagation of his cult. For Lindisfarne, obviously, he was an especial protector, and one who was identified with the restoration of the fortunes of the see and of the community after a period of great difficulty, in which it had faced threats from home and perhaps (in Iona) abroad. In response to these complex circumstances the monks of Lindisfarne initially produced a portrait of Cuthbert which gave due emphasis to the (Columba-like?) asceticism of the saint himself, but also threw his episcopal role into high relief. Their further reflections were recorded by Bede in a picture ultimately adapted to his own preoccupations with reform. In none of this writing is there much concern (it seems to me) to defend or propagate specifically 'Irish' or 'Roman' forms of observance. Though the spiritual life of the community at Lindisfarne continued to be shaped by a tradition derived at least partly from Iona, the monks cast their net widely in the search for means to advance their holy bishop, and like the Wilfridians themselves found an important model in the great episcopal cults of Gaul. Their own author used exemplars which may have seemed to him as much Gaulish as Irish. In the last resort, it was a conflict over church order and perhaps personalities which moulded Lindisfarne's traditions about Cuthbert.

PART TWO

Lindisfarne
and its Scriptorium

The Plan of the Early Christian Monastery on Lindisfarne: A Fresh Look at the Evidence

DEIRDRE O'SULLIVAN

This paper contains some of the fruits of a programme of fieldwork, excavation and research on Holy Island, Northumberland, which has been carried out as a joint project between the University of Leicester and St David's University College, Lampeter. Our programme started in 1977, when an excavation was undertaken on the site of the new museum.[1] A return visit in 1980 brought a number of interesting archaeological sites to light, and since 1983 our team has returned to the island twice yearly, and carried out a number of excavations, collections and site surveys (fig. 7). The search for the site of the monastery founded by St Aidan and closely linked to the career of St Cuthbert is only one aspect of this research, and this paper is best seen as a personal assessment of what can be concluded or reasonably inferred at present about the physical appearance of the early Christian monastic complex. Future fieldwork will hopefully add to our knowledge in terms both of detail and of general perspective.

The present programme is merely the most recent in a series of investigations. The earliest work on the ruined medieval priory, in the 1850s, was carried out when the property was in the care of the Ministry of Woods and Forests. Unfortunately it is completely undocumented but it is probable that some at least of the stone carvings now housed in the site museum were discovered in the course of this clearance. In the 1880s Sir William Crossman was responsible for excavation and consolidation in the priory cloister and on St Cuthbert's Island;[2] further clearance and consolidation took place under the overall supervision of Sir Charles Peers in the first quarter of this century;[3]

---

[1] D. M. O'Sullivan et al., 'An excavation in Holy Island village, 1977', Archaeologia Aeliana 5th series, 13 (1985), pp. 27 – 116.

[2] W. Crossman, 'The Recent Excavations at Holy Island Priory', History of the Berwickshire Naturalists' Club 13 (1892), pp. 225 – 40; W. Crossman, 'Chapel of St Cuthbert-in-the-Sea', ibid., pp. 241 – 2.

[3] C. R. Peers, 'The Inscribed and Sculptured Stones of Lindisfarne', Archaeologia 74 (1925), pp. 255 – 70.

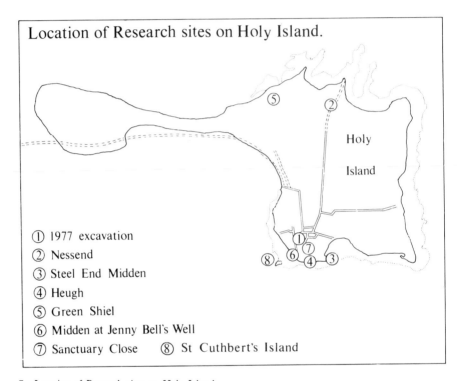

Location of Research sites on Holy Island.

Holy

Island

① 1977 excavation
② Nessend
③ Steel End Midden
④ Heugh
⑤ Green Shiel
⑥ Midden at Jenny Bell's Well
⑦ Sanctuary Close   ⑧ St Cuthbert's Island

7. Location of Research sites on Holy Island.

and Dr Brian Hope-Taylor carried out a series of small-scale excavations in the 1960s, which are as yet unpublished, outside the priory on the Heugh, the rocky ridge which overlooks it on the south, and in the field adjacent to the vicarage.[4]

[4] Brief reference to this work is made in M. Magnusson, *Lindisfarne, The Cradle Island* (Stocksfield, 1984), p. 49. The writer would also like to thank Prof. Richard Bailey, Ms Lisa Donel and Prof. Charles Thomas for providing information about this work.

Before describing and evaluating the results of all of this work, it seems appropriate to set some general parameters: one must ask what local factors will have influenced the siting and form of the early monastery, for example. The topography of the island imposes certain obvious limitations. The northern part of the island is not suitable for settlement or farming; it consists of a band of sand dunes, stretching all the way from the Snook, where the present causeway joins the island. However, within this band is an area of rig and furrow, which seems to indicate that the arable land of the village was once rather more extensive.[5] Most of the island is now given over to sheep farming, although there are some cattle in improved pasture and a small number of arable fields. Present settlement is concentrated in the village with only one or two outlying dwellings. The buildings, which can get rough treatment from the prevailing westerly winds, are usually stone built. Today there are two working farms on the island and a handful of full-time fishermen. The permanent population, at about 200, is now less than half the population of the nineteenth century.[6]

The island landscape is open and treeless, but natural resources include coal, iron ore, and building stone. Shellfish abound on the shoreline, especially that facing the mainland. Important topographical features include two prominent rocky eminences on the south coast: the Heugh, and the Castle Rock, Biblaw. A small tidal islet, St Cuthbert's Island, just west of the Heugh, is separated from the main island before this is cut off from the mainland. The island harbour allows shallow, safe anchorage although sandbars in the bay are a potential hazard to craft.

This is a description of the island today but most of these factors will have operated in the long term, affecting, even determining, the form and structure of settlement. It is also important to take account of how the recovery of information about the past is controlled: the absence of much arable, for example, severely restricts the potential for fieldwalking and the identification of cropmark sites. The dunes also conceal archaeology.

Before St Aidan's arrival Holy Island had been in the control of Anglo-Saxon kings for about a century, possibly even longer. It is not really appropriate to view the island as particularly inaccessible or previously uninhabited: apart from the accumulating evidence for prehistoric activity,[7] it must be also remembered that it can be reached easily and reasonably safely on foot from the mainland for a period of several hours every day at low tide. The nature of early settlement on the island is not yet known, however. It is visible from Bamburgh, and the tale of the besieging of the English on

[5] The Cambridge University Collection of air photographs contains a number of vertical photographs which show this feature clearly.
[6] R. A. and D. B. Cartwright, *The Holy Island of Lindisfarne and the Farne Islands* (Newton Abbot, 1976), pp. 89 – 92.
[7] P. Beavitt, D. O'Sullivan, and R. Young, *Recent Fieldwork on Lindisfarne* (University of Leicester, Department of Archaeology Occasional Paper No. 1, 1985), pp. 6 – 10.

Lindisfarne, reported in Nennius's *Historia Brittonum*,[8] may indicate that it was itself some kind of royal centre. Alternatively, it may have supported a population of peasant fishermen.

The monastery founded by St Aidan may reasonably be expected to mirror, at least in its initial stages, those ecclesiastical foundations with which he had come in contact: the Columban foundation on Iona, especially, would have been an important model. In very general terms, the initial comparison seems appropriate from a topographical point of view, although there are one or two points of difference. Iona is much more genuinely remote than Holy Island, the island can only be reached by sea, and it is also somewhat larger.

Unfortunately, the early monastery on Iona, like that on Lindisfarne, is not at all well known archaeologically. Adomnan's *Life of Columba* is our source of information for the existence of separate buildings with different functions.[9] These include a church,[10] a communal building,[11] and a number of huts which seem to have been utilised for a variety of purposes.[12] Excavations since the 1950s have confirmed the existence of timber buildings, although clear plans of these are another matter, and a number of industrial activities, including woodturning, leatherworking, bronze and glass-working, and possibly limeburning.[13] No masonry buildings of the early Christian period have as yet been found; and at least some of the early buildings were in the vicinity of the site of the later abbey.

The most striking early Christian feature visible on Iona is the monastic enclosure or *vallum monasterii*, which surrounds a D-shaped area approximately 300m × 200m. This survives partly as a visible boundary bank, on the western side, partly as a cropmark, on the north, and partly as a geophysical anomaly.[14] Comparable enclosures, although not always defined in quite this way and usually of more curvilinear form, are a feature of most major Irish monasteries.[15]

While Iona is the most useful site to consider as a prototype for Lindisfarne, the gradual severance of the Columban tie, and the undoubted contact which

---

[8] Nennius, *Historia Brittonum* ch. 63; ed. and trans. J. Morris, *British History and the Welsh Annals* (London and Chichester, 1980), pp. 38, 79.

[9] Adomnan, *Life of Columba*, ed. and trans. A. O. and M. O. Anderson (Edinburgh, 1961). A. D. S. MacDonald, 'Aspects of the Monastery and Monastic Life in Adomnán's Life of Columba', *Peritia* 3 (1984), pp. 271 – 302, is a comprehensive review of the documentary evidence for the monastic buildings on Iona.

[10] *Life of Columba*, ed. Anderson, pp. 112, 504 – 7.

[11] Ibid., pp. 113, 220 – 1.

[12] Ibid., pp. 109, 112 – 13, 258 – 9, 536 – 7.

[13] J. W. Barber, 'Excavations on Iona, 1979', *Proceedings of the Society of Antiquaries of Scotland* 111 (1981), pp. 282 – 380; R. Reece, *Excavations in Iona 1964 to 1974* (University of London Institute of Archaeology, Occasional Publication No. 5; London, 1980).

[14] The Royal Commission on the Ancient and Historical Monuments of Scotland, *Argyll: An Inventory of the Monuments*, vol. IV: *Iona* (Edinburgh, 1982), pp. 31 – 9.

[15] A number of examples are well illustrated from the air in E. R. Norman and J. K. S. St Joseph, *The Early Development of Irish Society: the Evidence of Aerial Photography* (Cambridge, 1969), pp. 92 – 121.

took place between Lindisfarne and monasteries with quite different traditions, not least that reflected in the cult of Cuthbert himself, must be kept in view. The development of the site, and the renewal and repair of buildings in the eighth and ninth centuries, may well have introduced new plans, materials, and ideas. As with Iona, there are a number of references in the surviving sources to specific buildings of St Cuthbert's time or earlier. These include a watchtower,[16] a guesthouse,[17] a dormitory[18] and two churches.[19] It is clear that the churches at least were originally built of wood. There is no clue in the sources as to the exact whereabouts of these buildings, however.

The belief that the principal monastic church, which had contained the original shrine of Cuthbert, was situated due east of the parish church presumably dates from the late eleventh century, when the priory church was constructed on its present site. It was not until the nineteenth century, however, that clearance in the priory and casual discoveries in the churchyard started to produce the first material evidence for the early monastery. Many of the early Christian carvings in the priory museum were discovered prior to Crossman's work in the late nineteenth century; Stuart refers to carved stones visible in the priory walls before 1866 – 7 and illustrates a number of these.[20] It is possible that they were removed from the walls slightly before this date, conceivably as a result of the clearance carried out under the auspices of the Commissioners for Woods, in the middle of the nineteenth century.

Sir William Crossman was the first to undertake serious archaeological work in the priory, and publish the results.[21] His activities were confined to the area of the cloisters, however, and he only received permission to remove deposits to the level of the floor of the church nave.[22] His published account makes no reference to any finds of Anglo-Saxon date, and while it is not really feasible to estimate the extent to which his work may have penetrated early deposits, it is quite possible that in fact these were little disturbed at this time.

The clearance works carried out under Charles Peers's direction in the years before and after the First World War clearly did penetrate to the foundations of the medieval priory, and the quantities of unstratified medieval pottery recovered certainly indicate that medieval levels were removed in some quantity.[23] There is some material of Saxo-Norman type in the collection, but finds of specifically Anglo-Saxon artefacts are not abundant,

---

[16] *VCP* 40.
[17] *VCA* IV, 16.
[18] *VCP* 16.
[19] *HE* III, 17 and 25.
[20] J. Stuart, ed., *Sculptured Stones of Scotland* (2 vols.; Aberdeen, 1856 – 67), II, 19 – 20, pl. XXVI.
[21] See above, n. 2.
[22] This information is contained in unpublished correspondence in the archives of The Historic Buildings and Monuments Commission for England.
[23] This pottery has never been fully studied. It is now temporarily housed in the Dept. of Archaeology, University of Durham.

and seem to consist only of a couple of coins and a small piece of metalwork, as well as the stone carvings published by Peers and stated by him all to have been found in secondary contexts.[24] A comparison with Whitby is illuminating at this point. Whatever the very real shortcomings of the programmes of work carried out at both Holy Island Priory and Whitby, there is a sense in which they may be said to have been excavated by the same method and director, but there is an enormous disparity in terms of both the number and quality of finds recovered: Whitby produced a very substantial range of both functional and decorative metalwork datable to the Middle Saxon period, as well as pottery and other finds.[25] If Peers's work on Holy Island did in fact disturb Anglo-Saxon buildings, these cannot have been artifact-rich. It seems, however, quite possible that no such disturbance took place.

As has already been noted, Peers's workmen did recover many fragments of Anglo-Saxon stone sculpture, but he provided almost no information about the context of this material in his published report. With regard to the small stones known as pillow-stones he observed that 'the stones occurred in various places — several being found within the area of the priory church, two close together in the parish churchyard just west of the western range of the priory buildings, and others in the area of the cloisters. But all occurred among building rubbish and loose stones in disturbed ground, and were in no case in a position which could give any evidence as to their original arrangement.'[26] His paper contains no other information about the circumstances of the discovery of other stones with one notable exception: a cross base, which he illustrates. He claims that this was found *in situ*, under the north-west crossing pier.[27] If he was correct about this then it is likely to have been out of doors, in which case the principal early Christian monastic church is presumably not sited within the area of the sanctuary of the priory church, in spite of early beliefs. However, an unpublished photograph in the Historic Buildings and Monuments Commission archives,[28] taken while work was in progress, seems to indicate that the piers of the nave were constructed on a continuous foundation, which would have removed all pre-existing stratigraphy. This implies that the cross base is simply one of a number of stones used in the construction of the foundations.

Peers found only one architectural foundation which he believed to antedate the priory construction, 'a foundation underlying the north aisle wall. This seems to have belonged to a plain rectangular building, whose east wall was a little to the west of the east end of this aisle; but its south and west walls have left no trace . . . it has no features from which a date could be deduced.'[29]

[24] Peers, *Archaeologia* 74, p. 259.
[25] C. R. Peers and C. A. R. Radford, 'The Saxon Monastery of Whitby', *Archaeologia* 89 (1943), pp. 27 – 88.
[26] See above, n. 24.
[27] Peers, *Archaeologia* 74, p. 269 and pl. LV, fig. 2.
[28] Thanks are due to Mr David Sherlock for locating this material.
[29] Peers, *Archaeologia* 74, p. 257.

Without more information it is impossible to offer a sensible interpretation of this evidence.[30] It is conceivable that the structure to which Peers refers was an earlier church on the site of the priory church, but other possibilities cannot be excluded. Peers himself offered no such interpretation, but it can be noted in this context that he was one of the first to draw serious attention to the east end of the nave of the parish church, and the possibility that it contains Saxon work.[31]

As part of our own survey programme we have carried out resistivity and magnetometer surveys inside the priory ruins, and in the pasture field to the east of it, known as Sanctuary Close (fig. 8). One of the name stones in the priory museum was found in this field, although the exact findspot is not known.[32] The magnetometer survey was not particularly useful, but the resistivity survey did reveal some interesting results.[33] The areas inside and outside the priory cannot be effectively compared in terms of absolute values, probably because drainage inside the Guardianship area is superior. Allowance must also be made for the natural slope of the ground, especially in the outer court; this tends to produce a pattern of high values at the top of a slope and low values at the bottom, which are not caused by buried features. When the data have been 'smoothed' to take these factors into account, however, a number of geophysical anomalies remain which may indicate the existence of buried structures. Some of these are hardly surprising; the south range of the cloister is now partly turfed over but the survey indicates a continuous range, which is no more than one would expect. The continuous foundation for the piers of the nave is also suggested by the readings inside the priory church. In the western part of the outer court, there is some indication of a range of buildings parallel with the enclosing wall, although these are not as clearly defined. They are presumably related to the standing walls, however, and may indicate structures of either medieval or post-medieval date. A number of other anomalies are present which may indicate hitherto unsuspected structures, less clearly aligned with the standing walls and therefore more likely to predate them, but unfortunately none of these are sufficiently clearly defined to make a tentative reconstruction of their plan possible.

In Sanctuary Close, some features can be explained in terms of topography and background noise. For example, the area of high resistance at the southern edge of the field is clearly caused by the rising basalt of the Heugh, and the high readings to the west are probably caused by the proximity of the wall foundations of the outer court of the priory. A massive bank of resistance

---

[30] An unpublished plan of Peers's excavations has recently (October 1987) come to light. It has not been possible to evaluate it fully in the context of this paper, but it is hoped to publish it separately elsewhere.

[31] Peers, *Archaeologia* 74, p. 258.

[32] *Corpus* I, p. 202.

[33] A simple introduction to the principles and methods of geophysical survey in archaeology is provided by K. Greene, *Archaeology, an Introduction* (London, 1983), pp. 48–54.

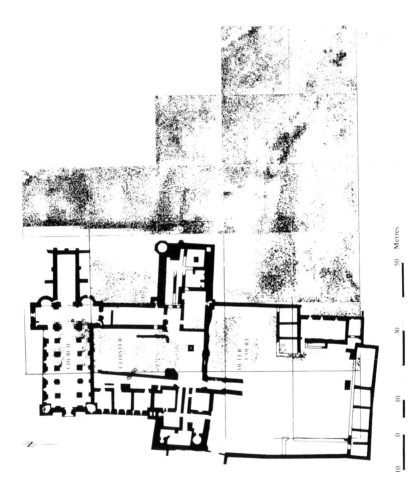

8. *Resistivity in the Priory and Sanctuary Close.*

running at an angle to the slope of the ground (fig. 8, a-b) cannot be caused by this phenomenon, and we must seek another explanation. Also, parallel with the boundary fence which separates the field from the eastern range of the cloister is a clearly defined linear feature. This may simply be caused by the cut for the enclosing wall of the priory, but there is undoubtedly a linear feature (fig. 8, c-d), quite conceivably a building, at right angles to this, and another linear feature (fig. 8, e-f), running east-southeast across the lower part of the field, which might possibly be a drain.

These features may seem rather ephemeral but the survey has been repeated in two successive years with similar results, and survive when the data is plotted at different values. However, features detected in resistivity survey cannot be dated without excavation, and the technique is of little use in detecting small or deeply buried features. This may be of some significance in the context of Sanctuary Close, as it is possible that there has been a considerable build-up of soil in the field as a result of successive clearances from the priory.

The excavation on the site of the new museum in 1977 revealed some early features which might be of the Anglo-Saxon period.[34] These consisted of an area of flat paving, and a shallow hearth. They were the earliest features, stratigraphically, on the site, and had been covered by a wind-blown deposit, but the contexts themselves produced no dateable finds. In the excavation report it was suggested that they might be internal features in a building, the more substantial parts of which had been obliterated by later pits. A couple of Anglo-Saxon finds were found residually in later contexts in the upper strata of the site.[35]

Attention has already been drawn to the Heugh, the rocky ridge overlooking the priory on the seaward side. A series of low turf banks and other earthwork features are visible here, running along the ridge between the coastguard station at the western end and the post-medieval redoubt known as Osborne's fort at Steel End. Attention was first drawn to these earthworks in an unpublished letter of 1897, now in the Northumberland Record Office, from one S. P. Blackwell, who commented on a number of features on the western part of the ridge.[36]

Blackwell's letter provided the inspiration for our own survey (fig. 9) which was carried out over two years and involved both conventional survey and resistivity survey. A number of the features noted by him are still apparent. The resistivity data, which is here plotted as contours rather than dot-densities, complements the features which were clearly visible and could be planned.

Starting from the west, the first visible feature (excluding the flagstaff base, fig. 9 A) is a low bank, to the west of the ruined look-out known as the

[34] O'Sullivan, *Arch. Ael.* 13, pp. 31 – 4.
[35] Ibid., pp. 101 – 3, 112.
[36] Northumberland Record Office 683/10/133.

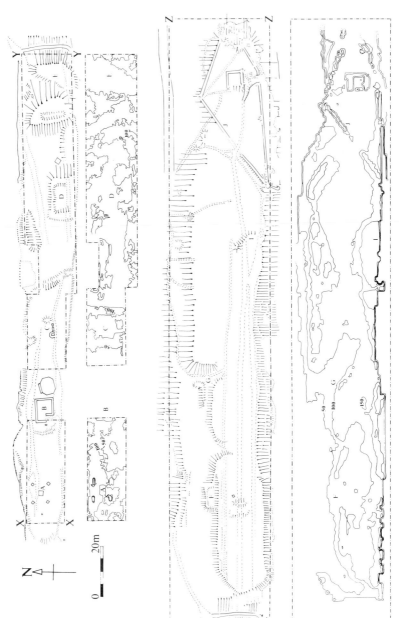

9. *Survey on the Heugh.*

'chapel', (fig. 9 B). This may simply represent rubble collapse, but it was noted by Blackwell. On the east of the present coastguard station is a rectangular feature (fig. 9 C), about 7m × 8m. This was clearly defined in two successive seasons by resistivity, but is only partly represented above ground, by a low mound. Further east (fig. 9 D) a rectangular building is clearly visible and is also apparent from the resistivity data. This measures about 5m × 10m, its long axis running east-west. The last feature worthy of note before the path is the curious curved bank or mound known as the 'Cockpit' (fig. 9 E). A rectangular trench with a suspiciously archaeological appearance has been cut through the western side. It is not known when this work was carried out, but it is apparently not the work of Dr Brian Hope-Taylor.

On the far side of the path, which bisects the ridge, structures are perhaps not so clear, but there are still items of interest. The sites excavated by Dr Hope-Taylor are located on the north-facing slope and may have included either or both of the small rectangular buildings visible at F and G. The results of his work are not known in detail but it is thought that he discovered the remains of at least two buildings. The excavations seem to have been confined to the removal of turf and topsoil and little dating evidence was forthcoming.[37] The low resistivity readings at G may imply that it is a filled-in, natural cleft in the rock. The low, irregular bank at (I) is of uncertain function but it also is definitely picked up by the resistivity meter. The banks of Osborne's Fort are also clearly shown (J).

Blackwell speculated that the western end of the Heugh was at least partly surrounded by a wall, but it is difficult to be sure if the higher readings around the perimeter are caused by something like a wall, or by the basalt bedrock which seems to be very close to the surface around the edges of the ridge.

Without excavation it is impossible to say much about the date and function of these buildings, but it seems quite probable that at least one of them may be the watchtower from which the monks of Lindisfarne watched for news of Cuthbert's death on Farne:

> 'Without delay one of them ran out and lit two torches: and holding one in each hand, he went on to some higher ground to show the brethren who were in the Lindisfarne monastery that his holy soul had gone to be with the Lord: for this was the sign they had agreed upon amongst themselves to notify his most holy death. When the brother had seen it, who had been keeping watch and awaiting the hour of this event far away in the watchtower of the island of Lindisfarne opposite, he quickly ran to the church where the whole assembly of the brethren were gathered.'[38]

The Heugh affords a good view of Inner Farne, although one must assume night-time and the absence of any mist at sea for the story to be true. A

---

[37] See above, n. 4.
[38] *VCP* 40. (*Two Lives*, p. 287).

watchtower or lookout would also have provided useful shelter when waiting for sea or land travellers on their way to the monastery. Advance notice of their arrival would have enabled important visitors to have been greeted with appropriate ceremony. There is no obvious need for a whole series of such lookouts, however, and the number of buildings situated along this exposed and windy ridge is rather surprising. Of course, as with the features detected in the resistivity survey in Sanctuary Close and the priory, there is no real dating evidence and there is also the possibility that the monks of the refounded priory would also have maintained a watchtower. In the latter context, the proximity of the rectangular foundation at C to a path which leads to a blocked doorway in the outer court may be significant. We are still left with a number of structures which have no obvious place in the post-conquest settlement plan of either the secular or monastic communities, but which can perhaps be fitted into a dispersed, early Christian monastic complex, as individual retreats, chapels or even 'stations'.[39]

The place most commonly seen as the setting for the solitary life of the Lindisfarne monks is St Cuthbert's Island. The visible remains were cleared and consolidated by Crossman in the late nineteenth century, but the site has never been in state care, and there does not appear to be any record of subsequent work. The most prominent feature on the island today is a T-shaped chapel (fig. 10 A) situated below the raised knoll on the southern side of the island and surrounded by a curious ditched feature (fig. 10 D). This chapel is presumably the chapel of St Cuthbert-in-the-Sea which was still in use in the later middle ages.[40] Although in its present form it is surely not pre-conquest, earlier remains may lie beneath. To the north-west of this is a low circular mound (fig. 10 C), previously identified as a cell but no longer clearly identifiable as such.[41] On the south-east of the islet is a small rectangular foundation, now rapidly disappearing into the sea, where one of the little name stones was found.[42] Resistivity survey added little to the evidence provided by the visible remains.

The remains on St Cuthbert's Island, even if they cannot be dated archaeologically, reflect an important strand in the tradition of insular monasticism, and the islet fulfilled an important need in providing the possibility of physical isolation within a monastic community. The more communal aspects of the monastic life would also have been apparent on the monastic plan, and it is in this context that that rather embarrassing omission from the island topography, the *vallum monasterii* can be considered.

The evidence for a monastic vallum on Holy Island is not strong, and much of what follows can be dismissed simply as speculation. However, in the context of the monastic tradition from which the Lindisfarne monks took their

[39] See Herity, above.
[40] Crossman, 'Chapel', *Berwicks. Nat. Club* 13, p. 241.
[41] Cartwright, *Holy Island*, p. 56.
[42] Peers, *Archaeologia* 74, p. 259.

ST CUTHBERT'S
ISLAND.

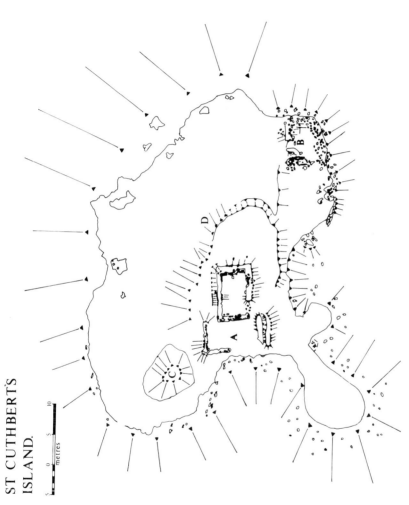

10. *St Cuthbert's Island.*

roots, the tradition of insular Irish monasticism, it is the absence, rather than the presence of this feature which should be considered noteworthy and minimalist approaches are not appropriate.

Dr Hope-Taylor seems to have had a very positive faith in the existence of a monastic vallum on Holy Island, and placing his muscle behind his commitment, excavated a section of the rather amorphous bank in the Vicar's field, east of the churchyard. Unfortunately the result proved to be wholly negative, the bank being revealed as post-medieval in date. There is no other excavated evidence which can be brought to bear on the problem, and the other major source of archaeological evidence about relict landscape features, aerial photography, has not provided much positive evidence either. The photographs in the Cambridge Air Photography collection have been scrutinized as part of our overall research programme, and although the collection contains a number of superb vertical photographs which provide overlapping coverage of the island, taken on a number of different occasions, and a series of oblique views which concentrate on the area around the village, the priory and the Heugh, there is only one area where it is even possible to speculate that there is any possibility of a monastic vallum. However, as noted at the beginning of this paper, the very small area of the island which is now used for arable farming, and the fact that there are grounds for believing that arable farming may have represented a much greater proportion of the farmed area in the past, are both factors which will have contributed to the limited utility of the technique at the present time. On the one hand, more intensive farming will have resulted in the obliteration of the type of evidence which might otherwise have survived as an earthwork; on the other, ploughed-out features will no longer be apparent from the air if these are now converted to permanent pasture.

The one feature which could be seen as indicating a segment of a banked enclosure is quite possibly a purely natural feature, but the slope of the ground in Sanctuary Close and the priory, already referred to,[43] is apparent in a number of published photographs of the priory as a visible bank running east-west across the northern part of the outer court and continuing into Sanctuary Close.[44] It is possible to interpret this as a low bank from the ground, but it is not possible to follow it for any distance or relate it to other topographic features.

We can, however, suggest some boundaries for the early monastic enclosure, partly by utilizing natural features and partly by considering the street patterns of the village (fig. 11). It is possible, for example, that the Heugh itself, and the line of raised beach along the east side of Sanctuary Close, might have formed southern and eastern limits respectively to the monastic enclosure. For the northern boundary, there are two possibilities.

---

[43] See above, pp. 131–3.
[44] E.g. the photograph published in L. Butler and C. Given-Wilson, *Medieval Monasteries of Great Britain* (London, 1979), p. 284.

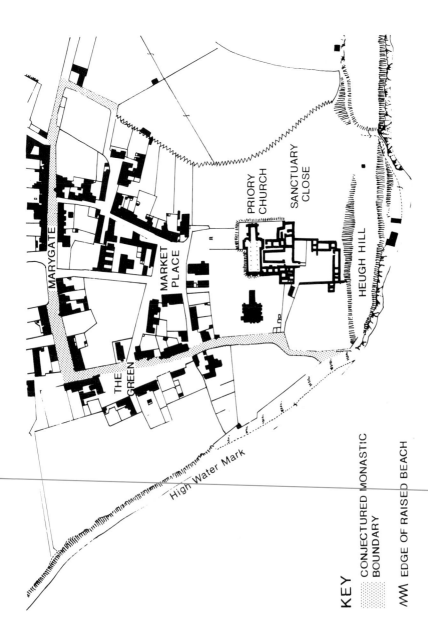

MARYGATE

THE GREEN

MARKET PLACE

PRIORY CHURCH

SANCTUARY CLOSE

HEUGH HILL

High Water Mark

KEY

░░░ CONJECTURED MONASTIC
BOUNDARY

ⱮⱮ EDGE OF RAISED BEACH

11. Suggested line of Monastic Vallum. Street lines taken from first edition survey map.

One is the northern street frontage of the market-place, which links up well with the eastern edge of Sanctuary Close and a possible western boundary along the road which runs past the west end of the parish church towards St Cuthbert's Island; but this would give rather a small enclosure. Alternatively, there is the line of Marygate, which would yield a much larger enclosure, comparable with that at Iona. These suggestions are not necessarily mutually exclusive, for it is possible that at Lindisfarne, as at Iona, the monastic enclosure was subject to alteration and extension.[45] It is also possible that the topography of the early Christian monastery was similar to that of a number of Irish early Christian sites, where a small enclosure is surrounded by a larger one.[46]

It is thus possible to make some attempt at reconstructing a monastic *vallum* or enclosure on Holy Island, although the evidence is woefully inadequate, and likely to remain so. More secure evidence of the importance of the link with Iona is provided by the commemoration of St Columba on the island. His name is found attached to the now disused St Coomb's farm on the Straight Lonnen, the inland track which leads to the dunes, and also, and much more significantly, in connection with a site called St Columba's Chapel or Chapel garth; there is also a St Columba's Street. These no longer survive above ground but are evidenced in a document of 1592 which itemizes burgage properties on Holy Island.[47] The location of the properties is given, but not all of the street names can now be certainly identified. However, the approximate, if not the precise siting of St Columba's Chapel can be ascertained: it was north of Marygate, and south of the King's Highway. Information about adjacent properties seems to indicate that it was somewhere in the area between what is now Lewin's Lane and the road to Berwick. No medieval reference to the chapel has as yet come to light,[48] and there are not any particularly promising candidates for the chapel itself among the surviving buildings in the area.

The two fields to the north of the zone within which the chapel site should be found are ploughed, and the farmer has reported a 'hard patch' at the southern end, although nothing is visible from the air. However, a significant pointer may be the fact that the westernmost plot is awarded to the Dean and Chapter of Durham on the enclosure award map.[49]

A number of reports of the finding of skeletons have taken place in the area north of Marygate, although not, in so far as is known, in any of the gardens

---

[45] RCHMS, *Iona*, pp. 31 – 9; Barber (as n. 13), pp. 361 – 4. Barber, however, suggests that the 'nucleus' of the earliest phase of the Columban monastery is to the south of the proposed southern line of the vallum, under Reilig Odhráin.

[46] A number of examples are illustrated in Norman and St Joseph, *Early Development of Irish Society*, loc. cit.

[47] Northumberland Record Office 683/10/103.

[48] It seems quite probable that some medieval documentation for this site will be found in the Durham Cathedral archives.

[49] Northumberland Record Office 683/9/2.

in the western part of the 'zone'. Human bones have, however, been discovered in the vicinity of Cambridge House, in the area of the present carpark, and at the back of one of the cottages opposite the carpark. The cottage finds were apparently associated with an undecorated stone slab.

With the exception of the Cambridge House finds, these discoveries were all made to the east of the possible site of St Columba's Chapel. It is difficult to evaluate them properly, as none were fully investigated at the time of discovery, and even the dates when the discoveries were made are no longer easy to establish, although all are within the memory span of living islanders. However, they do raise some interesting questions. One might speculate, for example, that the chapel enclosure had originally extended further to the west; or suspect that they constitute evidence for a reasonably extensive, additional burial ground. Alternatively, they might be unrelated to the early Christian monastery.

It is interesting that the evidence for the chapel and these graves is found to the north of the village. While any conclusions must be very tentative, the existence of a multiplicity of chapels and burial grounds is hinted at. While this is again, perhaps, no more than one might expect by analogy with other sites in the Irish tradition, it is useful to be able to offer some positive evidence for it. In the light of the speculations which have just been entered into with regard to the monastic enclosure, it is perhaps worth noting that on Iona Reilig Odhráin, the main burial ground, is found apparently outside, or at least as an annex to, the main monastic enclosure.[50] Perhaps the initial purpose of the plurality of sites may be a division between monastic and secular worship and/or burial. The existence of separate burial grounds is suggested by Bede's wording, to the effect that St Aidan was buried 'in the cemetery of the brothers.'[51] Although the evidence is slight and easily overstretched, the absence of finds which could be specifically linked with a monastic, literate community in the area north of the village may be an indication that the burials here were probably secular.

The evidence reviewed in this paper is clearly inadequate in providing any detailed picture of the monastery of which Cuthbert was prior, but there is nonetheless quite a surprising body of material which can be brought to bear on general issues. While only careful excavation is likely to add much certainty in terms of dating and plan details, it is possible to focus attention on key areas in terms of future work, and also to draw some conclusions, even if these must be based on probabilities rather than certainties. Whatever we may think about the evidence for a monastic enclosure, there is evidence for a number of stone buildings within the area of the priory and the Heugh which may belong to the Anglo-Saxon monastery. There is some evidence for more than one burial ground; and evidence for a rather more dispersed type of monastery than has perhaps hitherto been appreciated. This latter consideration is an

---

[50] See n. 45, above.
[51] *HE* III, 17.

important one, since any development inside Holy Island village may be potentially damaging to the early monastic remains. Holy Island is important archaeologically, not simply because it is important historically, but because it is a vital link between two different worlds, the 'Celtic' and the Anglo-Saxon. The quality and interest of its archaeological deposits has yet to be fully appreciated.[52]

[52] Acknowledgements: The writer would like to thank the following for discussion and assistance with illustrations, etc.: Mr P. Beavitt, Mr D. S. Hides, Mr A. Clark, Ms D. Miles, Mr D. Sherlock, Mr N. Tulip, and Dr R. Young. She would also like to acknowledge the help of students from Leicester who have assisted in the annual field survey courses which have made much of this work possible.

The Gospel Texts at Lindisfarne
at the Time of St Cuthbert

CHRISTOPHER D. VEREY

The textual evidence of certain Latin Gospel books, whose style or history suggest early connection with Lindisfarne though they may not necessarily derive from Lindisfarne, provides indications of the varying influences on Northumbrian culture no less significant than, and in many ways paralleling, those from script and ornament.[1]

With so much material lost, and much of that surviving having no precise origin, the fact that we can argue for a group of books having a Lindisfarne connection is, in no small part, because of the cult of Cuthbert himself. The Lindisfarne Gospels provide one of those rare fixed points for books of this period. This we owe to the circumstances of their production and to the recollection by Aldred of the same, both in honour of the saint. Moreover it is to the community of St Cuthbert and to its spiritual successors here in Durham that we owe the survival not only of the Lindisfarne Gospels (until the Dissolution), but also of other key books. Given the almost unique continuity of the Durham collection, an early Durham provenance can reinforce other evidence for a Lindisfarne connection.

Two of the books discussed here are from the Durham collection: the early fragments in Durham MS A.II.10 and elsewhere[2] and the Durham Gospels, MS A.II.17.[3] The Echternach[4] and Lindisfarne Gospels[5] and the Gospel book now divided between London, BL Cotton MS Otho C.V and Cambridge,

---

[1] This contribution is dedicated to the fond memory of Julian Brown. His scholarship so richly illuminated the significance of the manuscript evidence from early Christian Northumbria. I recall with thanks the early direction of my studies by Gerald Bonner, and I am grateful to him and his colleagues for the invitation to participate in this celebration of St Cuthbert. My particular thanks go also to Michelle Brown of the British Library; her infectious enthusiasm kept me to my task.
[2] *CLA* II, no. 147.
[3] *CLA* II, no. 149; see *The Durham Gospels*, ed. Christopher D. Verey, T. Julian Brown, Elizabeth Coatsworth (EEMF vol. 20, Copenhagen, 1980).
[4] Paris, Bibliothèque Nationale MS lat. 9389; *CLA* V, no. 578.
[5] *CLA* II, no. 187; see *Cod. Lind.*

Corpus Christi College MS 197B[6] will also be examined. Before turning to the particular, I offer a few comments on the nature of the evidence, not least its limitations.

The Gospels passed into the tradition of the Latin west through various translations and revisions; there was no single textual archetype.[7] The first three, so-called synoptic Gospels, provide further cause of textual confusion by their similar narrative of common substance. The Gospels were by far the best known and copied book in the early middle ages, and this familiarity was not always wholly conducive to the precise transcription of an exemplar; there was a widespread process of local editing or 'improving'. Finally, the majority of the evidence is lost. None of this makes for easy interpretation of the surviving material. It is only rarely that the evidence is sufficient to allow even tentative conclusions about direct textual dependence. For the most part it allows no more than the conclusion of family likenesses.

The concern of the missonary church will have been primarily with the availability of Gospels rather than with textual niceties. But as the church in Northumbria became more established, concern with the pedigree of texts will have featured more. Italy was the great provider of books in this period, and in at least some centres Italian Gospel books will have enjoyed intrinsic authority. Even so, prejudice towards the presumed pedigree of a book is not to be confused with informed judgement on textual substance. This latter will always have been the exception. In this period the only clear example is that of Wearmouth/Jarrow consciously emulating the earliest editorial efforts of Cassiodorus.[8]

If the evidence of the Gospel text proper is frequently difficult to interpret, that of the prefatory matter is far more amenable to classification. This material is, moreover, less susceptible to corruption in transmission. For example, scribal inattention or textual licence is unlikely to confuse the number of sections in a particular family of *capitula*, the 'chapter' divisions which vary according to family — to take the example of Matthew, between twenty-eight and ninety-one.[9] The other prefaces to individual Gospels are the so-called Monarchian Prologues and the decidedly Insular set of glosses on Hebrew names.[10] The texts of these will never have been so familiar and at significant risk of 'improvement'. But in other ways they did enjoy a familiarity which could influence their place in the scheme of things. There are clear indications of conscious preference for prefatory matter belonging to a particular family. Prefaces are found alongside Gospel texts from different

[6] *CLA* II, no. 125.

[7] For a convenient summary see Raphael Loewe, 'The Medieval History of the Latin Vulgate', in *The Cambridge History of the Bible*, vol. II, ed. G. W. H. Lampe (Cambridge, 1969), pp. 102 – 54.

[8] See B. Fischer, 'Codex Amiatinus und Cassiodor', *Biblische Zeitschrift*, neue Folge 6 (1962), pp. 57 – 79.

[9] See Patrick McGurk, *Latin Gospel Books from A.D. 400 to 800* (Les Publications de Scriptorium V; Paris and Brussels, 1961) for an indispensible survey of the early material.

[10] See also *The Durham Gospels*, pp. 18 – 25, on the nature of this prefatory matter.

traditions. One well-known example is found in the Books of Durrow and Kells, which share virtually identical prefaces in an otherwise unique configuration, but contain Gospel texts from fundamentally differing traditions.[11] The clear caution is never to judge a Gospel book by the family of its prefaces alone.

Finally, texts alone cannot prove the origins of books. There is nothing exclusively Irish or Northumbrian about a Gospel text.[12]

Palaeographical and art-historical evidence places the fragments in Durham MSS A.II.10, C.III.13 and C.III.20 (pl. 31) at a stage between the Cathach of St Columba and the Book of Durrow, some time around the middle of the seventh century. The Durham provenance would suggest a Northumbrian origin. This is Northumbria before Whitby; a period in which the influence of the Irish mission predominated. The evidence of the text is wholly consistent with this background. It seems also to tie in with the conclusions of Julian Brown in his unpublished Lyell Lectures that early Irish and Northumbrian book production reflected archaic and provincial practice.[13]

As to the 'architecture' of these fragments, no prefatory matter survives. There is no room for any between Matthew and Mark. It is possible that the book followed the anomalous arrangement found in the Books of Durrow and Kells in grouping all the prefaces before Matthew; calculation of the missing leaves might just about allow this.[14] Alternatively, there may have been none, as with some earlier Old Latin examples. The total absence of such prefatory matter is not uncommon in later Gospel books of Irish pedigree.[15]

The Gospel text itself is decidedly Old Latin in places. The character of the Old Latin is particularly distinct in the section Mark 2:12 – 6:6 (after which there is a break), where the text is almost identical with that of the slightly earlier fragments in Dublin, Trinity College MS 55 (*Usserianus Primus*).[16] Another pointer to the pre-Jerome tradition may be the complete absence of Eusebian divisions in Matthew, through either marginal numbers or the incidence of text initials. These divisions were introduced into the Latin Gospels by Jerome and their purpose described in his dedicatory letter to Pope

[11] See *Evangeliorum Quattuor Codex Durmachensis*, ed. A. A. Luce, G. O. Simms, Peter Meyer and Ludwig Bieler (2 vols.; Olten and Lausanne, 1960), II, 7 – 17.

[12] Burkitt was mistaken; see F. C. Burkitt, 'Kells, Durrow and Lindisfarne', *Antiquity* 9 (1935), pp. 33 – 7. Texts are the most portable of items; their legibility is all that is required for their adoption by new centres, whereas letter and ornament have to be acquired through lengthy training.

[13] Julian Brown, 'The oldest Irish manuscripts and their late antique background', in *Irland und Europa*, ed. P. Ní Chatháin and M. Richter (Stuttgart, 1984), pp. 311 – 27.

[14] C. D. Verey, 'A Collation of the Gospel texts contained in Durham Cathedral MSS A.II.10, A.II.16 and A.II.17' (unpublished M.A. thesis, University of Durham, 1969), pp. 149 – 50.

[15] McGurk, *Latin Gospel Books*, particularly Appendix II.

[16] For details see Verey, 'A Collation', pp. 137 – 242. Brief analysis of the textual evidence is published in C. D. Verey, 'Some Observations on the Texts of Durham Cathedral MSS A.II.10 and A.II.17', in *Studia Evangelica* 6, ed. E. A. Livingstone (*Texte und Untersuchungen zur Geschichte der altchristlichen Literatur*, Band 112, Berlin, 1973), pp. 575 – 9.

Damasus. In Mark there are Eusebian numbers in the margin, but the numbers of the relevant canon table and of the corresponding sections are omitted. This odd, and arguably unworkable, arrangement is also found in Paris, Bibliothèque Nationale MS lat. 11553, and may, like that particular manuscript, derive from an early tradition.[17] Finally, whilst there are no *capitula* numbers shown in the margins, the incidence of initials in Matthew appears to correspond to the divisions found in de Bruyne's family I.[18] The same family is found also in *Usserianus Primus*, and is associated with the Old Latin, for example in the very early uncial *Codex Corbeiensis*.[19] It is the family closely associated with Gospel books of Irish provenance; indeed in the early period there seems to be no evidence of any other family of *capitula* within the Irish tradition.

In Durham MS A.II.10 there appears little of the influence of sixth- and seventh-century Italian texts and practice which so influenced Northumbria within the following half-century. The character of the book is very much what the young Cuthbert might have found at Melrose.

With the Durham Gospels we move on some fifty years; we are in the realm of the great codices *de luxe*. There are strong arguments in favour of a Lindisfarne origin, and on the basis of the textual evidence I remain of the opinion that Durham predates the Lindisfarne Gospels, though probably not by long.[20] The Durham Gospels are very different in appearance from Durham MS A.II.10. Much of the order of Italian book production has rubbed off on Durham. But there are clear indications of other influences. The text is written in long lines and not *per cola et commata*, as in Lindisfarne and Echternach. But perhaps the most distinct 'tell tale' of the Irish mission is the inclusion of the gloss on Hebrew names before each Gospel. Only that for Mark survives. The inclusion of this list of Hebrew names is decidedly Insular.[21] Eight out of ten of the pre-ninth-century examples are of Insular

---

[17] See B. Fischer, 'Bibelausgaben des frühen Mittelalters', *Settimane di Studio del Centro Italiano di Studi sull' Alto Medioevo* 10 (Spoleto, 1963), p. 578.

[18] The classification of the *Capitula* families is found in Donatien de Bruyne, *Sommaires, divisions et rubriques de la Bible latine* (Namur, 1914).

[19] Paris, Bibliothèque Nationale MS lat. 17225; *CLA* V, no. 666.

[20] The close palaeographical and artistic relationships with the Lindisfarne Gospels, and other arguments for the Lindisfarne origin of the Durham Gospels, are discussed fully in *Cod. Lind.* II and *The Durham Gospels*. The significance of the art-historical evidence is further discussed in this volume by Rupert Bruce-Mitford (pp. 175 – 88). I continue to find it difficult to reconcile the textual evidence with the conclusions of the art historians, who would place the production of Durham later, possibly significantly so, than that of Lindisfarne. The palaeographical evidence seems less conclusive; Julian Brown consistently regarded the 'Durham-Echternach Calligrapher' as the older contemporary of Eadfrith. My own conclusion on the circumstances of the revision of the Durham Gospels towards the text and punctuation of the Lindisfarne Gospels is given in *The Durham Gospels*, pp. 106 – 8.

[21] See *The Durham Gospels*, pp. 23 – 4.

origin, and all the earliest from an Irish tradition — *Usserianus Primus* and Durrow before Durham. But in the Durham Gospels they sit in a textual context which otherwise enjoys no obvious Irish affinity.

The rest of the prefatory matter belongs to a different tradition. The *capitula* are not of family I, and the text of the Monarchian Prologues does not correspond to the quite distinct type found in Irish books (and which was also known in Northumbria). The text of the Prologues in Durham is particularly close to that found in two uncial Gospel books, Oxford, Bodleian Library MS Auct. D.2.14 (O),[22] and Cambridge, Corpus Christi College MS 286 (X).[23] The affinity with O is most marked. The *capitula* in Durham belong to de Bruyne's family B, which is also that found in O and X. The Gospel text type in Durham is that found in O and X, referred to by Wordsworth and White as the mixed Italian text.[24] These two Italian uncial books are well known to the historian of the Anglo-Saxon church. Both contain evidence of being in England by the eighth century. Tradition ascribes to both the distinction of having been amongst the books brought by Augustine from Rome to Canterbury; this is held by many to be plausible in the case of the Corpus book. O is slightly later, seventh century. A late eighth-century inscription refers to Chad. Later corrections to the Gospel text in O incorporate readings of the Italo-Northumbrian text, whose principal witnesses are Lindisfarne and *Codex Amiatinus*.

It is not necessary to conclude that the Durham Gospels are in direct line of descent from O itself; the type of text in OX was widespread and could well have arrived in the British Isles through exemplars other than those which have survived. Equally, direct descent is not excluded by the textual evidence; indeed the nature of some of the evidence would tend to encourage such a conclusion and I am prepared to hold it a possibility.

Might the text-type found in Durham have been introduced into Anglo-Saxon England via Ireland? There is no evidence which would positively exclude this route. But the balance of argument tends against it. That the Irish had access to good Vulgate texts is not doubted.[25] With the exception of the gloss on Hebrew names, the textual matter in Durham finds no obvious parallels in the surviving early Irish material. In no early Irish books does the family B *capitula* break the seeming stranglehold of family I. Family B is found

---

[22] *CLA* II, no. 230.

[23] *CLA* II, no. 126. The *sigla* for this book, 'X', and the Bodleian one, 'O', are those assigned in *Nouum Testamentum Domini Nostri Iesu Christi Latine secundum editionem Sancti Hieronymi: pars prior, Quattuor Euangelia*, ed. J. Wordsworth and H. J. White (Oxford, 1889 – 98).

[24] *Nouum Testamentum Latine* I, 710. The texts of these two books were described as 'first cousins' by John Chapman, *Notes on the Early History of the Vulgate Gospels* (Oxford, 1908), p. 213.

[25] There seems respectable argument to conclude an Irish origin for the Book of Durrow, which contains a relatively pure Vulgate text. It is a matter of greater uncertainty as to whether that text came directly to Ireland, for example the *libellus* of Finnian, or via Anglo-Saxon England.

in several Anglo-Saxon books.[26] The family of the Gospel text survives in several early examples on this side of the Irish Sea, but I know of only one, and that rather interesting, on the other. John in Kells is the exception; here I believe the affinity with Durham is sufficient to allow the possibility of direct descent.[27] The Gospel text type is found in Northumbria in the corrections in BL, Royal MS 1.B.VII,[28] and in Mark in Durham MS A.II.16.[29] The latter is quite close to the text in the Durham Gospels. The same Gospel text type features in southern England, in BL, Royal MS 1.E.VI.[30]

Since preparing my contribution to the facsimile edition of the Durham Gospels I have compared the text of Durham with that of the contemporary book now divided between Cambridge, Corpus Christi MS 197B and London, BL Cotton MS Otho C.V. This is generally held to be of Northumbrian origin. More specifically it enjoys close artistic affinity with the Echternach Gospels, and affinity in certain scribal tricks with both Echternach and Durham.[31] The relationship with Durham extends to the text. The text of Luke in the Corpus leaves is exceptionally close to that in Durham, even in the peculiarities of orthography. The relationship extends also to Mark in the Cotton leaves, though following extensive damage in the Ashburnham House fire the remains are fragmentary. The relationship does not appear to hold good for John. But John in the Corpus leaves contains two surviving *capitula* numbers in the margin, and these belong to family B. Likewise there is one in the margin of Luke.[32] In complete contrast the extant prefatory matter (before Mark, in the Cotton leaves) belongs to a different tradition. The gloss on Hebrew names is found together with the family I *capitula lectionum*. Here, in the prefatory matter, is the Irish tradition.

The same juxtaposition is found in the Echternach Gospels. In Echternach the Gospel text of the first hand is a relatively good Vulgate written *per cola et commata*, not wholly inconsistent with the suggestion of Italian pedigree in the colophon which claims for an ancestor the distinction of having been corrected against a text reputedly the property of Jerome in the library of Eugippius,

---

[26] McGurk, *Latin Gospel Books*, Appendix IV.

[27] From Durham to Kells, that is! *The Durham Gospels*, p. 73.

[28] *CLA* II, no. 213.

[29] For details see Verey, 'A Collation', pp. 411 – 14.

[30] *CLA* II, no. 214. See H. H. Glunz, *History of the Vulgate in England from Alcuin to Roger Bacon* (Cambridge, 1933), pp. 29 – 30.

[31] For a readily accessible discussion see George Henderson, *From Durrow to Kells* (London, 1987), chapter 3. This book was published after the preparation of this paper. See also Janet Backhouse's observations in this volume (pp. 169 – 73).

[32] The manuscript has been rebound recently and far more of the inner margins is now visible, but there are no other *capitula* numbers. There is part of one *capitula* number visible in the Cotton leaves, at fol. 16[r], and this indicates membership of family B.

abbot of Lucullanum near Naples.[33] But the prefaces belong to the tradition of *Usserianus Primus*, Durrow and Kells: family I *capitula lectionum*, the gloss on Hebrew names and the distinct 'Irish' text of the Monarchian Prologues. In both Echternach and in the Corpus/Otho leaves there appears to have been a conscious preference for familiar prefatory matter included alongside Gospel texts from a different tradition. In Durham this preference extended only to the gloss on Hebrew names.

What of the origins of Echternach? Is it a Lindisfarne book? The textual evidence can neither prove nor disprove the origin. It will require some fairly convincing new argument to overturn Julian Brown's conclusion that Durham and Echternach were written by the same scribe.[34] Textual differences cannot disprove this. Given that the Frisian mission of Willibrord was very much Irish based, it would not be surprising to find a Gospel book for Willibrord or one of his followers containing familiar Irish prefatory matter. As for the Gospel text itself, the exemplar claiming good Italian origins may have had some particular significance; possibly a gift to Willibrord in the course of one of his visits to Rome; possibly from Wilfrid's collection when he consecrated Swithberht (692/3). It was at a later date that Echternach was amended extensively to incorporate readings of the so-called Irish family. It is not unreasonable to think of Echternach as a Lindisfarne book, even though we can no longer establish the precise historical circumstances of its production and export to the mainland of Europe. There is nothing unreasonable in an Irish missionary of Northumbrian birth commissioning or receiving as a gift a book from Lindisfarne; the scriptorium of this great royal foundation around the turn of the seventh century must have offered a centre of rare excellence to judge from the Durham and Lindisfarne Gospels — a place to go for the best.[35]

Around the turn of the seventh century the Lindisfarne Gospels, at least textually, were uncompromising in the transmission of the Italian tradition imported in the archetype of the Italo-Northumbrian text.[36] There is no gloss on Hebrew names. The *capitula lectionum*, with their distinct integral Neapolitan lections, belong to a family which is uniquely associated with the

---

[33] Wordsworth and White included the text of the first hand in their list of witnesses of the 'first class' (*Nouum Testamentum Latine* I, 707, 712). There are those who argue, as did Dáibhí Ó Cróinín at the Conference, that the textual admixture found in the first hand is essentially of the 'Irish' family. That of the main, near contemporary, corrector is generally ascribed to the 'Irish' family. Whilst it is clear that the text of the first hand is fairly mixed, there does seem to be a qualitative difference between it and the full flower of the 'Irish' textual tradition. See also *The Durham Gospels*, pp. 70 – 1.

[34] *Cod. Lind.* II, 95 – 100.

[35] The alternative views of Dáibhí Ó Cróinín, 'Pride and Prejudice', *Peritia* 1 (1982), pp. 352 – 62, and in this volume, pp. 189 – 201, clearly need further assimilation. But the various palaeographical, artistic and even textual links between the three great Gospel books, Lindisfarne, Durham, and Echternach, remain too strong simply to hive off one or two to some largely unknown centre such as Rath Melsigi, or a daughter house of Lindisfarne.

[36] The textual aspects of the Lindisfarne Gospels are comprehensively reviewed in *Cod. Lind.* II.

particular Gospel text-type found in Lindisfarne. The same text is found in *Codex Amiatinus* and other surviving Wearmouth/Jarrow products. In the course of editing texts for the three great pandects the monks of Wearmouth/Jarrow would seem to have made a value judgement about the authority of the Italo-Northumbrian text, and it is as if that judgement had passed to Lindisfarne when Eadfrith came to produce the great Gospel book in honour of St Cuthbert. At about the same time, and seemingly not much divorced from the date of its own production, Durham was comprehensively punctuated *per cola et commata* with divisions very close to those in Lindisfarne; and in the same hand, found also in Lindisfarne, amended to include numerous Italo-Northumbrian readings.[37]

Julian Brown used to speak of the Northumbrian 'love affair' with Italian book production.[38] Such an association, if not 'affair', is evident also in the textual material. In the early period — accepting of course the dangers of drawing conclusions from a statistical sample of only one — the predominant influences in Durham MS A.II.10 are from the Irish mission, the Old Latin and the sort of prefatory matter found in *Usserianus Primus*. Half a century later we find in the Lindisfarne Gospels a textual near 'clone' of its Italian source. But other evidence, e.g. in Durham, Echternach and the Corpus/Otho leaves, would suggest that the first 'mistress' was by no means wholly abandoned. The Gospel texts proper point to Italian sources imported into Anglo-Saxon England, though they quickly absorbed some local 'improvements', doubtless including readings familiar from the Irish tradition. More obvious elements of this Irish tradition were retained in the gloss on Hebrew names and the family of *capitula lectionum*. There is nothing mutually exclusive about the Irish and Italian Gospel traditions in Northumbria. There is no need to set the two traditions against each other. Such a conclusion is hardly surprising when we consider the ministry of Cuthbert himself.

---

[37] *The Durham Gospels*, pp. 17, 74–5. See above, note 20, for my views on the relative chronology of the two books. At the Conference William O'Sullivan advised that towards the end of his life Julian Brown expressed reservations about the identity of hand between the two books. Unfortunately we are unable to probe any such change of judgement by Julian, and other colleagues, notably Michelle Brown, do not recall any such changed perceptions. Identity of hand in this period, particularly on relatively little evidence, is difficult to prove. But even if precise identity were excluded, the similarities are sufficiently striking to argue common, and near contemporary training. Such a conclusion would not significantly affect the conclusions about the association between the work of the main corrector in the Durham and Lindisfarne Gospels, which go well beyond identity of hand. See also Janet Backhouse's observations at p. 172, n. 31, below.

[38] See, for example, 'The oldest Irish manuscripts and their late antique background', p. 325.

The Lindisfarne Scriptorium from the
Late Seventh to the Early Ninth Century

MICHELLE P. BROWN

The title of this paper was first proposed by Julian Brown, in whose stead I was, sadly, given the honour of being invited to contribute to these proceedings. To cover so wide a span in so short a space will obviously require brevity and selectivity; nonetheless it is undoubtedly a worthwhile exercise, for too often discussion of Lindisfarne and its manuscripts has focused almost exclusively upon the big triad of the Lindisfarne, Durham, and Echternach Gospels,[1] with an uncomfortable glance backwards at the Book of Durrow and a nervous peek forwards at the Book of Kells.[2] Discussion as to which of these key manuscripts were produced at or influenced by the Lindisfarne scriptorium is obviously a central issue, but, many of their minutiae having already received much attention, it now seems appropriate to place them within a wider context and to look at some other material. This may in turn enable a re-evaluation of the key manuscripts and their inter-relationships.

Lindisfarne has for some time been recognized as one of the most important and influential Insular scriptoria. The only others to enjoy a reputation of similar magnitude, although other major centres are known or thought to have existed,[3] are the twin centres of Wearmouth/Jarrow, and Canterbury.

---

[1] References to manuscripts are accompanied by their numbers in Alexander and in *CLA*. The Lindisfarne Gospels: London, BL, Cotton MS Nero D. IV; Alexander no. 9; *CLA* II, no. 187. The Durham Gospels: Durham, Cathedral Library, MS A.II.17; Alexander no. 10; *CLA* II, no. 149. The Echternach Gospels: Paris, Bibliothèque nationale, lat. 9389; Alexander no. 11; *CLA* V, no. 578.

[2] The Book of Durrow: Dublin, Trinity College Library, MS 57; Alexander no. 6; *CLA* II, no. 273. The Book of Kells: Dublin, Trinity College Library, MS 58; Alexander no. 52; *CLA* II, no. 274.

[3] For example, Boniface's correspondence with Abbess Eadburh indicates that a scriptorium, staffed by female scribes, was active at Minster in Thanet during the 730s; see *EHD*, pp. 811–12. York was certainly a major source of supply, and probably of production, as evinced by letters requesting books from Lul to Archbishop Ethelbert (767–78), *EHD*, pp. 834–5, and from

These are comparatively well documented, the fame of the Northumbrian centres owing much to Cuthbert and Bede. This information, along with the assignation of several extremely important manuscripts to these scriptoria, has inevitably meant that for many scholars they have acted as giant magnets, inexorably drawing other tantalizingly unprovenanced works into their orbit. This is, perhaps, a natural consequence when dealing with a body of material, Insular manuscripts, which although known to be woefully fragmentary and incomplete, still presents us with a rich selection of items, many of which may be seen to inter-relate but few of which contain any firm indicators of their place of origin. The perennial academic debate of what was actually produced where, and notably of what was produced in Anglo-Saxon centres under Irish influence, or Irish centres under Germanic influence, largely stems from this situation.[4] The term 'Insular', which was coined to overcome the difficulties of culturally distinguishing northern Britain from Ireland at a period when, although major differences obviously existed, they were broadly part of the same cultural milieu, or in manuscript terms, part of the same *irische Schriftprovinz*, has apparently failed to satisfy the needs of many scholars, although others still find it extremely useful, especially in avoiding artificial and over-rigid segregation.

The first question one needs to ask is whether any manuscripts may be securely placed at Lindisfarne? Unsurprisingly, the foremost candidate is the Lindisfarne Gospels. The colophon by Aldred, provost of Chester-le-Street in 970, and a slightly later repetitive prayer, naming himself, Eadfrith and Aethelwold (both bishops of Lindisfarne) and Billfrith the anchorite as those responsible for constructing the Gospels 'for God and for St Cuthbert', is our firmest evidence of a Lindisfarne origin.[5] There is no apparent reason to doubt the colophon. The dates of the two bishops accord with the stylistic dating of the manuscript and its stylistic and textual affinities all point to Lindisfarne as a likely place of production.[6] The colophon presumably embodies a well-preserved piece of community folklore. Eadfrith and Aethelwold were probably well-known figures in Anglo-Saxon England; but Billfrith would otherwise have passed into the mists of oblivion, his very obscurity lending

---

Lupus of Ferrières to Abbot Ealdsige (852), *EHD*, pp. 877–8. The list of books owned by Archbishop Aelberht and bequeathed to Alcuin (*c*.778) also indicates the presence of a major library at York: see M. Lapidge, 'Booklists from Anglo-Saxon England', in *Learning and Literature in Anglo-Saxon England, Studies Presented to Peter Clemoes*, ed. M. Lapidge and H. Gneuss (Cambridge, 1985), at pp. 45–9. Other, less tangible evidence may be adduced in favour of other possible centres of production.
[4] For a recent discussion of some of the central issues see the various contributions to *Ireland and Insular Art A.D. 500–1200*, ed. M. Ryan (Royal Irish Academy, Dublin, 1987).
[5] Aldred's colophon occurs on fol. 259[r] and the prayer on fol. 89[v]; see *Cod. Lind.*, II, 5.
[6] Eadfrith was bishop of Lindisfarne 698–721, followed by Aethelwold, 721–40: see *Cod. Lind.*, II, 17–20.

credibility to the 'creation' story.[7] The early Chester-le-Street/Durham provenance is also corroborative. An early provenance may often be taken as an indication of possible origin, although caution should be exercised here. A tradition preserved in the twelfth century by Symeon of Durham tells us that, following the flight of the community from Lindisfarne in 875, emigration to Ireland was attempted.[8] Had the Lindisfarne Gospels not immediately 'jumped ship', thereby preventing the voyage, they would in all likelihood have ended up with an early Irish provenance and the course of subsequent academic debate might have been quite different.

The early history of the community's library is most interesting. Several manuscripts which were apparently in the library at an early date contain evidence of a Wearmouth/Jarrow origin; and the fourteenth-century inscriptions conveying the impressive statement 'written by Bede' which occur in some of them may well represent the fossilized recognition of a tradition of Wearmouth/Jarrow origin.[9] The manuscripts would have reached the community by gift — the probable presentation of the Stonyhurst Gospel of St John for inclusion in Cuthbert's coffin is a prime witness to this[10] — or by force of subsequent circumstances. Other early manuscripts now in Durham Cathedral Library may well have reached the community as a result of the cult of Cuthbert, especially under the patronage of King Athelstan in the tenth century (this excess of princely interest perhaps relating to his devastation of the north and attempts to bring it under West Saxon rule).[11]

---

[7] For details of Aethelwold's career and literary references to him see *Cod. Lind.*, II, 18 – 19. There is good reason, however, to doubt any specific relationship between him and the Bishop Aethelwald of the Book of Cerne: see M. P. Brown, 'Cambridge, University Library MS LI.1.10, the Book of Cerne' (unpublished Ph.D. thesis, University of London, forthcoming).

[8] See *HDE* II, 11 – 12; *Sym. Op.*, I, 63 – 8.

[9] The *de manu Bedae* inscriptions occur in the following Insular MSS from Durham Cathedral Library: A.II.16, Gospels: B.II.30, Cassiodorus *In psalmos*; Cambridge, Trinity College, MS B.105 and London, BL Cotton Vitell. C.VIII, Pauline Epistles, also formerly in Durham Cathedral Library. See *DCM*, pp. 13 – 21. It is interesting that these MSS bear no obvious stylistic relationship to each other which might have led a later librarian to link them in this manner. This may lend credibility to the possibility that they were linked by the recollection of a common point of acquisition, indicating that they were obtained from Wearmouth/Jarrow. If they were simply linked by their appearance of antiquity it is surprising that similar inscriptions do not occur in other Insular manuscripts from the Durham Library.

[10] Stonyhurst College Library, s.n. (on loan to the BL); *CLA* II, no. 260: see *The Stonyhurst Gospel of St John*, ed. T. J. Brown (Roxburgh Club; Oxford, 1969). Benedicta Ward (see above, pp. 69 – 71) has indicated the significant role of the Gospel of St John in Cuthbert's life, which may well account for the probable inclusion of the MS within Cuthbert's tomb. One may speculate whether this manuscript might even have been intended to represent the so-called 'book of St. Boisil master of St. Cuthbert', kept among the relics in Durham Cathedral and now assumed lost. See *DCM*, 14. Boisil's manuscript is said to have contained seven quires, or gatherings (*VCP* 8), whereas the Stonyhurst Gospel has eleven, so they cannot be one and the same.

[11] See S. Keynes, 'King Athelstan's Books', in *Learning and Literature* (as n. 3 above), pp. 143 – 201.

His sanctity having been acclaimed during his lifetime, the cult of Cuthbert was soon well under way, the elevation of 698 representing a major landmark in the community's history. The manufacture of works of art to commemorate and participate in this event may be seen as a suitable context for a work such as Lindisfarne and the career of Eadfrith who is accredited with writing and illuminating it has also been cited in support of this date.[12] In 698 Eadfrith became bishop and heir of Cuthbert, a post which he occupied until 721. It may be that, as was often the case during the middle ages, the attribution to Eadfrith in fact refers to his patronage; it is certainly improbable that he would have found time to undertake the task himself during the busy period of his episcopate. The minimum estimated time required to complete Lindisfarne, if working more-or-less full-time, is two years. Those burdened with high-powered administrative duties will appreciate the limitations imposed upon Eadfrith after 698, in addition to a demanding monastic timetable. The case for actual participation by Eadfrith becomes tenable if he undertook the work in preparation for the elevation of 698. One might even go a step further and, without detracting in the least from the concept of a work of devotion, envisage involvement in the manufacture of a prestigious cult item as a significant career move. The community at Lindisfarne certainly witnessed some major shifts in personnel around the time of the elevation. Eadfrith acquired the plum post of bishop and Aethelwold, allegedly responsible for binding and impressing the Gospels,[13] was promoted in 699 to the position of prior of Melrose, an important daughter house, eventually succeeding Eadfrith as bishop of Lindisfarne in 721. We do not know what became of Billfrith, the craftsman responsible for the metalwork adornment of the binding or its *cumdach*. Perhaps we might assume that as an anchorite he was less concerned with a career structure. Aldred himself indicates that work on Lindisfarne might carry such implications. His colophon states that his addition of the glossed translation of the Gospels into English carried special intentions: Matthew was glossed for God and St Cuthbert, Mark for the bishop, Luke for the community (with eight ores of silver for his own induction), and John for his own soul (with four ores of silver for God and St Cuthbert). This indicates that his work on the manuscript, which is presented

---

[12] For details of Eadfrith's career, see *Cod. Lind.*, II, 17 – 18.

[13] The references to Aethelwold having bound and impressed the MS, prior to its adornment with metalwork by Billfrith, raise the intriguing possibility that the MS may have received a contemporary *cumdach* or book-shrine, perhaps similar to the 8th-century example found in 1986 at Lough Kinale, Co. Longford (now in the National Museum of Ireland). The 'impressing' of the binding would seem to suggest tooling or stamping, resulting in the sort of highly skilled decoration found upon the contemporary covers of the Stonyhurst Gospel. Billfrith's metalwork may have formed part of such a binding, as applied plaques etc., but the possibility of a *cumdach* cannot be ruled out.

as its completion, was designed to establish the new priest in the Chester-le-Street community.[14] By 970 Aldred had attained the position of provost.

This glimpse of the possible implications of scriptorium politics may relate to an apparent house-feature of the Lindisfarne Gospels and other probable major Lindisfarne manuscripts. Despite the length and complexity of Lindisfarne, both the script of the text and the decoration are the work of one gifted artist/scribe, the only other involvement prior to binding being that of the rubricator/corrector and a second corrector.[15] With the possible exception of the Hereford Gospels, produced in western England or Wales, the only other surviving Insular manuscripts *de luxe* which may be considered as more than fragmentary and which similarly embody the work of one main artist/scribe are the Book of Durrow, the Echternach Gospels, and the Durham Gospels, all of which have been proposed as Lindisfarne manuscripts.[16] The admittedly much heftier Codex Amiatinus from Wearmouth/Jarrow employed seven scribes and one artist;[17] the Macregol Gospels employed two scribes and one artist and the St Gall Gospels were the work of one scribe and two artists: both are important Irish manuscripts;[18] the Vespasian Psalter from Canterbury employed one artist/scribe (although two major scribes may well be represented) and a team of five correcting proof-readers;[19] the Stockholm Codex Aureus, probably also from Canterbury, employed two artists;[20] the Royal Bible, a later work from St Augustine's, Canterbury, employed one artist/scribe and four other scribes, some of whom were pupils;[21] the Leningrad Gospels, an as yet unplaced English manuscript exhibiting strong Northumbrian influence, employed three artists and several scribes;[22] the Barberini Gospels, again English but unplaced, but which I am inclined to attribute to Mercia, or perhaps York, employed four scribes and three

---

[14] See J. Backhouse, *The Lindisfarne Gospels* (Oxford, 1981), p. 16. I am indebted to Susan Kruse for pointing out that Aldred's colophon and his gloss to Luke 19:13 are amongst the earliest occurrences of the term 'ore', which probably represents a Danelaw loan-word. Aldred's work, as a priest, on the Lindisfarne Gospels may be dated before 970, but which time he had become provost, and probably after 950: see *Cod. Lind.*, II, book ii, p. 32.

[15] For details of the work-team, see *Cod. Lind.*, II, 104 – 8.

[16] The Hereford Gospels: Hereford, Cathedral Library MS P.I.2; Alexander no. 38; *CLA* II, no. 157. I would not favour a direct association of the Book of Durrow with Lindisfarne. The broader attribution of the manuscript to Northumbria or Ireland remains a major source of controversy. For some of the arguments see Alexander no. 6; and *Ireland and Insular Art*, ed. Ryan, pp. 1 – 6, 23 – 9, 40 – 3, 44 – 55.

[17] Florence, Biblioteca Medicea-Laurenziana, Amiatinus I; Alexander no. 7; *CLA* III, no. 299.

[18] The Macregol Gospels: Oxford, Bodleian Library, Auct. D.2.19; Alexander no. 54; *CLA* II, no. 231. The St Gall Gospels: St Gall, Stiftsbibliothek, Cod.51; Alexander no. 44; *CLA* VII, no. 901.

[19] London, BL, Cotton Vesp. A.I; Alexander no. 29; *CLA* II, no. 193.

[20] Stockholm, Royal Library, MS A.135; Alexander no. 30; CLA XI, no. 1642.

[21] London, BL, Royal 1.E.VI; Alexander no. 32; *CLA* II, no. 214.

[22] Leningrad, Public Library, Cod. F.v.I.8; Alexander no. 39; *CLA* XI, no. 1605.

artists;[23] the Cutbercht Gospels, probably produced at Salzburg, boasts the Insular scribe, Cutbercht, amongst its production team;[24] the Lichfield Gospels, an unplaced manuscript showing close affinities with both the Lindisfarne Gospels and the Book of Kells, employed one artist and probably two scribes;[25] and the Book of Kells itself, again of hotly disputed origin, but which I am inclined to attribute to Iona, was produced by an extensive and complex team of four major artists plus ancilliaries and at least four scribes.[26]

This does not imply that all manuscripts employing one artist/scribe were produced at Lindisfarne, that this was the only work pattern in the scriptorium, or that there may not be other manuscripts with a similar structure; but it does appear significant that even a survey restricted to those manuscripts listed should yield such results. It may be possible to deduce something of the organization of the Lindisfarne scriptorium from these details: that unlike most Insular scriptoria it often adopted a practice in the manufacture of manuscripts *de luxe* whereby one master was responsible for the body of the work, perhaps implying a desire for homogeneity or that the work was seen as one person's *opus Dei*, embodying their own act of devotion. There are no signs here of a master allowing a trainee to take a hand in the work, as indicated by the specimen teaching passages in the Garland of Howth and the Royal Bible.[27] Curiously this pattern of work does not appear to apply to lesser undertakings of the scriptorium which elsewhere, for example at Wearmouth/Jarrow, might be allotted to one hand. One might, if feeling bold, go a step further and postulate the existence of a concept of the 'hero-scribe'. This may have owed much to Irish influence. Columcille himself enjoyed such a role and the *De abbatibus* refers to miraculous healings performed by the relics of a famous Irish scribe, working somewhere in England, called Ultan.[28] It is noteworthy that many early Irish manuscripts preserve contemporary colophons, unlike most of their English counterparts. Thus it is possible to attribute manuscripts to Armagh, Birr, Roscrea, and Tech Moling.[29] These colophons generally entreat prayers for the named scribe, although more than one scribe actually participated, for example, in the book of Armagh of *c.*807, in which three artist/scribes were each responsible for their own quires of the book, although only one, Ferdomnach, is cited in the colophon.[30] In these

---

[23] Vatican City, Biblioteca Apostolica Vaticana, MS Barberini Lat. 570; Alexander no. 36; *CLA* I, no. 63.

[24] Vienna, Nationalbibliothek, Cod. 1224; Alexander no. 37; *CLA* X, no. 1500.

[25] The Lichfield or Chad Gospels: Lichfield, Cathedral Library, s.n.; Alexander no. 21; *CLA* II, no. 159.

[26] See F. Henry, *The Book of Kells* (London, 1977), pp. 154–7 and 211–12. The work of four major scribes may be distinguished, rather than the three identified by Henry.

[27] The Garland of Howth: Dublin, Trinity College Library, MS 56; Alexander no. 59; *CLA* II, no. 272. Cf. pl. 17.

[28] Aethelwulf, *De abbatibus*, ch. 8; ed. and trans. A. Campbell (Oxford, 1967), pp. 20–3.

[29] For Irish places of origin see Alexander, p. 216.

[30] The Book of Armagh: Dublin, Trinity College Library, MS 52; Alexander no. 53; *CLA* II, no. 270.

cases the identity of 'scribe' is probably reserved for the master, perhaps the head of the scriptorium or co-ordinator of the work.

It has been noted that the Matthew portrait in the Lindisfarne Gospels (fol. 25^v) takes a Cassiodoran exemplar depicting Ezra as its model, this miniature also having been copied in the Codex Amiatinus (fol. V^r) at Wearmouth/ Jarrow. Art historians have been puzzled by the use and adaptation of this particular model in Lindisfarne when others were available.[31] Lindisfarne is the first extant Insular manuscript to choose to represent the evangelists as scribes, rather than the terrestrial animal symbols of Durrow, although these zoomorphic symbols are still used as identifiers. There is some possibility of a further missing exemplar,[32] but could it be that we are witnessing a sophisticated extension of the imagery seen in Amiatinus based upon the recognition that, within the model, Cassiodorus had had the image of Ezra modified by including the depiction of his own transcription of the Bible, the *Novem Codices*, thereby comparing 'his work in preparing copies of the Holy Scriptures with that of Ezra as scribe and preserver of the Law.'[33] The transference of this role to the evangelists, and notably to Matthew the man, is a logical one. If such imagery were understood then a further logical projection would be to the contemporary scribe himself.

The Durham Gospels are linked to the Lindisfarne Gospels stylistically, and also by their common correcting hand.[34] The artist/scribe responsible for them reveals both a progression in decorative vocabulary, implying a slightly later date, and an innate conservatism in decoration and script which led Julian Brown and Rupert Bruce-Mitford to view him as an older contemporary of Eadfrith's within the Lindisfarne scriptorium. Brown further identified his hand as being responsible for the Echternach Gospels and accordingly christened him the 'Durham-Echternach Calligrapher'.[35] The validity of this hypothesis has been challenged, although without any systematic attempt to disprove the identity of hands. The major criticism has focused upon discrediting the false assumption that St Willibrord's Frisian mission, which led to the foundation of Echternach in 698, was a satellite of Northumbria, when in fact Willibrord had spent the years prior to his mission in Ireland.[36] This should not be taken, however, to necessitate an Irish origin for the

---

[31] See *Cod. Lind.*, II, 146 – 7.

[32] Copenhagen, Royal Library, MS G.K.S.10,2^o has been cited as possible evidence for a missing exemplar: see Alexander, p. 38 and E. Temple, *Anglo-Saxon Manuscripts 900 – 1066* (London, 1976), p. 69.

[33] See Alexander, p. 33.

[34] For a discussion of the correcting hand see C. D. Verey's appendix to T. J. Brown, 'Northumbria and the Book of Kells', *ASE* 1 (1972), at pp. 243 – 5. See also *The Durham Gospels*, ed. C. D. Verey, T. J. Brown, and E. Coatsworth (EEMF 20; Copenhagen, 1980), pp. 38, 69 and 74 – 6. For the problem of the different texts employed in the Lindisfarne and Durham Gospels see C. D. Verey's contribution to this volume.

[35] See *Cod. Lind.*, II, 100 – 2 and *Durham Gospels*, pp. 42 – 9.

[36] See D. Ó Cróinín, 'Rath Melsigi, Willibrord, and the earliest Echternach Manuscripts', *Peritia* 3 (1984), pp. 17 – 49.

Echternach Gospels and to preclude the possibility of gifts from Lindisfarne to the new foundation.[37] The instigator of the mission, Ecgberht, persuaded Iona to conform to Roman practices, and Echternach certainly preserved contact with Northumbria, whatever its Irish affiliations. A piece of evidence which has been inadequately utilized is the fragmentary Gospels preserved partly in Cambridge, Corpus Christi College MS 197B, and partly in the British Library, Cotton MS Otho C. V, a charred survivor of the Cottonian fire of 1731. The decoration of this manuscript bears a striking resemblance to that of the Echternach Gosepls and the scribe of the Corpus fragment has been compared to Laurentius, a scribe working at Echternach.[38] On the basis of this evidence alone one need only see the Echternach Gospels, be they Northumbrian or Irish, as the inspiration for this manuscript; but this ignores the unfortunate and neglected Cottonian fragment which includes the work of a second scribe who was undoubtedly influenced by the distinctive script of the Lindisfarne Gospels (see plates 15 and 22). This substantially reinforces the case for a Lindisfarne origin for this fragment and, by implication, for the Echternach Gospels. It is perhaps worth adding that the hand which added prayers to the Calendar and Martyrology of St Willibrord in the second half of the eighth century is undoubtedly that of a new Anglo-Saxon, rather than Irish, recruit.[39] There was undoubtedly a strong Irish element in the Frisian mission, but here, as elsewhere, the idea of 'ne'er the twain shall meet' in reference to both Irish and Anglo-Saxon personnel is untenable, and there is increasing evidence for collaboration between scribes from different backgrounds, both in Britain and on the continent.

I have made reference to the Cottonian fragment as exhibiting definite influence from the script of the Lindisfarne Gospels. This is possible owing to the distinctive nature of this script, which belongs to a grade termed 'Insular majuscule' by Lowe, but preferably 'Insular half-uncial' (T. J. Brown's 'Phase II Insular half-uncial').[40] In the past the most developed form of this script, found in the Lindisfarne Gospels, has been seen in a rather evolutionary context. The Irish are thought to have received a script known as cursive half-uncial, the hand of the educated man of late antiquity rather than

[37] For a discussion of the complexity of the Echternach scriptorium and the presence of Anglo-Saxon, Irish and continental traditions there see N. D. Netzer, 'The Trier Gospels (Trier Domschatz MS 61): Text, Construction, Script, and Illustration' (unpublished Ph.D. thesis, Harvard University, 1987), pp. 263 – 76, and below, pp. 203 – 12.

[38] Cambridge, Corpus Christi College, MS 197B and London, BL, Cotton Otho C. V; Alexander no. 12; *CLA* II, no. 125 (which includes the comparison with the hand of Laurentius).

[39] The Calendar and Martyrology of St Willibrord: Paris, Bibliothèque nationale, lat. 10837; *CLA* V, nos. 605 and 606a – b.

[40] For E. A. Lowe's terminology see *CLA*. The complexity of T. J. Brown's terminology, however, enables greater flexibility and precision. T. J. Brown's 'Insular System of Scripts' was included in his Lyell Lectures, Oxford, 1976 – 7. It is to be hoped that these will be published in the future. Some of the material appears in T. J. Brown, 'The Irish Element in the Insular System of Scripts to *circa* A.D. 850', in *Die Iren und Europa im früheren Mittelalter*, ed. H. Löwe (2 vols.; Stuttgart, 1982), I, 101 – 19.

a professional hand, as a result of their conversion and to have both gradually upgraded it to provide a formal bookhand culminating in a half-uncial similar to that of antiquity, and also to have downgraded it to provide a working minuscule script. The oldest Irish manuscripts employ cursive half-uncial, giving way to a hybrid minuscule. The Book of Durrow adopts a more settled stylistic canon of script which may be termed half-uncial and which reaches a degree of virtuoso perfection in the Lindisfarne Gospels. This fully developed script is then deemed to act as the formal Insular bookhand. In actual fact Lindisfarne was and remains rather unique. It represents an essay in conscious classicism almost as obvious as that of the uncial scripts of Wearmouth/Jarrow and Canterbury. Its introduction of a stately rounded aspect, its rigorous adherence to a uniform base and head line and its introduction of uncial features, especially at line ends, are as classicizing as its use of the antique punctuation *per cola et commata* (see plate 15). This reformed script is rather artificial, standing aside from any evolutionary line. It is, in effect, exotic. It is highly probable that hybrid minuscule, found in places in the Durham and Echternach Gospels (see plate 16), in fact remained the major Insular bookhand.[41] Certainly it continued to be used at Lindisfarne despite the innovations of Eadfrith, and it is frequently represented in Irish and Southumbrian manuscripts, an important and formal work such as the Royal Bible being largely in hybrid script.[42] The main body of the text in the Echternach Gospels, apparently written at speed, goes so far as to employ an even lower grade of script, set minuscule. The principle difference between hybrid minuscule and half-uncial is that the former is a slanted, rather than a straight pen script, with sloping minim heads, which tends to exhibit freer ductus (the way the letters are formed) and a lighter aspect (general appearance), and, although employing many half-uncial letter forms, exhibits a preference for minuscule forms. If hybrid minuscule remained the main Insular hand, then manuscripts written in it should not be seen as less formal, as rushed, or as embodying an earlier stage of development. If anything they might be viewed as the norm of formal book production. This having been said, reformed half-uncial of the classicizing Lindisfarne type was extremely influential, providing a distinctively Insular high-grade alternative to the blatantly romanizing uncial.

Irish half-uncial often differs from its English counterpart in several details: it inclines to angularity, stretches bows upwards to the left and tends not to

---

[41] The great debt owed to Julian Brown for his patient tuition and for discussion on this and many other topics is, and will continue to be, gratefully acknowledged and sorely missed.

[42] See M. O. Budny, 'London, British Library MS Royal 1.E.VI: The Anatomy of an Anglo-Saxon Bible Fragment' (unpublished Ph.D. thesis, London University, 1985), pp. 770–80 and passim. For a preliminary discussion of scripts in Southumbria see M. P. Brown, 'Paris, Bibliothèque nationale, lat. 10861 and the Scriptorium of Christ Church, Canterbury', *ASE* 15 (1987), pp. 119–37.

close them, is less concerned with regularity of minims and uniform height, lengthens descenders, and displays frequent use of a slanted pen with a leaning of ductus to left or right, and a preference for minuscule forms. Irish formal scripts tend to follow two lines of development from *c.*700, either essentially continuing the hybrid of the oldest Irish manuscripts with some overlay of half-uncial influence, resulting in the scripts of the Garland of Howth (see plate 17) and the Domnach Airgid,[43] or developing into a calligraphic display half-uncial seen in the Stowe Missal,[44] the Lichfield Gospels, and the Book of Kells. The latter manuscripts develop decorative calligraphic tendencies found in the Lindisfarne manuscripts to new heights, perhaps under the influence of, or themselves influencing calligraphic minuscule such as that of the Book of Armagh. However, the influence of Lindisfarne half-uncial was felt in Irish centres. The Rawlinson Gospels employ it in a modified form,[45] as do the Kells prefaces. Another tangible piece of evidence is a comparatively little-known piece of sculpture at Tullylease, County Cork (see plate 8), which commemorates Berechtuine, thought to be the Northumbrian princeling Berichter, who left his homeland, with others, following the synod of Whitby in 664 and who died around 700.[46] An eighth-century date would seem acceptable for the slab, which almost embodies in stone a carpet page of the Lindisfarne Gospels, both ornament, script (which is one of the closest approximations to a pen-script in stone that I have seen), and also the form of the stone exhibiting a familiarity with Northumbrian trends. It is noteworthy, however, that this piece apparently had but limited immediate impact upon local tradition, although it would appear to form a significant link between the name stones of Northumbria and the grave-slabs of Clonmacnois.[47]

The impact of Northumbrian half-uncial may be seen in Insular centres on the continent in the Cutbercht and Trier Gospels,[48] and may even have influenced the development of caroline minuscule. In England it may be found in several manuscripts, such as the Salaberga Psalter and Oxford, Lincoln College MS 92,[49] both probably written at Lindisfarne, and in a series of Northumbrian manuscripts of which the Lindisfarne group forms the focus.[50] Examples of its influence elsewhere in England may be seen in the

---

[43] The Domnach Airgid MS: Dublin, Royal Irish Academy, MS 24.Q.23; *CLA* II, no. 269.
[44] Dublin, Royal Irish Academy, MS D.II.3; Alexander no. 51; *CLA* II, no. 268.
[45] Oxford, Bodleian Library, Rawlinson G.167; Alexander no. 43; *CLA* II, no. 256.
[46] For a review of the literature on the Tullylease slab see P. Lionard, 'A Reconsideration of the Dating of the Slab of St. Berichter at Tullylease, Co. Cork', *Journal of the Cork Historical and Archaeological Society* 58 (1953), pp. 12 – 13, and P. Lionard, 'Early Irish Grave-Slabs', *Proceedings of the Royal Irish Academy* 61C (1961), pp. 154 – 5.
[47] See R. Cramp, below, p. 220.
[48] The Trier Gospels: Trier, Domschatz, MS 61 (134); Alexander no 26; *CLA* IX, no. 1364.
[49] The Salaberga Psalter: Berlin, Deutsche Staatsbibliothek, MS Hamilton 553; Alexander no. 14; *CLA* VIII, no. 1048. Oxford, Lincoln College, MS 92; *CLA* II, no. 258.
[50] For the Northumbrian groups see *Cod. Lind.*, II, 90 – 2.

Leningrad Gospels, the Worcester Cathedral Gregory,[51] and most notably in the Barberini Gospels. The latter is an extremely impressive manuscript, exhibiting strong Mediterranean influence, which has received limited attention and remains tantalizingly unplaced, although generally dated to the second half of the eighth century. Having spent some time studying its hands I have identified four scribes, two of whom write a respectable Northumbrian half-uncial of Lindisfarne type. The most proficient of these, Wigbald (see plate 7), is mentioned in a colophon and was probably the master scribe. It is interesting that Françoise Henry should have proposed an, as yet, unaccepted identification with Higbald, bishop of Lindisfarne (781 – 802).[52] The two remaining hands are more idiosyncratic. Although obviously influenced by Wigbald they practise ornamental variants. The decorative devices of one of the hands and a comparison with charter material leads one to conclude that it is probably a Mercian hand.[53] The fourth scribe produces a unique, highly calligraphic and elegant hand, which could well be Mercian too. The evidence suggests that Northumbrian scribes, probably from Lindisfarne, may have participated, probably as instuctors, in the production of Mercian manuscripts, of which Barberini is a major, if isolated, example.

The role of the Lindisfarne scriptorium in producing a new script, reformed high-grade half-uncial, and in influencing and perhaps guiding the development of similar scripts elsewhere in Britain, was obviously of major importance and is paralleled in its contribution to the development of Insular ornament. The repertoire of the scriptorium was not, however, confined to this script. Time precludes a discussion of its role in developing the forms of both major and minor initials and of its invention of an influential ornamental display script, formed of enlarged text letters, Roman square capitals, some Greek and runic forms, and of distinctive rectangular letters, possibly derived from local epigraphy on stone and wood.[54] We have seen that in addition to the new script a traditional, but developed, hybrid minuscule was also used within major works such as the Durham and Echternach Gospels. Further down the hierarchy of scripts was minuscule proper, with its set, cursive, and current variants. The most formal of these, set minuscule (see plate 16), was used for the body of the Echternach Gospels, one of the most prestigious Insular manuscripts despite the obvious haste of its production, showing the versatility and adaptability in approach to script at Lindisfarne.[55] However, the lower-grade minuscules were probably more commonly employed for non-

---

[51] The Worcester Gregory: Worcester, Cathedral Chapter Library, Addit. MS 3; *CLA* II, no. 264.

[52] See Henry, *Kells*, p. 214.

[53] For further details on Barberini see M. P. Brown, 'Book of Cerne' (as n. 7).

[54] For a discussion of the ornamental capitals and initials see *Cod. Lind.*, II, 75 – 8. On the significance of the use and reading of runes see R. I. Page, below, pp. 257 – 65 and R. D. Eaton, 'Anglo-Saxon Secrets: Run and the Runes of the Lindisfarne Gospels', in *Amsterdamer Beiträge zur älteren Germanistik*, ed. A. Quak and P. Vermeyden (Amsterdam, 1986), pp. 11 – 27.

[55] See *Cod. Lind.*, II, 100 – 2 and *Durham Gospels*, pp. 42 – 9.

liturgical texts of a less formal character. Informal Insular minuscule was undoubtedly an Irish invention and, with no antique or Mediterranean tradition of this sort in Britain, one would expect the Lindisfarne scriptorium to adopt and build exclusively upon Irish models.[56] In a forthcoming facsimile volume of Vatican MS Palatinus 235, a copy of the *Carmina* of Paulinus of Nola (see plate 6), Julian Brown identifies this manuscript and a copy of the same text in Leningrad as examples of schoolbooks written and used at Lindisfarne, *c.* 700 – 37 (under the textual influence of Wearmouth/Jarrow), on the basis of the affinities of their script, decoration, and codicology with the manuscripts already discussed.[57] The five scribes who worked on these Paulinus manuscripts and the Durham-Echternach Calligrapher all exhibit mastery and individuality in their use of the full minuscule range, the variations between these hands serving to reinforce the identity of hands in the Durham and Echternach Gospels. It is interesting to note that, along with the other hands already discussed, these scribes raise the number of personnel of the Lindisfarne scriptorium *c.* 700 to at least nine. These and other early Northumbrian minuscule manuscripts most clearly embody the Irish background in the area and indicate that conservatism, as well as innovation, was a feature of the Lindisfarne scriptorium. The development of a more distinctive Northumbrian minuscule during the 730s – 40s would appear to have been largely the work of Wearmouth/Jarrow, although this Phase II minuscule spread rapidly throughout Northumbria and in turn exerted a profound influence upon Southumbrian, and, to a lesser extent, Irish minuscule.[58]

We have little evidence for the activities of the Lindisfarne scriptorium after the mid eighth century, although many subsequent manuscripts exhibit a strong Lindisfarne influence. The next manuscript capable of a possible Lindisfarne attribution is the Durham *Liber vitae*, the community's confraternity book of *c.* 840, which employs a half-uncial of Lindisfarne type, with some indications of Southumbrian influence. It is, however, possible that the manuscript was written elsewhere, Wearmouth/Jarrow being a likely alternative.[59] Perhaps the focus shifted from the northern centres along with the tide of political events, other scriptoria arising to challenge their leading role. Perhaps Scandinavian activity played a part in diminishing production, but more likely there has been a great subsequent loss of material, reflecting the varied fortunes of the north. Certain of those manuscripts which have not

---

[56] See T. J. Brown, 'Irish Element', pp. 101 – 19.

[57] The Vatican Paulinus: Vatican City, Biblioteca Apostolica Vaticana, Pal. Lat. 235; *CLA* I, no. 87. The Leningrad Paulinus: Leningrad, Public Library, Cod. Q.v.XIV.1; Alexander no. 42; *CLA* XI, no. 1622. See the facsimile edition of *Codex Palatinus Latinus 235, Paulinus Nolanus*, ed. T. J. Brown and T. MacKay (Armarium Codicum Insignium; Turnhout, forthcoming).

[58] See M. B. Parkes, *The Scriptorium of Wearmouth-Jarrow* (Jarrow Lecture 1982), pp. 3 – 32.

[59] BL, Cotton MS Domitian VII. For a most interesting reassessment of the *Liber vitae* and its possible connection with Wearmouth/Jarrow, see Dr Jean Gerchow, 'Die Gedenküberlieferung der Angelsachsen' (unpublished Ph.D. thesis, Albert-Ludwigs-Universität, Freiburg, 1987), pp. 140 – 93.

been satisfactorily placed may in fact be Lindisfarne products. A brief review of the surviving Insular manuscripts listed by Lowe and by Gneuss reveals forty-eight of probable 'Northumbrian' origin (many others hovering ambiguously somewhere over the Irish Sea or the Channel).[60] Of these, twenty-four represent liturgical volumes, twelve biblical commentaries and patristic works, and twelve miscellaneous texts, including works by Bede, Isidore, Paulinus, Orosius, and Pliny. Some of these may eventually be brought to ground at Lindisfarne; others will undoubtedly continue to 'float'. We might expect Lindisfarne and Wearmouth/Jarrow to emerge as principal Northumbrian centres of learning and book production; but we should remember to spare a thought for Hild's Whitby, Wilfrid's Ripon and Hexham, Alcuin's York, and for Melrose, Hartlepool, Coldingham, and other now dimly perceived lights in Cuthbert's Northumbria, and of course Lindisfarne's own mother house, Columcille's Iona.

Finally, the picture which emerges of the Lindisfarne scriptorium in this period is one of great innovation and conservatism, of spirituality and ecclesiastical 'politicking', and the attainment of a successful fusion of Celtic and Roman, Irish and Anglo-Saxon, which is in many ways reminiscent of the contradictions and outstanding achievements of Cuthbert's own career.

[60] See Lowe, *CLA* and H. Gneuss, 'A preliminary list of manuscripts written or owned in England up to 1100', *ASE* 9 (1981), pp. 1 – 60.

Birds, Beasts and Initials in Lindisfarne's Gospel Books

JANET BACKHOUSE

The Lindisfarne Gospels — unless one is prepared entirely to disregard the evidence of the colophon added to it by Aldred in the middle of the tenth century (pl. 32) — is one of the best documented and most closely dated of all medieval manuscripts. In spite of the fact that the monks of Durham lost this incomparable treasure to Henry VIII's commissioners more than four-and-a-half centuries ago, it is still regarded throughout the north-east of England with something akin to proprietorial pride. In honour of the thirteen-hundredth anniversary of the death of the saint in whose name it was made, the book was therefore permitted to leave the British Museum building in Bloomsbury for only the third time since the Cotton manuscripts were transferred there in the mid eighteenth century, to become for some ten weeks the centrepiece of a special exhibition in the Treasury of Durham Cathedral.[1] The presence of the Gospels in the cathedral precinct, symbolized by the fact that the floodlighting remained on throughout the night, provided a focal point within the blend of religious and secular celebrations dedicated to St Cuthbert during the 1987 anniversary. It was welcomed with great warmth and wide publicity throughout the region. The four members of the British Library staff who accompanied the manuscript on its journey were additionally privileged to pay a direct mark of respect to St Cuthbert by placing it for a short while on his tomb slab in the cathedral (frontispiece).[2]

---

[1] The relics of St Cuthbert and Durham's own manuscripts were supplemented for the occasion by related manuscripts now owned by the Society of Jesus, Corpus Christi College, Cambridge, the Bodleian Library and University College, Oxford, and the British Library. See the exhibition catalogue *St Cuthbert's Heritage*, ed. R. C. Coppin (Durham: the Dean and Chapter, 1987).

[2] The British Library was represented by Pamela Porter and Shelley Jones (Western Manuscripts), Tony Parker (Preservation) and myself. The Lindisfarne Gospels arrived in Durham on the evening of Tuesday, 16 June and the exhibition was opened by Rosemary Cramp on Friday, 19 June. It closed on Tuesday, 1 September and the manuscript left Durham on the evening of the following Monday, 7 September. Three visits were paid to St Cuthbert's tomb.

Thanks largely to the facsimile edition published by Urs Graf Verlag in 1956 and supplemented in 1960 by a five-hundred-page volume of scholarly discussion, the Lindisfarne Gospels is to date the most extensively studied medieval book in the world. More recent contributions to its bibliography have concentrated on specific aspects of its decoration, and in particular on the mathematical principles and concepts lying behind the complex structure of its five great carpet pages.[3] Less attention has been paid to the straightforward mechanics of the six major initial pages in the manuscript, where a tremendous variety of small asymmetrical spaces pose particularly difficult problems which Eadfrith seems always to solve with fluent and deceptive ease. A particularly good example occurs on the opening page of St Matthew's Gospel (fol. 27[r]), where the four unequal arms of a cross-shape, formed where the 'L' of 'Liber' passes over the 'I', are filled with four matching 'ducks' of completely different sizes. In circumstances such as these as much must certainly be due to the keenness of the artist's eye and the steadiness of his hand as to his mathematical talents.

Animal and bird forms are a particular feature of the decoration of the Lindisfarne Gospels. The modern visitor to the Northumbrian coast and its islands can hardly fail to be aware of the richness of the wildlife of the region, and many past writers on the manuscript have tried to equate the creatures employed by Eadfrith in the ornamentation of his pages with the birds and animals which he might be expected to have seen around him there at the end of the seventh century. In particular the long-necked, long-beaked birds which are intertwined on all the initial and carpet pages have been related to the cormorant and its cousin, the shag. This obviously attractive idea was challenged by Rupert Bruce-Mitford in his fundamental study of the decoration of the Gospels, and he enlisted the help of a colleague from the Natural History Museum in studying physical details of Eadfrith's birds.[4] He concluded that no natural model had been followed and stressed the incidence of processions of birds in Mediterranean art, whence an Italo-Syrian or Italo-Greek Gospels providing inspiration for the Lindisfarne canon tables might most probably have come. He was furthermore convinced that Eadfrith 'did not copy nature, as the artist of the Book of Kells, who put in moths, cats with mice, an otter with a salmon, and other vignettes, copied it'.

While not for a moment suggesting that Eadfrith was conscientiously trying to produce accurate representations of local wildlife in a modern and scientific

---

The manuscript was unpacked there immediately upon arrival on 16 June. On the following morning the visit was repeated so that unofficial photographs could be taken. On Thursday, 3 September, before and during Matins, a final visit was made and the cathedral's official photographer recorded the event. One of his photographs is used here.
[3] See J. Guilmain, 'The Geometry of the Cross-Carpet Pages in the Lindisfarne Gospels', *Speculum* 62 (1987), pp. 21 – 52; R. Stevick, 'The Design of the Lindisfarne Gospels folio 138v', *Gesta* 22 (1983), pp. 3 – 12 and idem, 'The 4 × 3 Crosses in the Lindisfarne and Lichfield Gospels', *Gesta* 25 (1986), pp. 171 – 84. Earlier references are given in Alexander, no. 9.
[4] *Cod. Lind.*, II, pp. 199 – 201.

sense, I find myself in strong disagreement with Bruce-Mitford's overall conclusions on this subject and am inclined to revert in some degree to the earlier view. I do not doubt that Eadfrith is likely to have seen and been inspired by a Mediterranean model which supplied a prototype for the bird-filled canon table arcades, but I feel quite certain that his birds were no mere adaptation of the birds appropriate to the experience of the original artist. They clearly have characteristics with which he himself felt at home. The chronology of the Lindisfarne Gospels and the group of manuscripts most closely related to it is still a matter of some controversy, and it is therefore impossible to say with certainty whether it was Eadfrith himself or his brilliant contemporary, the Durham-Echternach Calligrapher, who first introduced the characteristic Lindisfarne bird into the illuminator's repertory.[5] But as far as surviving manuscripts are concerned, it is certainly in the Lindisfarne Gosepls that the birds are first extensively used. It has been objected that Eadfrith's birds lack the webbed feet of the cormorant family.[6] On the other hand, it is worth noting that, when depicting their wings, he almost invariably employs the convention of overlapping scales in varying colours. A striking and unusual feature of the cormorant clan is the strongly marked 'tiled' texture of their wings (pl. 11).[7]

Naturalistic features on the evangelist portrait pages are more immediately obvious. The evangelist figures themselves, demonstrably based on Mediter-ranean models, display realistic human characteristics to a degree unparalleled in the Durrow, Durham, Echternach and Lichfield Gospels, to mention only those manuscripts most closely related to Lindisfarne. Even more interesting in this context is Eadfrith's treatment of the evangelist's symbols. St John's eagle (fol. 209[v]) has recently been described by an ornithologist as having plumage so accurately rendered that it can hardly have been achieved save

---

[5] For the Durham birds see E. Coatsworth in *The Durham Gospels*, ed. C. D. Verey, T. J. Brown and E. Coatsworth (EEMF 20; Copenhagen, 1980), pp. 57 – 8.

[6] *Cod. Lind.* II, p. 201.

[7] The National Trust's illustrated souvenir booklet on the Farne Islands (1983) includes good photographs of both the common cormorant (*Phalacrocorax carbo*) and the shag (*Phalacrocorax aristotelis*). The characteristic features and attitudes of both birds are depicted in P. Hayman and P. Burton, *The Birdlife of Britain* (London, 1976), pp. 244 and 245 respectively. It is instructive to see how more recent bird painters have viewed them. T. Lambert, *Birds of Shore and Estuary* (London, 1979), pp. 50 – 3, stresses the pattern of the feathers on the wings of both species. C. F. Tunnicliffe, *A Sketchbook of Birds* (London, 1979), also stresses this pattern on his shag (pl. 7) and provides a sketch of the very large and strong toes of a nestling cormorant (pl. 8). In the immature bird these toes are much darker in colour than the intervening web, a feature which is anyway inappropriate in the construction of an interlaced design. H. E. Dresser, in a plate from his *Birds of Europe* (1871), reused in J. L. Bonhote, *Birds of Britain* (London, 1907), p. 221, characterizes the shag as having strongly-patterned wings, very large and horny legs and toes, and a very prominent and forward-facing crest, which it would be tempting to equate with the lappets on the Durham and Otho/Corpus bird heads, were lappets not so standard a feature of zoomorphic ornament. The line-drawing offered in *Cod. Lind.* I, p. 199 fails to convey the sinuous quality of the bird, cf. Tunnicliffe, pl. 7.

through direct observation.[8] Both St Mark's lion (fol. 93ᵛ) and St Luke's
vitulus (fol. 138ᵛ) are shown as credible animals,[9] and both are given stylized
hairy pelts, carefully distinguished in texture. The lion is painted a tawny
yellow ochre that appears nowhere else in the manuscript and is in marked
contrast to the sunshine yellow of the parti-coloured Echternach lion.[10] Is it
possible that this was the deliberate result of descriptive information?

Perhaps the most significant evidence of Eadfrith's tendency towards
naturalism is to be seen in his treatment of the cat. Cats are found on two
pages of the Lindisfarne Gospels. Two small specimens are contained within
the framing lines of the 'M' at the beginning of the Matthew *argumentum* (folio
18ᵛ).[11] They are so delicately drawn and coloured that they do not immediately
attract the eye, but when isolated from their surroundings they are seen to be
crouched as if waiting outside a mousehole. More obvious is the cat that forms
the right-hand margin of the initial page to Luke (folio 139ʳ, pl. 11). No one
seems to have noticed that this creature, however stylized and distorted, is
quite distinctly provided with whiskers. These whiskers, which make no
contribution to the general design of the page, are so very delicately drawn
that they are virtually invisible on the appropriate page of the Urs Graf
fascimile and have been entirely ignored by the artist of the line-drawing
provided for the introductory volume.[12] It may be true that Eadfrith made no
attempt to incorporate into his masterpiece any of the little animal groups that
are to be found in Kells, but there seems every indication that he observed
with some care the animals and birds whose characteristics he planned to adopt
in his decorative schemes.

A parallel may surely be drawn between Eadfrith's use of directly observed
naturalistic features in the animal decoration of the Lindisfarne Gospels and
the well-known animal stories in the contemporary lives of St Cuthbert, in
whose name the manuscript was made. Cuthbert is the only English saint of
the time to be credited with incidents of this type, though their relationship to

---

[8] B. Yapp, *Birds in Medieval Manuscripts* (London, 1981), p. 84. He writes: 'The distinction
between breast feathers, under wing-coverts and primaries is correct, and the line dividing the
small feathers of the neck, which are not individually shown, from the breast is nearly in the right
place. The detail of the feathers, each with a rachis and two rows of barbs (especially good in the
coverts) could hardly have been invented. The beak is more or less correct, but the eye is too far
forward. This eagle is in contrast to most Johnian eagles, which are merely conventional birds
with hooked beaks.'

[9] A yet more realistic *vitulus*, of comparable date, has recently come to light in the shape of a clay
mould from excavations at Hartlepool, see R. J. Cramp and R. Daniels, 'New finds from the
Anglo-Saxon monastery at Hartlepool, Cleveland', *Antiquity* 61 (1987), pp. 430 – 1 and below,
pp. 219 – 21 and pl. 39a. This must once have been part of a set of four, representing the four
evangelist symbols, and would clearly be very much at home in the context of the ornamental
binding of a manuscript such as the Lindisfarne Gospels.

[10] *Cod. Lind.* II, p. 270.

[11] Ibid., fig. 42 m.

[12] Ibid., fig. 42 n. The realistic pads and claws of the Lindisfarne animals have recently attracted
comment, see G. Haseloff, 'Insular animal styles with special reference to Irish art in the early
medieval period', *Ireland and Insular Art*, ed. M. Ryan (Dublin, 1987), p. 48.

the tradition found in such earlier sources as the *Life of St Antony* or the
biographies of some of the Irish saints is undeniable.[13] However, the animal
stories told of Cuthbert by the anonymous monk of Lindisfarne, and
incorporated into both his prose *Life* and the appropriate part of the
Ecclesiastical History by the Venerable Bede, although they follow very closely
the pattern set in the earlier sources, do involve animals and birds credible in a
Northumbrian setting. Both the anonymous and Bede produced their
biographies of Cuthbert in the time, and apparently at the behest, of Eadfrith.
These are not the only Cuthbert animal stories. The unknown draft of Bede's
verse life of the saint, recently identified by Michael Lapidge,[14] offers a
hitherto unknown incident of the same kind, this time involving seals. The
popular view of Cuthbert as the friend of 'the angels, the otters and the eider
duck',[15] so attractive in our own day, is very firmly rooted in the time of
Cuthbert himself and there is no reason to suppose that it does not reflect the
saint's own attitude.

The Lindisfarne Gospels and the illuminated manuscripts most closely
related to it have been extensively studied over a very long period. It is
unusual to be in a position to add anything to the corpus of relevant material
and thus especially gratifying to be able to do so in the context of a paper
honouring so distinguished an occasion as the thirteen-hundredth anniversary
of St Cuthbert's death. The least well known of the related manuscripts is now
divided between the Cotton collection in the British Library and Corpus
Christi College, Cambridge.[16] Now very imperfect, and never as grand and
elaborate a book as either the Lindisfarne or the Durham Gospels (Durham,
MS A.II.17), it is further disadvantaged through the severe mutilation of
much of its surviving decoration as a result of the Ashburnham House fire in
1731.[17] In her contribution to the present volume, Michelle Brown has
underlined the relationship between the script of this manuscript and that of
the Lindisfarne Gospels itself.[18] Its two surviving evangelist symbol pages are
close cousins of the ones in the Echternach Gospels (Paris, BN., MS lat.9389),
and the initial page to John has been compared particularly to similar work in
the Durham Gospels.[19] In his recent study of the Insular Gospel books, George
Henderson has been the first to draw attention to a further, albeit lesser, form
of decoration featured in the book, in the shape of a line of display capitals

---

[13] See B. Colgrave, 'Bede's Miracle Stories', in *Bede, His Life, Times and Writings*, ed. A. H.
Thompson (Oxford, 1935), pp. 223–4.
[14] Above, pp. 78–85, esp. p. 80.
[15] So expressed in the intercessions composed by Rev. Kate Tristram for use in the parish church
of Holy Island at a Eucharist in Thanksgiving for St Cuthbert Year, 5 September 1987. 'Eadfrith,
artist of the Lindisfarne Gospels' was specifically commemorated on the same occasion.
[16] Alexander, no. 12.
[17] See E. Miller, *That Noble Cabinet* (London, 1973), pp. 34–6, for an account of the disaster.
[18] See above, p. 158.
[19] Alexander, loc. cit.

introducing the glossary of Hebrew names in the preliminaries to Mark, now part of the Cottonian fragment.[20] This he has reproduced from a very clear and detailed engraving, published in 1784 by Thomas Astle,[21] relating it to a similar feature in the Durham Gospels (pl. 12) and commenting on the contrast between its somewhat rigid and rectilinear letters and the rounded forms used in the latter book.

The original page from which Astle's plate is derived does in fact survive in BL Cotton MS Otho C. V (pl. 14). Although it has been very badly singed and distorted by fire, seven of the ten capitals seen in the engraving are still clearly visible, together with much of the accompanying text, testifying to the accuracy of the eighteenth-century image. The letters are coloured yellow, outlined in dark brown ink, which is in turn edged with small red dots. The central portions of the capitals 'A' and 'V' are missing. At the bottom of the same page, and more seriously damaged, is a further line of display capitals designed to introduce the preface to Mark. These are in dark brown ink on a ground of red dots, with yellow patches in the interstices of the letters.

The handpainted fascimiles from which Astle's engraver worked also survive in the British Library.[22] Among them is a copy of the whole of this page of Otho C. V as it appeared before 1731 (pl. 13).[23] This reveals not only details of the red, green and yellow colouring of the large initial 'C' that appears on the engraving but also an impressive initial 'M' belonging to the lower line of capitals. Both have now entirely disappeared. The bows of the second large initial letter enclose a pair of birds' heads, with long curved beaks and elaborate extended lappets, very like the arrangement in the corresponding Durham initial. The letter itself was dark brown, outlined and filled with red dots. The birds' heads were uncoloured but the areas covered by the interlaced lines extending from the lappets were filled with yellow paint. Those portions of the accompanying display capitals now missing from the original were apparently once coloured green. The lower line of capitals, far from echoing the squared off form of the upper one, is very close indeed in general appearance to the corresponding line in Durham, consolidating the general impression of a close relationship between the two books. A similar form of capital 'M' also occurs in Lindisfarne (pl. 22), where it forms part of the 'MA' monogram at the beginning of the Matthew *argumentum* (folio 18ᵛ). In the

[20] G. Henderson, *From Durrow to Kells. The Insular Gospel-books 650 – 800* (London, 1987), p. 70.

[21] T. Astle, *The Origin and Progress of Writing* (London, 1784; 2nd ed. 1803), pl. XV.

[22] Stowe MS 1061; mostly on paper but with a few specimens, including four pages from the Lindisfarne Gospels (fols. 42 and 43), on vellum. The quality of many of these copies is astonishing.

[23] Fol. 36. The sad fate of the original is noted both in Astle's published text and at the foot of the facsimile page itself. According to a footnote by Astle, 'the drawing was taken at the expence of Edward Earl of Oxford.' This suggests that the facsimile from which the watercolour supplied to the engraver was taken may have been made by Elizabeth Elstob, famed for her work on Anglo-Saxon manuscripts and well known both to Edward Harley and to his librarian, Humfrey Wanley. For her career see G. B. Richardson, *William and Elizabeth Elstob, the learned Saxonists* (Reprints of Rare Tracts etc.; Newcastle-on-Tyne, 1847).

Lindisfarne example the birds' heads are replaced by somewhat smaller dogs, but in other respects the form and treatment of the letter is closely akin to the Durham and Otho examples. Small decorative initials of this kind are not a universal feature of Insular Gospel books, though a comparable series is to be seen in a volume of canons, now in Cologne.[24] They stand at the very beginning of the development of the highly decorated text initial, an aspect of illumination that was to become one of the great strengths of English book painting.

One further decorated leaf in Cotton MS Otho C. V has also escaped detailed attention and should therefore be recorded here.[25] It (fol. 22) marks the transition between the Gospels of Matthew and Mark. On the recto the last two verses of Matthew are expanded to fill more than six long lines by the introduction of elongated decorative extensions to the bows of such minuscule letters as 'b', 'd' and 'm'. Some of these extensions are filled with yellow pigment. In the lower right-hand corner of the page the explicit/incipit of Matthew and Mark is written in red within dark brown framing lines.[26] The remaining space on the page is filled with little decorative trails of red dots and lines. On the reverse side the Mark *capitula* begins with *Erat Iohannes* in an impressive line of decorative capitals similar in style to those of the Mark *argumentum* on fol. 25ᵛ. These too are carried out in dark brown ink against a ground of red dots, with decorative patches of yellow inside the letters. Equivalent areas of missing vellum suggest that there were once also patches of green.

Had the Otho/Corpus Gospels survived in a less defective form, and in particular had the British Library portion escaped the Ashburnham House fire (as did the Lindisfarne Gospels), it would without doubt have enjoyed far more attention than has hitherto been the case. The variety of decoration which it contains (if not its quality) would have exceeded that found in the Echternach Gospels, which lacks the lesser initials and lines of display capitals discussed above. If the arcaded canon tables of which faint traces are to be seen in BL, Royal MS 7. C. XII, fols. 2 and 3, are indeed to be associated with this particular manuscript,[27] it was a relatively ambitious undertaking, and on a physical scale equivalent to that of the three great Gospel books — Lindisfarne, Durham and Echternach — with which it is usually compared.[28] It is unfortunate that so little is known of its history, though the Corpus

---

[24] Alexander, no. 13.

[25] These decorative initials are in fact included in the general description of the manuscript in P. McGurk, *Latin Gospel Books from A.D. 400 to A.D. 800* (Les Publications de Scriptorium V; Paris and Brussels, 1961), no. 2, but have escaped the notice of art historians.

[26] For a discussion of the use of frames for passages of text see Henderson, op. cit., pp. 57 – 60.

[27] Ibid., p. 71.

[28] Lindisfarne measures 340 × 240 mm., Durham (A.II.17) is 344 × 265 mm., Echternach is 335 × 255 mm. Otho/Corpus is now only 285 × 212 mm. but has been severely trimmed on two sides. It should probably measure about 50 mm. more in both directions.

portion is circumstantially connected with Canterbury in the sixteenth century.[29] The Canterbury connection is reinforced by an erroneous tradition, recorded in the 1696 Cotton catalogue and in an inscription added on fol. 1 of the Corpus fragment, that the book was the property of St Augustine.[30]

The various links between the decoration of the Otho/Corpus Gospels and the Lindisfarne, Durham and Echternach Gospels strengthen the ties which bind this group of manuscripts together. The Lindisfarne scriptorium is the obvious claimant for the entire group.[31] The group of four may be divided into two pairs — the extremely elaborate Lindisfarne and Durham books and the much less ambitiously decorated Echternach and Otho/Corpus manuscripts. The second pair is also distinguished by a much less extensive range of pigments. It is worth considering whether this subdivision reflects a simple difference in purpose between the two pairs of manuscripts. Available evidence strongly suggests that the first two remained within the community itself. Lindisfarne is directly associated with the name of Cuthbert, which is generally taken to mean that it had some specific connection with the relics of the saint. Maybe the Durham manuscript had a more regular liturgical function. Both manuscripts were certainly among the early treasures preserved by the community at Chester-le-Street in the tenth century. By contrast the history of both the other manuscripts seems to lie outside Northumbria. The Echternach Gospels was certainly available to local Echternach scribes and illuminators at the beginning of the eighth century,[32] whether or not its acquisition is to be directly connected with the foundation of Willibrord's abbey in or about 698.[33] As already noted, there are substantial, if much later, reasons to connect the Otho/Corpus fragments with Canterbury, most probably St Augustine's, presided over in the early years of the eighth century first by Archbishop Theodore's friend and companion Hadrian

---

[29] The Corpus fragment was presented to the college by Archbishop Matthew Parker (d. 1575).

[30] T. Smith, *Catalogus Librorum Manuscriptorum Bibliothecae Cottoniae* (Oxford, 1696). A photographic reprint from Robert Harley's copy, annotated by Humfrey Wanley, and with additional material relating to the fire of 1731, was edited by C. G. C. Tite in 1984. Smith reveals that the Otho fragment originally included an evangelist symbol page for Matthew, but this has completely disappeared.

[31] One of the links which has been put forward involves a suggested identity between the main corrector of the Durham Gospels and a hand which contributed one or two very small corrections to Lindisfarne. Details are given in C. D. Verey's appendix to T. J. Brown, 'Northumbria and the Book of Kells', *ASE* 1 (1972), pp. 43–5, pl. VI a-c. This has aroused considerable controversy which was voiced during the Durham conference. It was therefore decided to take the opportunity offered by the presence of Lindisfarne in Durham to make a direct comparison between the two manuscripts. This took place on Wednesday, 2 September 1987 in the Cathedral Library. The British Library couriers and members of the cathedral library staff were joined by Alan Piper and Gerald Bonner. No clear-cut conclusion was reached. The additions to Lindisfarne seem less decisively written than those in Durham and the ink is weaker. This may account for some of the variations noted. I am myself prepared to accept that the two are by the same hand.

[32] See N. Netzer, below, pp. 207–12.

[33] *Cod. Lind.* II, pp. 103–4.

(d. 708) and then by Hadrian's own disciple Albinus, the friend of Bede.[34] Both men maintained close contact with the north of England and either would be a perfectly feasible recipient of a Northumbrian Gospel book. Can it be that the Echternach and Otho/Corpus volumes represent a less ambitious and, in particular, a less time-consuming type of work produced either as a gift or on request for the use of some community other than Lindisfarne itself? Julian Brown has drawn attention to aspects of the Echternach book which suggests that it was written and illuminated in some haste, perhaps to meet a deadline.[35] There are no obvious signs of haste in Otho/Corpus, but its relative simplicity would have been economic in terms of working time. The very modest range of pigments used in the comparatively restrained decoration of both books can also be regarded as deliberately economic when contrasted with the amazing variety of colours found in Durham and, especially, in Lindisfarne.[36]

There is no lack of evidence for the movement of books during the seventh and eighth centuries, as developing communities sought a nucleus for their libraries and individuals in the mission field sent to their friends and colleagues for particular texts to aid in their presentation of the Christian message.[37] The letters of St Boniface include several such requests.[38] Parallel references to gifts which he himself sent to his correspondents reflect a mild form of barter for the everyday type of book. But on one occasion he did ask Abbess Eadburh for something rather more spectacular, a copy of the Epistles of St Peter written out in letters of gold.[39] This was specifically intended to make a visual impression on the congregations in whose presence he might use it.[40] Furthermore, Boniface himself sent Eadburh materials to be used in its making.[41] Although this volume was not a copy of the Gospels, it was clearly designed to have a similarly public function. It has long been recognized that the Echternach Gospels is written on vellum prepared by the continental rather than the insular method. Is it possible that this too is due to the supply of materials by or on behalf of the intended recipient?

Illuminated copies of the Gospels were the ultimate showpieces among the decorated books produced in the British Isles in the late seventh and early eighth centuries. Of some thirty manuscripts of the period listed by Alexander in his survey, almost two-thirds are Gospels, including of course all the

---

[34] *HE* (Colgrave and Mynors), preface.

[35] *Cod. Lind.* II, p. 104.

[36] Ibid., pp. 263 – 77.

[37] W. Levison, *England and the Continent in the Eighth Century* (Oxford, 1946), ch. 6.

[38] C. H. Talbot, *The Anglo-Saxon Missionaries in Germany* (London, 1954), pp. 65 – 149 passim.

[39] Ibid., pp. 91 – 2; *EHD*, pp. 811 – 2.

[40] *EHD* renders Boniface's request as: '. . . to write for me in gold the epistles of my lord, St Peter the Apostle, to secure honour and reverence for the Holy Scriptures when they are preached from before the eyes of the heathen; and because I particularly wish to have always with me the words of him who guided me to this course.'

[41] It is usually assumed that Boniface was sending Eadburh the gold required for the manuscript; but this is not actually specified.

magnificent examples mentioned in the present paper.[42] These books, besides honouring the word of God through the increasing splendour of their decoration within and without, were clearly intended to be visually impressive to the congregations — often not far from pagan and certainly largely illiterate — which they served. This function is clearly implied in the description of the Gospels which Wilfrid commissioned for his church at Ripon, which was written in letters of gold on purple parchment, illuminated, and covered in gold and gems.[43] Their status lies somewhere between the relic and the liturgical object and is far removed from that of an ordinary library book. Of all the surviving books in this class, the Lindisfarne Gospels best illustrates its special function and indeed retains something of its relic status even into the present day.

---

[42] Alexander, nos. 1 – 31, comprising 19 Gospels (many of them now fragmentary), 5 Psalters, the Codex Amiatinus, the Leningrad Bede, the Cologne Canons, and single copies of Jerome on Isaiah, the *Chronicon* of Orosius, Cassiodorus on the Psalms, and Pliny's *Natural History.*
[43] *VW* 17.

The Durham-Echternach Calligrapher

R. BRUCE-MITFORD

In his preface to the commentary volume of *Codex Lindisfarnensis*, the Swiss facsimile edition of the Lindisfarne Gospels, published in 1960, Sir Thomas Kendrick, himself expert in these matters, said of the commentary volume that in it the Lindisfarne scriptorium 'had been raised to an unexpected new importance.' What he had in mind, I am sure, was Julian Brown's claim (and mine, for I gave him my full backing) that, in addition to the Lindisfarne Gospels, two other exceptional and particularly important codices *de luxe* — the Echternach Gospels (Paris Bibl. Nat. MS lat. 9389) and the Durham Gospels, here in the Cathedral Library (MS A.II.17), were both the work of the same artist-scribe and were also made in the Lindisfarne scriptorium.[1]

The Durham Gospels is sadly incomplete. It originally had an elaborate scheme of decoration approaching in complexity those of the Gospels of St Chad and the Book of Kells. It now preserves only the monogram page at the beginning of St John (*In principio*), a number of major initials introducing text passages of importance, some small decorative initials in the running text, a frame of broad panels of interlace executed in red dots round the end of the text of St Matthew, and, on the verso of that leaf, a badly worn full-page miniature of the crucifixion, rendered less easy to interpret by the showing through of the interlace-filled framework from the recto. The Echternach Gospels, virtually complete with no evidence of any major lost decoration on its few missing leaves, preserves its canon tables, with plain, unembellished bordering-strips; the major monograms opening the texts of Mark, Luke and John; some small text initials; and the four remarkable and well-known pages each depicting one of the evangelist symbols.[2]

Although this is all the decoration, or illustration, that the Durham Gospels now has to show, it can be inferred from internal evidence that it originally possessed in addition either evangelist portraits or carpet-pages at the beginning, and miniatures at the end, of each Gospel.[3] This more complex architecture or decorative scheme which we can reconstruct follows the trend

---

[1] *Cod. Lind.* II, pp. 89 – 106 ('The Lindisfarne Scriptorium') and 246 – 50.
[2] Alexander, no. 10, pp. 40 – 1 and no. 11, pp. 42 – 3.
[3] Ibid., p. 41, col. 1.

of elaboration and overloading which climaxes in the Gospels of St Chad and the Book of Kells. This is a factor which alone suggests a date for the making of the Durham Gospels appreciably later than that of Lindisfarne (698, or shortly before).

At first sight these two manuscripts, Echternach and Durham, appear as different as chalk from cheese. Indeed, I do not think that it would have occurred to me, from the decorative viewpoint, that they could be the work of the same hand (artist and scribe being in each case the same person, as Julian Brown and I believed), had not Julian Brown come to this conclusion on palaeographical grounds, and asked me whether I thought from the point of view of decoration that it could be so. But after careful consideration I gave his theory my full support, having, of course, like Julian Brown, studied both manuscripts in the original. Professor Brown himself ventured into the art-historical field, circumspectly, by making a detailed comparison, which was accurately observed, between the Matthew symbol in Echternach and the Durham Gospels' crucifixion miniature, and concluded that both were by the same hand.[4]

Should the claim that the Echternach Gospels and the Durham Gospels are the work of the same man prove true, then the credit for a brilliant piece of perception, that behind evident differences lay none the less a single creative identity, is Julian Brown's. He is the 'onlie begetter' of the man he dubbed 'the Durham-Echternach calligrapher'. Let us remind ourselves that the two Gospel books thus joined are not any run-of-the-mill manuscripts. The great palaeographer, E. A. Lowe (not an art-historian, or archaeologist, but intimately familiar with the corpus of material) wrote of the Durham Gospels:

> Decorated by an artist of superb skill and ingenuity with a remarkable sense of form and composition.[5]

Of the Echternach Gospels' evangelist symbols, Dr J. J. G. Alexander has written:

> The illumination is one of the high points of Insular calligraphic virtuosity applied to the stylization of natural objects.[6]

Taking the two manuscripts together Professor Brown called the Durham-Echternach calligrapher:

---

[4] *Cod. Lind.* II, p. 102.
[5] *CLA* V, no. 587.
[6] Alexander, p. 42, col. 2.

One of the greatest masters of formal and informal handwriting in the history of Europe.[7]

I, in turn, designated him, as creator of both manuscripts:

One of the greatest masters of decorative art, greater than Eadfrith [the artist-scribe of the Lindisfarne Gospels] in spite of the latter's remarkable willingness to absorb invent modify amalgamate and create afresh.[8]

It can only be said of these claims: 'them's fighting words'; for what must we not conclude about the Lindisfarne community, that Irish foundation, if it could produce, at the same time, in its poorly lit, draughty island scriptorium on the North Sea, two such great yet different personalities as Eadfrith, the master of the Lindisfarne Gospels, and the Durham-Echternach calligrapher, in the days of Cuthbert and Bede?

The question, whether Julian Brown and I were right, is the subject I should like to consider briefly tonight, in general terms. It reduces essentially to three points, matters which should depend on evidence rather than any theory of probabilities:

(i)   Are artist and scribe in fact, in the case of each of the manuscripts, one and the same individual?
(ii)   Are the two codices really by the same hand?[9]
(iii) If so, can either be assigned to Lindisfarne, rather than to anywhere else?

The claim put forward by Julian Brown and supported by me has naturally been contested, and rightly so. Such are the implications, not only for the status of Lindisfarne but in the fields of palaeography and art, and for the historical process, that it seems essential that serious critical analysis should be brought to bear on it.

It is indeed sad that Julian Brown is not here, where he would so much have liked to be, to honour St Cuthbert and to speak, with his own great authority, for himself. May I say at the outset that it does not seem to me particularly helpful, or indeed helpful at all, in assessing his case, to accuse him of

---

[7] *Cod. Lind.* II, pp. 104 – 5.

[8] Ibid., pp. 246 – 7.

[9] See *Cod. Lind.* II, p. 247, where I wrote: 'If however one looks at D[urham] and E[chternach] closely, making allowances for the speed with which E was done and for possible differences in the scale attempted and in date, it seems that there can be no doubt that the two MSS were decorated by the same hand. So many details, matters of taste or idiosyncracy, recur in both, and the same touch and special skills and predilections are manifest, so that one cannot fail to recognize the artist's individuality. It is also clear, on arguments similar in general to those that apply in the case of L[indisfarne] (pp. 123 – 5) that in both cases the scribe was responsible for the decoration.'

prejudice.[10] Julian Brown was far too good a scholar to let himself be either proud or prejudiced. He was, however, convinced; and that conviction was based upon deep knowledge of the whole field within his speciality, combined with exceptional powers of observation and an acute critical, and self-critical sense. Perhaps he over-persuaded himself of his case, as which of us, at some time or another, has not? But to think in terms of prejudice fails to read correctly both the substance of his case and his personal scrupulousness.

Before referring to the manuscripts themselves, I would wish to make three further points:

(i) There are, I believe, times and places, and Northumbria from around AD 650 – 750 is one of them, when archaeological or art-historical evidence is more decisive than that of handwriting or text, in the relative dating of manuscripts. This is so when decoration, ornament and illustration, as applied to the codex, are evolving rapidly, while the pace of change in handwriting or text is less perceptible, hardly perceptible at all, or of uncertain interpretation.

---

[10] Dáibhí Ó Cróinín, 'Pride and Prejudice', *Peritia* 1 (1982), pp. 352 – 62. Ó Cróinín, 'Rath Melsigi, Willibrord, and the earliest Echternach Manuscripts', *Peritia* 3 (1984), p. 19, says of the claim that both the Echternach Gospels and the Durham Gospels were produced at Lindisfarne at roughly the same time, that it is not new but a refinement and elaboration of the thesis of Masai, in which 'the whole corpus of important early Insular illuminated manuscripts was claimed for Northumbria' (ibid., p. 18). W. J. O'Sullivan also says that Julian Brown's 'very substantial contributions have been obscured, especially for Irish scholars, by his having fallen early under the spell of François Masai who propounded the theory of the Northumbrian origin of most of the surviving majuscule manuscripts' (O'Sullivan, 'Insular Calligraphy: Current State and Problems', *Peritia* 4 (1985), p. 351). The mention of F. Masai, Keeper of Manuscripts in the Royal Library, Brussels, founder of the review *Scriptorium*, inventor of the term 'codicology', and his book *Essai sur les Origines de la Miniature dite Irlandaise*, is like a red rag to a bull to supporters of the traditional view of the essentially Irish creation in Ireland of Irish or Hiberno-Saxon art. In fact, he was a brilliant advocate who let a breath of fresh air into the subject of Insular illuminated manuscripts which was full of dogma and complacency. His essay, however, was written during the German occupation of his country, without access to any of the original materials, or to the latest research and opinion, and so suffered from numerous shortcomings and inaccuracies. Julian Brown was perfectly well aware of these errors and limitations. In my own review of Masai's book (*The Connoisseur*, June 1949), I said that 'his barrage largely fell on positions from which the enemy had already withdrawn.' Julian Brown was greatly stimulated by Masai's iconoclastic and eloquent book, and by many of the sound original points that he made; but it is wrong to overestimate the influence that Masai had upon him (acknowledged by T. J. Brown, 'Northumbria and the Book of Kells', *ASE* 1 (1972), pp. 219 – 20). In no sense was Brown's discovery or recognition of the 'Durham-Echternach Calligrapher' or his attribution of both Echternach and the Durham Gospels to the Lindisfarne scriptorium, or my support of his case, based upon anything that Masai had said. It was a wholly new, independent, and direct assessment of the works in question. My interest in the problem of Insular illumination of this period was excited primarily by Sir Alfred Clapham's pioneer paper, 'The Origins of Hiberno-Saxon Art' (*Antiquity* 8 (1934), pp. 43 – 57) and by F. C. Burkitt, 'Kells, Durrow and Lindisfarne' (*Antiquity* 9 (1935), pp. 33 – 7). That does not prevent me from seeing them now, in the light of advances in the subject, as out of date and wrong in not a few respects. Let us hope that we shall not hear any more of Julian Brown's dependence on Masai.

(ii) I speak only from the point of view of the decoration, not being competent to pronounce on textual or palaeographical matters.

(iii) It is not possible here in the short time at my disposal to go into the case in any sort of depth. What I offer is a short summary, a few comments, and a plea for closer investigation than it seems has yet been accorded to the detailed case we put forward.

To consider now briefly the two manuscripts principally concerned, we are at once faced with a factor which troubled Julian Brown more than it troubled me; or shall I say, one which troubled me particularly initially, namely the manifest difference decoratively between the two manuscripts. It is my view that these differences are to be explained, or could well be explicable, by a number of factors, one of which — a substantial difference in date — Brown, from his study of the script, was reluctant to accept, but which seems inevitable from the archaeological or art-historical angle. Durham MS A.II.17 seems to me some twenty or twenty-five years later than Echternach, because of the degree of ornamental development both in detail of ornamental execution and style and in the profusion and extension of its application to the Gospel codex.

The other factors which explain, or might explain, the main obvious decorative and script differences are the layout chosen for Echternach — set out in two columns on the page, in sections intended for ease of reading, *per cola et commata*, resulting in half-scale monograms; and the very clear evidence, seen both in text and decoration, that Echternach was written in some haste, as if for a deadline, and left unfinished, while Durham MS A.II.17 was dwelt upon and finished at leisure with no limits at all imposed upon the artist-scribe. The limits imposed on the creator of Echternach were clearly set out by Julian Brown and as clearly reinforced by myself.[11]

The evangelist symbol pages, in particular, provide evidence that the manuscript was left incomplete. The man symbol of St Matthew (pl. 9) does appear complete. Its frames are filled with finely set out painted interlace, and the letters of the inscription in capitals in the field (*imago hominis*) not only have the bowls or loops of the letters tinted in, but the fields between and around the letters are sown with red dots in spaced clusters of three. In the Luke symbol the frames are empty and though the bowls of the letters in the inscription are tinted, the background of red dots is lacking. In the lion symbol the beautifully designed frames, of purple and of red lead, are empty and neither tinting nor red dots have been applied to the inscription; and the same applies to the St John symbol. These pages, so brilliant otherwise in concept and execution, were clearly never finished.

The *Quoniam quidem* monograph in Echternach (pl. 18) and the *Initium* monogram in St Mark[12] both show some acceptance of the panelled style, so

---

[11] *Cod. Lind.* II, pp. 96, 97 and 246 – 9.

[12] George Henderson, *From Durrow to Kells: The Insular Gospel-books 650 – 800* (London, 1987), figs. 97 and 98 and Alexander, pl. 53.

characteristic of the Lindisfarne Gospels and of the Durham Cassiodorus miniature-frames,[13] but they are exceptions. Neither the remaining monograms (e.g. the *In principio*, and *Liber generationis* and *Christi autem* monograms of John and Matthew),[14] nor the frames of the four symbol pages (or, in Durham MS A.II.17, the great *INP* monogram of St John[15]) show any flirtation with the panelled style. This general absence of panelling suits the fluency and movement in which the artist of both these manuscripts revelled.

A major decorative difference between the two manuscripts is the absence of animal ornament in Echternach, in sharp contrast to its lavish and enthusiastic use in A.II.17. It cannot be supposed that a top-class scribe-illuminator of the Lindisfarne Gospels/Durham Gospels horizon, to which the Echternach Gospels belong, was unfamiliar with zoomorphic ornament. It was clearly omitted deliberately. Moreover, while an expert handler of Celtic curvilinear trumpet-spiral ornament, the Echternach painter used it with great restraint. It occurs only in the informal curvilinear shapes that bubble out of the uprights of the monograms into free space (e.g. pl. 18 in the Q of *Quoniam*, at top and bottom and within the bow of the Q). The reason for this, as for the omission of animal ornament, is compatible with the other signs of haste in the completion of the manuscript, pointed out by Julian Brown, since, as the study of the mechanics of the decoration in *Codex Lindisfarnensis* showed,[16] these types of ornament are much more complicated and time-consuming to execute than is interlace.

Shared between Durham and Echternach is a relatively inconspicuous use of ornamental devices, not seen in the Lindisfarne Gospels, such as circular spots (small bare vellum 'holes' in black-ink backgrounds) and of concave-sided spikey triangles that appear here and there in background spaces as fill-ups. These latter can be seen for example in the fields, defined by hair-lines, joining the terminal spiral-flourishes of the serifs at the top of the F and the U of *Fuit* on folio 2^v of the Durham Gospels (plate 19), and in Echternach at the top of the U of *Quoniam* of folio 116^r and in the innermost ornamental development within the bow of the Q (pl. 18). It is not so much that these devices are used (they occur in Durrow and many later manuscripts), but the way and style in which they are used. A particular link between the two manuscripts is also the exquisitely delicate penwork in spirals and other shapes seen in both (here pl. 18, and fig. 12; in *Cod. Lind.* II, pl. 50, a-d and h, fig 61 A), and especially in the beautiful handling of open interlace associated with initials (pls. 18, 19). Plate 20 illustrates the development in the Durham Gospels of zoomorphic finials inside the pen-spirals in passages of Celtic curvilinear ornaments, a feature not seen in the Lindisfarne Gospels or the Book of Durrow (and of course not in Echternach, which avoids animal

---

[13] Alexander, pls. 74 and 75.
[14] Both well seen in *Cod. Lind.* II, pl. 7, Alexander, pls. 48, 51 and 52.
[15] Full size in *Cod. Lind.* II, pl. 6; also Alexander, pls. 48, 51 and 52.
[16] *Cod. Lind.* II, ch. 8 and figs. 58 and 59.

12. Maze-design in ink from the ornament at the bottom of the double-vertical stroke to the left of the IN monogram on fol. 177r of the Echternach Gospels. (Approximately 6:1.)

ornament altogether). It is a zoomorphization evolved from the 'ragged' interior terminals, often with zoomorphic touches, seen in Celtic metalwork of around AD 600 as in hanging-bowl escutcheons.[17] This is among the late features of A.II.17, as is the development (from its relatively naturalistic stage in the Lindisfarne Gospels) of the bird theme, with long stringy necks and other stylizations, which adds to the picture of Durham as a manuscript appreciably later than Lindisfarne.

[17] E.g. Rupert Bruce-Mitford, *The Sutton Hoo Ship-burial*, vol. III, i (London, 1983), figs. 162 163, 169; Richard B. Warner, 'Ireland and the Origins of Escutcheon Art,' in *Ireland and Insular Art A.D. 500 – 1200*, ed. Michael Ryan (Dublin: Royal Irish Academy, 1987), pp. 19 – 22, esp. fig. 1. Also the well-known disc from Lougham Island, River Bann, Co. Derry (ibid., p. 18, pl. III).

Finally there is the claim made by Brown and myself jointly that the man symbol (*imago hominis*) of Echternach and the Crucifixion miniature in Durham A.II.17 are by the same hand (pls. 9, 10).[18] There is no point in repeating here the detailed case for this made out in the facsimile edition of the Lindisfarne Gospels, which seems to me unaffected by such criticism, if we can call it that, as has yet appeared. The two miniatures need to be studied in the original. The fine pen-work and delicate drawing is particularly compelling (*Cod. Lind.* II, pls. 8 and 9). Dr Coatsworth, in her account of the decoration of A.II.17 in the fine facsimile edition of the Durham Gospels, wrote of the Crucifixion miniature:

> Every feather, strip, or fold, as well as the frames and borders of the cross, is edged with a fine double contour, within which the vellum is unpainted. The fine drawing and pen and ink work are more prominent and detailed than in many insular illustrations; and the miniature is better regarded as a pen-and-ink drawing to which colour has been added than primarily as a painting.[19]

Apart from the fact that double contouring is used in Durham and single in Echternach, this can also be said of the Echternach man symbol. George Henderson, in an important new book, says of these two miniatures:

> The extraordinary faces and features and tiny feet of the *Imago hominis* of Echternach and the Christ on the Cross in Durham are the same; and so, too, is the abstract treatment of dress. There is in these two images, Matthew's man, and Christ Crucified, the same intensely spiritual quality of illustration.[20]

On the question of whether the two manuscripts are by the same hand he seems to preserve an open mind. To Brown's detailed commentary on the two miniatures, I added a series of further points, and concluded:

> It is very difficult, after intimate study, for anyone who is sensitive to individuality and to touch, to feel that these two figures are not the work of the same hand. I accept the argument that the two miniatures are by the same artist.[21]

It cannot be said that this potentially important discovery, or claim, has been received with much enthusiasm. It was too much for my friend Françoise Henry, to whom Nordenfalk has referred, because of her passionate belief in

---

[18] *Cod. Lind.* II, pp. 102, 247; see also the full-page illustrations of the two pages *en face*, pls. 8 and 9.

[19] *The Durham Gospels*, ed. C. D. Verey, T. J. Brown and E. Coatsworth, with an appendix by R. Powell (EEMF 20; Copenhagen, 1980). Maze, spiral and rhomboid patterns are well illustrated in *Cod. Lind.* II, pl. 50 a-c, e; also Henderson (see note 12), figs. 79, 85.

[20] Henderson, op. cit., pp. 76–8.

[21] *Cod. Lind.* II, p. 247, col. 2.

the primacy of Ireland, as the *Jeanne d'Arc* of Irish Art.[22] In her review-article on the commentary volume of *Codex Lindisfarnensis* she wrote:

> Here intervenes one of those disastrous comparisons which can ruin an argument. We are shown, on two opposite pages, the Echternach Matthew symbol and the Durham Crucifixion and are asked to believe that they are by the same hand. Though small details are cited, it is enough to stand back and view the two illuminations in their general appearance to be convinced that they cannot possibly be due to the same man.[23]

Reading these words again I am reminded of Nordenfalk's own response to Meyer Schapiro's detailed critique of his derivation of the Echternach Gospels evangelist symbols from those of the Florence *Diatessaron*, 'his sophisticated arguments fail to make me distrust the simple evidence of my own eyes.'[24]

Dr Henry's gut reaction is not unlike that of one who might find himself looking at, side by side, a painting of Picasso's Blue Period and one of his guitar-player series — or *Guernica*, or *Les Demoiselles d'Avignon*, dismissing out of hand that they could be the work of the same artist. It is a pity that Dr Henry only 'stood back' and never got to grips with the substance of the matter. Other eminent commentators have disagreed more judiciously. Dr J. J. G. Alexander wrote:

> [Brown] suggests that scribe and artist [of Echternach] are one, and the close connection between script and illumination, for example the script on the Man's book (f. 18ᵛ), and the inscriptions on all the symbol pages, makes this plausible (cf. Eadfrith, the scribe/artist of the Lindisfarne Gospels, no. 9). It is less easy, however, to accept that the artist of the Durham Gospel Book is the same as the artist here.[25]

And

> though the crucifixion miniature is so damaged that its original style and quality are not easy to judge . . . it seems to lack the taut dynamism of the Echternach Gospel Book's symbol pages . . . . It is difficult to accept that both are by the same artist.[26]

The 'taut dynamism' of the Echternach symbols lies largely in the clever design of the frames around the creatures, a factor that does not apply to the

---

[22] C. Nordenfalk, 'One Hundred and Fifty Years of Varying Views on the Early Insular Gospel-books', *Ireland and Insular Art A.D. 500–1200* (see note 17), p. 2, col. 2.

[23] F. Henry, 'The Lindisfarne Gospels', *Antiquity* 37 (1963), p. 104.

[24] Nordenfalk, art. cit., p. 5.

[25] Alexander, p. 43, col. 1.

[26] Ibid., p. 41, col. 2.

Crucifixion miniature because of the subject and the quite different iconographic milieu from which it was taken.

Nordenfalk has commented:

> . . . apart from the symbol of St Matthew in the Echternach Gospels being probably by a different artist than those of the other Evangelists, the two [the Echternach symbol and the Durham Crucifixion] differ too obviously in style, particularly in the treatment of the drapery, to be by the same hand.[27]

This seems to me to beg the question. There is, I believe, nothing in the claim that the man symbol is by a different hand from the other symbols,[28] and 'obvious differences' are what we started from. The matter is better concentrated in arguments such as Julian Brown's, that the majuscule, the display script, the decorative drawing and the figure drawing in Echternach and Durham 'show a degree of likeness better explained by identity of hand than by mere community of training',[29] and upon the details of the evidence for the identity of scribe and illuminator in both manuscripts, adduced by both Julian Brown and myself.[30] Reconsideration in 1987 leaves me with the conviction that our case for the identity of hand in the Durham and Echternach Gospels remains sound. If this be so, then the 'Durham-Echternach Calligrapher', as a personality, survives also. Whether he worked at Iona, or at 'Rath Melsigi' or Lindisfarne, or Echternach itself, or elsewhere, is a different issue.

There is a proviso I would wish to insert here. Our two manuscripts should be subjected also to close comparison with certain other manuscripts which Julian Brown, I think, and certainly I myself, had not the time, amongst the pressure of official duties and from the publisher, to subject to as close an examination as we would have wished. Françoise Henry made the point in her

---

[27] Nordenfalk, art. cit., p. 3.

[28] The uncharacteristic use of dark red and purple in the man figure, making a strong structural pattern, employs the purple *'folium'* (*Cod. Lind.* II, pp. 268 – 70) seen on the lion symbol folio. But the pen work is identical in all four symbols. The treatment of the drapery may be explained by the treatment of man as symbol, and the use of an entirely different sort of model and approach for the Crucifixion (cf. the difference in drapery treatment and style between the Ezra figure in the Codex Amiatinus and that of the figures in the Christ-majesty miniature, both by the same hand: R. Bruce-Mitford, 'The Art of the Codex Amiatinus', *Journal of the British Archaeological Association* 32 (1969) = Jarrow Lecture 1968). The man symbol model could well have been a sculptured figure from the Roman Wall: cf. the Tullie House Museum, Carlisle, mother-goddess figure (*Cod. Lind.* II, pl. 19a) for heavy schematization of dress; even the cluster of fruit held by the mother-goddess figure is akin to the otherwise incongruous rosette in the lap of the Echternach figure. See also the striking analogy between the Durrow man symbol from the four-symbol page which (*pace* Henderson, *From Durrow to Kells*, p. 43, and Meyer cit. ibid. in note 106) never had feet, and the Neptune figure from the Roman pavement from Withington, Gloucestershire, which shares also the inset sideways profile of the arm in a fully frontal figure.

[29] Brown, *ASE* 1, p. 227.

[30] *Cod. Lind.*, loc. cit.

review-article on *Codex Lindisfarnensis*,[31] in relation to our view of the Lindisfarne scriptorium; though from the point of view of establishing the existence, or otherwise, of the 'Durham-Echternach calligrapher' some of the comparisons she urged (e.g. of the Lindisfarne Gospels with the Gospels of St Chad (Lichfield) and the monogram-leaf Rawlinson MS G 167 in the Bodleian) seem less relevant to our purpose than Cologne, Dombibliotek MS 213 and the Gospel book, Cambridge, Corpus Christi College MS 197 together with London, British Library, Cotton MS Otho C.V, which has a very close relationship with the Durham Gospels.[32]

It seems to me that the existence (or otherwise) of the 'Durham-Echternach calligrapher' is not a matter of predilection, or probabilities, or gut reaction, or the construction of more plausible scenarios, but of evidence. Either the observations so carefully made on palaeographical and art-historical detail, by so careful and experienced an expert as Julian Brown, supported by myself, stand; or they do not. It is a matter for the exacting application of the palaeographical and art-historical disciplines and criteria. The case should not be cold-shouldered,[33] but either refuted, or else accepted, in its own terms.

Lastly, is there adequate ground for attributing either of our manuscripts to Lindisfarne? This seems to me less strongly based or certain than that the two are by the same hand. We know that the Durham Gospels was with the Lindisfarne community by the tenth century[34] which of itself proves nothing; but to this we add Christopher Verey's observation that the Lindisfarne Gospels and the Durham Gospels were both corrected by the same hand, before the Durham Gospels were rubricated. In making this claim Verey himself pointed out that it did not of itself prove that the manuscripts were originally written in the same scriptorium.[35] Correctors and manuscripts may both be itinerant. Nevertheless, combined with the early ownership of the

---

[31] Henry, *Antiquity* 37. Her comments on p. 104 suggest that Dr Henry did not grasp the reason for the inclusion in *Cod. Lind.* of a colour plate (pl. XVII) devoted to details from items in the Sutton Hoo treasure (cf. also Henderson, op. cit., illns. 27 – 31). The purpose was to show the vigour and trend of the metalworking tradition and the remarkable skills and design sense to be found in an Anglo-Saxon royal context already eighty or more years before the production of the Lindisfarne Gospels (the prevailing view at the time of writing was that the ship-burial dated from the 650s, not *c.*625 as is now established). Françoise Henry might have noted that five of the illustrations were of details of the large hanging-bowl, a piece which she was convinced was of Irish manufacture — a provenance which I did not exclude in my subsequent study of the bowl in *The Sutton Hoo Ship-burial* III, i, pp. 293 – 5, though I thought a north-British origin more likely. The plate and commentary were also used to show that the process of fusion of Celtic and Germanic craft-traditions had already begun as early as the first quarter of the century, in a pagan context.

[32] For illustrations see Alexander, and Henderson, *From Durrow to Kells*. The MSS are well surveyed in Henderson, op. cit., ch. 3 (pp. 57 – 97), 'The Durham Corpus and Echternach Gospels with minor fragments', but a more minute and detailed analysis of the originals is called for.

[33] Cf. Brown, *ASE* 1, p. 224.

[34] Cf. Alexander, p. 41, col. 2.

[35] Appendix to Brown, 'Northumbria and the Book of Kells' (*ASE* 1), p. 244.

manuscripts by the community, and the demonstration by Verey that the text of A.II.17 is a good Vulgate text belonging to the mixed Italian tradition and that Lowe was incorrect in describing it as Irish, and the strong palaeographical and art-historical links already discussed, the probability is surely that the Durham Gospels was there when the corrections were made.[36]

With regard to the Echternach Gospels and its origins, if the date of AD *c.*690 – 700 or shortly after for its creation is correct,[37] then we can at least say that it was not made at Iona. The very unusual and careful depiction in its man symbol of the Roman tonsure (pl. 9) certainly could not have been carried out there before 716 – 18 when Ecgberht, Willibrord's sponsor (for whom Henderson claims a key role in the cultural development of the period[38]), persuaded this last-ditch centre of resistance to change over to the Roman Easter and the Roman tonsure. As it happens, however, at precisely the date envisaged by Julian Brown as a context for the making of the Echternach Gospels (698, the year of Echternach's foundation), we find the Roman tonsure depicted in the same restrained style on St Peter, alone amongst the apostles and archangels, on St Cuthbert's coffin.[39]

We do not know what purity or mix of scribal traditions may have been maintained or developed in the essentially Anglo-Saxon monastic community at Rath Melsigi from which Willibrord, trained initially at Ripon under Wilfrid, set out on his Frisian mission;[40] nor do we have the full picture of the links which Ecgberht and his community there, as we know, maintained with Northumbria. But this monastery in County Carlow, if correctly identified,[41]

---

[36] Though manuscripts may have travelled, the Lindisfarne Gospels at least never left Lindisfarne. W. J. O'Sullivan has expressed his disagreement with Verey over the identity of the correcting hands, as well as otherwise criticizing the cases for the 'Durham/Echternach Calligrapher' and the attribution of either MS to Lindisfarne (William O'Sullivan, 'Insular Calligraphy, Current State and Problems', *Peritia* 4 (1985), pp. 346 – 59). A great deal has recently appeared on these matters, most notably the historian's revision by Ó Cróinín of the affiliations of the Echternach foundation and of Willibrord, and the status and affinities of the monastery (identified as Rath Melsigi) from which Willibrord set out on his Frisian mission. I cannot review the relevant part of this body of literature here, but I am fully cognizant of it.

[37] As concluded by Julian Brown and myself (*Cod. Lind.*, loc. cit.) and I think as generally accepted.

[38] Op. cit., pp. 91 ff.

[39] See E. Kitzinger, 'The Coffin-Reliquary', in *Relics*, pp. 202 – 304, esp. pp. 265 – 7. See also Henderson, op. cit., pp. 75, 95 – 6 and pls. 166 – 8; and J. Higgitt, below, pp. 267 – 85, and plate 44 and figs. 19, 21, this volume.

[40] Dáibhí Ó Cróinín, 'Rath Melsigi, Willibrord and the Earliest Echternach Manuscripts', *Peritia* 3 (1984), pp. 17 – 49; cf. pp. 32 – 3: 'Hence Rath Melsigi emerges clearly as the real source of inspiration for this Anglo-Saxon missionary effort in the seventh and eighth centuries. But not only did it provide the personnel for these undertakings, it must also have provided at least a few of the manuscripts for the initial missionaries and the scribal expertise required to produce further ones.'

[41] Henderson, *From Durrow to Kells*, p. 94, col. 1, prefers the hitherto-accepted view that it was Mayo where the Anglo-Saxon contingent which left Lindisfarne in 664 settled. (See also his footnote 79).

would hardly have been exposed to the direct and fresh Wearmouth/Jarrow influences that made so strong an impact at Lindisfarne. The Italianate features of the Echternach Gospels, among them its setting out the text in two columns to the page, *per cola et commata* (like the Lindisfarne Gospels and the Codex Amiatinus), the palaeographical links between it and the Lindisfarne Gospels shown up by Julian Brown,[42] its Pictish elements, stressed by Henderson (for Lindisfarne also had its Pictish connections); its delicate pastel colours and pigmentation for the *c.*690 – 700 date, the unfaltering discipline and 'sobriety' (Lowe's expression) of its ornament, and even its a-typical vellum,[43] make a Northumbrian origin for the Echternach Gospels much more plausible than one in County Carlow. To this we may add its observed close affinities with the Durham Gospels, whose links with St Cuthbert's community of Lindisfarne have been discussed above. Altogether, a Lindisfarne provenance for the Echternach Gospels seems to me entirely likely.

Henderson has envisaged the Irishman Ultan, referred to in a ninth-century poem *De abbatibus*, as creator of the Lichfield Gospels, otherwise known as the Gospels of St Chad.[44] To suit this proposition he is inclined to give the Lichfield Gospels a date earlier than the AD 730 suggested by Wendy Stein in her doctoral thesis devoted to this manuscript. I see that, when the whole subject was fresh in my mind, 730 was the date I too preferred for St Chad's Gospels.[45] It now seems to me, from the advanced degree of its decorative evolution,[46] that 730 would be the very earliest date for it. I have not had the benefit of reading Dr Stein's thesis. I feel, however, because of what I take to be a certain slackness or lack of quality in the decoration of St Chad's Gospels, in spite of its richness and ambitious planning, that it is simply not good enough to qualify for the accolade given to Ultan, if this be taken at its face value. Chad seems to me well below the level of artistic achievement of the Durham Gospels. It shows a tendency to run to seed. Stein was quite right in noticing a provincial quality about it. If one is to match up Ultan, the super-

---

[42] *Cod. Lind.* II, e.g. pp. 97 – 9.

[43] Not referred to in Alexander. There seems to be some confusion on the subject of Insular or continental vellum and its preparation and significance. Both the Lindisfarne Gospels and the Codex Amiatinus are calfskin, not sheepskin as stated by O'Sullivan, *Peritia* 4, p. 353: see R. Bruce-Mitford, *The Art of the Codex Amiatinus* (Jarrow Lecture 1968, published also in *Journal of the British Archaeological Association* 32 (1969), pp. 1 – 25), pp. 1, 2.

[44] *From Durrow to Kells*, p. 126.

[45] R. L. S. Bruce-Mitford, 'The early Gospel Book in the British Isles with special reference to the Gospels of St Chad', *30th Annual Report of the Friends of Llandaff Cathedral*, April 1962 – March 1963, pp. 16 – 20, esp. p. 18. Dr W. A. Stein's thesis ('The Lichfield Gospels', unpublished Ph.D. thesis, University of California, Berkeley, 1980) is cited by Henderson, op. cit., pp. 126 – 7.

[46] *Cod. Lind.* II, pp. 257 – 8 and pls. 50g, 53d and 54.

scribe, with such manuscripts as survive, I would think it more appropriate to attribute to him the Durham Gospels,[47] and so pose the question, if our Durham-Echternach Calligrapher existed, as I believe he did, could he not be Ultan?[48] Like the Irish Tuda, bishop of Lindisfarne, he would be an Irishman who had accepted the Roman usage.[49]

[47] The decoration of the Lichfield Gospels, it seems to me, like that of Kells, is not all by one hand. Apart from this, in spite of its fine carpet-page, it seems to lack the inspiration that there is in every line and every ornamental detail in the Echternach and Durham Gospels. It seems to me, by comparison, derivative, and repetitive of established formulas without feeling. Stein speaks of 'provincial qualities in the book's excessively regular script and slightly clumsy figures' (*absit* Ultan!) (Henderson, loc. cit). Alexander, weighing options with regard to the provenance of the Durham Gospels, says of the latter: 'The interlaced lacertine animals can be compared to those in the Lindisfarne Gospels, however, and support the attribution . . . to the Lindisfarne scriptorium made on paleographical and textual grounds' (p. 41). More significant perhaps for a Northumbrian origin (rather than Iona) may be the appearance, in Anglian contexts, of stylistic prototypes or embryonic forms of this Durham animal type, e.g. on the Franks Casket, with the distinctive knob on the end of the jaws, and in the long straight jaws of the animal heads on the porch doorway at Monkwearmouth (Henderson, illns. 38 – 9). The simple canon tables of the Echternach Gospels with their delicate and subtly-balanced use of the yellow and orange colours employed, are reminiscent in this respect of the tables, of quite different form (architectural arcades) of the Codex Amiatinus (*Cod. Lind.* II, pl. 34; Bruce-Mitford, *The Art of the Codex Amiatinus* (as n. 42 above)). As Alexander rightly says (p. 42): 'The aesthetic seems comparable to the Book of Lindisfarne.'
[48] Ultan, the Irishman — in a new monastery near Lindisfarne, founded in the eighth century — whose mastery of the illuminative art was such that no modern scribe could equal him (according to Aethelwulf's poem *De abbatibus*, composed between 802 and 821), is on the crest of a wave just now. Apart from Dr Henry's earlier championship of him, see now Ó Cróinín, 'Pride and Prejudice', p. 362; Ó Cróinín, 'Rath Melsigi', p. 37; Henderson, op. cit., p. 97. The founder of the new, unidentified, monastic house went for advice to Eadfrith, bishop of Lindisfarne, himself the master scribe-illuminator of the Lindisfarne Gospels, and obtained from him, *inter alia*, a teacher to instruct his monks (Ó Cróinín, 'Rath Melsigi', p. 36). I can see no objection to the scenario that Ultan might have moved to the new house from Lindisfarne on the recommendation of Eadfrith, perhaps to take charge of its scriptorium; that the Echternach Gospels was an early Lindisfarne example of his skills; that he produced the Durham Gospels in the new scriptorium in the 720s; and that the mother-house might have commissioned from Ultan this masterpiece, or later, in circumstances of which we are ignorant, re-absorbed the library of its daughter-house. The corrector could have worked in both establishments. On this showing, Ultan would himself be the 'Durham-Echternach Calligrapher'. That he should be an Irishman is of no particular consequence. He must have been a man of exceptional talent and sensibility; but beyond that it is essentially a matter of scriptorium tradition, discipline, training and technique. As I light-heartedly expressed it in my study of the methods and principles of construction of the Insular ornament in *Cod. Lind.*, 'once the principles have been absorbed, anyone (with sufficient will and application) whether Celt, Saxon or Australian aborigine, can achieve the most complex-looking Hiberno-Saxon designs of every type' (*Cod. Lind.* II, ch. 8, quoted by F. Henry, *Antiquity* 37, p. 105). The racial issue seems irrelevant. There is really no reason to postulate that Ultan was sent to his new cell of Lindisfarne by Ecgberht from Rath Melsigi (Henderson, p. 129), and it is surely more likely that he came from the great scriptorium of the mother-house, at the peak of excellence and creativity demonstrated by the Lindisfarne Gospels, on the advice and with the encouragement of Eadfrith.
[49] Henderson, *From Durrow to Kells*, p. 54.

Is the Augsburg Gospel Codex
a Northumbrian Manuscript?

DÁIBHÍ Ó CRÓINÍN

In the famous essay which he prefaced to his description of Insular manuscripts from before AD 800 now in Insular libraries, E. A. Lowe remarked that 'the historic struggle between Irish and Roman parties over liturgical questions which came to a head at the Council of Whitby in 664 resulted in a victory for Rome, but the less spectacular victory went to the Irish. It is indelibly inscribed upon the manuscripts of England, for the script which was destined to remain for centuries the national hand of England is not immediately Roman but Irish in origin.'[1] Although the debate still goes on about the respective contributions of the Irish and the Anglo-Saxons to the development of Insular art and manuscript illumination, that basic underlying point of Lowe's remains sound; in the words of the late (and sorely missed) Julian Brown: 'Until 669, then, Anglo-Saxon England was a cultural province of Ireland, and evidently a province in which Latin learning flourished much less vigorously than in Ireland itself.'[2]

This was the cultural and social climate into which Cuthbert was born and in which he received his early education, and the churches in Northumbria during his youth were very like the churches in Ireland in their organization, their interests, and their aims.[3] Indeed, so similar were some aspects of the common experience that some Irishmen in the twelfth century seem to have convinced themselves that Cuthbert was one of their own, and tried to

---

[1] E. A. Lowe, *CLA* II, p. xiv.

[2] T. J. Brown, 'An historical introduction to the use of classical Latin authors in the British Isles from the fifth to the eleventh century', in *La Cultura antica nell'occidente latino dal VII all' XI secolo: Settimane di Studio del Centro Italiano di Studi sull' Alto Medioevo* 22 (2 vols.; Spoleto, 1975), pp. 237 – 299, at pp. 253 – 4. (A very valuable study.)

[3] See especially Eric John, 'The social and political problems of the early English church', in *Land, church, and people: essays for H. P. R. Finberg*, ed. Joan Thirsk (*Agricultural History Review* 18, supplement; Reading, 1970), pp. 39 – 63.

persuade fellow churchmen in England that this was so.[4] In this Cuthbert commemorative volume, therefore, it is entirely appropriate that another look be taken at that particular aspect of the Hiberno-Saxon world and its culture, namely its script, which Lowe discussed but never, unfortunately, elaborated on. It is greatly to be regretted that neither he nor Lindsay before him ever presented their views on the subject in substantial monograph form, and that their successor in the field, Julian Brown, was denied the opportunity to publish a synthesis of the researches with which he had done so much to reshape and refine the earlier picture.[5]

The modern critical study of Insular manuscript illumination, and of the Insular Gospel books in particular, can be traced back to the publication of Ernst Heinrich Zimmermann's great collection *Vorkarolingische Miniaturen*, which appeared in four portfolio volumes at Berlin in 1916.[6] Many of the received opinions which are still being published concerning early Insular manuscripts and their histories were first voiced by Zimmermann, and I think it is fair to say that the rough chronology of these manuscripts mapped out by Zimmermann is that which still holds the field to this day.[7] Some emendations and corrections of his views have, of course, been made in the seventy years since his work appeared, but for the most part, Zimmermann's survey set a decisive pattern and its influence is to be seen particularly in E. A. Lowe's great multi-volume survey of Latin manuscripts before AD 800.

---

[4] See the 'Irish' Life of St Cuthbert by Laurence of Durham, *Libellus de nativitate sancti Cuthberti*, preface and chs. 1 and 29; ed. James Raine in *Miscellanea Biographica* (SS 8; London and Edinburgh, 1838), pp. 63 – 5, 86 – 7: 'Quia maximis viris et nonnullis Hybernensium episcopis perorantibus de beati Cuthberti natalibus praeclara quaedam audivimus . . . Eugenius Hardmoniae episcopus quaedam distinctius annexuit; sed et duo alii episcopi quorum jam nomina exciderunt, una cum sociis ipsorum presbyteris et clericis sub diverso tempore nostris uberius in auribus infuderunt.' This was taken by Laurence 'de Scottorum paginis et scriptis'. Text cited and discussed by Denis Bethell, 'English Monks and Irish Reform in the Eleventh and Twelfth Centuries', in T. D. Williams (ed.), *Historical Studies: Papers read before the Irish Conference of Historians* 8 (Dublin, 1971), pp. 111 – 135 at p. 123 and n. 79. Such claims for Cuthbert's Irish birth were still being made in the august pages of the *Irish Ecclesiastical Record* a century ago! See John Healy, 'Was St. Cuthbert an Irishman?', *Irish Ecclesiastical Record* 9 (1888), pp. 1 – 16, 110 – 118. For more recent treatment of the question, see Paul Grosjean, 'The alleged Irish origin of St Cuthbert', in *Relics*, pp. 144 – 54, and Richard Sharpe, 'Were the Irish annals known to a twelfth-century Northumbrian writer?', *Peritia* 2 (1983), pp. 137 – 39. Sharpe seems to think the author was Reginald of Durham.

[5] See W. M. Lindsay, 'Irish cursive script', *Zeitschrift für celtische Philologie* 9 (1913), pp. 301 – 8. Brown presented his views in the James P. R. Lyell Lectures in Bibliography, delivered to the University of Oxford in 1977 under the title 'The Insular System of Scripts, circa 600 – circa 850'; unfortunately, the lectures were never published in their entirety.

[6] E. H. Zimmermann, *Vorkarolingische Miniaturen*. Denkmäler Deutscher Kunst 3/1, Sektion Malerei (4 vols. of plates + 1 vol. text; Berlin, 1916).

[7] It is perhaps worth pointing out that the potentially revolutionary proposal by William O'Sullivan, 'Insular calligraphy: current state and problems', *Peritia* 4 (1985), pp. 346 – 359 at pp. 353 – 354, that the Book of Durrow be redated to the eighth century, was anticipated by Zimmermann; cf. *Vorkarolingische Miniaturen*, p. 95.

It was Zimmermann who first drew scholarly attention to the corpus of manuscripts from Echternach (in Luxembourg),[8] now housed mainly at Paris,[9] and demonstrated the existence at Echternach in the eighth century of a lively, thoroughly Insular production which survived even up to Carolingian times. The evidence for this lay in two great Gospel codices, the so-called Echternach Gospels (Paris, Bibl. Nat., MS lat. 9389) and the Harburg/Maihingen Gospels (now at Augsburg), together with a dozen or so other manuscripts of the same provenance and a third Gospel book, Trier, Domschatz, MS 61 (134),[10] written in part by an artist-scribe brought up in Echternach traditions.

Zimmermann was criticized, however, by another great scholar, Carl Nordenfalk, for discussing this corpus under the rubric of 'pre-Carolingian illuminating in Echternach', maintaining — correctly, as it happens — that this terminology was misleading in so far as 'it suppresses the important fact that the school was founded on the other side of the Channel'.[11] More importantly, Nordenfalk took issue with Zimmermann's proposed dating of these manuscripts, on the very good grounds that Zimmermann made the whole chronology of Insular illumination dependent upon that of the Echternach manuscripts — a fatal decision, which has dogged all subsequent discussion of the problem. Zimmermann, for example, proposed a date in the latter third of the eighth century[12] for the Augsburg Gospels, a date which I think most would agree is hopelessly late.[13] On the other hand, Nordenfalk's alternative dating, to the 730s,[14] is, I think, still out by roughly a generation.

These Echternach manuscripts are doubly important because they provide the crucial link between the earliest Irish codices and the group of Insular illuminated Gospel books known to us as the Book of Durrow, the Book of Lindisfarne, the Lichfield/Chad Gospels, the Durham Gospels, and the Book

---

[8] *Vorkarolingische Miniaturen*, pp. 122 – 9.

[9] See Hermann Degering, 'Handschriften aus Echternach und Orval in Paris', in *Aufsätze Fritz Milkau gewidmet*, ed. Georg Ley (Leipzig, 1921), pp. 48 – 85.

[10] See now Nancy D. Netzer, 'The Trier Gospels (Trier Domschatz MS 61): Text, Construction, Script, and Illustration' (unpublished Ph.D. thesis, Harvard University, 1987; available from University Microfilms International). This is the most important contribution to the debate for a decade or more.

[11] Carl Nordenfalk, 'On the age of the earliest Echternach manuscripts', *Acta Archaeologica* 3 (Copenhagen, 1932), pp. 57 – 62 at p. 59.

[12] *Vorkarolingische Miniaturen*, p. 126: 'Die karolingischen Vögel auf den unteren Ablauf der Initiale *In* und dem Akrostichon sollten allein schon davon abhalten, den Kodex früh zu datieren', contra Lindsay, whom he cites as proposing an early date on account of the double abbreviation stroke used throughout the Augsburg Gospels.

[13] Lowe's date in *CLA* VIII, no. 1215, is '*saec.* VIII[1]'.

[14] 'To us a dating of the Maihingen [Gospels] to the 730's is most satisfactory, and therefore of Paris [i.e. the Echternach Gospels] to the period before or about 700, the Book of Durrow to the middle of the 600's'. ('The earliest Echternach MSS', p. 60.)

of Kells.[15] What singles out the Echternach manuscripts in this field is the fact that the most important of them can be securely dated. Four in particular form a group within this corpus and I give here the brief description of them published by Julian Brown in the facsimile volume of the Lindisfarne Gospels.[16]

1. *The Kalendar of St. Willibrord*, Paris, B.N. lat. 10837, ff. 34 to 41, 44; *CLA* V, no. 606a. This was Willibrord's personal Kalendar and contains a note in his own hand written in 728 (f. 39[v]) . . . In the Paschal Table for the years 703 – 21 written by the first hand on f. 40[v], the year 717 is marked with a cross, but Wilson [the editor] shows that to judge by certain additions to the Kalendar it was probably written between 703 and *circa* 710. Lowe describes it as 'written at an Anglo-Saxon centre on the Continent, probably at Echternach by the scribe of the Maihingen Gospels'.

2. *The Maihingen Gospels*, once at Maihingen, now at Harburg, Fürstlich Öttingen-Wallersteinsche Bibl. I.2.4°2; Zimmermann, pp. 125 – 6, 279 – 80, pls. 260 – 6. This Gospel-book appears, as Lowe says, to have been written by the same hand as Willibrord's Kalendar, and certainly came from Echternach. The date can hardly be later than about 730 – 40, and may well be earlier, if the Kalendar dates from 703 to *circa* 710. An acrostic (f. 157[v]) on the words 'Laurentius uiuat senio' could refer, as W. M. Lindsay saw [*Notae Latinae* (Cambridge 1915) 473], either to the scribe or to the head of the scriptorium.

3. *The Echternach Martyrology*, Paris, B.N. lat. 10837, ff. 2 to 33; *CLA* V, no. 605. Dated by Lowe '*saec. VIII in.*', and certainly written before the death and deposition of St Willibrord in 739, which are recorded in the margin of f. 28[v]. The scribe, Laurentius, signed the MS. on f. 32[v].

4. *Prophets* (Jeremiah-Malachi), Paris, B.N. lat. 9382; *CLA* V, no. 577. Lowe dates the MS. '*saec. VIII in.*' and says that it was 'written doubtless in the same centre as the [Kalendar] and the Maihingen Gospels, presumably at Echternach'. A colophon in verse by a scribe named Vergilius is on f. 45[v].

These four manuscripts were classified by Brown (and by Lowe before him) as quintessentially Northumbrian, and one of them, the Calendar of Willibrord, was singled out by Lowe as providing a touchstone for Northumbrian calligraphy at the turn of the eighth century: 'If [the student] wants examples of authentic English performance [he wrote] he must go to the Lindisfarne Gospels and the Codex Epternachensis, to St. Willibrord's Calendar and Martyrology . . . and to the Moore Bede. There he will find his criteria for Northumbrian calligraphy'.[17] The reasons for regarding the group as Northumbrian, according to Brown, were of three kinds: 'First, Willibrord's own background was almost purely Northumbrian, and in the

---

[15] On the importance of the Echternach manuscripts, and of Northumbrian manuscripts generally, for the establishment of developments in Irish script in the seventh century, see O'Sullivan, 'Insular calligraphy', cited n. 7 above.

[16] *Cod. Lind.* II, pp. 90 – 1.

[17] *CLA* II, pp. xvi – xvii.

early days of his mission close contact with Northumbria was maintained. Secondly, much of the contents of the Kalendar and Martyrology are derived from Northumbria. Thirdly, the Echternach MSS. are palaeographically linked to certain Northumbrian MSS'.[18]

At this point I must interpolate a bit of personal history. I published a review of the Durham Gospels facsimile some five years ago in *Peritia*, Journal of the Medieval Academy of Ireland,[19] a review which in hindsight I realize had too much criticism and too little praise for the very fine work that went into that volume.[20] Nevertheless, the basic points which were advanced in the review as a critique of the 'Lindisfarne theory' seemed valid to me then, and still seem so now. I elaborated on my views in a subsequent article in the same journal,[21] and since one recent writer has described my views as 'interesting but tendentious'[22] I suppose I am expected to say something by way of reply. There are some things which I think it is necessary to say, and I shall try to say them as dispassionately as I can.

The gist of my argument was (and is) that the community at Echternach came to that monastery not from England — as Lowe and others persistently stated — but from Ireland. The fact of the matter is that Willibrord and his eleven companions reached Frisia from Ireland, where Willibrord at least had been resident for twelve years prior to his departure on the continental mission. The Frisian mission of the English was an Irish-based undertaking from the start, for the earliest missionary from Rath Melsigi was Wihtberht, who left Ireland sometime in the 680s and after two years' unsuccessful labour returned there (not to Northumbria).[23] Contrary to what Brown stated in the *Lindisfarne* commentary volume, Willibrord's and Wihtberht's background was *not* 'almost purely Northumbrian'; most of their formative years were spent in Ireland. Furthermore, it is clear from Bede's account that the earliest recruits for the continental mission (such as the two Hewalds) also came from

---

[18] *Cod. Lind.* II, p. 91. The 'Northumbrian MSS.' referred to are Cambridge, Corpus Christi College, MS 197, Durham, Cathedral Library, MS A.II.17, and the Echternach Gospels. For the palaeographical criteria on which Brown's argument is based, see further below.

[19] D. Ó Cróinín, 'Pride and Prejudice', *Peritia* 1 (1982), pp. 352 – 62.

[20] In conversation with Julian Brown on the subject we had agreed (in principle, at least!) that his proposed reply should be called 'Sense and Sensibility', while my rejoinder was to be called 'Persuasion'! It was characteristic of the man and the scholar that, even in the face of vigorous criticism, he could still see the humorous side of things.

[21] D. Ó Cróinín, 'Rath Melsigi, Willibrord, and the earliest Echternach manuscripts', *Peritia* 3 (1984), pp. 17 – 49.

[22] D. N. Dumville, 'Late seventh- or early eighth-century evidence for the British transmission of Pelagius', *Cambridge Medieval Celtic Studies* 10 (Winter 1985), pp. 39 – 52 at p. 40 n. 9.

[23] For a slightly different interpretation of some of the evidence see Hermann Moisl, 'Das Kloster Iona und seine Verbindungen mit dem Kontinent im siebenten und achten Jahrhundert', in *Virgil von Salzburg: Missionar und Gelehrter*, ed. Heinz Dopsch and Roswitha Juffinger (Salzburg, 1985), pp. 27 – 37. However, Moisl's case for Ecgberht's connection with Mayo seems to me to strain the evidence. That Ecgberht was in some association with the Anglo-Saxon house there can be readily accepted, but Moisl understates the importance of Rath Melsigi.

Ireland, not from Northumbria. Hence I wrote in my review of the Durham Gospels that 'If I were looking for a source of spiritual and material supply for Echternach I would look not to Lindisfarne but to the English settlement at Ráth Maélsigi in Ireland.'[24]

These views seem to have caused something of a stir,[25] but the material concerning Rath Melsigi is almost all in Bede and is not the product of my imagination. Indeed, the principal of Rath Melsigi, Bishop Ecgberht, could be described as one of the leading characters in Bede's *History*, and Bede relates in considerable detail how Ecgberht had spent many years already in Ireland when the Great Plague struck in AD 664. Ecgberht vowed that, if he were spared, he would never again return to his homeland but would devote the remaining years of his life to a spiritual and physical exile. Ecgberht was saved, as it happens, and he lived to the grand old age of ninety, dying on 24 April 729 on Iona.

Bede tells how Ecgberht had conceived the desire to go and preach the Gospel to the continental Germans, but then two prophetic visions were revealed to him by a member of the Rath Melsigi community, who had been instructed in his dreams to warn Ecgberht against his plans for the German mission. Ecgberht twice ignored these warnings, but when finally the ship which he had provisioned for the journey was wrecked in a storm he reluctantly decided that his destiny lay elsewhere. He chose instead another of his companions at Rath Melsigi, a certain Wihtberht, who likewise (according to Bede) had spent many years' exile in Ireland. Wihtberht took ship sometime in the 680s (as I remarked above) and after reaching Frisia 'preached the word of life to that nation and to its king, Radbod'. But Radbod was not impressed, and Wihtberht met with no success; after two years he packed it in and returned to Rath Melsigi. Undeterred by this second setback, Ecgberht chose a third candidate, Willibrord, who left Ireland with eleven companions in the year AD 690.[26] 'The rest is history'.

By the time of Willibrord's departure, therefore, Ecgberht had spent at least thirty years in Ireland, and others of the missionary group (such as Wihtberht) may have been there equally long. Willibrord himself had been twelve years there up to AD 690. On the basis of this predominantly Bedan evidence, therefore, I argued that the earliest so-called Echternach manuscripts could quite conceivably have been written at Rath Melsigi rather than at Echternach (or Northumbria, as some would have it). Certainly, the early Echternach scribes must have received their training there. Given that Echternach was founded only in AD 699, and that these early manuscripts, dating from the

---

[24] 'Pride and Prejudice', p. 359.

[25] They have been accepted, however, in Bernhard Bischoff, *Paläographie des römischen Altertums und des abendländischen Mittelalters* (Grundlagen der Germanistik 24; 2nd rev. edn. Berlin, 1986), p. 126.

[26] *HE* III, 27; V, 22; V, 9 (Plummer I, 192 – 3, 346 – 7, 296 – 8; C and M, pp. 312, 552 – 4, 474 – 8).

first years of the eighth century, already display fully-developed Insular half-uncial and minuscule hands, it is impossible to conceive of that script as an indigenous, locally-developed Echternach script. In other words, the Echternach hand is an imported hand; but the question is: imported from where? My answer still is: from Rath Melsigi.

In support of this argument I was able to draw on evidence which is not normally called into play by art historians or archaeologists, that is the evidence of computistics or Easter tables. If we turn to the first item on Brown's list of four Echternach manuscripts, the famous Calendar of Willibrord, we get a good example of this script. Lowe dated the main hand of this manuscript to between the years AD 703 and 721, and pointed out that the hand that wrote the main entries in the Calendar also wrote the Augsburg Gospels; so we have a rough date for that codex as well, i.e. AD 703 – 721.

It is possible, however, to narrow those limits somewhat. Since the *prima manus* commemorates Pope Sergius I (d. 7 September 701) the manuscript clearly cannot have been penned before that date. Absent from the Calendar, on the other hand, is the name of Willibrord's first teacher and mentor, Wilfrid (d. 12 October 709). It is hard to believe that Wilfrid would not be mentioned in Willibrord's own calendar when Wilfrid's biographer, Eddius, describes Willibrord as 'filius eius, in Hripis nutritus, gratia Dei episcopus'.[27] It seems reasonable to infer, therefore, that the main text of the Calendar was penned in the first decade of the eighth century.[28] But we can go one better: bound in with Willibrord's Calendar, on a separate single folio, is an Easter table for the nineteen-year cycle AD 684 – 702. This is found on the recto side of the leaf; there is no continuation of the cycle on the verso, which was originally left blank. To anyone remotely familiar with Easter tables, the only reasonable assumption which can be made is that this one must have been written in or before its initial year, AD 684. Lowe never explained why an Echternach scribe, writing (as he claimed) in the early years of the eighth century, should have bothered to include an outdated Easter table. What possible purpose could such a retrospective cycle have served? The answer, as I stated in my article, is that the table must have been written around AD 684 — in which case it must have been written in Ireland, for Willibrord and his companions were at Rath Melsigi until AD 690. In my review of the Durham Gospels I further conjectured that, given the dates of the table, and its probable provenance, it may in fact have been written for Wihtberht, Willibrord's predecessor on the Frisian mission, who left Rath Melsigi

---

[27] *VW* 26.

[28] A dating technique which I proposed at the Durham conference turned out, on further examination, to be invalid. I wish to thank here especially Dr Jan Gerchow, Historisches Seminar der Albert-Ludwigs Universität, Freiburg im Breisgau, for discussing the question with me and for saving me from error.

sometime in the 680s, only to return two years later, perhaps with this very table. The initial years of the table and of Wihtberht's mission coincide exactly. This still seems to me a reasonable interpretation of the evidence, and nobody to date has produced any plausible argument against it.[29]

If the Easter table for AD 684 – 702 was written at Rath Melsigi we would have an explanation for its inclusion with Willibrord's Calendar, for the table was still valid in AD 690, when Willibrord and his companions left for Frisia; in fact it still had twelve more years to run. But what is most important from our point of view is that the distinctive features of the Echternach script are all there already; the peculiar letter-forms which allowed Lowe, Julian Brown, and others to talk of a 'school' are there to be seen in the headings of the table.[30] Given the obvious family relationship between this hand and the hand of the Calendar and Gospels, it seemed to me five years ago, and it still seems to me now, that this must be the script of Rath Melsigi. That this subsequently became the script of Echternach as well is not in dispute; it seems beyond doubt that some at least of the Rath Melsigi scribes transferred to Echternach, but it may be significant that the names of the two principal scribes, Laurentius and Virgilius, do not appear in charters there before AD 704 and 709 respectively. But what is crucial, to my mind, is that the historical background to these manuscripts, *pace* Lowe and Brown, was *not* 'almost purely Northumbrian'; indeed, I would go so far as to say that there is no evidence to prove that *any* of the Echternach manuscripts was written in Northumbria. If the presumption of Northumbrian origin for the early Echternach manuscripts is seen to rest on little more than an ignorance of the true historical background to the establishment of that monastery (note Lowe's statement, for example, that Willibrord brought the so-called Echternach Gospels with him from England),[31] then the way is left open to the manuscripts to speak for themselves; to my mind they speak for Rath

---

[29] In order to correct a possible misunderstanding, I should state here that I do not now (and never did) maintain that the early Echternach manuscripts were all written at Rath Melsigi. I merely stress that the *script* of those manuscripts must have been developed and perfected there. Given what we know about the personnel there and their place of origin, the only conceivable alternative would seem to be that the script might have come to Rath Melsigi from Ripon, or some other Northumbrian monastery. But there is no evidence to support such a theory. All the evidence, as we have it, points to Rath Melsigi.

[30] Brown, *Cod. Lind.* II, 91 n. 6, referred in particular to the theta-shaped *e*, usually conjoint with the next letter (*CLA* II, no. 125), which occurs in CCCC 197, the Calendar, the Augsburg Gospels, and the Prophets MS.; the open *q* (*CLA* V, no. 605), and the elaborate *q* (*The Calendar of St. Willibrord*, ed. H. A. Wilson (London, 1918), pls. 3, 4) found in the 'decorative minuscule' of Durham A.II.17, the Echternach Gospels, the Martyrology, and the Calendar; and the vertical space-fillers in the Calendar (*CLA* V, no. 606a, Wilson, pl. 5, etc.) and in Durrow (*CLA* II, no. 273): below, plates 24 – 6. (Brown did not mention the identical space-filler in the Augsburg Gospels, fol. 128[v]: plate 26 below.) For a plate of the Easter table see below, plate 24.

[31] *CLA* II, p. xvii.

Melsigi.[32] It remains, in the limited space available here, to examine the textual evidence of the Augsburg Gospels, to see whether that manuscript has any bearing on this theory.

Given what has been said about the physical location of the Rath Melsigi community in Ireland prior to its removal to Echternach, one would expect that Irish environment to show through in the text of the Augsburg Gospels. In other words, we would expect the text to show clear traces of affinity with the so-called 'Irish' family of biblical manuscripts: DE EpLQR (Armagh, Egerton 609, the Echternach Gospels, the Lichfield/Chad Gospels, the Book of Kells, and the Rushworth/Macregol Gospels.)[33] There is space here only to summarize the results of my collation, but the conclusion is exactly as we would expect it to be in the circumstances: the Bible text in Augsburg belongs to the Irish family.[34]

The detailed statistics are set out below; I summarize them here under four main headings:

(1) The total number of variations from the Vulgate text in Wordsworth-White is 4852. This comprises *all* variants, textual and orthographical.

(2) Readings (other than merely orthographical ones) which are unique to Augsburg (i.e. variants which are not listed in the apparatus of Wordsworth-White either for the Vulgate or for Vetus Latina MSS) number 813. (I emphasize that these and the following figures are based on the selection of what I considered to be substantial textual variations, eliminating the obviously orthographical ones, which are only of limited value).

(3) By far the largest number of variants follows the 'Irish' family, DE EpLQR. Augsburg has 52 readings which it shares with Armagh alone; 44

---

[32] One additional computistical argument which possibly speaks in favour of an Irish background is the occurrence at the bottom of fol. 40[v] in the Calendar of the Dionysiac/Alexandrian Easter limits, including the *luna prima primi mensis. Uiii Id. Mar.* [8 March]. This rubric does not normally occur in Dionysiac tables, but the southern Irish cleric Cummian, writing to Abbot Ségéne of Iona *c.* 633 concerning the Easter question, refers to precisely these data in the tables he was using. See the new edition, *Cummian's Letter 'De controversia Paschali', together with a related Irish computistical tract, 'De ratione conputandi',* ed. Maura Walsh and Dáibhí Ó Cróinín (Pontifical Institute of Mediaeval Studies (Toronto), Studies and Texts 86; Toronto, 1988) pp. 44–6.

[33] The sigla are those used in *Nouum Testamentum Domini Nostri Iesu Christi latine secundum editionem Sancti Hieronymi* 1, Gospels, ed. John Wordsworth and H. J. White (Oxford, 1898). I should point out that for the purposes of this comparison I make no distinction between the readings of the main text in Ep (which is usually taken to represent a fairly pure Northumbrian type Vulgate) and the marginal readings (usually regarded as typically Irish), because of the recent and startling discovery by Fr Martin MacNamara, announced in a paper read by him at the 1st Irish Conference of Medievalists, Maynooth June 1987, that the main text in Ep has over 100 variants from the Vulgate which are found nowhere else but in the Mac Durnan Gospels and in two other twelfth-century Irish Gospel books of Armagh provenance. It should be clear that I still believe in the existence of an identifiable Irish family of Gospel texts. Attempts to deny the existence of such a grouping have not been convincing, in my view.

[34] For a more detailed account of the Augsburg Gospels and its text, see my introduction to the facsimile edition, *Evangeliar aus Echternach (Universitätsbibliothek Augsburg, Cod. I.2.4°2), Codices Illuminati Medii Aevi,* ed. Dáibhí Ó Cróinín (Edition Helga Lengenfelder, München, 1988). I hope to publish an exhaustive study of the Bible text in Augsburg elsewhere.

which it shares with Egerton 609 alone; 13 which it shares with the Echternach Gospels alone; 14 which it shares with the Lichfield Gospels; 38 which it shares with Kells alone, and 31 which it has in common with the Mac Regol/ Rushworth Gospels. The total of DE EpLQR readings is over 450, and combinations of all DE EpLQR readings number over 900.

In stark contrast with these figures is the fact that Augsburg has no more than half-a-dozen readings in common with the Codex Amiatinus and the Lindisfarne Gospels, the two roughly contemporary representatives of the so-called Italo-Northumbrian text (and those are only of an orthographical nature).

(4) Vetus Latina readings are few in Matthew and Mark, but increase markedly in Luke and John. John in particular shows very strong Old Latin traces.

	Mt	Mc	Lc	Io	
D	1	10	12	29	(52)
E	7	0	23	14	(44)
Ep	4	2	7	0	(13)
L	4	9	1	0	(14)
Q	10	15	9	4	(38)
R	12	6	5	8	(31)

Variant Readings (Total)	4852
Unique Readings in Aug	813
Vetus Latina Readings	2(Mt) 9(Mc)
	125(Lc) 232(Io)
DE EpLQR Readings (Indiv.)	453
All combinations of D	152 (204)
All combinations of E	88 (132)
All combinations of Ep	115 (128)
All combinations of L	77 (91)
All combinations of Q	120 (158)
All combinations of R	161 (192)

The overall impression left by these figures is of a manuscript with strong Irish connections, the closest connection being with the Gospel text in the Book of Armagh — a manuscript whose Irish origin is not in doubt. It is perhaps of additional significance that Augsburg contains the oldest and most accurate copy of the verses on the Eusebian canons, *Quam in primo speciosa quadriga*, composed by Ailerán, a scholar of Clonard in Co. Meath (d. AD 665).[35] And there is also the interesting fact, noted above, that the vertical

---

[35] For the particular significance of the Ailerán poem, and its unique relationship with the canon tables in the Augsburg Gospels, see Nancy Netzer, 'The Trier Gospels', pp. 113 – 14, 119 – 20, and below pp. 207 – 7.

space-fillers which figure so prominently in Willibrord's Calendar, and on one page of the Augsburg codex, also appear on three pages of the Book of Durrow, and in Paris, Bibl. Nat., MS lat. 9538, fol. 7ᵛ, another Echternach manuscript.[36] (See plate 27.)

To sum up our findings then: the Augsburg Gospels were written *c.* AD 705 by the scribe who penned Willibrord's Calendar.[37] This scribe was trained at Rath Melsigi (wherever he may have been at time of writing). There is nothing new in this concept of Irishmen and Anglo-Saxons working in the same milieu. All I have been trying to do is to make scholars aware of the fact that this cultural interchange need not have been confined to Northumbria (and certainly not to Lindisfarne). In a famous passage in his *History* (III, 27) Bede related how 'large numbers of the English race' (*multi nobilium simul et mediocrium de gente Anglorum*) had taken themselves to Ireland in the first half of the seventh century, some as political refugees, others in order to study at the feet of Irish masters. Many of these returned to England in due course and rose to positions of power in the Anglo-Saxon churches. Some visited Ireland more than once. The southern English bishop and scholar Aldhelm of Sherborne wrote a letter, the text of which survives,[38] addressed to a fellow countryman who had studied in Ireland and who was about to set out once again for another stint there. Aethelwulf, an eighth-century Northumbrian writer,[39] apparently spent some time himself in Ireland and seems even to have had an Anglo-Saxon teacher during his stay. Bede himself names a dozen or so others who had spent some parts of their careers in Ireland, and we can supplement his picture by reference to various Irish sources.

Berchert (or Berichter) of Tullylease (Co. Cork) is perhaps the best known of these. He is commemorated on a stone slab still standing at the site, in an inscription whose importance for palaeographical purposes is pointed out elsewhere in this volume.[40] (Plate 8.) Apparently a different Berchert is commemorated at a place called St Berchert's Kyle, situated in the townland of Ardane, parish of Templeneiry (Co. Tipperary), directly at the foot of the Galtee Mountains, to the south of the road that leads through the Glen of Aherlow. There are at present over seventy slabs, crosses, and inscribed stones

---

[36] Professor Bernhard Bischoff pointed out to me that a debased version of this space-filler is found also in ninth-century Freising manuscripts written by the Insular scribe Peregrinus. Peregrinus may, therefore, have been associated with Echternach.

[37] The statement by Nancy Netzer, 'Trier Gospels', p. 267, that the manuscript was written by the Echternach scribe Virgilius, is a slip. I am grateful to P. Édouard Jeauneau and M. Jean Vezin, Paris, for examining both the Calendar and the Prophets MS. (written in part by Virgilius), and for assuring me that Virgilius was, in their view, not the scribe of the Calendar (nor, by inference, of the Augsburg Gospels).

[38] Ep. 5 (ad Ehfridum), ed. Rudolf Ehwald, *Aldhelmi opera*, MGH, Auctores Antiquissimi 15 (Berlin, 1919/München, 1984), pp. 488–94.

[39] Aethelwulf, *De abbatibus*, ed. A. Campbell (Oxford, 1967).

[40] See Michelle Brown, above, p. 160.

surviving at this site, one of them a very impressive sandstone cross-head.[41] When the Irish abandoned Lindisfarne in AD 664 they brought with them some thirty English inmates of the monastery for whom a separate house was eventually established at Mayo, referred to as *Magh Eo na Sacsan* as late as the fifteenth century.[42] Mayo continued to recruit directly from Northumbria in the seventh and eighth centuries, and the so-called 'Northumbrian Annals' preserved by Byrhtferth of Ramsey[43] (*sub anno* AD 768) refer to an Eadwuine as newly-ordained bishop of Mayo, and mention his successor Leodfrith as well (*sub anno* AD 773).[44] A further Mayo bishop, Aldwulf, is mentioned in the same source *sub anno* AD 786, and he seems to have attended an English synod in that capacity.[45] Alcuin was in correspondence with Mayo more than once,[46] and his contacts with the *Mugensis ecclesia* remained strong even after his departure from York to the Carolingian court.

Other, more shadowy Anglo-Saxons figure from time to time in Irish sources. The notes to the *Martyrology of Oengus* mention a 'Bendict Tailcha Leis na Saxsan' (i.e. Tullylease, Co. Cork?) and a brother of his, Cuthbert, otherwise unknown.[47] We can also deduce from placename evidence that isolated Englishmen were to be found scattered here and there throughout the country: at Tech Saxan, a church of the Tuam diocese to this day; and Inis an Ghaill Chráibhthigh ('The island of the pious foreigner', Inchagill) in Loch Corrib, near Cong (Co. Mayo). These and other such placenames bear witness to a fairly widespread (if sporadic) Anglo-Saxon presence in Ireland throughout this period, so that any talk of Hiberno-Saxon cultural contacts cannot be confined to Northumbria.

In the past, when archaeologists and art historians talked about that active interplay of Irish and other Insular elements that we call Hiberno-Saxon art, they tacitly assumed that this interplay can only have taken place in Northumbria, believing that only there could such a strong Anglo-Saxon contribution have been possible. But this view underestimates the role played by the Anglo-Saxons in this formative period. The presence of numerous Anglo-Saxons in Ireland, sometimes for prolonged periods, provides a

---

[41] See Pádraig Ó hÉalaidhe, 'The crosses and slabs at St. Berrihert's Kyle, in the Glen of Aherlow', in *North Munster Studies: Essays in commemoration of Monsignor Michael Moloney*, ed. Etienne Rynne (Limerick, 1967), pp. 102 – 26.

[42] Bede, *HE* IV, 4.

[43] See Cyril Hart, 'Byrhtferth's Northumbrian Chronicle', *EHR* 97 (1982), pp. 558 – 82; Michael Lapidge, 'Byrhtferth of Ramsey and the early sections of the *Historia Regum* attributed to Symeon of Durham', *ASE* 10 (1982), pp. 97 – 122.

[44] *HR* 46, 47.

[45] *HR* 53. *Councils and Ecclesiastical Documents relating to Great Britain and Ireland*, ed. A. W. Haddan and W. Stubbs (3 vols., Oxford, 1869 – 71), III, 460.

[46] J. F. Kenney, *Sources for the early history of Ireland*, I, Ecclesiastical (New York, 1929/Dublin, 1979), p. 534, no. 340. See Hermann Moisl (as n. 23), 'Das Kloster Iona', pp. 29 – 31.

[47] *Félire Óengusso Céli Dé, The Martyrology of Oengus*, ed. Whitley Stokes (Henry Bradshaw Society 29; London, 1905), p. 258, mentions a Cuthbert among a group of Anglo-Saxons resident in Ireland; see further below.

perfectly plausible alternative context for the development of Hiberno-Saxon art forms, and the stones at Tullylease — to name just one example — indicate the degree of skill in monumental sculpture which could result from such an admixture.

The monastery at Rath Melsigi was only one of several such foundations in Ireland, where Englishmen and Irishmen were to be found together. It is the most important of them, to be sure, since we can locate there a thriving and highly-skilled scriptorium which in time produced the only securely datable illuminated Gospel codex in the Insular style,[48] and therefore it constitutes an important landmark in the otherwise poorly charted terrain of Hiberno-Saxon art.[49]

[48] I cannot understand the comment by Rupert Bruce-Mitford, *Cod. Lind.* II, 293, that 'at Echternach, even in the Maihingen Gospels, the atmosphere is one of primitive and provincial simplicity, almost wholly Insular and largely dependant (*sic*) for what elegance it could muster on models from the Northumbrian homeland'. Lowe, *CLA* V, no. 1215, seems to have had a greater appreciation of the quality of the workmanship to judge by his reference to its 'dignified simplicity', marred by the intrusions of the tenth-century Master of the *Registrum Gregorii*.

[49] I acknowledge with thanks a Travel Grant from the Royal Irish Academy, which made possible some of the research for this paper.

Willibrord's Scriptorium at Echternach
and Its Relationship to Ireland and Lindisfarne*

NANCY NETZER

When Willibrord, a native Northumbrian and emigré to Ireland, crossed the English Channel with eleven companions to convert the Frisians in 690,[1] he must have brought with him manuscripts and scribe-artists trained in the Insular tradition. At his monastery at Echternach, founded in 697 or 698, at least some of these scribe-artists were to meet with others trained in the local Merovingian tradition and to see manuscripts from the Mediterranean world.[2] It is the clash of traditions and the resulting amalgamation of foreign styles in the manuscripts produced at Echternach that distinguish Willibrord's scriptorium from other Insular centres of the period, and it is the sorting out of the various traditions reflected in Echternach manuscripts that bears on the current debate surrounding the production of the great scriptorium at Lindisfarne. First, a brief review of the Lindisfarne question and the suppositions that have been made about its relationship to Echternach; then a discussion of the evidence provided by the Echternach manuscripts.

In 1960, in the commentary volume to the Lindisfarne Gospels, T. Julian Brown and Rupert Bruce-Mitford assigned four Gospel books to the scriptorium at Lindisfarne in about 700.[3] The first and most securely placed was the Lindisfarne Gospels[4] itself. Preserved in the middle ages with the relics of St Cuthbert at Chester-le-Street and Durham, the manuscript contains a colophon in Anglo-Saxon by Aldred, provost of Chester-le-Street in

---

* For Ernst Kitzinger on his seventy-fifth birthday, from whose ideas and guidance the author's work on the scriptorium at Echternach has benefited greatly and whose exemplary work on the art of Lindisfarne serves as inspiration for all who follow.

[1] *HE* V, 10.

[2] Willibrord travelled to Rome in 690 and 695 and probably brought back manuscripts with him. According to Bede (*HE* V, 11), the purpose of the first trip was to obtain the sanction of Pope Sergius and to collect relics of Roman apostles and martyrs for use in the churches he would later construct in Frisia.

[3] *Cod. Lind.* II, pp. 97 – 108.

[4] London, British Library, Cotton MS Nero D. IV. See *CLA* II, no. 187; P. McGurk, *Latin Gospel Books from A.D. 400 to A.D. 800* (Brussels, 1961), no. 22; Alexander, no. 9; *Cod. Lind.*

970, stating that Eadfrith and Aethelwold, bishops of Lindisfarne, and Billfrith, the anchorite, were responsible for the manuscript. The fragmentary Durham Gospels[5] is the second codex. Also preserved at Chester-le-Street and Durham, it has corrections to the text, punctuation, and Eusebian apparatus by a corrector of the Lindisfarne Gospels.[6] The third, the Echternach Gospels,[7] preserved until the end of the eighteenth century in the monastery from which it takes its name, is thought to have been produced by the scribe-artist responsible for the Durham Gospels, coined the Durham-Echternach calligrapher.[8] Finally, two folia in Oxford from another Gospel book have been related to the other three on the basis of their script.[9] According to Brown, these four *de luxe* Gospel books all contain examples of a distinctive script called Insular half-uncial of phase II. Rigidly confined by base and head lines, this heavy, round script is thought to have been invented by the Durham-Echternach calligrapher in about 700 as the result of new Italian influence at Lindisfarne.[10] The four Gospel books containing this classicizing script share some decorative motifs but, surprisingly, display little agreement in their texts, layout, quire arrangements and choice of miniatures;[11] in other words, assuming that the four manuscripts are products of the Lindisfarne scriptorium, the scribe-artists responsible for them did not share models for either text or illustration. Should it be surprising that a monastery with such wealth and resources should produce diverse works of this kind?

For at least one historian, Dáibhí Ó Cróinín, the assumption seemed implausible. In recent years, and again at the proceedings of this conference, he challenged the established picture of the Lindisfarne scriptorium. Without adducing positive evidence for connecting either manuscript to an Irish scriptorium, he suggested an origin in Ireland for the Durham and Echternach Gospels.[12] Ó Cróinín correctly observes that the identification of correctors in the Lindisfarne and Durham Gospels does not preclude the Durham Gospels' composition in Ireland and correction at Lindisfarne in the early eighth

---

[5] Durham, Cathedral Library, MS A.II.17, fols. 2 – 102; and Cambridge, Magdalene College Pepysian, MS 2981 (19). *CLA* II, no. 149; McGurk, *Latin Gospel Books*, no. 13; Alexander, no. 10; *The Durham Gospels*, ed. C. D. Verey, T. J. Brown and E. Coatsworth (EEMF 20; Copenhagen, 1980).

[6] See C. D. Verey's appendix to T. J. Brown, 'Northumbria and the Book of Kells,' *ASE* 1 (1972), pp. 243 – 5; *Durham Gospels*, pp. 38, 44, 74 – 6.

[7] Paris, Bibliothèque Nationale, lat. 9389. *CLA* V, no. 578; McGurk, *Latin Gospel Books*, no. 59; Alexander, no. 11; *Cod. Lind.* II, pp. 89 – 97, 103 – 4, 158, 187, 246 – 9.

[8] See *Cod. Lind.* II, pp. 100 – 2; *Durham Gospels*, pp. 42 – 9.

[9] Oxford, Lincoln College, MS 92, fols. 165 – 6. *CLA* II, no. 258; McGurk, *Latin Gospel Books*, no. 36; Alexander, no. 11; *Cod. Lind.* II, pp. 95 – 6, 98, 103.

[10] See *Cod. Lind.* II, pp. 64 – 70, 97 – 108; *Durham Gospels*, pp. 36 – 49; T. J. Brown, 'The Irish Element in the Insular System of Scripts to circa A.D. 850', in *Die Iren und Europa im früheren Mittelalter*, ed. H. Löwe (2 vols.; Stuttgart, 1982), I, 101 – 19.

[11] See *Cod. Lind.* II, pp. 97 – 108, 246 – 250; *Durham Gospels*, pp. 42 – 9, 68 – 76.

[12] D. Ó Cróinín, 'Pride and Prejudice', *Peritia* 1 (1982), pp. 352 – 362; 'Rath Melsigi, Willibrord and the Earliest Echternach Manuscripts', *Peritia* 3 (1984), pp. 17 – 49.

century (the date to which the corrector's script may be assigned).[13] He fails, however, to consider that it is highly unlikely that such a *de luxe* codex would have been finished in any eighth-century scriptorium without having been corrected, punctuated, or supplied with Eusebian apparatus. Moreover, to suppose that the Durham Gospels was written in Ireland in a script nearly identical to that employed by Eadfrith at Lindisfarne for the Lindisfarne Gospels and that this Irish manuscript was then sent to Lindisfarne and there corrected by the same scribe who corrected the Lindisfarne Gospels seems unnecessarily complicated. Rather, the confluence of evidence supplied by the similarity of main hands and that of correctors in the Lindisfarne and Durham Gospels argues strongly that both were made in the same scriptorium, i.e., Lindisfarne.

The remaining source of controversy is the Echternach Gospels. Here Ó Cróinín rejects origin at Lindisfarne on historical grounds: 'there is no evidence to suggest . . . that Echternach was a kind of daughter house of Lindisfarne and consequently no reason to suppose that Lindisfarne would automatically provide a decorated Gospel codex as a "gift from the old to the new foundation." '[14]

This point is indeed well taken. Echternach was not, as has been assumed, an exclusively Northumbrian foundation on the continent.[15] Although Willibrord was born in Deira (Northumbria) and spent his early years at Ripon under the tutelage of Bishop Wilfrid of York, his background was not 'purely Northumbrian.'[16] He spent the twelve years prior to his Frisian mission in Ireland at the monastery of Rath Melsigi, and Bede leaves little doubt that Willibrord's mission to the continent was undertaken from Ireland at the request of Rath Melsigi's abbot, Ecgberht.[17] As Ó Cróinín points out, it comes as no surprise that the earliest manuscripts produced in a scriptorium founded by Willibrord should have Irish connections.[18]

That such a scriptorium existed at Echternach in the early eighth century is attested by four manuscripts all written and decorated in the Insular style and signed by scribes whose names appear on Echternach charters from the first two decades of the eighth century. The first, a Book of Prophets, was copied at least in part by a scribe called Virgilius[19] who gave his name in verse at the

---

[13] Ó Cróinín, 'Pride and Prejudice', p. 355.

[14] Ó Cróinín, 'Pride and Prejudice', p. 359.

[15] For this previously accepted view of Echternach, see W. Levison, *England and the Continent in the Eighth Century* (Oxford, 1946), pp. 53 – 69; *Cod. Lind.* II, pp. 90 – 1, 103 – 4.

[16] *Cod. Lind.* II, p. 91.

[17] *HE* V, 10.

[18] Ó Cróinín, 'Rath Melsigi', p. 42.

[19] Paris, Bibliothèque Nationale, lat. 9382. *CLA* V, no. 577. On fol. 45[v]: *falso qui fungor Vergili nomine.* Lowe thought the manuscript to be written in a similar half-uncial by several scribes, but did not distinguish hands. On the four MSS see also above, p. 192.

end of Jeremiah. This is undoubtedly the latinized name of an Irishman called Fergal and the same Virgilius who wrote and signed charters for Willibrord in 709 and 721 – 722.[20] Virgilius's script and decorated initials in the Prophets manuscript parallel closely those in two other codices possibly by the same hand: the Calendar of Saint Willibrord containing a note written by Willibrord in 728[21] and the *de luxe* Augsburg Gospels.[22] The latter codex contains an acrostic, the first and last letters of which read vertically: *Laurentius vivat senio*. This elderly venerated Laurentius, to whom the manuscript was dedicated, is most likely the scribe of the same name who wrote four charters conveying properties to Willibrord in 704, 710, 718, and 721 – 722,[23] and the same Laurentius who signed the Hieronymian Martyrology, which has been bound with the Calendar since the eighth century.[24] The Prophets and Calendar manuscripts, and the Augsburg Gospels reveal similar half uncials of advanced phase I that were considered to be of Northumbrian origin,[25] until Ó Cróinín pointed out that the earliest Paschal table in Willibrord's Calendar (fol. 44[r]), a single leaf added to one of the Calendar's quires, covers the Easters of the nineteen-year cycle 684 – 702. The best explanation for the origin of this leaf probably written about 684, therefore, is that it was produced at Rath Melsigi, where Willibrord was then living, and brought by him to the continent in 690.[26] As its half-uncial script displays the distinctive features of that in the three early Echternach manuscripts, the background of the earliest script practised in the Echternach scriptorium may well be Irish.

Examination of the canon tables in the Augsburg Gospels and a poem preceding them (fol. 1[v]) supports this hypothesis. Written by the Irish poet Ailerán, who died in the plague of 665, the poem describes a discourse among (or between) the appropriate evangelist symbols for each of Eusebius's canon tables and mentions the number of comparative passages belonging to

[20] C. Wampach, *Geschichte der Grundherrschaft Echternach im Frühmittelalter*, I, 2 (Luxembourg, 1930), nos. 16, 31, 32. For Fergal see Ó Cróinín, 'Rath Melsigi', p. 28 n. 1; and Levison, *England and the Continent*, pp. 59 – 60, for Latin names signifying reception into the Roman community.

[21] Paris, Bibliothèque Nationale, lat. 10837, fols. 34 – 41. *CLA* V, no. 606a; H. A. Wilson, *The Calendar of St. Willibrord* (Henry Bradshaw Society 55; London, 1918); below, plates 24 and 26a, c.

[22] Augsburg, Universitätsbibliothek (formerly Harburg, Öttingen-Wallersteinsche Bibliothek, Cod. I.2.4°2). *CLA* VIII, no. 1215; McGurk, *Latin Gospel Books*, no. 72; Alexander, no. 24; below, plates 25 and 26d.

[23] Wampach, *Grundherrschaft Echternach*, nos. 8, 17, 28, 32.

[24] Paris, Bibliothèque Nationale, lat. 10837, fols. 1 – 33. *CLA* V, no. 605.

[25] See *Cod. Lind.* II, p. 91: 'The general appearance of the majuscule in these Echternach MSS. is more disciplined and compact that that of the early Irish and Northumbrian majuscule . . ., but it is still comparatively free and spontaneous and is not so rigidly confined between head-line and base-line.' Specifically noted were two unusual forms, an open *q* and elaborate *q*, in the decorative minuscule of Durham and Echternach, which also appear in the Martyrology and Calendar.

[26] Ó Cróinín, 'Rath Melsigi', pp. 29 – 30; above, pp. 195 – 6 and plate 24.

most canons.[27] The number of passages cited in the poem matches the number of numerals in the Augsburg canon tables (fols. $7^r - 12^v$). The one apparent exception — twenty passages in canon X for Luke (fol. 12^r) when, according to the poem, it should have nineteen — is a discrepancy that can be resolved in the fact that the final passage, written between two ruled lines, appears to be a correction. Most significant is that the poem mentions ninety-seven passages proper to John in canon X, a number unique among early canon series to the Augsburg tables.[28] Ailerán's poem, then, must have been written for a Gospel book containing a set of canon tables of the same recension as those in the Augsburg Gospels. Although the decoration of the Augsburg tables reveals origin of its model in the Mediterranean world, correspondence between numerical text and that mentioned in the Irish poem leaves little doubt that the exemplar, either a Mediterranean Gospel book or, more likely, a faithful Irish copy of such a book, came to Echternach via Ireland, probably with Willibrord.[29] Thus, both text and script tie the earliest Echternach manuscripts to Ireland.[30]

This, however, does not reflect the whole story of the Echternach scriptorium in the eighth century and is certainly not sufficient for establishing origin of the Echternach Gospels in Ireland. The Augsburg codex is only one of four Gospel books that can be shown, primarily through a complex sharing of textual and artistic models, to have been produced at Echternach in the eighth century.[31] The others are a manuscript in Maeseyck (pl. 30);[32] a codex in Trier (pls. 27, 28), written and decorated by two scribe-artists, one Insular and the other Merovingian;[33] and a bifolium in Freiburg-im-Breisgau (pl. 29) containing the prologue and some of the chapter summaries for the Gospel of

---

[27] For the critical edition of this poem, see D. De Bruyne, *Préfaces de la bible latine* (Namur, 1920), p. 185.

[28] For a more detailed discussion and tables showing the layout of canon tables on twelve pages in early Gospel books, see N. Netzer, 'The Trier Gospels (Trier Domschatz MS 61): Text, Construction, Script, and Illustration' (Ph.D. thesis, Harvard University, 1987; published by University Microfilms, UMI no. 8711524), pp. 109 – 14, 118 – 20, appendix O.

[29] In either case the exemplar provides evidence of Irish contact with and artistic receptivity to manuscripts from the Mediterranean world.

[30] An additional connection between Ireland and Echternach has been suggested by Ó Cróinín in 'Pride and Prejudice', pp. 360 – 1; and 'Rath Melsigi', pp. 26 – 8. Arguing that Pseudo-Anatolius was a computistical work known almost exclusively in Ireland, he proposes that three fragments preserved in the middle ages at Echternach, one of which actually contains an Old Irish gloss, are of Irish origin: Dionysiac Paschal tables and Pseudo-Anatolius *De Pascha* (Paris, Bibliothèque Nationale, lat. 10399, fols. 35 – 36 and lat. 9527, fol. 201, *CLA* V, nos. 595, 585).

[31] For reasons involving text, script, construction, and illustration, see Netzer, 'Trier Gospels', esp. pp. 263 – 6.

[32] Maeseyck, Church of St Catherine, s.n. *CLA* X, no. 1558; McGurk, *Latin Gospel Books*, no. 14; Alexander, no. 23.

[33] Trier, Cathedral Treasury, MS 61. *CLA* IX, no. 1364; McGurk, *Latin Gospel Books*, no. 76; Alexander, no. 26; Netzer, 'Trier Gospels'.

Luke.[34] Two exemplars seem to have been used for these four Gospel books. Containing a unique series of canon tables, the first, as described above, came from Ireland and was copied for the Augsburg Gospels and for the text of the Maeseyck Gospels. The nearly identical dimensions (*c.* 245 × 180 mm.) and sets of quires (both including fifteen quaternions, one ternion, and at least two quinions) of these two manuscripts may reflect those of the exemplar. Considerably larger (*c.* 305 × 252 mm.), the Trier Gospels derives some of its text (principally portions written *per cola et commata*) from this same exemplar, and some from another that was copied page for page.[35] Because it most likely contained a set of canon tables with apostle portraits, the frames and numerals of which are most closely paralleled in Roman examples of the sixth century, this second exemplar is probably of Roman origin. The Roman canon tables were copied faithfully in the Trier Gospels and less so in the Maeseyck Gospels and the incomplete set of canon tables bound with it.[36] Of nearly identical size to the Trier Gospels, the Freiburg Fragment contains texts from the second exemplar.[37]

The chronology of these four Gospel books is significant in assessing the relationship of the Echternach scriptorium to Ireland and Lindisfarne. The Augsburg Gospels, with a script close to that of Virgilius, known to have been active at Echternach between 709 and 722, is datable to the first quarter of the eighth century.[38] The presence of Willibrord at Aldeneyck, where the Maeseyck Gospels was preserved in the middle ages, suggests that he presented the book to Harlindis, the abbess whom he consecrated, either at the

---

[34] Freiburg-im-Breisgau, Universitätsbibliothek, Cod. 702. *CLA* VIII, no. 1195; McGurk, *Latin Gospel Books*, no. 76; Alexander, no. 25. Finding close parallels between initials in another Gospel book in Gotha (Forschungsbibliothek Cod. Memb. I. 18; *CLA* VIII, no. 1205; McGurk, *Latin Gospel Books*, no. 69; Alexander, no. 27) and the Trier Gospels, Carl Nordenfalk ('On the Age of the Earliest Echternach Manuscripts', *Acta Archaeologica* 3 (1932), p. 57 n. 1) has associated the former codex with Echternach. To the author's eye, however, this resemblance is only superficial. On the contrary, the Gotha Gospels shares no textual peculiarities with any of the other Echternach manuscripts. Rather, it contains general prologues and tables of lections — including Neapolitan feasts and chapter lists of Family C paralleled in two Northumbrian manuscripts: the Lindisfarne Gospels and the Royal Gospels (London, British Library, Royal MS 1.B.vii; *CLA* II, no. 213; McGurk, *Latin Gospel Books*, no. 28; Alexander, no. 20). Moreover, the script of the Gotha Gospels relates most closely to the Durham Cassiodorus (Durham, Cathedral Library, B.II.30; *CLA* II, no. 149; Alexander, no. 10), usually assigned to Lindisfarne in the second quarter of the eighth century.

[35] See Netzer, 'Trier Gospels', pp. 29 – 78.

[36] Bound with the Maeseyck Gospels is an incomplete series of canon tables and a single Evangelist portrait (*CLA* X, no. 1559; Alexander, no. 22) that have always been assumed to be all that remain of another Gospel book. It is more likely that these canon tables were an unacceptable first attempt at creating a series of canon tables for Maeseyck. In any case, these canon tables can be shown to have been produced at Echternach. See Netzer, 'Trier Gospels', pp. 109 – 70.

[37] For discussion of the two exemplars see Netzer, 'Trier Gospels', pp. 29 – 170; 272 – 4.

[38] See n. 19.

founding of the abbey or on one of his subsequent visits.[39] Thus, a date before Willibrord's death in 739 emerges as likely for the Maeseyck Gospels. Similar guides for absolute dates do not exist for the other two. Analysis of texts in the four codices, conclusions of which may only be summarized here,[40] supplies the most significant clues to their relative chronology. Although closeness between contents of the Augsburg and Maeseyck Gospels suggests that they are roughly contemporary, textual variants among their general prefaces indicate the Maeseyck Gospels to be later than the Augsburg Gospels and the Trier Gospels to be the latest of the three. Finally, the close relationship between the Trier Gospels and extant portions of the Freiburg Fragment suggests, as do their similar half-uncial scripts, that these two Gospel books belong together in the sequence. What emerges then among the Gospel books produced at Echternach is a chronology beginning with the Augsburg Gospels and followed by the Maeseyck Gospels, Trier Gospels, and Freiburg Fragment.[41] While the earliest Gospel book appears to be closely tied to Ireland, other influences, both Mediterranean and Insular, are introduced in the later codices.

Both the Trier Gospels (pl. 27) and Freiburg Fragment (pl. 29) contain Insular half-uncial scripts that can be shown to derive from the half-uncial of phase II thought to have been invented at Lindisfarne.[42] Horizontal wedges on vertical strokes indicate that letters were written with a straight (or, in some cases, nearly straight) pen, and the ductus matches in nearly every feature that in the Lindisfarne, Durham, Echternach, and Oxford Gospels. Furthermore, all ligatures, monograms, and abbreviations in the half-uncial script of the Trier Gospels may be found in both the Durham and Lindisfarne Gospels. Although the scribe of the Trier codex, who identified himself on three folios as Thomas, wrote a script whose proportions and general appearance most closely resemble that in the Lindisfarne Gospels, he failed to incorporate several of the latter's basic components. Using a thinner pen, Thomas and the scribe of the Freiburg Fragment produced more compressed, slimmer, and less substantial scripts. Not confined between two lines like those in the Lindisfarne Gospels, the letters vary slightly in height, and the spacing between letters may be uneven. Such deficiencies reveal a limited and superficial understanding of the Lindisfarne script — precisely the failing one

---

[39] The Maeseyck Gospels is first recorded in the *Vita Harlindis et Relindis* at Aldeneyck in the second half of the ninth century. It was transferred to Maeseyck in 1571, when the canons of Aldeneyck moved to the church of St Catherine in Maeseyck. For Willibrord's presence at Aldeneyck, see A. Dierkens, 'Les origines de l'abbaye d'Aldeneick, première moitié du VIIIe siècle', *Le Moyen Age* 85 (1979), pp. 389–531; M. Budny, 'The Anglo-Saxon Embroideries at Maaseik: Their Historical and Art-Historical Context', *Academiae Analecta* 45 (1984), pp. 98–9, 103.

[40] See Netzer, 'Trier Gospels', pp. 29–68, 266–9.

[41] For further discussion, see Netzer, 'Trier Gospels', pp. 266–9.

[42] According to D. Wright (*Traditio*, 1961, p. 448), the English uncial script of the Freiburg Fragment is distantly related to that of the Codex Amiatinus.

might expect of a second-generation practitioner trained in a provincial centre like Echternach.[43]

Unlike the script of the earliest Echternach manuscripts, which may be tied to Ireland, that of the later ones derives from Lindisfarne.[44] The shift to a Lindisfarne script is paralleled by the introduction in the Maeseyck, Trier, and Freiburg Gospel books of decorative and figural motifs closely matched in objects produced at Lindisfarne. A few examples will illustrate the point.

Showing seated evangelists in front of ladder thrones with half-length winged symbols holding books in the upper right, the unusual portraits of Mark and Luke (pl. 28) in the Trier Gospels reflect either a type of evangelist portrait devised at Lindisfarne or, more likely, Thomas's combination of Insular and Mediterranean sources.[45] Whatever the case, there can be little doubt that the evangelist symbols at least have their roots at Lindisfarne. Features of the calf in the Luke portrait are most closely paralleled in the Lindisfarne Gospels and on the Cuthbert coffin.[46] Contemporary products of the same monastery, these two monuments present the only examples of full-length symbols with wings, books, and haloes from the pre-Carolingian period. Both show the mild calf (instead of the muscular ox of the Mediterranean tradition) found also in the Durrow and Echternach Gospels.[47] They differ, however, from the latter examples in the illogical addition of horns and the turning of the head to face the viewer. Found on the Trier Luke portrait as well, both features are thought to have been devised at Lindisfarne.[48] Moreover, the shape, proportions, and rendering of the calf's head in the Trier Gospels are so close to those in the Lindisfarne Gospels (cf. especially the large circles around the eyes) that the former symbol must be indebted either to the latter or to a common model.

Similar arguments may be found for the flat stepped bases on two canon tables in the Maeseyck (fols. 10^r and 10^v) and Trier (fols. 11^r and 11^v) Gospels, which match those in the Lindisfarne Gospels, and for the frame of the Four-Symbols page in the Trier Gospels (fol. 1^v) comprising a central medallion and semicircular terminals mitred into the frame. Although unmatched on extant Insular miniatures, this design occurs on several Northumbrian grave

---

[43] Two other manuscripts — a *de luxe* edition of the *Collectio canonum* (Cologne, Dombibliothek Cod. 213; *CLA* VIII, no. 1163, Alexander, no. 13) and an *Epistulae Pauli* (Colmar, Bibliothèque Municipale MS 38, fols. 173 – 238) — contain a similar slender version of Phase II half-uncial, and thus may be tentatively attributed to Echternach. For more detailed discussion of this script, see Netzer, 'Trier Gospels', pp. 81 – 96.

[44] The Maeseyck Gospels are written in a set of minuscule of phase I that is similar to that in the Hieronymian Martyrology. The relationship of this script to England and Ireland needs to be studied. For the most recent discussion of Insular minuscule, see M. Parkes, *The Scriptorium of Wearmouth-Jarrow* (Jarrow Lecture 1982).

[45] See Netzer, 'Trier Gospels', pp. 211 – 30.

[46] See E. Kitzinger, 'The Coffin Reliquary', in *Relics*, pp. 202 – 304.

[47] Dublin, Trinity College, MS A.4.5 (57). *CLA* II, no. 273; McGurk, *Latin Gospel Books*, no. 86; Alexander, no. 6.

[48] Kitzinger, 'The Coffin Reliquary', *Relics*, pp. 230 – 3, 237 – 8.

markers of carved stone from Hartlepool and Lindisfarne datable from the middle of the seventh to the eighth century (pl. 39d, e).[49]

While apostle portraits on the canon tables in the Trier Gospels reflect a Roman model of the sixth century with remarkable accuracy, those on the tables of the Maeseyck Gospels (pl. 30) combine aspects of the Roman model with another source for such portraits probably from Lindisfarne.[50] The first five Maeseyck portraits (fols. 6^r-8^r) are waist length, like those on Cuthbert's coffin. As on the coffin, all hold their right hands open on their chests, and, with the exception of Peter's, left hands are covered by the pallium. The Maeseyck John and James Alphaeus have one end of the pallium draped over the right arm — the same convention found on the coffin apostles — and the heads depend on various sources: Andrew and James Alphaeus, for instance, have cascading curls on one side, as on the coffin (pl. 44, fig. 19), and Bartholomew's jagged beard (pl. 30) matches Paul's on the coffin (pl. 44, fig. 19). Faces, too, are drawn to a fixed Northumbrian formula. Heavy dark brown lines form eyebrows, the right one extending to form the contour of the three-quarter nose. This S-stroke with a hook for the nostril appears on the coffin figures and in the portrait of St Augustine of Canterbury in the Leningrad Bede (pl. 21), a manuscript written at Wearmouth/Jarrow in 746.[51] The shallow foreheads, delicate three-quarter noses, small, pursed mouths, prominent eyes, broad cheekbones, and narrow jaws find parallels in the Lindisfarne Gospels and the Leningrad Bede.

Finally, decorative motifs found in the fragmentary set of canon tables in the Maeseyck Gospels are tied to the Lindisfarne Gospels as well. The Maeseyck bird friezes have been attributed to an imported Mediterranean model and are thought to have been Northumbrian precursors of animal friezes in the Lindisfarne tables.[52] However, now that these Maeseyck tables can be attributed to Echternach, the argument cannot be defended. That the influence went the other way is undeniable. The plump interlaced birds on fol. 2^r and the left side of fol. 5^v (like those in the initial L on fol. 1^r of the Freiburg Fragment) derive from processions of birds developed at Lindisfarne.

These few examples leave little doubt that Lindisfarne played a key role in determining styles of script and decoration employed by the second generation of scribe-artists at Echternach. Moreover, this influx from Lindisfarne coincides with use of the Echternach Gospels as a source for decoration in the Trier Gospels. Here Thomas excerpted the frame and part of the inscription from the Echternach Matthew (fol. 18^v, pl. 9) for his Matthew portrait (fol. 19^v). For his Four-Symbols page (fol. 1^v), he adopted with varying degrees of fidelity the Echternach full-page lion, calf, and eagle (fols. 75^v, 115^v, 176^v),

---

[49] See *Corpus* I, nos. 437, 446, 1119, 1125 – 7.
[50] For more detailed discussion, see Netzer, 'Trier Gospels', pp. 121 – 42.
[51] Leningrad, Public Library, Cod. Q.v.I.18, fol. 26^v; *CLA* XI, no. 1621; Alexander, no. 19; M. Schapiro, 'The Decoration of the Leningrad Manuscript of Bede', *Scriptorium* 12 (1958), pp. 191 – 207.
[52] *Cod. Lind.* II, pp. 193 – 4.

and the layout of his *Liber generationis* (pl. 27) depends on that in the Echternach Gospels (fol. 20ʳ).[53]

Clearly, Echternach must have been in contact with Lindisfarne, most likely after the production of its earliest manuscripts. T. J. Brown has already cited an entry in the anonymous and Bedan lives of St Cuthbert indicating that between 698 and 705 one of Willibrord's companions visited Lindisfarne briefly, fell ill, was cured at Cuthbert's tomb and then was on his way again.[54] Whether this man was the courier for the Echternach Gospels is impossible to determine. One might expect a somewhat later date for the arrival of the manuscript on the continent based on the place of the Trier Gospels in the chronology of Echternach manuscripts.

In any case, such questions are not central to the origin of the Echternach Gospels. Neither are discussions about whether or not Echternach was a daughter house of Lindisfarne, because the Maeseyck, Trier and Freiburg Gospels provide sufficient evidence for contact between Lindisfarne and Echternach. Such historical arguments only divert attention from the manuscripts themselves to factors that surround them, as if the issue were the setting and not the jewels.

---

[53] For more detailed discussion, see Netzer, 'Trier Gospels', pp. 95, 207 – 8, 246 – 8.
[54] *Durham Gospels*, p. 44.

The Artistic Influence of Lindisfarne within Northumbria

ROSEMARY CRAMP

My initial assumption was that since Lindisfarne was a centre strategically placed in Northumbria; the primary foundation of the Columban church in Anglo-Saxon England; a major and well-endowed monastic site whose land holdings were not just the only Bernician group to survive the holocaust of the Viking invasions and settlements of Northumbria, but the only one to be augmented, it must have been influential. It also seemed reasonable to suppose that this influence should be detectable in the evidence, albeit partial, which survives today, but I found it more difficult to document than I had anticipated.

The strategic position of the island, with its natural rock fortress, which could have served as a strong point or lookout point in many ages, and its half-island protection twice a day by the sea, are important factors in its development. But it is important to remember that this was not a remote place in the days of coastal trade and offshore travel. Lindisfarne has a good natural harbour, and several times in its history it is mentioned as a place from which people set off to sail to the Picts. Its fortress character is mentioned in the story of Urbgen's siege of the Angles for three days and three nights as told in the *Historia Brittonum*,[1] but it is also near to the much larger fortress of Bamburgh and its harbour entry is overlooked by that royal site.

When Aidan chose the island as his centre in 635 (it is often assumed for its topographical likeness to Iona), he put his community under the direct protection or control of the ruling Bernician house based on the rock fortress of Bamburgh. This period of idyllic church and state relationship, according to the evidence which we have, is nevertheless clearly one of close contact. If, as Bede tells, kings did not expect lavish entertainment when they visited the island, they nevertheless expected to have a bishop who was closely identified with the tribe/emergent state and who ate and travelled with them. Aidan, Finan, and Colman were generously treated by the Northumbrian kings in

---

[1] The island is called *Metcaud* in the British source, Nennius's *Historia Brittonum*, ch. 63; ed. and trans. J. Morris, *British History and the Welsh Annals* (London and Chichester, 1980), p. 79.

terms of endowments, and built up, in the Irish manner, a colony of
dependent or allied foundations; but, until Theodore took the matter in hand,
the Northumbrian church councils were presided over by the kings. This was
of course a tradition long established in the continental church and adopted in
Northumbria by Edwin when he prepared himself by thorough theological
study to lead his people from paganism to Christianity. Perhaps there was a
certain wariness of another nearby race in this practice, but the Irish abbots
and bishops of Lindisfarne were also detached from their secular kin, and
hence from their feuds with a royal patron — and this could have been seen as
an advantage by any Northumbrian ruler. Likewise, during the rule of the
immediate English successors to the Irish, Eata, Cuthbert, Eadfrith, and
Aethelwold, in what I shall describe as phase two — the period of assimilation
and integration into one Northumbrian church — there seems to have been
considerable harmony between church and state.

Yet despite the apparent success of the community in imposing their own
standards on the secular rulers in the first generations of abbots and bishops,
by the mid eighth century (phase three), things had changed. The change may
have come about when an ex-king, Ceolwulf, became a member of the
community in 737, and even if he gave the community more land, customs
changed, and it must have become difficult to keep the world at bay.

In 750, King Eadberht took Bishop Cynewulf as a prisoner to Bamburgh
and had the church of St Peter besieged. One cannot imagine any king daring
to do that to Finan or indeed Cuthbert, but then perhaps neither of these
clerics would have sheltered the king's enemies. The *Historia regum* goes on to
tell us that 'Offa son of Aldfrith, who had been forced to flee to the relics of the
holy bishop Cuthbert, though innocent, was dragged unarmed from the
church, almost dead with hunger'.[2] Unless this is a conscious anachronism on
the author's part, it demonstrates that by this time the island furnished
another type of protection — religious sanctuary. Yet, as we all know, this
protection failed, when the Vikings came: the Vikings were presumably
ignorant of it. But Alcuin's shocked letter to Higbald after the 793 raid, 'What
assurance is there for the churches of Britain, if St Cuthbert, with so great a
number of saints, defends not his own',[3] assumed this new type of non-secular
protection, even though it is hinted elsewhere in the letter that the secular
activities were absorbing too much of the attention of the monks. Indeed, the
community continued to be involved in the troubled and checkered histories of
the Northumbrian royal house throughout this phase. The *Historia regum* tells
us how in 796 the patrician Osbald, pretender to the throne, was put to flight
and banished. '[He] retired with a few followers to the island of Lindisfarne,
and from there he went by ship to the king of the Picts with certain of the
brothers.'[4]

---

[2] *HR sub anno* 750; trans. *EHD*, p. 265.
[3] Letter of Alcuin to Higbald, bishop of Lindisfarne, in 793: *EHD*, p. 845.
[4] *HR sub anno* 796; trans. *EHD*, p. 274.

Yet the community continued to attract major land grants during the ninth century, and some of these estates, such as Wycliffe and Billingham along the Tees valley, seem earlier to have been independent monasteries.[5] Just before the major Viking invasions and settlements of the mid ninth century, King Aella of Northumbria in 862 – 7 seized several estates back, including Billingham, and is said to have occupied the monastery of Crayke, one of the earliest Lindisfarne possessions, because of his hatred of St Cuthbert (the landowner). The final flight from Lindisfarne of a section of the community was preceded by the moving not only of the bodies of Cuthbert and King Ceolwulf but also of Aidan's wooden church.[6] In the light of the later history of the community while at Lindisfarne, the activities of the Chester-le-Street/Durham community in proposing a king to the Danish host and the later involvement with, and dependence on, the Northumbrian earls such as Uhtred, seem only a natural continuation of an established pattern of behaviour.

The map of the landholdings of the community prepared by Christopher Morris in his update of Craster's work on the patrimony of St Cuthbert gives some indication of the community's influence at various stages of its history.[7] Such properties provided an outlet to the west in the area around Bowness on Solway and Furness which could have provided important trading and staging points in relation to the western seaways. There were also staging points to the major Northumbrian trading centre and gateway to the Humber, York. The Leader/Adder territories, which in the first land grants stretched to the Firth of Forth, were held as a bastion of Anglian influence north of the Tweed until 971. The eastern group, given by Ceolwulf in 737, of Brinkburn, Edlingham, Eglingham, Warkworth, and Woodhorn, covered a significant area of the prosperous coastal strip in central Bernicia, while vills consolidated by Bishop Ecgred between 830 and 845 established Lindisfarne's power in the south of the province on the border with Deira. Some of these vills were, as already noted, seemingly first independent monastic centres. Some were closely linked monastic colonies such as Melrose, Tyningham, and Abercorn, and may have remained closely linked with Lindisfarne traditions throughout their history. Some monasteries, which owed their foundation to the first stage of the Ionan mission, probably remained loyal to its early traditions for a time but later went their own way, such as Hartlepool or Whitby. Many would only have

---

[5] *HDE* II, 5 (= ch. 20 in *CHE*, p. 653). The gift in question was from Bishop Ecgred who donated the vill of Gainford with the church which he had built, and its appurtenances, and also Wycliffe, *Ileclif* and Billingham. Symeon says of these last, 'of which he had been the founder', but funerary sculpture from both Billingham and Wycliffe indicates that there were Christian burial grounds, if not stone churches, before that.
[6] There is a difference between the account in *HDE* 5 and *HSC* 9 (*Sym. Op.* I, pp. 52, 201). In the former Ecgred is first credited with building a church at Norham and then moving the body of Ceolwulf. In the latter he is credited with moving the church built by Aidan, and rebuilding it at Norham to house the bodies of both Ceolwulf and Cuthbert.
[7] C. D. Morris, 'Northumbria and the Viking Settlement: the evidence for land-holding' *Archaeologia Aeliana* 5th series, 5 (1977), pp. 81 – 103, at p. 89.

come under the influence of the episcopal monastery when it too had developed under wider influences both in customary monastic life and in cultural connections. One should therefore not expect to find a homogeneous Lindisfarne influence.

There is no doubt that in most facets of Northumbrian art there is an unambiguous swing to southern English fashions by the early ninth century. By this time the peripheral areas of Northumbria had developed their own artistic identity, after a period when they had been something like the flagships for displaying the continental styles of Northumbria on its borders. This is particularly obvious in stone crosses when monuments of the eighth century such as the Ruthwell cross, or the Hoddam crosses in Dumfries, are part of the same stylistic traditions as are to be found east of the Pennines; but by the ninth century the Solway area, whether in Kirkcudbright or Cumbria, has developed its own styles and monument types.[8] Likewise, in the hinterland of the Forth, by the ninth century there is a perceptible difference in styles between monuments such as those from Tyningham or Jedburgh and those elsewhere in Northumbria.

One should not forget that the phase of Irish supremacy and direct influence at Lindisfarne was only about fifty years, and it is difficult to assign any artefacts to that period. In the second phase, which was longer — from *c.*685 – 750 — the documentary sources indicate that the community was anxious to assimilate the new English culture of the age, as promulgated in Bernicia through the foundations at Hexham (a centre which might at one stage have superseded Lindisfarne as the episcopal centre of Bernicia); and Wearmouth/Jarrow, whose influence is well known in the Bedan *Lives* of Cuthbert and in manuscript art. But the final phase or phases of Lindisfarne's history and potential influence could be seen as lasting more than a hundred years. In that time, other than the political events which I have already mentioned, we know very little of how the community interacted with other centres.

Yet surviving documents demonstrate that there was something special about the Lindisfarne church even in its decline, so that a Deiran and international scholar like Alcuin, trained in the metropolitan centre of York, could still call it not only the mother church of the Bernicians but also 'a place more venerable than all in Britain'.[9]

Now what does one expect from the influence of such a place? I think that the nature of the influence may differ during the various identifiable phases of its history. In the period of the Irish bishops in which the first customs of the house and the nature of the bishopric were established, we might assume, as I believe is implicit in many of the discussions about Lindisfarne's artistic

---

[8] An analysis of the crosses of Dumfries and Kirkcudbright has recently been undertaken by Derek Craig as part of a Ph.D. thesis at the University of Durham. The later Anglian crosses of Cumbria are discussed in *Corpus* II, p. 15 – 23.

[9] *EHD*, p. 842.

influence, that there was a close identity between Lindisfarne and its daughter foundations in customs and ideals, and also that these replicated those of Iona.

It is important, though, to remember that these customs were capable of being maintained in very different environments which could have affected the peripheries of life, and it is these peripheries which are most detectable today. Mayr-Harting said that for thirty years 'Lindisfarne superseded Canterbury as the effective ecclesiastical centre . . . because of the calibre of its monks and the Northumbrian *bretwaldaship* which lay behind it',[10] but these are very intangible qualities to detect in the archaeological record. The calibre of its monks and their learning, perhaps also the books they took with them, do indeed seem to be the most influential export, and these Lindisfarne-trained people were exported not only to Northumbrian monasteries such as Melrose, Gilling or Lastingham, Ripon, Gateshead or Tynemouth, but also, through the mission to the Middle Angles and the East Saxons, to areas as far away as Bradwell on Sea, Essex. It is this mobility of the members of the early communities, which existed even after Theodore's decrees of 672,[11] which must have served as a vehicle for transmission of culture to and fro across the Irish sea and throughout mainland Britain. Nevertheless we do not have a complete picture and it would be over-simplistic to assign all Insular motifs to the direct influence of Lindisfarne. There were other important centres in England, notably Glastonbury. Some of these Insular motifs could derive from the migrations of monks or just from the migration of books, others could reflect the influence of other centres, and we should not let that miraculously surviving manuscript, the Lindisfarne Gospels, blind us to what has been lost in other potentially influential works of art from Lindisfarne or from centres elsewhere.

One might in searching for evidence for the influence of Lindisfarne assume that there could be some reflection in the form or layout of buildings on related sites. Any comparison is of course hampered by the lack of excavated evidence from Lindisfarne itself. There has however been sufficient excavation elsewhere to know that an identity of rule did not produce an identity of layout. At Monkwearmouth and Jarrow, which were twinned in the minds of their founders, the excavated plans do not reveal the sort of identity the excavation of two Cistercian or later Benedictine houses would produce.[12] Nevertheless there is an identity in the use of stone for the major buildings on these sites, and in all that went with the mortared stone tradition such as painted plaster, *opus signinum* floor and coloured window glass. In these buildings the founders may be seen as consciously breaking away from the traditions of the Irish church, traditions of wood building which Bede

---

[10] H. Mayr-Harting, *The Coming of Christianity to Anglo-Saxon England* (London, 1972), pp. 94 – 5.
[11] *HE* IV, 5.
[12] R. Cramp, 'Monastic Sites', in *The Archaeology of Anglo-Saxon England*, ed. D. M. Wilson (London, 1976), pp. 201 – 52; and R. Cramp, 'Proceedings', *Archaeological Journal* 133 (1976), pp. 230 – 7, figs. 34 and 35.

described in passages which are quoted ad nauseam. First, even as late as the time of Colman, Bede tells us there were very few buildings there except for the church, 'in fact only those without which the life of a community was impossible', and 'they had no need to . . . provide dwellings for the reception of worldly and powerful men'.[13] We know that the first church that Aidan built was of wood, like the chapel on the estate near Bamburgh against whose external buttress he leant to die.[14]

The first Lindisfarne church was replaced by Finan with one suitable for an episcopal see. He built it in the Irish method, not of stone but of hewn oak, and thatched it with reeds. This was the church which Archbishop Theodore then consecrated to St Peter (we do not know the dedication of Aidan's church), and whose roof and walls were covered with sheets of lead by Eadberht in the assimilation of Anglian traditions.[15] This strange treatment — a sort of enshrining of the church — seems to be unparalleled elsewhere although there is plenty of evidence for the lead sheeting of roofs on Northumbrian churches.[16] Either this church or Aidan's may have been moved to Norham as mentioned above, but we have no record of the building of a stone church at Lindisfarne nor any architectural sculpture which might serve as a clue to its existence. Nevertheless it seems odd, when Bishop Ecgred (830 – 845) is credited with building or rebuilding so many churches, that he did not build one at Lindisfarne. Perhaps part of the present parish church dates from the ninth century and the old timber and the new stone church originally stood in a line as at the ancient Celtic foundation of Glastonbury.[17]

The tradition of wooden church building is a difficult one to assess. The 'Irish' tradition of building in wood may have been quite specific in the eyes of Bede and his contemporaries, in a way we do not perceive today, since the tradition of the English and of the Britons was also to build in wood. It is difficult today to imagine the subtleties of superstructure from surviving post-pits. One may remember the timber buildings of Yeavering, amongst which was one identified by the excavator as a church, and claimed by him as belonging in the Roman-British tradition,[18] although others since have interpreted the Yeavering evidence as part of the common Anglo-Saxon tradition. Certainly, in contrast to Wearmouth/Jarrow, the sites of Hartlepool and Tynemouth — both of which were founded while the Irish influence at Lindisfarne was strong — do have timber buildings, although in neither place has a church been found, and only at Hartlepool are we reasonably certain

---

[13] *HE* III, 26 (C and M, pp. 310 – 11).

[14] *HE* III, 17.

[15] *HE* III, 25.

[16] R. Cramp, 'Excavations at the Saxon monastic sites of Wearmouth and Jarrow, Co. Durham: an interim report', *Medieval Archaeology* 13 (1969), fig. 24, 3a-b.

[17] H. M. & J. Taylor, *Anglo-Saxon Architecture* (3 vols.; Cambridge, 1965), I, 253, fig. 110.

[18] B. Hope-Taylor, *Yeavering, An Anglo-British Centre of Early Northumbria* (London, 1977), pp. 232 – 7, and cf. pp. 73 – 8 for building B, the possible church.

that the structures belong to the early monastery.[19] The type of structure found at these sites however would be quite at home in a secular Anglo-Saxon site, thus supporting the idea that there was initially no distinctive monastic architectural tradition.

Since we have no excavated structures of the early period, only the generalized traditional descriptions, what else may be considered to be the indigenous tradition of Lindisfarne? There should surely be Lindisfarne traditions of metalworking, and of manuscript production and decoration, and possibly also of the sculptured and incised memorial stones which survive. Others in this conference are talking about the manuscripts which have been assigned to the Lindisfarne scriptorium, and also the individual items which have survived from within St Cuthbert's coffin, which constitute the evidence for the decoration of metalwork and wood work at this centre. I shall therefore try not to impinge on their subjects. But there are some general comments which must be made. First, it is difficult to isolate the earliest imported traditions. Other than in manuscripts everything we have is potentially to be dated after the synod of Whitby and indeed after Cuthbert's death: the second phase, when it is obvious from the textual evidence that the community was intent on bringing itself up to date. Secondly, we should remember Hope-Taylor's long essay on the art of Bernicia as it might have been at the time when the Irish monks arrived, which included La Tène spirals and peltas, as well as Roman and Anglo-Saxon motifs, such as the little foil beast which he discovered at Bamburgh.[20] Important sites on the northern shores of the Solway such as the Mote of Mark have demonstrated how the metalworkers of the native strongholds used metalworking techniques common to both sides of the Irish sea, and copied Anglo-Saxon ornament.[21] There is no reason why the citadel of Bamburgh should not have housed smiths who were similarly employed. We have not the smith's waste from the early monastic site of Lindisfarne which would enable us to know rather than guess how influential metalworking techniques were on the decoration of manuscripts. But luckily we have recently gained some insight into the metalwork produced in one of the Lindisfarne colonies — Hartlepool.

Hartlepool has a claim to be the primary female monastery in Northumbria since it was founded by Heiu, the first Northumbrian woman to take the vows and habit of a nun in the episcopate of Bishop Aidan.[22] It formed one of an important coastal network from Coldingham to Whitby. Recent excavations have produced the plans of several timber buildings and some nineteen fragments of two-piece moulds which were part of the fill of a boundary ditch

---

[19] Cramp, 'Monastic Sites', fig. 5.5; and below, n. 23.

[20] Hope-Taylor, *Yeavering*, pp. 313 – 24.

[21] L. Laing, *The Archaeology of Late Celtic Britain and Ireland c. 400 – 1200 AD* (London, 1975), pp. 33 – 6.

[22] *HE* IV, 23 (21).

(plate 39 a-c).[23] These moulds demonstrate a close resemblance between their motifs, and those which are traditionally associated with Lindisfarne. One fragment (b) shows a ribbon animal with a ribbed body and back-bent head, which (with its closed pointed jaws) is very like the animals in the Durham manuscript A.II.17. It has not a rolled-back nostril like so many Insular pieces (see below), but it could have been part of a brooch or shrine, the best parallels of which survive in the Celtic world.[24]

Even more interesting is the mould (a) which shows a square impression of an animal which stands rather like an apocalyptic Lamb, with stiff legs and back-turned head, but betrays itself as one of the evangelist symbols by its trumpet attribute. Its stance may be determined by the desire of the artist to fit it into a square shape. This then is an apocalyptic animal/evangelist symbol of the naked type, i.e. without halo or book. It is thus more like the symbols of the Book of Durrow rather than the Cuthbert coffin or Lindisfarne Gospels; but it *is* like two of the Lindisfarne Gospels' creatures in that it has a trumpet. Rupert Bruce-Mitford, in a full description of the Lindisfarne Gospels' symbols, noted the use of two sets of models for the evangelist symbols in that manuscript, indicated by St Matthew's man/angel and St Mark's lion with trumpets, and St Luke's calf and St John's eagle without trumpets.[25] Until this discovery at Hartlepool, only the much later Copenhagen Gospels' bull and angel provided parallels for the Lindisfarne Gospels' trumpeting beasts. The Hartlepool unhorned *vitulus* is not identical with the Lindisfarne type and is more like the animal in the Trier or Durrow Gospels, but its apocalyptic attribute is closely similar to Lindisfarne. Presumably both centres drew on a set of models in which all the evangelist symbols were shown in this guise and each used the models individually.

The other decorated mould (c) from Hartlepool depicts a fan-armed cross decorated with interlace. This may be compared with similar pieces from Whitby where the round-ended arm shape is popular in metalwork in simple and highly elaborate forms.[26] This link between St Hilda's two monastic houses is worthy of note.

Now these moulds, together with fragments of plain moulds and crucibles, are very like those found on British and Irish sites, and whether one considers that this is the work of one mobile smith imported to make the plaques and fitments for a shrine or book-cover, or the work of a smith resident in Hartlepool, the decorative features are an important addition to the repertoire of Insular art motifs, and potentially provide some hint about Lindisfarne workshop practices. The decoration on these moulds appears to have been

[23] R. J. Cramp and R. Daniels, 'New Finds from the Anglo-Saxon monastery at Hartlepool, Cleveland', *Antiquity* 61 (1987), pp. 424–32.
[24] R. B. K. Stevenson, 'The Hunterston Brooch and its Significance', *Medieval Archaeology* 18 (1974), pp. 16–42.
[25] R. L. S. Bruce-Mitford, 'Decoration and Miniatures', in *Cod. Lind.* II, esp. pp. 158–73.
[26] C. R. Peers and C. A. R. Radford, 'The Saxon Monastery of Whitby', *Archaeologia* 89 (1943), fig. 10, 6 and pl. XXVI.

impressed and there is on the animal mould a rim surround which might indicate the use of a motif piece. It is unfortunate that no motif pieces have been found at Hartlepool or elsewhere in Northumbria, since they would clearly point to an Insular Celtic tradition, and are important indicators of cultural diffusion both from one craft production centre to another and perhaps from one craft to another. Moreover they are, I think, one explanation of the compartmentalized layout of Insular art. It may be of interest to note here that what does indeed seem to be a Lindisfarne tradition, namely the completion of an image by calligraphy, is found on moulds from Scotland (Dunadd and Blanes) as well as at Nendrum in Northern Ireland. O'Meadhra, who has published the most recent and detailed summary of their use, makes the tantalizing suggestion that the origin of motif pieces might have been Pictish.[27] At Lindisfarne, the combination of image and inscription is common to the evangelist portraits in the Gospels, the metal covering for the altar, the wooden coffin, and the stone name stones. It is, then, a tradition clearly established in the first or second phases of Lindisfarne life.

The other widely accepted attributes of Insular art are formally the use of instruments for constructing geometric patterns, particularly spiral form and curved patterns, and the use of grids, for forming basic layouts. It is true that these are used in many cultures as a drawing aid, but they seem to be in continuous use in the British Isles from La Tène times onwards. To these commonly accepted attributes I would add layout into discrete panels of ornament — a feature which has been linked by O'Meadhra to the use of motif pieces. Motifs themselves are more difficult to discriminate between. Ribbon animals may have derived from Germanic art but a rolled-back snout seems to be a 'Celtic' rather than Germanic Insular feature. The animals which are derived from Germanic style II ornament have either closed sling-like jaws or squared off jaws with or without a little knob. The cat and dog and bird creatures of Lindisfarne have so far I believe no satisfactory derivation, and seem to be an individual response to the well-recorded contact with naturalistic Mediterranean art in the late seventh/early eighth centuries. Key patterns, although classically derived, are another important element in Insular art, as is also geometrically conceived interlace.

If one looks for fine quality Insular elements in early sculpture one finds them not amongst the surviving pieces from Lindisfarne but at Monkwearmouth, where despite the documentary evidence for the church's construction by Gaulish workmen, there is a strong Insular element in the sculptural decoration. Some interior decoration such as the splendid lion arm-rests which supported the abbot's throne and clergy benches, also the lathe-turned balusters can be seen as having a continental ancestry. But clearly Insular are the twisted beasts on the jambs of the west entrance. Perhaps even more strikingly Insular is the panel which seems to be part of a closure screen for the

---

[27] Uaininn O'Meadhra, *Early Christian, Viking and Romanesque Art. Motif-pieces from Ireland* (Stockholm, 1979).

altar. This is divided into small panels, one with a composition of ribbon animals, and the others with small neat interlace roundels of a type repeated on other excavated fragments from the site.[28] These have been compared by Gwenda Adcock with the Book of Durrow interlaces on folio 85^v and with Pictish art, for example the stone at Meigle (no 5).[29] It is possible that the Monkwearmouth foundation was influenced by Christian art already in existence in Northumbria, and it is interesting that in the sister foundation of Jarrow, founded eight years later, no such Insular ornament is found, only severely classical ornament comparable with that at Hexham.

Also excavated at Monkwearmouth is part of a tiny gravestone inscribed with Anglo-Saxon names in runic letters and in well-formed Insular capitals and with a cross which closely resembles one of the cruciform pages of the Lindisfarne Gospels. Such name stones are otherwise only found at sites which are closely associated with the Irish church — namely Lindisfarne itself, Hartlepool, and Billingham (plate 39).[30] The Monkwearmouth piece has inscriptions with runic texts and Insular majuscule on the same stone, as is also occasionally found at Lindisfarne. At Hartlepool the runic and the manuscript letters only occur on different stones whilst at Billingham and on some free-standing pyramidal stones from York, the cross types are similar but there are no runic texts.

These stones have been variously dated and have also been compared with many examples on Irish monastic sites as well as Iona where the incised cross and the lettering are inscribed on roughly shaped stones. Lionard notes that where the Irish stones can be referred to datable individuals, they largely date from the ninth/tenth centuries, although the tradition had certainly started by the eighth century.[31] Such stones may span a long period of time at Lindisfarne also since the crosses are sometimes incised, sometimes carved in relief. I would nevertheless suggest that these memorials are a phenomenon of the early, rather than the later Northumbrian church. They are an extension of calligraphy and of the incised ornament of the late Roman tradition, and, like the altar of St Cuthbert, such inscriptions may originally have been inscribed on wood and placed in the graves. The expanded or round-armed crosses can be paralleled on the early carpet pages of the Lindisfarne Gospels, but this is only one of several types of crosses on these pages. Nevertheless I feel that such small incised stones were superseded by inscribed slabs with relief ornament at the more sculptural centres, such as Wearmouth/Jarrow, and Hexham. At Lindisfarne they are the only types of gravestone which bear inscriptions, though there are later slabs carved in low relief.

[28] *Corpus* I, pp. 125 – 6; pls. 113 – 16, and 121 (656).
[29] G. Adcock, 'A study of the types of interlace on Northumbrian sculpture' (unpublished M.Phil. thesis, University of Durham, 1974), pp. 68 – 9.
[30] Billingham: *Corpus* I, pl. 17 (85); Hartlepool: pls. 84 – 5; Lindisfarne: pl. 199 – 201; Monkwearmouth: pl. 110 (600).
[31] P. Lionard, 'Early Irish grave-slabs', *Proceedings of the Royal Irish Academy* 61C (1961), pp. 95 – 169, at pp. 125 – 36.

At Ripon there is an extraordinarily important monument which combines the form of the recumbent name stone with that of a plain cross, and seems to represent a monument type transitional between the incised name stone and the cross.[32] At Hilda's second establishment after Hartlepool — Whitby — the type of monument to bear inscriptions is a plain cross, whose form reminds one of a wooden cross, especially in the incised ornament of the base of the shaft.[33] Such plain cross shafts have also been found at Hexham, Jarrow, Escomb, and Lindisfarne so we should beware of considering them only as an adjunct to the 'Celtic' church, but their number at Whitby is striking and so is their absence from Lindisfarne. It seems therefore that the period from the late seventh to the early eighth centuries was one of intense and swift experimentation.

Bede tells us quite unambiguously that the first cross to be raised in Bernicia was the wooden cross raised by Oswald before the battle of Heavenfield in 633/4, and it is indeed possible that the tradition of putting up wooden crosses was maintained by the Ionan church for some time. One may remember that the magnificent carved crosses of St Oran's and St John's on Iona were constructed with mortised joints as in wood.[34] The tradition of mortising parts of crosses together is also found on other Northumbrian crosses such as Ruthwell, Jedburgh, Rothbury, and Lowther. It might be assumed that the free-standing carved stone cross was accepted at Lindisfarne by the end of the seventh century since before St Cuthbert died on Farne he said that he wished to be buried near to the (stone) cross to the south of his oratory.[35] In the light of the simplicity of his life there and the fact that Aethelwold is supposed to have had the first stone cross on Lindisfarne carved before his death in 740 it is unlikely that the cross, if of stone, would have been elaborately carved, but it could have been something like the simple slab-like shape which was found on the island hermitage of Ardwall Island off the west coast of Scotland.[36] This may have been replaced later by a piece thought to be more seemly, at the period when the cult of St Cuthbert was being developed by the Lindisfarne monks in the time of Eadfrith and Aethelwold. The surviving fragment of a cross from Farne is housed today in Durham (plate 40c). This cross is badly damaged but it is possible to see that it is like a group of crosses at Lindisfarne with panels of ornament interlace, key patterns and ribbon animals.[37] In fact it is so like that it must have been carved in the same workshop, but it is clearly not as early as Cuthbert's death.

---

[32] W. G. Collingwood, *Northumbrian Crosses of the Pre-Norman Age* (London, 1927), fig. 117.

[33] Peers and Radford, *Archaeologia* 89, pl. XXIX, a.

[34] The Royal Commission on the Ancient and Historical Monuments of Scotland, *Argyll: An Inventory of the Monuments*, vol. IV: *Iona* (Edinburgh, 1982), pp. 192 – 204.

[35] *VCP* 37 (*Two Lives*, pp. 272 – 3).

[36] C. Thomas, 'An Early Christian cemetery and chapel on Ardwall Isle, Kirkudbright', *Medieval Archaeology* 11 (1967), pp. 127 – 88 at p. 156, fig. 31, 9/16.

[37] *Corpus* I, pls. 189 and 193.

The monument which may have been the earliest Lindisfarne stone cross and which was certainly the most influential is the one already mentioned which Aethelwold caused to be made *c.*740, in honour of St Cuthbert, directing that his own name should be engraved on it. This cross was damaged, possibly in the 793 Viking raid, but was mended with lead and 'subsequently to this it was constantly carried about along with the body of St Cuthbert, and honourably regarded by the people of Northumbria out of regard to these two holy men. And at the present day it stands erect in the cemetery of this church (that is, the church of Durham) and exhibits to all who look upon it a memorial of these two bishops'.[38] This cross must have been an extremely influential monument — not so much perhaps at the time it was erected but as it was carried round amongst the Lindisfarne dependencies in Northumbria during the community's seven years of wanderings and when it was finally erected at Durham. It was the most visible memorial of Lindisfarne in the new location and I will return to what I think is its influence later.

Because so many crosses and other fragments of stone sculpture have survived from Northumbria in comparison with other artefacts such as manuscripts or fine metalwork or textiles, it is tempting to think that they must provide a correspondingly greater insight into the tastes and relationships of the individual centres. Sculpture is, however, very difficult to date and the interrelationships of the various centres are extremely complex. I suggested, more than twenty years ago, that the development of the elaborately carved stone cross was to be located in those centres where other types of carving (i.e. architectural and furnishing) occur, and where there were major stone churches. At Jarrow there is an identity in the ornamental repertoire of some of the friezes and crosses, whilst at Hexham there is not, but the latter site was obviously an important centre for developing a type of cross, without panel divisions but with continuous vinescroll as its main ornament in a classical rather than an Insular layout. Yet how many centres maintained specialized stone masons in this period when all secular buildings and many small churches were of wood? It has recently been suggested by Eric Cambridge that there is for County Durham a close correspondence between monastic sites and those with stone churches or sculpture.[39] This does not mean that every site with stone sculpture must have had stone buildings as well; in fact at Chester-le-Street this correlation certainly did not apply. Nor does one need to rule out the hiring of workmen from major centres. Nevertheless some of the sites of the early Ionan church such as Cedd's site of Lastingham have produced elaborate architectural sculpture which is quite distinctive.[40] This could mean that by the mid eighth century many monastic

---

[38] *HDE* I, 12, trans. *CHE*, pp. 642 – 3.
[39] E. Cambridge, 'The Early Church in County Durham: A Reassessment', *Journal of the British Archaeological Association* 137 (1984), pp. 81 – 2.
[40] W. G. Collingwood, 'Anglian and Anglo-Danish Sculpture in the North Riding of Yorkshire', *Yorkshire Archaeological Journal* 19 (1907), pp. 265 – 7.

houses would have supported skilled stonemasons; but it is at least possible that Aethelwold's cross was carved by craftsmen imported for the occasion, just as the elegant crosses from Abercorn and Aberlady north of the Tweed[41] could have been commissioned by the communities. The Lindisfarne tradition of relief carving then need not have pre-dated 740, and indeed could have been fully established later.

The finest Bernician crosses in quality of carving and design such as Bewcastle have many parallels with Insular manuscripts in their panelled format and fondness for geometric interlace. They do, however, incorporate other motifs which are not found in the earlier Insular tradition, namely plant scrolls. Such monuments could well be seen as later than the Lindisfarne Gospels, and, although worked in the old panelled tradition, as recipients of a wider repertoire of motifs popular in England during the eighth century. The Bewcastle cross interlace patterns, for instance, have been convincingly compared with those on the Durham manuscript of Cassiodorus's *Commentary on the Psalms*.[42] On the Ruthwell cross in Dumfries, where two figures are strictly comparable with Bewcastle, the layout is different with figures and inscriptions on its broad faces in the same way as on the Cuthbert coffin — and indeed the figure of Christ on the lid is very similar — and the inscriptions on the Ruthwell cross have been seen as closely related to Lindisfarne scripts.[43] But it is difficult to believe that these crosses were carved by Lindisfarne masons since there is no surviving stone carving at Lindisfarne which is anything like them in motifs or style of cutting. It is possible that the major works from Lindisfarne have been lost, but it is as reasonable to suggest that the coffin and these crosses were copying similar models, in the way that the Lindisfarne Gospels' Matthew portrait and the Codex Amiatinus' Ezra portrait seem to have done.

What crosses are there then at Lindisfarne to set beside the grave-markers already mentioned? The grave-markers are usually thought to be monastic although one has a female name (plate 39 d), but it is interesting to note that none of the crosses which survive have inscriptions, as do many from other centres in the north. The only one which bears any resemblance to manuscript art, other than a very worn interlace head, is a shaft with two animals interlaced on one side and a single animal enmeshed in interlace on the other (plate 40 a, b). I have elsewhere compared the animal with fine interlace (a) with Lindisfarne Gospels, fol. 211[r], and the other with the MacDurnan Gospels. Neither animal is really closely similar to the creatures on early Insular manuscripts, although they may be more like later Northumbrian manuscript productions, of which we know very little, but they seem to belong

---

[41] *Corpus* I, pls. 265 – 7.
[42] Adcock, 'Types of interlace' (as n. 29). Durham Cath, MS. B.II.30 fol. 81[v] is discussed on pp. 158 – 165.
[43] Bonner and Higgitt forthcoming, as part of a detailed study of Ruthwell and Bewcastle.

to a similar debased Hiberno-Saxon tradition as a bird built into the late Saxon tower at Billingham (plate 40 d).

Another Lindisfarne group of three crosses, which I would date to the ninth century, includes a ribbon animal with a coiled haunch and rolled-back jaws which looks rather Pictish, as well as a pair of confronted animals such as are found at Jedburgh or in a very much grander form at Hackness in Yorkshire.[44] In fact the Lindisfarne stone crosses are not in any way the best of their region, but are very similar to what I would see as a later group of Northumbrian sculpture.

On the north-eastern boundary of the Anglian kingdom there is a group of crosses which show a certain independence from Lindisfarne although they would be assumed to be within the sphere of influence of that centre.[45] The early monuments are amongst the finest surviving Northumbrian carvings. A cross from Aberlady[46] has been compared by Bruce-Mitford with the Lindisfarne Gospels in its motifs of interlaced birds,[47] but they are different types of birds and do not have the plumed head extensions of the Lindisfarne manuscript, while the sculpted key patterns, the blunt-headed reptilian beast, and the elegant vinescrolls are more like those of other manuscripts. Abercorn's vinescrolls are very like some from Hexham and the little birds with displayed wings as well as the interlace would fit well alongside ninth-century crosses in Yorkshire. At Jedburgh, another Lindisfarne land-holding in the ninth century, there is some very good vinescroll both inhabited and uninhabited, as well as a cross head which, like one from Edzel, has some affiliation to Pictish art.[48]

In fact, in this region of the original landholdings of the Lindisfarne church there is a clear movement away from Anglian art in the ninth century; and yet the work, even in the ninth century, remains distinct from that of the Picts. The strange bird from Tyningham, a monastery which survived until 941, is a good representative of the type. Yet there are links between centres in this area. The animal-headed interlace of the Bamburgh chair is reflected in a cruder form at Coldingham, as is Lindisfarne geometric interlace. In other words it seems as though a regional style develops, and in this Lindisfarne plays a part.

---

[44] *Corpus* I, pl. 189 (1044 – 7); 191 (1055 – 7); 193 (1071 – 4).

[45] *Corpus* I, pls. 265 – 7.

[46] *Corpus* I, pl. 265 (1430 – 3).

[47] Bruce-Mitford in *Cod. Lind.* II, 255. An alternative parallel with the Lichfield Gospels is provided by G. Henderson, *From Durrow to Kells. The Insular Gospel-books, 650 – 800* (London, 1987), p. 124.

[48] For these pieces from the border territories between England and Scotland see R. B. K. Stevenson, 'The Inchyra stone and other Unpublished Early Christian Monuments', *Proceedings of the Society of Antiquaries of Scotland* 92 (1958 – 9), pp. 33 – 55; R. Cramp, 'The Anglian Sculptures from Jedburgh', in ed. A. O'Connor and D. V. Clarke, *From the Stone Age to the 'Forty-Five* (Edinburgh, 1983), pp. 269 – 84; I. Henderson, 'Pictish Vine-Scroll Ornament', in ibid. pp. 243 – 68.

If a stone church was built at Norham in the ninth century it is possible that stone carvers were imported to the area and that they may have introduced south Northumbrian styles. The remarkable group of fragmentary crosses which survive from that site seems to represent the most up-to-date ninth-century taste of a strongly Deiran type. It is indeed noteworthy that the ornamental repertoire of the crosses from Norham includes as well as confident carvings of vinescrolls and figures also excellent Insular key patterns which make everything at Lindisfarne look so tentative that the Lindisfarne crosses may well be copies. What may be the latest piece of all is, however, an inept ribbon animal which is remotely copying old manuscript models.

So far I have looked at Lindisfarne's influence mainly in eastern Bernicia; but Lindisfarne, as already noted, had its landholdings west of the Pennines, also, and in Carlisle there are crosses which may be closely compared with a newly discovered cross head from Norham.[49] Insular taste is apparent in the confidently carved key and fret patterns, and plant scrolls very like that on the Stonyhurst Gospels cover, which are to be found on a cross shaft from Penrith.[50] In the west the key and fret patterns normally seem to have a complementary distribution to distinctive elegant plant scrolls, as if there were two different patterns of contact. It is the plant scroll motif, however, which is taken over by the Anglo-Viking carvers of Cumbria in the post-monastic phase, and there, as in the Yorkshire Danelaw, the new Scandinavian overlords obviously felt it was a prestigious matter to have a memorial cross. In the early period of Scandinavian supremacy, stone monuments were used as a propaganda vehicle for Scandinavian and Anglian traditions; but by the later tenth century monuments were localized in style and ornament. In eastern Bernicia, there was something of a revival of competence in the tenth/eleventh centuries, but there was a marked difference in the extent of the acceptance of purely Scandinavian styles as compared with areas west and south. The variety in the sculptural repertoire is diminished, and the tradition of Insular ornament dominates.

I have written elsewhere about the artistic effect of the survival of the Lindisfarne community as the only organized religious body in Northumbria from about the mid ninth century. I have also noted how the collection of crosses at Chester-le-Street indicates contact with ninth-century Jarrow traditions as well as with Lindisfarne, and there are close links in the motifs favoured at Tynemouth, Aycliffe, and Durham.[51] It is almost as though the maintenance of Insular patterns became a necessary banner for St Cuthbert's people. All the centres mentioned betray some knowledge of the new Viking Age art of Deira and Cumbria, but on the whole they are remarkably true to

---

[49] Carlisle: *Corpus* II, illustr. 202 – 7; Norham: *Corpus* II, illustr. 675.
[50] *Corpus* II, illustr. 476 – 9.
[51] R. Cramp, 'The Pre-Conquest Sculptural Tradition in Durham', in *Medieval Art and Architecture in Durham Cathedral*, ed. N. Coldstream and P. Draper (The British Archaeological Association, Conference Transactions for 1977; British Arch. Assoc. 1980), p. 1 – 10.

the eighth-century Lindisfarne tradition of panels of precise geometric interlace, of animals and birds. It is only in the fashionable twisted lips of the beasts and the new closed-circuit interlace patterns that a later generation of ornament is betrayed. Was it manuscripts, pattern books, or the visible monument, St Aethelwold's cross, which inspired these patterns? A detailed survey of Northumbrian crosses of this period reveals several monuments which appear to have exerted an influence on lesser monuments nearby, and it is indeed possible that Aethelwold's cross was an important model.

When the cross from St Oswald's Church, Durham (plate 40 e,f,g,) was first discovered and written about by Canon Greenwell, some thought that it might be Aethelwold's cross itself. I prefer to think, as Gwenda Adcock did,[52] that the warped panel of interlace on one of the broad faces of the cross indicates the template copying of some model here, and one can then see the Aycliffe crosses and the Durham grave-cover as part of a conscious revival. Not for nothing did the Anglo-Saxons call their crosses *becun* — distinguishing sign or mark; such monuments made many statements as well as serving as memorials for the dead. In bringing with them from Lindisfarne their first great stone monument and implanting it in the cemetery at Durham the hard-pressed community of St Cuthbert proclaimed their heritage. As we have seen in other papers in this conference the light of the Lindisfarne tradition burnt brighter through time as other competing illuminations flickered and died.

[52] Adcock, 'Types of Interlace', pp. 209 – 19.

PART THREE

The Coffin
and its Treasures

St Cuthbert's Relics: Some Neglected Evidence

RICHARD N. BAILEY

I

Dr James Raine, librarian of Durham Cathedral and rector of Meldon, opened St Cuthbert's tomb in the feretory on 17 May 1827.[1] In an editorial published two days later *The Durham Advertiser* gave a brief description of the event which had 'occasioned a great sensation in the town'. Drawing upon information supplied by the Reverend W. N. Darnell, sub-dean at the cathedral, the *Advertiser* claimed that the discoveries had been made in 'carrying into effect certain alterations and improvements at the eastern end of the church'.[2] This explanation of the work was not, however, 'credited by the greater part of the inhabitants' according to the Durham correspondent of *The Tyne Mercury*, writing on 22 May, and he went on to report that the excavation had caused great offence to the Roman Catholic congregation in the city.

The sectarian background revealed here is crucial to a proper understanding both of Raine's initiative in opening the tomb and of the subsequent account given in his *St Cuthbert*. Although Roman Catholics had been granted freedom of worship in 1791, the struggle for complete emancipation continued to arouse deep religious and political antagonisms throughout the first three decades of the nineteenth century. The editorial and correspondence columns of *The Durham Advertiser* clearly reveal these divisions at local level. On 10 December 1825, for example, a Durham freeholder demands a parliamentary candidate for the county to oppose Catholic emancipation; on 7 October 1826 a 'Protestant' writes of the 'struggle between the Church of England and the Church of Rome becoming in this country more and more serious' whilst on 10 March 1827 an editorial asserts the need to 'take a stand against Catholic claims . . . otherwise Roman Catholic ambitions will take to the throne itself'.

Both locally and nationally, these sectarian tensions were particularly acute during the period between April and June of 1827. Canning's administration had come to power in April with a strong commitment to Catholic emancipation whilst at the end of May two Roman Catholic churches were to

---

[1] *St Cuthbert*, p. 183.
[2] Darnell's authorship is confirmed by Raine's notes in his annotated copy of *St Cuthbert* (Durham Cathedral Library, Additional MS 148).

be consecrated in County Durham. The first was St Augustine's at Darlington, whose completion had been delayed by Protestant vandalism.[3] More immediately relevant here however was the opening of a new Roman Catholic church in the Old Elvet area of Durham itself. This building was dedicated on 31 May — and dedicated to St Cuthbert.[4] Raine's decision to investigate the saint's tomb a fortnight earlier could not be seen as mere coincidence. The two events were clearly connected, the one a discrediting preface to the other.[5]

It is this background which, at least in part, explains why the excavation took place when it did. It also accounts for the tone and the curiously selective emphasis of the subsequent report in *St Cuthbert*. Much of the motivation for the inquiry sprang from the need to demonstrate that it was in an *Anglican* cathedral where lay the saint to whom the city's new Roman Catholic church was to be dedicated. And to demonstrate moreover that what the cathedral sheltered were the *bones* of Cuthbert and not a miraculously preserved body. And finally the excavation was designed to lay to rest persistent Roman Catholic traditions that St Cuthbert's body had been removed by monks at the time of the Reformation and a substitute put in its place. Whilst recognizing the very real academic achievement of Raine's *St Cuthbert*, therefore, it must be read as a partisan document. It is perhaps only fair to record that Raine himself later regretted the manner in which he had written, recognizing that he had been particularly injudicious in deleting paragraphs which took a more positive view of Durham's pre-Reformation clergy than emerged in his published text.[6]

II

Hitherto it has been assumed that Raine's book is the only source available for examining the 1827 excavations. Other records have, however, survived unnoticed and provide their own interesting commentary on Raine's report. These sources suggest, first, that the excavation may not have been fully authorized, for it is probably significant that the matter was never discussed (on the evidence of the minute book) by the cathedral chapter. Secondly, it is clear that the whole operation was a highly contentious issue among the cathedral clergy. Darnell, who as sub-dean was the responsible cleric, clearly did not approve of the project (at least in retrospect) and his relations with Raine were strained. This emerges in a letter dated 30 July 1827 preserved in Raine's own annotated copy of *St Cuthbert* (Durham Cathedral Additional MS 148). In it Darnell sent Raine the drawing of St Cuthbert's skull, used so

---

[3] See accounts in *The Northern Catholic Calendar* reprinted in *Parish Histories from the Northern Catholic Calendar*, ed. G. Milburn (Durham, 1986).

[4] See accounts in *Parish Histories* and J. W. Tweedy, *Popish Elvet* (Durham, 1981), pp. 120 – 1.

[5] See the informed comment in W. Brown, 'Where is St Cuthbert's Body?', *The Ushaw Magazine* 6 (1896), p. 212.

[6] Ibid., p. 212 and Raine's annotation to p. 172 of his copy of *St Cuthbert*.

dramatically on p. 214 of the report, but ended his missive: 'I wish no evil may befall you for having been engaged in this wicked spoliation of the dead'. None of this dissension of course leaked out beyond the cathedral — as witness the opening of an attack on Raine published in *Andrew's Penny Orthodox Journal* for 1833:

> It's good to be rector of Meldon
> Hand in glove with a Chapter and Dean
> Whatsoever one does, then, is well done
> Though in others, 'twere wicked or mean.[7]

More significant for evaluating the reliability of Raine's report is the evidence supplied by other sources about the conduct of the excavation. Thus Raine lists sixteen witnesses to the investigation as though this group had kept a constant monitoring watch on the work. Yet one of the workmen, Joseph Taylor (d. 1875), recalled later that even Raine was not actually present when the covering slabs were removed.[8] Raine himself acknowledges this fact in a pencilled note in his copy of *St Cuthbert* — and also admits absence later in the day when decisions about re-coffinning took place.

The fullest 'alternative' account of the excavation however is to be found among the letters of John Lingard (1771 – 1851) preserved in the Library of Ushaw College, near Durham. Lingard was a distinguished Roman Catholic historian who had published in 1828, anonymously, a critique of Raine's book, exposing some of the inconsistencies and special pleadings of its argument.[9] He had a wide circle of friends with whom he conducted a voluminous correspondence from his home at Hornby in Lancashire.[10] One of these friends was Dr W. S. Gilly, a member of the cathedral chapter at the time of Raine's investigation, who became vicar of Norham and there campaigned vigorously to improve the lot of Northumberland's agricultural workers. Gilly visited Lingard in 1841 and they discussed the Cuthbert excavations. In three letters written immediately afterwards, Lingard gives Gilly's version of the events of 17 May 1827, most fully in a letter to Dr G. Oliver dated 14 October 1841:

> Yesterday Dr Gilly, prebendary of Durham, called. He was according to the extract from Raine in the little book which I sent you one of the openers of St

---

[7] The poem is transcribed in Durham Cathedral Additional MS 148 by Raine and the magazine is there described as 'containing other silly articles on the same subject'. I have not been able to trace a copy of this work.

[8] Newspaper cutting pasted into Newcastle City Library copy of J. Lingard, *Remarks on the 'St Cuthbert' of the Rev. James Raine* (Newcastle, 1828).

[9] See n. 8 above. Lingard's text was altered after it was submitted to the president of Ushaw College so as to delete statements in which he accepted that the body discovered in 1827 really was that of St Cuthbert: see Ushaw College, Lingard letters, nos. 531 and 370 and *Notes and Queries* 11 (1855), p. 255. Lingard was later introduced to Raine by an unknowing hostess and the pair became friends; see Lingard letters, nos. 31 and 647. (Lingard's correspondence is cited according to the numbering of the transcripts.)

[10] M. Haile and E. Bonney, *Life and Letters of John Lingard, 1771 – 1851* (London, 1911).

Cuthbert's tomb. He tells me that he was not: but hearing in the choir a strange noise in the feretory, the moment the service was over he ran there in his surplice to see what was going on, and there found Darnell and Raine with two workmen, the latter actually standing within the coffin and trampling on the contents. He ordered them out, remonstrated with Darnell and requested that witnesses might be sent for out of the town and someone from Ushaw. Darnell was sub-dean and seemed very nervous, but refused. He wished to finish the investigation as quickly as possible and to prevent any crowd assembling. Gilly then went down himself and discovered two stoles and maniple, the altar of oak covered with silver, the gold cross on the breast and the paten lying by it. Now this is contrary to Raine who says there was no paten discovered. They removed all the bones into a new chest and buried them in the same place. He will send me some of the silk in which the saint's body was enveloped . . .[11]

No doubt this account is biased. One notes for example that Gilly is credited with most of the important discoveries. No doubt also it contains inaccuracies; the alleged 'paten' may well have been a misinterpretation of the silver disc at the centre of the portable altar. Yet is must be recognized as evidence for a marked degree of chaos attending the original excavation. Raine's record and observations must clearly be read with Lingard's letter in mind.

One final piece of untapped information about the 1827 excavations should also be recorded. Among the Durham Cathedral manuscripts are some coloured illustrations, with annotations in Raine's hand, which may originally have been intended for use in *St Cuthbert*. One is a large-scale drawing, inserted into Raine's own copy of his work, showing the clasps or 'bandages' which he describes as attached to the outer coffin. The others are found in a separate manuscript (Durham Cathedral Additional MS 149) and show (a) the outer coffin, (b) a plan of the relationship between the three coffins and (c) a drawing of Cuthbert's skeleton, clad in its vestments, together with attendant skulls (see plate 45). Unfortunately it is very doubtful if these can be treated as eye-witness records of what was actually found, drawn at the time of discovery. Firstly there was little time in which to complete such drawings and secondly the illustrations and the written account contradict each other. Thus the mouldings of the outer coffin are described in the text as being broken and the lid as 'dished' upwards.[12] The presence of two skulls by Cuthbert's feet also sits awkwardly with Raine's uncertainty about the precise location of this group of material in relation to the different coffins.[13]

The value of these drawings is therefore as evidence of what Raine *believed* (on the basis of his excavation) to have been the original state of the outer coffin and the post-Reformation appearance of St Cuthbert; their testimony undoubtedly clarifies some muddy sections of his text.

---

[11] Ushaw College, Lingard letters, no. 429. Other letters give shorter versions of the same event: nos. 149, 754a.

[12] *St Cuthbert*, p. 185.

[13] *St Cuthbert*, pp. 186 – 7.

III

The tomb was re-opened in 1899, at the instigation of the indefatigable Canon Greenwell. The purpose of this excavation was twofold: to obtain a proper anatomical examination of the skeleton and to recover those items which had been thrown back into the tomb by Raine. On this occasion Father William Brown was present as a representative of the Roman Catholic church. Despite this, Greenwell was attacked for the desecration of the grave at a meeting of the Newcastle Society of Antiquaries; he defended himself with characteristic vigour.[14]

Three accounts were published of this work: a fully illustrated article by J. T. Fowler in *Archaeologia*; a chapter section by Dean Kitchin in the *Victoria County History*; an article by Father Brown in *The Ushaw Magazine*.[15] To these can be added the anatomical report contributed by Dr Selby Plummer to the *Northumberland and Durham Medical Journal* (pp. 231 – 45) for July 1899. There are minor variations in these papers but it will suffice here to draw attention to one additional neglected source — a series of letters by Brown which appeared in *The Durham Advertiser* during 1908 and which were subsequently printed in *The Ushaw Magazine* for 1909. Brown was a convinced adherent of the theory that Cuthbert's body had been removed from the cathedral at the Reformation, and although he acknowledged that the 1899 excavations had been carried out as reverently as was possible he felt obliged to recall:

> something that occurred on 2 March 1899. A careful attempt was being made to raise from the vault the 'new coffin' in which Canon Raine had placed the remains found by him on 17 May 1827. The shoddy thing collapsed, and the contents, consisting chiefly of his 'skeleton of St Cuthbert', fell out, and were scattered among a mass of bones and broken wood that lay at the bottom of the grave. However, with the least possible delay the vault was cleared, and human remains, sufficient not only for a skeleton, but with about 180 bones to spare, were brought to light. The collection included three lower jaws, about twenty ribs, thirty-five bones of feet, twenty-six portions of backbone, seven left shin bones, etc., in addition to those selected to form a skeleton, which during the following fortnight was pieced together from the abundant material at hand . . .[16]

As with the Gilly/Lingard account of the earlier excavation we are here dealing with a particular viewpoint. Nevertheless Brown's record needs to be

[14] *Proceedings of the Society of Antiquaries of Newcastle upon Tyne* 9 (1901), pp. 18 – 21.

[15] J. T. Fowler, 'On an Examination of the Grave of St Cuthbert', *Archaeologia* 57 (1) (1900), pp. 11 – 28; G. W. Kitchin, 'The Contents of St Cuthbert's Shrine', *The Victoria History of the Counties of England: Durham*, I (London, 1905), pp. 241 – 58; W. Brown, 'St Cuthbert's Grave and Coffin', *The Ushaw Magazine* 9 (1899), pp. 124 – 32.

[16] W. Brown, 'St Cuthbert's Remains', *The Ushaw Magazine* 19 (1909), pp. 28 – 9. His earlier analysis of the Cuthbert body problem can be found in: *The Ushaw Magazine* 6 (1896), pp. 211 – 46; ibid., 9 (1899), pp. 74 – 88 and 117 – 32.

set against Plummer's confident reconstructions of the skeletal remains of both Cuthbert and Oswald.

IV

Relics of St Cuthbert were scattered early. Bede records one of his hairs being used for a miraculous cure in the eighth century and the relic lists of many medieval foundations include material associated with the saint.[17] At the Reformation other items strayed away from Durham: this is probably the time when the Ushaw ring, the front tooth preserved until the French Revolution in Paris, and the (alleged) griffin's claw, now in the British Museum, left the cathedral.[18] Our concern here, however, is with the dispersal of material found in 1827 and 1899; a preliminary attempt to list this evidence is presented at the end of this paper (pp. 243 – 6). What follows is a discussion of the channels through which it was dispersed.

Some of the 1827 finds began to leak away from the main holding at an early date. Raine describes, for example, a small linen bag or burse: 'Its size may be compared to that of a duodecimo book, or perhaps it was somewhat larger'. By the time he wrote his account this could not be found and in a pencilled note in the index to his copy he ruefully gives the explanation: 'lost in Darnell's house'.[19] One of the other canons present at the excavation seems to have been another channel by which material disappeared. Raine notes that 'Mr Gilly, as it appeared afterwards, took possession of one of the teeth of St Cuthbert . . . It is now in his possession'.[20] Gilly, however, removed far more than a single tooth for in a letter in Ushaw College we are told that 'Gilly had several large bits of vestment, which he doled out to his friends'.[21] One of those friends was John Lingard who, in turn, provided offcuts for his own correspondents (see below p. 243).

Another route for dispersal emerges from the records of Ushaw College. The College now possesses several fragments of fabric which were contained in a booklet presented to it on 21 July 1858 by William Trueman, a Durham chemist with antiquarian interests. In the booklet was a certificate attesting that the fragments had come from Matthew Thompson, a Durham upholsterer who was used by Raine as one of his illustrators.[22] They

---

[17] *HE* IV, 32 (30). On relic-lists, see I. G. Thomas, 'The Cult of Saints' Relics in Medieval England' (unpublished Ph.D. thesis, University of London, 1974), Appendix I, s.n.
[18] For these items see: A. B. Tonnochy, 'The Ring Preserved at Ushaw College', in *Relics*, pp. 526 – 7; *The Ushaw Magazine* 35 (1925), pp. 38 – 40, 73 – 80; ibid., 58 (1948), pp. 37 – 40; C. Eyre, *The History of St Cuthbert* (3rd edn., London, 1887), p. 307. The griffin's claw will be the subject of a forthcoming paper.
[19] Durham Cathedral Additional MS 148, index.
[20] Ibid., facing p. 3 of Appendix.
[21] Ushaw College, Lingard letters, no. 149 to F. C. Husenbeth dated 3 November 1842.
[22] I owe this information to notes supplied by Dr I. A. Doyle who examined the booklet in 1957.

presumably reached Thompson as a gift from Raine and it is known that others present at the opening were similarly rewarded (see below).

Throughout the nineteenth century and into the early years of the twentieth, small fragments of the vestments and the coffins continued to be presented to individuals and institutions. The story of one piece of silk is typical (see below p. 245). When, in 1847, Sir E. H. Alderson was acting as assize judge in Durham he was taken on a tour of the cathedral by the dean. On expressing interest in the fabrics he was promptly offered a small piece of the Nature Goddess silk. This was inherited by the judge's daughter who passed it on to a friend who finally presented it, at some date in the 1920s, to the church of St Cuthbert and St Matthias in Philbeach Gardens, London. In this case the fragment has survived and the record is clear; in many other instances, however, material has disappeared without trace. Small as they are, these scattered fragments often provide vital evidence; in particular they frequently survive in a better state of preservation than material still at Durham and thus furnish valuable supplementary information about the original appearance of these pieces.

V

This paper has concentrated so far on documentary evidence which has been neglected and on fragments of scattered Cuthbertiana which have been ignored. This final section highlights three items associated with the saint which have not hitherto had the attention they merit: a fragment of the stole from Ushaw College, a piece of decorated silver now in the British Museum, and a cross-incised board which is still in the Durham Cathedral collection.

a) Stole fragment now at Ushaw College (see below p. 245)

This fragment, which is 3.3 cm long, carries the characteristic border pattern of the stole together with the letters 'BA' set vertically one below the other. The accompanying label in the Ushaw display identifies these as the opening letters of the name 'BARUCH' — a prophet who is not otherwise represented among the stole's figures. It is, however, almost certain that the Ushaw fragment preserves the fourth and fifth letters of 'ABABACVC' (Habakkuk). The reasoning is set out below but I am encouraged in this identification by the fact that Dr Ian Doyle has independently reached the same conclusion.

The starting point for the argument lies in Raine's *St Cuthbert*. On p. 204 he records the presence on the stole, when found, of a complete inscription 'ABABACVC'. By the time he came to write his account however 'the first three letters only now remain'. These three letters can still be seen on the stole in Durham, together with the remains of the prophet's halo, in the section below 'Joel'. The rest of the figure has now disappeared. The proposal here is that the Ushaw letters represent the 'BA' continuation of the name, following directly after the Durham letters 'ABA'. The 'BARUCH' suggestion must be rejected on the grounds that the Ushaw letters are set *vertically*; the evidence of all of the other stole inscriptions shows that the opening letters of names are always arranged in a *horizontal* sequence, whatever patterns they adopt at later points in the name. Figure 13 shows a possible arrangement of the surviving Durham and Ushaw letters around a restored Habakkuk figure.

b) Silver fragment now in the British Museum (Acc. No. 1858, 10 – 23, 1).

This small fragment (3.75 cm by 2.25 cm) was presented to the British Museum in 1858 by the Reverend F. W. Lee; the register entry records that it was 'said to come from the tomb of St Cuthbert'.

Lee was a remarkable theologian, controversialist and antiquary who was also responsible for the gift to the national collection of a silver fragment from Hexham.[23] As Radford noted, it is difficult to identify the lightly incised decoration on this damaged Cuthbert fragment and it clearly deserves a more extended study than is possible here.[24] What can be distinguished however is an acanthus type of leaf with a lightly rolled tip and three detached buds contained within a curved 'bite' in the outline of the leaf. In some details this decoration can be compared with the foliage on the stole from the shrine and it seems reasonable to assign the fragment to the tenth century. Since the piece does not figure in Raine's inventory there is no need to assume that it came from the 1827 opening of the coffin. More likely, if it does have genuine Cuthbert links, it was part of the treasure associated with the shrine in its pre-Reformation stage, though not necessarily placed within the coffins.

c) The cross-incised board

Various fragments from all three coffins were recovered during the re-excavation of the tomb in 1899. It was possible to use some in the display mounting of the 698 coffin-reliquary but over 4,000 other pieces are now stored in boxes in the cathedral. Among these are a large number of mouldings, an 'arcade', and fragments from a board decorated with an incised cross.[25] In a future paper I hope to discuss the relationship between the 'arcade', mouldings, the illustrations of the Cuthbert shrine appearing in the *Life of St Cuthbert* in Oxford, University College MS 165, and Reginald of Durham's description of the 1104 translation — notably his reference to *ostiola* (small apertures/doorways).[26] The present discussion is restricted to the cross-incised board (fig. 14).

The fragments from this board were assembled after 1899 and fixed to a display base. As now arranged the fragments make up a board which is *c.*28 cm broad and 75.4 cm long. There is, of course, no reason to infer that these

---

[23] See R. N. Bailey, 'The Anglo-Saxon Metalwork from Hexham', in *St Wilfrid at Hexham*, ed. D. P. Kirby (Newcastle upon Tyne, 1974), at pp. 155 – 8.

[24] C. A. R. Radford, 'The Portable Altar of St Cuthbert', in *Relics* p. 335.

[25] F. J. Haverfield and W. Greenwell, *Catalogue of the Sculptured and Inscribed Stones in the Cathedral Library, Durham* (Durham, 1899), pp. 154 – 5; Kitchin, *Victoria History: Durham*, I, p. 243.

[26] *St Cuthbert*, appendix p. 6 and p. 92; *Relics*, p. 112.

13. *Possible reconstruction of 'ABABACVC' figure on stole including surviving fragments from Durham Cathedral (1) and Ushaw College (2).*

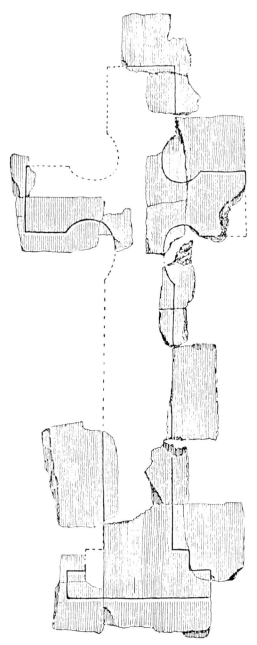

14. The cross-incised board fragments (after Haverfield and Greenwell, Catalogue
1899).

were the original dimensions of the board; the stem of the cross, in particular, could have been much longer than now reconstructed. Despite these doubts about size the original decoration is clear: an incised free-armed outline cross standing on a stepped base.

When Kitzinger commented on these pieces he noted that the wood resembled that of the 698 coffin in both its thickness and its grain.[27] He felt obliged nevertheless to reject the possibility that these fragments had formed part of the original coffin because he believed that stepped bases were not a feature of free-standing pre-Norman sculpture. As a general observation this is undoubtedly correct, though one could point to examples from Lindisfarne, Gosforth (Cumbria), and Halton (Lancashire) where stepped bases survive in a pre-Norman context.[28] None of these, however, belong to a date before the Viking period.

Despite this, an art-historical case *can* be advanced for assigning this incised cross to an early Anglo-Saxon date. Firstly the shape of head is one which occurs early in the development of Anglo-Saxon sculpture, for example on 'Acca's Cross' at Hexham, and secondly it may not be irrelevant to note that this type of base is used in Irish sculpture in the course of the eighth century.[29] Neither of these parallels, of course, offers convincing proof that the Durham fragments must be of seventh-century date but they do suggest that a pre-Viking period context is not wholly impossible. Much more crucial to the argument is the fact that crosses with stepped bases can be found on coins circulating in seventh-century England. Such crosses are a persistent motif on Byzantine issues of the period and the Wilton pendant, incorporating one such coin, shows that the relevant types were known here.[30] A more likely setting in which it would be familiar in England however is on the imitations of Byzantine coins produced in the Merovingian and Visigothic west; finds from sites like Sutton Hoo and Crondall show that these reached England in some quantities.[31] It is presumably this Merovingian coinage which is responsible for the occurrence of the stepped cross on some of the earliest English issues. In a paper published in 1953 Grierson was able to identify three specimens

---

[27] E. Kitzinger, 'The Coffin-reliquary', in *Relics*, p. 218.

[28] *Corpus* I, pl. 199, 1110; T. D. Kendrick, *Late Saxon and Viking Art* (London, 1949), pl. XLII; *Corpus* II, *s.n.* 'Gosforth'.

[29] E.g., F. Henry, *Irish Art in the Early Christian Period to A.D. 800* (London, 1965), pls. 78, 80, 83, 84, 86.

[30] D. M. Wilson, *Anglo-Saxon Art* (London, 1984), pl. 18. See also: P. D. Whitting, 'The Byzantine Empire and the Coinage of the Anglo-Saxons', in *Anglo-Saxon Coins*, ed. M. Dolley (London, 1961), pp. 28–9; P. D. Whitting, *Byzantine Coins* (London, 1973), passim.

[31] C. H. V. Sutherland, *Anglo-Saxon Gold Coinage in the Light of the Crondall Hoard* (Oxford, 1948); J. P. C. Kent, 'The Coins and the Date of the Burial', in *The Sutton Hoo Ship Burial*, I (London, 1975), ed. R. L. S. Bruce-Mitford, pp. 578–678; M. Prou, *Les monnaies mérovingiennes* (Paris, 1896), passim.

minted in England using this form of cross on their reverse face. To these can
be added the 'benu:tigo' runic coin from Dorchester.[32]

Seventh-century England, and particularly those centres with overseas
contacts, must therefore have been acquainted with the notion of the stepped-
base cross. A 698 dating of the incised board from Durham would
consequently not be impossible and would be consonant with the evidence of
the wood's grain and dimensions. This was the proposal with which I came
armed to the 1987 Cuthbert conference only to discover that, independently,
Janey Cronyn had reached the same conclusion using the more convincing
armoury of dendrochronology (see below pp. 247 – 56). The case must now be
accepted; this cross-incised board was once part of the original
coffin-reliquary.

But to which part of the coffin did it belong? We have two possibilities. It
could be part of the inner lid whose former existence is attested by the
anonymous account of the 1104 translation and by the survival of mortises on
the side panels of the coffin.[33] Since there is no pressing argument for
assuming that this lid was a later addition, this must provide one solution for
the board's function. Alternatively, the fragments may be the remains of the
bottom of the coffin which, according to Reginald's account, required
attention at the time of the translation.[34] The grounds for this identification
can be found in Raine's description, for on three occasions (twice in italics) he
claimed that one of the bottom boards of one of the coffins carried
decoration.[35] Obviously the implications of the opening sections of this essay
are that Raine's observations need to be treated with extreme caution, and,
indeed, he himself admitted that he could not properly distinguish the order or
number of bottom boards available.[36] He could therefore have misinterpreted
incised fragments from the sides or ends of the coffin-reliquary which had
fallen inwards during the excavation. Yet it should be noticed that he lifted out
all of the bottom boards, along with the skeleton, in one single operation; he
could thus have been in a position to recognize the presence of carving on *a*
bottom board, even if he was incapable of distinguishing which of the three
coffins was involved.[37]

Whatever the original function of this cross-incised fragment it must now be
seen as part of the coffin-reliquary of AD 698. This conclusion has important
ramifications since it implies that free-standing crosses of this shape were
familiar objects in late-seventh-century Northumbria. It is but another
measure of the abiding significance of the Cuthbert material that this

---

[32] P. Grierson, 'A New Anglo-Saxon Solidus', *Numismatic Chronicle* 6th series 13 (1953), pp. 88 – 91; R. Page, *An Introduction to English Runes* (London, 1973), p. 123.

[33] J. M. Cronyn and C. V. Horie, *St. Cuthbert's Coffin* (Durham, 1985), pp. 65 – 7; *Relics*, p. 101.

[34] *Relics*, p. 108.

[35] *St. Cuthbert*, pp. 189, 191, 216.

[36] Ibid., p. 215.

[37] Ibid., pp. 192 – 3.

deduction has radical implications for the study of the chronology of Anglo-Saxon sculpture.

APPENDIX

THE SCATTERED FRAGMENTS: A CHECKLIST

A) The Gilly/Lingard fragments (now lost)

In a letter to Dr G. Oliver of 14 October 1841 describing Gilly's visit (see above p. 234) Lingard records that Gilly 'will send me some of the silk in which the saint's body was enveloped'.[38] More than one fragment eventually reached him as is evident from a letter of 2 November 1841 to J. G. Rokewood, now part of the Hengrave Hall deposit 21 (13) in the University Library, Cambridge, where he states that 'I have received from Dr Gilly two little bits of silk taken out of St Cuthbert's coffin'. A year later he wrote to Dr F. C. Husenbeth: 'I will send you in this letter, but only to look at, and with the strict injunction that you send it back, a bit of the vestment of St Cuthbert'.[39] By December he seems to have succumbed to entreaties and writes (2 December 1842): 'I can spare only a small part of St Cuthbert's vestment. It was originally twice the size of what you saw but has been diminished by the distribution of pieces to those who wished to have them. I have enclosed you half of the smaller piece'.[40] On 18 1843 May he wrote to Oliver, 'I send for your inspection, and veneration if you think proper, a portion of his vestments, as you will see by the paper in which it is enclosed (taken from the coffin in 1827 and presented to Dr Lingard by Dr Gilly 26 October 1841. One red silk with a black glory cross. The other a drab silk)'.[41] A later but undated letter to Miss Hannah Joyce, the adopted daughter of his Lancashire friend Dr William Shepherd, shows yet another fragment being sent out for inspection: 'I add two curiosities for your ladyship to look at, — one is a specimen of a difficult French manuscript — the other, the silk from St Cuthbert's coffin, must be 1200 years old'.[42]

Gilly therefore had at least two different types of fabric, portions of which he gave to friends. Despite intensive searches none of these fragments can now be traced. Lingard's will, preserved in Ushaw College, was drawn up before Gilly's visit and understandably therefore does not mention these pieces; the

---

[38] Ushaw College, Lingard letters, no. 429.
[39] Ibid., no. 149, dated 3 November 1842.
[40] Ibid., no. 150.
[41] Ibid., no. 438.
[42] Ibid., no. 763.

instructions to his executors, though written later, also omit all reference to them. It is just possible, however, that one of the Ushaw College fragments may stem from the Lingard holding, since most of his library and personal effects were bequeathed to the College (see below p. 245).

B) Alnmouth, Northumberland: Society of St Francis

i.   Fragment of Nature Goddess silk (8 cm by 6.5 cm) preserving part of the twist pattern flanking the fruit-laden border motif. This was presented to the Alnmouth Community by Father Trevor Huddlestone of Mirfield at some date after 1963. He had received it as a gift from Lady Howick who kindly informs me that her mother, Lady Gray, believed that it originally belonged to her aunt Lady Sophie de Franqueville (d. 1915). Though letters in the Durham Department of Palaeography indicate that Dr Gilly had correspondence with both the 2nd and 3rd Earls Gray in 1829 and 1837, there is no reason to assume that the fragment reached the Gray/Howick family by that route.

C) Durham: St Cuthbert's Roman Catholic Church

i.   Fragment of coffin (length *c*. 11 cm) now set in a gilt reliquary. This can probably be identified with the fragment recorded in 1896 by Father William Brown.[43] There is no indication of how it reached the church but Raine developed close links with the Very Reverend Ralph Platt of St Cuthbert's in the middle years of the century; this friendship suggests one possible route.

ii.   Fragment of coffin (12 cm by 8 cm by 1.5 cm). Part of a peg hole is still visible on this fragment.

iii.   Textile fragment, now lost. An envelope with a label in the hand of Father William Brown (priest at St Cuthbert's from 1874 – 1924) still survives; the textile fragment kept in it and described on the label was, according to the priest-in-charge, still in existence in the 1960s. It has now disappeared.

D) London: British Museum, Department of Medieval and Later Antiquities

The Department holds a set of textile fragments mounted in a glass-fronted display case (Acc. No. 1896, 5-1, 96). The accession book shows that they were presented in 1896 to A. W. Franks by Greenwell who had purchased them in a sale. I am very grateful to Hero Granger-Taylor and Clare Higgins for their help in identifying these fragments as follows:

i.   Two fragments of brick red tabby weave (5.7 cm by 2 cm; 4.3 cm by 2 cm).

ii.   Fragment of the Rider silk (9.5 cm by 2.7 cm). No decoration visible.

iii.   Fragment of Nature Goddess silk (13 cm by 3.5 cm).

---

[43] W. Brown, 'Where is St Cuthbert's Body?', *The Ushaw Magazine* 6 (1896), p. 235.

iv.   Two fragments of Central Asian silk (5.5 cm by 3.7 cm).

v.   Several small fragments of weft-patterned silk.

E) London: St Cuthbert with St Matthias Church, Philbeach Gardens, SW5

The church now possesses five fragments from the tomb. The only information about their provenance is provided by the *Guide* to the church; this is undated but, on internal evidence, was written in the late 1930s.

i.   Fragment from the Nature Goddess silk (4 cm by 4 cm) showing part of the fruit-bearing border together with a fish from the sea beneath the figure.

ii.   Fragment from the Nature Goddess silk (2.5 cm by 5 cm). This piece is currently in too fragile and folded a state to be certain about its pattern.

According to the *Guide* one of these fragments was given in 1847 to Baron Alderson by the dean of Durham (see above p. 237). It was presented to the church during the 1920s. The other piece was donated at about the same time by the grandson of one of those present at the 1827 opening.

iii. Fragment of silk cord, possibly from the fringe of the maniple (length 7.5 cm). No known provenance; probably presented with either Ei or Eii above.

iv.   Fragment of 698 coffin (1.5 cm by 1.8 cm by 5 cm).

v.   Fragment of 698 coffin (1.9 cm by 1.7 cm by 5 cm)

These two pieces of wood were presented to the church in 1927, the donor having received them from a relation.

F) Ushaw College, near Durham

The following textile fragments are now placed in a glass-fronted display case. They represent two distinct gifts, though it is now impossible to distinguish between them. The majority came from a small booklet with an inscription of gift to the College, dated 21 July 1858, from William Trueman. With this booklet was Matthew Thompson's certification, dated 15 March 1859, discussed above p. 236. There was, however, another separate fragment which was recorded in the 1922 description of the Ushaw Museum as being the gift of President Dr Lennon in 1898.[44] It is just possible that Lennon's fragment represents part of Lingard's bequest (see above).

i.   Fragment with inscription from stole (3.3 cm by 1.7 cm). See above p. 237.

ii.   Three fragments from the Rider silk (7 cm by 6 cm; 6 cm by 4 cm; 2 cm by 3 cm) showing the beaded border and adjacent section.

iii. Three fragments of stole braid (largest 4.6 cm by .97 cm).

iv.   Fragment of weft-patterned silk (7.5 cm by 6 cm).

[44] J. McCormack, 'Church Plate and Vestments at Ushaw', *The Ushaw Magazine* 32 (1922), pp. 122 – 3.

v.   Fragment of Nature Goddess silk (greatest width 8.5 cm) showing the leaf from the potted floriate motif which appears between the roundels.
vi.   Fragment of Nature Goddess silk (8 cm by 5.5 cm) showing part of the beaded tassel on the end of the figure's scarf.
vii.   Fragment of Soumak weave (7 cm by 3.5 cm).
viii. Four silk threads (*c*.8 cm long), presumably from the maniple fringe.

I am deeply indebted to Dr Ian Doyle for his notes on the Trueman/Thompson record.

G) Cleadon (private possession)

i.   Iron ring from the outer coffin (diameter 9.2 cm).
ii.   Fragment of the outer coffin (6.5 cm by 4 cm).
       These fragments were presented to Archibald Brown, Clerk of Works to Durham Cathedral, on his retirement and are now held by a member of his family. Brown was present at the 1899 opening.

H) Wallsend (private possession)

i.   Fragment of 698 coffin (4.8 cm by 3 cm by 1.5 cm). This fragment was presented to George William Welch in 1900 after long service in the choir of the cathedral. It passed to his daughter Mrs. A. E. Hunter and thence as a gift in 1968 to the present owner.

Several fragments have been returned to the cathedral in recent years and now form part of the reserve collection. Details of the items held in private possession are recorded in the cathedral's archives.

Acknowledgements

I gratefully acknowledge the help afforded in this project by Dr Ian Doyle; he had trodden part of this road before me and generously made available his notes on the Ushaw material as well as his deep knowledge of nineteenth-century Durham. I also thank the following institutions and individuals who allowed me to examine material in their care: The Dean and Chapter of Durham and Roger Norris; Ushaw College and Father Michael Sharratt; The British Museum and Leslie Webster; Alnmouth Friary and Brother Colin Wilfrid; St Cuthbert's RC Church, Durham and Father John James; St Cuthbert and St Matthias' Church, Philbeach Gardens and Father John Vine; Mrs D. Lake; Mrs McCann. For information, and illustrations used in the lecture, I here thank: Denis Briggs; Eric Cambridge; Elisabeth Crowfoot; Janey Cronyn; Robin Gard; Hero Granger-Taylor; Clare Higgins; Victoria Tudor; Father John Tweedy. My wife helped in the survey of nineteenth-century sources and I thank her for her help in yet another investigation.

The Anglo-Saxon Coffin:
Further Investigations[1]

J. M. CRONYN, C. V. HORIE

INTRODUCTION

In 1827 the Relics of St Cuthbert were removed from the tomb behind the high altar of Durham Cathedral by the Cathedral Librarian James Raine.[2] The Relics included the fragmentary remains of up to four wooden coffins which had contained the body of St Cuthbert. In 1899 Dr Greenwell cleared the tomb and recovered further fragments.[3] From this mass of about 6,000 pieces of oak, c.169 engraved fragments were extracted over the ensuing four decades. These formed the basis in 1939 of a reconstruction by Kitzinger of the Anglo-Saxon coffin originally built during the elevation of St Cuthbert in 698.[4] An isolated single plank making up a stepped cross was also reconstructed at this time (fig. 15). However, its relationship to the Anglo-Saxon coffin remained tentative. Conservation treatment of the coffin fragments was required in 1978. This process enabled some modification and additions to Kitzinger's reconstruction.[5] (Plate 43).

As with all objects, the conservation of the coffin required close examination. As a result, new facts and insights into its technology and history were elicited, in part by observation but also by applying modern scientific analytical techniques. Of particular importance here were the tree-ring

[1] Acknowledgements: The Dean and Chapter and staff of Durham Cathedral, through Canon Coppin, have provided generous access and help in enabling us to study the coffin and associated fragments. Mr M. Bond carried out the recent dendrochronology work as an undergraduate project with the generous assistance of Miss J. Hillam of the University of Sheffield. Mr Alan Piper and Dr Ian Doyle, University of Durham, kindly helped with the deciphering of the fragmentary inscriptions while Mr R. Norris, the Chapter Deputy Librarian, has always given us encouragement. Mrs Y. Beadnell ably prepared the drawings.
[2] *St Cuthbert*.
[3] F. J. Haverfield and W. Greenwell, *Catalogue of the Sculptured and Inscribed Stones in the Cathedral Library, Durham* (Durham, 1899), pp. 133 – 56.
[4] E. Kitzinger, 'The Coffin Reliquary', in *Relics*, pp. 202 – 304.
[5] J. M. Cronyn and C. V. Horie, *St. Cuthbert's Coffin: The history, technology and conservation* (Durham, 1985).

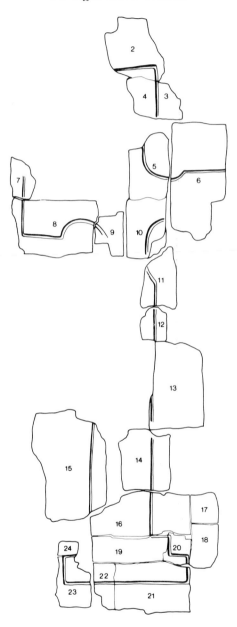

15. Line drawing of the Stepped Cross panel. Fragments have been identified by numbers, nominally preceded by 'SC' as identifier. It is possible that the panel, and thus the shaft of the cross, was longer as the joins do not inspire confidence. Present dimensions are 74 cm long, 28 cm wide (at its widest).

studies.[6] The oak coffin had been constructed of six planks, of which five were identified — the two sides, the two ends and the lid. The five planks were shown, by dendrochronological study, to have been taken from one tree 300 – 400 years old. Unfortunately, owing to the fragmentary and degraded state of the wood, it was not possible to establish a complete dendrochronological sequence but two overlapping sequences were obtained. Nor was it possible to match these sequences with any of the sequences from other sources which have been firmly dated. The wood of the coffin therefore remains undated by this means. A previous radiocarbon study[7] of a fragment whose position in the dendrochronological sequence is unknown puts the date of the felling of the tree in the range AD 420 – 1170, using recent calibration data.[8] Scientific evidence of an Anglo-Saxon date of the coffin is therefore lacking.

RECENT RECOVERIES AND PLACING OF FRAGMENTS

In 1987 we felt that a further examination of the *c.* 6,000 pieces, currently held in the triforium of Durham Cathedral, would be profitable — by drawing on the familiarity and expertise gained during the 1978 study. The fragments were sorted by eye into groups that appeared to come from the Anglo-Saxon coffin. From these, a total of thirty-one fragments with engraved decoration (fig. 16) and nine fragments with incised lettering (fig. 17) were recovered. In addition, fragments that appeared similar in wood grain to those of the reconstructed coffin were extracted. Some of these were edge pieces and one is probably the only identified fragment from the base. Undoubtedly, further portions of this coffin remain to be discovered in the mass of stored fragments.

The placing of fragments in the reconstruction has been achieved in the past by using various clues as one would for a jigsaw puzzle, the line of the pattern, the grain of the wood, the thickness of the fragment and the gaps left in the whole. In the latest study, microscopic examination of the tree rings has established the orientation of the fragments (using late and early wood) and, where possible, the relative placing of the fragments in the tree ring sequence. Time has not allowed the reliable placing of the engraved fragments in the reconstruction.

However, at the time of writing, placings (fig. 18) of inscribed fragments have been proposed. These fragments have been allocated identifiers following those given in our recent book (as note 5): i.e. each fragment is given a number preceded by a panel abbreviation: AS for Archangel Side, AP for Apostles' Side, AE for Archangel End, V & C for Virgin and Child End and L for Lid. On the Apostles' Side (fig. 19: cf. fig. 21 for the previous

[6] J. Hillam, 'Tree ring analysis', in Cronyn and Horie, op. cit., pp. 72 – 80.
[7] H. Barker and C. J. Mackey, 'British Museum Radiocarbon Measurements 1', *American Journal of Science Radiocarbon*, Suppl. 1 (1959), pp. 81 – 6.
[8] G. W. Pearson and M. G. C. Bailie, 'High-precision C14 measurement of Irish oaks to show the natural C14 variations of the AD time period', *Radiocarbon* 25 no. 2 (1983), pp. 187 – 96.

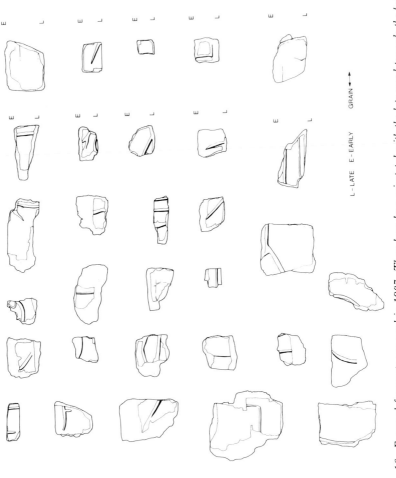

L – LATE   E – EARLY   GRAIN

16. *Engraved fragments recovered in 1987. These have been orientated with the late wood towards the bottom, so as to assist in comparing the fragments with the panels whose orientation is already known.*

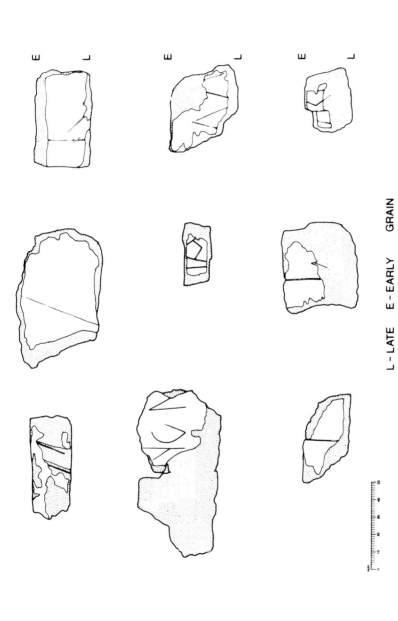

L – LATE   E – EARLY   GRAIN

17. Incised fragments recovered in 1987.

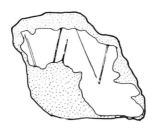

AP 48

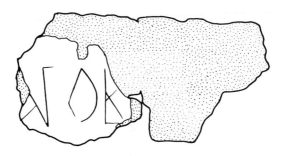

AP 49

AS 77 78 79

18. The placed incised fragments: scale 1:1. Where a position on a panel has been postulated, the appropriate fragment identifiers are indicated (see figures 19 and 20).

reconstruction) AP f.48 can be added to extend the name of the apostle on the right end of the second row, to form

PAULU[S]

In the reconstruction, the adjacent apostle has up to now lacked an inscribed name next to his halo. This figure has been assumed to represent James and now there is an inscription to support this. Using tree ring studies and the grain pattern, it is proposed that this is the only position in which AP f.49 can be placed. The inscription reads

[I]ACOB[US]

Two inscribed fragments, AS f.78 and 79, have been joined along a break caused by a peg hole, and must be placed along the edge of a plank. Combining this information and the tree ring data they can be placed on only one plank, the Archangel Side (fig. 20), where there are two archangels whose identity is in some doubt.[9] From an examination of the grain, it appears that the inscription lay alongside the angel third from the left. The inscription is damaged but can be interpreted as

V̱ṞI̱[.]I̱A

A third fragment, AS f.77, may join onto the left of f.78. If this is the case the reading becomes

A̱[.]V̱ṞI̱[.]I̱A

with no room for any other letter between the halo of the archangel and the first A. To date approaches to a number of scholars have not revealed the identity of this archangel.

CROSS PANEL

Consideration was also given to the mounted but unpublished panel made up as a stepped cross (figure 15). The tree rings of two fragments on this panel, identified by numbers prefixed by SC, were examined to assess their relationship to the wood of the reconstructed coffin.[10] The statistical analysis strongly suggests that the wood of the cross panel and of the coffin are contemporary. When taken with a comparison of the grain, it appears likely that this plank was cut from the same tree as was used to make the coffin and therefore that it was probably part of the original coffin. In our previous study, we concluded that the inner lid, described following the translation of 1104,[11] had been inserted into the coffin some time after the original construction, possibly during periods of travel of the congregation with the coffin. This inference was drawn from the crude cutting of the mortises which were necessary to house the three transverse bars which supported the inner lid. It is unlikely that a plank from the group originally used for the coffin would be retained for more

---

[9] Kitzinger, art. cit.

[10] M. Bond, 'St. Cuthbert's Coffin: further tree ring analysis', submitted as part of the requirements for the degree of B.Sc. at the Department of Archaeology, University of Durham (1987).

[11] C. F. Battiscombe, 'Historical introduction', in *Relics*, pp. 1 – 114.

19. *Apostles' Side fragments, AP f. 48 and 49, inserted into the 1978 reconstruction.*

20. *Archangel Side fragments, AS f. 77, 78 and 79, inserted into the 1978 reconstruction.*

than a century before being used as the inner lid. If this is the case, the other likely position for the cross panel is as the original base. Examination of the fragments lends support to this view. The thickness of the fragments varies between 13 – 19 mm, about within the range of thickness estimated in 1978 for the missing base, 14 – 25 mm. The cross was carved out with a round end gouge, similar to that used on the coffin. However, the workmanship is considerably rougher than that exhibited in the other panels of the coffin, both in outline and in the grooves themselves — as though the cross had been engraved after the narrow coffin had been constructed. On initial examination, there is no evidence of the excessive decay or addition of the consolidant described for the 1104 translation. As an extension of this argument, it appears that the engraving on the coffin was carried out after its construction.

The tree ring data from SC f.16 has made the tentative placing of the overlap between the two sequences from the coffin[12] more secure but not certain.[13]

FURTHER WORK

The radiocarbon dating of two fragments which have been placed in the dendrochronological sequence has been arranged with the Oxford Radiocarbon Laboratory,[14] with the assistance of a grant from the Science and Engineering Research Council.

The following areas for further study have been identified:

a) The cross panel: This is extremely dirty, fragile and coming away from its 1939 mount. It requires conservation treatment. Analytical work on this panel is needed to clarify its relationship to the coffin.

b) Location of missing fragments: The further sorting of the remaining 6,000 fragments for pieces of the Anglo-Saxon coffin will assist in confirming its current reconstruction but, more importantly, will enable the tentative reconstruction of the cross panel to be enlarged and improved.

c) Restoration of the Anglo-Saxon coffin: The incorporation of the newly found fragments into the reconstruction of the coffin on display will add to the perceived integrity of the coffin.

d) The other coffins: The many thousands of wood fragments hold clues of up to three coffins placed in the tomb with the Anglo-Saxon coffin. The sorting, study and reconstruction of the other coffins should provide evidence both of the care of St Cuthbert and of the technology at the time.

[12] See n. 6 above.
[13] J. Hillam, personal communication, 1987.
[14] The findings will be published in *Archaeometry: radiocarbon list* in due course.

Roman and Runic on St Cuthbert's Coffin

R. I. PAGE

Among the contents of the new runic periodical *Nytt om Runer* is a running bibliography, its final section headed *Fantas(t)isk litteratur*.[1] This lists writings that show runes as an occult script, one suited to oracular pronouncement in modern as well as medieval life. The recent past has seen a good deal of this sort of writing, and occult bookshops can usually be expected to have a shelf or two of books on runes. They have no scholarly value, and serve only to document that fascination with fantasy, that flight from reason that is such a sad feature of the modern world.

Occasionally, however, a book in this field has claims to scholarship, and therefore merits more formal consideration. One such book is *The Way of Wyrd* which its author, in the preface, describes as 'a report of a major research project'.[2] Though written in narrative form as a series of connected 'tales of an Anglo-Saxon sorcerer', the material is 'reconstructed from research evidence', and each episode has been subjected to 'a process of rigorous analysis'. The events are set in the later seventh century, the principal episode in 674. The hero, a young man with the slightly unusual Anglo-Saxon name of Wat Brand, is a Christian who learns the practices and beliefs of paganism, and in the course of this makes acquaintance with runes, 'the mysterious writings of the pagans.' The author comments on the Christian attitude to this script:

> In Mercia runes were now officially outlawed, though peasants still unlawfully carved them on sticks and threw them as lotteries, foretelling the future. Brother Eappa knew how to read and write runic inscriptions, but they were forbidden to initiates in the scriptorium for they were sacriligious (*sic*).[3]

Weird though this is, it nevertheless calls for comment. It has often been asserted even in scholarly works that the runic script was intimately linked with paganism, with the implication that its employment conflicted with Christian teaching and so was unacceptable in Christian times. In fact there

---

[1] *Nytt om Runer: Meldingsblad om Runeforskning* 1 (1986), p. 30.
[2] B. Bates, *The Way of Wyrd: Tales of an Anglo-Saxon Sorcerer* (London, 1983, repr. 1984), p. 9.
[3] Bates, *Way of Wyrd*, p.78.

is, as far as I know, nothing from Anglo-Saxon England to support this contention. Some twenty years ago I summed up the English evidence for the magical or cult use of runes, and concluded that it was unconvincing.[4] I have seen no reason to change my opinion.

It is particularly difficult to support any assertion about runes in seventh-century Mercia, for there is little known directly from that time and place Nor is there, to my knowledge, any survival anywhere in England of wooden stick charms or lotteries such as the author of *The Way of Wyrd* predicates. From its text and decoration the copper-coated wooden shrine now at Mortain, département Manche, France, may have been made in Mercia *c*.700, though the evidence is not at all conclusive.[5] The shrine is decorated with figures of Christ and the archangels Michael and Gabriel, yet its maker formula is in runes. By the second half of the eighth century runes were certainly acceptable for formal use in Mercia since Offa allowed them on some of his coins.[6] The later Anglo-Saxon period shows runes used for a Christian memorial inscription on a carved stone from Overchurch in the Wirral.[7] So whatever sacrilegious content officials found in the script in late seventh-century Mercia does not seem to have lasted long.

Nor is there any general reason to believe that runes were kept out of the scriptorium. Indeed, by the eighth century two runic graphs, *thorn* and *wynn*, had penetrated English bookhand, and would presumably be taught to initiates.[8] In more sophisticated work, as Michelle Brown has reminded me, occasional runic forms were used in display scripts. A clear case is in the Chad Gospels (Lichfield Cathedral Library), tentatively ascribed to the West Midlands and the early eighth century.[9] Its formal scripts show runic influence, and even the borrowing of individual runic graphs, sometimes correctly used, sometimes not. Examples are on the openings of the Gospels of Mark (in XpI, using runic 'p') and Luke (in QUONIAm, the 'm' runic).[10]

---

[4] R. I. Page, 'Anglo-Saxon Runes and Magic', *Journal of the British Archaeological Association* 3rd ser. 27 (1964), pp. 14 – 31.

[5] The first monograph on this piece, M. Cahen and M. Olsen, *L'inscription runique du coffret de Mortain* (Collection linguistique publiée par la société de linguistique de Paris 32; Paris, 1930), gives a date '660 – 700 (725), vraisemblablement vers 680' (at p. 50), but more recently the casket has been put rather later; I. Dahl, for instance, suggests '8th – 9th c.', *Substantival Inflexion in Early Old English* (Lund Studies in English 7; Lund, 1938), p. 28. I agree with Dahl in finding the only clear evidence of dialect to be the stem vowel of the verb *gewarahtæ*, which suggests the West Midlands.

[6] C. E. Blunt, 'The Coinage of Offa', in *Anglo-Saxon Coins*, ed. R. H. M. Dolley (London, 1961), at p. 49.

[7] For the Anglo-Saxon runic inscriptions cited in this article see R. I. Page, *An Introduction to English Runes* (London, 1973).

[8] A. Campbell, *Old English Grammar* (Oxford, 1959), p. 25.

[9] G. Henderson, *From Durrow to Kells: the Insular Gospel-books 650 – 800* (London, 1987), pp. 126 – 9.

[10] Illustrated in Alexander, pls. 50, 78. In fact, the Mark page has an unusual form of 'p', doubled as in the futhark of the Breza, Jugoslavia, stone. In the word *scriptum* on the same page, *p* is given by the rune 'm' (or 'd'). The doubled 'p' represents *m* in *multi* on the Luke page.

Runica manuscripta, English manuscript accounts of the runic script, are quite common in the later Anglo-Saxon period, but none of them, to my knowledge, comments that runes are pagan or sacrilegious.[11] Indeed, some scribes put the Anglo-Saxon rune-row alongside Hebrew, Greek and other esoteric alphabets, so they seem to have thought there was nothing specially sacrilegious about it. Earlier than these manuscripts is a bit of concrete evidence direct from the scriptorium, though it is neither Mercian nor seventh century. This is the (?) eighth-century writing tablet of bone found at Blythburgh, Suffolk, early this century (British Museum accession no. 1902.3.15.1).[12] Though the tablet has been known for decades, its runes were spotted only recently, by Professor Martin Biddle. On the recessed surface, which in use would be covered by a wax layer, there are irregular lines of engraved marks which, under the binocular microscope, reveal themselves as runes. Parts of three lines can be traced, though in general they make no sense and are perhaps the epigraphical equivalent of *probationes pennae*: 1, '[ ] o g (or should this be read 'n'?) u a t [-2-] þ [ ]'; 2, '[ ] s u n t [ ]' (is this intended as the Latin word?); 3, '[ ] m a m æ m æ m [ ]'. In case anyone should argue that these, being ordinarily covered by wax, were secret or surreptitious letters which would escape the critical eye of the writing master, I point to a fragment of a runic text on the raised rim, just by a break in the surface, 'u n þ ['.[13]

I have dwelt on this point because the function of the runes on the coffin of St Cuthbert is at first sight puzzling. If runes were essentially pagan/cultic/magical/sacrilegious, it is hard to explain why the monks of Lindisfarne used them on a public piece of tomb furniture for their revered saint in 698, a couple of decades only after Wat Brand's adventures with the mystical. Clearly at Lindisfarne at the end of the seventh century runes were not 'officially outlawed', nor were they thought unsuited to professional Christian or learned use. There could be a geographical distinction, with Northumbria showing — as was to be expected — a more balanced and sensible view of the script than regions further south. But I think it more likely that this reflects a general attitude in Anglo-Saxon England, that runes were a script as any other; if they had been employed for pagan practices, all the more reason for

[11] R. Derolez, *Runica Manuscripta: the English Tradition* (Rijksuniversiteit te Gent, Werken Uitgegeven door de Faculteit van de Wijsbegeerte en Letteren 118; Brugge, 1954).

[12] J. G. Waller in *Proceedings of the Society of Antiquaries of London*, 2nd ser. 19 (1901 – 3), pp. 40 – 2.

[13] For Anglo-Saxon runes I use the system of transliteration defined in R. I. Page, 'On the Transliteration of English Runes', *Medieval Archaeology* 28 (1984), pp. 22 – 45. It is interesting to note that runic parallels to the Blythburgh tablet — though rather later — have come to light in Scandinavia in recent years: so, a rune-inscribed wooden tablet from Bergen (A. Liestøl, *Runer frå Bryggen* (Særtrykk av *Viking* 1963; Bergen, 1964), pp. 11 – 12) and a similar though less well preserved example from Trondheim (J. R. Hagland, *Runefunna: ei Kjelde til Handelen si Historie* (Fortiden i Trondheim Bygrunn: Folkebibliotekstomten, Meddelelser 8; Trondheim, 1986), pp. 7 – 10). More distant is a rune-inscribed stylus from Lödöse, Västergötland, Sweden (E. Svärdström, *Runfynden i Gamla Lödöse* (Lödöse — Västsvensk Medeltidsstad IV:5; Stockholm, 1982), pp. 30 – 3).

applying them to Christianity, so that people accustomed to using them might be reconciled to a new religion. Whatever else the later history of Anglo-Saxon runes shows, it makes clear that the church, far from discouraging writing in runes, exploited the script.

The inscriptions on St Cuthbert's coffin, and in particular the runes, are poorly preserved. This is partly because of the condition of the wood, attacked as it is by a fungoid infection that has made it crack both in the line of the grain and at right angles to it. But the carvers of the runes must take some responsibility for the difficulty in reading them. Runes were originally devised for cutting on wood, and their shapes are such as can properly be made in a grained material. The forms are made up of straight lines, vertical and sloping; the verticals cut the grain at right angles, while the sloping lines cut it at oblique angles. Thus the staves stand clear of the grain. The Lindisfarne rune-cutters did not observe these rules. On the coffin the rune stems run parallel to the grain and can easily be lost in it. And it may be this that renders parts of, for instance, the name *Iohannis* and the Jesus form *ihs* illegible. From this we might deduce that the Lindisfarne carvers were unused to cutting the characters, at any rate in their traditional way on wood. Even though Lindisfarne had other saints to honour, it is likely that St Cuthbert's coffin was a unique piece. There was no direct model to copy, and the rune carvers were left to their own devices.

Because of the difficulties in reading the texts on the coffin, it is advisable to make use of early drawings that show the inscriptions when they were more accessible. There are, I think, only two publications that give first-hand information on the inscriptions before the work that led to Battiscombe's 1956 volume on the relics. These are the ones of James Raine (1828) and William Greenwell (1899). Other drawings before 1947 derive, I think, from these. Bruce Dickins saw the coffin in the 1920s and made notes on it which unfortunately do not survive. By 1956 he was already able to say that the inscriptions 'have become decidedly more difficult to read' because of the effect of the preservatives applied. It is this condition that McIntyre's 1947 drawings record. Presumably Dickins's readings for the 1956 volume depend to some degree on his earlier notes, so they have independent importance. My own detailed examination of the coffin was in 1967, since when it experienced, in 1978, further conservation and cleaning, the then condition recorded in the Dickinson drawings published in 1985.[14] A brief recent examination suggests to me that the inscriptions are now slightly easier to see than in 1967. Moreover, there are a few newly identified pieces of the coffin with fragments of inscriptions on them which will fill out, though not significantly change, the

---

[14] *St Cuthbert*, pls. II, III; F. J. Haverfield and W. Greenwell, *A Catalogue of the Sculptured and Inscribed Stones in the Cathedral Library, Durham* (Durham, 1899), pls. 9 – 13, supported by pls. 1 – 5; B. Dickins, 'The Inscriptions upon the Coffin' in *Relics* at pp. 305 – 7, together with the McIntyre plates VII – X; J. M. Cronyn and C. V. Horie, *St. Cuthbert's Coffin: the History, Technology and Conservation* (Durham, 1985), pp. 92 – 100.

present readings. Clearly there is need for yet another detailed examination of the inscriptions.

Raine's drawings reproduce the inscriptions: ANDREAS, THOMAS, 'x p s',]PVS, MATHEAS (pl. II), PETRVS, LVCAS, RAR[, SMICH[(pl. III). Greenwell shows: on the lid, 'mātheus' ('t' inverted), 'mārcus', LVCAS, 'iohannis' (pl. 9); on the archangel side *RAP*[*h*]AEL, SCS VRIA[, S*C*S and]VmIA[(pl. 10); on the apostle side PETR*V*S, I*A*COB*V*S, IOHANNIS, ANDREAS,]PVS, BAR[, THOMAS, PA[and MATHEÆ͡S (which Greenwell read as MATHEAS) (pls. 11, 12); on the Christ and Mary end]AR[and 'i h s x p s'; on the other end]*C*SmICHÆL and]ABRIÆL (pl. 13).

Dickins has:

(i) '*m*/*atheus*', '*m*/*arcus*', LVCAS, '*iohann*[*i*]s'.[15] Of these I would comment on: (a) the ending of the Matthew name, for I can see only three stave bases between '*h*' and '*s*'; which could imply that '*e*' and '*u*' here formed a bind-rune. Greenwell confirms the three bases as does Dickinson, while McIntyre is obscure here. (b) the Mark name shows some damage in the drawings from McIntyre onwards. Greenwell gives it intact. (c) LVCAS is clear and generally accepted. (d) the John name. Greenwell has this complete save that his second rune looks nearer 'æ' than 'o'. Dickins remarks that 'the short verticals that rise from the ends of the main twigs of the second character are just discernible', and both McIntyre and Dickinson show them, though I could not see them. Nor could I see either of the 'i' runes — both McIntyre and Dickinson had difficulty with these — and only the centres of the 'n' runes.

(ii) defective names of two archangels at the head end. Dickins reads [*S*]*C*S MICH[Æ]L. The final letter is on a separate fragment absent from Greenwell's drawing of the coffin end, though implied in his transcript of the name (which, it will be noted, contains a runic '*m*' for which there is no justification, and which is not on the general drawing). Raine misses the end of this name, so the fragment probably appeared in the 1899 excavation. The vowel preceding *L* cannot be supplied from what survives now or from any known drawing. Dickins must be conjecturing here. He reads the second name [*SCS G*]ABR[*I*]ÆL. McIntyre does not show the two vowels before L. Dickinson shows only the top of the second vowel, which is all that I could see. Greenwell records clearly IÆ, the second vowel having a shape divergent from that of the apostle name MATHEÆ͡S.

(iii) at the foot end Mary and Christ. For Mary, Dickins gives [*M*]AR. McIntyre shows only A and a stave of R, while Dickinson shows nothing on his main drawing, but A on the smaller version. I saw the final stave of M (or

this could be the rune 'm'), A and the top of R. Greenwell, Dickins, McIntyre
and Dickinson coincide in giving the Christ name and title entire:
'i h s x p s'. Of 'h' and 's' I could see only staves, but 'x p s' remains clear.
Raine did not note 'i h s' at all.

(iv) on the archangel side are parts of three names and forms of *sanctus*.
Though not listed at all by Raine, all are confirmed by Greenwell, McIntyre
and Dickinson. Dickins reads (a) *RAPHAEL*. I cannot see the letter H, nor
could Greenwell, for he supplies it as the runic form 'h'. McIntyre and
Dickinson confirm that the letter is almost completely lost, as indeed is the
preceding P. The name is to the right of the archangel's halo; to its left I
thought I saw very faint traces which might have been [*S*]*CS*, not recorded by
anyone else. (b) SCS VRIA[*EL*]. Greenwell confirms that the last two letters
are entirely Dickins's conjecture. (c) *S*CS, which Dickins combines with an
otherwise unplaced [*R*]VmIA[*EL*]. Again it is clear from Greenwell that what
is visible of the name now,]VmIA[, was all that remained in 1899.

(v) on the apostle side names and fragments of ten of the twelve apostles.
Raine has six of the names. Greenwell, McIntyre and Dickinson agree in what
survives, and Dickins completes some of the names. I give the order reading in
pairs from right to left, and Kitzinger points out that this represents the litany
of the canon of the mass.[16] (a) PETRVS. (b) P*A*[, which Dickins completes as
Paulus. Greenwell shows the A entire in his transcript, though not in his
general drawing of the side. (c) ANDREAS. (d) Here should be a form of
Iacobus, which indeed Dickins supplies, and see now Cronyn and Horie above,
p. 253 and figures 18 – 19. (e) IOHANNIS. (f) THOMAS. (g) Dickins reads
I*A*[*CO*]*B*VS, corresponding to Greenwell. There is no trace of the *CO* in
modern times. (h)]*P*VS. Greenwell omits. Raine suggests the bow of a
preceding P. Dickins reads [*PHILIP*]*P*VS. (i) BAR[, as Greenwell, corresponding to Raine's RAR. In this case Dickins does not complete the name,
perhaps being uncertain whether it was *Bartholomaeus* or *Barnabas*. (j)
MATHE*Æ*S. This used to be read MATHE*Æ*, which Kitzinger took to be a
vocative appropriate to a litany form. Dickins drew attention to the base line
of the last letter (which Raine had tentatively, and Greenwell confidently
recorded) which converts *Æ* to *Æ̃S*, but accepted that the form is an odd one,
presumably for *Matheus*. Yet the evangelist's name (in (i) above) also has some
sort of ambiguity in its ending. (k)]*N*VS, apparently what Greenwell meant
by his angular P + VS. Dickins leaves the name incomplete. Kitzinger notes
that Simon Cananaeus fills the litany at this point, and suggests a form *Simonus*
if not an irregular spelling of *Cananaeus*. (l) a lost name, which should be
Thaddaeus, which Dickins does not supply.

Though there are these minor uncertainties (as well as the additions that
must be made from the newly found fragments), the inscriptions show no
serious problem of meaning, only of form. Epigraphically they are of some

---

[16] E. Kitzinger, 'The Coffin-reliquary', in *Relics*, at p. 269.

interest. The Roman characters are what Dr Okasha calls, rather uninforma-tively, 'AS capitals',[17] but which perhaps should be called mixed Insular 'display' letter forms. They are mainly angular, but here and there, in O, P, the carver condescended to curves. There are variant forms of some of the letters used, A, H, for instance. Whether this points to more than one carver I do not know.

The runes are neatly and carefully incised, and though there are a couple of rare forms, the only unorthodox usage is the inverted 't' of *Matheus*. For this there may be an artistic rather than an epigraphical explanation: the desire to set an arm of 't' neatly beneath those of the preceding 'a'. The 'o', if that is what it is, of *Iohannis* has its side staves set unusually far apart, but not unrecognizably so. The rune 'x' is rare in inscriptions, simply because Old English does not need the character. The only other epigraphical example with the certain value 'x' is on a group of related coins of Beonna of East Anglia, where it occurs in the title 'r e x'.[18] Otherwise it appears in an uncertain context on the York spoon, and in its proper place in the futhorc of the ninth-century Thames (Battersea) scramasax, where it has no ascertainable value.[19] However, 'x' is a standard equivalent for this character in Anglo-Saxon manuscript accounts of runes.[20] The 's' form of St Cuthbert's coffin is ᚻ, for which Dickins here uses the distinctive transliteration 'ʃ', deriving it from the Insular minuscule character.[21] It is not common elsewhere in inscriptions, though it appears on the Thames scramasax, and on an amulet ring from Kingmoor, Cumbria, where the related ring from Bramham Moor, Yorkshire, has the more common *s*-rune. It is also recorded in a pair of manuscript rune-rows. Besides its 's', the Thames scramasax has a couple of other runic forms which suggest manuscript inspiration for its futhorc — 'œ', and perhaps 'j' and 'y'. There is a suggestion here, then, that the St Cuthbert's coffin runes derive directly from manuscript tradition rather than epigraphical, but I admit it remains unproven.

The intrusive 'm' in]VmIA[is to be noted. There are several epigraphical examples of this rune in otherwise Roman contexts, probably because of its similarity to the Roman letter. So, the memorial stone at Chester-le-Street has the name EADm | VnD (plate 48a), while 'm' occurs in legends in Roman characters on Anglo-Saxon coins, as mONE (for *moneta*), DAIEmOND for the

---

[17] E. Okasha, *Hand-list of Anglo-Saxon Non-runic Inscriptions* (Cambridge, 1971), p. 68.

[18] M. M. Archibald, 'The Coinage of Beonna in the Light of the Middle Harling Hoard', *British Numismatic Journal* 55 (1985), p. 39.

[19] In 1932 Dickins suggested that this rune was 'a fossil in Old English', and placed its transcription in brackets to signal the fact: as '(x)' (B. Dickins, 'A System of Transliteration for Old English Runic Inscriptions', *Leeds Studies in English* 1 (1932), pp. 16 – 17). Presumably he changed his mind for in 1956 he abandoned the brackets for his transliteration of the coffin text. See on this Page, 'Transliteration of English Runes', pp. 30 – 1.

[20] As in Derolez, *Runica Manuscripta*, pp. 9, 59.

[21] This derivation is not at all certain: see Page, 'Transliteration of English Runes', p. 32.

moneyer's name *Dægmund*, and often in the royal name on the St Edmund memorial coinage.[22]

I cannot discern any pattern behind the differential employment of runes and Roman script on the coffin. Why Matthew, Mark and John are runic, but Luke Roman. Why Christ's monogram is runic but, as far as it survives, Mary's name is Roman. I classify this piece alongside such an object as the Franks casket, which has on one of its sides the description of the scene carved nearby, part in Roman, HIC FUGIANT HIERUSALIM, and the rest in runes, 'a f i t a t o r e s': 'here the inhabitants flee from Jerusalem'. There is, however, a significant difference. In the case of the Franks casket, words in Roman script are also classical in form, more or less. The word in runes uses a different form, with the spelling based on contemporary pronunciation. On the coffin of St Cuthbert, the runes give texts in classical form, more or less. Particularly important is the sequence 'i h s x p s', for that is a straight transliteration from Roman, with no basis in pronunciation at all. It could not exist without a precedent Roman form: that is, the runes are secondary, dependent on a pre-existent Roman. This tends to confirm the general impression that the coffin runes are learned letters, deriving perhaps from manuscript sources. The carvers were not at home in the script; hence its peculiarities.

This poses a further question: why are there runes on the coffin at all? And to this there is the supplementary question: who was supposed to read them? To take the supplementary first. It is a proper question for all runic texts, but particularly cogent for St Cuthbert's coffin. The coffin-reliquary stood above ground as an object of veneration. From some early date unknown, it was swathed in linen cloth covering the whole surface and obscuring the carving. Even in its earliest days the faint inscriptions would have been hard to see in a dimly lit church, for their incisions are slight, considerably thinner than those of the decoration.[23] Theoretically this could have meant that the inscriptions preceded the figures, and were intended to direct the carvers as to the designs to be cut. But this cannot be so in one case — if my observations are correct — for the figure of *Scs Raphael* has precedence over the text, with the two parts of its inscription falling one on each side of the saint.

Moreover, I have shown that the runes are a secondary script at Lindisfarne, and it is odd that directions to carvers should arbitrarily employ two scripts, one of them a specialist one. Professor R. W. V. Elliott suggested that Christians used runes on their tomb furniture because an old belief survived of their efficacy 'for the dead man's salvation or against his haunting his survivors';[24] but it seems unlikely that the Lindisfarne monks who honoured

[22] C. F. Keary, *A Catalogue of English Coins in the British Museum: Anglo-Saxon Series* I, ed. R. S. Poole (London, 1887), pp. 91 – 2, 114.

[23] The same problem affects dry-point glosses in Anglo-Saxon manuscripts, which are, at any rate now, almost illegible save with careful side lighting, but presumably were readable in Anglo-Saxon lighting conditions.

[24] R. W. V. Elliott, *Runes: an Introduction* (Manchester, 1959), p. 71.

their great saint had so little faith in him as to have recourse to such adventitious aids.

A casual mixture of the two scripts is not all that uncommon in Anglo-Saxon England: witness the legends on the rings from Manchester (Lancashire) and Llysfaen: + æDRED MEC AH EAnRED MEC agROf, 'Ædred owns me, Eanred engraved me', and + ALHSTAn, a personal name. The St Cuthbert's coffin case is something different. Yet there is also, in the east of Northumbria, an extended tradition of the use of the two scripts side by side but distinct. Examples can be found elsewhere at Lindisfarne, at Monkwearmouth and at Falstone. Lindisfarne I, a name stone, has *Osgyth* written twice on it, once in runes in the quadrants above an incised cross, once in Roman below (plate 39d). A similar stone, Lindisfarne V, seems to have two names, both with the second element *-wini*: '[.] a m | w i n i' and]*A*[*D*] | WINI. There are other cases, though the names are damaged on other Lindisfarne stones. The second Monkwearmouth stone is only a fragment, but it preserves two name openings, 'e o [' and *ALD*[, giving two distinct first elements of personal names. Most revealing is the Falstone stone which has a double inscription, virtually the same text in both Roman and runes. The stone is in poor condition, but enough of the two inscriptions survives to show it is a memorial to one *Hroethberht*. The name form in the two cases is significant. In Roman it is HROETHBERHTÆ with the vowel of the first element — which represents the *i*-mutation of *ō* — given by the two graphs OE. The runic form is badly damaged, but it has the first element vowel represented by two runes 'oe'. This is clearly copied from the Roman. The self-evident way of representing the vowel *ō*. . .*i* in runes is to use the single rune 'œ' which, by virtue of its name *oeþil*, must give this sound. Here again, then, there is runic and Roman on the same object with the Roman predominant. To these examples we may add — though they are not so convincing — the groups of stones of related design, some of which have runic and some Roman legends; as the name stones from Hartlepool. Here there is a further refinement. Hartlepool I has a runic text 'h i l d i | þ r y þ', but the letters are carefully seriffed, as though Roman (plate 39e). Again a link between the scripts, with Roman convention imposed upon the runic. As if to stress the learned background, Hartlepool I also has the letters *alpha* and *omega* cut in the quadrants above its incised cross.

Thus, while I can give no reason for the mixture of runic and Roman on St Cuthbert's coffin, I can at least set its inscriptions into a context that is both local and learned. It seems there was a north country practice — and one which the Christian church approved — of using runic script in the company of Roman, either mixed in with it or side by side with it. The coffin shows this was in operation by the end of the seventh century, some two generations after Edwin accepted Christianity at his council held near York. Already runes had lost any sinister associations they may have had. They had become an esoteric script, regarded perhaps with antiquarian affection by the learned and religious.

The Iconography of St Peter in Anglo-Saxon England, and St Cuthbert's Coffin

JOHN HIGGITT

In Anglo-Saxon England St Peter, the prince of the apostles, was almost always represented as clean-shaven. Elsewhere he was almost always shown with a characteristic short, bushy beard. Why was this? In the middle of the last century Mrs Jameson commented on this 'curious exception' to the 'predominant, almost universal type'. Since then one or two other writers have noticed this feature but it has attracted surprisingly little comment.[1]

A typical Anglo-Saxon St Peter can be seen flanking Christ in the *Liber vitae* of the New Minster in Winchester (pl. 42). He is tonsured and beardless and holds a pair of keys (or a double key) against his left shoulder. The surviving examples of this Anglo-Saxon type are mostly of the tenth and eleventh centuries but it seems already to be fully formed as early as the end of the

---

[1] The following abbreviation will be used in the footnotes below: *DACL* = *Dictionnaire d'archéologie chrétienne et de liturgie*, ed. F. Cabrol and H. Leclercq (15 vols., Paris, 1907 – 53).

Mrs (A.) Jameson, *Sacred and Legendary Art* (2 vols.; new edn, London, 1890), I, 187 – 8; A. Homburger, 'Die Anfänge der Malschule von Winchester im X. Jahrhundert', *Studien über christliche Denkmäler* 13 (1912), p. 21, n. 3; M. Schapiro, 'The Decoration of the Leningrad Manuscript of Bede' in M. Schapiro, *Late Antique, Early Christian and Mediaeval Art Selected Papers* (London, 1980), p. 214; J. E. Rosenthal, 'The Historiated Canon Tables of the Arenberg Gospels' (unpublished Ph.D. thesis, Columbia University, 1975), p. 249; C. K. Carr, 'Aspects of the Iconography of Saint Peter in Medieval Art of Western Europe to the Early Thirteenth Century' (unpublished Ph.D. thesis, Case Western Reserve University, 1978), p. 11. (I am very grateful to Mr Raymond McCluskey for this last reference.)

For general studies of the iconography of St Peter see *inter alia*: Carr, op. cit.; *Lexikon der christlichen Ikonographie*, ed. E. Kirschbaum and W. Braunfels (1976), VIII, cols 158 – 74; *Bibliotheca Sanctorum* (Istituto Giovanni XXIII della Pontificia Università Lateranense, Roma, 1961 – 70) X, col. 588 – 650; *DACL* XIV.1, cols. 935 – 73; J. Vielliard, 'Notes sur l'iconographie de Saint Pierre', *Le moyen âge* 2e série, 30 (1929), pp. 1 – 16; C. Cecchelli, *San Pietro* (= *Iconografia dei papi*, I) (Giunta Centrale per gli Studi Storici, Roma, *c.*1939); E. Mâle, *Les saints compagnons du Christ* (Paris, 1958), pp. 87 – 108; K. Weitzmann, *The St. Peter Icon of Dumbarton Oaks* (Washington, D.C., 1983), pp. 21 – 8. (Weitzmann's theory that Byzantine art 'consciously avoided a Peter type associated with Rome' after 1054 and again after 1204 provides an interesting analogue to the ideologically charged Peter iconography argued for in this paper.).

seventh century in the damaged figure identified by an inscription as
'PETRVS' on 'St Cuthbert's coffin' (pl. 44 and fig. 21).[2] Here St Peter
appears carrying what was probably intended as a pair of keys against his right
shoulder and holding a book in his draped left hand. He is clean-shaven and
the two concentric arcs on the top of his head of short hair are most probably
the artist's rendering of a Roman tonsure.

Schapiro in an acute aside described this type as 'the Roman Peter of the
Durham work' and noted that the type 'remained traditional in Anglo-Saxon
art'.[3] In what sense, if at all, is it 'Roman'? St Peter was the most powerful
saint of the Latin church. For the west he was, through Christ's gift of the
keys, the first pope, the gate-keeper of heaven, and, in the words of St
Wilfrid's epitaph, *arbiter orbis*. Bede's *Ecclesiastical History* shows vividly the
extraordinary powers attributed to the supposed body of St Peter, which drew
kings and numerous lesser pilgrims from England to Rome.[4] It has even been
claimed, by Sir Richard Southern, that 'for the western church from the
seventh to the eleventh century the existence of the tomb of St Peter was the
most significant fact in Christendom'. Devotion to St Peter seems to have
been particularly intense in the early Anglo-Saxon church.[5] In these
circumstances the consistent use in Anglo-Saxon England from the seventh to
the eleventh centuries of a distinctive and very unusual portrait type for St
Peter is likely to have been deliberate and significant. As we shall see, the type
may have been used elsewhere in Britain and in Ireland. It may possibly be
more accurate to think of it as Insular rather than simply Anglo-Saxon. The
evidence outside England, however, is much sparser and is also less consistent.

St Cuthbert's coffin is one of the very few works of art of the early middle
ages that can be both dated and localized with a fair degree of confidence. It is
almost certain that it is the *levis theca*, or light chest, into which, according to
Bede, the monks of Lindisfarne placed the incorrupt body of St Cuthbert and
other relics at the translation of 698.[6]

This coffin-reliquary is an unsophisticated oak box which bears a series of
incised figures on its top and its vertical faces. Kitzinger analysed these very
fully in 1956. He convincingly demonstrated that the Lindisfarne artist or
artists were following and adapting a variety of models from the Mediterranean world for the figures of Christ, the evangelist symbols, the Virgin and
Child, the archangels and the twelve apostles. He interpreted the series of
figures, identified by inscriptions in Roman and runic lettering, as forming a

---

[2] *Relics*, pp. 266–8, pl. V and VIII; J. M. Cronyn and C. V. Horie, *St. Cuthbert's Coffin*
(Durham, 1985), foldout 1d.
[3] Schapiro, op. cit., p. 214.
[4] Matthew 16:19; *HE* V, 19; V, 7 etc.; W. Levison, *England and the Continent in the Eighth Century*
(Oxford, 1946), pp. 36–42.
[5] R. W. Southern, *Western Society and the Church in the Middle Ages* (Harmondsworth, 1970), p. 94;
Levison, op. cit.; T. Zwölfer, *Sankt Peter Apostelfürst und Himmelspförtner: seine Verehrung bei den
Angelsachsen und Franken* (Stuttgart, 1929), pp. 20–63.
[6] *VCP* 42, p. 294; *Relics*, pp. 221–3; Cronyn and Horie, *St. Cuthbert's Coffin*, pp. 1–8.

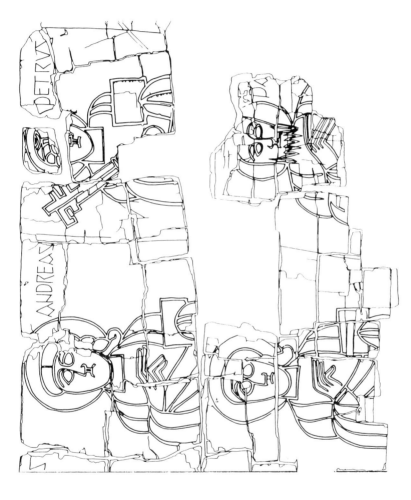

21. *St Cuthbert's coffin (detail of one of the long sides). Upper row: Sts Andrew and Peter; lower row: unidentified apostle and St Paul. (Cf. now fig. 19.)*

litany in pictures, designed to invoke the protection of those represented for
the collection of relics.[7]

The twelve apostles occupy one of the long sides and are shown in two tiers
of six half-length figures. Some of the loose fragments of the coffin were
rearranged in a reconstruction in 1939. This reordering very plausibly placed
the individualized figures of Sts Peter and Paul at the right end of the series of
apostles, with Peter placed above Paul. (This arrangement was followed in the
1978 remounting.[8]) The other ten apostles are identified only by their
inscriptions. They seem all to have been of the same long-haired, beardless,
book-holding type. Kitzinger argued that the artist was not copying a
complete imported set of apostles, like, for example, the series of paintings
brought back from Rome to Monkwearmouth by Benedict Biscop, but that
instead he adapted, twelve times over, the same model as was used for the
archangels on the coffin. On to this type he grafted the characteristics derived
from Mediterranean representations of Peter and Paul. According to this
argument the keys and the distinctive hair-style, which consists of a roll of hair
over the forehead and a tonsure-like feature above, would have been taken
over from Mediterranean art but the beardless face would be an accidental
survival from the archangel prototype.[9] More recently new, but not totally
conclusive, evidence has been put forward to support the view that the coffin
copies an imported model (or models) with a complete set of twelve apostles.[10]

There is no scriptural evidence for the appearance of the apostles, but
already by the later fourth century, for example in paintings in the Catacomb
of Sts Peter and Marcellinus in Rome, Peter and Paul are portrayed with
features which proved remarkably persistent, although those of Peter were
subject to more variation. Most representations of Peter, both in the east and
the west, are nevertheless consistent with the disapproving description by
Epiphanius of Salamis in the late fourth century of images of Peter as 'an old
man with hair and beard cut short'. According again to Epiphanius some
showed Paul 'with receding hair', whilst others showed him as 'bald and
bearded'. The tradition is still preserved in the early eighteenth-century
Painter's Manual from Mount Athos in Greece, which has been translated as
describing Peter as 'an old man with a rounded beard' and Paul as 'bald, with
a brown, rush-like beard and grey hair'.[11]

In the Catacomb of Sts Peter and Marcellinus, as often later, St Peter is
given a squarish slightly combative face framed by a short white beard and

---

[7] E. Kitzinger in *Relics*, pp. 228 – 80.

[8] *Relics*, p. 49; Cronyn and Horie, *St. Cuthbert's Coffin*, p. 207.

[9] *Relics*, pp. 265 – 8, 278; K. Weitzmann, *The St. Peter Icon of Dumbarton Oaks* (Washington, D.C., 1983), pp. 21 – 6 (for Petrine hair-styles).

[10] L. Nees, 'The Iconographic Program of Decorated Chancel Barriers in the pre-Iconoclastic Period', *Zeitschrift für Kunstgeschichte* 46 (1983), pp. 15 – 26.

[11] P. du Bourguet, *Early Christian Art* (London, 1972), pl. on p. 171 (Sts Peter and Marcellinus); C. Mango, *The Art of the Byzantine Empire 312 – 1453* (Englewood Cliffs, 1972), pp. 41 – 2; P. Hetherington, *The 'Painter's Manual' of Dionysius of Fourna* (London, revised edn., 1981), p. 52.

hair. His features contrast effectively with the long face and long, dark beard of St Paul. (Paul's hair ranges between a receding hairline and advanced, but not total baldness.) During the fifth and sixth centuries Peter begins to be shown with varying numbers of keys, from one to three, as an attribute, in reference to Christ's gift of the keys (Matthew 16:19). He has three, for example, on the sixth-century icon of St Peter on Mount Sinai, on which he also carries a cross-staff. In Rome and elsewhere in the west in the sixth century Peter is shown with a roll of hair above his face and apparently much shorter hair above and behind this. An example can be seen in the mosaics of the church of Sts Cosmas and Damian in Rome. The hair above and behind the roll looks distinctly close-cropped and stubbly on the early ninth-century reliquary made for Pope Paschal I. Kitzinger carefully calls this hairstyle 'a distinctive crown of hair reminiscent of a tonsure'. As he implies, it is not the same thing as the true clerical or 'Roman' tonsure used and represented in Italy from the sixth century, for example in San Vitale in Ravenna (on the Gospel-holding attendant of Maximian) or, in the 640s, in the Chapel of St Venantius in St John Lateran in Rome. This tonsure appears to have consisted of a roughly circular area of clean-shaven scalp on the top of the head surrounded by a ring of hair. James may, nevertheless, be right to suggest that the iconographic type of Peter with the roll of hair may have been responsible for the idea that the crown tonsure originated with St Peter.[12]

There are a number of early representations of St Peter without a beard in Mediterranean art. These are most frequent in those early Christian works that show Christ and the apostles as beardless youths.[13] Peter and Paul appear beardless on one or two of the fourth-century 'gold glass' bowls from Rome.[14] The beardless type very occasionally survives later, perhaps in more out-of-the-way places. A pair of ivory plaques from Kranenburg, attributed by Volbach to fifth-century Gaul, show Peter, holding two keys in his veiled hands, and Paul, holding a book. Neither has a beard. There is another example on the silver casket from San Nazaro in Milan. Christ and the apostles are beardless in the sixth-century Italian Gospel book, which was, by tradition, the one brought by St Augustine of Canterbury to England. It was already in England by the eighth century and perhaps earlier.[15] An imported

---

[12] Du Bourguet, loc. cit. (Sts Peter and Marcellinus); E. Kitzinger, *Byzantine Art in the Making* (Cambridge, Mass., 1977), pl. VIII (Mount Sinai icon), fig. 160 (Sts Cosmas and Damian), fig. 158 (San Vitale), pl. VI (Chapel of St Venantius); Weitzmann, *St. Peter Icon*, fig. 19 (Paschal I reliquary). Kitzinger's discussion of this hair-style is in *Relics*, p. 266, n. 4. See also E. James, 'Bede and the Tonsure Question', *Peritia* 3 (1984), pp. 85 – 98 at p. 86.

[13] A. Grabar, *Christian Iconography: a Study of Its Origins* (Princeton, 1968), pp. 33 – 4.

[14] *Age of Spirituality*, ed. K. Weitzmann (exhibition catalogue, Metropolitan Museum of Art, New York, 1979), pp. 569 – 70; C. R. Morey, *Early Christian Art* (Princeton, 1942), pp. 176 – 7.

[15] *Relics*, p. 267, n. 2; Morey, loc. cit.; J. Hubert, J. Porcher and W. F. Volbach, *Europe in the Dark Ages* (London, 1967), ill. 216 – 7 (Kranenburg diptych); W. F. Volbach, *Early Christian Art* (London, 1961), pl. 111 (San Nazaro); F. Wormald, *Collected Writings* I, *Studies in Medieval Art from the Sixth to the Twelfth Centuries* (London, 1984), pp. 13 – 35 and illustrations (St Augustine's Gospels = Cambridge, Corpus Christi College, MS 286).

model with a beardless Peter might, therefore, have been available. I do not, however, know of any early medieval images of Peter from the Mediterranean world which show him both without a beard and with a true 'Roman' tonsure.

Interestingly the mosaics commissioned by Pope John VII in the first decade of the eighth century, just a year or so after the making of the coffin-reliquary, for his chapel in St Peter's in Rome seem from Grimaldi's sketch and the surviving fragment of one of the figures of St Peter to have shown him bearded and tonsureless. To judge from surviving early medieval representations in mosaics and paintings in Rome the 'Anglo-Saxon' type of Peter, as it appears on the coffin, was certainly not canonical in Rome.[16]

The type, however, seems to have had some currency in England, as it appears to be the image that underlies Bede's story of the vision of Sts Peter and Paul experienced by a young English boy on his deathbed at Selsey.[17] The saints introduced themselves to him as Peter and Paul and he described the former as *attonsus . . . ut clericus*, that is with hair like a cleric, and the latter as having a *barbam prolixam*, a flowing beard. It is important in this context to remember that *tonsura* and related forms in Latin referred generally to the cutting, shearing and shaving of hair and were not restricted to the 'tonsure' in the modern sense. To be *attonsus* like a cleric may well have involved being clean-shaven as well as tonsured at this time in England. Constable, in his fascinating study of beards in the middle ages, argues that from the seventh century onwards it was probably normal in the west for monks to cut their beards. Unambiguous evidence for decrees against the wearing of beards by the clergy in general seems, however, only to come later.[18] Furthermore, whilst the boy described Paul's beard, his description of Peter makes no mention of a beard. So the Selsey St Peter seems to have been both tonsured and beardless like the Peter of St Cuthbert's coffin.

Kitzinger wrote that he could not help 'wondering whether a seventh-century artist at Lindisfarne who depicted St Peter with a very distinctive crown of hair of the Roman type was merely applying an iconographic convention or whether he was consciously displaying a symbol of a topical cause.'[19] As we have seen, there is apparently no evidence that the beardless, tonsured and clerical-looking St Peter was a current iconography on the continent at that time. It is worth therefore considering the possibility that the type was invented, and not just taken up, as a visual slogan in the ecclesiastical

---

[16] C. G. Paluzzi, *La Basilica di San Pietro* (Roma Cristiana, XVII; Bologna, 1975), fig. 57 and 59. See also n. 40 below.

[17] *HE* IV, 14; Morey, *Early Christian Art*, p. 176; Schapiro, op. cit. in n. 1 above, p. 214, n. 67.

[18] G. Constable, 'Introduction on Beards in the Middle Ages', in *Apologiae Duae*, ed. R. B. C. Huygens (*Corpus Christianorum: Continuatio Medievalis* 62 (Turnhout, 1985), pp. 47 – 130, especially 103 – 7, 115 and (for the term *barba prolixa*) 120; *Enciclopedia Cattolica* (12 vols.; Città del Vaticano, 1948 – 54), II, *s.v. barba*, cols. 798 – 801.

[19] *Relics*, p. 266, n. 4; James, *Peritia* 3, pp. 97 – 8.

disputes which came to a head in the second half of the seventh century in Northumbria and which may to some extent have been anticipated earlier in the century in Ireland. The debate in Ireland seems, however, to have been conducted with rather less bitterness.[20]

St Peter was the authority and justification cited by the Roman party of Wilfrid and his allies. Peter and Rome were almost syonymous terms in these disputes. Wilfrid attributed the Roman method of calculating the date of Easter to St Peter in Bede's account of the synod of Whitby, whilst Colman, the spokesman for the Irish party, claimed St John's authority for Irish practice.[21]

The debate over the correct form of the clerical tonsure was almost as controversial and St Peter's authority was again invoked. The Roman party insisted on the form widely used by the church in the west from the sixth century, in which the hair on the top of the head is cut very short or shaved and a circle of longer hair like a crown is left around the head below. This type of tonsure was current by the sixth century, when Gregory of Tours referred to it as a *corona*. It is presumably also the form which, according to another passage by Gregory, St Peter adopted as an example of humility.[22] The fourth council of Toledo in 633 tried to enforce the wearing of this form of tonsure by all clerics. The tonsure is described quite clearly in order to distinguish it from another form: *detonso superius toto capite inferius solam circuli coronam relinquant* (the clerics are to have the whole of the upper part of the head shorn and are to leave only an encircling crown of hair).[23]

The letter of Abbot Ceolfrith of Monkwearmouth to Nechtan, king of the Picts, claims that Peter wore his tonsure in memory of Christ's Passion and that its form imitated the crown of thorns. At about the same time the Petrine tonsure is again associated with the Crown of Thorns by the anonymous *Life of St Cuthbert* (*tonsurae . . . Petri formam in modum corone spineae capud Christi cingentis*) and in almost identical words by Eddius in his *Life of Bishop Wilfrid.*[24] The

[20] K. Hughes, *The Church in Early Irish Society* (London, 1966), pp. 102 – 10, especially 109 – 10; J. Ryan, 'The Early Irish Church and the See of Peter', in *Medieval Studies Presented to Aubrey Gwynn, S.J.*, ed. J. A. Watt, J. B. Morrall and F. X. Martin (Dublin, 1961), pp. 3 – 18; J. F. Kenney, *The Sources for the Early History of Ireland*, I, *Ecclesiastical* (New York, 1929), no. 57, pp. 220 – 1; H. Mayr-Harting, *The Coming of Christianity to Anglo-Saxon England* (London, 1972).
[21] *HE* III, 25.
[22] James, in *Peritia* 3; Gregory of Tours, *Life of the Fathers*, XVII, 1, trans. E. James (Liverpool, 1985), pp. 114, 153 – 4; Gregory of Tours, *Liber in gloria martyrum* I, 27 (MGH, Scriptores Rerum Merovingicarum, 1, ii (Hannover, 1885), p. 503 (and, for *Vita patrum* XVII, 1, p. 728)).
[23] J. Vives, *Concilios Visigoticos e Hispano-Romanos* (Barcelona-Madrid, 1963), pp. 22 – 3.
[24] *HE* V, 21 (C and M pp. 548 – 9); *VCA* II, 2; *VW* 6. (The tonsure of St Peter is also mentioned in Felix's *Life of Saint Guthlac*, ed. and trans. B. Colgrave (Cambridge, 1956, repr. 1985), pp. 84 – 5). The tonsure was compared to the crown of thorns in Ireland at about the same time. (See below and see references in n. 45.)

Roman party maintained that the Irish tonsure, whatever its exact form was, had been invented by no less a villain than St Peter's arch-enemy, Simon Magus, thereby giving a further Petrine reinforcement to their views.[25]

The anonymous *Life of St Cuthbert* takes us back to the community at Lindisfarne in the years immediately after the translation for which the coffin was almost certainly made. The author writes that St Cuthbert received the Petrine tonsure at Ripon.[26] This looks like a rewriting of history to conform with the Romanist point of view. It is probable that Cuthbert was initially tonsured in the Irish manner, whether he received the tonsure at Ripon, as the anonymous monk of Lindisfarne maintains, or at Melrose, as Bede has it. Eata and Cuthbert were among those followers of the Irish party who left Ripon rather than conform to Roman usages, when the monastery was handed over to Wilfrid.[27] After the Roman victory at Whitby Lindisfarne itself was romanized. Abbot Colman and others who would not accept the changes left and returned to Iona. Shortly afterwards the church at Lindisfarne was dedicated to St Peter.[28]

If the 'Anglo-Saxon' type of Peter originated as a partisan statement about ecclesiastical organization in general and the tonsure in particular, is it possible that the type was influenced by pictures of the popes? It is certainly true that the drawing of a saint in one of the initials in the Leningrad copy of Bede's *Ecclesiastical History* is very like the St Peter on the coffin-reliquary, although it is a little less stylized (pl. 21). This figure, identified by a later inscription as *Augustinus*, has been interpreted very plausibly by Meyvaert as showing Pope Gregory the Great.[29] The two figures (fig. 21 and pl. 21) are cut off at the waist and the lines of their drapery are very similar. Both carry books in their draped left hands and lean against their right shoulders sceptre-like objects (the keys and the cross) which they hold in their right hands. Neither head is totally frontal: St Peter appears from the cut of his chin to have turned slightly to his left and St Gregory turns a little to his right. Both have the crown-like roll of hair. Both seem to be tonsured, although Gregory's tonsure appears to be larger.

What was the relationship between the two images? Schapiro suggested that the Gregory, which he took to be Augustine, was modelled 'with some

[25] *HE* loc. cit.; Aldhelm, *Epistola I. Aldhelmi ad Geruntium* (PL 89, cols. 87 – 92); L. Gougaud, *Les chrétientés celtiques* (Paris, 1911), pp. 193 – 200; Plummer II, pp. 353 – 4; J. Dowden, 'An Examination of Original Documents on the Question of the Celtic Tonsure', *Proceedings of the Society of Antiquaries of Scotland* 30 (1895 – 6), pp. 325 – 37.

[26] *VCA* II, 2.

[27] *VCP* 6 and 8; Plummer, II, pp. 192 – 3.

[28] *HE* III, 26; III, 25; Plummer I, pp. 189, 181 and II, p. 188.

[29] Alexander, p. 47; P. Meyvaert, *Bede and Gregory the Great* (Jarrow Lecture 1964, Jarrow, reprinted 1976), pp. 3 – 4; G. B. Ladner, *I ritratti dei papi nell'antichità e nel medioevo* (Città del Vaticano, 1940), I, pp. 70 – 7.

religious intent' on the coffin type of Peter.[30] Alternatively an imported picture of Gregory or of some other pope or ecclesiastic may lie behind the unusual representation of Peter. Similar beardless tonsured heads appear in a number of mid-seventh-century mosaics in the Chapel of St Venantius in the Lateran.[31] The Gregory of the initial differs from early documented representations of Gregory in Rome in lacking a beard. Gregory was shown with a slight beard in addition to the tonsure (*corona rotunda et spatiosa*) in a portrait painted in Rome during his lifetime according to the detailed description in the late ninth-century *Life of St Gregory* by John the Deacon. He seems to have worn a beard in two other roughly contemporary portraits.[32] Incidentally James in his recent and very useful paper on 'Bede and the Tonsure Question' points out that Gregory seems to have favoured a short hair-cut rather than the Roman *corona* for priests.[33]

Whatever its sources, it looks as if this 'Roman' or Romanist iconography of St Peter gained currency and was perhaps invented among the Roman party in the Anglo-Saxon church. The type, as we shall see, was thought of as Roman, although it does not seem to have been used in Rome — a case, and perhaps not the only one, of the Roman party being more Roman than the Romans. This portrait type of St Peter may then have been created in order to resolve the contradiction between the Romanist claim that St Peter instituted and wore the Petrine tonsure and an imported pictorial tradition that failed to corroborate this view.

If the coffin did indeed show St Peter with the Petrine tonsure, might it not also have shown St Paul with the tonsure attributed to him? The first tonsure of Theodore of Tarsus, who was later to consecrate the church at Lindisfarne, was so short that he had to let his hair grow for four months before it was long enough to be cut into the Roman crown tonsure. His earlier tonsure, called by Bede *tonsura more orientalium sancti apostoli Pauli*, has been reasonably interpreted as the shaving or close cropping of the whole head. What is unusual about the St Paul on the coffin is that he seems to have been shown with no hair at all apart from the customary beard. Normally he has hair on the sides of his head, however far the hair on top recedes. Bede does not indicate whether the Pauline tonsure was compatible with a beard, but, if it was, that may be what is shown above Paul's *barba prolixa* in the Lindisfarne carving.[34]

[30] Schapiro, op. cit. in n. 1 above, p. 214.

[31] W. Oakeshott, *The Mosaics of Rome from the third to the fourteenth centuries* (London, 1967), pl. XVII, pp. 95, 102 – 4.

[32] Ladner, loc. cit.; Paul the Deacon, *Sancti Gregorii Magni vita*, in PL 75, cols. 229 – 31; Meyvaert, *Bede and Gregory*, pp. 3 – 4 and n. 17.

[33] James, *Peritia* 3, p. 96.

[34] *HE* IV, 1 and Plummer II, pp. 353 – 4; *DACL*, XV.2, cols. 2433 – 4. See Constable (op. cit. in n. 18 above, p. 120, n. 359) for the *barba prolixa*.

There is nothing specifically Insular about the two large keys that the Lindisfarne Peter carries sceptre-like across his right shoulder. Kitzinger did suggest that the model might have shown Peter carrying a cross rather than keys, as do the Mount Sinai Peter and the Leningrad Gregory. This triumphal manner of carrying a pair of large keys need not, however, be a Northumbrian invention. The Grimaldi drawings of the (slightly later) early eighth-century mosaics of John VII in St Peter's in Rome seem to show Peter carrying his keys this way three times over.[35]

Christ's figurative gift of the keys to St Peter featured dramatically in accounts of the synod of Whitby. Wilfrid disparagingly compared the authority of St Columba invoked by the Irish party to that of the prince of the apostles, St Peter, to whom Christ said in Matthew 16:18 – 19: 'Thou art Peter, and upon this rock I will build my church; and the gates of hell shall not prevail against it. And I will give unto thee the keys of the kingdom of heaven.' King Oswiu, who was presiding at the council, seems to have been as impressed by a very literal interpretation of these metaphors as by their use to support the argument for Roman primacy. According to Bede Oswiu decided in favour of the Roman party in a much-quoted passage: 'Then, I tell you, since he [Peter] is the doorkeeper I will not contradict him; but I intend to obey his commands in everything to the best of my knowledge and ability, otherwise when I come to the gates of the kingdom of heaven, there may be no one to open them because the one who . . . holds the keys has turned his back on me.'[36]

Then, as now, in the popular and secular imagination St Peter was first and foremost the saint who controlled access to heaven. Aldhelm uses the threat of the doorkeeper's displeasure to press home his argument in favour of conformity with Roman practice in his letter to King Geraint. More than three centuries later King Cnut seems to have been impressed with a similar view of the practical advantage of having St Peter on one's side. In late seventh-century Northumbria the primary purpose of the keys in an image of St Peter would be to identify him as 'the one who holds the keys', that is as the keeper of the gates of heaven. In a sermon on this passage of Matthew Bede interprets the keys of the kingdom of heaven as a symbol for the knowledge and power needed to decide (*discernendi sciĕntiam potentiamque*) who should be admitted to and who excluded from heaven.[37]

It is now time to look at a very interesting short text of about this time which includes a two-word description of how St Peter appeared, it is claimed, in

[35] Carr, op. cit. in n. 1 above; *Relics*, p. 266, n. 4 and p. 267, n. 2; Paluzzi, *La Basilica di San Pietro*, fig. 57; J. Wilpert, *Die römischen Mosaiken und Malereien der kirchlichen Bauten vom IV. bis XIII. Jahrhundert* (4 vols., Freiburg im Breisgau, 1924), I, pp. 399 – 400.

[36] *HE* III, 25 (trans. C and M, p. 307).

[37] Aldhelm in PL 89, cols. 87 – 92; F. Barlow, *The English Church 1000 – 1066* (2nd edn., London and New York, 1979), p. 291 (Cnut); Bede, *Homelia* I, 20, ed. D. Hurst, CCSL 122, p. 145.

Roman painting (or, less probably, in a single Roman painting).[38] Its title, *De tonsura apostolorum*, which could be translated as *Concerning the Hair-styles of the Apostles*, suggests that the tonsure question was still a live issue when this document was compiled. The text appears in two manuscripts in the company of an exegetical work, the 'Reference Bible' or '*Biblelwerk*', which seems to have been written in Irish circles on the continent in the late eighth century.[39] It begins: 'In (a?) Roman painting the apostles are depicted in the following way' (*Romanorum pictura apostolorum imagines sic depinguit*). Each of eleven apostles is briefly described in terms of hair colour and of special features of hair-style including beards. (St Paul is not included.) Six of the apostles are said to be bearded and four of the others are said to be tonsured (*coronatus*). Beards and tonsures do not go together here. Peter is grey-haired and tonsured but no beard is mentioned (*Petrus canus coronatusque*). The author must have in mind the beardless and tonsured St Peter. The text is good evidence that some people thought, consciously, of the Lindisfarne type of St Peter as Roman and also that the type was known beyond Northumbria.

The *De tonsura apostolorum* as we have it may be an embroidered, even whimsical, version of a more sober original. The apostles' tunics are described as multicoloured and Andrew is given 'a grey beard and the sign of the cross in his hair' (*in crine crucis imaginem habens*). This sounds like a cruciform tonsure, but it is not clear whether the hair cross was a positive or negative image. Four of the apostles (Peter, James the son of Zebedee, Thomas and Thaddaeus) have the crown tonsure, which, if it appears at all in depictions of the apostles, is normally the distinguishing mark of St Peter alone. As far as I know, there are no beardless apostles with crown tonsures or apostles with cruciform tonsures in the early medieval art of Rome itself.[40] It is in fact very unlikely that these descriptions were in any sense modelled on what paintings of the apostles looked like in Rome itself. The iconographies are Roman in the ideological sense only.

---

[38] A. Wilmart, 'Effigies des apôtres vers le début du moyen âge', *Revue bénédictine* 42 (1930), p. 76; B. Bischoff, 'Regensburger Beiträge zur mittelalterlichen Dramatik und Ikonographie', in his *Mittelalterliche Studien* (3 vols.; Stuttgart, 1966–81), II, pp. 156–68; C. Davis-Weyer, *Early Medieval Art 300–1150* (Sources and Documents in the History of Art Series, Englewood Cliffs, New Jersey, 1971), pp. 78–9 (translation). This and related texts are discussed in a very interesting forthcoming paper by Dáibhí Ó Cróinín: 'Cummianus Longus and the Iconography of Christ and the Apostles in Early Irish Literature', in *Sages, Saints and Storytellers, Celtic Studies in Honour of Professor James Carney*, ed. L. Breatnach, K. McCone and D. Ó Corráin (Maynooth, forthcoming). I am very grateful to Dr Ó Cróinín for allowing me to read this paper before publication.

[39] Bischoff, art. cit., p. 166.

[40] I would like to thank Professor John Osborne for confirming (in a letter) my impression that there appears to be no example of a clean-shaven and tonsured Peter in surviving art from the Rome of this period. An exception to the rule that only St Peter appears with a tonsure can be found in an eighth-century Northumbrian (or Northumbrian-influenced) Gospel book at Maeseyck, in which at least one other apostle was tonsured. (See Alexander, no. 23, p. 51.) The features of the apostles in this manuscript do not coincide with those described in the *De tonsura*.

The *De tonsura apostolorum* and some other comparable descriptions of the apostles have been studied by Bischoff and are the subject of a forthcoming paper by Ó Cróinín.[41] The *De tonsura apostolorum* is edited by Bischoff from three manuscripts, the oldest of which, as we have seen, comes from a context with Irish associations and is dated by Lapidge and Sharpe, following Bischoff, to the early ninth century. This text seems to lie behind one in a Regensburg manuscript of the late twelfth century, which Bischoff thought was intended as a guide for dressing the participants in liturgical dramas. Bischoff published another analogous set of brief descriptions of the apostles, *De figuris apostolorum*, which he knew from nine manuscripts, the oldest of which he dated to *c.*1000. The individual descriptions in this set are unrelated to those of the *De tonsura apostolorum*. Peter is described in this set as 'grey-haired with a short beard' (*canutus non longa barba*). He has a short beard and no tonsure and therefore he has nothing to do with the 'Anglo-Saxon' type. A twelfth-century copy of the *De figuris apostolorum* is followed by the name *Comianus longus*, probably the seventh-century Irish Cummianus Longus. This text or its source also exists in versions in Irish. Ó Cróinín's paper investigates a possible context in which these descriptions could have been written by Cummianus Longus in Ireland.[42]

To summarize: the *De tonsura apostolorum*, which describes the 'Anglo-Saxon' type of St Peter and which claims to represent 'Roman' practice, is first found on the continent in a context with Irish associations in a ninth-century manuscript; the analogous but independent *De figuris apostolorum*, in which the St Peter is not of the 'Anglo-Saxon' type, appears first in a continental manuscript of *c.*1000, is found once in the company of the name of its possible seventh-century Irish author and exists in Irish versions. Both sets of descriptions suggest an Irish interest in the appearances of the apostles but neither is primary evidence for how St Peter was represented in Ireland in the seventh and eighth centuries.

The *De figuris apostolorum*, which has the stronger Irish connexions, does not have St Peter in his 'Anglo-Saxon' guise. It would be very interesting to know whether the Insular Romanist viewpoint implied in the *De tonsura apostolorum* is of Anglo-Saxon or Irish origin. It is worth considering the possibility that the 'Anglo-Saxon' type of Peter might have originated among the Roman party in Ireland in the seventh century. It might in that case have been introduced into Northumbria from Ireland. It is certainly simplistic to see the dispute as one between the Irish church in general and the Anglo-Saxon Roman party. Early in the seventh century St Columbanus could describe the Irish as disciples of Sts Peter and Paul and from *c.*632 the southern Irish seem to have conformed

[41] Bischoff, loc. cit.; Ó Cróinín, art. cit.
[42] M. Lapidge and R. Sharpe, *A Bibliography of Celtic-Latin Literature 400–1200* (Royal Irish Academy Dictionary of Medieval Latin from Celtic Sources, Ancillary Publications 1; Dublin, 1985), p. 205, no. 762; Bischoff, art. cit., pp. 164–8; Ó Cróinín, art. cit.

to Roman practice on the Easter question and probably in other matters.[43] It is important too in this context to notice that Bede seems to say that the Roman tonsure was in use among the southern Irish by 664 and was worn by Bishop Tuda when he became bishop of the Northumbrians following Colman's withdrawal to Iona. Colgrave's translation assumes that the province (*prouincia*) spoken of by Bede as observing the crown tonsure must have been Northumbria; but the immediate antecedent in the original is the reference to Tuda's ordination among the southern Irish. Plummer, however, had earlier read the passage as meaning that Tuda had received the Roman tonsure in the south of Ireland.[44] If this is right, the southern Irish might well have developed the iconography of the tonsured and beardless Peter. Ireland was probably in much less frequent direct contact with Rome than was England in the seventh century and there were likely to be fewer works of art imported from Rome into Ireland. It might therefore have been easier in Ireland than in England to think of the new type as Roman.

St Peter no doubt played an important part in the arguments of the Roman party in Ireland as well as in England. The section on the tonsure in the *Collectio canonum hibernensis* calls for the excommunication of any cleric who does not wear the Roman tonsure. It quotes the view of the *Romani*, probably the Roman party, that this tonsure was first worn by Peter and that its form was an 'image' of the crown of thorns. The *Romani* also saw this tonsure as distinguishing its wearer from Simon Magus, whose tonsure is described. The *Collectio* was probably put together in the eighth century, but the sections attributed to the *Romani* may well go back to the seventh. Muirchu, who wrote his *Life of St Patrick* in the later seventh century, seems also to have been influenced by the Romanist point of view. In the *Life* Patrick's contest with King Lóegaire's wizard, Lochru, is explicitly compared to the victory of Peter and Paul over Simon Magus in their contest before Nero.[45]

The fall of Simon Magus is one of the two or three Petrine subjects shown on the tenth-century high crosses in Ireland. The first documented illustration

[43] K. Hughes, 'The Celtic Church and the Papacy', in *The English Church and the Papacy in the Middle Ages*, ed. C. H. Lawrence and D. Knowles (New York, 1965), pp. 3–28; J. Ryan, 'The Early Irish Church and the See of Peter', in *Medieval Studies Presented to Aubrey Gwynn, S.J.*, ed. J. A. Watt, J. B. Morrall and F. X. Martin (Dublin, 1961), pp. 3–18; Columbanus, *ep.* 5, 3, ed. G. S. M. Walter, *Sancti Columbani opera* (Scriptores Latini Hiberniae 2; Dublin, 1957), pp. 38–9; Kenney, *Sources*, no. 57, pp. 220–1.

[44] *HE* III, 26 (C and M, pp. 308–9); Plummer, II, p. 125. (Plummer's reading is hidden in a note to another passage.) I am very grateful to my colleague, Dr Allan Hood, who has examined the passage and confirms my view that Plummer's reading is the more natural one. '*Prouincia*' followed by the name of a people is often used by Bede, e.g. *septentrionalis Scottorum prouincia* (*HE* III, 3). See many examples in P. F. Jones, *A Concordance to the Historia Ecclesiastica of Bede* (Cambridge, Massachusetts, 1929), pp. 429–31. See the next paragraph below for seventh- or eighth-century Irish legislation aimed at enforcing the Roman tonsure.

[45] Hughes, *CEIS*, pp. 107, 125–6; H. Wasserschleben, *Die irische Kanonensammlung* 52, 7(Giessen, 1874), pp. 241–3; Kenney, *Sources*, no. 82 (*Collectio canonum hibernensis*), pp. 247–50; Muirchu, *Life of St Patrick*, 17; ed. and trans. A. B. E. Hood, *St. Patrick: His Writings and Muirchu's Life* (London and Chichester, 1978), pp. 69 and 89–90.

of this scene was in the destroyed mosaics of the Chapel of Pope John VII (705 – 7) in St Peter's in Rome.[46] The fall of Simon Magus and the scene of Christ and Peter walking on the water are shown on the West Cross at Monasterboice. The fall of Simon Magus also appears on the Market Cross at Kells and perhaps on the North Cross at Castledermot. Muiredach's Cross at Monasterboice and the Cross of the Scriptures at Clonmacnois have the scene of Christ giving the keys to Peter and a book to Paul. This is no longer a literal illustration of the giving of the keys in Matthew 16 but has taken over the symmetrical arrangement and presence of St Paul from the early Christian '*traditio legis*', a symbolic rather than historical scene in which a central figure of Christ hands the scroll of the Law to Peter in the presence of Paul. The earliest surviving example of this form of the giving of the keys is in the Carolingian paintings at Müstair.[47] Verses written for a scene of this sort have been attributed to an origin late in the seventh century in the Irish foundation of Péronne, although the evidence for the attribution does not seem to amount to proof:[48]

> Iustus apostolicos aequat Salvator amicos:
> Clavibus hic Petrum, hic Paulum legibus ornat.

I have not so far examined the Irish crosses systematically to find whether the 'Anglo-Saxon' type of Peter occurs. Weathering has generally obscured the issue. Peter and Paul appear from photographs to wear impressive and un-Roman moustaches on Muiredach's cross at Monasterboice; but in the scene of the fall of Simon Magus on the West Cross at Monasterboice, on which Peter and Paul carry croziers, they look as if they might have been clean-shaven and possibly tonsured with the *corona*.[49]

Too little remains of the possible figure of St Peter on the added silver cladding on the portable altar of St Cuthbert for it to contribute to the discussion of the St Peter on the coffin. The confident reconstruction of it as a seated figure of St Peter in *The Relics of Saint Cuthbert* is largely conjectural. When Raine found the altar in 1827, much of the silver on this face had already gone, but he thought that there was evidence for 'the full length figure of a priest in his robes, with a glory over his head' and an inscription. Only

[46] Paluzzi, *La Basilica di San Pietro*, fig. 57.

[47] F. Henry, *Irish Art during the Viking Invasions (800 – 1020 A.D.)* (London, 1967), pp. 157 – 8, 184 – 5, 187 – 8, fig. 35, pls. 82 and 111; H. M. Roe, *The High Crosses of Kells* (Meath Archaeological and Historical Society, 1975), p. 39; H. M. Roe, *Monasterboice and its Monuments* (County Louth Archaeological and Historical Society, 1981), pp. 31, 52, 55 – 7. For Müstair see Carr, op. cit. in n. 1 above, pp. 83 – 4 and J. Hubert, J. Porcher and W. F. Volbach, *Carolingian Art* (London, 1970), ill. 21.

[48] P. Grosjean, 'Notes d'hagiographie celtique', *Analecta Bollandiana* 78 (1960), pp. 369 – 70; F. Henry, op. cit., p. 185.

[49] F. Henry, op. cit., pl. 82 and 111.

small fragments of the halo, drapery and a few letters remain. The head has entirely disappeared.[50]

There is room here only for a rapid and selective survey of the role of St Peter in the art of early medieval Britain. The Anglo-Saxon enthusiasm for St Peter, demonstrated, for example, by the large number of early church dedications in his name in England, is well known.[51] Bede's *Ecclesiastical History* and Alcuin's poem on the *Bishops, Kings, and Saints of York* contain or refer to strongly visual images of St Peter's interventions in wordly affairs. In verses on St Balthere in the York poem Alcuin reflects belief in Peter as the great and powerful protective patron. St Balthere protects the soul of a sinful deacon from devils in a way that perhaps derives from Peter's role at the Last Judgement. The devils taunt the sinner that he will not escape them, even if St Peter held him in his arms (*nec si tenearis in ulnis Petri*). St Balthere acknowledges that St Peter is one hundred times more worthy than he and his miracle of walking on the water is compared to that of St Peter. Two striking visions of St Peter are recounted in the *Ecclesiastical History*. He appeared along with St Paul, as we have already seen, to the boy on his deathbed at Selsey. St Peter also intervened in a dream of Laurence, archbishop of Canterbury, and scourged him vigorously for planning to leave the mission in England.[52]

Given the importance of St Peter for the English church it is surprising that he does not seem to have appeared very often in Anglo-Saxon sculpture. His crucifixion head-downwards is shown on the cross at Aycliffe and he appeared on the destroyed cross at Reculver in Kent carrying the text from Matthew 16:16 (*Tu es Christus filius Dei vivi*), which comes shortly before the gift of the keys to Peter. As Christ and Paul were also shown, this was possibly a form of the *traditio legis* or of the giving of the keys. The surviving fragment which has been identified as showing parts of the figures of Christ and Peter could not belong, however, to a group of Christ giving both the keys to Peter and a book to Paul because Christ's surviving hand is holding a scroll in front of him. Representations of Peter may also have been intended in a number of now anonymous beardless and tonsured figures, for example on the crosses of Auckland St Andrew and Hoddom. The figure of Peter on the Hedda Stone at Peterborough is very worn. It might have been bearded but no clear indication of a tonsure now remains.[53]

---

[50] Radford in *Relics*, pp. 229 – 32, fig. 2 and pls. XVIII and XIX; *St Cuthbert*, p. 200. (Radford's reconstruction of the figure as seated does not necessarily contradict Raine's description of it in *St Cuthbert* as 'full length'.)

[51] Zwölfer, *Sankt Peter*, pp. 20 – 63; Levison, *England and the Continent*, pp. 35 – 42, 259 – 61.

[52] Alcuin, *The Bishops, Kings, and Saints of York*, ed. P. Godman (Oxford, 1982), pp. 106 – 9; *HE* II, 6 and IV, 14.

[53] *Corpus* I, i and I, ii, p. 42 and pl. 8.28 (Aycliffe), pl. 5.13 and 5.15 (Auckland St Andrew); R. Kozodoy, 'The Reculver Cross', *Archaeologia* 108 (1986), pp. 67 – 94, especially pp. 68 – 71 and pl. XXXI; J. R. Allen and J. Anderson, *The Early Christian Monuments of Scotland* (Edinburgh, 1903), p. 439, fig. 461B and 461C (Hoddom); *The Anglo-Saxons*, ed. J. Campbell (Oxford, 1982), pl. 103 (Hedda Stone). I would like to thank Dr Carole Farr for an excellent slide of the Hedda Stone.

In Scotland worn figures of Peter and Paul stand side by side below the Virgin and Child on the perhaps ninth-century cross-slab at Brechin. Peter's face, which is broad in distinction to the long head of Paul, appears to be beardless but untonsured. He carries a key (or keys).[54]

The St Peters in two continental Gospel books of the eighth century decorated in the Anglo-Saxon style can perhaps be interpreted as a compromise between the 'Anglo-Saxon' and the normal bearded types. In the Maeseyck and Trier Gospels Peter appears with a Roman tonsure, which is probably based on Anglo-Saxon models, but he also has a beard. In the early ninth-century Sedulius manuscript in Antwerp, which reflects a slightly earlier Anglo-Saxon copy, Peter seems to be tonsured and sometimes has a beard and sometimes not.[55]

The 'Anglo-Saxon' type of Peter re-emerges vigorously in southern English manuscripts of the tenth and eleventh centuries, the earliest instance being in the Athelstan Psalter. This is one of the most striking examples of iconographic continuity between early and later Anglo-Saxon art, which suggests that this was already a common and widely revered image in England before the Viking invasion of the ninth century. The iconography was taken up enthusiastically by artists of the period of the Monastic Reform. The 'Anglo-Saxon' Peter appears, for example, as one of the patrons of the New Minster in Winchester in the New Minster Charter, and later in the New Minster *Liber vitae* (pl. 42), as well as in several scenes, including his crucifixion, in the Benedictional of St Aethelwold.[56] An already venerable English tradition of the tonsured Peter would have had a renewed relevance and a special appeal for the reforming English Benedictines of the tenth century. The New Minster prayerbook of the 1020s or 1030s contains a picture of St Peter enthroned in which the artist went as far as to borrow certain elements from images of Christ in Majesty: the globe-and-arc throne, the foot-stool and the book.[57]

Peter's power as the gate-keeper of heaven at the Last Judgement was vividly illustrated in the *Liber vitae* of the New Minster in the 1020s. The iconography is in part quite closely related to that in the ninth-century mosaics in Santa Prassede in Rome, a possible indication of continued interest in developments in Rome. The Anglo-Saxon picture heightens the drama and makes Peter into the leading actor in his two appearances. St Peter was of course one of the patrons of the New Minster, which may have contributed to his special treatment here.[58]

The rather menacing image of St Peter with stubbly tonsure and face in the eleventh-century Sacramentary of Robert of Jumièges may serve as a graphic

[54] Allen and Anderson, op. cit., pp. 249 – 50 and fig. 261.

[55] Alexander, ills. 96, 108, 298 – 301.

[56] E. Temple, *Anglo-Saxon Manuscripts 900 – 1066* (London, 1976), ills. 32 and 84; G. F. Warner and H. A. Wilson, *The Benedictional of St. Aethelwold, Bishop of Winchester, 963 – 984* (Roxburghe Club, Oxford, 1910), passim.

[57] Temple, op. cit., ill. 243. (Compare with ills. 84 and 245.)

[58] Temple, op. cit., ills. 247 – 8; Oakeshott, *Mosaics of Rome*, pl. 121 – 2.

illustration of the infrequency and perhaps also inefficiency of monastic hair-cutting and shaving. As the shaving seems to have taken place at intervals of weeks rather than days, clerical beardlessness and tonsures must have been relative rather than absolute most of the time.[59]

The one exception that I know to the general beardlessness of St Peter in art attributed to later Anglo-Saxon England is in the two leaves of unknown provenance from a Gospel lectionary formerly at Damme in Belgium and now in Malibu. This fragment is an oddity in iconographic terms and is not closely connected to the mainstream of late Anglo-Saxon art.[60]

Depictions of St Peter shown as both beardless and tonsured seem to have been very rare on the continent. There is a Carolingian example on the ivory handle of the Tournus flabellum. At about the time that that was carved Ratramnus of Corbie wrote, in a polemical text against the Greek church, that there were pictures that showed St Peter with shaved beard and shaved (tonsured?) head.[61] In the Ottonian Gospel book of Bernward of Hildesheim a tonsured Peter appears both with and without a beard. A beardless and tonsured figure on the ivory bucket at Aachen has been identified as St Peter. The type also appears in French Romanesque sculpture at Vézelay. Its appearance in the stubbly variant in the Saint-Bertin Gospels of *c*. 1000 in New York is an example of the well-known direct Anglo-Saxon influences to be seen in Saint-Bertin manuscripts.[62] Knowledge of Anglo-Saxon art may perhaps be responsible for the other examples, but they could also be due to an independent development. It is of course possible that some reflect a rare early medieval continental type (tonsured and beardless), the early examples of which are now perhaps lost. In that case the 'Anglo-Saxon' type might also derive from it. The type could of course have carried a 'Roman' meaning regardless of whether it originated in England, or in Ireland, or on the continent.

The type is replaced in England after the Norman Conquest by the continental convention of the bearded Peter, often but not always tonsured.

---

[59] H. A. Wilson, *The Missal of Robert of Jumièges* (Henry Bradshaw Society 11; London, 1896), pl. XI; Constable, op. cit. in n. 18 above, pp. 55 (n. 29) and 116 – 21; J. Higgitt, 'Glastonbury, Dunstan, monasticism and manuscripts', *Art History* 2 (1979), p. 286 and n. 40.

[60] Temple, op. cit., pp. 72 – 3, ills. 173 – 6.

[61] A. Goldschmidt, *Die Elfenbeinskulpturen aus der Zeit der karolingischen und sächsischen Kaiser VIII. – XI. Jahrhundert* I, (reprint, Berlin and Oxford, 1969), p. 76 and Taf. LXVIc. For Ratramnus see Constable, op. cit. in n. 18 above, pp. 74 and 111 and PL 121, col. 324C.

[62] F. J. Tschan, *Saint Bernward of Hildesheim* (3 vols., Notre Dame, Indiana, 1942 – 52) III, pls. 65 and 70; E. G. Grimme, 'Der Aachener Domschatz', *Aachener Kunstblätter* 42 (2nd edn., 1973), Taf. VI and 24; E. Mâle, *Religious Art in France in the Twelfth Century* (Bollingen Series 90, i; Princeton, 1978), p. 253 (Vézelay); A. K. Porter, *Romanesque Sculpture of the Pilgrimage Roads* (reissue, New York, 1985) I, ill. 36 (Vézelay); F. Salet, *La Madeleine de Vézelay* (Melun, 1948), pp. 136, 196 – 7, pl. 45 (Vézelay); H. Swarzenski, *Monuments of Romanesque Art* (London, 1954), pl. 161 (Saint-Bertin Gospels). There are also beardless Peters without tonsures in Carolingian and Romanesque art, e.g.: A. Boinet, *La miniature carolingienne* (Paris, 1913), pl. II; E. T. De Wald, *The Illustrations of the Utrecht Psalter* (Princeton, n.d.), pl. XXXI (fol. 19ʳ); G. de Francovich, 'Il ciclo pittorico della chiesa di San Giovanni a Münster (Müstair) nei Grigioni', *Arte Lombarda* 2 (1956), pp. 28 – 50, fig. 11; Mâle, op. cit., p. 253 and fig. 42.

The beardless and tonsured type continues to appear here and there, showing perhaps that Anglo-Saxon models went on exerting some influence. It is used in a copy of the *Prayers and Meditations of St Anselm* and in sculpture at Daglingworth, Stoneleigh and Malmesbury. In the early twelfth century at Wentworth in Cambridgeshire Peter, clearly identified by an inscription, holds a book and keys, wears a papal pallium and is beardless and tonsured (pl. 41). A century later in nearby Ely Cathedral, dedicated to St Peter, he appears in a vaulting boss in the presbytery in a monastic cowl (as on the capital at Vézelay) holding a key and a church. Does this represent the entire Christian church or simply Peter's church at Ely? Perhaps there was still in the thirteenth century a popular pre-Conquest image of St Peter at Ely.[63] An 'Anglo-Saxon' St Peter welcomes the blessed into heaven in the fourteenth-century Taymouth Hours. A model like the New Minster *Liber vitae* seems still to have been available.[64]

The later examples were no doubt sometimes due to local conservatism or nostalgia, but in some cases at least the intention may rather have been to underline St Peter's role as the first and leading priest, after Christ. The *Gemma animae* of Honorius Augustodunensis, written early in the twelfth century, and the *Golden Legend* and Durandus's *Rationale*, both of the second half of the thirteenth century, state that while Peter was preaching in Antioch the top of his head was shaved by his opponents in mockery of the Christians. (The *Gemma animae* adds that his beard was shaved as well.) The first work implies and the other two state that this mark of shame is now worn as a sign of honour by all of the clergy. In the later middle ages St Peter was also increasingly shown as pope by dressing him in pontifical robes and a tiara, which would hide any tonsure. The fourteenth-century alabaster statue of Peter at Flawford is a beardless version of this papal Peter.[65]

The image of St Peter on St Cuthbert's coffin lacks any specifically papal attributes. He is shown rather as one of the two princes of the apostles (along with and above St Paul) and as gate-keeper of heaven. He is also depicted as

---

[63] C. M. Kauffmann, *Romanesque Manuscripts 1066–1190* (London, 1975), ills. 77, 147 and 218; D. T. Rice, *English Art 871–1100* (The Oxford History of English Art, Oxford, 1952), pl. 14b (Daglingworth); L. Musset, *Angleterre romane* (La Pierre-qui-Vire, 1983), pl. 106 (Malmesbury); N. Pevsner, *Cambridgeshire* (The Buildings of England; Harmondsworth, 2nd edn., 1970), pl. 12a (Wentworth); M. Roberts, 'The Effigy of Bishop Hugh de Northwold in Ely Cathedral', *The Burlington Magazine* 130 (1988), pp. 77–84 at p. 83 and fig. 18.

[64] J. Harthan, *Books of Hours and their Owners* (London, 1977), p. 47; Temple, *Anglo-Saxon Manuscripts*, ills. 247–8.

[65] Honorius Augustodunensis, *Gemma animae* 1, 195–7 in PL 172, cols. 603–4; Jacques de Voragine, *La légende dorée*, trans. J.-B. M. Roze (2 vols., Paris, 1967) I, p. 213 (Chaire de Saint Pierre, apôtre); *Rationale divinorum officiorum a Gulielmo Durando . . . concinnatum* (Venice, 1609) 2, 1.29, p. 32b; J. Alexander and P. Binski, *Age of Chivalry: Art in Plantagenet England 1200–1400* (exhibition catalogue, Royal Academy of Arts, London, 1987), pp. 511–2 (Flawford). St Peter is already shown as pope with a conical mitre in coins (AD 905–11) of Pope Sergius III. (See C. Serafini, *Le monete e le bolle plumbee ponitificie del medagliere vaticano* (4 vols.) I (Milan, 1910), p. 18 and pl. IV, 18–19.)

the first wearer of the crown tonsure, which was almost certainly already thought of as an image of the crown of thorns. He is *attonsus ut clericus* and is therefore a priest.[66] He is portrayed in fact as he was pictured by the Roman party in England and Ireland. It is appropriate that the earliest surviving example of this 'Roman' iconography of St Peter should appear on the reliquary of the most famous Anglo-Saxon churchman to change his allegiance from the 'Irish' to the 'Roman' party, St Cuthbert. The connotations of the image were, however, Roman rather than Anglo-Saxon and it might even have been invented in the (Roman) south of Ireland. The Lindisfarne type of St Peter should in any case have been quite acceptable to the Irish Romanists in 698, but the still un-romanized Iona and north of Ireland might well have found this partisan image of the prince of the apostles rather offensive.[67]

[66] Abbot Ceolfrith of Wearmouth and Jarrow explicitly states (*HE* V, 21, C and M, pp. 548–9) that the tonsure is to be used by both monks and priests (*uel monachi uotum uel gradum clericatus habentes*).

[67] Acknowledgements: I would very much like to thank a number of people for advice, references, or help of various sorts that they have very kindly given while I was preparing this paper: Professor Jonathan Alexander; Mr Michael Bury; Dr Brendan Cassidy; Dr Janey Cronyn; Dr Gary Dickson; Dr Carole Farr; Professor William Gillies; Mrs I. Hariades; Mrs Jane Hawkes; Mrs Caroline Higgitt; Dr Allan Hood; Mr Raymond McCluskey; Dr Dáibhí Ó Cróinín; Professor John Osborne; Dr Clare Stancliffe.

The Pectoral Cross and Portable Altar from the Tomb of St Cuthbert

ELIZABETH COATSWORTH

Near contemporary descriptions of St Cuthbert's death and burial in 687, and his translation into a shrine above the church floor at Lindisfarne in 698, lend no support to the idea that he was buried with any objects other than vestments and other textiles, apart from *oblata*, the unconsecrated elements, which we are told were placed on his breast in 687.[1] The twelfth-century accounts of the opening of the tomb, however, are important for the dating of the cross, not because they mention it, but because they do not.[2] This silence seems reasonably explained by descriptions of the state of the body and its wrappings, which show that the garments nearest the body were not really disturbed at this time.[3] Raine's account of the 1827 investigation shows that the cross was found among the garments close to the body. The cross was broken but the fragments, and apparently some of the rivets from one of the repairs which had been carried out in antiquity, were found together and I would agree with Battiscombe that this indicates that the cross could not have been disturbed by any of the earlier investigations.[4]

---

[1] *VCA* IV, 13 details a waxed shroud, a head cloth, priestly garments, and shoes, as well as *oblata*. Bede tells us that the outer garments were removed in 698, and replaced with fresh garments: *VCP* 42.

[2] *De miraculis* 7 lists the objects found, including a chalice which is described in detail sufficient for identification if it had survived Henry VIII's commissioners. The other objects were the ivory comb, a pair of scissors, a silver altar 'as becomes a priest', a linen cloth to cover the consecrated elements, and a paten. *Libellus* lists the same objects (42); and adds details of a gilded and jewelled head ornament or fillet (41).

[3] Reginald's account seems to hover uneasily between the need to affirm the proofs of incorruption, and the need to show respect for the remains of the saint, which actually appear from his description to have been in a fragile condition. Although he maintains that the incorrupt flesh was seen and touched, he makes it quite clear that some of the undergarments were not seen, and that some were irremovable: *Libellus* 41. Interestingly, Bede (*VCP* 42) says that at the translation of 698, only the original outer garments were taken away, the monks not daring to take away what was nearest the skin.

[4] *St Cuthbert*, p. 211; *Relics*, p. 17, n. 2.

A silver altar was mentioned but not described in the twelfth century when, we are told, it was replaced.[5] Its relationship to the body was not recorded, however; it could not, for example, have been found on the saint's breast, for he was found lying on his side to accommodate all the other remains and objects found with him.[6] The object identified as a portable altar was removed by Raine in 1827.[7] Moreover, the altar and the two parts of its silver covering were not necessarily put together at one time. Its dating and even its connection with St Cuthbert is therefore less secure than is the case for the cross.

However, although the effect of Christianity on burial practices is well known, there are certainly pointers to a long transitional period in the sixth and seventh centuries. The evidence from secular contexts includes cross pendants, such as the example from Winster Moor,[8] and the more disputable evidence, such as the cross patterns which can be discovered on, for example, the Sutton Hoo scabbard mounts,[9] or disc brooches such as the Kingston brooch.[10] There are scattered fragments of evidence from Ireland and Britain to suggest that portable altars may sometimes have been buried with bishops or priests,[11] but plenty to show that many were preserved in church

[5] *Libellus* 7 says it was replaced on a shelf above the saint, and may imply that it and the other objects mentioned in n. 2 were found in such a position. *De miraculis* says only that a copy of the Gospels was found on this shelf, and does not say where in the coffin they were replaced.

[6] *De miraculis* 7 gives a convincing description of the position of St Cuthbert and the relics which were packed around him.

[7] *St Cuthbert*, p. 199.

[8] J. Campbell, ed. *The Anglo-Saxons* (Oxford, 1982), pl. 41.

[9] R. L. S. Bruce-Mitford, *Aspects of Anglo-Saxon Archaeology* (London, 1974), pp. 26 – 35, and pls. 5c, and 8, in which evidence for Christianity at Sutton Hoo is discussed. See also R. L. S. Bruce-Mitford, *The Sutton Hoo Ship Burial* II, *Arms, Armour, and Regalia* (London, 1978), pl. 202a – f and pp. 294 – 7, 304 – 5. R. B. K. Stevenson, 'Aspects of Ambiguity in Crosses and Interlace', *Ulster Journal of Archaeology* 44 – 5 (1981 – 2), pp. 1 – 27, makes a strong case for the importance and ubiquity of the cross as a motif. R. Avent, *Anglo-Saxon Disc and Composite Brooches* (British Archaeological Reports, British Series, 11; 2 vols., Oxford, 1975), on the other hand thought that only a few even of cross-shaped designs could be regarded as crosses.

[10] Campbell, *The Anglo-Saxons*, pl. 48.

[11] What there is is summarized by C. Thomas, *The Early Christian Archaeology of North Britain* (Oxford, 1971), pp. 190 – 8. Particularly interesting is his account of what may have been a 'burial' portable altar from Ardwall Isle. R. N. Bailey, *Viking Age Sculpture* (London, 1980), pp. 231 – 3, takes a critical look at the depiction of puzzling objects in (later) sculpture. An inscribed wooden object in two parts, joined by silver nails, said to be an altar, was reported in the twelfth century to have been discovered in the grave of Bishop Acca of Hexham over 300 years after his death in 740: *HR* 36. The passage is an interpolation stressing the importance of Hexham, but it may have been a genuine discovery. See P. Hunter Blair, 'Observations on the *Historia Regum*', in *Celt and Saxon: Studies in the Early British Border*, ed. N. K. Chadwick (Cambridge, 1964), pp. 70 – 1, 87 – 90; R. N. Bailey, 'The Anglo-Saxon Metalwork from Hexham', in *Saint Wilfrid at Hexham*, ed. D. P. Kirby (Newcastle upon Tyne, 1974), pp. 141 – 67, esp. p. 141.

treasuries.[12] However, there is some evidence, though only from nineteenth-century accounts, that the small stones known as name stones, at the early monastic site of Hartlepool at least, were found in, rather than on, graves.[13]

I

As I have suggested, the cross at least seems to have been buried in 687 or perhaps 698, but if one then asks how much before these dates it was made, or what light it throws on the history of gold and garnet jewellery in England, one is thrown back completely on to stylistic dating criteria (plate 35). The first thorough discussion of the cross denied that it was Anglo-Saxon at all. This was by T. D. Kendrick in 1937, who thought it was too unlike what was known about Kentish gold and garnet jewellery at the time.[14] He placed it very early, in his words, 'the solitary example remaining to us of the goldsmith's work of the Britons in fifth-century Strathclyde'. Given the influence of the British church on Northumbria, particularly Lindisfarne, and the fact that Strathclyde was brought under Northumbrian rule in the 670s by Ecgfrith, this theory has its attractions, and certainly there is nothing inherently improbable about influence from this area. On the other hand, I cannot find any parallel in early work from the north which bears more than the passing resemblance one might expect, given that the *crux gemmata* was the ultimate model for many variant forms of the cross in the sixth and seventh centuries, while modern research has tended to confirm the influence of Anglo-Saxon *cloisonné* jewellery on the rest of Britain.[15]

---

[12] J. Braun, *Der christliche Altar in seiner geschichtlichen Entwicklung*, vol. I (Munich, 1924), lists and illustrates many of the surviving examples in continental treasuries. C. Oman, *English Church Plate 597 – 1830* (London, 1957), pp. 63 – 5, 96 – 7, also discusses some of the documentary sources for England.

[13] *Corpus* I, i, p. 97.

[14] T. D. Kendrick, 'St Cuthbert's Pectoral Cross and the Wilton and Ixworth Crosses', *Antiquaries Journal* 17 (1937), pp. 283 – 93, esp. p. 288.

[15] A cross at Golgotha had been replaced by a gem-studded cross by the Emperor Theodosius by *c.*440, and became a focus of pilgrimage. See H. Pétré, *Éthérie: Journal de Voyage* (SC 21, 1948). This theme was taken up in art, and some developments from areas far from Northumbria have features comparable with the Cuthbert cross: for example, on a sixth-century silver paten of Byzantine origin in Leningrad two angels adore a cross which has arms expanded through a slight curve, with the crossing and terminals elaborated by circular loops (G. Schiller, *Iconography of Christian Art*, vol. II: *The Passion of Jesus Christ* (trans. J. Seligman, Gutersloh/London, 1972), pl. 6). The most similar carving from Scotland that I can find is a crude carving of three apparently jewelled crosses from Whithorn: see C. A. R. Radford and G. Donaldson, *Whithorn and Kirkmadrine* (Edinburgh, 1953), p. 40, where however it is dated to the ninth century and said to be the result of Anglian influence. I concluded that it could be seventh century, but dependent on Merovingian influence, for which there is other evidence (E. Coatsworth, 'The Iconography of the Crucifixion in pre-Conquest Sculpture in England' (unpubl. Ph.D. thesis, Durham University, 1979), pp. 28 – 30). See also R. B. K. Stevenson, 'The Hunterston Brooch and its Significance', *Mediaeval Archaeology* 18 (1974), pp. 16 – 42.

Kendrick's early and unusual placing of the cross, in any case, preceded the discoveries at Sutton Hoo, which changed perceptions of the Anglo-Saxon jeweller-craftsman. In studies based on this discovery Bruce-Mitford has been able to show that the cross was not so out of line as Kendrick thought.[16] Its narrow rectangular and trapezoidal cells,[17] and versions of the dogtooth ornament,[18] are all found in Anglo-Saxon jewellery from the south of England, and even the absence of gold foil can be paralleled.[19] Bruce-Mitford also showed that the centre of the cross, a large, flat-topped garnet set into the top of a gold tube, and surrounded by several collars of gold filigree and anchored in a setting of white material, is an exact parallel of the central settings of some disc and composite brooches, perhaps even cut down and adapted from the centre of one such brooch.[20] This is a very interesting suggestion, for if a standard setting for a disc brooch was cut down and used to make up a brooch of a new form, that not only gives us a horizon for the date of the cross, but also an insight into its experimental nature.[21]

This is important, because while Bruce-Mitford's study underpins the current view that the cross is related to Anglo-Saxon garnet and gold jewellery of the seventh century, it has so far only been defined in relation to southern work of the early part of this period, in comparison with which it has been described as 'arid', and as a coarsening of the style found at Sutton Hoo, an example of a long-lived tradition in its decline.[22] It is certainly different from the only two other comparable cross pendants, the Wilton and the Ixworth brooches, both of which have broader spreads of garnets, an enlarged circular setting which overwhelms the crossing, and a gold setting visible only as cell walls between garnets. These crosses have been shown to be very closely related to the jewellery from Sutton Hoo, and therefore to share its early seventh-century date.[23] This is, however, a negative way of looking at the Cuthbert cross itself. If we accept that the cross is indeed a development, but was also buried with the saint at the end of the century, then it is a uniquely important piece in providing us with a glimpse of a traditional jewellery style

---

[16] For a full study of the Sutton Hoo jewellery, see Bruce-Mitford, *The Sutton Hoo Ship Burial*, II. The evidence from Sutton Hoo is taken into account by the same author, 'The Pectoral Cross', in *Relics*, pp. 308 – 25.

[17] For example, on the edge of the Sutton Hoo shoulder clasps, illustrated in Campbell, *The Anglo-Saxons*, pl. 77; or the brooch incorporated into the Egbert reliquary, Bruce-Mitford, *Aspects*, pp. 31 – 2 and pl. 9b,c. See also n. 19 below.

[18] The solid moulding on the cross is really unparalleled, Bruce-Mitford, 'The Pectoral Cross', pp. 318, 321; but see the gold-foil teeth gripping the central stone on, for example, the Sarre brooch (*Relics*, pl. XVI, 8).

[19] Bruce-Mitford, 'The Pectoral Cross', p. 318 and pl. XVII, 4, for a strap end from Faversham, Kent, which also has lines of plain cells and a terminal with a heart-shaped filigree motif, as on the cross's suspension loop. This piece is unusual among Kentish jewellery.

[20] See, for example, the Sarre brooch, *Relics*, pl. XVI, 8. Other examples are from Faversham and Dover, both Kent: see Avent, *Anglo-Saxon Disc and Composite Brooches* I, 16, 20.

[21] Bruce-Mitford, 'The Pectoral Cross', pp. 318 – 21.

[22] Ibid., p. 319. D. M. Wilson, *Anglo-Saxon Art* (London, 1984), p. 29.

[23] Bruce-Mitford, *Aspects*, pp. 28 – 33.

developing alongside the new monastic arts of manuscript illumination and sculpture. It is frequently said that Hiberno-Saxon manuscripts such as Durrow and Lindisfarne show the influence of contemporary metalwork design, but there is very little discussion of what this means when the surviving manuscripts are from Northumbria, if from anywhere in England, and the metalwork with which they are compared is from the south.

If we look again at the Wilton and Ixworth examples it is easy to see that the design is based on a compass-drawn circle, and the curves of the arms are arcs of circles for which the centres are spaced around the main circle according to some regular formula (fig. 22). It is worth dwelling for a moment on the geometric design structure underlying these two pendants. The Ixworth cross is the simpler of the two. It is based on two concentric circles with the same centre as an equal-armed cross. The arms are arcs of circles of the same radius as the larger circle, centred on the points at which the construction cross breaks this circle (fig. 22a). The cross, or a grid of four equal squares, provides all the necessary working lines. The Wilton cross is rather more complex, though it retains the two concentric circles and the equal-armed cross. The inner circle is larger, however, at two-thirds the radius of the outer circle. The arcs of the arms imply a complete small circle in each quadrant of the main square. The circles are two-thirds the diameter of the quadrant. The centres of these circles could have been found by dividing each square diagonally, but an original grid of sixteen squares provides both the working lines and also all the relative proportions (fig. 22b). The pattern has been varied by making the upper arm straight, but the herringbone pattern in the *cloisonné* seems to refer to the central line of the underlying grid. The regular cross-patterns could not have been drawn free-hand, so it is interesting to see that the crosses themselves provide evidence for a method of design stretching back to the period before the great Hiberno-Saxon manuscripts.[24]

That favourite form the disc brooch is not too far away, many of them with cross designs with equally exaggerated centres and arms.[25] The artist of the Lindisfarne Gospels shows familiarity with this form, for one folio depicts perfectly clearly several circular settings with their characteristic surrounds of white material.[26] The sides of the Cuthbert cross are also quite reminiscent of the structure of some composite brooches, particularly the multiple edging of gold filigree, although the dummy rivets which punctuate the sides are an unusual feature. Visually this multiple dotted edging is one of the features which link metalwork with manuscript art,[27] and is also found as we shall see in related sculpture. Disc brooches were not necessarily very strong structures, and examples survive which appear to have become distorted or broken in

---

[24] For example Wilson, *Anglo-Saxon Art*, p. 34; Campbell, *The Anglo-Saxons*, p. 93 and pls. 76, 77.
[25] Avent, *Anglo-Saxon Disc and Composite Brooches*, II, pls. 18 – 20, 63, 64 – 72, 102, 109 – 24, 126, 128 – 31, etc.
[26] *Cod. Lind.* I, fol. 26ᵛ.
[27] But the dotted outlines in manuscripts seem to have been inherited from earlier manuscript sources: see Alexander, pp. 11 – 12.

Ixworth

Wilton

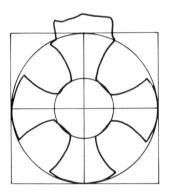

Fig. a

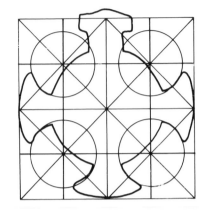

Fig. b

Cuthbert

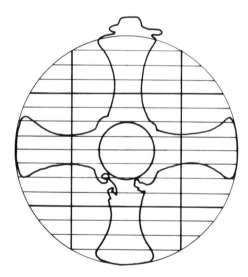

Fig. c

22. Design geometry of Anglo-Saxon gold and garnet crosses: a) Ixworth cross, British Museum (height 4.5 cm); b) Wilton cross, British Museum (height 5.6 cm); c) St Cuthbert's pectoral cross, Durham Cathedral Treasury (height 6 cm).

wear.[28] The Cuthbert cross's history of breakage suggests that the application of old technology to new or developed design was not particularly successful. The narrowness of the arms, of course, means that the front plate has been reduced merely to the narrow *cloisonné* trays.

The underlying design principle of the Cuthbert cross is the same as for the Wilton and Ixworth pendants, but it is clearly a new development, for the narrower arms give greater emphasis to the form of the cross, and examination reveals a number of further refinements. Using the three complete arms it is possible to show that the Cuthbert cross is based on a compass-drawn circle, and with a concentric central circle. The arms are also based on arcs of circles but eight circles, not four, are needed to achieve them (fig. 22c). Additionally, the lobes of the setting if one turns the cross over and looks at the back (pl. 36) are based on a square of which the edges are also equidistant from the centre of the circle. The medial lines which divide some of the cells in the widest part of the arms can also be produced to form a cross, with the crossing point again at the centre of the main circle. The medial line is also crossed by other cell walls, forming a crosslet at the end of each arm; and the centre both has a cross formed in this way, and another cross set diagonally, composed of the central setting and the lobes. This underlying geometry, already obviously more complex when compared with the Wilton and Ixworth crosses, assumes even greater interest when it is compared to the other works of seventh- to eighth-century Northumbria.

The design technique of grids and compass-drawn circles is immediately comparable to manuscript art, on which a great deal of work has been done showing the technical virtuosity of the Anglo-Saxon draughtsman-painters.[29] In the Lindisfarne Gospels the working lines for many of the designs can still be seen, and by a great piece of good luck one of the most famous examples of those surviving provides all the working lines necessary for the Cuthbert cross, including formulae for calculating the size and position of the central circle and square and the centres and diameters of the circles for the arms. This is the circular grid for the very different pattern from the centre of folio 94[v].[30] In fact the same lines are important in establishing the proportions in both designs (fig 22c and pl. 37). It is interesting that this central circle measures 4.8 cm, so that there is no incompatibility of scale between it and any of the metalwork examples. In the manuscript example all the measures are based on a grid of sixteen units square, thus giving a circle with a radius of eight units. The same grid applied to the cross giving a circle of the same radius shows that the central setting has a radius of two units fitting tightly into a surrounding frame, four units square. The circle forming the arms works out at six units (three-quarters of the radius of the main circle), with the compasses centred at

[28] Avent, *Anglo-Saxon Disc and Composite Brooches* I, pp. 3–4; II, pls. 79, 192.

[29] *Cod. Lind.* II, 226–30. For recent work in this field, see R. D. Stevick, 'The 4×3 Crosses in the Lindisfarne and Lichfield Gospels', *Gesta* 25 (1986), pp. 171–84.

[30] Illustrated in Wilson, *Anglo-Saxon Art*, pl. 29.

the point where the line marking off the fourth and the twelfth unit of each side of the square crosses the circumference. If the point of the compasses is then moved to the next grid inside the circle on the same line, the neatly parallel inner line of the *cloisonné* tray is achieved. (Of course the actual grid used for the cross may have been divided into a square of only eight units, which would achieve the same proportions.) The cross is not of course a neatly squared off piece of vellum, so that although the proportions are as I have described them, each individual measurement is probably not quite true, and it is slightly distorted both by wear and by its several breakages and repairs. Nevertheless, the design geometry is not merely close, or derivative, as we might say in comparing it to the earlier Wilton and Ixworth crosses: it is identical with that used in the manuscript. I am not saying that the artist of Lindisfarne and the designer of the cross were the same person, but it is possible to see a very direct transfer of design technique between goldsmith and illuminator.

Moreover the use of grids and circles as a basis for the elaborate patterns in the Lindisfarne Gospels produces some of that manuscript's most characteristic features, some of which are also reproduced in the cross. The form of the cross (of both the Wilton/Ixworth and Cuthbert types) is found again and again in Lindisfarne, sometimes appearing as the void between four circles or roundels placed symmetrically.[31] It thus appears as a result of the methods employed.[32] Allowing for the difference of the medium, the geometry I have described and the motifs to which it gives rise are expressed particularly clearly in the carpet-page, folio 94^v, for which the same circular grid was used. The centre has a stepped pattern but the underlying grid comes through in the central cross, which is also depicted as a medial line with a crosslet at each end. The lines four units from the centre are also featured in the design. The central circle is enclosed within a square relating to the larger grid of the whole page, and this is the centre of a cross which again has crosslets at the end of the arms.

When we turn to sculpture in more detail the impression of a regional metalwork style now almost lost to us, but which must have had many of the features of the Cuthbert cross, including its draughtsman-like design technique, is very much reinforced. A cross treated like a metalwork cross with its arms fixed to the background by ornamental studs is found at Jarrow, for example.[33] The relationship between name stones and carpet-pages has been pointed out before.[34] Sometimes this extends to details of construction lines extended into the design, as well as the more obvious one of the types of cross themselves. For example one from Lindisfarne incorporates a St Cuthbert's type cross at the centre, and the cross also has medial lines related to the

---

[31] *Cod. Lind.* II, fig. 57, shows how closely related is this form of the cross to the underlying geometry.
[32] See also Stevenson, art. cit. in n. 9, above.
[33] *Corpus* I, pl. 94, 505.
[34] E. Coatsworth, 'The Decoration of the Durham Gospels', in *The Durham Gospels*, ed. C. D. Verey, T. J. Brown, and E. Coatsworth (EEMF 20; Copenhagen, 1980), pp. 53–63, esp. p. 60.

original working grid.[35] On larger free-armed crosses there are also strong hints of an important connection with a metalwork style. For example the head on one of the earliest crosses from Hexham, often called Acca's Cross, is clearly set in a collar in which alternate pelleted and square-cut mouldings cover the join between shaft and head. On the one surviving face itself, enlarged pellets surround a cross with the same expanded terminal and narrow-waisted arm as on the jewelled cross.[36] Fragments from Jarrow imitate jewelled crosses surrounded by a dogtooth border, one of these pieces with baluster ornament punctuating an otherwise plain side.[37] A fragment from Northallerton seems to show a development of the jewelled cross with a more decoratively treated centre, and this too has sides featuring the upright balusters set amid horizontal strips.[38] The opposite face of the Northallerton head shows the same cross framed by pellets. The ornament on the sides is also found on architectural sculptures, from Hexham, for example,[39] and I am reminded that Bruce-Mitford saw the Cuthbert cross as architectural in its conception.[40] On larger metalwork crosses, such as we know existed, large functional rivets may have been needed as part of the construction, although there is no sign of this on a fifteenth-century painting of a now destroyed large garnet and gold cross from St Denis.[41] Even the heart-shaped motif from the filigree detail on the suspension loop appears as a terminal on a design from Hexham.[42] The closeness in conception between architectural fragments, sculpture, manuscript painting and metalwork seems indicative of the small, closely-knit monastic milieu which produced them all.

In the area of iconography there are other features of the St Cuthbert cross which ought to be discussed. I have already pointed out the play of crosses within the cross. As it is made of garnets it is perhaps inevitably red; but, as we know, one at least, and possibly one other of the stones, are not garnets but red glass.[43] The centre also features five stones, and each arm is carefully subdivided into twelve. It is hard to know what this means, but twelve stands for the twelve apostles and also for the twelve foundations of the heavenly Jerusalem, in the exegesis of which, redness was associated with martyrdom and particularly the Crucifixion. This association was commented on by Bede, who wrote at length on the meaning of the stones of the Holy City, and who was drawing on earlier sources although his emphasis seems to have been a

[35] *Corpus* I, pl. 200, no. 1122.

[36] Ibid., pl. 169, nos. 900 – 3.

[37] Ibid., pl. 93, nos. 497 – 500.

[38] *St Wilfrid at Hexham*, ed. Kirby, pl. XXII, c,d,e.

[39] *Corpus* I, pls. 182 – 3.

[40] Bruce-Mitford, 'The Pectoral Cross', p. 318.

[41] The cross attributed to St Eligius is illustrated in J. Hubert, J. Porcher and W. F. Volbach, *Europe in the Dark Ages* (London, 1969), pl. 267. The painting is in the National Gallery, London.

[42] *Corpus* I, pl. 176, nos. 929, 931.

[43] H. J. Plenderleith, 'Examination of the Gem Stones in the Cuthbert Cross', *Relics*, pp. 542 – 4.

new development at this period.[44] Blood, gold and jewels are also associated in the opening of *The Dream of the Rood*, although we only know this in the form in which it was set down in the tenth century.[45] Early in the poem, the cross is sometimes red with blood, sometimes adorned with treasure, changing even as the observer looks at it.[46] The cross of the Crucifixion in the Durham Gospels, a Lindisfarne manuscript (plate 10), is red painted over yellow, like garnets over gold,[47] and there is evidence of red paint on stone crosses.[48] In its treasure-laden aspect it is overlaid with gold and set with jewels, in particular five jewels on the *eaxlgespanne*, which has been translated both as cross beam and crossing.[49] The pervasive strength of this imagery can be seen as well on the Bischofshofen cross[50] or on the back of the Lindau Gospels.[51] The five-fold centre, which is repeated in the crosses at the ends of the arms, finds numerous echoes in sculptured crosses, and in other jewelled examples.[52] I find it difficult to believe that the St Cuthbert cross, which if anything is overdesigned, did not carry some, if not all, of these connotations for contemporaries.

II

The altar presents rather different problems since there is no date relevant to it except for 1104, which provides a *terminus* if we accept that the fragments now under consideration represent the silver altar mentioned in the twelfth-century accounts of the translation. A further problem, which I have already mentioned, is that the altar was made in three stages, and that it is possible that these represent three different dates. These are the wooden altar itself,

---

[44] For Bede's exegesis of the Book of Revelation 21:19 – 20, see PL 93, cols. 197 – 204. For a discussion of the background to Bede's interest, see P. Kitson, 'Lapidary Traditions in Anglo-Saxon England: part I, the background; the Old English Lapidary', *ASE* 7 (1978), pp. 9 – 60; and *idem*, 'Lapidary Traditions in Anglo-Saxon England: part II, Bede's *Explanatio Apocalypsis* and related works', *ASE* 12 (1983), pp. 73 – 123. See also P. Dronke, 'Tradition and Innovation in Medieval Western Colour Imagery', *Eranos Jahrbuch* 41 (1972), pp. 51 – 106, esp. pp. 77 – 9.

[45] *The Dream of the Rood*, ed. M. J. Swanton (Manchester, 1970), pp. 1 – 2.

[46] Ibid. lines 21 – 3, pp. 89 – 90.

[47] Coatsworth, 'The Decoration of the Durham Gospels', in *The Durham Gospels*, p. 59.

[48] See Bailey, *Viking Age Sculpture*, pp. 25 – 7. But much of the red paint which survives may have represented a 'primer' or base for other colours.

[49] Cf. the glossary of B. Dickins and A. S. C. Ross's edition, *The Dream of the Rood* (London, 1934), with that in Swanton, *The Dream of the Rood*.

[50] Campbell, *The Anglo-Saxons*, pl. 101.

[51] Illustrated in D. Matthew, *Atlas of Medieval Europe* (London, 1983), p. 57.

[52] See the Northallerton cross-head, cited above, p. 295. Other appropriate crosses are mentioned below, in connection with the altar. B. Raw, '*The Dream of the Rood* and its Connection with early Christian Art', *Medium Aevum* 39 (1970), pp. 239 – 56, esp. pp. 240 – 1, sees the literature and the iconography as connected in only the most general way, however. For other literary and documentary references, see R. Woolf, 'Doctrinal Influences on the *Dream of the Rood*', *Medium Aevum* 27 (1958), pp. 137 – 53. See also R. L. S. Bruce-Mitford, 'The Gold Cross from Thurnham, Kent', *Antiquaries Journal* 47 (1967), pp. 290 – 1.

completely plain except for five crosses, one at the centre and one at each corner, and on the same side, an inscription. That inscription runs along one long side of the board and translates as 'In honour of St Peter'.[53] There seems to be agreement that the inscription could have been made in the seventh century.[54] At a second stage, the altar was turned around so that the short sides became the top and bottom; the back was covered by a silver plate incorporating a figure, possibly of St Peter, and the reverse by a plate including corner-ornaments of conventional foliage around an inscription set in a circle round the centre. This centre was either left open or covered by a roundel, but not necessarily the same one which now occupies that position, which is clearly separate and represents the third stage in the decoration of this piece.

The front has been discussed in greatest detail by Radford, who reconstructed it as showing a seated figure of St Peter;[55] but the fragmentary remains make it impossible to feel confidence in this ascription, and the evidence of Raine who saw it in 1827 and described it as having a standing figure cannot be lightly dismissed.[56] The only feature which clearly survives is the nimbus with its marked pattern of radiating lines, and that can be compared to eighth-ninth century Carolingian works such as the fragment of a silver altar frontal from Conques, or the gold altar of Volvinio in Sant' Ambrogio, Milan,[57] more easily than to the plain halo of the only piece of seventh-eighth century Northumbrian silver, the plaque from Hexham. The remains seem to me to be too few for much confidence, however, and it is to the reverse we must turn for any real meat for discussion (plate 38).

This was again discussed by Radford, who dated the second stage by comparing the corner ornaments of conventional foliage with an openwork mount from Whitby, said by Haseloff to be eighth century; and who thought it might have been early enough to have been done for the reburial of St Cuthbert in 698.[58] Unfortunately the openwork mount has since been shown to be a work of the thirteenth century.[59] More recently, David Hinton has suggested that the altar is related to ninth-century Winchester art in a

---

[53] E. Okasha, *Hand-List of Anglo-Saxon Non-Runic Inscriptions* (Cambridge, 1971), pp. 69–70.

[54] Ibid.; and C. A. R. Radford, 'The Portable Altar of St Cuthbert', *Relics*, pp. 326–35, esp. p. 327.

[55] Radford, 'The Portable Altar of St Cuthbert', pp. 330–2.

[56] *St. Cuthbert*, pp. 200–1.

[57] D. Bullough, *The Age of Charlemagne* (London, 1965), pls. 47–9.

[58] G. Haseloff, 'An Anglo-Saxon Openwork Mount from Whitby Abbey', *Antiquaries Journal* 30 (1950), pp. 170–4; Radford, 'Portable Altar', pp. 333–4.

[59] G. Zarnecki, *English Romanesque Lead Sculpture* (London, 1957), pp. 3–4, 42–3. G. B. Brown, *The Arts in Early England* (6 vols.; London, 1903–37), vol. VI, *Completion of the Study of the Monuments of the Great Period in the Art of Anglo-Saxon Northumbria*, pp. 16–17, describes the ornament as unparalleled in Anglo-Saxon art, but related to motifs in Merovingian manuscripts of *c.*700.

comparison with a reliquary discovered in Winchester in 1976.[60] The parallel is based on a comparison with the plant scroll, which on the Winchester reliquary is formed from a tree or bush motif originally forming a continuous strip, which has been cut up and applied more or less haphazardly to the back of the reliquary.[61] The long and short leaves on the Durham altar plant and the flat triangular bindings might also be compared to this and other southern works of the ninth century, such as the sculptures in the church tower at Barnack, Northamptonshire, and the back of the Alfred Jewel.[62] But the Durham plant looks much simpler than any of these, both in its leaf forms, in the simplicity of its arrangement, and in the treatment of the binding. The central leaf looks almost like one of the earliest appearances of plant decoration in Northumbrian art, that in the Leningrad Bede, while plants springing from trumpet bindings are, after all, also a feature of the Northumbrian vine scroll.[63] Certainly these motifs would not have looked particularly exotic to people who knew the plant ornaments of eighth-century manuscripts such as the Maeseyck Gospels,[64] or southern manuscripts like the Vespasian Psalter.[65] While it appears that this theme did not emerge in Lindisfarne sculpture before that site was abandoned in 875, it certainly appears in one other work associated with Lindisfarne, and that is the cover of the Stonyhurst Gospel, where it is handled confidently though rather differently.[66]

A second possible point of comparison with the Winchester reliquary is the format, with a figure on one face balanced by plant motifs on the other.[67] But at Durham the back has four motifs placed symmetrically round the centre. This symmetrical layout has a close parallel in the centre of the Bischofshofen Cross which is thought to be Northumbrian work of the eighth century.[68] The cross is 1.58m high, which makes its rectangular centre rather larger than the altar. The plant forms have a similarly fleshy spear-shaped leaf springing up in the centre, though without any kind of binding, but some of the leaves curl round to form birds' heads. The plants on the crossing are arranged symmetrically around a circular void which in this case would have held a setting. On the other hand, a tenth-century book plate which has been linked to tenth-century southern English art preserves the same layout and similar motifs but in this case carried out in filigree.[69] There is still room for doubt,

---

[60] D. Hinton, S. Keene, and K. Qualman, 'The Winchester Reliquary', *Medieval Archaeology* 25 (1981), pp. 45–77.
[61] Ibid. pp. 54–7 and figs. 3 and 4.
[62] *Tenth Century Studies*, ed. D. Parsons (London and Chichester, 1975), figs. 19, 20.
[63] Leningrad, State Publ. Lib. MS. Q. v. 1.18, fol. 3ᵛ. See Alexander, pl. 83.
[64] Maeseyck, Church of St Catherine, Trésor, *s.n.*, ff. 3ʳ, 3ᵛ, 5ʳ, 5ᵛ; Alexander, pls. 88–91.
[65] London, BL, Cotton Vespasian A.1, fol. 30ᵛ; ibid. pl. 146.
[66] *Relics*, pl. XXIII.
[67] Hinton, Keene, and Qualman, 'The Winchester Reliquary', pp. 70–1.
[68] Wilson, *Anglo-Saxon Art*, p. 134.
[69] D. M. Wilson, 'Tenth Century Metalwork', in *Tenth Century Studies*, ed. Parsons, pp. 200–7 and pl. XXIV.

but technique and layout and the details of the plant motif argue at least as strongly for an eighth-century as for a later date.

It is not unlikely that originally the centre was left open, as was common in other altar reliquaries, and perhaps also in rich altars intended for use.[70] If it were, this suggests that the altar was an object of veneration, and perhaps the centre was added, as Charles Thomas suggested, to deter relic hunters.[71] The decoration of the completing roundel is very worn, and very difficult to read. There are many roundels with which it could be compared in Northumbrian art, both in sculpture and on metalwork. The centre of the Northallerton head, for example, which was mentioned in connection with the cross;[72] or the two roundels inside and outside the Ormside bowl.[73] There are undoubtedly also connections with the name stones and the cross-carpet pages already mentioned, since the central motif is clearly a cross with thin arms and an expanded centre and expanded terminals. A series of detached metal roundels of Anglo-Saxon workmanship, perhaps book plates or elements from similar shrines or altars, which have been found, for example in Scandinavia,[74] and Whitby,[75] show how close this is to the complex cross designs of the seventh to eighth centuries.

There is a difference, however, in that many of these early Northumbrian examples exhibit a cross of interlace spaced by bosses in a cross pattern, whereas on the altar the interlace is in the spandrels of the cross. The design at Durham is more like a pin-head from Kegworth in Leicestershire, which does have this feature, or the pins from the river Witham, in which the animal interlace is also in the spandrels, not the cross itself.[76] The inturned, clubbed terminals of the cross on the Durham roundel are at least comparable to the scrolled terminals of the interlace on the Witham pins and its parallels, which include cross designs combining interlace and plant motifs.[77] These correspondences might suggest that the completing roundel was made in the late eighth/early ninth century, at a time when Mercian influence was strong.

The plant motifs on the Durham roundel are, however, difficult to read (Radford described them as 'delicate scrolled patterns'), but appear to me to

---

[70] Examples illustrated in Braun, *Der christliche Altar*, I. For Anglo-Saxon examples, see Wilson, *Anglo-Saxon Art*, pls. 156, 239.

[71] Thomas, *The Early Christian Archaeology of North Britain*, pp. 193–4.

[72] See above, p. 295.

[73] G. Baldwin Brown, *The Arts in Early England*, V, *The Ruthwell and Bewcastle Crosses, The Gospels of Lindisfarne, and other Christian Monuments of Northumbria*, pl. XXX.

[74] D. M. Wilson, *Anglo-Saxon Ornamental Metalwork 700–1100 in the British Museum* (London, 1964), pl. Ic, and see below, n. 77.

[75] Ibid., pls. XXXVIII, 105–6; XXIX, 107.

[76] Ibid., pl. IIc.

[77] The Witham pins: ibid., pl. XVIII. For an important parallel combining an elaborate cross, interlace with clubbed terminals, animal and plant ornament, see the metal plaque from Bjorke, ibid., pl. Ic. The Northumbrian vine scroll includes some large flower and leaf compositions, but always with a rather tight outer line to the cupping leaves: for example, the north face, Bewcastle cross: Baldwin Brown, *The Ruthwell and Bewcastle Crosses*, pl. XXVIII.

be ragged, hollow leaves in profile with curling tips, from which strands or some other element emerge to trail across between the paired leaves: quite like the development of acanthus leaves of early tenth-century southern English art, in fact, especially in the early phase where this was still sometimes combined with motifs such as interlace drawn from the Northumbrian and Mercian past. The type is strikingly represented in the embroideries presented to the shrine of St Cuthbert *c.*934 by King Athelstan, perhaps the girdle (maniple II) even more than with the stole and maniple I, if this is accepted as part of the same gift. Related motifs appear quite clearly in manuscripts associated with the king such as the Chester-le-Street Gospels (where they are combined with interlace), and also in the Corpus Cambridge manuscript of the *Lives* of St Cuthbert, both of which the king also presented to the shrine.[78]

The roundel, therefore, because it is a detachable piece, possibly out of context and because its detail is blurred by damage and wear, seems to me to be a somewhat enigmatic piece. The only certain thing is that it is an addition to the silver casing. There is evidence for a considerable artistic revival in the Durham community of St Cuthbert in the late tenth and eleventh centuries, based partly on earlier Northumbrian/Mercian traditions, and partly on newer ideas closer to those of the contemporary south of England.[79] This revival is particularly manifest in the sculpture of the community. For example, there are some affinities in style, and in interlace pattern, between the roundel and a cross from St Oswald's Durham, now in the Cathedral collection (plate 40). The Chapter House heads in the same collection are in a harder, more controlled, style but still have some features in common.[80] The way the interlace patterns are shaped into the spandrels on the roundel, and their general treatment, is not unlike the head and shaft of the Woodhorn Cross, Northumberland, which is thought to be another expression of this late revival of Northumbrian art.[81]

The altar is undoubtedly a more puzzling piece than the cross, but it seems clear that this was a hallowed piece refurbished on at least two occasions. The original seventh-century altar, which may possibly have been associated with St Cuthbert, is the plain wooden one, decorated only with incised crosses and an inscription. This was later covered in silver, probably in the mid eighth century, since this is where its strongest parallels in technique, layout, and plant ornament, lie. Unfortunately, the figure scene is too fragmentary to support this dating, but the little there is does not contradict it. It may have been intended to leave an area of the original wooden altar open to view, as in

---

[78] BL, Cotton MS Otho B.IX; Cambridge, Corpus Christi College, MS 183. *The Golden Age of Anglo-Saxon Art 966 – 1066*, ed. J. Backhouse, D. H. Turner and L. Webster (London, 1984), nos. 5 and 6, pp. 24 – 7.

[79] E. Coatsworth, 'The Four Cross-Heads from the Chapter House Durham', in *Anglo-Saxon and Viking Age Sculpture*, ed. J. T. Lang (British Archaeological Reports, Brit. ser. 49; Oxford, 1978), pp. 85 – 96.

[80] *Corpus* I, pls. 37 – 8, 43 – 7.

[81] Ibid., pls. 230 – 2.

surviving altars, but at some stage it was decided to close this off. The design of the closing roundel relates it to Anglian/Mercian work of the eighth to ninth centuries, but another possibility is the revival of late Northumbrian art partly under the influence of southern English art of the Reform period. In spite of this somewhat inconclusive ending, the two objects, the cross and the altar, rather interestingly tell us much between them of the development of metalwork design over a long period of the community's history.

The Weft-patterned Silks and their Braid:
The Remains of an Anglo-Saxon Dalmatic of c. 800?

HERO GRANGER-TAYLOR

Among the textiles recovered from the tomb of St Cuthbert are some fragments from a piece of clothing.[1] They are at present mostly mounted within one frame (*Relics*, pl. LI, A.);[2] slightly rearranged they are shown here in fig. 23. Four different types of textile are represented:

(a) two weft-patterned tabby silks, from which the garment was principally made

(b) two plain tabby silks

(c) two weft-faced compound twill silks used as binding strips for seams and facings on the inside edges

(d) and (e) two braids, the Soumak braid decorating the edges of the garment, and the Unique braid, probably used in the same way.

These will be examined in turn before the form of the complete garment from which they came is considered.

(a) THE WEFT-PATTERNED TABBY SILKS (formerly termed Tissued-Taffetas)

(i) *Technique*

The two silks in question are identical in weave but they have different designs (A and B) and must therefore have been cut from two different lengths of cloth

[1] This paper differs from J. F. Flanagan and Grace Crowfoot's work in the 1956 *Relics* volume really only in the dating and provenance given for some of the textiles, and in the understanding of their relationship to each other. For guiding me through northern territory previously unknown to me, I would like to thank especially Frances Pritchard and Elisabeth Crowfoot, Michelle Brown, Katherine East, Lise Bender Jørgensen, Inger Raknes Pedersen and Leslie Webster, as well as others too many to name. I owe a special debt to Anna Muthesius for permission to use her unpublished thesis (cited below, n. 30), and to the Pasold Research Fund, for their generous grant towards the cost of Susan Bird's drawing, figure 23.

[2] I have only examined them through the glass of the frame; the frame itself is at present in the Monk's Dormitory at Durham Cathedral while the box in the Library has the loose fragments from the coffin. My thanks to Roger Norris and Jill Ivy for arranging access and photographs.

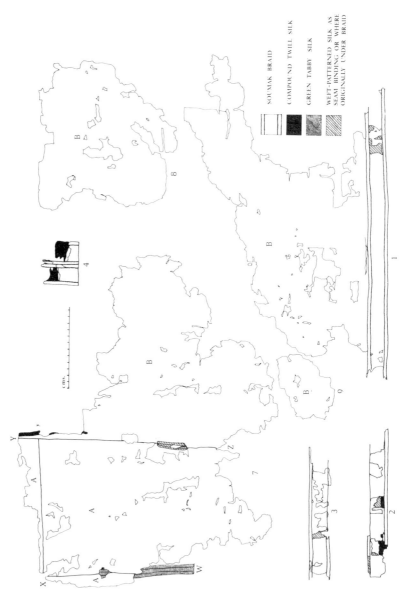

SOUMAK BRAID

COMPOUND TWILL SILK

GREEN TABBY SILK

WEFT-PATTERNED SILK AS
SEAM BINDING, OR WHERE
ORIGINALLY UNDER BRAID

23. The Weft-patterned silks and Soumak braid; the fragments at present in the frame, slightly rearranged (the numbering of the fragments follows on from the numbers given by Grace Crowfoot to the braid fragments).

(pl. 54 and *Relics*, pl.LI).[3] In colour, they are not 'amber' as Raine thought; darker areas are the result of discolouration only. Originally they were white or, strictly speaking, the natural light cream of undyed silk. The effect of the weft-patterned weave in monochrome is quite subtle, requiring an oblique light to show up the design. Given that this is so, the use of the two different designs in one garment may simply reflect what was to hand.

The weave, shown correctly in Flanagan's fig. 4,[4] consists of a tabby or 1-over-1 ground, with additional pattern weft threads, in alternate sheds, floating to form the design; where floating, the pattern threads are bound by every sixth warp thread, where not required they are bound together with the main weft threads. The best English term, and the one adopted here, is 'weft-patterned tabby'; as so often with pattern weaves, the French term, *taffetas lancé*, is rather more precise.[5]

This weave is superficially similar to a class of weave called 'lampas'. J. F. Flanagan, in naming these two textiles 'Tissued-Taffeta', erroneously places them within the lampas class ('tissue' is the old term for 'proto-' or 'pseudo-lampas'; see his fig. 2). The lampases are better understood as growing out of weft-faced compound twill (the weave of the Nature Goddess and Peacock silks) and they did not appear until the late tenth century. The fact that they are products of much more sophisticated looms is revealed by comparing Flanagan's fig. 4 with his figs. 2 and 3.[6] In the weft-patterned tabby the pattern weft always completes its float; on the lampases, the floats are often curtailed to suit the design, a detail which shows the design to have been controlled by a mechanism separated from the shafts responsible for the two bindings.

In an article of 1978,[7] Daniel De Jonghe and Marcel Tavernier group the variant of weft-patterned tabby seen at Durham, called by them Structure 4, with three other early medieval weaves: Structure 3 has the same repeating binding points as Structure 4 but is a 'brocaded tabby', that is to say, the pattern weft turns back on itself at the edges of the motifs instead of travelling the full width of the textile; Structure 2 is once more a weft-patterned tabby but with a bricked pattern effect due to staggered binding points; Structure 1 is a 'self-patterned tabby' without a supplementary weft and so is the least like Structure 4 in appearance. The authors conclude that all four weaves were

---

[3] Both have Z-twisted warp threads, and weft threads without twist but A is generally finer, with 35 – 38 threads per cm in the warp and 25 – 38 threads per cm in the weft, while B has *c*.28 threads per cm in both warp and weft (Flanagan's figure for the warp of B seems to be a mistake, *Relics*, p. 500).
[4] *Relics*, p. 499.
[5] For terminology throughout see the *Vocabulary of Technical Terms* (Centre International d'Étude des Textiles Anciens, Lyon (hereafter CIETA); Lyon, 1964); also Dorothy K. Burnham, *A Textile Terminology: Warp and Weft* (London, 1981).
[6] *Relics*, p. 498.
[7] 'Met selectieroeden geweven koptische Weefsels', *Bulletin van de Koninklijke Musea voor Kunst en Geschiedenis* 50 (1978), pp. 75 – 105.

woven on related, comparatively simple looms. They reconstruct the loom used for the Structure 4 silks by means of an analysis of a fragment at Utrecht, a *pars de vestimenta dni. nri.*[8] They point out in particular that some of the details of the design do not exactly repeat and conclude that the design was not selected in advance as it would have been on a draw-loom, but instead was 'picked up', with the aid of pattern rods, as weaving progressed. Although they did not come to Durham, the authors refer to the faults in the repeats that Flanagan found on Textile A, particularly in the little crosses, and conclude that the Durham silks were made in exactly the same way.

The earliest dated example of Structure 4, a simple cross and stripe design in wool on a linen loin-cloth found at Halabiyeh in Syria, was in use at the time of the destruction of the town in AD 610.[9] Thus although the weave is relatively simple, it is not particularly old. The silk examples, indeed, could be considered as belonging to a sort of second rank of silk textiles. None of the surviving examples are especially fine, and with their long weft floats, they would have been particularly vulnerable to damage (and there are places on the Durham fragments where the pattern has worn away but where the ground weave is still solid). In a way, the weft-patterned and brocaded tabby silks fill the gap between twill damask, an earlier but more sophisticated weave which had mostly also been used in white silk, and the two lampases already mentioned, many early examples of which are again in white on white.

(ii) *Provenance*

Because large numbers of wool and linen weft-patterned tabbies have been found in Egypt, people have often assigned to Egypt the silk examples preserved in European churches.[10] However, the climate in Egypt has allowed the survival of large numbers of many different types of textile and quantities thus become meaningless. Some silk weft-patterned tabbies of De Jonghe and Tavernier's Structure 2 have been found in Egypt, but the present author knows of no Egyptian example of Structure 4 in silk. Their comparative

---

[8] Cf. *Relics*, p. 505, 'Note'. The fragment is Rijksmuseum Het Catharijneconvent St.81. The other fragment of Structure 4 silk mentioned by Flanagan (*Relics*, p. 496) as being at Utrecht no longer appears to be there. A fragment of weft-faced compound twill weave, *de panno serico in quo corpus sancti Willibrordi in sepulchro involutum fuit* (St.85), has with it a fragment of cream silk, but this is plain, and there is no record of either ever having been part of a chasuble, as Flanagan claims. But Flanagan is right to call the compound twill textile 'early Byzantine' (*Relics*, p. 504). In dark red and greeny-gold, it has a trellis design with repeating cross-monograms in circles at the intersections; the monogram has not yet been read but in many ways the silk resembles the fragments with the monogram of Heraclius (610 – 41) at Liège (*Splendeur de Byzance*, exhib. cat. (Musées Royaux d'Art et d'Histoire; Brussels, 1982), p. 207). My thanks to Tuuk Stam and Sieske Binnendijk of Het Catharijneconvent for showing me these textiles.

[9] R. Pfister, *Textiles de Halabiyeh (Zenobia)* (Paris, 1951), no. 53.

[10] De Jonghe and Tavernier, art. cit., p. 101; Brigitta Schmedding assigns the three Chur fragments to Egypt but the Saint-Maurice fragment to the Near East (*Mittelalterliche Textilien in Kirchen und Klöstern der Schweiz* (Bern, 1978), nos. 62 – 4 and 135).

technical simplicity would tend to the conclusion that such textiles were being produced in a number of different places. One can say at least that most of these places were Christian, as a common feature of virtually all the designs of the Structure 4 textiles is a number of Greek crosses.[11] The Durham weft-patterned tabbies illustrate this well, as both have as their main motif an adaptation of the Byzantine cross monogram enclosing at its centre a small barred cross.[12] Several of the small group of Structure 4 silks preserved in western European churches are likely to be Byzantine, but we do not know this definitely. One of the group of six Structure 2 *mappae* from the Sancta Sanctorum in Rome has a woven Greek inscription but another very similar cloth has an inscription in Latin and W. F. Volbach plausibly assigns the whole group to Rome.[13]

In one case there is more definite evidence of an Italian origin. This is a *mappa* from the sarcophagus of an archbishop of Ravenna in the church of Sant'Apollinare in Classe, Ravenna. With a field in Structure 4 and some Structure 3 brocading, this also has six contrasting bands in tapestry weave.[14] Four of these tapestry bands have woven inscriptions; two are verses from Psalms, but the other two are a dedication:

+ *SUSCIPE DME HANC OBLATIONEM QUE TIBI OFFERT JOHAN*
+ *NES ET MARIA PER MAN[um s]ACERDOTIS UT INPINGUATA*

Mappae, the forerunners of ecclesiastical maniples, were little cloths carried by the owner to wipe his or her hands on.[15] The donors referred to, John and Mary, who must have been members of the archbishop's congregation,

---

[11] For an Islamic example see *Early Islamic Textiles*, ed. Clive Rogers (Brighton, 1983), p. 19, but in writing the captions for this work I had not noticed the extent to which the designs of two others depended on crosses, op. cit., pp. 13 and 15 (I would not now date either of these as late as 11th-century).

[12] *Relics*, p. 502.

[13] W. F. Volbach, 'I Tessuti', *Catalogo del Museo Sacro della Biblioteca Apostolica Vaticana*, III, i (Vatican City, 1941), nos. T.19 – T.23 and T.131. Note that the inscriptions on T.19 and T.21 (not 'embroidered') are weft-patterned and thus necessarily more rectilinear than the tapestry-weave inscriptions on the Ravenna *mappa*. The Structure 2 weave of these *mappae* is not the same as Flanagan's Fig. 5 (*Relics*, p. 501); Flanagan omitted the main weft threads which accompany the pattern weft in every other shed (though in some of the stripes of T.20, at least, the weave does change to Structure 1, self-patterned tabby).

[14] Museo Arcivescovile, Ravenna. Mario Mazzotti, 'Antiche Stoffe Liturgiche Ravennati', *Felix Ravenna* 53 (1950), pp. 40 – 6; for a clearer photo, see Idem, *La Basilica di Sant'Apollinare in Classe* (Vatican City, 1954), Fig. 76. The *mappa* measures 95 x *c*.50 cms, either end is in Structure 2 weft-patterned tabby. Note that the tapestry bands are woven integrally, not sewn on as stated by Schmedding (*Mittelalterliche Textilien*, p. 166).

[15] Joseph Braun S.J., *Die liturgische Gewandung* (Freiburg, 1907), p. 517. *Mappae* are of course the forerunners of *mappulae* or maniples (this one seems too wide to be a *mappula* yet). For an early version, see R. N. Soler Villabella, 'Una Stoffa Romana Bimillenario: La 'Mappa' dell'Antiquarium del Governatorato di Roma', *Bullettino della Commissione Archeologica Comunale di Roma* 65 (1937), pp. 73 – 82.

presumably themselves ordered and paid for the textile. The likelihood is that it was made locally in Ravenna or perhaps Bologna. That it was made somewhere in Italy is confirmed by the Italian character of the letter forms.[16] It has not previously been recognized that Italy had a silk-weaving industry at this period.[17] The Ravenna *mappa* establishes this and makes Italy a possible source for some of the other Structure 4 weft-patterned tabbies. In the author's opinion, the Durham textiles are much more likely to be Italian than Egyptian, but their origin cannot be established with certainty.

(iii) *Date*

The only weft-patterned tabby silks from Europe from an approximately datable context (that is, examples not preserved with relics or reliquaries) are the *mappa* just mentioned and two other Structure 4 silks at Ravenna.[18] The Ravenna *mappa* is not very similar to either of the Durham silks in design, though the hook forms of the wave borders do recall the hooks on Durham design B and the scale of the trellis design, with a repeat of *c.* 11 cms, is almost the same as design B. But it is a good parallel with the Durham textiles for two other reasons. The first is that the two tapestry bands without inscriptions have a repeating stylized vegetable design which derives ultimately from the same group of Central Asian silks as the design of the Durham Soumak braid (compare fig. 24, A with fig. 24, F). The second is that another braid with soumak brocading was found in the same tomb (see below, (d), (ii)).

The sarcophagus from which the braid and *mappa* come is the second on the left in the north aisle of Sant'Apollinare in Classe. Unfortunately, it does not record the name of the archbishop buried in it and it may be an older sarcophagus re-used (the carving on the front, of lambs flanking a cross and wreath is sixth-century in composition if not necessarily in style). Experts agree, however, that the carving on the two ends must be contemporary with the ultimate burial.[19] These have double horse-shoe arched niches, decorated with pearls, each enclosing two circular helix motifs of rotating leaves. A cross

---

[16] Working only from sketches of the inscription, this is the opinion of Michelle Brown; she points out in particular the downwards curve of the cross-stroke of F: see A. Petrucci, 'L'onciale romana', *Studi Medievali*, 3rd ser. 12 (1971), pp. 75 – 80.

[17] But this fact is not surprising considering the extent of the earlier, Roman silk-weaving industry, based on imported Far Eastern fibre (H. Granger-Taylor, 'Two Silk Textiles from Rome', *CIETA Bulletin de Liaison* 65 – 6 (1987), forthcoming 1988).

[18] Schmedding, op. cit., pp. 165 – 6 reviews the examples known to her, including all those mentioned by Flanagan. A piece was recently found at Augsburg cathedral, with a design very like that of the Ravenna *mappa*; see *Textile Grabfunde aus der Sepultur des Bamberger Domkapitels* (International Colloquium, Schloss Seehof, April 1985), *Bayerisches Landesamt für Denkmalpflege*, *Arbeitsheft* 33 (Munich, 1987), p. 69, Fig. 14.

[19] Mazotti, 'Antiche Stoffe', p. 40; G. Valenti Zucchini and M. Bucci, 'I sarcofagi a figure e a carattere simbolico', *'Corpus' della scultura paleocristiana bizantina ed altomedioevale di Ravenna*, ed. G. Bovini (Rome, 1968), II, no. 47; also illustrated in H. Peirce and R. Tyler, *L'Art Byzantin* II (Paris, 1934), Pl. 152.

from Budrio near Bologna with helix motifs very similar to those on the sarcophagus is dated 827.[20] Where it occurs in churches at Rome, the helix style has been considered to be characteristic of the period 795 – 867.[21]

The sarcophagus's horse-shoe niches are apparently unique in sculpture but C. Cechelli has pointed out their similarity to manuscript canon tables.[22] Such tables are of various dates but it is notable that the arches of fol. 13 in the Anglo-Saxon Leningrad Gospel book, of the late eighth century, like those of the sarcophagus, also finish in small volutes.[23] G. De Francovich observed in addition the influence of Oriental silks on the niches.[24] Horse-shoe forms are not found on textiles, but niches decorated with pearls are (see fig. 24, A, D and F). The fact that the octagonal forms in the tapestry bands of the *mappa* can be seen to have their origins in the same sort of pearled arch provides a link between the sarcophagus and the *mappa* found within it. Since the carving of the sarcophagus can be dated to the first half of the ninth century, the *mappa* would appear to be of the early ninth or possibly the late eighth century. Neither the *mappa* nor the associated braid show any real sign of wear.

The other two Ravenna Structure 4 weft-patterned tabbies are fragments from another archbishop's burial at Sant'Apollinare in Classe.[25] The sarcophagus here, 'with six niches', is definitely a sixth-century one re-used, without any further carving.[26] A guide to its date, however, is a list of the burials of archbishops in the church. According to Mazzotti, these occurred between 648 and 788, with an isolated later burial, that of Archbishop Petronax, in 834.[27] If the sarcophagus containing the *mappa* and the braid is that of Petronax, which it could be, then these other fragments are likely to come from the burial of either John VI (d.784) or Leo (d.777). Going further back, the next archbishop without an inscribed sarcophagus is Damian (d.705). 705 would seem to be too early when one considers that the design repeat on the thicker of the two textiles is 60 cms;[28] as a general rule repeat

---

[20] R. Kautzsch, 'Die langobardische Schmuckkunst in Oberitalien', *Römisches Jahrbuch für Kunstgeschichte* 5 (1951), p. 30, Fig. 29.

[21] Idem, 'Die römische Schmuckkunst in Stein vom 6. bis zum 10. Jahrhundert', *Röm. Jahrb. für Kunstgesch.* 3 (1939), p. 48, table.

[22] 'La decorazione paleocristiana e del alto medio evo nelle chiese d'Italia', *Atti de IV Congresso Internazionale di Archeologia Cristiana: Città del Vaticano, 1938*, II (Rome, 1948), pp. 173 – 6.

[23] Alexander, no. 39, Fig. 189.

[24] 'Studi sulla Scultura Ravennate: I Sarcofagi', *Felix Ravenna* (1959), pp. 119 – 25.

[25] These fragments are now in the Museo Nazionale, Ravenna. Mazzotti, 'Antiche Stoffe', p. 45.

[26] Valenti Zucchini and Bucci, op. cit., no. 28.

[27] *Sant'Apollinare in Classe*, pp. 189 – 90. But N.B., it has not been possible to check Mazzotti's manuscript sources. Mazzotti himself ('Antiche Stoffe', p. 44) identifies the sarcophagus with the *mappa* and braid as that of Damian (d.705), a date that does not fit in at all with the style of the carving.

[28] But please note that the figure given here is for the full lengthways pattern repeat; unlike the weft-faced compound twill silks, all these weft-patterned silks have reverse repeats lengthways as well as widthways, thus in weaving terms the repeat is really only 30 cms.

sizes were all relatively small in the seventh century and none reached this scale before the mid eighth century.[29]

These Ravenna fragments are also particularly relevant to Durham since they are white and are the remains of a vestment. The combination of two Structure 4 silks with different designs in one piece of clothing, again as at Durham, is explained at Ravenna by the fact that the thicker textile, which has a long weft pile on the reverse for warmth, could only be practically used in the more central areas of the garment. In her unpublished study of these textiles Anna Muthesius has pointed out some stylistic resemblances with the Structure 4 silks at Chur and Saint-Maurice d'Agaune.[30] The design of the thinner textile, although in negative on a patterned ground, is also similar in its details and general layout to Durham design A.

(b) TWO PLAIN TABBY SILKS

One of the strips from the seams in Durham Fragment 7 (fig. 23) is of pale green silk in simple tabby weave.[31] Flanagan doubted whether this was 'ancient, at least anything like so ancient as the material to which it is attached'.[32] All one can say in response is that it is impossible to be certain of the dates of completely plain textiles. The combination here of warp yarn with Z-twist and weft yarn without twist does seem to have been standard for early medieval European plain silks and is found, for instance, in the fragments of a blue tunic of the sixth to eighth century, still 'woven to shape' in the ancient Mediterranean manner, from Santa Cecilia in Rome.[33]

A similar plain silk, but brick red in colour, is not represented among the framed pieces.[34] This must, however, be associated with the garment since it survives sewn to the back of the separated length of the Soumak braid called Fragment 5 by Grace Crowfoot (*Relics*, pl.XLIV, fig. 3) and as a minute scrap still attached to the end of a loose strip of seam binding in the box of bits in the cathedral library. Three small pieces are among Dr Greenwell's collection in the British Museum.[35]

---

[29] The earliest of the large-scale silks, with a vertical repeat of *c*.80 cms., is the compound twill with paired huntsmen-emperors from Mozac, probably given to the shrine of St Austremoine by Pepin the Short in 761 (M. Martiniani-Reber, *Lyon, Musée Historique des Tissus: Soieries sassanides, coptes et byzantines Ve – XIe siècles* (Inventaire des collections publiques françaises 30; Paris, 1986), no. 96.

[30] 'Eastern Silks in Western Shrines and Treasuries before 1200' (unpublished Ph.D. thesis, University of London (Courtauld Institute), 1982), pp. 237 – 45; Schmedding, op. cit., nos. 62 – 64 and 135.

[31] The technical details are these: warp, Z-twisted, *c*.30 threads per cm; weft, without twist, *c*.45 threads per cm.

[32] *Relics*, p. 504.

[33] Volbach, op. cit., T.2 (it cannot be linen, as Volbach says, because the weft is without twist).

[34] Warp, Z-twisted tabby, *c*.45 threads per cm; weft, without twist, *c*.36 threads per cm (based on the fragments in the BM. Grace Crowfoot counted 32 and 34 threads per cm in the pieces attached to the back of braid Fragment 5, *Relics*, p. 454).

[35] BM M&LA 1896,5-1,96. One of these has part of a guilloche plait still attached by sewing.

(c) TWO WEFT-FACED COMPOUND TWILL SILKS

A two-coloured silk occurs both as binding strips for seams and as wider facings at the back of the Soumak braid (three little bits have been flattened out and are mounted separately in the frame). Now mostly brown and cream, the original weft colours are purple and what seems to have been yellow; the warp threads must have been yellow or undyed (the strip in the box in the library, just mentioned in relation to the red tabby silk, has the best preserved colour). The weave is 1:2 weft-faced compound twill, the main warp paired.[36] Both warp yarns are without twist, and the decoupure is four in both warp and weft (the decoupure, called by Flanagan 'scaling', is the unit of threads — here paired main warp threads and weft passes — in which the outline of the design progresses). The weave is thus basically the same as the Nature Goddess and Peacock silks, but with the important distinction that there are large decoupures and that the warp threads are *grège* (the correct term for silk warp yarn without twist).

Just visible through the decayed Soumak braid of Fragment 2 is a small area of another compound twill silk. This has the same general character as the last but clearly derives from a different length of cloth; the direction of the line of twill is Z instead of S and there are three weft colours including perhaps pink and pale blue: the warp yarn is apparently pink.[37]

The purple and yellow textile may have resembled a silk at Essen cathedral with the same technical characteristics, that is with *grège* warp yarn and large decoupures, also in mainly yellow and purple; this has a design of paired simplified horses in roundels of about 45 cms across.[38] The Essen silk is listed by Dorothy Shepherd under her 'Zandanıji II' heading, a category to which we can now add the two Durham examples.[39] 'Zandaniji', a term for a type of cloth made in the area of Bukhara, need not be taken too literally for this group. Although certainly Central Asian products, it seems likely that they were made somewhere further to the east; *grège* warp threads are also a characteristic of Chinese textiles. None of Zandaniji II silks from Europe are accurately dated but examples recently excavated in the northern Caucasus can be shown by context to belong to the eighth and ninth centuries.[40] The

---

[36] The direction of the line of twill S. There are *c*.20 pairs of thread and *c*.20 single threads of each warp respectively per cm. The weft yarns are also without twist and there are *c*.22 weft passes per cm.

[37] Though note that some of this pinkness may be due to the madder dye leeching out of the Soumak braid in damp conditions.

[38] J. Lessing, *Die Gewebe-Sammlung des königlichen Kunstgewerbe-Museums* (Berlin, 1900), I, Pl. 33.

[39] 'Zandaniji Revisited', *Documenta Textilia: Festschrift für Sigrid Müller-Christensen*, ed. M. Flury-Lemberg and K. Stolleis (Munich, 1981), p. 120, no. 55.

[40] Shepherd, op. cit., p. 118; A Jeroussamlimskaja, 'On the Formation of the Sogdian School of Artistic Weaving' [in Russian], *Sredniaia Azii i Iran* (Gosudarstvennogo Ermitazha, 1972), pp. 5–46.

grouping of the main warp threads, when found in Asiatic silks, does not seem to have the same significance for dating as in Byzantine compound twills.[41]

At this point a third Zandaniji silk also from St Cuthbert's coffin should be mentioned. Now very faded, it seems originally to have been dark blue, yellow and white and can probably be identified as Battiscombe's textile f), with 'a very large animal or monster as its design'.[42] The fragments add up to only about 200 square centimetres, but because there are no traces of sewing they cannot have been facings for the weft-patterned tabby garment. This textile may have been the main silk of a separate but probably contemporary garment, such as a chasuble.

(d) THE SOUMAK BRAID

(i) *Design and Date.*

The design down the centre of the Soumak braid (fig. 24, C here, and *Relics*, pl.XLIV) measures just over 2 cm across. Pinky-red and purple now predominate, but six different colours were actually used (*Relics*, fig. 16).[43] The closest parallels for the Durham braid's design are integrally-woven borders on two compound twill silks, one from relics of Saint Amon, Toul, now in the Musée Lorrain, Nancy, the other in the church at Faremoutiers, Seine-et-Marne (fig. 24, E and D).[44] A braid, from Salzburg, has a related but not quite so similar design (fig. 24, B and *Relics*, pl.XLIV, fig. 6). This braid is another example of soumak brocading and will be mainly discussed under the heading of technique. It should be pointed out now, however, that the Salzburg braid has its own parallel in a compound twill border design, on a silk from the shrine of St Lambert, Liège, now in the Musée Diocésain, Liège (fig. 24, F).[45]

The similarity between the palmettes of the Durham braid (fig. 24, C) and the Faremoutiers border (fig. 24, D) is clear. Also to be noted are the two dots on the Durham petals which recur on the petals of the Toul/Nancy silk (fig.

---

[41] See below, p. 336.

[42] *Relics*, p. 12. The 'monster' sounds like an informed guess; it is doubtful whether enough was ever recovered to show the whole design. The Greenwell fragments in the BM include some of this silk.

[43] P. 458. Note that the colours given are as they look now, for example, the 'brownish purple' would have been a good rich purple originally. R. Pfister found that the pinky-red was dyed with madder, the light brown possibly with walnut (*Relics*, p. 454).

[44] For the Nancy silk see K. Riboud and G. Vial, 'Quelques considérations techniques concernant quatre soieries connues', *Documenta Textilia*, pp. 129 – 55, Fig. 10. For the Faremoutiers silk, J-P. Laporte and N. Moore, 'Tissus médiévaux de Chelles et Faremoutiers', in *Tissu et vêtement: 5000 ans de savoir-faire* (Musée Archéologique Départmental du Val d'Oise; Guiry-en-Vexin, 1986).

[45] *Rhin-Meuse: Art et Civilisation 800 – 1400* (exhib. cat.) (Musée d'Art et d'Histoire; Brussels, 1972), p. 173, B.4.

24, E). The Durham braid in fact uses alternately as its main motifs a five-branched palmette and a rose petal.[46] The Toul/Nancy and Faremoutiers borders, as well as the Liège border and Salzburg braid design are all represented as if they were strips cut from a textile with an all-over repeating pattern — in each case, the motif at the side is half the central motif.[47] On the Durham braid, however, while one of the repeating side shapes could be an elongated bisected petal, the other, with purple at the top, is less clear. This uncertainty is important to bear in mind when considering the origin of the braid itself.

The Toul/Nancy and the Liège silks both belong to Dorothy Shepherd's Zandaniji I category.[48] Technically, they are weft-faced compound twill silks with twisted warp yarns, with the unusual feature that the threads of the main warp are grouped into threes or more (the Faremoutiers silk, only recently published, has the main warp threads in pairs, rather than threes, but on account of its style and colours can probably also be described as Zandaniji I). The textile around which the Zandaniji I category is based, a silk at Huy cathedral with an ink inscription in Sogdian actually using the term 'Zandaniji', also has a border of the same bisected repeat type.[49] In the case of Shepherd's Zandaniji I, as opposed to her Zandaniji II, it does seem reasonable to believe that the place of manufacture was the Bukhara region of Sogdia, modern Uzbekistan. The Toul/Nancy and Liège silks have often been attributed to Persia, but while Sogdian silks were obviously influenced by Persian art, Persian textiles, where one can identify them, have more pictorial, less purely decorative designs than these (they are closer to Byzantine textiles).[50] The Toul/Nancy silk has paired stylized lions within flower-like roundels. The main design of the Faremoutiers silk, only partially preserved, seems, like the Liège silk, to have consisted principally of large round flower forms.

The dating of the Zandaniji I silks is controversial. Shepherd herself puts them all before about 720, believing them to precede in time her second group, Zandaniji II. But the considerable technical as well as stylistic

---

[46] For the movement of palmettes from the Mediterranean eastwards see J. Rawson, *Chinese Ornament: The Lotus and the Dragon* (London, 1984), p. 222 and passim. Flanagan states that the flower petal or bud cannot be from a rose because, when seen from above it has four petals, not five (*Relics*, p. 464, n. 1). The Romans very often depict roses with only four petals (see W. Jashemski, *The Gardens of Pompeii* (New York, 1979), passim). But by this date such petals, often separated from their original garlands, had become confused with a Persian heart-shaped motif.

[47] They resemble earlier silks with smaller main designs, cf. Martiniani-Reber, *Soieries sassanides, coptes et byzantines*, nos. 44, 57, 69, 71. For the use in Sogdia of strips cut from silks with large repeating designs (often apparently Persian rather than locally woven) see the 8th-century wall paintings from Pendzhikent (A. M. Belenizki, *Mittelasien: Kunst der Sogden* (Leipzig, 1980)).

[48] Op. cit., p. 119, nos. 1 and 13.

[49] D. G. Shepherd and W. B. Henning, 'Zandaniji Identified?', in *Aus der Welt der islamischen Kunst: Festschrift für Ernst Kühnel* (Berlin, 1959), pp. 15–40.

[50] A silk of roughly this period which is probably Persian is that with paired mounted emperors from St Ursula, Cologne; see O. von Falke, *Kunstgeschichte der Seidenweberei* (Berlin, 1913), Abb. 73.

A   B   C

24. *Border and braid designs: A) the decorative tapestry bands on the Ravenna* mappa; *B) the Salzburg braid; C) the Durham Soumak braid, the colours in the blanket stitaching only partly reconstructed.*

D E F

D – F) borders on three weft-faced compound twill silks, D at Faremoutiers, E at Nancy, F at Liège. The decoupures are only indicated on the Faremoutiers silk (after Laporte and Moore). The Durham braid is 3.2 cm wide; the Salzburg braid is 5 cm wide in total and the other designs are shown on this scale.

differences between the two groups (Zandaniji I has neither the *grège* warp yarns nor the large decoupures of Zandaniji II) would tend to the conclusion that they are the products of two different areas. And if this is the case, Zandaniji I probably spread over a much longer period. The historical evidence for the Toul/Nancy silk points to it having been placed with the relics of St Amon in 820.[51] At this date it need not have been new but in the opinion of this author it probably was; the aspects that made Shepherd put it at the beginning of the group, 'its elegance and elaborateness of design', speak more strongly for its relatively late date.[52] In comparison with the Toul/Nancy silk, the Faremoutiers and Liège silks are simpler. They have fewer colours (four instead of five), and do not use double outlining. For these reasons they are likely to have been made before the Toul/Nancy silk, probably at some point in the second half of the eighth century.

The similarity of the Salzburg braid to the Liège silk (fig. 24, B and F) lies in the central flower form and in the columns. Stylistically, however, the Salzburg design is close to the Toul/Nancy border; both have double outlining as well as an additional flower form sitting above the main motif. One can deduce that the Salzburg braid's design must derive from a compound twill silk closer in date to that at Nancy than that at Liège. In a similar manner, but vice versa, the Durham braid (fig. 24, C) shares its rose petal with the Toul/Nancy silk, but is generally less detailed. The Durham braid is therefore likely to be copying a compound twill border of around the date of the Faremoutiers silk, perhaps one itself combining palmettes with petals. 'Copying' is the appropriate term here because, although the design of the Durham braid is of Asiatic origin, when technique is taken into account it becomes obvious that neither the Durham braid nor the Salzburg braid can have been made in Central Asia.

(ii) *Technique*

The constituent parts of the Soumak braid are well illustrated by Grace Crowfoot's figure 14.[53] The ground weave is a simple tabby. The central area is covered by supplementary weft threads, brocaded in a method known as soumak. At the borders, the ground is covered by decoration that is embroidered, rather than woven, closely-spaced blanket stitching.[54] At both

[51] D. King, 'Patterned Silks in the Carolingian Empire', *CIETA Bulletin de Liaison* 23a (1966), pp. 47–9.

[52] 'Zananiji Identified?', Fig. 18 and text; Riboud and Vial, op. cit., pp. 137, 143 and 153–4 (but note that the enormous figure of 12,000 lacs, or warp manipulations, per repeat seems to have been calculated omitting the weft decoupure of '2 passées?'; if this decoupure is right the figure should be *c.*6,000).

[53] *Relics*, p. 454.

[54] 'Blanket stitch' is used here in preference to 'buttonhole stitch' because the stitches here do not have the extra loop or knot peculiar to buttonholing.

outside edges there are sewn-on guilloche plaits. Some connection with tablet weaving is proved by the two double 'twists', each made with two four-hole tablets, running just inside the blanket stitching. The tabby ground weave itself may have been produced on a device such as a rigid heddle. But the evidence of the 'Unique' braid, where the centre is all certainly tablet-woven and tabby only occurs under the buttonholing in the borders, supports the view that the ground of the Soumak braid was made with two-hole tablets (54 tablets would have been needed).

Since Grace Crowfoot's exemplary work on the Durham braids, many more examples of tablet weaving have been published. A few early finds are from the Mediterranean region, but the majority are from northern and western Europe, where they go back to at least 500 BC.[55] According to Peter Collingwood, the braid from Fort Miran in Chinese Turkestan, dated AD 750 – 900, is the oldest example of tablet weaving found in the East. Recently-published examples of soumak brocading seem to suggest that it too was originally a European rather than an Oriental technique; soumak brocading appears not to occur before the fifth century AD.

Grace Crowfoot's figure 15 shows the exact form of the soumak brocading on the Durham braid. It is important to note that at Durham the short 'wraps' are on the face of the textile. In most other examples longer wraps are used on the front side; these longer wraps overlap creating reversing rows of little diagonals (pl. 56). The Durham braid is also exceptional in that the brocading weft completely covers the ground weave of the braid. But these are differences of appearance, not significant technical differences. On the reverse of the Durham braid, untidy threads stretching between areas of the same colour show that, from the beginning, the braid was intended to be sewn to another textile.

The most common early form of soumak is outline 'eccentric' brocading, on textiles of wool or wool and linen, mostly decorated in tapestry weave. Examples range from the tapestries of the Oseberg ship burial in Norway, of *c.*850,[56] to some of the later 'Coptic' tapestries from Egypt (in pl. 53, for example, all the outlining is in soumak). There are many fewer instances of soumak brocading on full-width textiles where the soumak is used in parallel rows, itself making solid blocks of colour. Three textiles, all fragments of wool on linen, are from England, two from Sutton Hoo and one from the barrow at

[55] See Peter Collingwood's list of early finds in his *The Techniques of Tablet-Weaving* (London, 1982), pp. 14 – 16 (it is not known for certain that simple starting borders based on one, two or three cords or 'twists', such as that found at the Kerameikos, were made with tablets).

[56] B. Hougen, 'Oserbergfunnets billedvev', *Viking* 4 (1940), pp. 87 – 91. Hougen's full-length work on the Oseberg material is not yet published; he apparently does not say that soumak was also used for solid areas of decoration (my thanks to Anne Kjellberg of the Norsk Folkemuseum for checking this point in the manuscript).

Taplow (both sites of early seventh-century date).[57] The Taplow textile, the finest of the three, is believed by Elisabeth Crowfoot to be the remains of a reversible couch cover. In a church context, solid soumak on full-width textiles occurs apparently only in the limited form of Greek crosses. The crosses are on: two otherwise plain-weave silk dalmatics at Ravenna, again from archbishops' sarcophagi;[58] a fragment at Sion which must be from something very similar to the Ravenna dalmatics;[59] on three of the Structure 2 silk *mappae* from the Sancta Sanctorum, Rome.[60]

Looking for soumak brocading actually on braids, one must first mention three examples where all that remains is the brocading thread, of gold. Listed by Elisabeth Crowfoot and Sonia Chadwick Hawkes, these have been found: on the brow of the body of a Frankish princess at Cologne cathedral buried in the second quarter of the sixth century; in a burial of *c.*600 at Kärlich, near Koblenz; in a burial of the first half of the seventh century at Saint-Denis.[61]

Besides Durham, only three instances are known of soumak brocading on intact braids. In each case, the braid is tablet woven. The earliest of these is a wool braid from a chieftain's burial, of the second half of the fifth century, at Evebø in Norway; here the soumak is restricted to bars at either end of panels otherwise in a sort of tapestry weave.[62] The second certain example is the silk braid mentioned earlier from the same sarcophagus at Ravenna as the weft-

---

[57] SH7 where the design is all soumak, with short and long wraps used on both sides, probably part of a reversible bed cover, and SH14 where the design is mainly tapestry outlined in soumak, but which has 'intersecting lattices' in solid soumak. E. Crowfoot, 'The Textiles', in *The Sutton Hoo Ship Burial*, ed. R. Bruce-Mitford, III, i (London, 1983), pp. 428–38 and 475–8. The Taplow fragments will be published more fully by E. Crowfoot in the forthcoming BM catalogue of the Taplow finds, ed. K. East. Fragments at Dover may have been decorated with soumak brocading (E. Crowfoot in V. I. Evison, ed., *Historical Buildings and Monuments Commission for England, Archaeological Report* 3 (1987), 194–5). The textile from Valsgärde 6 (*c.*750), also mentioned by Grace Crowfoot (*Relic*), p. 459, n. 6) appears never to have soumak more than a few rows deep.

[58] Mazzotti, 'Antiche Stoffe', p. 45. One of the dalmatics came from the sarcophagus 'with the six niches', and seems to have been on the body over the dalmatic of weft-patterned silk; the other comes from the sarcophagus 'of the twelve apostles', another re-used 6th-century one without a later inscription or carving (Valenti Zucchini and Bucci, op. cit., no. 16).

[59] Schmedding, *Mittelalterliche Textilien*, no. 223.

[60] Volbach, 'Tessuti', T.19, 21 and 131. An 11th-century Islamic wool textile from the caves of Murabba'at in Jordan is the earliest recorded non-European example of soumak brocading (G. and E. Crowfoot, 'The Textiles and Basketry', in P. Benoit et al., *Les Grottes de Murabba'at*, (Discoveries in the Judaean Desert, II; Oxford, 1961), Fig. 21, Pl. XVI.

[61] 'Early Anglo-Saxon Gold Braids', *Medieval Archaeology* 11 (1987), cat. nos. 34, 52 and 56. In these, the loops of the gold thread show that the technique was soumak, while the narrow extent of the thread shows that the textile was a braid.

[62] Collingwood, op. cit., p. 350; B. Magnus, 'Om folkedrakt og hovdingklede', *Jul I Nordfjord* (1982), pp. 22–5. Fragments of braid recently recovered from a similar burial at Veiem in Norway also appear from photos to have soumak brocading but this is not confirmed in any publication (L. Bender Jørgensen, *Forhistoriske textiler in Skandinavien* (Copenhagen, 1986), p. 66, lower photo, and p. 256, no. 91).

patterned *mappa*.[63] This (pl. 56) was woven on thirty-six four-hole tablets grouped in fours. The soumak brocading, mostly in pairs of rows, seems to pass over three warp 'twists' on the front of the braid, and over two twists on the back, creating overlapping wraps on both sides. By this means the design is made reversible and clearly the braid was never intended to be sewn down. Its narrow width (1.5 cms) fits with the identification by Mazzotti as an ecclesiastical girdle (Braid 1 at Durham, 2 cms wide, is also believed to be a girdle).[64] The seven surviving fragments add up with their fringes to a length of *c*.150 cms. The separated warp twists which Mazzotti believed to be the fringes proper to a girdle in fact result from the decay of the main weft, probably of linen.[65] Where held together by the silk brocading, however, the condition of the fragments is good. The colour of the warp, that is the ground, is now a yellowy brown but was probably once lighter and greener. Most of the decoration is in wine red, but some of the geometric motifs are violet or white.

The similarity of the Ravenna braid to the Durham Soumak braid lies in the principle of its technique. Its decoration nevertheless has its own relevance. It is based on verses from Psalm 127.[66] Michelle Brown remarks on the script that 'in many respects it resembles the display capitals favoured by Insular scribes'.[67] In support of this she points to the wedges on the letters, particularly heavy on the S, the double cross-stroke on the N, and the upwards cross-stroke of the U, as well as the 'points' in the interstices between letters. She adds that, 'A resemblance to pre-Carolingian Frankish manuscripts is suggested' by, for example, the 'cross'-shaped infill of the O and the division by horizontal bars of the I, but that 'these features may be found within an Insular milieu'. Michelle Browne concludes that the evidence of the script would 'tend to suggest an origin for the braid within Britain, or an Insular centre on the continent, in the late seventh or eighth centuries'.

Besides text, the braid is decorated with five different geometric motifs separated by blocks of little chequers. These motifs, all variations on crosses, also have parallels in Insular art. For instance, that on the left of pl. 56

---

[63] Museo Arcivescovile, Ravenna. Mazzotti, 'Antiche Stoffe', pp. 41 – 2 and Pl.; for a photograph of all the fragments see idem, *Sant' Apollinare in Classe*, Fig. 77 (the gold thread here must come from another textile, perhaps another braid, the square cross is one of the crosses in soumak from the plain dalmatics, see below (g)).

[64] *Relics*, pp. 435 – 8.

[65] The silk weft floats visible in the little chequer design are probably not the main weft, but another kind of brocading.

[66] Verses 5 and 6. Mazzotti ('Antiche Stoffe', p. 42) gives the fragments of text. They include at least one unusual variant, *ut* instead of *et* in Verse 5. The variants may be some guide to the braid's place of manufacture, but so far it has not been possible to follow them up. One of the two lines from psalms on the *mappa* is verse 1 of Psalm 127 (the other is 19, 2).

[67] It is much regretted that there is not space here to give Michelle Brown's analysis of the script in full. A separate publication on the Ravenna braid and *mappa* is planned where full references for the script's parallels will be given.

resembles the framing of the evangelist's eagle in Cambridge Corpus Christi College MS 197, and the outlined cross with wedge-shaped arms on the right of pl. 56 recalls the motif in the bottom-right corner of fol. 78 of the Leningrad Gospel book.[68] Given what we know of the history of decorated tablet weaving, that it is a development of Germanic rather than Celtic areas, the description 'Insular' here can probably be narrowed to 'Anglo-Saxon'. It is not surprising that such a braid should have reached Ravenna considering the high regard in which Anglo-Saxon products were held at the period; an Anglo-Saxon ring of the ninth century has been found not far away, in the river at Bologna.[69]

The third and last braid with soumak is the silk braid from Salzburg already mentioned for its design (fig. 24B, and *Relics*, pl.XLIV, fig. 6). This is wider than that at Ravenna (it used *c.*120 four-hole tablets), it has no patterning at all in the warp, and the majority of its brocading is in gold thread. But in other respects its technique is just the same as the Ravenna braid's. Its warp colour is also a greeny yellow (besides gold, the brocaded colours are dark pink, purple, light blue and white).

The Salzburg braid survives as *infulae* sewn to a mitre. Until the 1930s in the abbey of St Peter, Salzburg, the mitre now belongs to the Abegg Stiftung, near Bern, while a cut piece of the braid is in the Los Angeles County Museum.[70] The mitre itself is probably of the twelfth or early thirteenth century,[71] and Flanagan's conclusion that the braid was considerably older has been overlooked by more recent authors.[72] But when one takes into account both the similarity of the its design with the Zandaniji I silks and the similarity of its technique with the Ravenna braid, there can be no doubt of this (a date for it close to the Toul/Nancy silk, deposited probably in 820, was suggested above).

---

[68] Alexander, Figs. 58 and 193.

[69] R. Bruce-Mitford, *Aspects of Anglo-Saxon Archaeology* (London, 1974), p. 315, Pl. 101 b – d.

[70] M. Lemberg and B. Schmedding, *Abegg Stiftung in Riggisberg: Textilien* (Schweizer Heimatbücher 173/4; Bern, 1973), Pl. 15. The mitre was sold to Werner Abegg by the Los Angeles dealer, Adolph Loewi. According to Mrs Loewi Robertson, Mr Loewi's daughter, the piece given to Los Angeles County Museum by her had been cut off the *infulae* or fanons in order to make them both the same length. However in a photograph published in 1913, the *infulae* are longer but of an equal length (H. Tietze, *Die Denkmale des benedicktinerstiftes St Peter in Salzburg* (Österreichische Kunsttopographie 12; Vienna, 1913), Pls. XIII & XIV). There might, therefore, be a second separated length somewhere, perhaps still at St Peter's. I am very grateful to Mrs Robertson for informing me on the recent history of this object.

[71] L. von Wilckens, 'Überlegungen zu den fünf Salzburger Mitren des hohen Mittelalters', *Anzeiger der Germanischen Nationalmuseums* (1984), pp. 13 – 20. Mitres were not generally worn by bishops until the 11th century and not by abbots before 1200 (see also *Relics*, p. 42). The main silk, however, a white proto-lampas, could be as old as the 11th century (Muthesius, 'Eastern silks', p. 279).

[72] *Relics*, p. 468. This was also suggested by Tietze, op. cit., p. 83.

The gold threads from soumak brocading found elsewhere on the continent are a warning not to jump to the conclusion that the Salzburg braid is Anglo-Saxon. Yet two additional details seem to support this. The first is the plait sewn to its edges, of the same greeny colour as the warp. This looks like a sennit, similar in principle if not appearance to the tiny sennits sewn to the Durham Braids 1 and 4.[73] The second detail is the little hollow silver hemispheres sewn to the plait. The only parallel for these so far found are little gilded copper cones on the *velamen* of St Harlindis at Maeseyck; the *velamen*, part of a collection of relics which includes Anglo-Saxon embroideries, may itself be an Anglo-Saxon composite textile.[74] The excellent execution of the Salzburg braid also tells for, rather than against, an English origin; the Ravenna and Durham braids are equally beautifully made. An Anglo-Saxon connection with Salzburg is already known from the presence there in the late eighth century of the Northumbrian scribe Cutbercht.[75] The Rupertus Cross, of the same period, at Bishofshofen outside Salzburg, may have been imported from England.[76]

The re-use of the braid on the mitre can be explained partly by its condition, which, very good now, must have been even better in the twelfth century.[77] Its original purpose may have been as a maniple since, like Durham Maniple II, it is reversible and, like both Durham maniples, it is finished with tablet-woven fringes.[78]

Doubters may feel that the Asiatic design of the Salzburg braid has still not yet been accounted for. But there is no problem here. We know that the Central Asian silks were reaching western Europe, and this is where they mostly survive. The tapestry bands of the Ravenna *mappa* prove that the border designs of the Zandaniji I silks were being borrowed and adapted by weavers in Europe. Also relevant is one of the wool tapestries from the Oseberg ship burial, thought by Bjørn Hougen to be inspired by Mediterranean silks, but where the pronounced stepping of certain areas of the design (not a technical requirement in tapestry) recall more strongly the Zandaniji II silks with their large decoupures.[79]

---

[73] *Relics*, p. 447, Fig. 13.

[74] M. Budny and D. Tweddle, 'The Early Medieval Textiles at Maaseik, Belgium', *Antiquaries Journal* 65 (1985), pp. 373 – 4, Pls. LVII and LXVIIa. Bosses of this sort should be turning up in excavations.

[75] Alexander, no. 37.

[76] D. M. Wilson, *Anglo-Saxon Art from the 7th Century to the Norman Conquest* (London, 1984), pp. 133 – 5.

[77] Some little bosses also occur on the crown of the mitre, but these may just have been unpicked from the braid, perhaps from the back.

[78] Allowing for two bits cut off, its original length would have been *c.*110 cms; with the plaits the width is 5 cms. Thus it falls between the two Durham maniples (I is 82.5 × 6 cms, II is 126 × 2.5 cms).

[79] 'Oserbergfunnets billedvev', Fig. 8; *Relics*, p. 460.

(iii) *The Blanket Stitching and Guilloche Plaits.*

The blanket-stitched border of the Durham Soumak braid is in the same yarn and colours as the soumak brocading. Clearly it was envisaged at the time of weaving because the ground weave of the braid extends out under it. The changing of colours in the border, in bars, from red to yellow, purple or blue, is best preserved on the fragment at Ushaw College;[80] it may have been inspired by the *latté* effect of the Central Asian silks (fig. 24, C, D, and F).[81] The blanket stitching is mostly purely decorative. At one point it becomes functional, however, across the bottom of the fragment with paired lengths of braid (pl. 55); presumably the two bits of braid had been cut off and the blanket stitching here serves to secure their raw edges.

The only parallel for the purely decorative use of blanket stitching remains the finds from the Swedish site of Birka, in particular the front of a man's garment from a tenth-century grave, where alternate parallel braids are edged with blanket stitching in a thick silk thread.[82] But there are at least two examples of braids where blanket stitching has been used to finish the cut ends: one is a sixth-century woman's cuff found at Mitchell's Hill and now in Oxford;[83] the other, at Utrecht, is a little *bursa* made of braid, from the relics of St Willibrord (*Relics*, pl. XLIII, e). On the Mitchell's Hill cuff, the sewing would have been covered by a metal wrist clasp; on the *bursa*, however, the stitching is in contrasting colour and is obviously partly decorative.[84]

Widely spaced blanket stitching occurs on three well known compound twill silks of about the eighth century[85] and seems for a time to have been a standard method in Europe of securing raw edges of precious textiles. Significantly it is not however found among textiles from Egypt. From an earlier period, the Evebø fragments, mentioned above for their braid with soumak brocading, are again an interesting precedent. Here double rows of blanket stitching finish cut edges, while a running thread forms seams by picking up the outer

---

[80] See above, p. 246.

[81] A *latté* effect is where one or more of the weft lats changes colour without reference to the design.

[82] A. Geijer, 'Die Textilfunde', *Birka* III (Uppsala, 1938), B 12, grave 735, p. 144, Pls. 14, 15, and 18, Abb. 48.

[83] G. Crowfoot, 'Anglo-Saxon Tablet-Woven Braids', *Antiquaries Journal* 32 (1932), pp. 189 – 91.

[84] I have not seen the *bursa*. These comments are based only on the photographs in *Relics*, Pl.XLIII.

[85] The three are: the Mozac silk, probably a gift of Pepin the Short in 761, Martiniani-Reber, *Soieries sassanides, coptes et byzantines*, no. 96 (the blanket stitching is just visible on the bottom right of the front cover); the Chur Lion-Strangler silk, Schmedding, *Mittelalterliche Textilien*, no. 89 (for some reason known only to themselves the V&A have unpicked the sewing from their fragment of this silk, cf. A. F. Kendrick, *Victoria and Albert Museum: Catalogue of Early Medieval Woven Fabrics* (London, 1925), no. 1001, Pl.II); the Sancta Sanctorum Lion silk, Volbach, 'Tessuti', T.114 (the blanket stitching is on the cut edges covered by the excellently-preserved tablet-woven braids, the five different braids are mainly in wool and gold thread but have some silk).

loops of the blanket stitching; the sewing is functional, but it is also very neat.[86]

The red 'guilloche plaits' attached to the edges of the Durham braid appear to be of the same thick yarn with a slight S-twist as the soumak brocading and blanket stitching. The role of the plaits is to disguise the join with the other textiles; they were first sewn to the braid, and then to the weft-patterned silks and their facings beneath. Grace Crowfoot emphasizes that the plaits are unlikely to have a different origin from the braid itself.[87] Nevertheless, an indication that they were only added at the point that the braid was sewn to the other textiles is the presence of only one plait down the middle of the two joined lengths of braid (pl. 55). Guilloche plaits also occur at Durham on the 'Unique' braid (see below) and on the outer edge of braids sewn to the tenth-century embroideries. Apparently, they are also found on some of the Birka braids.[88]

The same arguments that supported an Anglo-Saxon provenance for the Salzburg braid also apply to the Durham braid, where the context within England substantially strengthens the case. Two details, the blanket stitching across the cut ends of Fragment 4 (pl. 55) and the sewn-on guilloche plaits, in the same materials as the rest but apparently contemporary with the construction of the garment, tend to the conclusion that the braid was woven in the place where the garment itself was put together.[89]

(e) THE UNIQUE OR WARP-WEAVE BRAID

The last individual textile is a fragment of another silk braid, measuring 2.5 x 2 cms (*Relics*, pl. XLIV fig. 4). This is in the library, in a small glass frame labelled 'found sewn to the amber silk with the Soumak braid (note by Mrs Plenderleith)'. From the paired tablet twists outwards, the Unique braid is identical to the Soumak braid.[90] Grace Crowfoot's term 'warp-weave' refers to the central part of the braid (1.4 cms wide) where main warp threads of two

---

[86] Magnus, 'Om folkedrakt og hovdingklede', p. 25; I. Raknes Pedersen, 'The Analyses of the Textiles from Evebø/Eide, Gloppen, Norway', *Textilsymposium Neumünster: Archäologische Textilfunde*, ed. Textilmuseum (Neumünster, 1982), pp. 75 – 84. Judging by a photograph, the clothing fragments from similar Migration period grave at Snartemo also employ double rows of blanket stitch (L. Bender Jørgensen, *Forhistoriske Textiler i Skandinavien*, p. 163, Fig. 241 and p. 250, no. 28). For correspondences between clothing clasps found in Norway and those from England of the same period see John Hines, *The Scandinavian Character of Anglian England in the pre-Viking Period* (British Archaeological Reports 124; Oxford, 1984).

[87] *Relics*, p. 461.

[88] *Relics*, p. 460.

[89] Note that Grace Crowfoot, even though she did not know of the Ravenna braid or that there was soumak among the fragments from Sutton Hoo and Taplow, almost came to the same conclusion in 1956 (*Relics*, pp. 460 – 1).

[90] The ground tabby weave beneath the blanket stitching is better preserved here than on the Soumak braid.

colours, probably once red and yellow, change places with each other to form a design. Tablet-woven braids patterned by the warp are a major type; the uniqueness of this braid is due to the presence of supplementary brocading threads in the direction of the warp as well as the weft (floats in the direction of the warp almost cover the reverse of the braid).[91] The brocading threads are of the same sort of loosely twisted yarn used for the blanket-stitching and the soumak brocading on the other braid. The only part of the design still visible is a small diamond formed by the brocading threads binding with each other in tabby; the brocading threads are of different colours, again apparently red and yellow, and a tiny chequered effect is thus created within the diamond figure.

The colours used for blanket-stitched border of the Unique braid appear to be the same as for the Soumak braid; at least, a block of blue within the red is just visible. Nevertheless, with its narrower width and different design, it must be said that the Unique braid would have looked slightly odd sewn to the same garment as the Soumak braid. It is just possible that it came from another but contemporary item, perhaps the garment to which the loose fragments of Zandaniji II compound twill belonged.

(f) SEWING AND SEWN CONSTRUCTION

Three seams survive in the weft-patterned silks, all on Fragment 7; these are indicated in fig. 23. The seams ZY and WX roughly follow the direction of the warp in the pieces they join; Xy is parallel to the weft. Sewn from the outside, the seams are overcast in a fine white thread with no visible twist. A decorative feature is a thicker silk thread which has been laid down the centre of each seam and which is bound in along with the overcasting. On the inside of the seams, the turned-back cut edges of the weft-patterned silk are bound by separate strips of silk; these cut strips, with their edges turned under, were joined to the main silk down both sides in overcast stitching. The surviving strips are made of the green tabby silk, the (originally) purple and yellow compound twill silk, and of one of the white weft-patterned silks themselves.

The edges of the garment, decorated on the outside with the Soumak braid, are faced on the inside with the purple and yellow compound twill silk, and in one place, on Fragment 2, with the three-coloured silk with pink warp also already described.[92] These facings are the same width as the Soumak braid (3.2 cms) and appear to have been sewn on with the same red thread that

---

[91] One other example which (judging by its photograph) may have floats of a brocading warp is the braid from the Sancta Sanctorum mentioned by Grace Crowfoot in relation to the Durham girdle (Volbach, 'I Tessuti', T.172; *Relics*, p. 434).

[92] Flanagan (*Relics*, p. 504) thought that the compound twill silk was the main silk of the garment, the weft-patterned silks being its lining. But a) this does not fit the construction as it survives, and b), it is probably wrong to think of the Zandaniji II silk as having been all that expensive — even though it has travelled a long way, it does not compare in quality with many other silks in the same weave, for example the Nature Goddess silk.

passes through the guilloche plaits and which indirectly sews down the braid. The main or weft-patterned silk, at the centre of this sandwich of textiles, probably extends through to the outer guilloche plait.

The use of facings on inside edges is not a peculiarly northern feature and has parallels in two complete garments, geographically unrelated but both *c.*850. One, at Abbadia San Salvatore in Italy, is a compound twill silk chasuble which had facings inside the neck and curved hem of 11 cms deep cut from a good quality but probably somewhat earlier compound twill silk. The silk of the facings was also used in narrow strips to bind the inside of the lower seams in exactly the manner of the Durham seam bindings.[93] The other garment, a kaftan excavated at Moshchevaya Balka in the northern Caucasus, is also made of one compound twill silk with facings of another.[94]

At Durham, what is not clear is the role of the plain red silk. Writing of Fragment 5, Grace Crowfoot remarks 'the plain silk is in contact with the back of the braid and the twill [is] over it',[95] i.e. the position of the red silk here is exactly equivalent to the position of one or other of the weft-patterned silks in Fragments 1, 2 and 3. Similarly, the tiny scrap of red silk in the box in the library, attached to the part of a binding strip of compound twill, corresponds to the relationship of the weft-patterned silks with the seam bindings in Fragment 7. The conclusion seems to be that in some areas the red silk replaced the white weft-patterned silk as the main textile of the garment. If the red silk had come from a separate piece of clothing, it must have been one also decorated with the Soumak braid, using the same compound twill silk as seam bindings, and somehow this seems less likely.

(g) THE APPEARANCE OF THE GARMENT

On Fragments 1, 2 and 3 (fig. 23) the braid and facings are at right-angles to the warp of the weft-patterned tabby and it would be safe to assume that these fragments come either from the hem of the garment or from the bottom of sleeves. On Fragment 7, the slight convergence of the seams WX and YZ could represent some intentional shaping; if turned the other way up, the seams could have been at the side of a tunic. It is not possible to identify where the red silk or Unique braid belonged. The most interesting fragment from the point of view of the garment is Fragment 4 (pl. 55), the end of an embellishment with two bits of Soumak braid laid side by side. It was suggested by Grace Crowfoot that this came from the lower part of a central

[93] F. Mancinelli, 'La chasuble du Pape Saint-Marc à Abbadia S. Salvatore', *CIETA Bulletin de Liaison* 41/42 (1975), pp. 119 – 39.
[94] A. Jeroussalimskaja, 'Le cafetan aux Simourghs du tombeau de Mochtchevaja Balka (Caucase Septentrional)', *Studia Iranica* 7 (1978), pp. 183 – 211 and Pls. Coincidentally, the main silk of this garment has the same simurgh design as the Abbadia S. Salvatore chasuble.
[95] *Relics*, p. 454. She is in error in stating that the red silk at any point occurs together with the weft-patterned silks.

neck opening.[96] There are no equivalents among contemporary clothing fragments, but such neck openings do occur, for instance, on tunics belonging to a group of foreigners buried at Antinoë in Egypt, probably in the fifth and sixth centuries; here the ribbon or braid edging the neck opening continues for some way down the centre of the garment as two pieces side by side.[97] Judging by depictions of secular tunics in later Anglo-Saxon manuscripts, in England a neck opening of this type might have been closed at the top with tying strings.[98]

Grace Crowfoot's suggestion that the garment was a dalmatic is also very plausible. At this date, dalmatics were still white, and it is significant that the archbishop's garment of weft-patterned tabby which survives as fragments at Ravenna, in so far as it was a tunic of white silk, was also probably a dalmatic. The question arises, was the Durham garment similar to contemporary dalmatics worn in Italy or did it demonstrate in its overall form the antecedents, seen in its details, of the dress of northern chieftains? The answer must be that it was a compromise between the two influences.

The form of the dalmatic worn in eighth- and ninth-century Italy is quite clear. It was a long loose garment with wide sleeves, decorated with red vertical shoulder stripes, with similar stripes towards the ends of the sleeves. Good depictions are the figure of the deacon Peter in the Vercelli manuscript of St Gregory's Sermons on the Gospels of *c.*800 and the deacon in the apse mosaic of Santa Prassede in Rome (822 – 4).[99] The normal construction of these dalmatics is known from an example of *c.*700 from Moyen Moutier in France, and from the fragments of the two plainer dalmatics from Sant'Apollinare in Classe, Ravenna (those with crosses in soumak between the stripes);[100] in the old manner, these were 'woven to shape' in a single piece. What remains of the Ravenna weft-patterned dalmatic comes mostly from one sleeve, which narrows towards the wrist. This dalmatic, therefore, as well as having more sewing, also had more shaping, Nevertheless, its decoration consists of strips cut from a full-width textile, not a braid. The strips were also sewn on a little way in, not right at the end of the sleeve.

The practice of sewing braids along the outside edges of garments had its origins in northern European textile traditions; apparently it had not yet

[96] *Relics*, p. 454.

[97] Wulff and Volbach, *Spätantike und koptische Stoffe*, Pls. M. Tilke, *Costume Patterns and Designs* (London, 1956), Pl. 4, Fig. 4 (note how this tunic differs from the yellow one below it, Fig. 9, the Mediterranean type worn by Christians in Egypt until the 9th or 10th century).

[98] D. Owen-Crocker, *Dress in Anglo-Saxon England* (Manchester, 1986), pp. 158 – 9.

[99] J. Beckwith, *Early Christian and Byzantine Art* (Harmondsworth, 1979), Fig. 136; C. Faldi Guglielmi, *Roma: Santa Prassede* (Tesori d'Arte Christiana, 14; Bologna, 1966), pp. 373 & 375.

[100] Braun, *Liturgische Gewandung*, p. 260, Fig. 20. Mazzotti, 'Antiche Stoffe', p. 45. The construction of the Ravenna dalmatics, and presumably of that from Moyen Moutier, is in principle just like that of St Ambrose's plainer dalmatic (H. Granger-Taylor, 'The Two Dalmatics of St. Ambrose?', *CIETA Bulletin de Liaison* 57 – 58 (1983), pp. 127 – 73). See also H. Granger-Taylor, 'Weaving Clothes to Shape in the Ancient World', *Textile History* 13, i (1982), pp. 3 – 25.

spread to southern Europe, at least for vestments, though it would do so. The type of vertical neck opening represented by the paired piece of braid, Fragment 4, was also distinctly non-Mediterranean. We cannot know the original overall proportions of the Durham garment, but another way that northern clothing differed from Mediterranean dress was by being more fitted. One thinks of the close fit implied by metal wrist and, in some areas, ankle clasps.[101] And going back to the Roman period one has the evidence of the garments from Thorsbjerg, fitted trousers and a short narrow tunic.[102]

Probably the appearance of this dalmatic was close to those portrayed a hundred or so years later on Durham Maniple I (*Relics*, pls. XXV-XXVI). Looking at the two deacons, where the dalmatic is worn without a chasuble on top, one sees a fairly narrow garment ending just below the knees, with moderately wide sleeves (the longer narrow-sleeved tunic underneath is presumably the alb). A braid is clearly shown on the hem, but not, interestingly, around the sleeves. Both dalmatics have braids extending down from the neck opening, on Peter's below a square cut neck, on Lawrence's beneath a V.

From its richness, the tunic is likely to have been the dalmatic of a bishop, perhaps a bishop of Lindisfarne. It is impossible to know when it was put into St Cuthbert's coffin. As far as we know, the coffin was not opened between the elevation of 698 and the abandoning of Lindisfarne in 875. The tunic's date is roughly the same as the date of the Nature Goddess silk, which, as elsewhere explained, was probably not placed with the relics until 944. Ecclesiastical vestments have often been stored for a very long time, the Salzburg mitre with soumak braid as *infulae*, for instance, has never been buried or 'deposited' in the archaeological sense. The tunic therefore need not have been added until as late as the 1104 translation. What is unlikely, however, is that it was a secular garment since, made up, this would not have been handed down through generations (the Nature Goddess silk had remained a usable length of cloth).

---

[101] Such clasps depended on being attached to a tight band to stay done up. Owen-Crocker, op. cit., 40 – 1.
[102] Bender Jørgensen, *Forhistoriske Textiler i Skandinavien*, pp. 148 – 9; for their cut see K. Schlabow, *Textilfunde der Eisenzeit in Norddeutschland* (Göttingen, 1976), Figs. 165 – 7.

Some New Thoughts on the Nature Goddess Silk

CLARE HIGGINS

The first documentation of the Nature Goddess silk is given by Raine in his description of how at the opening of St Cuthbert's tomb in 1827, it was found as one of a number of inner shrouds or vestments of silk underneath the outer linen shroud.[1] He gives a clear indication of the decayed state of these textiles as they were removed from the coffin: 'It was quite impossible to detach them one by one, or to preserve any accurate account of their respective shapes or the order in which they occurred.'[2] Accordingly it is as a collection of fragments that the Nature Goddess silk survives today, with some areas of the design missing and unknown (in particular the head of the figure and the lower half of the decoration between the roundels). The whole has been further reduced by some fragments having been dispersed as gifts and relics,[3] and some deterioration is evident upon close comparison of old and recent photographs.

As shown in figure 25, the fragments are displayed stitched to a canvas on which roundels and the lower border have been drawn to achieve their appropriate relative positions. This allows each piece to be seen in isolation, but gives an unnecessarily scattered impression conveying neither the original size nor the design effectively.

As figure 26 shows, however, their present arrangement can be improved upon as three of the largest fragments can be combined, indeed fit exactly together to give a much clearer impression of the pattern unit.[4] Edges that have been cut can be found on fragments (a), (b), and (c). The cut between pieces (a) and (b) was no doubt made in the nineteenth century, but that on (c) I believe to be much earlier, perhaps dating from the time the silk was given to St Cuthbert's community: with a silk of this value it is likely that the piece given to the shrine was but a length cut at some stage from a longer cloth, and

---

[1] My thanks are due to Hero Granger-Taylor for initially directing my attention to this silk, and for her considerable help and support throughout its transformation from undergraduate dissertation to published paper.
[2] *St Cuthbert*, p. 193.
[3] For discussion of such fragments see Richard Bailey's paper, above pp. 236 – 7, 243 – 6.
[4] Flanagan has already linked these three. See photograph in J. F. Flanagan, 'The "Nature Goddess" Silk at Durham', *The Burlington Magazine* 88 (1946), p. 247, plate A.

25. Present arrangement of the Nature Goddess silk.

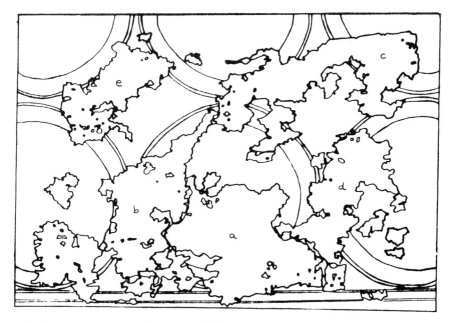

26. Suggested arrangement of the Nature Goddess silk.

not sufficient for a vestment. Indeed, on the remaining fragments there is no trace of stitching and, therefore, no evidence that the silk was ever intended as a garment.

Let us turn now to the design of the silk.[5] The pattern is based on roundels which have a diameter of approximately 60 cm. The lower portion of each roundel contains water, striped by waves in which six fish are swimming and on which two pairs of ducks are floating. In the centre is the top half of a female figure which dominates the roundel, her arms extended upwards holding a fruit-laden scarf which drapes across her chest. Also in each hand and on a level with the missing head are batons with decorated bulbous heads. The tunic ornamentation of diagonal beading is rich although rather flat. The hair is very long and is beaded as are the ends of the scarf. Now, it has been suggested that the decoration within the roundel is of a *calathos* or flaired fruit

---

[5] Cf. reconstructions in *St Cuthbert*, plate V, and J. F. Flanagan, 'The "Nature Goddess" Silk' in *Relics*, p. 506.

basket and not of a goddess figure.[6] Although the face is missing, the hair and arms at least are evident and from its shape it is unmistakably a human form.

The circular frames that contain this design are heavily ornamented with grapes and other fruit separated by their own stems. Around the outside edge there is a ring of twisting spirals. Between the roundels are tall baskets of grapes with large standing ducks facing these baskets from either side. Two fragments show a border of two horizontal rows of pearls separated by a yellow stripe.[7] Below the second row there is a short fringe marking the lower edge of the silk. The brightness of the original colours has faded, and as Flanagan points out, with a silk of this weave this can lead to parts of the design disappearing.[8] The background colour is red, the outlines are in dark blue and the other main colour is yellow. Green, the fourth main colour, has now faded and become indistinguishable from the blue. Extra colours such as purple and white were introduced intermittently for details but again are now indistinct.[9] The vertical repeat is slightly irregular, but is approximately 61 cm. As the design is symmetrical, the widthways repeat is a reverse repeat, halved to 30.5 cm.

A technical description of the weave would be that it is a weft-faced compound 1:2 twill.

— *weft-faced* indicates that the pattern is formed by the threads which transverse the cloth, and that the entire surface is covered by weft floats that hide the main warp ends or longitudinal threads.
— *compound* indicates that two or more weft colours are being used.
— *1:2 twill* indicates a weave in which each warp passes over one, then under the next two adjacent weft units. This gives an effect of diagonal lines as opposed to the grid-like appearance of plain weave.

A weave of this type requires two warps: firstly a pattern or main warp which creates the pattern or texture in the weft floats and is not visible on the surface, and secondly a binding warp which binds the weft floats to the fabric body. Significantly in this silk the pattern warp is paired and is in a two to one ratio with the binding warp. The thicker warp produced has the effect of magnifying the design and facilitates the production of large scale patterns. The sensitivity of the weave can be assessed by the decoupure or smallest gradation of design. This can be gauged approximately by looking at whether the curved lines in the design are smooth or are clumsily stepped. The smoother the slope the more manipulations of the loom and the more time-consuming to produce. In the Nature Goddess silk the weaver had a fine level

---

[6] *St Cuthbert*, p. 194, described the design as 'an urn, or some such receptacle'. See also M. and C. Picard, 'Observations sur la soierie de Durham trouvée dans le cercueil de Saint Cuthbert', *Revue Archéologique* 40 (1952), pp. 23–41.

[7] See also Hero Granger-Taylor's paper, below pp. 339–41.

[8] J. F. Flanagan, 'The "Nature Goddess" Silk', in *Relics*, pp. 510–11.

[9] These colours, in particular the green and the purple, can be seen more clearly on the underside of a fragment of the Nature Goddess silk in the British Museum, Reference 1896:5196.

of control: the design steps after each binding and pattern warp, and along the weft after every two weft units.

The primary sources for the history of St Cuthbert's shrine, although they detail the various openings of the tomb and the gifts of visiting monarchs, provide no details of the design or colour of the rich textiles mentioned. They do, however, provide a framework of possible monarchs and dates for these gifts, and an upper limit of 1104, when St Cuthbert was finally translated into the new Norman cathedral. In March 698 we are told that St Cuthbert's body was reclothed in fresh vestments. It is at this point, at the beginning of his cult, that Battiscombe suggests the Nature Goddess silk was placed in the tomb. For the next two hundred years there is no evidence to suggest that the tomb was opened.[10] By the tenth century the shrine, now at Chester-le-Street, began to attract royal benefactors. King Athelstan (925 – 39) endowed the shrine and monastery with many gifts, among which were seven *pallia*.[11] The usual translation of *pallium* is 'garment', but an alternative interpretation of the word is 'length of high quality cloth',[12] and so it is possible that this silk was one of these seven. Athelstan's visit is believed to have been in 934, when he was on his way to Scotland.[13] The *Historia de sancto Cuthberto* implies that the tomb was opened on this occasion, as we are told that Athelstan placed a *testamentum* at St Cuthbert's head.[14] The Nature Goddess silk, if one of the seven *pallia* mentioned, could either have been placed in the tomb at this point, or kept until a later date. A second possible donor is King Edmund who visited the shrine, also when on his way to Scotland, probably in 945. He gave both gold arm-rings and precious vestments, the latter described in the *Historia de sancto Cuthberto* as two *pallia Graeca* which Edmund placed on the saint's body.[15] The remaining possibility is that the silk was placed in the tomb on the translation of the relics in August 1104, when, according to Reginald of Durham, the body was re-vested and three of the uppermost cloths replaced with others 'much more beautiful and far more precious'.[16]

Accordingly the Nature Goddess silk could have been given to the shrine at any time between 698 and 1104, a period of over four hundred years. In any case, this can give little indication of the potentially much earlier date when the silk was woven, for textiles of such value were often stored for long after they were made and re-used at a later date. More precise results are to be gained by considering the design and technique of the silk and relating these to comparative material that is available. Flanagan undertook a thorough

---

[10] *HSC* 9 – 26; *Relics*, pp. 25 – 30. My thanks to Dr David Rollason for providing me with a working translation of the *HSC*.

[11] *HSC* 26.

[12] M. Hoffmann, *The Warp-weighted Loom: Studies in the History and Technology of an Ancient Implement* (Oslo, 1974), p. 230.

[13] *Relics*, p. 31.

[14] *HSC* 26.

[15] *HSC* 28, p. 212; and *Relics*, p. 34.

[16] *Libellus* 42; *Relics*, pp. 110 – 12.

analysis in the 1950s the conclusions of which, that it is a seventh-century Byzantine textile, have remained unchallenged.[17] I shall take his arguments as my starting point but on considering iconographic and technical details of the silk shall conclude that the textile is undoubtedly of a later date than the seventh century. That it is a fine example of Byzantine craftsmanship I do not dispute.

Flanagan compares the figure in the roundel with the Seasons and Earth figures in the fourth-century mosaics at Antioch,[18] and he shows clearly the classical origin of the motif. This link can also be seen in a watercolour of the now destroyed mosaics at Santa Costanza, Rome, which date from around AD 350.[18a] Here the central figure has her arms similarly raised and the water, fish, and ducks form a second parallel with the Nature Goddess silk. The vegetation that appears to sprout from the head of this mosaic figure can be compared to the leaves and branches on the silk around the area of the missing face (visible on fragment (c)). An impression of what the missing head would have looked like can be gained from an unpublished cuff decoration in the British Museum (EA 20430; see plate 53). The half-length figure, likewise in a roundel, has outstretched arms and is holding batons and a fruit-filled scarf. This is of wool and linen tapestry and is probably eighth- or ninth-century, although there is no secure basis for dating. Designs on tapestry were sometimes taken from silks with inevitable loss of detail, and it is possible that this might have been copied from a silk textile.

Now, Flanagan argues that the Nature Goddess silk is early Byzantine, first by emphasizing the similarity of the beaded decoration to decoration in sixth-century Byzantine mosaics, notably the portrait of Theodora in San Vitale, Ravenna, and secondly by remarking that so pagan a theme is unlikely to appear any later than the seventh century in the workshop of a Christian emperor. However, it appears that Byzantine emperors could be less scrupulous as regards pagan designs than this would lead us to believe. Certainly pagan motifs were used in ivories dating from the Macedonian dynasty.[19] Whereas it is true that bead-like patterns were popular in the seventh century, not only in mosaic but also in textiles, more dominant and unusual aspects of the Nature Goddess silk design press for comparisons of greater significance. The problem with Flanagan's work is that instead of searching for similar themes in other textiles, he cites nature goddesses from mosaic and stonework of an undoubtedly earlier era which make clear the origin of the design itself but detach it from its context within textile art.

The decoration of the frame of the roundel in the Nature Goddess silk provides the richest area for comparison. Two features are of particular importance. First, the motif of the fruit found there is unusual, but it does also occur on a smaller and less magnificent scale in a silk of peacock-tailed

---

[17] Flanagan, 'The "Nature Goddess" Silk', in *Relics*, pp. 505 – 13.

[18] Illustrated in *Relics*, Plate LIV.

[18a] Illustrated in H. Stern, 'Les mosaïques de l'église de Sainte-Constance à Rome', *Dumbarton Oaks Papers* 12 (1958), pp. 157 – 218.

[19] Illustrated in *Splendeur de Byzance*, Brussels exhibition catalogue (1982), pp. 118 – 19.

monsters of which there is a piece in the Victoria and Albert Museum.[20] Although this is a much less complex silk, it is closely comparable; the red fruit on a navy ground are separated from each other by their stems in similar manner to the Nature Goddess silk. The silk is attributed by Weibel to the eighth or ninth century.[21] Secondly, around the roundel's outer rim in the Nature Goddess silk is a band of twisting spirals. Several other examples of this can be found, the simplest being the Cock silk in the Vatican Museum.[22] In this case, however, comparison can contribute little as the stylized nature of the design marks it out as being earlier and of considerably less sophistication. Among silks closer in quality, this design is more common in those of eighth- and ninth-century date. The Lion Strangler silk at Sens which is believed to have been placed in the tomb of St Victor in 769 has a large spiral design in the roundel border.[23] Within the roundel is a full-length figure of a man grasping the throats of two lions that stand on either side of him while two more lions attack his feet. It is technically similar to the Nature Goddess silk, having a paired pattern warp,[24] and is stylistically similar, particularly in the treatment of the man's hair, the flat ornamentation of the tunic and the strikingly similar position of his arms. A more securely dated example with this spiral edging is at Sant' Ambrogio, Milan. In this silk, the roundels of 90 cm across contain a palm tree, two mounted hunting kings, and various animals. It is thought to be a Byzantine copy of a Sassanian theme, the legend of Bahram Gour.[25] The design is complex and well executed. This has been dated as eighth-century,[26] and it was used to cover the inner faces of the gold altar doors installed at Sant' Ambrogio in 835. A silk of the same pattern but in different colours was used to cover the relics of St Calais, in 837. A third example (in Cologne) is from the shrine of St Kunibert where it was probably used in the 830s to wrap relics.[27] That silk of this pattern was being used on at least two independent occasions in the 830s suggests that it was woven at a date not too far previous to this. Thus, as regards ornamentation, the Nature Goddess silk bears a close resemblance to several silks that can reliably be regarded as dating from the eighth and ninth centuries. This, when coupled with the general tendency

---

[20] Victoria and Albert Museum Reference 761 – 1893.110K5; illustrated in O. von Falke, *Decorative Silks* (London, 1936), No. 179. Fragment of same design in Brussels: Musées royaux d'Art et d'Histoire, Inv. Tx.609. *Splendeur de Byzance*, p. 216.

[21] A. C. Weibel, *Two Thousand Years of Textiles* (New York, 1952), No. 63.

[22] Illustrated in N. A. Reath and E. B. Sachs, *Persian Textiles* (New Haven, 1937), Example 45, Plate 45.

[23] A. M. Muthesius, 'Eastern silks in Western shrines and treasuries before 1200' (Ph.D. thesis, Courtauld Institute of Art, London University, 1982), p. 265. Illustrated in Falke, *Decorative Silks*, Fig. 100.

[24] Muthesius, 'Eastern Silks', pp. 491 – 2. I would like to thank Dr Muthesius for her assistance and for permission to use her Ph.D thesis.

[25] *Splendeur de Byzance*, p. 211.

[26] W. F. Volbach, *Early Decorative Textiles* (London, 1969), p. 100.

[27] Illustrated in Falke, *Decorative Silks*, Fig. 58.

evident in silks that with time the designs used become larger and more colourful, make a seventh-century dating too early to be likely.

A later date is also suggested by the structure of the weave, notably in the use of a paired pattern warp. The pairing of pattern warps was introduced for strength at a time when wider looms were producing heavier silks. The thicker warp magnified the design, rendering it slightly coarser and larger in scale. Flanagan noted this feature, which he refers to as 'scaling', when detailing the differences between textiles of the sixth and seventh centuries.[28] According to Flanagan, this method does not appear before the end of the seventh century, and he uses this to indicate that the silk was more likely to have been woven in the seventh century than the sixth. This however gives too early a date to this innovation in weaving technique. According to Beckwith, the earliest example of a paired warp is in a silk at Mozac, the Royal Hunter silk from the tomb of St Austremoine.[29] This is believed to have been given by the Emperor Constantine V (741 – 75) to Pepin the Short and used at the shrine in 761. Citing other examples, Beckwith concludes 'it would seem that by the middle of the eighth century the looms at Constantinople were producing a compound weft twill . . . strengthened by the pairing of the main or figure harness warp'.[30] This was not a technique being used in the previous century.

In conclusion, I have argued that the date currently accepted for the Nature Goddess silk is unsatisfactory in terms of the ornamentation and the structure of the silk, and more general trends in textile art.[31] By relating each of these aspects to comparable and more securely dated examples a more reliable assessment of date emerges. From a technical point of view the silk could not have been woven until the middle of the eighth century, and stylistic and iconographic parallels make either a late eighth- or early ninth-century date the most likely. And so it is not possible that the Nature Goddess silk was given to St Cuthbert during his life, nor placed in his tomb at his elevation in 698. Rather, in accordance with a ninth-century date, the silk was most probably a gift of either King Athelstan or King Edmund. The latter seems the most likely: it is recorded in the *Historia de sancto Cuthberto* that on his visit, thought to be in 945, he 'with his own hands placed . . . two robes of Graecian

[28] Flanagan, *Burlington Magazine* 88, p. 245.

[29] J. Beckwith, 'Byzantine Tissues', Actes du XIV[e] Congres International des Etudes Byzantines (Bucarest, 1971), pp. 343 – 53.

[30] Op. cit., p. 350.

[31] My conclusions are firmly at variance with those of F. W. Buckler, *Harunu'l Rashid and Charles the Great* (Massachusetts, 1931), and 'The Pallium of Saint Cuthbert', *Archaeologia Aeliana* 4th ser, 1 (1925), pp. 199 – 213. He argues that this silk originated from the court of the Abbasid Caliphs at Baghdad, and is not a Byzantine product. However, it appears that his analysis was made without having examined the Durham textiles, with the result that his description of the silk is confused and incorrect. Whilst noting the arrangement of the six fish, the ducks and the grapes, all clearly visible on the Nature Goddess silk, he makes obvious errors in describing the cloth as purple, heavily interwoven with gold thread, and containing a prominent kufic inscription 'There is no God save the One'.

workmanship upon the holy body';[32] whereas Athelstan, although a generous donor to the shrine, is not at any time described as having revested the body. However, it is also possible that a silk given to the shrine in the tenth century by Athelstan or some other donor could have been kept by the community and only placed in St Cuthbert's tomb at the time of the translation in 1104.

TECHNICAL ANALYSIS[33]

Vertical repeat of the design		61 cm
Widthways repeat of the design		61 cm
Description of weave		weft-faced compound 1:2 twill
		S direction of twill
Warp	*Proportion*	1 end binding warp
		2 ends pattern warp (paired)
	Fibre, yarn and colour	Z spun brown silk
	Decoupure	1 thread binding warp and 1 pair
		pattern warp
	Ends per cm	binding warp: 17 ends
		pattern warp: 17 paired ends
Weft	*Proportion*	4 lats = 1 pass
	Fibre, yarn and colour	silk, unspun to give greater lustre
		red, yellow, dark blue, green and others
	Decoupure	2 passes
	Picks or passes and lats	passes: 62 – 63
	per cm	lats: approximately 250
Interruptions and variations in the weave		none
Faults		none apparent
Selvedges		none
Other non-sewn edges		none
Sewing and use		There is no trace of stitching and therefore no evidence that the silk was used as a vestment or garment

[32] *HSC* 28.
[33] D. K. Burnham, *A Textile Terminology: Warp and Weft* (London, 1981).

The Inscription on the Nature Goddess Silk

HERO GRANGER-TAYLOR

Raine included in his 1829 drawing of the Nature Goddess silk the two rows of discs or pearls with which the design terminates.[1] Up till now, however, it has escaped notice that the pearls contain the remains of a Greek inscription. The layout of the border is as follows: the pink main ground ceases just below the lower roundels and is replaced by another ground colour, now much faded, probably originally purple; the weft forming the pearls has mostly rotted away but was clearly originally white; the two rows of pearls are separated by a plain stripe of faded yellow; below the lower row of pearls is a short fringe of warp threads, the original end of the cloth.

The letters were of the same colour as the border ground. Their remains can be traced to some extent by colour, the fact that the coloured weft threads are a bit thicker than the white threads partly overcoming the problem of fading. The best guide to their presence, however, is the structure of the weft-faced compound twill weave itself. Where the white weft or second lat goes through to the back of the cloth, to be replaced by the coloured first lat, tiny vertical valleys are formed that show up well in oblique light. Even where the contrasting white has disappeared completely, the vertical edge of the figure can still be detected. This is because, where the interruption in the darker colour is original and not due to damage, the float of every third weft thread is curtailed.

Plates 51 and 52 show as much as it is possible to trace of the inscription. Plate 52 is in fact an enlargement from an old negative made, it seems, shortly before the silk was remounted in the late 1940s or early 1950s.[2] Unfortunately, some of what is still visible in the old photo, notably the left-hand side of what appears to be an *eta*, must have been lost during the process of remounting. The parts of the inscription of which we can be reasonably certain are the cross, an empty pearl following the cross, the *theta* and the hooks at the top of the letter to the right of the *theta*. The lower row of pearls was empty.

---

[1] *St Cuthbert*, p. 194.
[2] Durham Dean and Chapter neg. no. 178; neg. no. 176 shows the cross in a more complete state.

The cross is on a different fragment of silk from the letters. Clare Higgins explains that a number of pieces are mounted wrongly; nevertheless, the two large fragments in question here do still seem to be in the right relationship with each other. From inscriptions on other Byzantine objects, it is clear that the cross marks the start of the text. On average each pearl measures 2.4 cms; thus there must have been twenty-one to twenty-three pearls between the cross and the *theta*. If the inscription was symmetrically arranged, and if the silk was four roundels wide, the complete inscription would have been about sixty-five pearls long.[3] The empty pearl immediately following the cross suggests that the style of the inscription was not very abbreviated — there may even have been spaces between words.

It is doubtful whether any of the missing letters could ever be restored with certainty.[4] The combination of *eta* followed by *theta* is distinctive, reminiscent of **BOHΘEI**, as in the invocation **KYPIE** (or **ΘEOTOKE**) **BOHΘEI TΩ ΣΩ ΔOYΛΩ** plus a name in the dative, that is 'O Lord, [or 'O Virgin'] save thy servant!'. But this phrase is usually found at the beginning of an inscription and there are too many pearls in front of the *eta* for it to fit the silk. From their position, the letters that survive are more likely to be part of someone's title. The letter with the hooks at the top, two pearls after the *theta*, looks at first like a *khi*, but is more likely to be an *upsilon*. It is just possible that it was an *upsilon* combined with an *omicron*, in which case one might be dealing with a masculine genitive ending, but the little one can see of the lower half of the letter does not seem to correspond to an O form.

In a recent article, Anna Muthesius discusses the six previously known inscribed Byzantine silks.[5] These show two forms of inscription. Five silks, those with large lion designs, had a cross and **EΠI** followed by the name of the emperor, or emperors, and 'the devout ruler(s)', all in the genitive. The second form has been found only on the Elephant silk from the tomb of Charlemagne at Aachen; here a cross and **EΠI** are followed by the abbreviated names and titles, not of emperors, but of officials under whom the silk was woven (the fact that the second official, Peter, was archon of the Zeuxippos, the old imperial bath building where dyeing perhaps took place, is

---

[3] A width of three roundels would have meant an inscription of about forty pearls long. Four roundels would give a width of 245 – 250 cms, including selvages, which may at first seem excessive for a textile of such complexity, but it corresponds with what we know of widths of Byzantine silks, see Anna Muthesius, 'A Practical Approach to the History of Byzantine Silk Weaving', *Jahrbuch der österreichischen Byzantinistik* 35 (1986), p. 240, n. 18; the silk of the Abbadia S. Salvatore chasuble, which is about 260 cms wide, may be Persian but is closer in date (*c*.850), F. Mancinelli, 'La chasuble du Pape Saint-Marc à Abbadia S. Salvatore', *Bulletin de Liaison du Centre International d'Etudes des Textiles Anciens* (Lyon) 41/42 (1975), pp. 119 – 39.

[4] My thanks to Mrs Charlotte Roueché, of King's College, London, and to Professor A. A. M. Bryer and the M.A. Think Tank at the Centre for Byzantine Studies, University of Birmingham, for their thoughts on the text.

[5] Art. cit.; the fourth lion silk, at Crépy St Arnoul has not been seen since the 18th century, while the fifth, once at Auxerre, is only known from a medieval description.

proof that the textile was woven in Constantinople).[6] Dating to around the early ninth century, however, the Nature Goddess silk is probably a hundred or so years older than the earliest of these silks (see above, pp. 333 – 6).

From the cross and the traces of Greek letters we at least know that the Nature Goddess silk is definitely Byzantine. This allows some closely related textiles also to be identified as probably Byzantine, including two of the examples mentioned by Clare Higgins, the Sens Lion-Strangler silk and the Simurgh silk in Brussels and London, both of which, at times, have been thought of as Persian.[7]

For the historian of St Cuthbert's shrine, the inscription confirms the very special quality of this textile gift. The inscribed silks elsewhere are also excellently woven with large-scale designs, almost certainly of the category of 'forbidden things' meant only to leave the Byzantine empire as diplomatic gifts or tributes.[8] It seems very likely that the Nature Goddess silk is one of the two *pallia Graeca*, or lengths of Greek cloth, which the *Historia de sancto Cuthberto* tells us King Edmund wrapped around the body of the saint *manu propria*, in 944.[9] The adjective *Graeca* is significantly specific considering that silks in the same weave were reaching England from a number of other sources.[10] The only object among Athelstan's gifts of 934 to be called *Greek*, one of the patens, is the type of object that is very likely to have carried an inscription, had it been Byzantine.[11] Luisella Simpson has argued elsewhere in this volume that the *Historia de sancto Cuthberto* was probably compiled at Chester-le-Street in 944 or shortly afterwards, that is, at a time when the events of Edmund's visit would still have been fresh in everyone's memory (below pp. 397 – 411).

[6] Robert S. Lopez, 'Silk Industry in the Byzantine Empire', *Speculum* 20 (1945), p. 7.
[7] Otto von Falke, *Kunstgeschichte der Seidenweberei* (Berlin, 1913), Abb. 129; *A Survey of Persian Art*, ed. A. Upham Pope and P. Ackerman (New York, 1938), I, Pl. 199B.
[8] Lopez, art. cit., pp. 20 – 4 and 35 – 8.
[9] *HSC* 28.
[10] See above, pp. 311 – 13.
[11] *HSC* 26.

Silks and Saints: The Rider and Peacock Silks from the Relics of St Cuthbert

ANNA MUTHESIUS

More than 2000 fragments of medieval silk survive in ecclesiastical treasuries and many of them have some connection with the cult of relics. Most of these fragments were taken from reliquaries in the nineteenth century, but unfortunately, records were rarely kept and today it is often no longer possible to associate particular silks with the reliquaries, which are more easily and more precisely datable. Also, much was lost in troubled times such as at the Dissolution of the Monasteries in Britain and during the Revolution in France, as well as by the natural deterioration over the centuries of the delicate fabrics themselves. In this country Durham Cathedral alongside Canterbury Cathedral has one of the finest collections of medieval silks to survive. On the continent the greatest number of splendid medieval silks is to be found in the treasuries of Aachen Cathedral, of St Servatius, Maastricht, and of Sens Cathedral.[1]

From the fourth century silks were considered appropriate for wrapping the

---

[1] More than 1000 of the surviving silks are studied in A. Muthesius, 'Eastern Silks in Western Shrines and Treasuries before 1200' (unpublished Ph.D. thesis, University of London (Courtauld Institute), 1982), hereafter referred to as Muthesius, 'Eastern Silks'. My introductory discussion on silks used for wrapping relics is taken from the thesis, pp. 264 – 8. Further liturgical uses of silk are discussed on pp. 268 – 305 of this thesis. The remainder of the thesis is incorporated into a *History of the Byzantine Silk Industry* (Vienna, forthcoming). For the silks in the treasuries of Aachen Cathedral, of St Servatius, Maastricht, and of Sens Cathedral treasury respectively, the reader is referred to the following publications:

Aachen Cathedral treasury — An incomplete catalogue of the silks appears in E. Grimme, 'Der Aachener Domschatz', *Aachener Kunstblätter* 42 (1972), pp. 1 – 400. Silks not described here appear in Muthesius, 'Eastern Silks', pp. 4, 69, 394, 405, 435, 470 – 1, 495, 509 – 10. There are thirty-one early medieval silks in the treasury at Aachen and several hundred later silks including vestments.

St Servatius, Maastricht — More than 450 silks survive in this treasury. As a whole the collection is unpublished but a preliminary catalogue with photographs has been prepared by the author. Some of the early medieval examples are in Muthesius, 'Eastern Silks', pp. 51ff., 93ff., 217ff., 236ff., 392 – 3, 396, 411, 423, 426, 433, 435, 437, 454, 482 – 3, 500, 553, 564, 577. Reference to literature on a few individual silks of the collection which have been published is included amongst the pages cited above.

bones of saints, and the sarcophagus of St Paulinus of Trier (d. 358) has
yielded two examples. Naturally the possession of major relics enhanced the
prestige of ecclesiastical centres and encouraged the beneficial growth of
pilgrimage.[2] Before 1200 it was rare to have a special room set aside as a
treasury for housing the numerous precious reliquaries and shrines in which
the relics of the saints were preserved. Instead, they were normally associated
with particular altars and housed in special chapels in churches, monasteries
and cathedrals. For example, at Chur Cathedral,[3] and at the chapel of St
Michel at Le Puy, before the twelfth century, the area beneath the main altar
served as a treasury for reliquaries.[4] At Chur and at Le Puy there was an altar
slab, which was placed above a sizeable hollow structure that held reliquaries,
relics and silks. The Sancta Sanctorum in the Lateran Palace in Rome had a
wooden cupboard with a grille front, through which a variety of wooden and
metalwork reliquaries enclosing relics and silks could be seen. This wooden
structure was inscribed with the name of Pope Leo III (795 – 816).[5] At the
abbey of St Pierre, Sens, there was a silver shrine into which relics including
those of St Peter, donated by the Emperor Charlemagne (d. 814), were placed
by Archbishop Magnus in 809.[6] Many of the small silk fragments at Sens
datable eighth- to ninth-century, may originally have served as wrappings for
relics in this silver shrine.[7] In 1106 the shrine is documented as being behind
the main altar at St Pierre, Sens, but today it and numerous other shrines once

---

Sens Cathedral treasury — More than 500 silks, most datable before 1200, survive in this major
medieval treasury. The silks in part were listed and described (without technical detail) by E.
Chartraire, 'Les tissus anciens du trésor de la cathédrale de Sens', *Revue de l'Art Chrétien* 61 (Paris,
1911), pp. 261 – 80, 370 – 86. A fuller preliminary catalogue of the entire collection at Sens
Cathedral has been made by the author.
The Durham Cathedral silks from the relics of St Cuthbert were briefly described by Raine, *St
Cuthbert*, pp. 194 – 7. Flanagan and Brett discussed the silks in greater detail in *Relics*, pp.
484 – 525, 470 – 83. The medieval silks at Canterbury Caathedral were published by G.
Robinson and H. Urquhart with weaving notes by A. Hindson, 'Seal Bags in the Treasury of the
Cathedral Church of Canterbury', *Archaeologia* 84 (1934), pp. 163 – 211.
[2] On the cult of relics in general there are interesting points in J. Sumption, *Pilgrimage: An Image of
Medieval Religion* (London, 1975), pp. 22 – 53. A short essay on medieval treasuries by F. J.
Rönig, 'Die Schatz und Heiltumskammern', is in the exhibition catalogue *Rhein und Maas* (2
vols.; Köln, 1972), II, 134 – 41. The St Paulinus silks are in W. Reusch, *Frühchristliche Zeugnisse im
Einzugsgebiet von Rhein und Mosel* (Trier, 1965), p. 179, pls. 3a, b.
[3] The altar at Chur was studied by C. Caminada, 'Der Hochalter der Kathedrale von Chur',
Zeitschrift für Schweizerische Archäologie und Kunstgeschichte 7 (1945), p. 23 ff.
[4] The altar at Le Puy was detailed by F. Enaud, 'Découverte d'objets et de reliquaires à Saint
Michel d'Aiguilhe (Haute-Loire)', *Les Monuments Historiques de la France* n.s. 7 (1961).
[5] The wooden reliquary structure at the Sancta Sanctorum was examined by H. Grisar in *Die
römische Kapelle Sancta Sanctorum und ihr Schatz* (Freiburg, 1908), pp. 1ff., pl. 1, 15, 55ff., pl. 29.
[6] See Chartraire, op. cit., p. 268. The report was made by Archbishop Guy of Nogers in 1192.
[7] For example, ibid., nos. 1 and 2 on p. 270. Chartraire does not list the majority of the tiny
patterned silk scraps at Sens Cathedral treasury. Cf. Muthesius, 'Eastern Silks', pp. 445 – 7,
458 – 9, 464, 490 – 1, 516, 532, 540 – 1, 555, 566 – 7, 569 – 71, 575 for fuller discussion of some
of the Sens silks. Others are briefly listed on pp. 382 – 90, 393, 397 – 400, 413 – 14, 423 – 4, 436,
438.

at Sens are lost.[8] The relics of St Victor came to St Pierre, Sens, from St
Maurice d'Agaune in 769 with Archbishop Willicaire of Sens. Subsequently
they were wrapped in an eighth- to ninth-century Byzantine silk and enclosed
in a shrine no longer extant. The relics of St Siviard, which are said to have
reached St Pierre in the ninth century, were translated into a shrine in 1029
and at this time it is likely that the tenth- to eleventh-century Byzantine griffin
silk, which is still at Sens, was added. The relics of the Holy Innocents were
wrapped in an eighth- to ninth-century Central Asian silk at St Pierre and a
later Islamic silk was used to shroud the relics of St Potentien there. At St
Columbe, Sens, important relics were also enveloped in silk and placed into
shrines long since lost. The relics of St Columbe and of St Loup were shrouded
in two pieces of a Central Asian lion silk datable to the seventh or eighth
century. This silk must have been cut into two at the time of the simultaneous
translation of the relics of the saints under Archbishop Wenilon in 853.[9]

Magnificent golden shrines studded with precious gems and enamels were
built in the twelfth century to receive the relics of newly-canonized saints. At
St Servatius, Maastricht, for instance, the Servatius shrine held many silks
alongside the relics of the patron saint. An eighth- to ninth-century Byzantine
silk with 'Dioscurides' design, an Islamic silk with lion pattern datable tenth-
to eleventh-century, and other silks including a Central Asian piece of the
eighth to ninth century were found in the shrine in the late nineteenth century.
The twelfth-century shrine of St Heribert, archbishop of Cologne (d. 1021) at
St Heribert, Cologne-Deutz, held an imperial Byzantine lion silk. This has an
inscription yielding the date 976 – 1025 for the fabric. Another Byzantine silk
of the same period with birds and trees was also found in the shrine in the late
nineteenth century. From a third twelfth-century shrine, that of Anno,
archbishop of Cologne (d. 1075), at St Servatius, Siegburg, came an imperial
Byzantine lion silk. This is precisely datable to 921 – 31 by its inscription. The
shrine of the Emperor Charlemagne himself (d. 814), which was finished early
in the thirteenth century, held a variety of impressive silks including two
magnificent imperial Byzantine pieces, an eighth- to ninth-century example
with charioteer design, and a silk of around 1000 with medallions enclosing

[8] The thirteenth-century account of the relics at St Pierre, Sens, by Geoffrey de Courlon was
published as *Libellus super reliquiis monasteri Sancti Gaufridi de Gellone*, in *Documents publiés par la Société
Archéologique de Sens*, no. 1 (Sens, 1876).
[9] At the time of the French Revolution relics and silks of St Columbe were deposited in Sens
Cathedral. In 1844 a casket containing anonymous relics were taken from the abbey of St Pierre,
Sens, to Sens Cathedral treasury. It was from this casket that in 1896 many silks were taken. They
had been used to envelop the individual relics. The vast collection of medieval silks at Sens
Cathedral today therefore represents pieces originally in the abbey of St Pierre, a few silks from St
Columbe, Sens, and pieces belonging to the cathedral itself.

large elephant motifs.[10]

For lesser relics it appears to have been usual to cut small patterned squares of silk. Examples survive at Sens, in a number of Swiss treasuries including Chur and St Maurice, and at St Servatius in Maastricht.[11] For reliquary pouches, pieces of patterned silks and plain silks were used, some of the latter being embroidered. Sens Cathedral has one pouch made from a small piece of a purple and olive green lion silk, which is probably tenth-century, Byzantine. The Museo Sacro in Rome has a silk reliquary pouch with the design of a figure, perhaps Samson, in combat with a lion, and this belongs to an extensive group of Samson silks, most probably Byzantine in origin, which reached the west in the eighth to ninth centuries.[12] St Servatius, Maastricht, has twenty silk reliquary pouches, most of fourteenth- to fifteenth-century Italian velvet.[13] Beromünster in Switzerland has a pouch with embroidered foliate design that may be eleventh-century Byzantine work,[14] and a lion silk pouch, perhaps a ninth- to tenth-century Byzantine textile sewn in the west.[15] Smaller silk purses at Canterbury Cathedral treasury were probably used for seals.[16] A very small purse from the Viking dig at Coppergate in York was

[10] The canonization of saints in the twelfth century led to a spurt in the growth of some major continental treasuries, at which time elaborate and costly shrines were built to receive their relics. Impressive, inscribed imperial Byzantine lion silks were used for the relics of important saints, such as Heribert, archbishop of Cologne (d.1021) and Anno, archbishop of Cologne (d.1075). The silks were added to the relics at the time of the translation of the respective relics into magnificent twelfth-century shrines. These and related lion silks are described in A. Muthesius, 'A Practical Approach to the History of Byzantine Silk Weaving', *Jahrbuch der österreichischen byzantinistik Gesellschaft* 34 (1984), pp. 235 – 54.

[11] At Sens Cathedral there is a mass of unpublished relics wrapped in silks. Each silk originally bore an identifying vellum label. Today the labels survive but they have become detached from the silks and the relics. In Swiss church treasuries relics still wrapped in small scraps of silk have also been discovered, for example at Beromünster. See B. Schmedding, *Mittelalterliche Textilien in Kirchen und Klostern der Schweiz* (Bern, 1978), nos. 42, 43, on pp. 52 – 3. At an unknown date in the nineteenth century small 'silk-enveloped' relics were stored in a large glass jar at St Servatius, Maastricht. Today a photograph of the jar, but not the container itself, can be seen at the treasury.

[12] For the reliquary pouch see W. F. Volbach, *Catalogo del Museo Sacro della Biblioteca apostolica Vaticana*, 3, Fasc. I Tessuti (Vatican City, 1942), T103. The largest fragment of silk to survive with the pattern of 'Samson and the lion' is at Ottobeuren. It is published in the exhibition catalogue, *Suevia Sacra, Frühe Kunst in Schwaben* (Augsburg, 1973), no. 200, pp. 192 – 3, pls. 188, 189.

[13] The reliquary pouches at Maastricht are unpublished. They are briefly described in Muthesius, 'Eastern Silks', p. 100. One unpatterned example, on technical grounds, may be dated eleventh- to twelfth-century. The more elaborately patterned fifteenth- and sixteenth-century Italian silk pouches may have replaced earlier unpatterned ones.

[14] Schmedding, op. cit., no. 14, pp. 29 – 30. On technical and stylistic grounds it would be possible to argue for an earlier date for this piece. The twill weave described by Schmedding is characteristic of pieces dating up to the ninth century. Only extremely rarely is it found in the twelfth century. The twill has only one main warp as opposed to two, characteristic of twills dating from the eighth to ninth century onwards; see further note 49 below.

[15] Ibid., no. 11, pp. 25 – 6.

[16] Robinson and Urquhart, op. cit., no. 32, p. 32.

made from a purple silk, perhaps Byzantine, and this suggests that relics may have been carried on the persons of their owners in England in the tenth century.[17]

Thirteenth-century ecclesiastical inventories indicate the existence of quite a few reliquary pouches in churches and cathedrals in England at that time. These were termed *theca*, *bursa* and *marsupium* in different inventories. Amongst the churches with such pouches were Adbury and Brent Pelham. At Clopton a small silk *bursa* was used as a cover for the host.[18] A splendid silk reliquary pouch in the Germanisches Nationalmuseum, Nuremberg, is thought to be eleventh-century Byzantine work,[19] and possibly some Byzantine pouches together with relics did reach the west from Byzantium. However, the careless stitching that is evident on most of the surviving reliquary pouches suggests that they were 'home-sewn' using imported silks.

Sometimes relics wrapped in silks were placed in smaller reliquaries instead of in larger shrines. For instance, an early thirteenth-century head reliquary of St Eustace from Basle Cathedral, now in the British Museum, enclosed several relics wrapped in silk. The head itself consists of a wooden carving with a silver gilt casing. Also, a small enamel cross at St Servatius, Maastricht, of the late tenth to mid eleventh century, contained a relic wrapped in a scrap of the Dioscurides silk, a larger piece of which came from the shrine of St Servatius at Maastricht.[20] No doubt, many unopened metalwork shrines and reliquaries still house both silks and relics, and of course those reliquaries which are empty today did originally contain relics, probably wrapped in silks. At Durham it is fortunate that the coffin-reliquary of St Cuthbert exists alongside silks from the relics of the saint.

The use of silks for the relics of St Cuthbert can be fully understood only in the context of the widespread use of silks for the relics of saints on the continent in the medieval period. Close parallels between Durham and the continent can be drawn in three respects:

[17] The archaeological context of the find suggests a tenth-century date for the silk. It is discussed by the author and by P. Walton in conjunction, in *Interim: Bulletin of the York Archaeological Trust* 6, no. 2 (York, 1979), pp. 5 – 6, as 'A Silk Reliquary Pouch from Coppergate'.

[18] Otto Lehmann-Brockhaus, *Lateinische Schriftquellen zur Kunst in England, Wales und Schottland vom Jahre 901 bis zum Jahre 1307* (5 vols.; München, 1955), I, no. 1064.

[19] A. Schönberger, *Germanisches Nationalmuseum, Ausgewählte Werke* (Nürnberg, 1971), pl. 14 (not mentioned in the short text preceding the plates). See also S. Müller-Christensen, *Sakrale Gewänder* (Munich, 1955), no. 43, p. 27. Pilgrims do appear to have transported relics. For example, Richard, abbot of St Vanne, in 1026 – 7 travelled to Jerusalem and Constantinople and he returned with two relics of the True Cross and with a precious purple fabric. This is discussed by E. Lesne, *Histoire de la propriété ecclésiastique en France*, vol. III (Paris, 1936), p. 249, n. 1 and p. 249, n. 2 with source references.

[20] In the early 1960s under the direction of Peter Lasko, the metal casing was removed from the wooden core. Eleven relics wrapped in a variety of silks and linen fabrics were discovered in the head. These were opened out and flattened down. They are now in the Department of Medieval and Later Antiquities at the British Museum. Vellum labels attached to the relics named each in turn, and a complete description of all eleven is given in Muthesius, 'Eastern Silks', p. 309. For the Servatius cross see *Rhein und Maas*, I, 179.

i. At Durham and abroad silks were considered appropriate for enveloping the relics of distinguished saints.

ii. At Durham just as on the continent, a splendid twelfth-century translation of the relics of the patron saint was seen as an occasion for the addition of further magnificent silks to the relics.

iii. At Durham in the same way as at Chur, at Sens, in the Rhineland, and in Rome, reliquaries and shrines housing precious relics wrapped in magnificent silks were set near high altars, where they formed a focal point for the attention of visiting pilgrims.

It is beyond the scope of this introductory discussion to describe in detail the many and varied ecclesiastical uses of silk in the medieval church, but it should be mentioned that the main impetus for the widespread appearance of silks in the Latin church undoubtedly came from the medieval papacy.[21] The popes donated thousands of patterned silks to the churches of Rome for use as hangings, furnishings, vestments, and for decorating manuscript bindings. There can be little doubt that the 'silken churches of Rome' in the eighth and ninth centuries especially set an enviable example to major ecclesiastical centres in the rest of Europe.

Of the silks removed from the relics of St Cuthbert in 1827 and briefly described by Raine, I wish to concentrate upon two particular examples.[22] These are the Rider silk and the Peacock silk, which are examined separately below.

1. THE RIDER SILK

In 1956 Gerard Brett published the silk with falconer design at Durham under the title of 'the Rider silk' (*Relics*, pp.470 – 83). Relying on stylistic, iconographic, and technical evidence he assigned it to a workshop in Persia and dated it to the late tenth or early eleventh century. While it is possible to agree with his dating of the silk, an entirely different centre for its weaving will be proposed.

The main problem in reconstructing the design on the silk lies in the fact that much of the pattern has worn away as it was printed onto the surface of the fabric and not woven in. Brett relied on a painted photograph of 1888 (Victoria and Albert Museum no. 1626 – 1888) for reconstructing the design on the silk but this has misleadingly hard outlines and may have led him to draw unsatisfactory stylistic parallels with other works of art as will be discussed below. My reconstruction of the design (figs. 27 and 28) has been

---

[21] For the shrine of St Cuthbert behind the main altar see *Rites of Durham*, ed. J. T. Fowler (SS 107; Durham, 1903), p. 73, and *Relics*, p. 58. For full discussion of silks donated by the papacy and source references see Muthesius, 'Eastern Silks', pp. 280 – 7.

[22] Raine, *St Cuthbert*, pp. 194 – 7, listed five silks that he said were found with the relics of St Cuthbert in 1827. A purple silk listed as no. 4 by Raine, seems lost today. The Rider silk and the Peacock silk at Durham appear as nos. 1 and 5 respectively in Raine's list.

SCALE IN INCHES

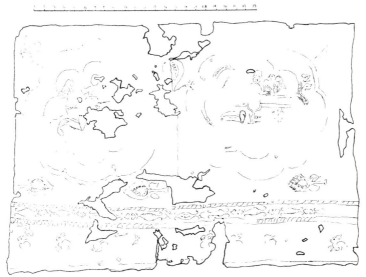

27. *The Durham Rider silk. Design as it appears on photograph MS157, Victoria and Albert Museum, London, reproduced as pl. 57, this volume. (Main areas of loss within the textile are indicated by a thicker black outline than that used to show the pattern itself.)*

28. *The Durham Rider silk: Sketch of main part of the design. Cf. pl. 58.*

drawn using a particularly clear photograph of the silk at the Victoria and Albert Museum (M2157) in conjunction with what I have observed from the remaining sections of pattern on the silk itself in the Monks' Dormitory at Durham Cathedral. See also plates 57 and 58.

On a pastiche of six fragments which make up the Rider silk, two lobed octagonal shapes enclosing a mounted falconer appear. The octagons have pearl edging and are set side by side across the silk. They are separated by a tear-shaped, foliate, decorative motif that also occurs on its side at intervals in the area below the two octagons. Beneath are two horizontal bands of ornament. The upper band with guilloche edging encloses a series of linear ornaments. The lower band shows small hares facing to the left in a repeated series. The falconer within the lobed octagon faces to the left and carries the bird of prey on his raised left arm. He wears a short tunic that reaches just below the knee. His horse has a complicated bridle and decorative trappings that are hung with jewels and studded with pearls. The joints of the limbs of the animal are marked by small circular designs.

The origin of the falconer motif is probably Near Eastern, although the sport itself was known from the fifth century onwards in Byzantium as well as in the Arab and the Latin worlds. The widespread popularity of the sport perhaps explains why falconer scenes were represented in the art of many cultures from an early date.[23] At Argos in the Peloponnese for example, there is a falconer mosaic on the floor of a villa, and this has been dated to *c.*500 on stylistic grounds. In this mosaic it is a small standing figure who carries the falcon. At Klinte Oland on a carved stone the hunter is mounted and further mounted falconers appear on Viking sculptures situated in the north of England.[24] Brett draws particular attention to the iconography of the falconer as it appears on works of art that he considers to be Persian, but the parallels he draws are not always wholly convincing.

Brett describes a series of eight metal plates thought to be Persian, one from Outemilski, one from an unknown site and today lost, the rest from the Perm region. Brett freely admits that there is no firm evidence for dating any of these.[25] He relies on the fact that two were excavated in Central Asian sites to suggest Persian provenance for all eight dishes, but this seems a poor

[23] For a full survey of the early history of the falconer the reader is referred to H. Epstein, 'The Origins and Earliest History of Falconry', *Isis* 34 (1943), pp. 497 – 509. Also see J. C. Harting, *Essays on Sport and Natural History* (London, 1883), and F. M. Allen, *Falconry in Arabia* (London, 1980). There is a valuable discussion in C. Hicks, 'The Bird on the Sutton Hoo Purse', *ASE* 15 (1986), pp. 153 – 65, esp. 162 – 5. The latter author distinguishes between falcons with long wings and hawks with short wings, but for the purpose of this paper I have not tried to determine which was represented on the works of art cited.

[24] Hicks, op. cit., p. 164, notes 54 and 56. She also draws attention to an early example on a Lombardic panel at San Saba in Rome. For the Argos mosaics she mentions see G. Akerstrom-Hougen, 'The Calendar and Hunting Mosaics of the Villa of the Falconer in Argos', *Skrifter utgivna av Svenska institutet i Athen* 23 (1974).

[25] Brett in *Relics*, pp. 47 – 8, pl. 49, figs. 1, 3 – 6 and pl. 48, figs. 1 – 3 with pp. 472 – 3.

argument, as they may be imported works rather than dishes produced locally. No details of the excavations at Outemilski or in the Perm region are discussed to allow the reader to reach a firm conclusion on this question, but quite apart from the lack of circumstantial evidence the iconographic and stylistic parallels that can be drawn between the Durham falconer motif and the falconer designs on the dishes are of little real value. This is because the falconer motif as it appears on the dishes presents a rendering a great deal cruder than that of the motif on the Durham silk. The dishes from the Perm area (figs. 3 and 4 on pl. XLIX in Brett) show very disproportionate and distorted riders on horses rendered as no more than flat 'wooden' creatures. The horses show none of the bridle or decorative trappings found on the Durham falconer design. The falcons held by the hunters on the dishes are portrayed in a scanty manner with none of the detail found on the Durham silk, where individual feathers are indicated. The falconer in figure 5 of Brett's plate XLIX is shown with more detail but the piece is labelled 'provenance and present owner unknown', so there is no information that can help either with date or provenance for the Durham silk. The Outemilski silver dish, now in the Hermitage in Leningrad, is the finest of the dishes (Brett's pl. XLVIII), but even here the proportions of the mounted falconer are different from those on the Durham silk, the rider being much larger than on the silk. Also his falcon appears in profile whereas the bird is shown in three-quarter view on the silk. The decorative trappings on the horse of this silver dish do not specifically show jewels including pearls, and they are unlike those on the Durham silk.

The most significant difference between the Durham and the Outemilski iconography, a point overlooked by Brett, is the fact that only the latter shows a rider with stirrups. There are no stirrups on the design of the silk at Durham. Stirrups were used from the sixth century onwards but it is curious that artists very rarely depicted them on works of art before the thirteenth century. The large group of Byzantine and Islamic hunter silks of the eighth to ninth century, with one exception only, show mounted hunters without stirrups.[26] Stirrups occur only on an imperial Byzantine hunter silk of the eighth century from Mozac, now in the Textile Museum at Lyons.[27] Perhaps the artists thought it would have been inappropriate to show their emperor mounted on a horse without this vital piece of fighting equipment.

[26] The date of the introduction of the stirrup is discussed in detail in L. White, *Medieval Technology and Social Change* (Oxford, 1971), pp. 20ff., p. 144 and n. 5. There are silks patterned with hunter motifs at Sant' Ambrogio, Milan, at Prague Cathedral Library, at St Calais, Sarthe, at St Cunibert, Cologne, at Nuremberg, Germanischesmuseum, at St Ursula, Cologne, at St Fridolin, Säckingen, and at St Servatius, Maastricht. These silks are described and dated in Muthesius, 'Eastern Silks', pp. 131 – 2, 136 – 45. Five of them have been catalogued on pp. 468 and 474 – 9, as nos. 27, and 31 – 4, in a catalogue of 120 silks that appears as an appendix to the thesis.

[27] The Lyons silk came from the church of St Austremoine, Mozac, in 1904. The silk shows a Byzantine emperor as a mounted hunter wearing stirrups. He plunges a spear into the throat of a lion rearing up from below. In 764 the relics of St Austremoine were carefully taken from her burial place at Issoire (Puy de Dôme) to the church of St Calais at Mozac wrapped in a silk donated by Pepin and this bore the royal seal. Bishop Robert of Clermont saw the silk with its seal

Returning to the silver dishes described by Brett, it has to be said that a firmer chronology for the series is required before useful parallels with the Durham silk can be made. Perhaps Brett was misled into comparing some of the cruder dishes with the silk because he worked from the painted photograph of 1888 and here the Durham Rider does have a somewhat crude outline. A falconer silk in the Detroit Institute of Fine Arts (another piece of it is at Columbia Textile museum and a third is housed at the Abegg Stiftung in Bern) is also cited by Brett as a parallel for the Durham Rider silk.[28] This silk does show a stirrup and stylistically as well as technically it belongs no earlier than the late twelfth to early thirteenth century. Before discussing the design on this silk some explanation of its weave is necessary. The Detroit/Columbia/Abegg Falconer silk is woven in what has been termed a *triple weave*.[29] The weave of the Rider silk is *twill* with paired main warps.[30] The triple weave divides the warp into three parts so that three textiles each above the other are produced simultaneously. The three textiles change position as required by the pattern. The twill weave of the Durham Rider silk is typical of eastern Mediterranean silks of the eighth or ninth to twelfth centuries. A twill is a weave based on three or more ends (warp or vertical threads) and three or more adjacent picks (weft or horizontal threads). Each end passes over two or more adjacent picks and under the next one or more, or under two or more adjacent picks and over the next one or more. The twill is termed weft-faced if the ends predominate on the surface of the weave and warp faced if the picks take precedence. The Durham silk is a weft-faced twill. Twills of the Durham type are 'one layer' fabrics, but between the two sides of the textile there are paired vertical threads which do not appear either on the obverse or on the reverse of the fabric. These are called *main warps*. They are indicated in a diagram of twill weave (fig. 29). The main warps were raised or lowered to allow the correct passage of the weft to the front or the back of the textile

in the shrine of St Austremoine on 10 April 1197 at the time of a later 'recognition' of the relics. In 1904 the silk was taken from a seventeenth-century shrine of the saint and sold to the museum at Lyons. There was no sign of the seal at that time, but there is no evidence to show that the silk presented by Pepin was ever subsequently replaced. Stylistically and technically the silk does belong to the eighth century. It acts as a pivot for dating the other hunter silks that survive. The silk and the source material are discussed more fully in Muthesius, 'Eastern Silks', pp. 132 – 5. The silk has more recently appeared in brief catalogue form in M. Martiniani-Reber, *Lyon, Musée Historique des Tissus, soieries sassanides, coptes et byzantines V – XI siècles*, (Paris, 1986) in the series Inventaire des collections publiques françaises, as no. 30. See pp. 109 – 11, no. 96. A review of this publication by the author is published by the Byzantine Institute of the University of Vienna in the *Jahrbuch der österreichischen byzantinistik Gesellschaft* 37 (1987), pp. 399 – 402.
[28] M. Lemberg and B. Schmedding, *Abegg Stiftung Bern in Riggisberg Textilien*, Schweizer Heimatbücher 173/4 (Bern, 1973), page unnumbered and colour plate 10, opposite this.
[29] All definitions used conform to the standard International CIETA format published by the international centre for the study of medieval textiles at Lyon (cf. above, p. 305, n. 5). See *Vocabulary of Technical Terms, Fabrics, English, French, Italian, Spanish* (Lyon, 1964), pp. 14, 52.
[30] Ibid., pp. 52 – 3.

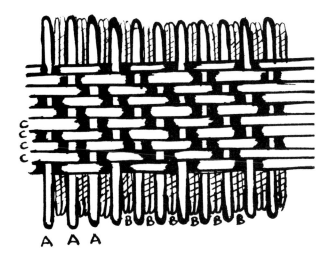

29. *Twill weave with paired main warps. A = Binding warp; B = Paired main wraps; C = Weft.*

according to the requirements of the design. A special pattern-producing device attached to the loom was operated by one or more weaving assistants, and this controlled the main warps.

Double and triple cloths were the speciality of Persian weavers in the middle ages, judging by the extant material.[31] Double cloths are related to triple cloths previously described. Just as triple cloths have three layers above one another, double cloths have two textiles one above the other. An example of a double cloth said to have come from a grave in Teheran is now in the Abegg Stiftung in Bern and this shows a falconer.[32] The latter silk, like the Detroit/Columbia/ Abegg Falconer silk discussed above, shows a mounted falconer with bird depicted in profile. Neither shows the type of three-quarter falcon with outspread wings noted on the Durham Rider silk. The falconers on the Persian examples are unlike the Durham Falconer, in that they wear more elaborate costumes with patterned boots and they are larger in proportion to their horses than is the rider on thé Durham silk. The stirrup appears on both Persian Falconer silks but, as was noted earlier, it does not appear on the Durham silk. The saddle cloths on the Persian silks are heavily patterned and they are large saddles in comparison to the small, unpatterned saddle of the Durham Rider silk. The treatment of individual features of the Persian horses differs from that found on the Durham Rider silk. For example, the tail of the

[31] The Persian material as a whole has been studied by P. Ackermann, *Survey of Persian Art* I (London and New York, 1938), section 10, chapter 52 ('Textiles of the Islamic Periods'), pp. 2033 ff., for example nos. 20, 21, 29, 30, 31 for double and triple cloths.
[32] M. Lemberg and B. Schmedding, op. cit., page unnumbered and coloured plate 9 opposite this.

horse on the Durham silk is tied but left to hang whereas on the Persian piece the horses' tails are tied up high. The entire setting of the falconer scene is different on the Persian silks from the setting of the Durham Rider silk. The lobed octagons filled with the falconer motif on the Durham silk contrast with the paired falconers that mirror image one another about a central tree motif on the Persian silks. The Persian triple cloth has an octagonal border but it is not of the lobed type found at Durham. The Persian double cloth places the whole scene in an irregular, angular geometric border, quite unlike what is found on the Durham silk. The elaborate foliage that accompanies the scenes on the Persian silks finds no counterpart on the Durham silk.

The iconography and style of the Persian Falconer silks described above is not close enough to conclude that either has a direct bearing on the date or provenance of the Durham silk. Indeed, a not inconsiderable number of so-called Persian silks at the Abegg Foundation have been tested and it is believed that traces of nineteenth-century anilin dye have been found on them, so that some authorities have declared them to be forgeries.[33]

Parallels for the falconer iconography outside Persia are not hard to find. For example, there is a splendid vestment with embroidered falconer motifs at Bamberg Cathedral treasury, which is thought to be Byzantine work of the eleventh century.[34] Here the crowned Byzantine emperor holds a falcon shown in three-quarter view with its wings outspread. The bird on the Durham silk is in the same pose. The pearled and jewelled trappings of the imperial horse bring to mind those on the Durham silk and the small dog shown on the Bamburg embroidery in the area in front of the fore-legs of the horse finds a parallel on the Durham silk. Although the dog is a feature hard to see with the naked eye on the silk itself in its present state of conservation, it has been painted on the photograph at the Victoria and Albert Museum (1626 – 1888) and it must have been more visible in 1888 when the photograph was taken. On the Durham silk the hunting dog appears in the area between the fore and the hind legs of the horse. On a Spanish embroidery in Fermo the falconer with his hunting dog appears in a number of slightly differing versions, each in some way comparable to the falconer motif of the Durham silk. Indeed the art of Spain furnishes many close parallels for the Durham falconer iconography.[35]

---

[33] M. Fleury-Lemberg has argued that the silks are forgeries but D. Shepherd has replied that she remains unconvinced in spite of the scientific findings. See a variety of discussions in *CIETA Bulletin* 37 (1973), pp. 28 – 54, 70 – 117, 120 – 33 and 143 – 5.
[34] In 1127 fifteen embroidered silk chasubles were extant in the treasury at Bamberg Cathedral. Today several examples survive in the Diocesan Museum, Bamburg. See S. Müller-Christensen, *Sakrale Gewänder* (Munich, 1955), nos. 18 – 25. The Emperor Henry II (d.1024) and Queen Cunigunde were the prinicpal patrons at Bamberg. See Muthesius, 'Eastern Silks', pp. 329 – 32 on this point.
[35] See D. Storm Rice, 'The Fermo Chasuble of St. Thomas à Becket (d.1170) revealed as the Earliest Fully Dated and Localised Major Islamic Embroidery Known', *Illustrated London News* 225 (3 October, 1959), pp. 356 – 8.

The elaborately embroidered chasuble at Fermo has an inscription that says it was made in Almeira in 1116. The significance of Almeira as a silk-weaving centre of Spain will be discussed more fully below as a conclusion to this article. At present it is sufficient to point out the close iconographic and stylistic similarities between this Spanish piece and the Durham Rider silk. Both the printed silk and the embroidered piece have designs that give the impression of being almost 'cut out' of a precious gold metal. The riders on the embroidery as on the silk are in proportion to their horses, and these are sturdy creatures like the Durham Rider silk's horse. The falconers in all cases wear short tunics and show no sign of having stirrups. They carry their birds of prey in their left hands. The Fermo falcons are nevertheless shown in profile and not in three-quarter pose as on the Durham silk. The lobed octagonal setting of the Durham silk cannot be paralleled on the Fermo chasuble either. The embroidery is set with interlinking medallions. Another Spanish embroidery less refined in style, with the falconer set in lobed octagons, came from St Lazare in Autun, and on stylistic grounds it has been dated to the eleventh century.[36] This embroidery shows a mounted falconer wearing a short tunic and a pointed hat. His falcon appears in profile and he holds a stick in one hand. His horse has a distorted and over-elongated, thickly set body and head, and it wears jewelled, decorative trappings like those of the Durham Rider silk.

The most convincing parallels for the 'falconer in lobed octagonal setting' iconography that I have discovered so far are on a series of tenth- to eleventh-century Spanish ivory caskets. These are particularly valuable works of art to use for comparative purposes because they are precisely datable through their various inscriptions. The inscriptions also suggest where some were made. One of these caskets is in Pamplona Cathedral treasury and its inscription proves that it was made for Abd al-Malik, son of al-Mansur, in 1104 – 5.[37] Another of these caskets, today in the Victoria and Albert Museum, London (368 – 1880), was made for Ziyad ibn Aflah, the prefect of police at Cordoba in 969 – 70.[38] A third casket with the falconer iconography was made for the prince al-Mughira, son of the caliph Abd al-Rahman III, in 968, and this today is in the Louvre Museum in Paris.[39] All three caskets portray a mounted falconer carrying a bird of prey on his raised left arm. The bird appears in strict profile on the Ziyad ibn Aflah casket but it is turned towards the spectator on the other two caskets and the wings are extended instead of at rest, particularly on the casket made for Prince al-Mughira in 968. There were probably two iconographical traditions for the pose of the falcon, one that showed the bird in profile with wings at rest and the other that showed a three-

---

[36] E. Baer, 'The Suaire de St Lazare: An Early Datable Hispano-Islamic Embroidery', *Oriental Art* n.s. 13 (1967), pp. 36 – 49.
[37] J. Beckwith, *Caskets from Cordoba* (London, 1960), p. 61, pl. 23.
[38] Ibid., pls. 20 – 21 on pp. 58 – 9.
[39] Ibid., pp. 54 – 5, pls. 16 and 17.

quarter view with wings outspread. These two types of bird are found on Byzantine examples of the falconer iconography. The falcon with outspread wings is seen on the embroidered chasuble at Bamberg Cathedral, which has already been described. A falcon in profile with lowered wings occurs on a Byzantine enamel plaque, stylistically datable to the early eleventh century. This plaque is from the Pala d'Oro at St Mark's in Venice.[40]

The actual placing of the falconer motif in the lobed octagons is very similar on the Durham Rider silk and on the Spanish ivory caskets under discussion. In both cases the rider fills up the entire octagon, the bird's head touching one of the edges of the lobed structure itself. On the caskets as on the silk the rider is rendered in proportion to his mount. The horses of the caskets and of the Durham Rider silk are close in type, with sturdy bodies and thick-set necks and they are similarly decorated with ornamental jewelled trappings. The extensive mane combed down over the neck of the horse on the Louvre casket and its looped, hanging tail are features particularly closely comparable with the Durham Rider silk. On the Durham silk and the caskets alike the riders themselves wear short tunics and do not have stirrups.

The Spanish ivory caskets are intimately connected with the caliphs of the Umayyad house of southern Spain. The Louvre casket was made for the son of the Umayyad caliph Abd al-Rahman III (929 – 61) in 968 in a palace workshop of Cordoba, according to its inscription. The casket of the prefect of police in the Victoria and Albert Museum has an inscription that yields a date of 969 – 70 for its manufacture, but Beckwith assigned this piece not to a court workshop, but to a commercial workshop of Cordoba, basing his view on the fact that the style of the carvings is coarser than that of the royal caskets.[41] He also noted that the scene on the casket showing the sovereign enthroned on a divan and surrounded by attendants was an adaptation of a Persian scene familar on Sassanian metalwork. The concept of Persian influence in Spain is interesting in the light of Brett's attribution of the Durham Rider silk to Persia. Might it not be argued that the Persian elements detected by Brett represent no more than Persian influence in Spain? Indeed several authors have pointed to specific Persian influences in Spain not least in silk weaving workshops themselves. Certainly Spanish weavers were not above falsely attributing to Baghdad the silks that they wove locally. No doubt Persia had its tradition of falconer iconography, as demonstrated by the appearance of this motif, albeit in somewhat crude form on the tenth-century pottery dishes of Nishapur, but neither Persian plates nor Persian silks provide as convincing a parallel for the Durham Rider motif as do the designs of the Spanish ivory caskets under discussion.[42] The Victoria and Albert Museum casket and the

---

[40] K. Wessel, *Byzantine Enamels* (Shannon, Ireland, 1969), pp. 149 – 50 and fig. 46 v – x, on p. 151.

[41] Beckwith, op. cit., pp. 20 – 1.

[42] Considerable Persian iconographic influence is noticeable on a number of Spanish silks. Moreover, an elephant silk from Leon, inscribed 'Made in Baghdad', has been shown to belong

Louvre caskets were made in Cordoba and the possibility of the Durham silk being made in a workshop of that city will be discussed more fully below.[43]

The technique of the Durham Rider silk cannot be closely examined whilst the silk remains under glass but it has been thought by Brett that the gold was printed onto a resinous base. Accepting that this is so it must be said that few gold printed silks of any kind survive, although the technique was known in ancient times in China and later in Persia, in Egypt and elsewhere. In China a splendid silk garment decorated in 'gold and silver dust' came from a Han tomb datable between 193 and 141 BC at Changsha. The funerary ornaments from the tomb recorded the family name Tai, and three generations of this family are recorded between the dates 193 – 141 BC. Unfortunately, the silk is only scantily published.[44] At Astana seventh- to eighth-century block printed silks were excavated.[45] There is a literary reference to printed stuffs from Tabaristan dated 1025, as Brett remarked, and there are printed silks from the Cave of the Thousand Buddhas at Tun-huang, walled up in the early eleventh century.[46] In Coptic Egypt resist-dye techniques incorporated printing on

to Spain itself. The inscription was probably intended to add false value to the piece. See A. F. Kendrick and A. Guest, 'A Silk Fabric Woven at Baghdad', *Burlington Magazine* 49 (1926), pp. 261 – 7. Cf. F. May, *Silk Textiles of Spain* (New York, 1957), p. 24, and fig. 14. Also C. D. Shepherd, 'A Dated Hispano-Islamic Silk', *Ars Orientalis* 2 (1957), p. 380. She makes relevant notes also in 'The Hispano-Islamic Textiles in the Cooper Union Collection', *Chronicle of the Museum for the Arts of the Cooper Union* 1, no. 10 (Dec. 1943), pp. 357 – 401, especially p. 365. See F. Day, 'The Inscription of the Boston Baghdad Silk', *Ars Orientalis* 1 (1954), pp. 190 – 4, especially pp. 190 – 1. A pottery bowl from Nishapur is shown in D. Talbot-Rice, *Islamic Art* (Norwich, 1975), pp. 51 – 2, pl. 43.

[43] May, op. cit., pp. 5, 11. The first *tiraz* silk weaving factory in Spain, weaving fabrics with official inscriptions, was established in Cordoba. The founder of the first factory may have been Abd al-Rahman II (821 – 52), although this is not documented. Certainly, the factory is documented at the time of Abd al-Rahman III (912 – 61) and the page Khalaf the elder, a court official, was in charge of it. May gives the source for this information on p. 250 in note 11. Fine *tiraz* silks of Cordoba are documented in the tenth century and described also in the 1090s. See May, op. cit., p. 9, note. 7.

[44] The Chinese finds have been published only very summarily in a booklet with unnumbered pages and without named editor called *New Archaeological finds in China* (Peking, 1974). Here a section of coloured plates of finds from the tomb of Magwangtui Changsha is included. The garment in question is a long-sleeved gown with a cross-over front. The body of the gown, which seems to reach well below the knees, is a deep pink silk. On the cuff, neck and lower hem areas is a golden yellow silk. Both the pink and the golden yellow silks appear to be decorated in gold and silver with a small repeating geometric motif. A detail of the design on the pink silk shows small swirling circular motifs representing clouds. The silver looks dark due to oxidization. The author speaks of 'painted' cloud design.

[45] For printed and other silks found in Central Asia see in particular the work of Sir Aurel Stein, including *Serindia* (Oxford, 1921) and *Innermost Asia* (Oxford, 1928). Brett, op. cit., p. 480, refers to printed silks described in *Innermost Asia*, on pp. 672 ff., pls. 82, 86, 88, cf. p. 618, pl. 82. For trading and other links between China and Central Asia see J. Needham's foreword to *Silk Roads, China Ships: An Exhibition of East-West Trade*, Royal Ontario Museum (Toronto, 1984), esp. pp. 26 – 44. On the silk road from ancient times there is interesting information in H. Uhlig, *Die Seidenstrasse: Antike Weltkultur zwischen China und Rom* (Bergisch Gladbach, 1986), pp. 72 – 101. Also I. Franck and D. Brownstone, *The Silk Road* (New York, 1986), pp. 59 ff.

[46] Brett, op. cit., p. 480. The silks from the caves were published by Stein, *Serindia*, pp. 901 ff. and 986 ff.

occasion.[47] There is one enigmatic printed medieval fabric from Halberstadt Cathedral with a peculiar iconography showing a figure being carried aloft by an eagle. Lessing identified the subject with a scene from the legend of Ganymede and assigned the piece to sixth- to seventh-century Sassanian Persia. Herzfeld and Migeon also drew parallels with Persian subject matter and Migeon agreed with Lessing that the fabric was a Sassanian textile. However, it may be profitable to compare the printed Halberstadt piece with a silk of the Cluny Museum (21.872) showing a prince carried aloft by an eagle, as Ackermann has done more recently. In style and technique the latter silk cannot be seen as a Sassanian piece and it and the Halberstadt fabric probably belong to the eleventh to twelfth century rather than earlier. Persian provenance has been suggested by Ackermann for the Cluny silk on technical and stylistic grounds but whether the Halberstadt piece was printed in Persia or in a centre under Persian influence remains to be seen.[48]

The actual weave of the Durham Rider silk, a paired main warp twill, is not useful for fine dating of the piece, for as discussed earlier twills of this nature were widely woven from the ninth to the twelfth century. Nevertheless, the pairing of the main warp as opposed to the use of single main warp should be noted as a development of the eighth to ninth century and it may be linked to a desire for weaving more complex patterns on wider looms when additional strengthening of these warps would be required.[49]

A final point on technique is that Brett noted uncertainties in the printing on the Durham Rider silk. He concluded that the silk was a pre-Seljuk piece, bearing 'all the marks of an experiment by a provincial craftsman in an unaccustomed technique'.[50] Such a conclusion would accord equally well with the hypothesis that the silk was produced in Spain in the tenth to eleventh century at a time when in all probability the technique of silk printing was a new introduction. It was most probably added to the relics of St Cuthbert at the time of the translation in 1104.

---

[47] Coptic textiles in the wax-resist technique were sometimes hand-painted, sometimes printed. For explanation of the technique and further information see V. Illgen, 'Zweifarbige reservetechnisch eingefärbte Leinenstoffe mit grossfigurigen biblischen Darstellungen aus Ägypten' (Inaugural Dissertation, J. Gutenberg, Universität, Mainz, 1968), pp. 59 – 62 ('Die Technik und Formgebung des Reservauftrages') with bibliography on pp. 80 – 2.

[48] The Halberstadt fabric was described by J. Lessing, 'Mittelalterliche Zeugdrucke im Kunstgewerbemuseum zu Berlin', *Jahrbuch der königlich preussischen Kunstsammlungen* 1 (1880), pp. 119 – 24. Cf. E. Herzfeld, 'Der Thron der Khosro', in the same periodical, 41 (1920), pp. 132 – 3, fig. 28. Also G. Migeon, *Les arts du tissu* (Paris, 1929), p. 20. See Ackermann, op. cit., p. 2014, fig. 649 for Cluny Museum (21.872).

[49] There were five main weaving types before 1200. These were tabby (also with extra pattern floats), damask, twill, lampas and tapestry weaves. These are defined and illustrated in Muthesius, 'Eastern Silks', Appendix A ('Weaving types'), pp. 357 – 62. The significance of the different groupings of the main warps in twills, whether singly, in pairs (gummed or degummed), and in threes to fours, is explained fully there.

[50] Brett, op. cit., p. 482.

2. THE PEACOCK SILK (pls. 59 – 60)

The design on the Peacock silk is woven rather than printed and for this reason it has survived more clearly than that of the Rider silk. Even so it is helpful to refer to a nineteenth-century drawing of the Department of Textiles in the Victoria and Albert Museum, London.[51] The colours of the Peacock silk, now all but faded to brownish tones, were originally blue, red, and yellow so that the overall effect must have been quite brilliant. The silk has a frontal view of double-headed peacocks as its motif. These nimbed birds are set in oval shapes with pairs of seated griffins in the interspaces. Flanagan, who published an account of the silk in 1956, freely admitted that there was little evidence for assigning a date or provenance to it. On grounds of its stylistic affinities with Byzantine silks, especially those of the eleventh century, he was inclined to regard it as a Byzantine silk woven at that period. The occurrence of a pseudo-Kufic inscription on the breasts of the peacocks (pl. 60) seemed to corroborate this insofar as it seemed to him to make an Islamic provenance unlikely.[52] In fact both pseudo-Kufic and legible Kufic inscriptions occur on Byzantine as well as Islamic works of art as several authors have demonstrated.[53] Also, I have found pseudo-Kufic inscriptions on silk from the tomb of Archbishop Hubert Walter (d.1205) at Canterbury Cathedral Chapter Library, and this stylistically and technically belongs with an extensive group of twelfth- to thirteenth-century Spanish silks.[54]

Iconographically speaking there are only two silks that can be compared with the Durham Peacock silk and both can be shown to be Spanish (see fig. 30). Only on these two silks are double-headed peacocks depicted. They are:

i. a Peacock silk from the grave of Alfonso VII, king of Castile (1126 – 57), at Toledo;[55]

ii. a Peacock silk fragment in the Museum of Historical Textiles in Lyons, probably from the larger Peacock silk in the parish church of Thuir in the French Pyrenees.[56]

On both silks the double-headed birds clasp captive gazelles in their talons and distinctive ogee foliate motifs occur between rows of the design. It is a

---

[51] Victoria and Albert Museum 425 – 1887. I wish to thank L. Wooley for kindly making this and other photos available to me.

[52] *Relics*, pp. 513 – 25, especially pp. 514 and 516. I am indebted to Dr Bivar of the School of Oriental and African Studies, University of London, for his advice concerning the inscription on the Durham Peacock silk. He considers that this is a pseudo-Kufic inscription and it cannot be read.

[53] See, for example, S. D. T. Spittle, 'Cufic Lettering in Christian Art', *Archaeological Journal* 111 (1955), pp. 138 – 52.

[54] A. Muthesius, 'The Silks from the Tomb', in *Medieval Art and Architecture at Canterbury before 1220*, ed. N. Coldstream and P. Draper (British Archaeological Association; London, 1982), pp. 81 – 7, pls. 18 – 23.

[55] M. Gomez-Moreno, *Ars Hispaniae: Historia universal del arte Hispánico* (Madrid, 1951), pp. 350 – 1, fig. 408b.

[56] May, op. cit., pp. 41 – 2, 45, pl. 27.

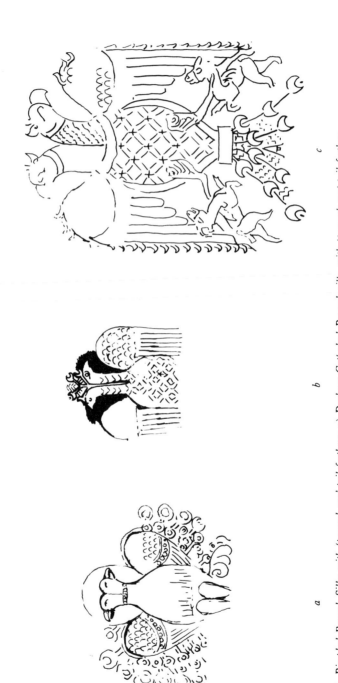

c

b

a

30. *Bicephal Peacock Silks with 'peacock eye' tail feathers: a) Durham Cathedral Peacock silk, with 'peacock eye' tail feathers surrounding the bird's body; b) Silk from the tomb of Alfonso VII, Toledo Cathedral, showing 'peacock eye' feathers in tail held above heads of the birds; c) Lyons, Musée Historique des Tissus and Thuir parish chruch, showing 'peacock eye' feathers in tail.*

characteristic 'peacock eye' tail feather which marks out the double-headed birds on the two silks as peacocks. This feather occurs above the heads of the birds on the Toledo silk as if the tail is held up. On the Lyons/Thuir silk the distinctive 'peacock eye' tail feathers appear on the extensive tail which is extended down below the body of the bird. These feathers have small circular eye markings. On the Durham Peacock silk the peacock tail is fanned out and forms a semi-circular shape encompassing the bird. The 'peacock eye' tail feathers are very prominent and the small circular eyes of the feathers are joined together by narrow shafts representing the spines of the feathers. The 'peacock eye' tail feathers on the Toledo and the Lyons/Thuir silks have been quite overlooked by textile historians so that these birds have incorrectly been identified as eagles.

The fact that the Toledo and the Lyons/Thuir silks were found on or near Spanish soil suggests they may well be locally woven pieces. This idea is supported by the fact that they belong to an extensive group of silks, found chiefly on Spanish soil, which display a peculiarly Spanish iconography. The group of silks to which they belong has as the design motif double-headed eagles (the tail feathers are oblong without the 'peacock eye' marking) and these birds of prey clasp captive gazelles in their talons. Amongst silks of the group are the following pieces:

a. A silk from the reliquary of the early Christian martyr St Librada at Siguenza;[57]

b. a silk from the shrine of St Anno (d.1075), whose relics were translated into a splendid twelfth-century shrine at St Servatius, Siegburg;
and closely related:

c. a silk of the Kunstgewerbemuseum, West Berlin (1881-474a and b);[58]

d. a silk today lost, once at Quedlinburg Cathedral, formerly Berlin (1882-1170).[59]

All these silks are woven in what is called a lampas weave with 'tabby, tabby' binding. This weave has been defined by the CIETA association as one 'used exclusively for figured textiles in which a pattern, composed of weft floats bound by a binding warp, is added to a ground fabric formed by a main warp and a main weft.' On the silks under discussion the ground is tabby weave and the wefts forming the pattern are bound by the ends of the binding warp in a

---

[57] Ibid., p. 39 and pl. 25 on p. 40.

[58] For the Siegburg piece see *Monumenta Annonis: Köln und Sieburg, Weltbild und Kunst im hohen Mittelalter*, Schnütgen Museum, Köln 30 April – 27 July 1975 (Köln, 1975), pp. 180 – 1 and fig. 22d (J. M. Plötzek, 'Textilfragmente aus Siegburger Schreinen'). Here an Islamic inscription on the Siegburg silk is translated 'Praise to the birth of Allah'. Also, P. Schmölz, *Der siegburger Servatius Schatz*, (Köln, 1952), p. 28, pl. 43. Both the Siegburg and the Berlin silks are in O. von Falke, *Kunstgeschichte der Seidenweberei* (Berlin, 1921 edition), figs. 155 – 6. In *Monumenta* the Siegburg silk is called 'perhaps Sicilian', but Schmölz prefers Spanish provenance for the piece. Neither Plötzek nor Schmölz cite iconographic parallels to support their views. Plötzek talks of 'Fatimid influence in Sicily'.

[59] May, op. cit., pp. 39 – 40, pl. 26.

tabby binding that is supplementary to the ground weave. Shepherd has brought together about fifty-five silks of this weave, of which she has published some fourteen examples and she calls them Spanish lampas weave silks on the basis of circumstantial, technical, stylistic, and iconographic evidence.[60]

The Spanish lampas weave silks that Shepherd described do not have bird and gazelle motifs exclusively. A great variety of designs including paired quadrupeds and foliate ornament are amongst the designs on the silks. Detailed publication of the 'double-headed eagle clasping gazelle' motif silks themselves has still to be made. Certainly Shepherd would assign these to Spain. Grönwoldt considers that the silk from the tomb of Peter Lombard (d.1160 or 1164) from St Marcel, Paris, now Cluny Museum (no. 13 286), a 'tabby, tabby' lampas weave silk with free-standing bird and free-standing gazelle motifs as well as foliate ogees, belongs with the group, but she is unwilling to commit herself to definite provenance for the silk.[61] Without drawing specific stylistic or iconographic parallels Plötzek suggests that the Siegburg 'double-headed eagle clasping gazelle' silk is a Sicilian piece, and perhaps this view was influenced by the presence of a bird and gazelle 'tabby, tabby' lampas weave silk in the tomb of Henry VI at Palermo (now British Museum, Department of Medieval and Later Antiquities 78,9-7, 4).[62] However, the latter silk, like the Peter Lombard silk described by Grönwoldt, shows only free-standing birds and free-standing gazelles and does not directly belong to the 'double-headed eagle grasping gazelle group'. The birds are not only free-standing on those silks but they have only one head. The evidence for Sicilian silk weaving is in any event problematic through there being a distinct lack of silks that can definitely or even reasonably be proved to have come from Sicily.

Only one silk, a brocaded twill fabric in the Kestner Museum Hanover (inv. 3875), can be reasonably proved to come from twelfth-century Sicily.[63]

---

[60] For 'lampas' see *Vocabulary of Technical Terms*, p. 28; for 'tabby', see p. 48. Consult Shepherd, *Ars Orientalis* 2, pp. 373 ff. for the Spanish lampas weave silks.

[61] R. Grönwoldt, 'Kaisergewänder und Paramente', in *Die Zeit der Staufer* (2 vols.; Stuttgart, 1977), I, no. 791 on pp. 627 – 8, and II, pl. 576.

[62] Plötzek, op. cit., p. 180. For the Palermo silk, see Grönwoldt, op. cit, in *Die Zeit der Staufer*, I, no. 776 on pp. 617 – 18, and II, pl. 567.

[63] For the Hanover textile (inv. 3875) see ibid., I, no. 780 on pp. 621 – 2, and pl. 571. Textile historians have put forward the view that Sicily specifically imported Spanish silks. See for example, F. Torrella Niubo, 'Problèmes posés par l'étude des tissus hispano-arabes', *CIETA Bulletin* 30 (1969), pp. 20 – 2. The author has read information from unpublished Spanish sources, but these are not specifically cited. Inventories and royal accounts of the houses of Catalonia and Aragon are said to yield much information about Hispano-Arab textiles. His prime concern is to show problems in using the term Hispano-Arab. Should this refer only to silks of Moslem southern Spain, and should silks related in style and technique thought to have been woven in the Christian north of Spain, whether by 'imported' Islamic or by Mozarab craftsmen, be given a different name? See also F. Volbach, 'Étoffes espagnoles du moyen-age et leur rapport avec Palerme et Byzance', *CIETA Bulletin* 30 (1969), pp. 23 – 5. Volbach also states that Spain imported Sicilian silks but cites no source references.

This fragmentary silk shows part of a medallion design with paired rearing quadrupeds, perhaps lions. It has a Latin inscription that reads 'made in a workshop of the realm' and this has been identified as the workshop of Roger II, established in Palermo in 1147 using Greek weavers captured in Athens, Thebes, and Corinth and probably also employing native Islamic silk weavers. The Hanover silk is quite distinct from other twelfth-century twills in its use of pale pastel shades, mainly light blue and purple. In no way does it bring to mind either the Durham Peacock silk or the Peacock silks of the lampas group studied by Shepherd. Serjeant has brought together the documentary evidence for silk weaving in Sicily and there was certainly much silk weaving in Palermo. There was an Islamic state weaving factory in Palermo in 978, and the first Latin silk weaving workshop was established by Roger II in the same city after his capture of the city in 1147. The city is further documented as having an Islamic *tiraz* factory in 1184.[64] The problem is that none of the silks woven there or elsewhere on the island were described in sufficient detail for surviving silks to be called Sicilian on the basis of their designs. On the available evidence there is no reason to assign the 'tabby, tabby' lampas weave silks to Sicily rather than to Spain, especially as the 'eagle grasping gazelle' motif is found on dated Spanish works of art. For instance it occurs on a marble basin in the Museo Arqueológico Nacional in Madrid, which came from Medina az Zahira, and which has an inscription that indicates it was made for Almanzor, the minister of Caliph Hisham II of Cordoba in 987 – 88.[65]

Single-headed peacocks are of course a common motif in all media from an early date. Examples are preserved: at San Vitale in Ravenna; on different pieces of Sassanian metalwork; on a seventh- to eighth-century Eastern Mediterranean silk at Aachen Cathedral; on a twelfth-century silk perhaps Islamic at Canterbury Cathedral; and on a tenth- to eleventh-century silk, perhaps Byzantine, at the Abegg Stiftung in Bern. The latter silk has been compared to the magnificent Byzantine Eagle silks at Auxerre and Brixen, which can be dated around 1000 on stylistic grounds.[66] In Spain a good

---

[64] The most systematic examination of Islamic sources was undertaken by R. B. Serjeant, 'Material for a History of Islamic Textiles up to the Mongol Conquest', which appeared as a series of chapters in different volumes of *Ars Islamica* 9 (1942), pp. 54 – 92, 10 (1943), pp. 71 – 104, 11 – 12 (1944 – 6), pp. 98 – 145, 15 – 16 (1951), pp. 29 – 85. Of this material specific references to Sicily with full references to source material are in chapter 19, vols. 15 – 16, pp. 55 – 6, under the heading 'Sicily'. Serjeant writes that according to Ibn Djubair, writing in the 1180s, Sicily traded with Spain. See Ibn Djubair, *Voyage en Sicile*, text and translation by Mamari in *Journal Asiatique* 19 (1845), pp. 35 ff.

[65] May, op. cit., p. 41, fig. 28 and p. 45.

[66] For San Vitale see coloured plate in S. Bettini, 'Les mosaiques de Ravenne à Saint-Vital', *Chefs d'Oeuvre de l'Art*, no. 10 (Paris, 1969), p. 23. For Sassanian metalwork see the exhibition catalogue, *Sassanian Silver* (University of Michigan Museum of Art, 1967), foreword by H. Sawyer; 'Historical Survey' by M. Carter on pp. 11 – 17; 'Introduction to Sassanian Silver' by O. Grabar on pp. 19 – 84; see also no. 42, pp. 126 – 7. Sassanian metalwork is difficult to date because museums tend to have no records of where the pieces were excavated or from where they came.

example of the frontal peacock, albeit without nimbus, occurs on one of the caskets discussed earlier in connection with the Durham Rider silk. This is the Louvre casket, which was made for the Prince al-Mughira, son of the Caliph Abd al-Rahman III in 968. This peacock is situated in an upper spandrel between lobed octagons of the casket. It is particularly close to the Durham Peacock silk motif in that it has a fanned-out tail that makes a large semi-circle enclosing the entire bird. Also the manner of depicting the 'peacock eye' feathers on the silk and on the ivory is very close. Circular patterns are joined by narrow shafts that represent the spine of the feathers both on the ivory and on the silk.[67] Apart from the lack of nimbus and second head the peacock on the Spanish casket is a perfect parallel for the Durham Peacock silk. I should like to propose that the weaver or weavers of the Durham Peacock silk followed an iconography that was an amalgamation of the frontal peacock with the double-headed eagle type, and that the development of the double-headed peacock motif was an essentially Spanish phenomenon. There is no sign from surviving works of art that the double-headed peacock was a type known in antiquity which had been transmitted down the ages.

The dating of the Durham Peacock silk must in part rely on the terminus ad quem of 1104, set by the fact that the coffin-reliquary does not seem to have been re-opened after the translation of the relics at that date. A late eleventh-century date for the Durham silk is not unacceptable, if one sees it as a silk added to the relics for the translation in 1104, but the presence of a thirteenth-century ring amongst the relics must open up the possibility that there was an undocumented thirteenth-century 'recognition' at Durham.[68] If further evidence should come to light in support of this idea, it would be possible to consider that the Durham Peacock silk might have been made later in the twelfth century. The question of where exactly it could have been woven forms the subject of my conclusion below.

Stylistic and iconographic evidence is used to date most pieces. The sculptures of Tak-i-Bustan showing Sassanian emperors prove useful for parallels. The sculptures were published by E. Herzfeld, *Am Tor von Asien* (Berlin, 1920), esp. figs. 32 – 43. The Sassanian silver with peacock Grabar admits is unusual, op. cit., p. 70. He assigns it to Sassanian Iran and suggests it may post-date the fall of the Sassanian Empire in 651 (Sassanian traditions were preserved in areas in the north of Iran for a considerable time before the coming of Islam, according to Carter, op. cit., pp. 16 – 17). See also Grimme, op. cit., no. 14 on pp. 20 – 21. Grimme has followed Falke's term 'Antinoë silks' as appeared in his *Kunstgeschichte* (2 vols.; 1913 edition), I, 35 – 6. Silks found in graves excavated at Antinoë, Falke dated to the 6th century. The Antinoë theory has fallen out of favour. Silks excavated there could anyway have been imported. For further discussion see A. Muthesius, 'Eastern Silks', pp. 174 – 5. This type of silk was probably produced in several centres of the Eastern Mediterranean simultaneously in the seventh to eighth century. For the Canterbury piece see Robinson and Urquhart, op. cit., pp. 182 – 4, pl. 55, fig. 2. The Abegg silk comes from Beromünster. See Schmedding, op. cit., no. 13, pp. 27 – 8 with colour plate. For the Byzantine eagle silks at Auxerre and Brixen see Muthesius, 'Eastern Silks', pp. 63 – 7. These date around 1000 on stylistic and technical grounds.

[67] Beckwith, *Caskets from Cordoba*, p. 55, pl. 17 and pp. 16 – 20.
[68] The ring with further references is discussed in *Relics*, pp. 85 – 6.

CONCLUSION

Assigning any textile provenance without the evidence of a woven inscription is difficult. In the case of the Durham Rider silk the close stylistic and iconographic parallels found with ivories from Cordoba makes it tempting to think that the Rider silk was made in a workshop of that city in the tenth to eleventh century. The Peacock silk, an eleventh- to twelfth-century fabric, may have been woven elsewhere. Serjeant has brought together the main references to silk weaving in Spain, which may be briefly considered here.[69] The origin of the state weaving factory or *tiraz* that produced inscribed silks, largely for distribution to distinguished civil servants, Serjeant saw as Persian. References to *tiraz* workshops in Spain under the Umayyads occur first in Ibn Khaldun (1332 – 1406), but the earliest such workshop was probably established in Cordoba under Abd al-Rahman I in 821. It certainly flourished there under Abd al-Rahman III (912 – 61) and May has found fine *tiraz* of Cordoba listed in a Portuguese document of 1090.[70] Sometimes *tiraz* robes of honour were presented to Christian princes who were guests in Cordoba during the time of the Umayyads. May cites the example of Ordono IV, King of Leon, Asturias and Galicia, at the court of al-Hakam II in 962, who received a tunic of 'gold tissue'. It is particularly interesting to note that in 970 the embassy of the count of Barcelona, Borrell I, to the caliph of Cordoba saw the exchange of silk gifts. Borrell presented beautiful silk clothes to the caliph and the latter gave sumptuous Cordoban silks to the Spanish ambassador on his return home in 971.[71] Evidently there was plenty of scope for the transmission of Cordoban artistic influence in Spain.

By the eleventh century Cordoba was no longer the leading silk weaving city of Spain. Almeira in particular had risen in prominence and silks were exported from Almeira to Christian countries. The Fermo chasuble mentioned above was a product of Almeira in 1116 and may well have reached Italy by way of trade. Otherwise it might have been captured as booty and later transported abroad when Almeira fell to the Christians in 1147. Shepherd has postulated that the 'tabby, tabby' lampas weave silks described above may have been woven in Almeira in the eleventh to twelfth century. This seems a possible centre also for the weaving of the Durham Peacock silk. There were *tiraz* factories at Basta, Finyana, Seville and Malaga, and Toledo had silk weavers, although there are not many references to the types of silk woven there.

In conjunction with the other silks discovered in the coffin-reliquary of St Cuthbert the Rider and the Peacock silks demonstrate the acquisition of impressive textiles, both Byzantine and Islamic, over a period spanning six centuries or more. The presence of an imperial Byzantine example, the

---

[69] Serjeant, *Ars Islamica* 15 – 16, pp. 29 – 40 ('Textiles and the *Tiraz* in Spain'), esp. pp. 34, 35, 37, 40.
[70] May, op. cit., p. 9 and n. 15 for source reference.
[71] Ibid., p. 9 and n. 17 for source reference.

Nature Goddess silk, which could have arrived only as a diplomatic gift, for such silks were forbidden to be exported, emphasizes the royal and other aristocratic patronage that the relics of St Cuthbert attracted. This silk at least must have been donated by a royal patron, who had received it as a gift from Byzantium.[72] The silks at Durham pay homage to the reverence in which the relics of St Cuthbert were held, and as magnificent works of art in their own right they deserve far greater attention than they have thus far received. The silks at Durham are truly amongst the most impressive medieval textiles to survive in Europe.[73]

WEAVE AND SIZE OF REPEAT ON THE DURHAM RIDER AND PEACOCK SILKS

Both silks are under glass and the lighting in the Monks' Dormitory, where the silks are housed, does not allow for a thorough technical analysis of the fabrics. Details that can be fairly accurately gauged only appear here. It is hoped a full technical analysis as recommended by CIETA may be made at a later stage if the silks are remounted.

Rider silk

Six fragments stuck down together measuring 87 x 62 cm (w. × l.)
Weave — Paired main warp twill 1.2, (Direction S)
Warps   1 binding, Z, silk, yellow.
            2 main, Z, silk, yellow.
Wefts Little twist, single, yellow, silk.
Selvedge 3 cord, linen.
Width of pattern repeat including lobed border 39 cm (31.5 + 7.5cm)
Length of repeat of hares 6 cm.
Width of border strip with guilloche edging 7.5 cm. Length of geometric repeat within this border *c*.11.5 cm.

Peacock silk

Total size 61 x 64 cm (w. × l.)
Weave — Paired main warp twill 1.2, (Direction S).
Warps   1 binding, firm Z, silk, yellow-brown.
            2 main, firm Z, silk, yellow-brown.
(*c*.14 pairs of main warps per cm.)
Wefts Little twist, single, red, greenish-blue, and perhaps originally golden yellow, silk.
Width of pattern repeat (half roundel) 13 cm and 14.5 cm (size varies)
Length of pattern repeat *c*.39 cm.
(Stepping over either 1 or 2 warps and across 4 wefts in most cases.)

---

[72] Imperial Byzantine silks were frequently sent as diplomatic gifts. See Muthesius, 'Eastern Silks', pp. 23 – 4.
[73] [Dr Muthesius is a fellow of Lucy Cavendish College, Cambridge. The editors would like to record their special gratitude to her for agreeing to modify her original paper in order to fit in with the volume as a whole. Ed.]

PART FOUR

St Cuthbert's Community at Chester-le-Street and Durham

Why did the Community of St Cuthbert Settle at Chester-le-Street?

ERIC CAMBRIDGE

Although the *Historia de sancto Cuthberto* and Symeon's *History of the Church of Durham* provide some information about the period during which the community of St Cuthbert was at Chester-le-Street, from 883 to 995, neither they nor any other written source explain what sort of a place Chester-le-Street was, nor why it was selected as the Cuthbertine community's base for more than a century; it is equally unclear what the community itself was like at that time. These questions are, nevertheless, crucial to an understanding of the community's history in the late ninth and tenth centuries. It is the purpose of this paper to cast light on them by means of a close analysis of the documentary, architectural, sculptural, and topographical evidence relating to Chester-le-Street in that period.[1]

It will be as well to begin by asking where exactly the church in which the Cuthbertine community established themselves in 883 was situated. It is generally supposed that its site is perpetuated by the present parish church. If that assumption can be substantiated, it will have much to tell us both about the subsequent architectural development of the church and about the relationship between the early church and the buildings of the Roman fort in which the present church is known to lie.

No traces of the early church have yet been discovered, but its location can be determined indirectly by considering the evidence for the way in which the place inside it, where Cuthbert's relics had rested from 883 to 995, was treated after their removal to Durham. The evidence for this is as follows. When the king's antiquary John Leland visited Chester-le-Street, probably in the 1530s, he noted that 'yn the Body of the Church is a Tumbe with the Image of a Bishop yn token that S Cuthberth ons was buried or remained in his Feretre there'.[2] What Leland apparently saw was a cenotaph marking the place where St Cuthbert's body was thought to have rested in the period 883 – 995. If we could be confident that its position in the sixteenth century really had not

---

[1] The numbers assigned to stones in *Corpus* I are used throughout the following paper.
[2] J. Leland, *The Itinerary*, ed. T. Hearne (9 vols., 3rd edn; Oxford, 1768), I, p. 77.

changed since the end of the ninth, this would be clear evidence that the later medieval church was on the site of the one used by the Cuthbertine community. It would be rash to accept this solely on the basis of the tradition recorded by Leland, but the case for continuity of site is supported by evidence showing how comparable holy places were treated at other churches. At Winchester Cathedral, for example, excavation has demonstrated that the precise site of St Swithun's original ninth-century grave was marked by a succession of structures up to the sixteenth century.[3] Furthermore, what is recorded about the Cuthbertine cenotaphs which formerly existed at two other places, at Holy Island Priory, and in the cloisters of Durham Cathedral, points in the same direction. Like Chester-le-Street, these are mentioned in sixteenth-century sources;[4] but references in the twelfth-century *Libellus* of Reginald of Durham demonstrate that cenotaphs had been established in both places much earlier.[5] Given that the interest in marking former resting places of Cuthbert's body is at least as old as the twelfth century, it is a reasonable guess that a cenotaph was also established at Chester-le-Street by this time. Indeed, the earliest evidence of an interest of this kind being displayed at any Cuthbertine site concerns Chester-le-Street where, according to Symeon of Durham (writing in the early twelfth century), the church, which hitherto had apparently been of timber, was replaced in stone by Aethelric, bishop of Durham (1041 – 56), 'because the body of the blessed Cuthbert had once rested there'.[6] As Cuthbert's relics had been moved to Durham only half a century earlier, the presumption that their previous location had been known and respected more or less continuously from 995 until the sixteenth century becomes a strong one. It seems likely therefore that any remains of the timber church used by the Cuthbertine community until 995 and of its mid-eleventh-century stone replacement must lie somewhere under the floor of the later medieval church we see today.

The exact position of these earlier churches in relation to the existing one cannot be determined at all precisely on the available evidence. The only hint

---

[3] See M. Biddle, 'Excavations at Winchester 1967: Sixth Interim Report', *Antiquaries Journal* 48 (1968), pp. 278 – 9, pls. 63 – 4, 68 – 9, and idem, 'Excavations at Winchester 1969: Eighth Interim Report', *Antiquaries Journal* 50 (1971), pp. 318 – 21, fig. 13.

[4] On Holy Island, see the muniments of the Dean and Chapter of Durham, Farne Island Accounts, 1519 – 20(A), dorse: *Status* 1520, *capella*. On Durham, see *Libellus*, p. xvii (where the MS reference should be to BL MS Harley 4843).

[5] On Holy Island, see *Libellus* 21, 22. On Durham, see ibid., 48. The Cuthbertine Cenotaphs are further discussed in E. Cambridge, 'The Anglo-Saxon Cathedral at Durham', in H. D. Briggs, E. Cambridge and R. N. Bailey, 'A New Approach to Church Archaeology: Dowsing, Excavation and Documentary Work at Woodhorn, Ponteland and the Pre-Norman Cathedral at Durham', *Archaeologia Aeliana*, 5th ser. 11 (1983), pp. 91 – 7.

[6] 'Placuerat eidem antistiti ecclesiam in Cunecacestre . . . de ligno factam destruere, et pro eo *quod aliquando beati Cuthberti corpus ibidem quieverat*, aliam de lapide fabricare.' (*HDE* III, 9; my italics).

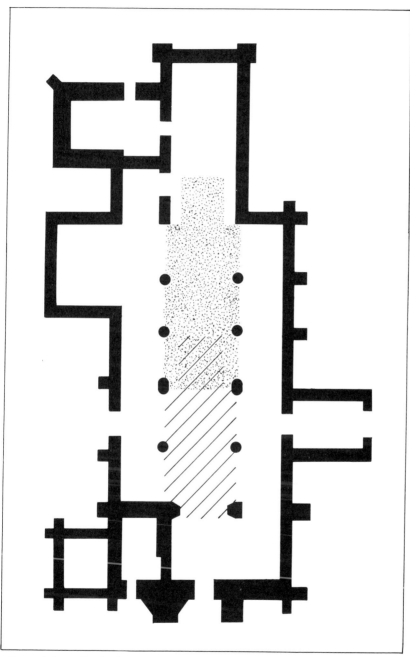

31. *Chester-le-Street church, sketch-plan showing possible locations of earlier church.*

comes from Leland's statement, quoted above, that the cenotaph stood in 'the body' of the church, which must mean in the nave;[7] so if the cenotaph indeed marked the position of the relics before 995, then it is under this western portion of the present church that remains of its predecessors are most likely to be found. Its fabric would therefore repay a more thorough investigation than it has yet received, or can be given here. The nave has aisles on both sides, divided from it by arcades or six bays, the western bay supporting a tower. Though none of these western parts seems to be earlier than the thirteenth century, they contain features which may betray an earlier phase of building (fig. 31). For one thing, there are the extraordinarily narrow proportions of the nave, its length being some five and a half times its width. This may be explained by supposing that the width was determined by the walls of an older church which was considerably lengthened by the thirteenth-century builders. The arrangement of the arcades seems to confirm this, for, instead of resting on a uniform series of columns, the three eastern bays are separated from those to the west by a rectangular pier on each side, suggesting that the arcades were erected in two stages, rather than in one continuous operation. These piers are most convincingly explained by supposing that they mark the junction between a phase in which the thirteenth-century builders were able to erect part of the arcades clear of an existing building, and one in which they were demolishing the walls of that building to erect the remaining arcades. Unfortunately, it is not clear which section marks the position of the earlier building (fig. 31), comparative evidence being of little help here, as examples of naves which have been expanded westwards and eastwards from an early nucleus can both be found.[8] All that can be hazarded therefore is that the width of the present nave has been determined by that of an earlier church, and that part of the existing arcades are on the lines of that church's walls.

When was the earlier church, which was later superseded by the existing thirteenth-century nave, itself constructed? It may be that the stone church erected by Bishop Aethelric in the mid eleventh century survived until that time, though the possibility that there may have been a rebuilding subsequent to Aethelric's but prior to the thirteenth century cannot be ruled out. At any rate, it is clear that none of the features of the existing church discussed above tells us anything about the form of the church used by the Cuthbertine community before 995. All we know about that building was that it was of timber. Yet, in view of the prestige of the community and of the relics which this church housed, even that fact seems to require some explanation.

---

[7] Cf. *Rites of Durham*, ed. J. T. Fowler (SS 107; Durham, 1903), pp. 32 – 40, passim.

[8] For an example of expansion westwards, see H. M. and J. Taylor, *Anglo-Saxon Architecture* (3 vols.; Cambridge 1965 – 78), II, 564 – 7, fig. 275; for an eastwards example, see J. Barmby, 'Pittington and its Church', *Transactions of the Architectural and Archaeological Societies of Durham and Northumberland* 3 (1890), pp. 19 – 20, fig. facing p. 32.

Admittedly, the church on Lindisfarne in which Cuthbert had been buried in 687 had been of timber. This structure survived into the ninth century, having been taken down and re-erected at Norham when the community moved there under Bishop Ecgred (830 – 45).[9] But it would be dangerous to argue on this basis that timber churches were somehow more acceptable to the Cuthbertine community in the ninth century. For one thing, the seventh-century timber church clearly came to be regarded as something of a special case; by the time of the move to Norham, it looks as though it was being treated as a kind of relic in itself. Besides, it is unlikely to have been the only church in the monastery by the ninth century; there might well have been others which were stone built.[10] This was possibly also the case at Norham during the community's time there to judge by two of the carved fragments from the site, which are probably of eighth- or early ninth-century date and may have had an architectural function.[11] Similarly, stone churches must have been reasonably familiar in County Durham by the time St Cuthbert's community arrived there.[12] It is true that none of our sources reveals anything about the date of construction of the timber church at Chester-le-Street, but it is a reasonable guess that it must have been there at least from 883; and even if it were a pre-existing structure taken over by the community in 883, it still seems odd that it was not replaced by a stone church during the community's occupation of the site. The choice of building material seems all the more curious, and all the more deliberate, given that the present church sits within a Roman fort (fig. 32);[13] for, if the above arguments in favour of continuity of site are accepted, the earlier timber church must have occupied the same position, surrounded by Roman ruins which would have supplied an easily accessible source of ready-cut building stone. Nor can its builders have been unaware of the Roman buildings, for the existing church still follows their alignment; and if the sequence of architectural development outlined above is right, its timber predecessor must have been placed right in the centre of the fort (fig. 32), probably overlying part of the cross-hall of the Roman

[9] *HSC* 9. The suggestion in N. Pevsner *et. al.*, *The Buildings of England, County Durham* (revised edn.; Harmondsworth, 1983), p. 125, note, that this church was moved again to Chester-le-Street in 883 seems unlikely, as its origin would surely have been known to Symeon (see above, n. 6).

[10] On the site of the parish church of St Mary, for example: see O'Sullivan, above, pp. 129 – 31.

[11] The pieces are too damaged to be sure that they tapered, so are not necessarily pieces of cross-shaft (*pace Corpus* I, pp. 210 – 11). Their general resemblance to a piece from Ruthwell, Dumfriesshire, which is almost certainly an impost, suggests an architectural function (W. G. Collingwood, *Northumbrian Crosses of the Pre-Norman Age* (London, 1927), p. 84, fig. 101).

[12] E. Cambridge, 'The Early Church in County Durham: A Reassessment', *Journal of the British Archaeological Association* 137 (1984), pp. 65 – 85.

[13] The precisely central location of the church within the fort is surely deliberate, though it is not clear what it means. It is paralleled in the north at Aldborough (R. K. Morris, *The Church in British Archaeology* (Council for British Archaeology Research Report 47; London, 1983), p. 43, fig. 14c).

headquarters building, and perhaps even reusing its wall lines as founda-tions.[14] Oddly ambivalent though this attitude to the most easily available building materials is, it can be paralleled at Rivenhall in Essex, where the foundations of a timber church were cut into the remains of a Roman villa and, indeed, in part built over its backfilled cellar. This phase at Rivenhall is not closely dated, but has been tentatively assigned to the tenth century, and would thus be roughly contemporary with the Cuthbertine community's occupation of Chester-le-Street.[15]

Why was there apparently no stone church at Chester-le-Street until the mid eleventh century? It is important to bear in mind that there are really two separate issues here: the failure to provide a stone church in 883; and the community's continuing use of a timber church for more than a century, until it moved to Durham in 995. Crucial to the former must have been the length of time the community expected to stay in Chester-le-Street when it first arrived there. It would certainly be unwise to assume that this was anything like as long as eventually turned out to be the case, for the community had been moving from place to place for the previous seven years,[16] and the political climate was uncertain, to say the least. A timber church might thus have been erected (or an existing one occupied) in the expectation that it would be a purely temporary expedient.[17] The evidence from Rivenhall offers a possible parallel here, as its excavators have tentatively suggested that the timber church there may also have been intended to be temporary.[18] Perhaps similar considerations of expediency dictated the occupation of the Roman fort, the defensive perimeter of which would presumably still have been complete enough to have provided badly needed security for the refugee community. But while the failure to provide a stone church in 883 may thus be explained as a consequence of the community's initial intention not to stay long, it is harder to explain in the same way the persistence of a timber church until long after the community had departed for Durham. Of course, the community may never have ceased to assume that their stay in Chester-le-Street would shortly be over; after all, this assumption was justified by the event in the end, though it took more than a century to come about. Or it may be that, by the time the realization dawned that their stay was going to be more protracted than first anticipated, the option to build a stone church was

---

[14] I am most grateful to Dr Jeremy Evans for his helpful advice on this point; as Morris has pointed out in discussing churches on Roman urban sites, it need not imply continuity of occupation, but rather that the Roman wall lines were more easily followed than ignored (Morris, *Church*, p. 41). For a summary of previous excavations at Chester-le- Street, see P. A. G. Clack, 'Chester-le-Street: A Report on the History and Archaeology of the Town' (Unpublished report, Archaeological Unit for North East England, Newcastle upon Tyne, 1980), pp. 1 – 4.

[15] W. J. and K. A. Rodwell, *Rivenhall: Investigations of a Villa, Church and Village, 1950 – 1977* (Council for British Archaeology Research Report 55; London, 1986), pp. 85 – 90, fig. 63.

[16] *HSC* 20.

[17] I am grateful to Mrs Enid Hart for this point.

[18] Rodwell and Rodwell, *Rivenhall*, p. 90.

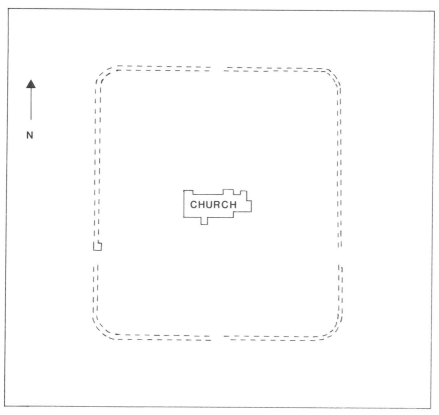

32. Chester-le-Street, church and Roman fort (after research by Dr J. Evans).

no longer feasible technologically. Certainly the lack of remains of stone churches in the region datable to the period between the late ninth and the early eleventh centuries is in striking contrast to the quantity surviving both from the pre-Viking period,[19] and from the early eleventh century onwards, when it looks very much as though the erection of a stone cathedral at Durham, after 995,[20] marked a new beginning in stone church building in the area. Thus, while the erection or take-over of a timber church in 883 is

[19] See above, n. 12.
[20] *Libellus* 16.

unlikely to imply anything about the state of contemporary stone building technology, the fact that the site continued to be served by a timber church for the next century and a half may well have something to tell us about that technology's subsequent decline in the region.

The only material remains actually surviving from the period of the Cuthbertine community's occupation of Chester-le-Street are a number of fragments of carved stone crosses, and these raise interpretative problems no less challenging than those relating to the use of a timber church. Just as the community's status might initially have led one to suppose that its church would have been of stone, so one might have expected that its long tradition of carving sophisticated stone monuments, to which the surviving Anglian carvings from Norham and Lindisfarne amply testify, would have been reflected in a series of comparatively high quality carvings at Chester-le-Street; here, if anywhere, the pre-Viking monastic craft traditions would seem most likely to have survived. Instead, we find a series of monuments which seem rather to indicate a complete break with the community's heritage, and which are also markedly inferior in quality both to carvings being produced contemporaneously at other sites in the region and to examples produced by the community itself after it moved to Durham in 995.

The Chester-le-Street carvings comprise twelve pieces and two recently discovered unpublished fragments, implying the existence of seven different monuments at the very least. For convenience they will be referred to in the following discussion by the numbers assigned to them in Rosemary Cramp's recently published catalogue.[21] One of the shafts, no. 3, is now lost, but is known from illustrations; several other stones seem to have disappeared without being drawn.[22] These carvings are not closely datable, but it seems reasonably clear on comparative grounds that none is likely to be earlier than the end of the ninth century, nor later than the first part of the eleventh. Some of the stones may therefore have been carved after the departure of the community of St Cuthbert for Durham, but it is highly unlikely that any was present on the site before its arrival; in other words, a case can be made for most of them having been carved while the community was at Chester-le-Street. Thus, the motif of an armed warrior on horseback on shaft no. 1 (pl. 48a) is likely, in this region at least, to reflect the influence of an early tenth-century Viking-age fashion, so can probably be assigned an early to mid tenth-century date.[23] This granted, stones which have other motifs in common with shaft no. 1 may have been carved at about the same time. For example, ring-knots (pl. 48a, middle) can also be found on one of the cross-bases (no. 11) and probably also on shaft no. 7. Again, several of the other motifs on shaft

[21] *Corpus* I, pp. 53–9. No. 13 has not been discussed here, as it is undatable.

[22] *Corpus* I, pp. 53–4 and 155; see below, pp. 377–8.

[23] The strength of the Scandinavian influence on this stone makes it difficult to see how it can be as early as the late 9th-century date proposed for it in *Corpus* I, p. 54. (See below, p. 377.)

no. 7 can be paralleled on further stones in the group. The general implication seems to be that the bulk of the material is probably tenth century.

These carvings are, in general, unlike anything that the community had produced earlier at Lindisfarne and Norham, though there are occasional similarities to sculptures probably produced at both of those sites after its move to Chester-le-Street. The shaft from the latter which shows the closest *prima facie* relationship to those at Lindisfarne is no. 5.[24] In its selection of ornament — interlace, ribbon animals, and fret pattern (pl. 47a) — it is the only one which resembles the typical Lindisfarne repertoire. But these motifs occur generally in the Durham area, so need not imply any direct link (see below); besides, there are some notable variations in the detailed arrangement, frets generally occurring on the broad faces of the Lindisfarne shafts, for example (pls. 47b, 47d).[25] Equally, some of the most distinctive features of the Lindisfarne material hardly occur at Chester-le-Street: for example, the division of ornament into panels, often separated by uncarved areas on the narrow sides.[26] There are even fewer parallels with Norham. The only shared interlace pattern is a Viking-age motif which occurs much more frequently south of Tyne than north of it, suggesting that, if a direct connection is involved at all, Chester-le-Street may have been the donor rather than the recipient in this instance.[27]

The only motif common to all three sites is fret pattern, so the possibility of a direct link must be taken more seriously here. The earliest surviving example is at Norham (pls. 46a-b), and indeed Rosemary Cramp has suggested that the series of frets at Lindisfarne derives from it.[28] But before assuming that the Chester-le-Street carving owes a similar direct debt to Norham, it is worth considering other evidence which suggests that the situation may be more complex. The fret on the broad face of that Norham cross (pl. 46a) also occurs on a later piece from Lindisfarne (pl. 47d); otherwise it is an uncommon pattern in Northumbria east of the Pennines, so it is notable that the only other example of it in Anglian-period sculpture occurs not far south of Chester-le-Street, on a fragment from Northallerton (fig. 33; pl. 47c).[29] This suggests that the motif's appearance in Viking-age contexts at Chester-le-Street and other neighbouring sites in the south Durham area may derive either from Northallerton itself or from another local Anglian carving which has since been lost, which would not rule out Lindisfarne as the ultimate source of the motif, but would entail moving the

---

[24] *Corpus* I, p. 56.

[25] Except for Lindisfarne no. 6D (*Corpus* I, pl. 193, ill. 1074).

[26] *Corpus* I, p. 27. Admittedly, too little of Chester-le-Street no. 5 remains to be sure how its ornament was laid out.

[27] *Corpus* I, pl. 205, ill. 1168, cf. pl. 20, ill. 105.

[28] *Corpus* I, p. 210.

[29] In northern Bernicia it also occurs at Old Melrose, Jedburgh, and Abercorn, all sites with documented Lindisfarne connections (see respectively *HSC* 3; *HSC* 9; *HR* 89), and at Aberlady.

period of its direct influence back to before the middle of the ninth century, rather than during the Viking age.[30]

Of course, it must be remembered that the repertoires of motifs on the surviving stones from Norham and Lindisfarne are very different from each other.[31] It is far from clear why this was so, but its implication seems to be that sculptural connections between Chester-le-Street and either site are not necessarily to be expected, and that divergence in the ornament or carving technique of its sculpture certainly cannot be taken to indicate lack of communication of any kind between Chester-le-Street and the two northern sites in the late ninth and tenth centuries. At any rate, if the carvers of the Chester-le-Street stones had any contact with the other two sites, it must have been at best occasional and, in the case of the fret motif, probably indirect. In contrast, the close relationship of the Chester-le-Street sculptures to the work of local carvers is immediately apparent. The motif much the most frequently employed is interlace, the limited repertoire of patterns being closely paralleled at neighbouring sites in County Durham and the northern part of Yorkshire.[32] The 'split plait' motif on shaft no. 1 (pl. 48a), for instance, has an exclusively local distribution, being found at Aycliffe, Jarrow, Durham, and (probably) Gainford.[33] Similarly, the fragmentary ribbon animal on shaft no. 5 is like examples from Aycliffe, which themselves are products of a vigorous local tradition.[34] The fret motif on the opposite face also occurs at Great Stainton and Sockburn.[35] Only occasionally do associations of motif appear to point to connections further afield. The figure style of cross-base no. 12, for instance, is comparable locally to Great Stainton, but also seems to be related to sites much further north.[36]

The similarities noted above might be taken to imply that the tenth-century Chester-le-Street carvers had influenced sculptures at neighbouring sites, but detailed comparisons suggest that the reverse is the case. Several of the interlace motifs, for example, are better executed at other sites, suggesting that the less competent Chester-le-Street examples are copied from them. The

[30] See below, pp. 380 – 3. If the motif on Chester-le-Street no. 9B is indeed a debased tree scroll (*Corpus* I, p. 57; pl. 25, ill. 132), the only known prototype in the area is another Anglian piece from Northallerton (W. G. Collingwood, 'Anglian and Anglo-Danish Sculpture in the North Riding of Yorkshire', *Yorkshire Archaeological Journal* 19 (1907), fig. on p. 373, c).

[31] *Corpus* I, p. 210, and for the interlaces, G. Adcock, 'A Study of the Types of Interlace on Northumbrian Sculpture' (Unpublished M. Phil. thesis, 2 vols., University of Durham, 1974), I, 270.

[32] Adcock, 'Interlace' I, 314 – 15, 322.

[33] *Corpus* I, p. 31.

[34] *Corpus* I, pp. 41 – 3, pl. 18, ill. 95, cf. pl. 8, ill. 28; and for a possible earlier 10th-century context, C. D. Morris, 'Aycliffe and its pre-Norman Sculpture', in *Anglo-Saxon and Viking Age Sculpture*, ed. J. T. Lang (British Archaeological Reports, Brit. series 49; Oxford, 1978), at p. 104.

[35] *Corpus* I, pl. 77, ill. 386, pl. 136, ill. 735. For the possible origins of this motif in the locality, see above, p. 375.

[36] *Corpus* I, p. 31, where a link to Lindisfarne is also suggested, though the resemblance does not seem to me to be specific enough to support this view.

'split plait' motif is the most obvious example.[37] Indeed, most of the Chester-le-Street interlaces seem to have been carved freehand or using a template, rather than following the more sophisticated Anglian technique of gridding, which survived into the early tenth century elsewhere in the region, notably on stones at Aycliffe (though their dating is, admittedly, controversial).[38] The horseman motif on shaft no. 1 tells a similar story, as it is apparently derived from well executed examples at centres of Scandinavian influence, such as those at Sockburn (pl. 48b), and Hart.[39] Indeed, the existence of Scandinavian influences at Chester-le-Street is in itself remarkable, given the generally vigorous resistance to them north of the Tees valley. One might have expected the Cuthbertine community to be in the vanguard of the maintenance of Anglian traditions; yet, although shaft no. 1 draws its interlace motifs from that tradition, the abandonment of the practice of dividing up the ornament into separate panels surrounded by moulded borders betrays the strength of Scandinavian influence much more tellingly than the adoption of the horseman motif as such (pl. 48a).[40] Thus, the use of motifs which probably originated at other centres, and their lack of technical competence in execution, make Chester-le-Street look much less like a regionally important centre of production and artistic influence than its status might have led one to expect.

Seen in the light of the preceding observations, the Chester-le-Street stones begin to look very odd indeed. Perhaps we can convincingly explain their inferiority to what had been produced earlier at Lindisfarne and Norham, and their apparent lack of contact with stones from those places, as in part reflecting a general decline in quality observable in Northumbrian sculpture from the late ninth century onwards and, more specifically, as the result of a hiatus in monastic craft traditions which is likely to have arisen during the upheavals which beset the community in the late ninth century. Perhaps also the superior monuments which were apparently commissioned by the community after it had moved to Durham should be seen as products of the same technological revival which enabled the new cathedral there to be built of stone, though another interpretation of them is possible, as will be explained below. But even if the foregoing suggestions are both correct, neither helps to explain why Chester-le-Street preserves no pieces comparable to the best that were being produced at other contemporary centres of production in the region. It may be that the impression of the site given by the surviving stones is misleading, and that more competent monuments remain to be discovered, or have been discovered and since lost. Indeed, as will be seen later, one nineteenth-century reference implies that a stone dating from before the community's arrival on the site formerly existed; and another made at the

---

[37] Adcock, 'Interlace' I, 305.
[38] Ibid., I, 315, and for the dating of Aycliffe, above, n. 34.
[39] *Corpus* I, pl. 79, ill. 394.
[40] R. N. Bailey, *Viking Age Sculpture in Northern England* (London, 1980), pp. 78–9.

beginning of the present century to the loss of 'the best piece' should put us on our guard against assuming that what we now have is necessarily representative of what was produced during the community's stay here.[41] It is even conceivable that some monuments may have been removed from the site in ancient times — perhaps some of the stones found at Durham Cathedral had been moved there after 995, having actually been carved earlier at Chester-le-Street.[42] There are difficulties in supposing that suggestions of this kind can entirely explain the characteristics of the surviving stones at Chester-le-Street, however. In either case, it seems odd that the numerous extant pieces show so few traces of the former presence of more elaborate carvings, or of a tradition of using more sophisticated carving techniques, in a way that can be seen at other nearby sites like Gainford or Brompton.[43] And there are good art-historical reasons for interpreting the high quality Durham sculptures as indicating a revival, and not a survival, of pre-Viking Lindisfarne traditions.[44]

Yet if, on the other hand, we accept that the surviving pieces from Chester-le-Street are not atypical of the original output from the site — if, that is, we are prepared to assume that little sculpture of substantially higher quality was ever carved there — how do we then account for the fact that the site's sculptural output was so unlike that of some of its contemporaries and apparently so inappropriate to a place of its importance? It may be that, if we could date the tenth-century sculpture from the region more precisely than is possible at present, the contrast between what was produced at Chester-le-Street and the comparatively high-quality sculpture from other sites would turn out to be more apparent than real. Thus, the Chester-le-Street stones may turn out not to have been atypical of what was being carved in the area by the later tenth century, given that there may be grounds for thinking that the better pieces in the region date from the earlier part of that century.[45] They might therefore be seen as dating from a period when competence in carving had declined generally — a decline parallel to that in building technology suggested above. But even if the contrast in quality could be explained in this way, the effect would be simply to intensify the anomalous character of the site, as it would then imply that little or nothing was being produced at Chester-le-Street while the higher quality pieces were being produced elsewhere. If, moreover, we were prepared to interpret such carvings as

---

[41] *Corpus* I, p. 53. Could this be identified with County Durham, Unknown Provenance no. 1, which has several ornamental links with the Chester-le-Street carvings, including fret pattern, but is of higher quality than any of them? (See *Corpus* I, pp. 146 – 7.)

[42] *Corpus* I, Durham, nos. 5 – 11.

[43] There is no discernible trace either of the presence of the eighth-century 'cross of Bishop Aethelwold', which the community allegedly brought with them from Lindisfarne (*HDE* I, 12). Was it, then, a plain, inscribed memorial cross of the Whitby type? Or, *pace* Symeon, was it brought from Lindisfarne direct to Durham only in the early 11th century, when the community's relic-hunting activity was at its height (*HDE* III, 7)?

[44] *Corpus* I, p. 33.

[45] For Aycliffe, see above, note 34. The Scandinavian-influenced stones from Sockburn must predate the end of the Viking kingdom of York in 954 at the latest.

memorials of some kind, we might then explain their absence from Chester-le-Street by supposing that the community had adopted different practices in this respect, which did not involve stone sculpture; but the production of so much high quality sculpture at both earlier and later stages of its history surely makes this unlikely. Or might the absence of high quality carving be seen as a consequence of the community's assumption that (especially in the years following 883) it would be leaving Chester-le-Street sooner rather than later? After all, the nature of its members' provision for their commemoration may have been determined by that assumption in just the same way as it has already been argued that their adoption of a timber church was. In that case, were they being commemorated elsewhere? If so, the best guess must be, at Lindisfarne itself; which may go some way to explaining the quantity and vigour of the tenth-century carvings from that site.[46] This may seem a surprising suggestion in view of the fact that the community, nevertheless, did not return there, but its failure to do so may be seen not so much as implying that Lindisfarne was inaccessible as that it was afraid of the consequences of leaving Chester-le-Street.[47] Given the uncertainties of the present evidence, however, the speculation that the sorts of carving produced at Chester-le-Street were affected by the exceptional circumstances of the community's occupation of the site, no less than was the sort of church it used, must remain pure guesswork.

So far, the discussion of Chester-le-Street has been confined to the period following the watershed in the Cuthbertine community's history marked by its arrival on the site in 883. This final section of the paper will consider what the nature and function of the place may have been before 883, and will suggest that its links with Lindisfarne may reach back far earlier than has hitherto been supposed. We have already seen that none of the surviving pre-Conquest stone carvings at Chester-le-Street can date from before the community's arrival in 883; but it is likely that one of the lost pieces did. Shortly after this stone was discovered in the 1860s, its ornament was compared by no less an authority than Dr William Greenwell to work at three other sites in the north: Hexham, Lowther, and Bewcastle.[48] The only motif which the carvings from these places have in common is plant scroll. Moreover, the carvings on which this motif is present at each of the three sites are all work of the highest quality, and none of them can be dated any later than the beginning of the ninth century; presumably then, the lost Chester-le-Street piece also dated from this earlier period. It is just conceivable that the community brought it with them

[46] *Corpus* I, nos. 3, 5 – 9, 11, 13, 15 – 17.

[47] See further below, pp. 385 – 6. There is no evidence that the community's possession of Lindisfarne was ever challenged; and the presence of the (surely friendly) Eadwulfing earls nearby at Bamburgh must have meant that it generally had access to the site at least. Tilred's purchase of the abbacy of Norham on joining the community in the early tenth century may suggest that at least one of its ancient estates in the north was under its control at that time (*HSC* 21).

[48] Reported in 'Meetings, 1864 – 68', *Transactions of the Architectural and Archaeological Societies of Durham and Northumberland* 1 (1870), p. xlv. See *Corpus* I, 53.

in 883, as they are alleged to have brought Aethelwold's cross from Lindisfarne.[49] If so, it is more likely to have migrated from Norham than Lindisfarne, as there is only the slenderest evidence that plant scroll was in the Lindisfarne repertoire at all, whereas it is well attested at Norham. Yet there is nothing about the surviving Norham plant scrolls which would prompt a comparison with the sites Greenwell names.[50] The possibility that this carving was already present at Chester-le-Street in 883 must therefore be taken seriously. Nor is the fact that scroll motifs scarcely appear in the Viking-age carvings from the site any reason to doubt this stone's proposed date and character. Precisely the same hiatus is observable at other sites where the dominant motif changes from scroll to interlace: compare Hart or Hexham.

If Greenwell's reference to this stone is correctly interpreted, it provides the only hint of an ecclesiastical presence at Chester-le-Street before 883. The date and character of the carving may be seen as suggesting that there had been some form of monastic community there, as I have argued elsewhere.[51] If so, it could have been associated with Wearmouth/Jarrow, especially as the lands granted to the incoming Cuthbertine community in 883 must have incorporated some of the estates of that monastery, including the sites of both its principal churches.[52] Alternatively, it is possible that the site had been under Lindisfarne's control for some considerable time before 883. There is no direct evidence for this, but it is suggested by considering the nature and function of a series of other sites which seem to have had a Lindisfarne connection.

Let us begin with the purpose for which, according to the *Historia de sancto Cuthberto*, the vill of Crayke was granted to St Cuthbert: 'so that he should have a *mansio* there whenever he should go to the city of York or return from it'.[53] The personal association of Cuthbert with this grant may be a later construct, which casts some doubt on its purported date; but there seems to be no other reason to doubt the explanation of its purpose. The implication is presumably that Crayke was to be used as a staging-post on the journey between York and Lindisfarne; indeed, it lies just off the Roman road (numbered 80 in I. D. Margary's catalogue) which ran northwards from Brough on Humber to join the Roman Wall at Newcastle upon Tyne (fig. 33).[54] If so, it was presumably only the southernmost in a series of such sites, others of which presumably lay on or near that road. The only material relic of the pre-Viking period at Crayke is a small piece of Anglian sculpture, decorated with plant scroll, and probably early ninth-century in date, now in

---

[49] But see above, n. 43.
[50] *Corpus* I, pp. 209 – 10, 212.
[51] Cambridge, *J. Brit. Archaeol. Assoc.* 137, pp. 65 – 85.
[52] Ibid., p. 73.
[53] *HSC* 5.
[54] I. D. Margary, *Roman Roads in Britain* (2nd edn.; London, 1967), no. 80.

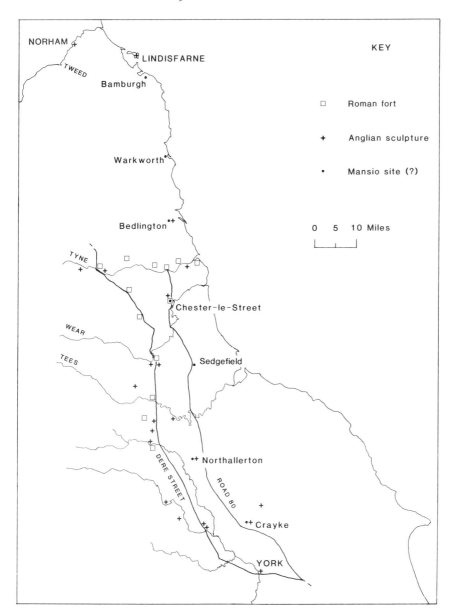

33. Eastern Northumbria: Roman roads, Anglian sculpture, and suggested Lindisfarne mansio sites.

the Yorkshire Museum.[55] One of the many intriguing features of the distribution of carvings of this period in Yorkshire is that they occur frequently at sites within five miles or so of Dere Street, the principal north-south Roman road on the west side of the Vale of York,[56] yet are much less frequently found on or near Road 80 (fig. 33).[57] From this perspective, it is worth considering the origins and function of Northallerton, another site close to Road 80 which has produced Anglian sculpture.[58] There is no evidence that this site was associated with the Cuthbertine community in the pre-Conquest period, though Brompton, later one of its chapelries, was apparently granted to Durham by Cnut.[59] The surrounding area of Allertonshire formed part of Durham priory's Yorkshire liberty from the late eleventh century, however.[60] Could this later interest have been in part prompted by the memory of a more ancient Cuthbertine community possession in this area which had subsequently been alienated or lost? If so, it may have originated in an episcopal *mansio*, serving as a staging-post as at Crayke. Given this possible context, the likely Lindisfarne associations of the fret pattern on the late eighth- or early ninth-century Northallerton fragment noted above assume an added significance.[61] The only other site beside this road for which there is any evidence of the presence of Anglian sculpture is Chester-le-Street itself. Might it have formed another link in this chain of *mansio* sites? If so, this need not have been inside the fort from the beginning; the arrival of the community in 883 may have prompted a reordering of the previous ecclesiastical organization involving the abandonment of an earlier site near by, from which the Anglian sculpture was transferred.[62]

The route which the bishops of Lindisfarne would have taken from York to Crayke is not clear, but must have involved a journey of some twelve to fourteen miles. From Crayke to Northallerton by the Roman road is about twenty miles; but it is nearly forty miles from there to Chester-le-Street, suggesting that an intervening staging-post may have existed (fig. 33). One possible candidate is Sedgefield, apparently purchased for the community only in the time of Bishop Cuthheard (899-*c*.915), but which also may have

[55] T. Sheppard, 'Viking and other Relics at Crayke, Yorkshire', *Yorkshire Archaeological Journal* 34 (1939), pp. 278 – 9, fig. VII.

[56] Margary, *Roman Roads*, no. 8.

[57] Sites with Viking-Age sculpture are much more evenly distributed in the vicinities of these two roads, at least in north Yorkshire and south Durham, suggesting that the contrast in the distributions of the Anglian material is not simply due to later losses or to the inaccessibility of a supply of suitable stone.

[58] Collingwood, *Yorks. Archaeol. Jnl.* 19, p. 372, fig. on p. 373, a – g.

[59] *HSC* 32; *Symeonis Dunelmensis Opera et collectanea* I, ed. H. Hinde (SS 51; Durham, 1868), p. 152, note p.

[60] *Durham Episcopal Charters 1071 – 1152*, ed. H. S. Offler (SS 179; Durham, 1968), pp. 50 – 3.

[61] See above, pp. 375 – 6.

[62] Ken Adams, in his important unpublished work on Crayke, suggests that the church site shifted during the Viking period. I am most grateful to Mr Adams for communicating his results to me.

represented the re-establishment of an earlier interest.[63] Potential sites north of the Tyne are harder to spot, as there is no longer the Roman road as a guide. Nevertheless, Bedlington, about twenty miles north of Chester-le-Street, is an obvious candidate. Intriguingly, this was also purchased for the community by Cuthheard,[64] and the church also preserves a piece of sculpture which is just conceivably of Anglian date.[65] The final stage of the journey to Lindisfarne could have been made from Bamburgh, where Bede's description of Aidan's residence makes it sound very much like other sites which he terms *mansiones* in the *Historia ecclesiastica* though, admittedly, he does not use that term of this site.[66] In this case also, the distance between Bedlington and Bamburgh, nearly forty miles, suggests that there was probably another site in between. Perhaps it was Warkworth, granted to Lindisfarne in the early eighth century.[67]

The hypothetical nature of the origin and function of the seven sites being proposed here must be frankly admitted. Nevertheless, before considering some more general implications, it is perhaps worth summarizing the evidence presented so far. Two of the seven, Crayke and Bamburgh, are documented as episcopal residences, and a third (Warkworth) was an early Lindisfarne acquisition. A Cuthbertine association is documented from the late ninth century at Chester-le-Street, and from the early tenth at Bedlington and Sedgefield. The documentation relating to Northallerton, however, dates only from the eleventh century. The ninth-century and later Cuthbertine community's interest in these sites can hardly be taken as conclusive in itself. After all, the community acquired many other estates in this period, particularly in the Durham area, for which it would be absurd to postulate an earlier Lindisfarne interest. On the other hand, the existence of cases such as Billingham, apparently granted to the monks of Durham by William Rufus in 1088 × 1091, yet documented as having come into the Lindisfarne community's hands in the second quarter of the ninth century, and having been wrested from them at least once in the intervening period,[68] suggests that other acquisitions may also conceal earlier interests for which documentation does not happen to survive, and that the impression of steady acquisition of lands from the tenth century presented by the writer of the *Historia de sancto Cuthberto* may conceal a much more complex pattern of alienation and recovery. The way in which some of those estates, most notably Bedlington, are conspicuously isolated from the main areas of the community's land-holdings

[63] *HSC* 21; *Symeonis Opera*, p. 147, note h. Great Stainton should perhaps also be considered.
[64] *HSC* 21.
[65] Dated to the tenth century (*Corpus* I, pp. 163 – 4; pl. 159, ill. 820) where, however, its affinities with the figures of the St Andrew Auckland cross of *c*.800 are noted.
[66] *HE* III, 17. Though constructed for different purposes, the components of Aidan's dwelling, an *ecclesia* and a *cubiculum*, sound similar to those of Cuthbert's hermitage on Farne, which is termed a *mansio*, and which comprised an *oratorium* and a *habitaculum* (*HE* IV, 28; *VCP* 17).
[67] *HSC* 8.
[68] *Durham Episcopal Charters*, pp. 9 – 10.

also makes more sense if they originated as links in a north-south sequence whose rationale predates the see's move to Chester-le-Street.[69] In terms of material remains earlier than the mid ninth century, two of the sites, Crayke and Northallerton, certainly have sculpture of this vintage. Chester-le-Street almost certainly once had, and it is possible that the enigmatic sculpture from Bedlington could also be early. What must be re-emphasized here is the scarcity of such sculpture along the line of Roman Road 80, compared to its abundance in the environs of Dere Street (fig. 33). Even so, some links in the chain (Sedgefield for example) remain weaker than others; and perhaps it is mistaken to assume either that there was ever a complete series of such sites, or that they have all been correctly identified.

Granted that the hypothesis at least deserves to be entertained, however, what are its general implications? First, it is a reasonable guess that, in most if not all cases, these sites were associated with royal estate centres.[70] Bamburgh demonstrably was in Aidan's time and, as Bede makes clear, there were others.[71] They may therefore be regarded as an ecclesiastical counterpart to the series of royal estate centres along one of the regular consumption routes of the Northumbrian kings, as recently postulated by Austin.[72] Initially they may have lacked any endowment of their own, as Bede's description of Aidan's circumstances implies.[73] According to the author of the *Historia de sancto Cuthberto*, Crayke had been granted to St Cuthbert together with an endowment, 'three miles around the vill itself', which sounds modest compared to the lavish endowment of some early monasteries;[74] further, he may have been guilty of an anachronism in dating the grant as early as the period of Cuthbert's own lifetime. On the other hand (if it is not another anachronistic interpretation by the writer of the *Historia de sancto Cuthberto*) others, like Warkworth, seem to have been provided with more substantial estates from the beginning.[75] The large medieval parishes which were later associated with, for example, Bedlington, Sedgefield, and Chester-le-Street itself, may preserve the approximate extent of some of those early estates in

---

[69] Map in C. D. Morris, 'Northumbria and the Viking Settlement: The Evidence for Landholding', *Archaeologia Aeliana*, 5th ser. 5 (1977), p. 89.

[70] Juxtaposition with a royal centre may have been one of the factors underlying the vulnerability of Warkworth and Crayke to royal confiscation in the later 9th century (*HSC* 10).

[71] 'in villa regia . . . habens ecclesiam et cubiculum . . . quod ipsum et in aliis villis regiis facere solebat' (*HE* III, 17).

[72] D. Austin, 'Central Place Theory and the Middle Ages', in *Central Places, Archaeology and History*, ed. E. Grant (Sheffield, 1986), at p. 101, fig. 9.2b (p. 99).

[73] 'nil propriae possessionis, excepta ecclesia sua et adiacentibus agellis habens' (*HE* III, 17). I am grateful to Clare Stancliffe for pointing out to me that the use of the possessive in *ecclesia sua* implies that Lindisfarne must be the church referred to here.

[74] 'et tria milliaria in circuitu ipsius villae' (*HSC* 5). David Hall has suggested that the present parish boundary approximately reflects the extent of this grant (D. J. Hall, 'The Community of St Cuthbert: its Properties, Rights and Claims from the Ninth Century to the Twelfth' (unpublished D. Phil. thesis, University of Oxford, 1984), pp. 63–4).

[75] *HSC* 8.

fossilized form; alternatively, they may only indicate the boundaries of the secular estates within which those churches were originally founded. In any event, it cannot be assumed that these sites all developed in the same way; differences may have emerged at an early stage. Initially, they may have been occupied only periodically, like the adjacent royal centres. Later, the better endowed sites at least may also have come to serve as continuously occupied minster centres, exercising pastoral functions over the surrounding areas. Others, such as Crayke, seem to have developed into fully fledged monastic communities;[76] to judge from its surviving sculpture, so may Northallerton.

If Chester-le-Street is permitted to take its place as a link in the chain of episcopal *mansio* sites suggested above, then the Cuthbertine community's settlement there in 883 becomes more comprehensible; it was not occupying a site completely new to it, but rather a place which had periodically accommodated the bishop of Lindisfarne and his *familia* for many years. Indeed, perhaps the community should be thought of already in 883 as more like a bishop's household and less as a large body of refugee monks; this might help to explain the break with earlier monastic craft traditions which the surviving sculpture appears to indicate. But why was this particular episcopal *mansio* selected? Firstly, because the existence of the Roman fort made it the only one of the series which had any potential defensive capability (fig. 32). Secondly, it was the best suited to function as a centre from which to retain control over the extensive estates which the community had recently acquired between the rivers Tyne and Tees, starting with two substantial blocks in the south-east and south-west of that area acquired under Bishop Ecgred (830 – 45), and extending into the north-east with the grant from King Guthred in 883.[77] Perhaps the community in 883 felt that its hold on these southern estates was the least secure of any of its properties. After all, they lay in an area which had already suffered during the Viking invasion of 875, and must have been felt to be under continued threat following permanent settlement by the Vikings from 876.[78] Similarly, it may have been the determination to hang on to these estates (which were again under threat during the troubled years of the early tenth century), rather than the insecurity or inaccessibility of Lindisfarne or Norham, which helped to keep the community at Chester-le-Street.[79] If that was indeed the underlying aim, it was achieved, by and large, remarkably successfully; and as the tenth century progressed, the increasing Scots dominance north of Tweed,[80] and the flow of

---

[76] It was perhaps a nunnery or double monastery, for when the community took shelter there shortly before 883, its head was apparently female (*HDE* II, 13; noted by D. Whitelock in her *English Historical Documents c.500 – 1042* (1st edn.; London, 1955), p. 93, note 2).

[77] *HSC* 9, 13.

[78] *ASC*, s.a. 875, 876.

[79] See above, note 47. D. W. Rollason, 'The Wanderings of St Cuthbert', in *Cuthbert Saint and Patron*, ed. D. W. Rollason (Durham, 1987), p. 50, has suggested that the wanderings preceding the community's arrival at Chester-le-Street may have fulfilled a similar function.

[80] G. W. S. Barrow, *The Kingdom of the Scots* (London, 1973), pp. 150 – 4.

benefactions in the Durham area which the community continued to attract (as attested by the *Historia de sancto Cuthberto*), must have combined to make a return to Lindisfarne seem less and less realistic. Perhaps the community's final move in 995, south to Durham rather than north to Lindisfarne, can be understood as a tacit admission that its strategy in settling at Chester-le-Street had turned out to be successful in ways which could never have been envisaged at the outset.

St Cuthbert at Chester-le-Street

GERALD BONNER

It may be said at the outset that anything like a comprehensive history of the community of St Cuthbert at Chester-le-Street between 883 and 995 is impossible; the sources are inadequate.[1] All that the historian can hope to do is to use the limited literary evidence, together with that provided by material objects which have survived the centuries, to see if the latter can, to some degree, supplement and illuminate that documentary evidence. Perhaps appropriately, in view of the literary traditions of Christian Northumbria, it is from manuscripts, considered not simply as written records but as objects, as pieces of material evidence in themselves, that we can draw a good deal of information, although there are other archaeological remains to illuminate the literary texts. We shall never have a complete picture; but it is possible, by careful evaluation of the evidence, to reach a more informed estimate of the community of St Cuthbert than the bare facts provide.

With regard to our sources, first and foremost comes, not the famous *Historia Dunelmensis ecclesiae* of Symeon, but the curious compilation called the *Historia de sancto Cuthberto*, an anonymous work apparently begun at Chester-le-Street in the mid tenth century. Symeon describes it as 'the charter-roll of the church, which shows the ancient munificence of kings and various persons in religion towards the saint',[2] while Thomas Arnold, its nineteenth-century editor, calls it 'an ancient estate-roll of the monks of St Cuthbert, with biographical and historical particulars interspersed.'[3] It constitutes the primary source for the history of the church of Chester-le-Street between 883 and 995.

Next comes Symeon's *Historia Dunelmensis ecclesiae*, which begins at Lindisfarne and carries the story of the fortunes of Cuthbert's community to 1096. In the course of the narration it deals with the period of the sojourn at Chester-le-Street, but in a cursory fashion — twelve chapters out of a total of sixty-nine. Furthermore, writing in the twelfth century, Symeon's knowledge of the earlier period was inevitably second-hand.

---

[1] It is difficult to improve upon the outline provided by C. F. Battiscombe in *Relics*, pp. 30 – 5.

[2] *HDE* II, 16.

[3] *Sym. Op.*, I, p. xxv.

Third comes the work entitled the *Historia regum*, popularly attributed to Symeon of Durham. This compilation, which has been carefully analysed by Peter Hunter Blair, is found in MS 139 of Corpus Christi College, Cambridge, folios 51^v – 129^v. It was copied at the Cistercian house of Sawley, in the West Riding of Yorkshire, probably about 1170. The attribution to Symeon comes from the Sawley scribe and is very doubtful. The *Historia regum* includes a brief chronicle of the years 888 – 957 which provides some information about the Norse rulers of York. In addition, there is a chronicle of the years 849 – 87 which strongly resembles the annals which formed the framework for Asser's *Life of Alfred*, though it supplies certain entries of Northumbrian interest not dependent upon Asser; and a longer chronicle spanning the years 848 – 1118 and giving some information about Chester-le-Street, concerning in particular the lands and sanctuary rights of the see.[4]

Finally there are a number of minor pieces, printed by Thomas Arnold in the Rolls Series edition of the works of Symeon of Durham, together with evidence afforded by charters and similar documents. Here, out of a mass of irrelevant information, a scrap of evidence may occasionally emerge.

Such are the literary sources; but before we start to exploit them, it is desirable to remind ourselves that the whole history of the stay of St Cuthbert at Chester-le-Street was conditioned by the fact that it took place during the period of the first Scandinavian invasion and settlement. Dr Rollason has recently observed that, in the light of what we know of the land-holdings of the Lindisfarne community, the period of wandering between 875 and 883 does not so much suggest the flight of a band of destitute refugees from the onset of the Vikings as of a community which retained its power and influence throughout the various moves described.[5] This is no doubt correct; but it remains true that the mere fact of being a landowner affords little security in the presence of a neighbour who disputes one's title and carries a battle-axe. The sojourn at Chester-le-Street was conditioned first by the Danish settlement, and subsequently by the West Saxon *reconquista*. Hence the significance of Danish figures like King Guthfrith, elected, it is said, at the command of St Cuthbert in a vision to Abbot Eadred, and of Onlafball, the pagan bully, who threatened the church of Chester-le-Street and was struck dead by St Cuthbert for his pains.[6] Danish patronage mattered; and there

[4] Peter Hunter Blair, 'Some Observations on the "Historia Regum" Attributed to Symeon of Durham', in *Celt and Saxon: Studies in the Early British Border*, ed. N. K. Chadwick (Cambridge, 1964), pp. 63 – 118. On the dating and attribution of the earlier sections, see M. Lapidge, 'Byrhtferth of Ramsey and the Early Sections of the *Historia Regum* Attributed to Symeon of Durham', *ASE* 10 (1982), pp. 97 – 122. The connection of the manuscript with Sawley is examined further by D. Baker, 'Scissors and Paste: CCCC 139 Again', *Studies in Church History* 11 (1975), pp. 83 – 123, where the possibility is raised that it might have been owned by Sawley but written at Fountains Abbey.

[5] 'The Wanderings of St Cuthbert', in *Cuthbert: Saint and Patron*, ed. D. W. Rollason (Durham, 1987), p. 50. See above, pp. 379 – 86.

[6] *HSC* 13 and 23.

seems to be no good reason for questioning the statement of the *Historia de sancto Cuthberto* that King Guthfrith did actually bestow a generous grant of land between the Tyne and the Wear on the bishop of Lindisfarne in 883.[7] This would explain why the community remained at Chester-le-Street after the Danish settlement, and did not seek to return to Lindisfarne, where it could have enjoyed the protection of the English nobleman Eadwulf, then ruling at Bamburgh: at Chester-le-Street it would have the protection of King Guthfrith, the votary of St Cuthbert, and since the episcopal succession at Hexham had come to an end in 821, when the see was united with Lindisfarne, there was no danger of any conflict of jurisdictions.

There is, however, another factor in the history of St Cuthbert at Chester-le-Street: the steadily increasing power of the rulers of Wessex during the first three-quarters of the tenth century, who were thus able to give their protection to the shrine. The bishops of Chester-le-Street were well aware of the importance of cultivating their southern patrons, and were prepared to do so retrospectively, by numbering King Alfred among the votaries of St Cuthbert. Whatever may be the truth of Alfred's alleged vision of Cuthbert in the marshes of Athelney,[8] it is clear that the veneration of St Cuthbert seems to have been diffused throughout England during the tenth century.

The church built at Chester-le-Street by Bishop Eardwulf and Abbot and Prior Eadred is said by Symeon of Durham to have been of wood; it was subsequently pulled down and replaced by one of stone by Bishop Aethelric of Durham (1041 – 56).[9] In the course of the thirty years following the settlement under Eardwulf and the reign of his successor Cuthheard, the land-holdings of the church of Chester-le-Street seem to have been enlarged, both by purchase and by gift. The situation of the community was not wholly secure. During the period 912 – 15 it was menaced by the Scandinavian adventurer Raegnald who, after defeating an army of Constantine of Scotland and Ealdred, earldorman of Bernicia, at Corbridge, divided the lands of St Cuthbert beyond the Tees between his followers, Scula and Onlafball, the second of whom came to a bad end after threatening the followers of St Cuthbert.[10] His death no doubt made a suitable impression, and St Cuthbert recovered his lands and showed himself a powerful defender of his own.

In the following years the kings of Wessex steadily extended their power beyond the frontiers of their kingdom, so that in 919 the kings of the Scots and of the Britons of Strathclyde; Raegnald the Viking, now king at York; and the

---

[7] Ibid., 13: 'Die etiam ei, postquam rex effectus fuerit, ut det mihi totam terram inter Tinam et Wirram, et quicunque ad me confugerit, vel pro homicidio, vel pro aliqua necessitate, habeat pacem per xxxvii dies et noctes.'

[8] *HSC* 14 – 17; *HDE* II, 10.

[9] *HDE* III, 9: 'Placuerat eidem antistiti [Egelrico] ecclesiam in Cunecaceastre, quae corrupte nunc Ceastre vocatur, de ligno factam destruere, et pro eo quod aliquando beati Cuthberti corpus ibidem quieverat, aliam de lapide fabricare.'

[10] *HSC* 23. See F. M. Stenton, 'The Danes in England', in *Studies in History: British Academy Lectures Selected and Introduced by Lucy S. Sutherland* (London, 1966), pp. 12 – 13.

sons of Earl Eadwulf accepted Edward as 'father and lord'. Edward's successes were maintained and extended by his son Athelstan in a series of operations which culminated in 937 in the great victory of Brunanburh, which set the seal on the work begun by Alfred at Edington.

It seems clear that before the campaign of 937 Athelstan had already visited the shrine of St Cuthbert at Chester-le-Street, of which he was to be the great benefactor in the year 934. His importance as a patron is made clear by the *Liber vitae* of Durham, commonly assumed to have been at Chester-le-Street (BL Cotton MS Domitian VII), which opens, as such compilations do, with the names of royal and noble benefactors in chronological order. By this arrangement, the name of Athelstan comes on the verso of the first leaf. This, however, seemed an inadequate tribute to so great a benefactor, and so on the first line of the recto, after the heading: *Nomina regum uel ducum*, a hand of the tenth century has added: *adelstan rex*.[11]

Athelstan was, indeed, a generous benefactor of Chester-le-Street. A list of his gifts has survived in the *Historia de sancto Cuthberto*, and these include books, vestments, church-furniture and sacred vessels and, in addition, the grant of 'my beloved vill of South Wearmouth [Bishop Wearmouth]' with its dependencies, including Uffertun [Offerton in the parish of Houghton-le-Spring] and the whole of the present parishes of Seaham and Dalton.[12] The fact that one of the books presented by Athelstan to Chester-le-Street has apparently survived (Cambridge, Corpus Christi College MS 183) and is a particularly fine example of tenth-century book-painting, has tended to overshadow his gift of land; but the material prosperity of Chester-le-Street, like other medieval religious houses, ultimately depended upon its land-holdings. Books, in themselves, were an expression of wealth, and not a source of income.

With this proviso, let us consider Athelstan's gift of books. It consisted of 'one missal, two texts of the Gospels, ornamented with gold and silver, and a life of St Cuthbert, written in verse and prose.' This last would seem to be the Corpus Christi manuscript. Of the other books, one of the Gospel texts survived to the eighteenth century, to be almost completely destroyed in the great fire at Ashburnham House, Westminster, in 1731. However, Humphrey Wanley, the great palaeographer, had previously examined the manuscript, which he believed to have been copied in France, and recorded an inscription: 'I Athelstan king gave this book unto St Cuthbert.' A picture was inserted before St Matthew's Gospel, showing the king presenting his gift to the saint.[13]

---

[11] *Liber vitae ecclesiae Dunelmensis: A Collotype Facsimile of the Original Manuscript with Introductory Essays and Notes: vol. I: Facsimile and General Introduction* (SS 136; Durham, 1923), p. 1.

[12] *HSC* 26.

[13] BL Cotton MS Otho B.IX. N. R. Ker, *Catalogue of Manuscripts containing Anglo-Saxon* (Oxford, 1957), no. 176; *The Golden Age of Anglo-Saxon Art*, ed. J. Backhouse, D. H. Turner and Leslie Webster (London: British Museum Publications, 1984), no. 5.

The Corpus Christi *Life of St Cuthbert* shows a similar scene. Athelstan presents his book, bowing before the saint, who is tonsured and vested in a chasuble and alb. Behind is depicted a church. Is this to be regarded as a representation of the church of Chester-le-Street? This seems improbable. One may compare an analagous painting in the Benedictional of St Aethelwold, of which Francis Wormald wrote: 'It would . . . be dangerous to assume that this miniature gives any certain indication of the appearance of the Saxon cathedral of Winchester.'[14] The same would be true, I suspect, as regards Chester-le-Street.

Athelstan's gifts to Chester-le-Street also included the stole and maniple, found when St Cuthbert's tomb was opened in 1827. They were made between 909 and 916, probably at Winchester. 'The vestments', wrote Margaret Rickert, 'are a priceless relic of an early manifestation of that English skill in embroidering which was famous later all over Europe by the name of *opus anglicanum*. They are also one of the earliest manifestations of the full and direct impact of the Carolingian Renaissance on English Art.'[15]

Athelstan's visit to Chester-le-Street was repeated by his brother, Edmund, who visited the shrine while on campaign in the north in 945, prayed before Cuthbert's tomb, and commended himself and his men to God and St Cuthbert. The army presented the shrine with an offering of sixty pounds, and the king with his own hands placed two golden bracelets and two Greek copes on the holy body. More importantly, he confirmed all the rights enjoyed by the church of St Cuthbert over its lands.[16] As with the gifts of his brother, Athelstan, this was, from the point of view of the community of Chester-le-Street, the most important part of the royal bounty. However desirable moveable property might be, it was upon land, and upon the rights which went with the ownership of land, that the prosperity of the shrine ultimately depended.

Let us, however, return to King Athelstan's gift of books to Chester-le-Street, since this raises the question of the library there in the period 883 – 995. No catalogue survives, if one ever existed, and except where we can decide upon historical grounds that a particular codex must have been there, our estimate must, of necessity, be conjectural. It is reasonable to assume that the earliest Hiberno-Northumbrian manuscripts in the Chapter Library at Durham (A.II.10, fols. 2 – 5, 338, 339 (plate 31); A.II.16, fols. 24 – 33, 87 – 101; and A.II.17, fols. 2 – 102)[17] were at Chester-le-Street, either in a library or preserved as relics in the church, and the same is no doubt true of uncial portions like A.II.16, fols. 1 – 23, 34 – 86, 102 and A.II.17, fols.

---

[14] *The Benedictional of St Ethelwold*, with an introduction and commentary by Francis Wormald (The Faber Library of Illuminated Manuscripts; London, 1959), p. 30.
[15] M. Rickert, *Painting in Britain: The Middle Ages* (The Pelican History of Art; London, 1954), p. 36.
[16] *HSC* 28.
[17] *CLA* II, nos. 147; 148b; 149.

103 – 11.[18] To these may plausibly be added the Cuthbert Gospels, discovered
when St Cuthbert's tomb was opened at the translation of 1104, and
manuscripts in Anglo-Saxon majuscule like A.II.16, fols. 103 – 34; A.IV.19,
pp. 177 – 8 and B.II.30.[19] In the case of A.II.17 the human propensity for
scribbling on books has provided us with evidence amounting to certainty,
with the famous Boge inscription on both parts of the present manuscript,
both half-uncial (plate 23a) and uncial, and the reference on folio 106[r] to
'aldred god biscop' (plate 23b), who may be indentified with the Ealdred who
was bishop of Chester-le-Street from 944 to 968.[20]

The practice of adorning the margin of a Chester-le-Street book with a
reference to one of the bishops was not confined to the writer of the Boge
inscription. On folio 75[v] (p. 136) of Durham A.IV.19, the famous Durham
Ritual, there is an inscription in a Carolingian hand: *Dominus saluet, honoret,*
amet aldhunum antistitem. Aldhun was consecrated bishop of Chester-le-Street in
990 and died in 1018. It was during his episcopate that the move to Durham
took place in 995. What motives inspired the inscription we do not know.

There was, however, at Chester-le-Street in the tenth century one
manuscript, not now at Durham but in the British Library, which is far better
known than any other product of the Lindisfarne scriptorium, the Lindisfarne
Gospels, and it is to a member of the Chester-le-Street community that we owe
our information about its origins. This was Aldred, priest and provost[21] of
Chester-le-Street who, about 950, provided the interlinear gloss on the Latin
Gospel text and a colophon describing the history of the manuscript (pl. 15,
32). Because of his annotations, we know something about the career of
Aldred, the son of Alfred. Besides the Lindisfarne Gospels examples of his
hand are to be found in two other books: Oxford, Bodleian Library, MS
Bodley 819 (plate 33) and Durham, Cathedral Library MS A.IV.19. The
Bodleian manuscript is a copy of Bede's *Commentary on Proverbs*, assigned by
E. A. Lowe to England, and probably to Northumbria, and to the late eighth
or early ninth century.[22] From this we can deduce that the library at Chester-
le-Street contained at least one work by Bede; and the fact that Aldred
provided a few glosses suggests that among the members of the community

---

[18] *CLA* II, nos. 148a; 150.

[19] *CLA* II, nos. 148c; 151; 152.

[20] See *The Durham Gospels (Durham, Cathedral Library MS A.II.17)*, ed. C. D. Verey, T. J. Brown
and E. Coatsworth (EEMF 20; Copenhagen, 1980), pp. 35, 51 – 52, 63 – 64.

[21] See the comment of A. Hamilton Thompson, *Rituale ecclesiae Dunelmensis: The Durham Collectar*,
ed. A. H. Thompson and U. Lindelöf (SS 140; Durham, 1927), p. xix: 'The title provost was
appropriate to the head of an establishment which, so far as we know anything of its constitution,
was at this date in the somewhat ambiguous condition, neither regular nor entirely secular, which
prevailed in tenth-century minsters untouched by the reforming influence of Dunstan and
Aethelwold.' It should, however, be remembered that the title *praepositus* occurs in the Benedictine
Rule (ch. 65) and would be appropriate at Chester-le-Street if the bishop were regarded as
equivalent to the abbot of the community.

[22] *CLA* II, no. 235.

were some who were literate, though not good Latinists, and required assistance in their studies.

The other manuscript, A.IV.19 (plate 34), is even more interesting, from the point of view of the historian of Chester-le-Street. Although traditionally called the Durham Ritual, it is in fact a collectar and capitular, which would have been used by the officiant at the daily offices. It will be remembered that Walcher, the first Norman bishop of Durham (1071 – 80), rebuked the married canons of Durham for using a monastic office,[23] while his successor, William of St Calais, turned them out and replaced them by a monastic chapter.[24] What the organization of the church of Chester-le-Street may have been in the last third of the tenth century, we do not know; but the existence of A.IV.19 may possibly indicate a concern for liturgical conformity, and thanks to Aldred we know where and when the Ritual was acquired: it was by Bishop Aelfsige on 10 August 970, at Oakley Down to the south of Woodyates in Dorset.[25] The manuscript is written in an Anglo-Saxon minuscule of the early tenth century, apparently in the south of England; but the text is that of a collectar of the community of Augustinian canons of St Quentin in Vermandois, in northern France. Is one to see its acquisition as an attempt by Bishop Aelfsige to bring his church into line with the liturgical practices of Europe? We cannot tell. Furthermore Aldred records in his annotation to A.IV.19 that he copied part of a mass in honour of St Cuthbert into the manuscript. The fact that he did so, in the bishop's tent at Woodyates, implies that these prayers were not familiar in Northumbria. But how did it come about that prayers in honour of St Cuthbert were unknown to a member of his own community? The answer may lie in the fact that three of Aldred's four prayers appear in the earliest-known sacramentary of Fulda, St Boniface's burial-place, in Germany.[26] St Boniface was a man of Wessex; and it is possible that his text represents a Wessex tradition with which Aldred would have been unfamiliar.

It is conceivable that southern England could have already affected the liturgical life of Chester-le-Street before 970, through the Corpus Christi manuscript presented by King Athelstan. Besides the two lives of Cuthbert composed by Bede, the manuscript also contains an office, with a special mass, for the deposition of St Cuthbert on 20 March and his translation (probably a translation from Lindisfarne to Norham in about 830, about which the medieval church of Durham preferred to remain silent). The office and special mass in the Cambridge manuscript seem to have been composed for the court

---

[23] *HDE* III, 18: 'Qui [Walcherus] cum clericos ibidem inveniret, clericorum morem in diurnis et nocturnis officiis eos servare docuit. Nam antea magis consuetudines monachorum in his imitati fuerant, sicut a progenitoribus suis, ut supradictum est, qui inter monachos nutriti et educati extiterant, haereditaria semper traditione didicerant.'

[24] *HDE* IV, 2 and 3.

[25] See *The Durham Ritual*, ed. T. J. Brown (EEMF 16; Copenhagen, 1969), p. 24; below, pl. 34.

[26] On this, see Christopher Hohler, 'The Durham Services in Honour of St. Cuthbert', in *Relics*, p. 158.

chapel of either King Athelstan or his father, Edward the Elder, and to have had a certain diffusion in Wessex. They cannot be proved to have been used in Northumbria before the Norman conquest, so we cannot say whether they did have any practical effect on the liturgical life of Chester-le-Street; but after the move to Durham they were rescued from oblivion by Walcher, the first Norman bishop, and although the mass was not finally accepted, the office was, being adapted for monastic use at some time between 1083 and 1150.[27]

Aldred's annotations to the Durham Ritual are not, however, solely of liturgical interest, for they raise the question: what was the bishop of Chester-le-Street doing in Wessex in 970? To attempt an answer, it is necessary to recollect the situation in England at that time. The kings of Wessex had by now established their authority over Northumbria. The expulsion of the Norse King Eric Bloodaxe from York in 954 left King Eadred ruler of all England, and may be said to mark the unification of England under a single monarch in a way which had never been known before. In 957, during the short reign of Eadred's nephew, Eadwig (955 – 9), a revolt of the Northumbrians and Mercians in favour of his brother Edgar left Eadwig the effective ruler of Wessex alone; but after Eadwig's death in 957, Edgar had no difficulty in asserting his authority over the whole of England.

King Edgar is famous in English ecclesiastical history as a reformer, the ally of Archbishop Dunstan and Bishop Aethelwold in their efforts to bring the English church into line with the reforms of the continent. It would therefore be not unlikely that he would have wished to avail himself of the counsel of the bishop of Chester-le-Street, which was, with the archbishopric of York, one of the two surviving sees in Northumbria. In so doing, Edgar would not have been an innovator: Aelfsige's predecessor Wigred had attended the great council held by King Athelstan at Colchester on 23 March 931.[28] Similar councils continued to be held during Athelstan's reign and under his successors.

There is, therefore, nothing surprising in finding Bishop Aelfsige in the south of England in August 970. It is reasonable to guess that he was summoned by King Edgar to offer advice on matters which could have been either sacred or secular. Can we go any further than this and try to suggest a reason? It is possible — and the possibility is no more than a hypothesis — that some significance can be found in the presence of Provost Aldred in attendance on his bishop, and in the acquisition of a liturgical manuscript by the latter. The year 970 is commonly regarded as the date of the council of Winchester, which led to the compilation of the *Regularis concordia*, in an attempt to provide a universal set of customs for all the religious houses of England following the Benedictine Rule. It is true that we have no evidence for the exact date of the council, and Abbot Thomas Symons has argued for

[27] Ibid., pp. 155, 157.
[28] *BCS*, no. 674. F. M. Stenton, *Anglo-Saxon England* (3rd edn.; Oxford, 1971), p. 352.

973 as a more probable date;[29] but even if this were the case, preparations for the council might well have been set in train at a much earlier date, and Aelfsige summoned with Aldred, the immediate superior of the community of Chester-le-Street, to offer such advice as might be expected from the bishop and the prior of a community which was monastic in origin and which had, according to the anonymous Lindisfarne biographer of St Cuthbert, already adopted the Benedictine Rule by his day, i.e. before 705.[30] Whether or not the Chester-le-Street community was truly monastic at this time is a matter of debate; but it is clear that even in their early days at Durham, St Cuthbert's folk did not forget their monastic heritage, and it is in this context that we can suppose Aelfsige's acquisition of the Durham Ritual to have been the demonstration of a desire to bring the community of St Cuthbert, at least in some degree, into liturgical conformity with development in the south.

The picture which thus emerges from our admittedly restricted evidence is that the community of Chester-le-Street in the second half of the tenth century, while not a creative community in the way that Lindisfarne had been creative in the days of Aidan and Cuthbert and, in another sense, in the days of Bishop Eadfrith and the scribe of Durham Cathedral MS A.II.17, was not unworthy of its heritage. It had apparently contrived to preserve at least part of the libraries of Lindisfarne and Wearmouth/Jarrow. It was aware of, and to some extent responsive to, liturgical reform in the south. In Aldred it had a scribe who, in the judgement of the late Neil Ker, had a 'mastery both of book-hand and of the smaller glossing hand,'[31] and who was, if not a profound scholar, at least a competent Latinist. Its bishops, even if they included a black sheep like Seaxhelm, whose avarice led him to exploit his flock and who was, for his sins, driven from his office in 944 by the threats of St Cuthbert, delivered in three successive dreams,[32] seem in general to have been competent and conscientious pastors, even if they made little mark on history. Altogether we may feel that the sojourn of St Cuthbert's *familia* at Chester-le-Street, even if it drew its glory from the corporeal presence of its great patron, rather than from any original contribution of its own, did not bring discredit upon the community which so devotedly honoured the greatest of the northern saints. Not all periods in the life of an institution can be equally creative. In some the main task of its members will be to keep the faith, and to hand on the tradition, so that more fortunate generations may build upon the foundations of the past. *Depositum custodi*.

---

[29] T. Symons, '*Regularis concordia*: History and Derivation', in *Tenth Century Studies*, ed. D. Parsons (London, 1975), at pp. 40–2.

[30] *VCA* III, 1: 'et nobis regularem vitam primum componentibus constituit [Cuthberhtus], quam usque hodie cum regula Benedicti observamus.'

[31] Ker, 'Aldred the Scribe', *Essays and Studies by Members of the English Association* 28 (1943 for 1942), p. 12.

[32] *HDE* II, 19.

The King Alfred/St Cuthbert Episode
in the Historia de sancto Cuthberto:
Its Significance for mid-tenth-century English History

LUISELLA SIMPSON

The purpose of this paper is to argue that the story of St Cuthbert's miracles for King Alfred, found in sections 14 – 19 of the *Historia de sancto Cuthberto*, originated in the mid tenth century and had a specific significance for that period of English history.[1] First we must establish, at least as a hypothesis, when the *Historia* itself originated. Sections 1 – 28 of the *Historia* are in essence a record of St Cuthbert's possessions from the time of the see's foundation in the seventh century, enriched by original information on Northumbrian events of particular importance to the see. Two themes run through these sections: on the one hand, that of the posthumous protection offered by St Cuthbert to his community and possessions; on the other hand that of royal patronage. With regard to the latter, it is striking that the *Historia*, after honouring the Northumbrian founders of the see, focuses almost exclusively on patrons of the West Saxon dynasty, beginning with King Alfred (871 – 99), and continuing with his descendants in unbroken succession down to his second ruling grandson, Edmund (939 – 46). The *Historia* gives no information about the fifty or so years after Edmund's time but the last five sections (29 – 33) record land transactions in favour of St Cuthbert's see datable to the first third of the eleventh century.[2] Sections 1 – 28 were almost certainly compiled *c.*945 and sections 29 – 33 added subsequently in the mid eleventh century. This dating

[1] I would like to thank Dr Rollason for the welcome he gave both to this article and to myself at Durham. I am also grateful to Dr Janet Nelson, Mr John Gillingham and the Early Medieval seminar at the Historical Institute, London, for their criticism of this study at an early stage and for their encouragement. *The Historia de sancto Cuthberto* will be referred to as the *Historia* in this paper. For the text, see *Sym. Op.* I, 196 – 214, where the editor has introduced numbered sections.
[2] The last grant recorded is a gift by King Cnut, probably in 1031. The presence of section 33 on the destruction of a Scots army, allegedly in the time of King Guthfrith (late 9th century), could be understood in the context of Durham's military preoccupations with the Scots in the 11th century. Section 29 begins with an invocation (*In nomine Dei* . . .), as section 1 did.

for sections 1 – 28 rests partly on the fact that one of the manuscripts, Cambridge University Library, MS Ff 1.27, pp. 195 – 202, contains only sections 1 – 28, in which the latest event recorded is a visit of King Edmund to St Cuthbert's see at Chester-le-Street, probably in 945. Although this manuscript is not the oldest extant, it would appear that it nevertheless contains an older version, i.e. the original mid-tenth-century compilation, lacking the eleventh-century additions represented by sections 29 – 33.[3] The dating of sections 1 – 28 to *c.*945 is corroborated by their chronological framework which, from section 14 to section 28, is provided by the reigns of the West Saxon kings, a frame of reference not found in sections 29 – 33. Moreover, section 28 concerns privileges granted to St Cuthbert's see by King Edmund on the occasion of his visit in 945 referred to above, and these may well have constituted the immediate incentive for the compilation of the work in its mid-tenth-century form.[4]

A persistent opinion has held, however, that sections 15 – 19, which contain the St Cuthbert/Alfred miracle story, form an eleventh-century interpolation in the earlier composition. This opinion goes back to Thomas Arnold. In the story the saint, in a nocturnal apparition to the king, promises Alfred decisive victory *apud montem Assandune.* The battle in question, Arnold suggested, was presumably that fought by Alfred in 878 at *Ethandune* (Edington), and the author of section 16 would seemingly have confused this battle with the one fought by Cnut at Ashingdon (*Assandune*) in 1016. Since such a confusion could hardly have arisen before the latter date, Arnold argued that sections 15 – 19 were to be seen as an eleventh-century interpolation (though he did not venture a date for the *Historia* itself).[5] While it cannot be discounted that *Assandune* may point to an eleventh-century scribe, Arnold's hypothesis cannot rest securely on this single instance. At this point, we must take a close look at the contours of the would-be interpolation.

It must be specified here that the numbered sections in the Rolls Series edition are, however useful, a nineteenth-century editorial creation. The purely narrative style and hagiographical tone of section 15 must have induced Arnold to take it as the beginning of an interpolation. However, this paragraph is prepared for by section 12 and especially by section 14, which concern the movements of the great Danish army both in northern and southern Anglo-Saxon territory and end with King Alfred's retreat to a Somerset marshland identified as Glastonbury. St Cuthbert's intervention in

---

[3] E. Craster, 'The Patrimony of St Cuthbert, *EHR* 69 (1954), pp. 177 – 99. See also J. Hinde, *Symeonis Dunelmensis Opera et collectanea* (SS 51; Durham, 1868), p. xxxvi; David Hall, 'The Community of St Cuthbert, Its Properties, Rights and Claims from the Ninth Century to the Twelfth' (unpublished D.Phil. thesis, University of Oxford, 1984). F. M. Stenton, *Anglo-Saxon England* (3rd edn.; Oxford, 1971), p. 262, n. 2, followed by Michael Lapidge, *The Annals of St Neots with the Vita prima sancti Neoti* (Cambridge, 1985), p. cv, ascribed the whole text to the eleventh century but offered no evidence for this.

[4] Hall, op. cit., p. 16.

[5] *Sym. Op.* I, 205, note a; p. 207, note a.

Alfred's favour follows thereupon: the saint penetrates the fen-fastness of Alfred's retreat in the guise of a pilgrim, where his needs are generously provided for by the king, before the pilgrim disappears; the same day Alfred's men bring back a miraculous catch of fish (section 15); during the night, the saint appears to Alfred in glorious and recognizable form. He promises the king victory (as we have seen), and the rulership of the whole of Britain for himself and his descendants (section 16). This apparition and promise are commented upon in the light of explicit parallels in the Psalms and in Bede (section 17), before Alfred's victory on the morrow and its consequences are recounted (section 18). Before his death, Alfred entrusts his son Edward with gifts for St Cuthbert (beginning of section 19). The 'Alfred passage' can thus be strictly defined as sections 14 to the first half of section 19.

At the extremities of this portion of the *Historia*, there are slight discrepancies in the chronological or subject-matter sequence which could point to an interpolation. Section 14 takes a step backwards in time, as King Alfred's resistance (in 878) follows Northumbrian events which led to the resettlement of the Cuthbertine community at Chester-le-Street (in the early 880s). Further on, the second half of section 19, concerning the territorial acquisitions of Abbot Eadred at Chester-le-Street, could be considered as a return to the Northumbrian and Cuthbertine scene of section 13. As we shall see, however, the 'Alfred passage' reveals an imperfect knowledge of West Saxon history and of its chronology, which could explain the position of section 14. As for the second half of section 19, it resembles the first half in recording accretions to St Cuthbert's possessions before the end of Alfred's reign. Moreover, if it really did represent the return to a mainstream narrative after an interpolation, it would find no smooth continuity in section 20, the episode of the abortive crossing of St Cuthbert's relics to Ireland. The latter episode returns to the time — *eodem tempore* — not of section 13, but of the beginning of the 'Alfred passage', to which it can hardly be anterior in composition.[6] The imperfections of the entire sequence were to find masterful correction in the early twelfth-century *Historia Dunelmensis ecclesiae*. However, just as the Alfred passage does not come unprepared, it is noticeable that section 25, which concerns Edward the Elder, makes an important reference to St Cuthbert's miracles in favour of Edward's father. Indeed, the very framework in which the fortunes of St Cuthbert's new patrimony at Chester-le-Street are recorded — the successive reigns of Alfred and of his immediate successors — seems in keeping with the story of the northern saint's miracle in favour of the West Saxon. At this point, to hypothesize a potential interpolation (or interpolations) in an ancestor text of the *Historia* as we preserve it seems less fruitful than to highlight the mid-tenth-century elements the King Alfred and St Cuthbert passage may reveal.

[6] Craster believed this miracle story to be anterior to the miracle for King Alfred, because it makes no mention of the loss and recovery of the (Lindisfarne) Gospels. But this element of the story can only be traced back to the early 12th-century *HDE*.

I shall focus therefore on a series of features which suggests that the 'Alfred passage' was politically meaningful *c*.945. It is noticeable first of all that St Cuthbert, as he assures Alfred of future rulership over all Britain, repeatedly extends his promise to *filiis tuis, et filiis filiorum tuorum*. Cuthbert presents himself as *amicus tuus, et defensor filiorum tuorum* (section 16). Someone writing in or after Cnut's time would hardly have insisted on this point. The author gives an authoritative parallel to these words in two biblical quotations: *de fructu ventris tui ponam super sedem tuam* and *filii tui, et filii filiorum tuorum sedebunt super sedem tuam*. These are both verses drawn from Psalm 131, 'Lord, remember David, and all his afflictions', a messianic psalm which ends with God's promise for David: 'upon him shall his diadem flourish'. Beyond the initial parallel with King Alfred's situation, I suggest that the promise is to be taken literally, in a mid-tenth-century context, as referring to Alfred's son Edward, and grandsons, Athelstan and Edmund, who ruled in turn in the years 899 – 946. These kings were clearly of special importance to the author of the *Historia*. First of all, Edward the Elder receives exceptional attention both in the 'Alfred passage' and in the *Historia* in general. King Alfred is first referred to as *patrem Edwardi regis* (section 14), and we are told that Edward was present at the battle of Edington, a statement to be found neither in the *Anglo-Saxon Chronicle* nor in Aethelweard's chronicle. Edward is said to have offered gifts to St Cuthbert on his father's behalf. Outside the 'Alfred passage', Edward's friendship with the Bernician lord of Bamburgh is evoked as a continuation of the friendship between their two fathers. Thus Edward's memory appears still to have been fresh in the author's time and his name was used as a prestigious reference: one could compare this with the poem on the battle of Brunanburh in alliterative verse preserved in the *Anglo-Saxon Chronicle s. a.* 937, which twice refers to the heroes of the day, King Athelstan and Edmund aetheling, as 'the sons of Edward' (*afaran Eadwardes*). The formula also occurs in another alliterative poem preserved in the *Chronicle s. a.* 942, which celebrates the redemption of the Five Boroughs by King Edmund. Here again, Edmund is honoured as *afera Eadwardes*. Now the entries in the A version of the *Chronicle* for the years 924 – 55 (that is, the record of the reigns of the three sons of Edward the Elder which includes the two alliterative poems) were written by a new scribe on a new quire, in a script typical of the 940s and 950s.[7] The 'son(s) of Edward' formula is not to be found, as far as I know, outside this and other documents of the mid tenth century. It therefore provides further corroboration for the dating of sections 1 – 28 of the *Historia*, including the 'Alfred passage', to the period *c*.945, if its similarity to the reference to Alfred as father of Edward in our passage is accepted.

Another feature which can help set the Alfred passage in a specific historical context is the *tu es electus rex totius Britanniae* formula in Cuthbert's promise to

---

[7] Cf. Janet Bately, *The Anglo-Saxon Chronicle MS A* (Woodbridge, 1986), pp. xxxiv – v. The important role given to Edmund aetheling in this poem could suggest that the piece was composed in Edmund's time.

Alfred (section 16). These words follow an equivalent promise: *tibi et filiis tuis data est tota Albion.* Now these formulae extolling West Saxon rulership over all Britain/Albion can be closely associated with a distinctive series of royal styles which were first elaborated for King Athelstan and developed by his tenth-century successors. Bede had of course voiced the concern of Rome and the English church for the *status . . . Brittaniae totius* — a Britain that he wished to see united in the Christian faith — in his *Ecclesiastical History;*[8] and King Alfred's biographer Asser was certainly setting himself on Bedan ground when he dedicated his biography to *Domino meo . . . omnium Brittanniae insulae Christianorum rectori, Aelfred, Anglorum Saxonum regi.*[9] Yet Britain as an ideal political entity received its widest publicity in the propaganda of the sons of Edward the Elder. From about 930, a coin bearing the style *rex to(tius) Brit(anniae)* was struck for King Athelstan at most mints south and west of Watling Street, and in the newly conquered York.[10] The formula also appears as a prominent element in a variety of styles given to Athelstan in his charters. An early example of these, in what is probably an original charter dated 29 April 930, qualifies Athelstan as *rex Anglorum . . . totius Bryttanniae regni solio sublimatus.*[11] Edmund's reign witnessed further innovations in royal styles around the same theme of the overlordship of Britain. The *rex totius Albionis* formula, for example, grew in favour in diplomas of his time.[12] As W. H. Stevenson argued, the fully 'imperial' style of the tenth-century English kings seems to have been introduced by King Edmund.[13] Though the political ideology underlying 'Britannic' styles reached a ceremonial peak with Edgar's 'imperial' coronation in 973,[14] and though these styles survived in charters up to the reign of Cnut, it is significant that Edgar had already adopted for his new coinage, in about 973, the less controversial and more quietly assured *rex Anglorum* title. The establishment by the West Saxons of a kingdom of England as distinct from mere symbolic lordship over the island, was indeed the chief goal and true achievement of the sons of Edward, an achievement which King Edgar could rest upon. At the immediate origin of Athelstan's new styles lay no doubt Athelstan's conquest of Northumbria in 927. Indeed, one could

---

[8] *HE* V, 23, and ch. heading. See also P. Wormald, 'Bede, the *Bretwaldas* and the Origins of the *Gens Anglorum*', in *Ideal and Reality in Frankish and Anglo-Saxon Society*, ed. P. Wormald (Oxford, 1983), at pp. 99 – 129.

[9] *Asser's Life of King Alfred*, ed. W. H. Stevenson (Oxford, 1904), p. 1.

[10] Cf. M. Dolley, *Anglo-Saxon Pennies* (London, 1964), p. 22 and plate xiii, and C. E. Blunt, 'The Coinage of Athelstan, 924 – 939: A Survey', *British Numismatic Journal* 42 (1974), pp. 39 – 60, esp. pp. 47 – 48 and p. 55.

[11] *The Crawford Collection of Early Charters and Documents*, ed. A. S. Napier and W. H. Stevenson (Oxford, 1895), pp. 5 – 9 and 65 – 80; and see P. H. Sawyer, *Anglo-Saxon Charters* (London, 1968), no. 405.

[12] For a table of the main types of royal styles used in charters from Alfred to Edgar (whatever the status of the surviving documents), see Harald Kleinschmidt, *Untersuchungen über das englische Königtum im 10. Jahrhundert* (Göttingen, 1979), pp. 40 – 42.

[13] Stevenson, *Crawford Charters*, p. 111.

[14] Cf. J. L. Nelson, 'Inauguration Rituals', in *Early Medieval Kingship*, ed. P. H. Sawyer and I. Wood (Leeds, 1977), at pp. 50 – 71.

connect the creative period of the *rex totius Britanniae* titles with that in which Northumbria, now gained, now lost, dominated West Saxon politics, that is from the reign of Athelstan to that of Eadred. In a word, St Cuthbert's promise to King Alfred in our passage of the *Historia*, allegedly fulfilled when Alfred *regnum Britanniae accepit* (section 18), would have borne a very precise meaning to a mid-tenth-century Cuthbertine author. I suggest it would have symbolized in essence the lawful entitlement of the house of Wessex to Northumbria.

Indeed, the 'Alfred passage' underlines the hereditary right of the West Saxon kings to rule Britain, and, as we shall see, northern England in particular. Cuthbert states forcibly to Alfred that God has delivered unto him and his successors *totam istam terram, et regnum haereditarium* (section 16). *Totam istam terram* refers to Albion and to the rulership of all Britain, as Cuthbert makes abundantly clear in the following sentences. Alfred repeats this to his troops before battle: Victory awaits them; *terram haereditario jure obtinerent* (section 18). Hereditary right, a hereditary realm: the question is certainly an important one to the author of the 'Alfred passage'. We find interesting parallels to these words, or at least to this notion, in three texts relating to the first half of the tenth century. In what is known as the 'Second English Coronation Order', the prayer marking the enthronement of the new king begins: 'Sta et retine amodo statum quem hucusque paterna suggestione tenuisti *hereditario iure* tibi delegatum.'[15] Now this Coronation Order was probably first elaborated for Edward the Elder's coronation at Pentecost 900, or at the latest for Athelstan's coronation on September 925, and remained in use with minimal variations throughout the tenth century. The original version of the ritual is lost, but the oldest surviving versions are likely to date from the reign of Athelstan or of his brothers, as various features including references to the throne of the *saxonum merciorum norhanimbrorum* or to the *regnum Albionis* would imply.[16]

My second and third texts reflect more precisely, I would suggest, West Saxon political propaganda in Athelstan's time. William of Malmesbury's *Gesta regum* contains a well-defined section derived, William informs us, from 'a very old book', which he believed to be from King Athelstan's reign, as he deduced from both its style and contents. Here the death in 927 of Sihtric, the

---

[15] 'Stand and hold fast now the position that you have held up to this time by your father's suggestion, and which is delegated to you by hereditary right'. For the text see P. L. Ward, 'An Early Version of the Anglo-Saxon Coronation Ceremony', *EHR* 57 (1942), pp. 345 – 58 at p. 357.

[16] Cf. J. L. Nelson, 'The Second English Coronation Ordo', in J. L. Nelson, *Politics and Ritual in Early Medieval Europe* (London, 1986), at pp. 361 – 374, and D. H. Turner, *The Claudius Pontificals* (Henry Bradshaw Society 97; Chichester, 1971), p. vii. The enthronement prayer may have been copied from a continental source (which survives in the so-called Seven-forms Ordo), but the possibility cannot be excluded that its allusion to hereditary right originated independently. Cf. C. A. Bowman, *Sacring and Crowning* (Groningen, Djakarta, 1957), p. 137 and n. 3.

Danish king of York, is commented upon thus: by his disappearance Sihtric 'gave Athelstan the opportunity of joining Northumbria . . . to his own part', Northumbria which belonged to Athelstan 'both by ancient right (*antiquo jure*) and by recent marriage alliance (*nova necessitudine*).[17] New and ancestral claims to the Northumbrian throne are thus joined in this passage which is allegedly based on materials from King Athelstan's time. Michael Lapidge has of course made the twelfth-century contribution to this whole section clear, but has further challenged not only its value for tenth-century history, but also the very existence of William's source.[18] Although there is no space here to argue the case in detail, I suggest that the Malmesbury librarian and historian was fooling neither himself nor his readers in this matter. William's rigorous and clearly-explained layout shows that he had first given his own account of Athelstan's reign, from beginning to end, then appended a series of documents, classified by their degree of trustworthiness. Of these this poem on King Athelstan was the first and essential piece. Aware of the contribution the Malmesbury archive was making to a reign so scantily documented elsewhere, he avoided here his usual amalgamation of sources into one narrative, so as to preserve their integrity. As William himself explains, however, he is giving a rendering of his source 'in plain style' (*familiari stylo*). Are the neatly balanced *et antiquo jure et nova necessitudine* merely William's own elaboration? I shall simply point out here that the hyperbolical praise of Edward the Elder, in the same section, has a very different ring from the standard twelfth-century historical comments on the king (including William's own, in his preceding account of Edward's reign) and suggests a close reproduction of a tenth-century source.[19]

My third text is contained in a book indubitably associated with Athelstan and with St Cuthbert's see. Cambridge, Corpus Christi College MS 183, the splendid volume offered by the king to the Cuthbertine community, contains, besides Bede's two lives of St Cuthbert and other material related to the saint, a series of royal genealogies. This is the first surviving manuscript in which the West Saxon genealogy appears side by side with the genealogies of the 'Anglian Collection', as defined by David Dumville.[20] Here we see the West Saxon pedigree linked, in its upper reaches, to the Bernician pedigree,

---

[17] William of Malmesbury, *De gestis regum Anglorum*, ed. W. Stubbs (2 vols., RS; London, 1887–89) I, 146, translated in *EHD*, p. 306.

[18] M. Lapidge, 'Some Latin Poems as Evidence for the Reign of Athelstan', *ASE* 9 (1981), pp. 61–98.

[19] Alluding to Athelstan's deceased father: 'His father, famed to every age, fulfilled his destiny, to conquer all ages with eternal fame' (*De gestis regum*, I, 146). The early 12th-century Worcester *Chronicon ex chronicis* states (s.a. 901) that Edward the Elder was 'litterarum cultu patre inferior, sed dignitate, potentia, pariter et gloria superior' (*Florentii Wigorniensis Monachi chronicon ex chronicis*, ed. B. Thorpe (2 vols.; London, 1848), I, 117). This comment was replicated thereafter by practically every medieval historiographer who covered Edward's reign, including William of Malmesbury (*De gestis regum*, I, 135).

[20] D. N. Dumville, 'The Anglian Collection of Royal Genealogies and Regnal lists', *ASE* 5 (1976), pp. 23–50.

through Brand and his father Baeldaeg, son of Woden. This invented link between the distant ancestors of the Bernician and West Saxon dynasties was not a novelty in the tenth century, for such a link can be seen in West Saxon genealogies contained in sources of King Alfred's time.[21] It could have been an Alfredian creation, or it could, as Dumville has hypothesized, have been invented as early as 635 to celebrate a Bernician and West Saxon alliance.[22] What is significant, I would suggest, is that Athelstan had it transcribed for the Bernician see of St Cuthbert. Maybe it was intended as a political weapon at a time when Athelstan was defending his Northumbrian conquest. In this case, the origins of the fabrication would be likely to lie in West Saxon ambitions in Northumbria a few generations earlier; moreover the presence of genealogies as an integral part of a volume devoted to St Cuthbert would take on its full sense. Certainly it would seem to reflect the same claims to rule by hereditary right as are found in the *Historia* and in the other texts discussed here.

The *Anglo-Saxon Chronicle*, which had publicized this genealogical link, could be used as a fourth comparative text.[23] The submission of the Northumbrians to the *Bretwalda* Ecgberht is noted there *s.a.* 829; Alfred's role as the leader of all the English people is of course put to the fore, in particular *s.a.* 886 and 900. As for Edward the Elder, we read *s.a.* 920 that he was chosen 'as father and lord' by the major rulers of northern Britain (the king of the Scots, the Danish king of York, the king of the Strathclyde Welsh and the English rulers of Bamburgh), although this may have been decidedly an overstatement.[24] The triumphant annal for 927 on Athelstan's achievement must be read with this background in mind. To summarize my last points: St Cuthbert's words to King Alfred in our passage of the *Historia* seem to carry an echo of claims of the earlier tenth century, and maybe of the later ninth century, to the lawful possession of Northumbria and of Britain beyond it, as expressed in royal styles, and arguably in genealogies and in histories of this period. The author of the 'Alfred passage', however, if I interpret his motives correctly, preferred to rely on more solid guarantees than the assertions of mortals. A saint as powerful as Cuthbert, making promises in God's own name, no doubt seemed to offer the ultimate ideological validation.

It is time to ask ourselves why, and from what time, the Cuthbertine community would have been anxious to support the cause of the West Saxons in Northumbria. Here the specific Bernician situation, as opposed to the Deiran around York, has to be fully understood. Our main source for this very obscure period of northern history is in fact the *Historia*, in passages of which the authentic basis has never been put in doubt.

---

[21] Cf. K. Sisam, 'Anglo-Saxon Royal Genealogies', *Proceedings of the British Academy* 39 (1953), pp. 287 – 348. Sisam demonstrated that the West-Saxon genealogy was modelled on the Bernician, but believed this to have originated in a scribal error.

[22] D. N. Dumville, 'Kingship, Genealogies and Regnal Lists', in *Early Medieval Kingship*, ed. Sawyer and Wood, pp. 72 – 104, at pp. 81 – 2.

[23] *ASC*, *s.a.* 547, 552, 597, 855.

[24] A. P. Smyth, *Warlords and Holy Men: Scotland 80 – 1000* (London, 1984), p. 199.

The Dane Halfdan's wintering on the Tyne with his army in 875 caused a seven-year period of peregrinations for St Cuthbert's community. After this trauma, however, the Bernicians and (near their southern border) St Cuthbert's new see at Chester-le-Street seem to have enjoyed a period of relative political autonomy and peace. Danish colonization does not seem to have extended north of the Tees or at least of the Wear,[25] and the community was on good terms with Guthfrith (the *Historia*'s *Guthredus*), the Danish king (d. 894?) probably based in York.[26] This peace was menaced when as a direct consequence of Edward the Elder's victory at Tettenhall (in 910) over the Danes of York, the Norse of Dublin stepped into the power-vacuum thus created and conquered York (*c.*911). Raegnald, their leader, labelled by the *Historia* as a *maledictus rex*, was victorious at the successive battles of Corbridge, not far from Chester-le-Street, in 914 and 918. These battles were a disaster for the Bernicians and for St Cuthbert's. According to the *Historia*, warriors holding land as *fideles* from the see had fought there, alongside the troops of the lord of Bamburgh, against Raegnald (sections 22 and 24). Friendship and alliances between the once royal Bernician family and the most powerful church in northern Northumbria were thus continuing long after the time in which the two could look at each other from Lindisfarne across to Bamburgh, and were to persist into the eleventh century.[27] Now the outcome of the Corbridge battles was an unprecedented alliance between the Scots and the new Norse masters of York, which left the Bernicians in an uncomfortable position between powerful and allied neighbours to the north and south, while St Cuthbert's was suffering territorial despoliations to the profit of some of Raegnald's followers (section 23). In these circumstances, it is understandable that St Cuthbert's community turned towards the kings of Wessex, who were English, Christian, and sufficiently unassured as yet to be courting allies in Northumbria. In the *Historia*'s cry of lament for the *Angli* killed at the battles of Corbridge, one can probably read support both for the Bernician cause and for the wider 'English' cause.[28]

The same political alliances, principally between the Scots and the Norse of York, spurred on Athelstan's successive campaigns in the north. During the second of these, in 934, he was welcomed at Chester-le-Street where he invoked Saint Cuthbert's help and made lavish gifts (sections 26–7). Athelstan was granted great victories. His brother Edmund, however, only three years after Brunanburh, was signing a disastrous treaty with the Irish-Norse leader Olaf Guthfrithson, who, we can notice in passing, appears on one of his coins as *rex to(tius) B.?(ritanniae)* — not an unjustified imitation of the

---

[25] Smyth, op. cit., p. 195 and Stenton, *Anglo-Saxon England*, p. 253.

[26] *HSC*, 13; also *HR* 98 and D. Hall, 'Community of St Cuthbert', p. 73.

[27] Cf. the tract *De obsessione Dunelmi* (in *Sym. Op.* I, 215–20), and the mention of leases of land by St Cuthbert's to earl Uhtred (of the family of Bamburgh) in *HSC* 31. Hall, op. cit., p. 78, sees St Cuthbert's with its Bernician allies as 'a spiritual and military counterbalance to York'.

[28] *HSC* sec. 22. *Angli* is used in the *HSC* in a narrower sense in sec. 3, in a broader sense in sec. 12 (in which the Danes *omnes prope Anglos in meridiana et aquilonari parte occiderunt*).

West Saxon style, for the master of Dublin and York.[29] The treaty of 940 between Edmund and Olaf marked a reverse in West Saxon fortunes unprecedented since King Alfred's darker days; and it left Olaf a free hand to ravage in Bernicia and as far as Tyningham in Lothian, a possession of St Cuthbert's community. For the latter, the spectre of the woes of Raegnald's time must have been aroused. With Olaf's death, the tide turned once again. Yet when Edmund regained control of Northumbria in 944, and when he stopped at Chester-le-Street (probably in 945), he still had good reasons to seek the support both of the saint and the see, by granting important privileges (section 28); and conversely, St Cuthbert's welcomed royal support.

As we have seen, the composition of the *Historia* may have stemmed from this event, and one further detail within the Alfred passage may point closely to Edmund's time. This is the mention of Glastonbury, not Athelney (as in the *Anglo-Saxon Chronicle*), as the place of King Alfred's marshland refuge, at the low ebb of his fortunes (*in Glesti⟨n⟩giensi palude*: section 14).[30] Now there is almost total silence in other extant sources about Glastonbury in the late ninth century. In Athelstan's time one of the royal gifts received by St Cuthbert's see, Corpus Christi College 183, may have been written at Glastonbury.[31] Yet it was during King Edmund's reign, under Edmund's active patronage and Dunstan's abbacy, that the reformed house emerged as an important religious and cultural centre, closely linked to the West Saxon rulers. This is the time, according to the most likely testimony, when Glastonbury received the relics of northern saints, including relics formerly in the possession of the Cuthbertines.[32] Thus Glastonbury would have been a prestigious name to the community at Chester-le-Street, not least through the personal contacts established between the community and Edmund and his entourage. The *Historia* seems to reflect this in the probably erroneous reference to Glastonbury as Alfred's place of refuge.

Three problems remain. First, why does King Alfred benefit from St Cuthbert's assistance in the *Historia*, rather than his grandson Athelstan, the first true conqueror of Northumbria and great benefactor of Northumbrian

---

[29] See C. F. Keary, *Catalogue of English Coins in the British Museum, Anglo-Saxon Series*, ed. R. S. Poole (vol. 1; London, 1887), p. 235. On Edmund and Olaf Guthfrithson, cf. M. L. Beaven, 'King Edmund I and the Danes of York', *EHR* 129 (1918), pp. 1 – 9.

[30] The adjective *glesti⟨n⟩giensi* represents an early form of the name Glastonbury, before *-byrig* was added (at an uncertain date). Cf. H. P. R. Finberg, 'Ynyswitrin', in his (ed.), *Lucerna* (London, 1964), p. 16.

[31] J. A. Robinson, *The Saxon Bishops of Wells: A Historical Study in the Tenth Century* (London, 1918), pp. 12 – 14, and S. Keynes, 'King Athelstan's Books', in *Learning and Literature in Anglo-Saxon England*, ed. M. Lapidge and H. Gneuss (Cambridge, 1985), pp. 143 – 201, at pp. 184 – 85. There is considerable evidence for Glastonbury scriptorial activity during Dunstan's abbacy, including its early period in the reign of Edmund. See C. Hart, 'Danelaw Charters and the Glastonbury Scriptorium', *Downside Review* 90 (1972), pp. 125 – 132.

[32] *De gestis pontificum*, ed. N. Hamilton (RS; London, 1870), p. 198. And see D. W. Rollason, 'Relic Cults as an Instrument of Royal Policy, *c.*900 – *c.*1050', *ASE* 15 (1986), pp. 91 – 103, at p. 95.

churches? One answer is that a king in such straits as Alfred was at the beginning of 878, who then won a memorable battle, is a subject begging for a miracle story. But more importantly, *c.*945 Athelstan would have been too recent a hero for such a miracle, and could have cast a shadow over his then reigning brother, Edmund. In sources of a somewhat later date, by contrast, we do find Athelstan as a beneficiary of miracles. Ailred abbot of Rievaulx (1147 – 67), in his *Genealogia regum anglorum*, wrote that St John of Beverley (the early eighth-century archbishop of York) appeared to Athelstan on the night before his battle with the Scots and his other northern enemies, thanked him for his devotion (the king had left his knife in token on the altar at Beverley) and promised him victory. It is striking that this miracle does not appear in Folcard's mid-eleventh-century life of the saint.[33] Moreover, in spite of the great attention the *Historia* lavishes on Athelstan's charter of donation, it does not reserve for the king quite the ovation which he enjoys in post-Conquest histories, especially in the north of England, as the 'first ruler' of the country. It is revealing that in evoking the King Alfred/St Cuthbert story, the author of the *Historia Dunelmensis ecclesiae* (written at the turn of the eleventh and twelfth centuries) felt the need of making a geopolitical clarification. St Cuthbert would have fulfilled his promise to Alfred in so far as the latter extended the frontiers of his realm (*imperii*) further than any of his predecessors, but these promises were only ultimately fulfilled when Athelstan, *primus regum Anglorum*, having received the submission of all his enemies, *totius Britanniae dominium obtinuit.*[34] Even a Durham *Chronica* of slightly earlier date (1071/88) does not fail to qualify Athelstan as *totius Angliae rex* (Anglia tending increasingly to replace Britannia in this formula in post-Conquest historiography).[35]

Secondly, is there any evidence that the St Cuthbert/Alfred legend was inspired by an actual link between King Alfred and the cult or community of St Cuthbert? The answer must be mainly in the negative. The *Historia* is seeing the late ninth century from a Cuthbertine viewpoint and the author associates Alfred's tribulations at the height of the Danish invasions with the terrible period of the peregrinations of St Cuthbert's community under Danish menace. This can be deduced from the broad placing of our episode, and maybe from the mention of Alfred remaining in hiding at Glastonbury for *three* years. Indeed, one suspects that this error may derive from a rough calculation of the time separating 875, the year in which the Cuthbertine wanderings began, from 878, the year of Alfred's victory at Edington. Other inexactitudes in our passage, such as the use of *terram Australium Saxonum* to refer not to Sussex but to the south of England, reveal both a northern and an

---

[33] The *Genealogia Regum Anglorum* is printed in *PL* 195, cols. 724 – 6. A near-identical account appears in a collection of miracles of St John of Beverley written shortly after, *c.*1170/80, printed in *The Historians of the Church of York and its Archbishops*, ed. J. Raine (RS; London, 1879), I, 263 – 64. For an edition of Folcard's Life of St John of Beverley, see pp. 239 – 60.

[34] *HDE* 10.

[35] Edited E. Craster, 'The Red Book of Durham', *EHR* 40 (1925), pp. 504 – 532, at p. 525.

ill-informed viewpoint. Is there other evidence, however, for Alfred intervening in Northumbria, or for a special relationship between the king and the cult or community of St Cuthbert? On this question, historical confusion has long reigned, stemming indirectly from the *Historia* itself and directly from eleventh- and twelfth-century expansions of its testimony. To the assertion in the *Historia* that Alfred was ever victorious after St Cuthbert's intervention and that he gained the *regnum Britanniae*, the author of the *Historia Dunelmensis ecclesiae* added, as we have seen, a reflexion on Athelstan's fulfilment of St Cuthbert's promise. In a further passage, he stated nevertheless that after his vision of St Cuthbert Alfred annexed to his West Saxon kingdom both Northumbria (after King Guthfrith's death) and East Anglia.[36] The author, probably Symeon of Durham, was anticipating tenth-century events here, as if he wanted to minimize discontinuities in Anglo-Saxon rulership over these territories. An earlier chronicle which was written in East Anglia around the year 1000, and which forms the first part of the *Historia regum*,[37] had been particularly messy on this point: the annal for 890 names Guthrum, not Guthfrith (*Guthredus*), as *rex Northanhymbrorum*, and adds that King Alfred stood sponsor to him at baptism, thus confusing him with the Danish king of East Anglia who died in 890.[38] Even William of Malmesbury seems to have been misled by his sources, for he states in his *Gesta regum* that King Alfred had given both East Anglia and Northumbria to his godson Guthrum, which the Dane did not hold faithfully from him but *tyrannico fastu*, transmitting them to his own successors.[39] Historiographical continuity is such that as late as 1828 James Raine (the Elder) could blandly write that 'after Guthred's death . . . Alfred at once united the kingdom of Northumberland (sic) to the other members of the Heptarchy over which he already bore rule, and thus became the first Monarch of England'.[40]

These views drew further support from the story of King Alfred's and King Guthfrith's joint legislation in favour of St Cuthbert's new see at Chester-le-Street, which appears not in the *Historia* but in Cuthbertine sources of the late eleventh and twelfth centuries — the *Chronica* mentioned above and the *Historia Dunelmensis ecclesiae* — and in a twelfth-century 'Lawson' life of St Cuthbert. All these texts allude to the *leges et consuetudines* or *statuta et donationes* decreed by the two kings, the 'Lawson' life even proclaiming defiantly: *Legat*

---

[36] *HDE* 14.

[37] Cf. M. Lapidge, 'Byrhtferth of Ramsey and the Early Sections of the *Historia regum* attributed to Symeon of Durham', *ASE* 10 (1982), pp. 97 – 122.

[38] *HR* 81.

[39] *De gestis regum* I, 126. In a preceding summary of East Anglian history (p. 98) copied from the Appendix to the Worcester *Chronicon ex chronicis*, William had stated clearly however that East Anglia was redeemed from the Danes by Edward the Elder.

[40] J. Raine, *Saint Cuthbert* (Durham, 1828), p. 49.

antiquas scripturas qui voluerit.[41] These scripturas, which are no longer extant, are likely in my opinion to have been forged in the aftermath of the Conquest. Among the references the three sources mentioned above make to them, the right of sanctuary is the only point to be authenticated by a reference in the *Historia*, where this right is said to have been granted by Guthfrith alone. Alfred would never have signed as *rex Australium Anglorum*, and yet this is the title he bears as legislator, in the passages of the *Chronica* and of the 'Lawson' life relative to the Guthfrith/Alfred statutes. The *Historia*'s *terram Australium Saxonum* (in section 14) may well have inspired this style. Professor Stenton was no doubt reacting to historiographical accretions such as this legislation when he affirmed that there is no evidence of Alfred's influence beyond the Humber comparable with Alfred's treaty with Guthrum and the East Anglian Danes.[42] This is not to say that there is no witness of general West Saxon influence in Northumbria in Alfred's time: the propagandist effort of the West Saxon dynasty has been evoked above, and new in particular is the evidence that these kings were attached to the cult of St Cuthbert.[43] But as far as the celestial intermediaries invoked by King Alfred at Athelney are concerned, the testimony of William of Malmesbury points away from Cuthbert. The monastery that the king built at Athelney in fulfilment of a vow was dedicated to St Eielwine, a saint of Alfred's own dynasty: an interesting instance of an ancestor cult, which William does not evoke without a smile.[44]

Thirdly, what was the literary source and subsequent influence of the St Cuthbert/Alfred miracle story? An explicit parallel within our passage (section 17) between Alfred's vision and King Edwin's vision in Bede (*HE* II, 12), reveals the author's immediate model and may suggest that the story originated no earlier than the *Historia* itself. According to Bede, King Edwin who had 'wandered secretly as a fugitive for many years' received a visit from a stranger whom the *Historia* identifies as St Peter. Thus Alfred takes the place of the Northumbrian *Bretwalda* in this episode, while Cuthbert is cast in the distinguished role of the prince of the apostles. As for the influence of the St Cuthbert/Alfred miracle story, the earliest direct evidence is provided by an epitome of it *s.a.* 877 in the first part of the *Historia regum*, composed *c.* 1000. As this entry seems to be derived from the *Historia*, it further confirms the

---

[41] E. Craster, 'Red Book of Durham', p. 524; *HDE* 13. The 'Lawson' manuscript of the life of St Cuthbert is BL Additional MS 39943. The reference it makes to the *antiquas scripturas* is printed in J. Raine, *The Priory of Hexham* (SS 44; Durham, 1864), appendix p. vii.
[42] Stenton, *Anglo-Saxon England*, p. 262.
[43] See below, pp. 415–17, 423; and P. H. Sawyer, 'Sources for the History of Viking Northumbria', in *Viking Age York and the North*, ed. R. A. Hall (CBA Research Report, 27; 1978), p. 6. On the ground of diplomatic relations, note that the pledges taken by Alfred from the Northumbrians, according to the Anglo-Saxon Chronicle (*s.a.* 894, in the C and D versions), are put into relation with the death of Guthfrith, the Danish king who protected St Cuthbert's see, by the author of the second part of the *Historia regum* (*Sym. Op.* II), *s.a.* 894.
[44] *De gestis pontificum*, p. 199.

mid-tenth-century dating both of the miracle story and of the *Historia* itself. Further, this episode of the *Historia* probably inspired the parallel story of St Neot and Alfred as it appears in the oldest life of Neot (the *Vita prima sancti Neoti*) written sometime after 980, at the new priory of St Neots in Huntingdonshire.[45] In this *Life* the account of St Neot's visit and subsequent appearance to King Alfred shares the same setting and general structure as the St Cuthbert/Alfred miracle in the *Historia*. Its message, however, is one of piety and not of politics; and the same can be said of the St Cuthbert/Alfred story as it appears in expanded form in the early twelfth-century *Miracles and Translations of St Cuthbert*.[46] Here, Cuthbert still promises Alfred *totius Britannie imperium* (the author is drawing heavily on the *Historia* and maybe on a draft of the *Historia Dunelmensis ecclesie*), but all mentions of hereditary right, allusions to Alfred's posterity, and some references to Edward the Elder are suppressed. Cuthbert has become the bishop figure (an apparition *pontificaliter infulatus*) familiar to post-Conquest hagiography, instead of the *senex sacerdos* of the *Historia*.[47] For his part, William of Malmesbury does not fail to make space for the story in his *Gesta pontificum*, skilfully introducing it as Cuthbert's miracle for an illustrious king, by which 'all England retrieved its liberty'. Yet he prefers to dwell on the saint's promise of a wondrous haul of fish, rather than on the promise of an empire.[48] The political issue is thus being played down within the narrative of the miracle retold, though its original conclusion was often retained. The theme of Alfred 'first monarch of England' was indeed to outgrow its origins, in competition with historiography supporting Athelstan or other West Saxon kings as candidates for this title.[49]

The miracle of St Cuthbert for Alfred in the *Historia* seems thus to have owed its birth less to hagiographical endeavour than to the specific desire to uphold the rights of the English kings in Northumbria, at a moment in which the creation of an English realm was a prime military and idealogical issue, both for the West Saxon dynasty and for the see of St Cuthbert. This common

---

[45] In his edition of the *Vita prima sancti Neoti* (*op. cit.*, in n. 3 above, p. cv), M. Lapidge considers the possibility of the anteriority of the St Cuthbert/Alfred legend but (as he ascribes the *Historia* to the 11th century) only in oral form. Details of this *Vita* which may have been inspired by the *Historia* are: *Domini . . . miles Neotus* (section 8) as compared to the famous *Cuthbertus Christi miles*, and perhaps the translation of St Neot's relics after seven years within the same church in Cornwall (section 10), as compared with the seven-year peregrinations of St Cuthbert's relics. The mention of Glastonbury as a *famosum cenobium* (section 2) may have an independent, West country origin.

[46] *De miraculis* I.

[47] On Cuthbert as a bishop-figure in the 12th century, see below, p. 452.

[48] *De gestis pontificum*, pp. 268 – 9. Alfred is simply promised *gloriose . . . in solio reponeris*.

[49] I hope to show this in detail in my doctoral thesis on the medieval historiography on King Alfred and particularly in a study on the issue of the *primus rex totius Angliae* in English medieval histories.

cause, enriched by personal links between St Cuthbert's community and King Athelstan, King Edmund and their entourage, would seem to have produced the St Cuthbert and King Alfred legend. The specificity of the political context of the miracle was rapidly lost to later historiography and hagiography, though it influenced the image of Alfred as the first ruler of England.

St Cuthbert and Wessex: The Evidence of Cambridge, Corpus Christi College MS 183

DAVID ROLLASON

Probably the earliest surviving source for the history of St Cuthbert's community in the ninth and tenth centuries is the *Historia de sancto Cuthberto*, a text which, although added to in the eleventh century, seems to have been written at Chester-le-Street in the middle of the tenth.[1] One of the main themes of this text is the interest taken by kings of the West Saxon house, and later by the Danish Cnut, in St Cuthbert and his community. Alfred is supposed to have attributed his victory at Edington to Cuthbert's intercession and to have recommended his son Edward the Elder to venerate the saint. Athelstan is said to have visited the shrine and to have made rich gifts, Edmund to have visited the shrine and Cnut to have given the wide estate of Staindrop to the community.[2] Of the attentions of the later tenth-century kings such as Edgar we hear nothing, but it should be remembered that the *Historia* does not deal with those decades which fell between its original composition in the mid tenth century and the addition of new material to it in the eleventh.[3] We need not of course accept the *Historia*'s testimony at face value, but there seems little doubt that its general assertion that the southern kings were especially anxious to pay their respects to Cuthbert is correct. Its account of Athelstan's interest is amply corroborated by the survival of the late ninth- or early tenth-century Gospel book, London, British Library, Cotton MS Otho B.IX, inscribed in Latin, 'Athelstan, the pious king of the English,

---

[1] *HSC*; discussed by E. Craster, 'The Patrimony of St Cuthbert', *EHR* 69 (1954), pp. 177–99, and above, pp. 397–9. My debt to Mr Christopher Hohler in this paper is immense, not only for his published works but also for the generosity with which he has informed and guided me over many years. His comments on this paper have done much to improve it and save me from errors: those that remain are of course my responsibility.

[2] *HSC* 14–19, 25–8 and 32, and above, pp. 389–95 and 404–11.

[3] Cf. D. J. Hall, 'The Community of St Cuthbert: Its Properties, Rights and Claims from the Ninth Century to the Twelfth' (unpublished D.Phil. thesis, University of Oxford, 1984), pp. 87–8.

gives this Gospel book to St Cuthbert, the bishop'.[4] Nor is there reason to doubt Cnut's interest, for the community's possession of Staindrop was real enough;[5] and even the *Historia's* account of King Alfred needs to be taken seriously as evidence for West Saxon royal interest in Cuthbert, although it in fact casts light on the early tenth rather than the late ninth century.[6]

This royal concern for St Cuthbert and his community needs explaining, especially if we compare it with the much more restricted largesse directed to what on the face of it might seem the more important ecclesiastical centre at York.[7] Three explanations, none of them mutually exclusive, seem possible. First, the kings may have been impressed by Cuthbert as a saint on their visits to the north and have thus acquired an enthusiasm for his cult. Secondly, they may have been responding to an enthusiasm for the saint which already existed in Wessex. Thirdly, they may have been deliberately fostering the cult and their association with it for political ends. Evidence of great importance for the evaluation of these possible explanations is provided by the tenth-century manuscript, Cambridge, Corpus Christi College, MS 183, which contains a remarkable collection of material devoted to Cuthbert: Bede's prose life, two chapters from his *Ecclesiastical History of the English People* dealing with Cuthbert's posthumous miracles, his metrical life of the saint together with a glossary of difficult words in it, and a liturgical section consisting of the hymn to Cuthbert, *Magnus miles mirabilis*, a proper mass with a preface beginning *Aeterne deus cuius misericordia inaestimabilis*, and a rhyming proper office. As first written, the only component of the book not connected with Cuthbert was a series of lists of popes, disciples, bishops and kings, together with a set of genealogies, placed just before the metrical life.[8] Of the bishop lists in this section, only those for West Saxon sees, apart from Canterbury itself, have been kept up to date and this, combined with the style of a miniature on folio 1ᵛ, provides evidence for the book having been produced in Wessex. Since the latest bishops represented are Aelfheah of Winchester and Aethelgar of Crediton, who both succeeded to their sees between June and December 934, the manuscript must have been written later than that. Assuming that these lists for West Saxon sees were all up to date, it must have been written before

---

[4] S. Keynes, 'King Athelstan's Books', in *Learning and Literature in Anglo-Saxon England: Studies Presented to Peter Clemoes on the Occasion of his Sixty-Fifth Birthday*, ed. M. Lapidge and H. Gneuss (Cambridge, 1985), pp. 170 – 9.

[5] Craster, *EHR* 69, pp. 195 – 6.

[6] See above, pp. 398 – 406.

[7] Only two grants to St Peter's, York, by the pre-Conquest English kings are known, that of Amounderness by Athelstan and that of Axminster by Edward the Confessor (*BCS* 703 and F. E. Harmer, *Anglo-Saxon Writs* (Manchester, 1952), no. 120; for references, see P. H. Sawyer, *Anglo-Saxon Charters: An Annotated List and Bibliography* (London, 1968), nos. 407 and 1161).

[8] M. R. James, *A Descriptive Catalogue of the Manuscripts in the Library of Corpus Christi College Cambridge* (2 vols.; Cambridge, 1909 – 12) I, 426 – 41. On the genealogies, see above, pp. 403 – 4.

937 × 8 when Aelfheah of Wells relinquished his see.[9] That the manuscript was produced under West Saxon patronage is shown by the miniature on folio 1ᵛ which represents a saint and a king. Neither can be definitely identified since there is no inscription and the figures have only general attributes; but, given the contents of the book, it is reasonable to identify the saint as Cuthbert while, in view of the dating evidence discussed above, the king is likely to be Athelstan (924 – 39).[10]

This royal patronage of CCCC 183 makes it very relevant to our inquiry. What light does it cast on the nature of the West Saxon kings' enthusiasm for Cuthbert? A study of the sources of those components of CCCC 183 which concern the saint suggests strongly that the collection was in every sense a West Saxon creation. It was not, in other words, a case of the English kings having collected Cuthbert texts from the saint's community at Chester-le-Street. The version of Bede's prose *Life of Cuthbert* which CCCC 183 contains is of particular interest because it diverges in significant respects from the version later known and copied in the Durham scriptorium, represented for example by the text in Oxford, University College MS 165. Colgrave believed that this Durham version was most likely to be authentic, based (he speculated) on a text brought to Durham by the Cuthbertine community in the tenth century.[11] This view was demolished by M. L. W. Laistner. The text with the greatest claim to authenticity is precisely that in CCCC 183 and related manuscripts.[12] This version of Bede's prose *Life of Cuthbert*, therefore, seems to have had no influence in the north in the later pre-Conquest period, and by the same token it is out of the question that it should have been derived from the north in the tenth century. The situation with regard to the text of Bede's metrical *Life* also to be found in CCCC 183 is in some ways similar. It is a version of high calibre since it avoids many of the errors of other manuscripts, but there is nothing to suggest that it was available in the north,

---

[9] For the dates see *Handbook of British Chronology*, ed. E. B. Fryde *et al.* (3rd edn.; London, 1986).
[10] On the dating, see Keynes, 'Athelstan's Books', pp. 181 – 5 and references. The identification of the king with Athelstan is provisionally accepted in this paper, but caution is needed. If the Wells episcopal list had not been updated, the king might equally well be identified with Edmund (939 – 46). Precise dating on palaeographical or stylistic grounds does not appear to be possible. E. Temple, *Anglo-Saxon Manuscripts 900 – 1066* (London, 1976), pp. 37 – 8 (no. 6), dates CCCC 183 to *c*.937, presumably on the evidence of the *terminus post quem* provided by the Wells bishop list in combination with the dubious belief that the book was given to Chester-le-Street by Athelstan who died in 939 (see below, pp. 421 – 2). In fact its scribe has been identified with one of those who wrote London, BL, MS Royal 7.D.XXIV (no. 4, p. 36), which she dates 'early tenth century to late tenth century'. As for the saint in the miniature, it should be noted that he is identified as a priest by tonsure, chasuble and alb but there is nothing to show him to have been bishop and monk, nor is there anything else to identify him with Cuthbert. I owe this point to Christopher Hohler.
[11] *Two Lives*, pp. 45 – 50.
[12] Review of *Two Lives* in *American Historical Review* 46 (1940 – 1), pp. 379 – 81.

at any rate in the tenth century. On the contrary its affinities do not lie with later Durham texts such as that in Oxford, Bodleian Library, Fairfax MS 6 and possibly Digby MS 175.[13]

As for the liturgical texts, the origins of the hymn, *Magnus miles mirabilis*, cannot be established but it is unlikely to have been written in the north, where there is no evidence of its use before it reached Durham probably in the late eleventh century and probably as part of a southern compilation. It is found in Durham, Cathedral Library, MS B.III.32 and London, British Library, Cotton MS Julius A.VI: both are southern books, the former certainly from Canterbury and the latter possibly, and both came into the Durham library, presumably in the late eleventh century.[14] The mass in CCCC 183 does not appear to have ever been used in the north at all and there is no evidence that the office was used at Durham before the late eleventh century and certainly none that it was composed in the north. The one element in these liturgical texts which might seem to point to derivation from the north is the rubric to the mass which declares that it is either for the feast of the deposition of Cuthbert on 20 March or for the feast of the translation on 4 September (fol. 93^r). This latter feast seems to have developed in some obscurity; its origins are lost and no clarification is offered by the *Historia de sancto Cuthberto*. The date was later chosen as that for the saint's translation into the new church at Durham in 998,[15] but the evidence of CCCC 183, together with that of the ninth-century calendar in Oxford, Bodleian Library, MS Digby 63 which has the feast in the original hand, shows that it must originally have been a celebration of an earlier translation.[16] As the 698 translation was performed on the day of the deposition, 20 March, the only options are the rather doubtful translation to Norham by Bishop Ecgred in the second quarter of the ninth century or the translation to Chester-le-Street in 883. The latter seems the more likely if only because it is at least certain that it took place even

---

[13] *VCM*, pp. 33 – 40. It is not clear how an eighth-century fragment of the metrical life from York, now preserved in the National Library at Budapest, will affect Jaager's interpretation: see M. L. W. Laistner and H. H. King, *A Hand-List of Bede Manuscripts* (Ithaca, 1943), pp. 88 – 9. On Digby 175 and Fairfax 6, see *Two Lives*, pp. 22 – 3; it is not in fact certain that the former is a Durham book and it is not listed as such in N. R. Ker, *Medieval Libraries of Great Britain: A List of Surviving Books: Supplement to the Second Edition*, ed. A. G. Watson (London, 1987), p. 31. On the *VCM* see above pp. 77 – 102.

[14] H. Gneuss, *Hymnar und Hymnen im englischen Mittelalter: Studien zur Überlieferung, Glossierung und Übersetzung lateinischer Hymnen in England* (Tübingen, 1968), pp. 85 – 7 and 340. Still useful but in need of correction with reference to Gneuss's work is J. Mearns, *Early Latin Hymnaries: An Index of Hymns in Hymnaries before 1100* (Cambridge, 1913), p. 53. Durham MS B.III.32 is printed as *The Latin Hymns of the Anglo-Saxon Church, with an Interlinear Gloss*, ed. J. Stevenson (SS 23; Durham, 1851).

[15] *HDE* III, 4.

[16] Printed in *English Kalendars before A.D. 1100*, ed. F. Wormald (Henry Bradshaw Society 72; London, 1934), pp. 1 – 13.

if no extant narrative source supplies its calendar date.[17] It might be supposed that knowledge of a feast so obscure in the historical record would not have been widely diffused outside the north by the tenth century. In fact, however, the calendar in Digby 63, which provides the earliest reference to it, has strong Flemish as well as Northumbrian features and the manuscript in which it is found may have had connections with St Bertin.[18] The compilers of CCCC 183 may therefore have learned of it from Flanders rather than direct from northern England, there being abundant evidence for contacts between Wessex and that area in the ninth and tenth centuries.[19]

In short, the sources of CCCC 183's Cuthbert materials provide no evidence for our first possible explanation of royal interest in Cuthbert, namely that the impetus came from Chester-le-Street, and support rather the second possibility, namely that the kings were influenced by an interest in the saint which was already general in Wessex. Even this, however, may be only part of the story, for CCCC 183 also yields evidence supporting our third possibility, that is that the kings themselves did much to stimulate interest in Cuthbert in Wessex. This evidence derives first from the influence exerted by the components of CCCC 183 relating to Cuthbert. The rhyming office represents a liturgical form that was novel in the early tenth century since it appears first in the work of Stephen of Liège, a contemporary of the late ninth-century liturgist Notker the Stammerer (*c.* 840 – 912).[20] Since the rhyming office for Cuthbert in CCCC 183 is thus an early example and indeed also one of the very few examples to have survived or perhaps to have existed, it must have been composed at somewhere closely in touch with continental developments. In view of this and of the fact that it was intended for a secular rather than a monastic church, Christopher Hohler may well be right in suggesting that the office itself was written under royal patronage and intended for the court chapel.[21] It is very striking that this office had a considerable influence on the development of Cuthbert's cult in Wessex. Hohler has shown that, at any rate after the Norman Conquest, the southern

---

[17] *VCP* 42 and *HSC* 9 and 20. The possibility that the mention of Cuthbert's translation to Norham is a later addition to *HSC* 9 is raised by I. G. Thomas, 'The Cult of Saints' Relics in Medieval England' (unpublished Ph.D. thesis, University of London, 1974), p. 74. Thomas argues that in *HSC* 9 in the part-sentence, '[Ecgred] illuc corpus sancti Cuthberti et Ceoluulfi regis transtulit', the singular form of *corpus* may mean that the words *Cuthberti et* are an interpolation. Moreover, Cuthbert is referred to subsequently as having been taken in 875 from Lindisfarne rather than Norham (*HSC* 20).

[18] For recent discussion with references, see D. N. Dumville, 'Motes and Beams: Two Insular Computistical Manuscripts', *Peritia* 2 (1983), pp. 248 – 56, especially pp. 252 – 3; and D. Ó Cróinín, 'Sticks and Stones — A Reply', ibid., pp. 257 – 60. Hohler points out (pers. comm.) that the 4 September feast is always likely to have been widely popular as an alternative to the 20 March feast which falls in Lent.

[19] P. Grierson, 'The Relations between England and Flanders before the Norman Conquest', *Transactions of the Royal Historical Society*, 4th ser. 23 (1941), pp. 71 – 112.

[20] R. Jonsson, *Historia: Études sur la genèse des offices versifiés* (Stockholm, 1968), pp. 115 – 76.

[21] C. Hohler and A. Hughes, 'The Durham Services in Honour of St Cuthbert', *Relics*, pp. 155 – 91, at pp. 156 – 8.

houses of Peterborough, Worcester and New Minster, Winchester, not only used this office but that their texts depend directly or indirectly on CCCC 183. This is because they omit the word *probis* before *operibus* in one of the responsories, an omission which derives from the fact that the scribe of CCCC 183 wrote *pro nobis* for *probis* and this was then deleted without a correction being inserted, so that the word simply fell out. Now, it was also missing from the post-Conquest Durham office which was based on CCCC 183's version, that manuscript having by then moved to Durham, so these southern offices could have derived their version from there in or after the late eleventh century.[22] It is also possible, however, that CCCC 183 had its influence before going north, as one may well envisage having happened especially in the case of New Minster in the royal city of Winchester. Another dimension is provided by those texts of this office which do not follow CCCC 183 in the omission of *probis*. As listed by Hohler, these are: an antiphoner-collectar of *c.*1200, probably from St Andrews but with close Ely connections (Paris, Bibliothèque nationale, MS lat. 12036); the thirteenth-century breviary of Ely Cathedral (Cambridge, University Library, MS Ii IV.20); the thirteenth-century breviary of Muchelney Abbey (London, British Library, Additional MS 43405/6); and, most interesting of all, the breviary supplement in the late tenth- or eleventh-century manuscript London, British Library, Harley MS 1117.[23] This last must derive from a monastic church since its version of the office has added antiphons (but scriptural and unrelated to those used at Durham). The style of its illuminated initials and the inclusion of a unique office for St Guthlac indicate a southern provenance, while the inclusion of a hymn for St Edward of Shaftesbury (fol. 1) together with the resemblance of the office text to that in the Muchelney breviary point to Wessex.[24] These manuscripts (with the possible exception of the Ely breviary which may derive from Durham since it includes the antiphons added to the office there) seem to provide evidence to show that the rhyming office had a wide influence in areas under West Saxon domination over and above the influence of CCCC 183 itself. If the office was indeed a product of royal patronage, we have here strong evidence for a royal role in stimulating veneration of Cuthbert.

CCCC 183's mass was never used in the north as far as is known, but it nevertheless enjoyed some diffusion in the south, appearing notably in Leofric

---

[22] Ibid., p. 157. On CCCC 183's move to Durham, see below, pp. 422 – 3.

[23] Ibid., p. 185 (note to section 83) and pp. 159 – 62. I am grateful to Mr C. Hohler for up-to-date information on Bib. nat. lat. 12036.

[24] See, for example, *Two Lives*, p. 28, and Temple, *Anglo-Saxon Manuscripts*, pp. 55 – 8. Further evidence for a Wessex provenance is provided by the fact that the book was given to Harley by John Anstis the Elder who came from Cornwall (C. E. Wright, *Fontes Harleiani* (London, 1972), pp. 50 – 2). Hohler tentatively suggests Sherborne as a possible home (*Relics*, p. 161). Despite a misleading pencil note inside the book, probably by Frederick Madden, it appears always to have been a single volume, the collation being I[8], II[8], III[8], IV[8], V[8], VI[4], VII[10], VIII[12]. I am grateful to Professor P. D. A. Harvey for his help with this manuscript.

C, the eleventh-century portion of the Leofric Missal.[25] The same may be true of the diffusion of the hymn *Magnus miles mirabilis*, the earliest text of which is to be found albeit imperfectly in CCCC 183.[26] It is notable for being almost the only hymn for an English saint to figure in manuscripts of the so-called 'new hymnal', introduced to the English church in the course of the tenth century through the agency of the reformed monasteries. All these manuscripts seem to be of southern extraction and, although it cannot be proved, it is tempting to see the influence of CCCC 183 or at least of material that lies behind it.[27] Here too we may be seeing the influence of royal patronage. The textual history of Bede's prose and metrical lives of Cuthbert as found in CCCC 183 points in the same direction. The same versions are to be found in two other manuscripts, the tenth-century London, British Library Cotton MS Vitellius A.XIX and the eleventh-century Harley 1117. Both contain the prose and metrical lives in versions close to that of CCCC 183, both contain the two chapters of posthumous miracles from Bede's *Ecclesiastical History*. The southern provenance suggested above for Harley 1117 would point to a similar provenance for Vitellius A.XIX, whose prose life was probably copied in Harley 1117.[28]

Finally, the diffusion of the 4 September translation feast in Wessex may have been assisted by the influence of CCCC 183, the mass in which was intended for that feast as well as for the deposition feast on 20 March. The 4 September feast certainly appeared prominently in later West Saxon calendars and there was even a proper mass for it, distinct from that devised in Durham, now to be found in the sacramentary of Bishop Giso of Wells (London, British Library, Cotton Vitellius MS A.XVIII).[29] Moreover the sequence of its appearance in West Saxon texts suggests that the impetus for its diffusion came from the royal city of Winchester, which would of course be consistent with royal influence. The feast is found first in Winchester calendars and those such as that in the Red Book of Darley (Cambridge, Corpus Christi College, MS 422) closely connected with Winchester. It does not occur in the calendar in London, British Library, Cotton MS Nero A.II, a tenth-century calendar from the west or south-west, nor in the other surviving tenth-century calendars from the south-west, those in Salisbury, Cathedral Library MS 150 and Oxford, Bodleian Library, MS Bodley 579, the 'B' section of the Leofric Missal from Glastonbury.[30]

---

[25] *Relics*, p. 157, and *The Leofric Missal*, ed. F. E. Warren (Oxford, 1883), pp. 205 – 6.

[26] Edited with notes in *Relics*, pp. 169 and 185.

[27] Gneuss, *Hymnar und Hymnen*, chapter 4.

[28] *Two Lives*, pp. 27 – 8 and 46 – 7; *VCM*, pp. 33 – 4; *Catalogue of the Harleian Manuscripts in the British Museum* (4 vols.; London, 1808 – 12) I, 556; and J. Planta, *A Catalogue of Manuscripts in the Cottonian Library Deposited in the British Museum* (London, 1802), p. 381.

[29] Printed *Leofric Missal*, ed. Warren, p. 306.

[30] *English Kalendars*, ed. Wormald, pp. 192, 38, 24 and 52 respectively. The feast does not occur in the Canterbury calendar (p. 66), influenced by Glastonbury, in the Bosworth Psalter (London, British Library, Additional MS 37517).

The influence exerted by CCCC 183, or at least of the texts it contains, was thus considerable in the south but, as we have seen, it appears to have been non-existent in the north in the pre-Conquest period. These conclusions are difficult to reconcile with the widely accepted interpretation of CCCC 183 as having been commissioned by King Athelstan as a gift to Chester-le-Street and presented to Cuthbert's community there soon after his visit in 934.[31] That interpretation, however, while possible, rests on evidence which is by no means incontrovertible. This consists first of all of the account of Athelstan's visit to Chester-le-Street in 934 in the *Historia de sancto Cuthberto*. After describing how the king placed a *testamentum* at the head of the saint, this goes on to give what purports to be the text of this document. It proves to be a list of gifts, including a volume containing the prose and verse lives of Cuthbert (*unam sancti Cuthberti vitam, metrice et prosaice scriptam*).[32] It may be that this is a reference to CCCC 183, although there is no means of proving it. In any case, whereas it is reasonable to believe the *Historia* to the extent that Athelstan visited the shrine, the details given are very suspect. The dating of CCCC 183 on the basis of the bishop lists shows that the *Historia*'s statement that Athelstan actually gave the book on the occasion of his visit must be incorrect.[33] It is of course possible that it was promised then and given later, but this is a dent in the *Historia*'s credibility as well as an awkwardness in any attempted reconstruction of events. Moreover the alleged *testamentum* was very probably based on a vernacular list of gifts, much of which has been lost through fire but which was once to be found in Otho B.IX.[34] It is thus very unlikely that the *Historia*'s *testamentum* ever existed as an independent document and, if this part of its account is fabricated, what credence can be placed in its list of gifts? Even if we are correct in identifying the book referred to as CCCC 183, it is entirely possible that whoever revised the *Historia* in eleventh-century Durham expanded the list of Athelstan's gifts with items which might have been received much later but which he considered would have been worthy of that king's largesse. (Exactly the same happened in the case of the Exeter relic list, in which relics of saints who had lived after Athelstan's time were included amongst the king's gifts.)[35] In the case of CCCC 183, if it was indeed Athelstan's book, the association would have been especially plausible although, as we shall see, very probably incorrect.

The second piece of evidence held to support the theory that Athelstan gave this book to Chester-le-Street is the miniature on folio 1[v]. This is held to be closely related to the miniature which was once in Otho B.IX and this alleged similarity is seen as proof that CCCC 183 was given to Chester-le-Street at more or less the same time. The Otho B.IX miniature has been completely

---

[31] See for example Keynes, 'Athelstan's Books', pp. 180 – 5.
[32] *HSC* 26 – 7.
[33] Keynes, art. cit., pp. 182 – 4.
[34] Ibid., pp. 177 – 8.
[35] M. Foerster, *Zur Geschichte des Reliquienkultus in Altengland* (Munich, 1943), p. 40.

destroyed by fire but descriptions of it were published before its loss. According to these the miniature showed Athelstan with crown and sceptre, kneeling and offering the book in his right hand to St Cuthbert, haloed and seated on his throne (*cathedra*), giving the blessing with his right hand and holding a book in his left hand. The descriptions also record the inscription identifying donor and recipient, as given in translation above.[36] Clearly, the CCCC 183 miniature resembles this in a general way, since it too shows a crowned king with a book and a haloed saint also with a book, but there are some very striking differences. It has no inscription; the saint is standing rather than seated and although he is raising his right hand the third and fourth fingers are not crooked in a way such as would show that he was blessing; and the king is neither kneeling nor actively offering the book to the saint — indeed he appears to have it open and to be reading it. It is thus by no means clear that this miniature was so closely related to the Otho B.IX miniature that it can be assumed that it too indicates that the manuscript in which it is found was a gift from Athelstan to Chester-le-Street.

There is in fact a strong possibility that the CCCC 183 miniature does not show Athelstan giving the book to the saint at all. The lack of an inscription is itself against the notion that it shows a gift. So is the fact that, although the miniature has been compared with Carolingian and Ottonian dedication or gift scenes,[37] it in fact differs from most of them in much the same way as it evidently differed from the Otho B.IX miniature.[38] In particular, standing recipients are very rare in such scenes. The only example earlier in date than CCCC 183 is on folio 12[v] of St Gall, Stiftsbibliothek MS 23, a psalter of *c.*870.[39] In this, however, the arrangement is quite different: donor and recipient are separated by arches (with scenes placed at the heads of columns) so that their standing posture is dictated by the space allocated to them. As for manuscripts later than CCCC 183, standing donors are found, for example in a Reichenau manuscript of after 1000 (formerly in the Brook Collection, Huddersfield), but they remain rare.[40] The CCCC 183 miniature also differs from these miniatures in so far as it is by no means obvious that the king is giving the book to the saint. On the contrary, he has it open in both hands and appears to be reading it: the saint does not look at him nor he at the saint and there is no suggestion of movement between them. In short, the CCCC 183 miniature may simply be intended to represent Athelstan's devotion to Cuthbert: the king reads the saint's *Lives* and Cuthbert is shown to illustrate

---

[36] Keynes, art. cit., pp. 173 – 4 and notes; above, pp. 413 – 14.
[37] See, for example, P. Bloch, 'Zum Dedikationsbild in Lob des Kreuzes des Hrabanus Maurus', in *Das erste Jahrtausend*, ed. K. Böhner *et al.* (2 vols.; Düsseldorf, 1961 – 2), I, 471 – 94, and II, pl. 246.
[38] Reference should be made to J. Prochno, *Das Schreiber- und Dedikationsbild in der deutschen Buchmalerei, I. Teil, bis zum Ende des 11. Jahrhunderts (800 – 1100)* (Leipzig and Berlin, 1929).
[39] Ibid., pp. 18* – 18.
[40] Ibid., pp. 38* – 38.

his meditation and devotion.[41] Such 'devotion' miniatures are found in continental art, for example on folios 38^v and 39^r of Munich, Residenz-museum, MS B.63 (the prayer-book of Charles the Bald) of after 850, showing Charles the Bald before the crucified Christ, and, from the late eleventh century, folio 2^r of a Gospel book, London, British Library, Harley MS 2821, showing the scribe or donor (there is no inscription) escorted by a saint and facing the enthroned Christ: as in the CCCC 183 miniature, the book is being held open.[42]

Such a re-interpretation of the miniature alters our perception of CCCC 183's purpose. Far from being Athelstan's gift to Chester-le-Street, it would seem to have been rather a token of the king's devotion to Cuthbert, a book perhaps intended for private meditation, perhaps also intended to publicize that devotion in the king's southern heartland. How and why it eventually reached Durham is no longer clear. All that is certain is that it was there by the time of Bishop Walcher (1071 – 80), a record of a lease by whom was entered on folio 96^v.[43] One feature of CCCC 183, however, does offer a clue, at least to the date of its arrival at Durham. Around the beginning of the eleventh century, someone added liturgical texts with neums to the margins of folio 93^{r-v}. Palaeographical study shows that the same person added the preface for a mass of St Cuthbert to folios 13^v – 14^v of the tenth-century West Saxon pontifical which is now Cambridge, Sidney Sussex College, MS 100. This book was at Durham in the later middle ages since it bears a Durham *ex libris*.[44] It is possible that the additions were made to both manuscripts there, but it is also possible that they were made while the manuscripts were in the south, since the mass represented in Sidney Sussex 100 is a rare one with Breton connections, probably deriving from the south-west of England.[45] It seems unlikely that such a mass was known in Durham and this line of argument

---

[41] I owe this suggestion to Professor George Henderson.

[42] Ibid., pp. 3* – 3 and pp. 52* – 52.

[43] T. A. M. Bishop, *English Caroline Miniscule* (Oxford, 1971), p. 14 (no. 16). Bishop's contention that the additions were made at Chester-le-Street or Durham is apparently based on the belief that CCCC 183 was given to the former by King Athelstan, on which, see below. For the *ex libris*, see *Medieval Libraries: Supplement*, ed. Watson, p. 18.

[44] Walcher's lease, which is printed and discussed in *Anglo-Saxon Charters*, ed. A. J. Robertson (Cambridge, 1939), pp. 230 – 1 and pp. 480 – 1, is preceded on fol. 96^v by an inventory (ibid., pp. 250 – 1). This is in the Northumbrian dialect (ibid., pp. 497 – 8) and features of it have been held to show that the book must have been in Northumbria by the tenth century (N. R. Ker, *Catalogue of Manuscripts containing Anglo-Saxon* (Oxford, 1957), p. 65). It is very doubtful that such a claim is justified. Some of the linguistic forms are certainly archaic and are found in tenth-century Northumbrian texts, but it is by no means clear that they did not persist through the eleventh century. See K. Luick, *Historische Grammatik der englischen Sprache* (2 vols.; Leipzig, 1921 – 40), I.i, section 119. It should be noted in any case that fol. 96 is not an integral part of the volume and may have been a flyleaf (Ker, *Catalogue*, loc. cit.).

[45] C. Hohler, 'Some Service-Books of the Later Saxon Church', in *Tenth Century Studies*, ed. D. Parsons (London and Chichester, 1975), at pp. 66 – 7 and n. 30 (pp. 221 – 2).

suggests strongly that both manuscripts were in the south until at least the early eleventh century, that they were in reasonably close spatial relationship to each other there, and even that they may have come north to Durham together.

The conclusion that Athelstan intended CCCC 183 for use in Wessex, probably by himself, makes the manuscript an even more impressive monument to the king's interest in Cuthbert than the interpretation that sees it as a gift to Chester-le-Street. There is no doubt that Cuthbert was a well known saint in the south from an early date. He had been given prominence by Bede and his deposition feast (20 March) occurs in virtually every English liturgical and quasi-liturgical text from the calendar of St Willibrord onwards.[46] The evidence of CCCC 183, however, suggests that Athelstan was instrumental in spreading and developing the saint's cult and associated himself closely with it. It seems likely that this lies behind his and Edmund's visits to Chester-le-Street, behind the story of how Cuthbert assisted Alfred at the battle of Edington,[47] and perhaps also behind the dedication of St Cuthbert's, Wells, which is close to the West Saxon royal palace at Cheddar.[48] What were the motives of this royal desire for association with Cuthbert? In view of the prominence given to the saint by Bede, Athelstan may well have been moved by religious feeling to honour such an important figure from the golden age of the English church, just as in the eleventh century the Evesham monks were to be inspired by Bede's writings to the extent of setting in motion a revival of northern monasteries which had flourished in his time.[49] We should not, however, rule out the possibility of political considerations. Luisella Simpson has shown how the account of Cuthbert's miracles for Alfred in the *Historia de sancto Cuthberto* is redolent of early tenth-century, West Saxon imperialist claims to rule the whole of Britain, including the north of England.[50] The royal devotion to St Cuthbert revealed by CCCC 183 may likewise have been intended to express the West Saxon kings' aspirations to rule the north where their power was by no means assured either in theory or in practice.[51] In Wessex such aspirations could hardly have been better represented than in the close association of the kings with the greatest of Northumbrian saints. That association may also have brought benefits in

---

[46] *The Calendar of St Willibrord from MS Paris Lat. 10837*, ed. H. A. Wilson (Henry Bradshaw Society 55; London, 1918), p. 5; and *English Kalendars*, ed. Wormald, passim.

[47] *HSC* 14 – 19; see above, pp. 413 – 14.

[48] Keynes, 'Athelstan's Books', p. 185.

[49] *HDE* III, 21; see also D. Knowles, *The Monastic Order in England* (2nd edn.; Cambridge, 1963), pp. 165 – 71.

[50] See above, pp. 400 – 4.

[51] See for example, D. Whitelock, 'The Dealings of the Kings of England with Northumbria in the Tenth and Eleventh Centuries', in *The Anglo-Saxons: Studies in Some Aspects of their History and Culture presented to Bruce Dickins*, ed. P. Clemoes (London, 1959), pp. 70 – 88.

Northumbria itself: a semblance of legitimacy for West Saxon rule and perhaps the active support of the saint's community which, to judge from the charters and territorial memoranda contained in the *Historia de sancto Cuthberto*, remained rich and powerful throughout the early middle ages, and may have been a useful counterbalance to the often rebellious church of York.[52]

[52] Craster, *EHR* 69, 177 – 99, and Hall, 'Community of St Cuthbert', pp. 72 – 92. See also D. W. Rollason, 'The Wanderings of St Cuthbert', in *Cuthbert: Saint and Patron*, ed. D. W. Rollason (Durham, 1987), pp. 45 – 61 at pp. 47 – 50.

The Sanctuary of St Cuthbert

DAVID HALL

> I also think that it will be more expedient for you that I should remain here, on account of the influx of fugitives and guilty men of every sort, who will perhaps flee to my body because, unworthy as I am, reports about me as a servant of God have nevertheless gone forth; and you will be compelled very frequently to intercede with the powers of this world on behalf of such men, and so will be put to much trouble on account of the presence of my body.[1]

Cuthbert's prophetic warning of the consequences of moving his body from Farne Island to Lindisfarne distinguishes the two elements of sanctuary: asylum and intercession. Providing as it did respite for fugitives and a brake upon uncontrolled bloodfeud, sanctuary developed along with, and complemented, royal power within the Anglo-Saxon system of fines, penalties and compensation. It is clear that there was a close link between royal and ecclesiastical status, and thus between the penalties for affronts to the same; and that royal intervention in legal matters was crucial to the definition and scope of sanctuary rights. Intervention by the church, in providing asylum, and intervention by the king, in mediating in disputes and exercising power over fugitives, were part of a single process by which centralized institutions intruded themselves into the legal process. By the tenth century, as Naomi Hurnard has argued, 'not only was there considerable scope for [royal] clemency but there was also a deliberate policy which involved it.'[2] This policy is apparent in the strict penalties for breaches of sanctuary. Kings were concerned both for the safety of the fugitive at a church and to preserve, or extend, their discretion to deal with the sanctuary seeker as they felt appropriate.[3] The violation of the protection afforded by a church, and thus disregard for the church's intercession, turned a man from a justified pursuer of his kinsman's murderer into a criminal whose life was forfeit. Only some special form of sanctuary and a merciful king could save his life.[4] Cuthbert, or

---

[1] *VCP* 37, *Two Lives*, pp. 278–9.
[2] N. Hurnard, *The King's Pardon for Homicide* (Oxford, 1969), p. 2.
[3] Ibid., p. 3.
[4] *VIII Aethelred* 1.1. References to the laws are to the edition in *The Laws of the Earliest English Kings*, ed. F. L. Attenborough (Cambridge, 1922) and *The Laws of the Kings of England from Edmund to Henry I*, ed. A. J. Robertson (Cambridge, 1925), unless otherwise stated, and are to chapters.

Bede, was fully aware of the implications for a church of possession of a sacred relic which would act as a magnet for those seeking protection, and the relationship this created with the 'powers of this world'.

By the end of the eleventh century a person seeking sanctuary at the shrine of St Cuthbert was afforded protection for thirty-seven days. Should his pursuers not respect this protection there may have been some consolation in the knowledge that, according to Symeon of Durham, violators of Cuthbert's peace faced a fine of £96, if they went so far as to kill the fugitive![5] A later Durham writer, Reginald, suggests that even an unsuccessful attempt to commit such a crime could lead to imprisonment, torture and horrible death for the perpetrator.[6] The majority of stories concerned with sanctuary at the shrine emphasize the miraculous and the likelihood of divine retribution. Such stories provide the basic evidence for the Cuthbertine sanctuary, which is traceable from Cuthbert's day to the twelfth century, but it is fortunate that we have other non-Cuthbertine sources that can help to flesh out this picture and place this sanctuary in a wider context.

As we have seen, Symeon records the bare fact that breach of the sanctuary at Durham was to be compensated by a fine of £96. Earlier a Durham chronicler of the 1070s had placed the fine at 1,200 ore, or about £80 to £100.[7] The importance of the figures is great, for by looking at Richard of Hexham's short account of the fines and structure of sanctuary at Hexham we can start to see how Cuthbert's sanctuary fitted into the general Anglo-Saxon scheme.[8] At Hexham, according to Richard, the sanctuary extended for a mile around the church, or in some places to the middle of the Tyne, and within the area furthest from the church (VI in fig. 34) a breach was compensated by two *hundred*, or £16, the *hundred* comprising £8. As the church was approached the fines increased. Within the walls of the church (III) it was twelve *hundred*, or £96, coinciding with that recorded by Symeon. In the choir, amendment could still be made for the sum of eighteen *hundred*, £144. Homicide at the site of the bishop's seat beside the altar, however, or at the shrine containing relics behind the altar, was an unemendable (*botolos*) crime for which the killer's life was forfeit. The bishop's seat, called the *friðstol* or *cathedra lapidea iuxta altare*, still remains at Hexham.

The trustworthiness of Richard's account is not easy to assess. There exists a dubious charter of Henry I purporting to confirm to St Peter's, York, just such a sanctuary as Richard describes at Hexham. The payments, gradation of fines and indeed the wording itself are all identical to those found in

---

[5] *HDE* II, 13.

[6] *Libellus* 60.

[7] *Cronica monasterii Dunelmensis*, ed. H. H. E. Craster, 'The Red Book of Durham', *EHR* 40 (1925), p. 524. *Domesday Book* (London, 1783) shows that the ore could equal between 16d. and 20d. (vol. I, fols. 269 – 70, 154), whilst the code *Edward and Guthrum* 3.1 would imply that 1,200 ore equalled £150.

[8] Richard of Hexham, *History of the Church of Hexham*, 14; *The Priory of Hexham*, ed. J. Raine (2 vols., SS 44, 46; Durham 1863 – 4), I, 61 – 2. See fig. 34.

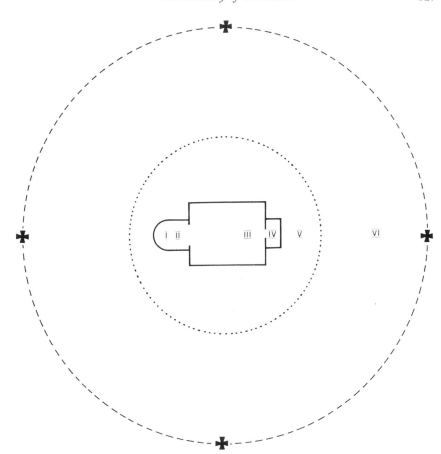

34. *Fines for breach of sanctuary (based upon Richard of Hexham):* I. In cathedra
lapidea iuxta altare, quem Angli vocant fridstol . . . vel etiam ad feretrum
sanctarum reliquiarum quod est post altare — *an unemendable or* botolos *crime;*
II. Infra valvas chori — *eighteen hundred, each of £8 (£144);* III. Infra ecclesiam
— *twelve hundred (£96);* IV. Infra muros atrii ecclesie *(perhaps within the
church's precinct walls rather than simply within the porch)* — *six hundred (£48);* V.
Infra villam — *four hundred (£32);* VI. Infra quatuor cruces extra villam —
two hundred (£16).

Richard's account.[9] If the charter can be accepted as genuine, it provides powerful corroboration. It appears to have been confirmed again by King Stephen, suggesting at least that it was believed at that time to be genuine. Another confirmation by King Stephen confirms the existence of a comparable sanctuary at Beverley. Although less detailed than the York charter, it does refer to 'pacem suam intra leugam suam et ejusdem violate pacis emendationem'.[10] Of course, these sources are all twelfth-century and open to doubt, not least because they are all associated with York and its satellites, but they nevertheless seem to provide general corroboration for Richard's account. Further corroboration is to be found in earlier sources. We have already seen that Symeon's early twelfth-century account of a £96 fine ties in with Richard's figure for the fine for breach of sanctuary inside the church. An early eleventh-century source, the tract *Norðhymbra cyricgrið* (*c.* 1015 – 50) takes us further back. Relating to the churches of St Peter (York), St Wilfrid (Ripon), and St John (Beverley), it confirms the existence at these places of a special sanctuary, based on fines calculated in *hundred*, although the amount does not tally with the twelfth-century evidence, nor is there a gradation of fines.[11] Richard's account finds more specific corroboration in the laws; the gradation of fines, and their amount, fits with the penalties described in the laws and elsewhere for breach of the church's sanctuary.

The relevance of the laws to the Cuthbertine sanctuary goes further, however, since both Symeon and the earlier Durham chronicler state that the fine for breach of the sanctuary at Durham was equal to that for breach of the king's peace.[12] This accords with the earliest English law code, that of Aethelberht of Kent, which provides an important indication of the church's special position as it was integrated into the existing system of status and compensation. Breach of *ciricfrið* (church peace) was to be compensated twofold, in the same way as *maethlfrið* (peace of a meeting place).[13] In Aethelberht's laws, as in the later laws of Wihtred (*c.* 695), the fine for breach of the king's *mundbyrd* (protection) was 50 shillings, and the later laws indicate that the breach of the church's *mundbyrd* called forth the same fine.[14] This

---

[9] *Regesta regum Anglo-Normannorum, 1100 – 1135*, ed. H. W. C. Davis, C. Johnson and H. A. Cronne (Oxford, 1956), no. 1083; cf. *Priory of Hexham*, I, 61.

[10] *Regesta regum Anglo-Normannorum, 1135 – 1154*, ed. H. A. Cronne and R. H. C. Davis (Oxford, 1968), nos. 99, 975.

[11] *Norðhymbra cyricgrið*, ed. F. Liebermann, *Die Gesetze der Angelsachsen* (3 vols., Halle 1903 – 16), I, 473.

[12] *HDE* II, 13; Craster, *EHR* 40, p. 524.

[13] *Aethelberht* 1.

[14] *Wihtred* 2; the laws of Ine of comparable date also mention sanctuary. Under Charlemagne 'the privilege of *mundbyrd* (*mundeburdis, tuitio, defensio*) [was] a special protection accorded by the king . . . The individual or ecclesiastical establishment enjoying the privilege was protected from any harm by the interdiction of the king, and if harm was done it involved the condemnation of the guilty party to a fine of sixty shillings for disobedience of the *bannum*.' (F. L. Ganshof, *Frankish Institutions Under Charlemagne* (trans. B. Lyon and M. Lyon; New York, 1968), p. 46.)

equating of the peace extended by a church with that extended by a king is common to the rest of the extant Anglo-Saxon laws, though from the tenth century it is more specifically the *cyricgrið binnan wagum* (peace within church walls) that is considered as inviolable as the king's *handgrið* (peace or protection).[15]

Further refinement is to be found in the later laws, where churches are divided according to their legal status. It was only the *heafodmynstre* (head or mother church) that enjoyed parity with the king in the matter of protection extended to fugitives, breach of its sanctuary being compensated by the same amount as breach of the king's *mund*.[16] The *Instituta Cnuti* in translating *heafodmynstre* uses *principales ecclesiae sicut episcopatus et abbatiae*, though one manuscript omits *abbatiae*.[17] It would seem likely on general grounds that Durham, Chester-le-Street (at least while the Cuthbertine community was there) and Hexham were in this category of church that enjoyed a status equal to that of the king; and this is confirmed by a comparison of the fines for breach of sanctuary specified by Symeon and Richard with fines for breach of the king's protection specified in Domesday Book. This tells us that the latter offence carried a fine of £144, of which £96 went to the king and £48 to the earl. Thus we find it stated in Yorkshire Domesday that:

> If the peace given by the hand of the king or his seal be broken, amend is to be made to the king alone by twelve *hundreds*; each *hundred* £8 . . . Peace given by the earl and broken by anyone is amended to the earl himself by six *hundreds*: each *hundred* £8.[18]

Entries in Domesday Book for Lincolnshire, Derbyshire and Nottinghamshire further explain the subdivision of the £144 fine paid by eighteen hundreds, as for example in the following passage:

> The king has two parts of this fine, the earl the third i.e. twelve *hundreds* pay the fine to the king, six to the earl.[19]

This tallies with the *Leis Willelme*, which give £144 as the fine for breaking the king's peace in the Danelaw, and with the laws of Aethelred II in which a

---

[15] For example, *Edward and Guthrum* 1, I *Cnut* 2.2. It should be noted that we are here concerned with the peace or protection afforded by the church building, and that the protection afforded by the various grades of ecclesiastic, and fines for breach thereof, depended upon their social and legal status: *Alfred* 15, 40. For the royal grant of sanctuary and privileges in Wales see H. Pryce, 'Ecclesiastical Sanctuary in Thirteenth-Century Welsh Law', *The Journal of Legal History* 5 (1984), pp. 7–8.

[16] VIII *Aethelred* 5.

[17] Robertson, *Laws*, p. 348. Cf. *Leges Henrici Primi*, ed. L. J. Downer (Oxford, 1972), 79.6, 'The penalty for *grithbreche* in the case of a mother or principal church [*matris et capitalis ecclesie*] is at least the same as the penalty for breach of the king's peace.'

[18] *Domesday Book*, vol. I, fol. 298v.

[19] Ibid., fols. 280, 336v.

breach of the ealdorman's or king's reeve's peace in the court of the Five Boroughs is amended by payment of £144 (admittedly in one borough by only half of this, £72). This information allows us to understand Richard's figure of £144 for breach of sanctuary in the choir and Symeon's of £96 for breach of sanctuary without further specification. The £144 was clearly equivalent to the total fine for breach of the king's peace including the earl's third. Athough Symeon's £96 would seem at first sight to have been equivalent to Richard's £96 fine for breach of sanctuary in the church, it is more likely that it represented the highest fine mentioned by Richard, £144, with the earl's third deducted on the same lines as described in Domesday Book. It would seem to have been uncommon for those who received the king's two thirds of the fine for breach of his peace also to have received the earl's third. In Nottingham and Derby, for instance, only three persons, the archbishop of York, Ulf Fenisc and the Countess Godiva enjoyed this right. Much the same may have happened with ecclesiastical sanctuary. This was certainly the case at York, and it seems likely that at Durham in Symeon's day the third not received by the church of Durham would have gone to the bishop, though to raise the question for any earlier periods leads to the thorny problem of the origin of the jurisdictional liberty of Durham.[20]

Symeon's and Richard's fines stand clearly in the tradition of Anglo-Saxon royal hand-given peace (*handgrið*) and church sanctuary. The Durham chronicle of the 1070s, with its twelve *hundred* ore, is also not out of place. The term *hundred* is, moreover, to be found in a directly Cuthbertine context as early as the mid tenth century. In the otherwise Latin text of the *Historia de sancto Cuthberto*, *XII hundred* appears as the sum of money donated to St Cuthbert by King Athelstan's army on the occasion of his visit to Chester-le-Street in 934. This has been interpreted as a reference to 1200 shillings, a king's thegn's wergild in the West Saxon laws, and it has been suggested that a group of thegns in Athelstan's army donated this sum.[21] The *Historia*, however, attributes the payment to the whole army and it is a strong possibility that the amount represents not a West Saxon wergild but rather a sum equivalent to the fine for breach of sanctuary.

The *Historia* also contains the earliest account of how, *c.*882, Bishop Eardwulf, Abbot Eadred and St Cuthbert's community helped the Danish Guthfrith to become king in Northumbria and how he granted the community not only a large section of what is now County Durham but also the right of asylum for thirty-seven days for anyone fleeing to the body of the saint. According to Symeon and the eleventh-century Durham *Cronica* this right was confirmed by King Alfred himself.[22] It is just possible that this latter tradition

---

[20] *Leis Willelme* 2.2; cf. III *Aethelred* 1; and *Domesday Book*, vol. I, fol. 280. I am grateful to Dr Ann Williams for drawing my attention to the important implications for the fines for breach of sanctuary, and jurisdiction generally, of this receipt by others of the king's portion and the reserving of the rest to the earl, except in exceptional cases.

[21] E. Barker, 'Two Lost Documents of King Athelstan', *ASE* 6 (1977), p. 142; *HSC* 27.

[22] *HSC* 13; Craster, *EHR* 40, p. 524; *HDE* II, 13.

is correct, for the law code of Alfred is the earliest to deal with sanctuary at any length, and to refer specifically to a period of thirty-seven days' protection allowed a fugitive.[23] Chapter 5 of this code gives a sanctuary seeker the right to remain unharmed for seven nights. Should he give up his weapons he is allowed thirty nights. It is likely that the thirty were in addition to the seven as another chapter reads, 'and then *after seven days*, if he will surrender and give up his weapons, he is to keep him unharmed for thirty days, and send notice about him to his kinsmen and his friends.'[24] Later codes do not mention the period of sanctuary to be allowed, except in the case of thieves whose ability to seek and remain in sanctuary was severely restricted. It is therefore tempting to suggest that not only was the Cuthbertine sanctuary influenced by Anglo-Saxon royal law, but that this influence is directly attributed to Alfred.[25]

The importance of royal intervention has quite rightly been emphasized, for it was the protection of a fugitive, allowing some respite, that 'set the stage for an amend settlement', promoting royal control and a general idea of non-violent legal process.[26] But it would be wrong to see either this intervention by the king or the actual institution of sanctuary as something outside or above the normal legal process. The criminal was not absolved from his crime simply by finding a church. Under Charlemagne there was a clear distinction between the man who was accused of a crime and the man who had been judged and condemned, and it was only to the former that sanctuary was afforded.[27] Much the same must have been true of the situation in England. The directions laid down by the laws all tend simply to suspend the feud and let the criminal be punished by the payment of fines and compensation, with the aid of his kin, or, as stated by one tract, by imprisonment or slavery (see below).

The laws provide for the proper supervision of the fugitive, even to the extent of limiting the number of doors any building should have if it became necessary to move him from the church itself. Pursuers who found it difficult to keep a proper guard upon the fugitive could call upon the king or ealdorman for assistance. Meanwhile the pursuers were to contact his kin and friends, in other words those who could arrange and pledge a money settlement.[28] The law code of Edmund concerning the bloodfeud details a procedure which is likely to have been also that followed, or at least promoted, where sanctuary

---

[23] *Alfred* 5.

[24] *Alfred* 42.1.

[25] E.g. IV *Athelstan* 6.1. For a contrary view, see above, pp. 404–9.

[26] C. Riggs, *Criminal Asylum in Anglo-Saxon Law* (Gainesville, Florida, 1963), p. 171; J. Goebel, *Felony and Misdemeanor* (Pennsylvania, 1976, originally pub. 1937), p. 375.

[27] *Capitulatio de partibus Saxoniae*, in *Capitularia Regum Francorum*, ed. A. Boretius and V. Klause (2 vols., MGH; 1883–97), I, 68; P. Timbal Duclaux de Martin, *Le Droit d'Asile* (Paris, 1939), p. 142. This last work, though now somewhat dated, provides one of the most wide-ranging and scholarly studies of sanctuary in the medieval period.

[28] *Alfred* 5 and 42.

had been sought. No one escaped scot-free by seeking sanctuary, though he might save his life, but was to submit to the law, only receiving continued protection as long as arrangements could be made to fulfil payment of fines and compensation and as long as these obligations were honoured.[29]

How often this procedure was followed cannot be decided on the meagre evidence we have. The repeated attempts by kings to impose and promote the same perhaps point to a disinclination to abandon violent measures. The few stories we have do seem to dwell more on the breach of sanctuary and divine, rather than human, intervention, although they do nevertheless suggest an awareness of the form, if not an eagerness to observe it.[30] Some stories, on the other hand, seem to show that the procedure was followed. In 750, for instance, Offa, son of Aldfrith, sought sanctuary in the church of Lindisfarne and was besieged there by King Eadberht, only to be dragged out 'almost dead with hunger'. There is no indication that Eadberht violated the sanctuary, only that Offa's time ran out.[31] In the incident described by Reginald of Durham in the twelfth century and referred to above, the guarding of the church doors is mentioned and the community obviously did not expect anyone to ignore the sanctuary rights of the church. In this case, however, the blood of the pursuers did not cool sufficiently to allow of a non-violent conclusion, though their actions were suitably punished.[32]

The fugitive at the body of St Cuthbert could then, in theory, feel safe for thirty-seven days; enough time to arrange pledges and prove a desire and ability to adhere to a monetary settlement. Any violators of the sanctuary, on the other hand, could be sure of swift punishment. But the system of fines described above refers to the extreme — homicide within a church or its environs. There is no reason to doubt that the Cuthbertine sanctuary also fitted into a broader system and was protected by a whole range of fines, dependent upon the nature of the crime and the status of the perpetrator. Lesser crimes, such as fighting with or injuring someone, are mentioned in the laws and all of these called forth appropriate fines, sometimes mutilation;[33] no doubt this was reflected in the penalties for breach of sanctuary.

Clearly homicide in breach of sanctuary was an exceptional crime. Immediately the whole substance of sanctuary was violated; God affronted, and the king, or his servants, deprived of any role in the process of justice,

---

[29] II *Edmund*: Goebel, loc. cit.; cf. Pryce, *Journal of Legal History* 5, p. 7.

[30] The materials available do not allow for the study of specific incidents to establish some kind of general pattern of 'case law', as opposed to prescriptive law — probably because by its very nature sanctuary is inextricably linked to royal pronouncements and their rigid application. Compare this to the approach being developed in other areas of Anglo-Saxon law: P. Wormald, 'Charters, Law and the Settlement of Disputes in Anglo-Saxon England', in *The Settlement of Disputes in Early Medieval Europe*, ed. W. Davies and P. Fouracre (Cambridge, 1986), at pp. 149 – 68.

[31] *HR s.a.* 750.

[32] *Libellus* 60.

[33] *Alfred* 5; VIII *Aethelred* 2 and 4; *Be griðe 7 be munde*, ed. Liebermann, *Die Gesetze* I, 470 – 3.

especially the exercise of any discretion. It was a grave sacrilege. It was a complete disregard for law and peace. To adjust to this special crime the laws show that kings further refined sanctuary rights in a way that restored the importance of non-violence in the settling of disputes and re-established the royal prerogative. Aethelred II declared homicide within church walls to be an unemendable crime.[34] The criminal was to be hounded 'unless he reaches such an inviolable sanctuary (*deope friðsocne*) that the king, because of that grant him his life, upon condition he make full amends (*fulre bote*) to God and man.' The tract *Be griðe 7 be munde* (*c.* 1028 – 70) confirms that 'on Norðengla lage' homicide within a church made a man *feorhscyldig* (liable in his life), and should such a man wish to save his live he must seek *friðstol*.[35] Clearly the *friðstol* was *deope friðsocne*. Aethelred reserved to the king the discretion as to whether, having sought an inviolable sanctuary, a man should be allowed to live, paying his wergild and thereby buying the right to offer compensation and pay the appropriate fines. *Be griðe 7 be munde* noted three ways a man might pay for his life: wergild, perpetual serfdom, or imprisonment. There was a *friðstol* at Hexham according to Prior Richard, the stone chair beside the altar which is still there and is traditionally associated with Wilfrid. For the purpose of Richard's scheme of sanctuary this was placed on a par with the *feretrum sanctarum reliquiarum quod est post altare* — presumably equivalent at Durham to the resting place of the body of St Cuthbert. It seems certain that these northern churches possessed Aethelred's special sanctuaries where, paradoxically, criminals could offer amends for unemendable crimes.[36]

The laws may, however, cast further light on these sanctuaries. The tract *Be griðe 7 be munde* offers the alternative of perpetual serfdom to the fugitive fleeing to one of them. It is possible that here we have the earliest indication of those residents at the sanctuaries called *grithmen*.[37] These were sanctuary seekers who were allowed to become servants of the church, though confined to the limits of the sanctuary within the precincts of the church. This was surely a form of perpetual serfdom such as is referred to in the tract. The evidence is perhaps slender, but there seems little else that might shed light upon the origin of this extraordinary group.

The evidence, therefore, places the Cuthbertine sanctuary firmly in the Anglo-Saxon legal context, probably influenced by West Saxon royal pronouncements and protected by fines associated with the Danelaw. Yet one element of Richard of Hexham's scheme, which can be shown to apply to other sanctuaries in England and to have parallels elsewhere, with some reflection in the laws, does not seem to figure in the evidence from the churches of St Cuthbert. As we have seen, the area of sanctuary around the

---

[34] VIII *Aethelred* 1.

[35] *Be griðe* 13, 16; Liebermann, *Die Gesetze* I, 471.

[36] It cannot be ruled out that all cathedrals and major abbeys enjoyed something like a special sanctuary because of their status, and possession of a *cathedra* or shrine.

[37] R. H. Forster, 'Notes on Durham and other North Country Sanctuaries', *Journal of the Archaeological Association* 61 (1905), p. 122.

church of Hexham was divided into a number of separate areas, ever more sacred as the altar was approached. Two of these, III and IV in the diagram, would seem to coincide with the sanctuary afforded within a church's walls and within a church's porch mentioned in the laws.[38] The specific mention of the church building, the porch and some areas associated with the church is to be found in continental sources, and the council of Toledo in 681 extended the area of sanctuary to a circuit of thirty paces from the doors of the church.[39] In Irish and Welsh accounts of sanctuary the delineation of sanctuaries for some distance around the church is found. Gerald of Wales noted in the twelfth century 'the fences and ditches marked out and set by the bishops to fix the sanctuary limits', and the Welsh laws confirm that the fine for breach of sanctuary was twice as much for the church itself as for the churchyard.[40] Also, in Ireland sanctuary limits were marked by crosses, banks and ditches. The precinct of the church (*termon*) was calculated by its status and, within the *termon*, areas of varying sanctity were recognized 'with the penalties for violation differing according to the area'. Full *díre* (fine) was incurred for violation of the church's innermost sanctuary, and half *díre* for violation of the *termon* land beyond the green.[41]

Anglo-Saxon sanctuary, and the scheme described by Richard of Hexham, does not stand outside the general pattern for western Europe. Further, as on the continent there was a close link between sanctuary and jurisdictional liberties or immunities. At Hexham, Beverley and Ripon the area of sanctuary became identified with the *banleuca*, or area in which the churches enjoyed special jurisdictional privileges, marked out by *bancruces* or *cruces Athelstani* after the alleged grantor of the privileges. Bury St Edmunds and a number of other churches in England, some likewise associated with Athelstan, also had distinguishable *banleucae*.[42] One commentator on the development of sanctuary on the continent has stated that 'à la fin de la période carolingienne, le circuit de l'asile se confond à peu près exactement avec le district de *l'immunité étroite* qu'il a contibuée à créer.'[43] Now, it is possible that Symeon's reference to the fine of £96 for breach of sanctuary may

[38] *Be griðe* 13; Leibermann, *Die Gesetze* I, 471.

[39] *Capitulare Carisiacense 873*, II, 346; Timbal Duclaux de Martin, *Droit d'Asile*, pp. 78 – 9, 122, 124, 173.

[40] Gerald of Wales, *Descriptio Kambriae* I, 18; trans. L. Thorpe, *Gerald of Wales: The Journey through Wales/The Description of Wales* (Harmondsworth, 1978), p. 254; *Venedotian Code* I, 43; II, 10 (printed in *Ancient Laws and Institutes of Wales*, ed. A. Owen (Record Commission; London, 1841)); and Pryce, *Journal of Legal History* 5, p. 5, notes the radius of sanctuary as the length of a legal acre, or 120 yards.

[41] K. Hughes, *The Church in Early Irish Society* (London, 1966), pp. 148 – 9. J. Ryan, 'The Cáin Adomnáin', in *Studies in Early Irish Law*, ed. R. Thurneysen et al. (London, 1936) at p. 273.

[42] M. D. Lobel, 'The Ecclesiastical Banleuca in England', in *Oxford Essays in Medieval History presented to H. E. Salter* (Oxford, 1934), pp. 123, 129; *Memorials of Ripon*, ed. J. Fowler (4 vols., SS 74, 78, 81, 115; Durham, 1882 – 1950) I, 33 – 5, 89 – 93; C. Cox, *The Sanctuaries and Sanctuary Seekers of Medieval England* (London, 1911), pp. 215 – 21.

[43] Timbal Duclaux de Martin, *Droit d'Asile*, p. 152. Cf. Ganshof, *Frankish Institutions*, p. 46.

imply some zoning of the sanctuary at Durham, but there is little else to indicate such a clearly definable *banleuca* as elsewhere. Of course, there has been speculation as to the existence of such an area and as to the identification of extant medieval crosses as markers of its boundary, but this is mere speculation.[44] Even if such markers existed there is no evidence that they enjoyed the prominence of those *bancruces* at, say, Ripon. But then these latter were also associated with jurisdictional limits. Durham's special jurisdictional liberty was not as restricted as Ripon's or Beverley's or Hexham's, but extended to the borders of County Durham. The confounding of sanctuarial and jurisdictional privileges within Durham's liberty would account for any lack of definition for a circuit of sanctuary around the church itself, whether at Durham or Chester-le-Street.[45]

The development of Durham's jurisdictional liberty is not the subject of this paper, but Cuthbert's prophetic death-bed warning has a particular poignancy when one considers the asylum that the whole county offered to all kinds of felons in the late middle ages.[46] There is doubt also that the community looked to the Anglo-Saxon period, and especially the tenth century, for the origin of its privileges. The community was a major force in the north from the seventh century onwards and it is no surprise to find one of the few references to asylum in the church of Lindisfarne relating to competing claimants to the Northumbrian throne, Offa and Aldfrith. That the West Saxons, probably from Alfred onwards, should have shown a keen interest in the rights, privileges and lands of this community is understandable.[47] Athelstan's name is associated with a number of churches and their privileges and he was both a benefactor of the church of St Cuthbert and a confirmer of its rights. His brother, Edmund, whose code concerning the bloodfeud relates so closely to the question of sanctuary, confirmed to the church *pacem vero et legem quam unquam habuit meliorem* ('peace and law better than it ever enjoyed'). This confirmation is paralleled by Edgar's later general injunction that *stande aelc ciricgriδ swa swa hit betst stod.*[48] The late ninth and tenth centuries were a watershed in the

[44] *Rites of Durham*, ed. J. T. Fowler (SS 107; Durham, 1903), pp. 226 – 7; crosses around Durham could indicate many kinds of boundary, including city and manor, as witnessed by an agreement of 1162 × 1189 between the monks of Durham and the lord of Houghall: *Feodarium prioratus Dunelmensis*, ed. W. Greenwell (SS 58; Durham, 1872), p. 203.

[45] There is however reference to *Cuthbertestones* in the fifteenth century, which marked the boundary of the liberty on the Tyne bridge: R. L. Storey, *Thomas Langley and the Bishopric of Durham 1406 – 1437* (London, 1961), p. 54.

[46] See, for instance, those who, in the reign of Edward I, committed burglary in Northumberland and then fled to safety at Farnacres in the liberty: *Three Early Assize Rolls for the County of Northumberland*, ed. W. Page (SS 88; Durham, 1891), p. 343. 'There are two great sanctuaries in Yorkshire, beside the bishopric of Durham, where all murderers and felons resort and have at least 100 miles compass', *Letters and Papers Foreign and Domestic of the Reign of Henry VIII*, VII (London, 1883), p. 617, for the year 1534.

[47] D. W. Rollason, 'Relic Cults as an Instrument of Royal Policy c.900 – 1050', *ASE* 15 (1986), pp. 91 – 103.

[48] *HSC* 28; II *Edgar* 5.3.

history of the community and not least in terms of its sanctuary, which mirrors
the royal legislation of that period.

The monks of Lindisfarne gathered around the dying Cuthbert were not
keen upon his body remaining on Farne,

> But after we had pleaded with him earnestly and long . . . at length the man of
> God spoke words of counsel. 'If', he said, 'you wish to set aside my plans and to
> take my body back there, it seems best that you entomb it in the interior of your
> church, so that while you yourselves can visit my sepulchre when you wish, it
> may be in your power to decide whether any of those who come thither should
> approach it.'[40]

Those who came were pilgrims, priests, kings, murderers and felons of all
kinds.

---

[40] *VCP* 37, *Two Lives*, pp. 278 – 81.

The First Generations of Durham Monks
and the Cult of St Cuthbert

A. J. PIPER

In 1083 Bishop William of St Calais brought together the monks from the recently refounded houses at Jarrow and Wearmouth to form the chapter of his cathedral in Durham. Only one of the secular canons from the existing community of St Cuthbert took on the monastic habit and remained;[1] the change in the cathedral's personnel was more nearly complete than on any other occasion in its history, and at a stroke the first monks of Durham became responsible for the major and long-established cult associated with the relics of St Cuthbert. This situation placed upon them a special obligation to show themselves worthy servants of the cult, and they responded with energy in a variety of ways. Insights into their thinking some twenty years after 1083 are afforded by the account of the church of Durham by the monk Symeon who joined the community in about 1090;[2] he presents an exceptionally carefully organized justification of the changes.

In 1092, on his return from exile, Bishop William ordered the replacement of the existing cathedral and on Thursday 11 August 1093 the foundation-stones of the present building were laid.[3] Although William died in 1096 and was only succeeded by Ranulf Flambard after a vacancy of over three years, work on the new building advanced rapidly and in 1104 the choir was sufficiently complete for Cuthbert's coffin to be translated to a shrine in the apse in the presence of Bishop Flambard, the king of Scotland's brother, and the abbots of Sées, St Albans, York and Selby; new liturgical forms were probably composed for the occasion.[4] Immediately beforehand the monks inspected the saint's body, reassuring themselves that it remained incorrupt, that the chief mark of its virtue had not been withdrawn. A public demonstration of the body's condition followed; the monks feared perhaps

---

[1] *HDE* IV, 3, pp. 122 – 3.
[2] He stands thirty-eighth in the list of monks prefixed to *HDE*; the first twenty-three represent the community formed in 1083: *HDE*, pp. 4 – 5; IV, 3, p. 122.
[3] *HDE* IV, 8, pp. 128 – 9.
[4] C. Hohler and A. Hughes, 'The Durham Services in Honour of St Cuthbert', *Relics*, pp. 156 – 7.

that this smacked of irreverence, for their account of the proceedings presents it as a response, unwillingly undertaken, to insinuations arising from the secrecy of the previous inspection, and the prior apparently allowed the body to be handled only by one outsider, the abbot of Sées. The very considerable length and circumstantial detail of the early account of the translation speak perhaps of a certain insecurity on the part of the monks.[5]

The events of 1104 provided the monks with one form of endorsement of their position. Within three years they had provided themselves with another, in the shape of the '*libellus* about the origin and development of this church, that is of Durham', generally known as the *History of the Church of Durham*, written by Symeon, at the direction of his superiors. He reports his commission as being 'to describe the origin (*exordium*) of this church of Durham'.[6] Although no mention is made of the intended audience, a powerful threefold admonition near the beginning urges the imitation of Cuthbert's virtues firstly on subjects and prelates, secondly on monks, and thirdly on priors; since it is 'ordinis observantiam' that is enjoined upon the first group, a virtue appropriate to those under a monastic rule, rather than diocesan clergy and bishops, it is clear that the whole admonition is addressed to monks and their monastic superiors.[7] Symeon's immediate audience was his community.

Symeon does not make it clear exactly what those who commissioned him intended. What he undertook was very much more ambitious than a mere continuation of the *Historia de sancto Cuthberto*, simply covering the transfer of the see to Durham and the introduction of the Benedictine community. In his opening sentences he proclaims:

> From the most fervent faith in Christ of Oswald, glorious former king of the Northumbrians and precious martyr, this holy church, which, in praise of God and his perpetual protection, keeps lodged in a single container (*loculus*) those relics of sacred veneration, the incorrupt body of the most holy father Cuthbert and the venerable head of that king and martyr, takes the origin of its position and sacred religion. Although from causes arising it is located elsewhere, nonetheless by stability of faith, by dignity and authority of a pontifical see, and by the fact of being the monastic dwelling instituted there by that king and Bishop Aidan, it endures as the self-same church founded with God as author.[8]

In Symeon's skilfully constructed chronological account of the see, from its foundation at Lindisfarne down to the death of Bishop William in 1096, the

---

[5] *De miraculis* 7.

[6] *HDE* I, 1 and preface, pp. 17, 3. H. S. Offler, 'Medieval Historians of Durham' (Inaugural lecture, Durham, 1958), pp. 6–8. A. Gransden, *Historical Writing in England c. 550 to c. 1307* (London, 1974), p. 116 is hesitant about the attribution to Symeon.

[7] *HDE* I, 6, p. 27; the passage concerns Cuthbert's virtues as a monastic superior. In the first person plurals used to describe the incorrupt state of the saint's body in 1104, *HDE* I, 10, pp. 34–5, the writer assumes that his audience are those who shared the experiences with him.

[8] *HDE* I, 1.

critical events unfold under Cuthbert's guidance. The onlookers on the shores of the Irish Sea bewail to the saint as the bearers prepare to carry the relics into exile, and a storm prevents the exodus.[9] Having left Chester-le-Street in 995, the saint's unwillingness to return there is expressed in the sudden immoveability of the vehicle transporting his relics, and the decision to settle in Durham follows; Symeon makes no mention of possible political considerations, nor, at this point, of the ready defensibility of the new site.[10]

Symeon did not pay quite the full price of a rigorously chronological treatment of the history of the see, bishop by bishop. That would have entailed a delay in introducing its tutelary saint, Cuthbert. Instead the young Cuthbert is introduced in the third chapter, following the death of Aidan.[11] In consequence the work starts with a most effective triptych of the saints at the heart of the Durham cult: Oswald, Aidan and Cuthbert. It brings Cuthbert into close association with both the founder of the see and its first bishop, his chronological disjunction from them smoothed away.

Symeon felt the need to repeat little of the available material on Cuthbert's life and only included what seemed apposite to his purpose. In his selection the emphasis on monasticism is very strong. First, at the point where Cuthbert is introduced, his monastic vocation is emphatically re-iterated: 'a monk completely (*plane*) a monk, a monk, I say'.[12] Cuthbert's move from Melrose to the monastery of Lindisfarne is the occasion for a quotation from Bede stressing that Aidan and his successors as bishop had all been monks, and the virtues of Cuthbert as a monastic superior are held up for imitation; Cuthbert's first period as a solitary on Farne is described in a distinctively high-flown passage on the contemplative life in which the most prominent image is that of the house of the Lord (*domus Domini*), an established synonym for a church or monastery.[13] For his brief time as bishop the only concrete details reproduced by Symeon concern gifts of property to the see; otherwise it is a matter of leaving a norm of the pontifical life for bishops to imitate.[14]

The intimate association of the monastic community with the see is further stressed in several of the elaborate dating-formulae employed in the earlier part of the work. For example:

> In year 664 from the incarnation of the Lord, year thirty from which the episcopal see on the island of Lindisfarne and the abode of monks were instituted by the most studious worshippers of Christ, King Oswald and Bishop Aidan.[15]

[9] *HDE* II, 11.
[10] *HDE* III, 1; *cf.* III, 2 'locum quidem natura munitum'.
[11] *HDE* I, 3.
[12] *HDE* I, 3.
[13] *HDE* I, 6 – 7. R. E. Latham and D. R. Howlett, *Dictionary of Medieval Latin from British Sources* (London, 1975 –   ), p. 720 *domus* defs. 6 – 7.
[14] *HDE* I, 9 – 10.
[15] *HDE* I, 7, also I, 10, p. 35; II, 5, p. 52; II, 6, p. 57.

Monastery and see together are thus treated as the threshold of an epoch, and it is significant that Symeon does not use such formulae for the period between 875 and 1083; with the final flight from Lindisfarne in 875 the fully monastic nature of the community was lost, only to be recovered in 1083.

Symeon did feel able to identify echoes of monasticism that persisted through the vicissitudes that followed the events of 875, and he prefaces his narrative of those events with the following statements. Eighty-three years earlier all the monks were killed, except a very few who somehow escaped; in 875 all disappeared, but those brought up and instructed among them in the clerical habit followed Cuthbert's body wherever it was taken, always maintaining the usage in the offices handed on to them by monks teaching, and the entire succession of their descendants observed by ancestral tradition the custom of singing the hours according to the institutes of monks rather than clerks, down to the time of Bishop Walcher. Nor until then did the body of Cuthbert, monk and bishop, ever lack the zeal and allegiance of monks: Bishop Eardwulf (d. 899), a monk like his predecessors, and Abbot Eadred kept close in undivided company as long as they lived, and after them the bishops down to Walcher are known to have been monks, never without two or three monks.[16]

These statements form one of Symeon's most striking passages, and his eagerness to emphasize the echoes of monasticism after 875 leads him close to tendentious obfuscation, as his own narrative subsequently reveals. The norm of the monk-bishop cannot be sustained in the case of the clerk Eadred (d. *c.* 1040), but he is struck down before he could perform the episcopal office, as a punishment for simony.[17] The account of Bishop Edmund's elevation in *c.* 1020 shows that it was not a matter of the choice of a bishop being restricted to a monk, but of the bishop-elect taking the monastic habit and renouncing the world, almost as an idiosyncratically extended consecration rite.[18] It requires careful reading to notice that Symeon's statement about the zeal of monks with which Cuthbert was served must refer to service by the bishops, not a monastic community.

Liturgical practice provided Symeon with a thread of continuity to link the observance of Cuthbert's community after 875 with its monastic past, a thread to which he returned more than once in the period up to 1083.[19] He stresses the way in which this had been learnt from the monks and faithfully handed down. But this was hardly very remarkable; matters could only have been otherwise if there had been alternative liturgical usages available at Lindisfarne before 875, or if there had subsequently been opportunity and a desire to adopt a usage from elsewhere, or if the later community, disregarding its prime function, had abandoned regular liturgical observance.

---

[16] *HDE* II, 6, pp. 57–8.
[17] *HDE* III, 9; III, 18, p. 106 lines 2–4.
[18] *HDE* III, 6.
[19] *HDE* III, 1, p. 80; III, 7, pp. 87–8.

In fact the community was less liturgically conservative than Symeon admits: in the later tenth century it took up a collectar from southern England and supplemented it with material favoured by the contemporary monastic reform movement, perhaps partly as a political gesture.[20]

A final striking feature of Symeon's account of 875 is his choice of words to describe the relationship of Bishop Eadwulf and Abbot Eadred: they kept close in undivided company (*individuo comitatu*). The same phrase is used both of Bishop Edmund and his monk-companion, and of the bearers of the coffin.[21] By 1100 *comitatus* had gone a long way in England to shifting from its general classical meaning of a company of people to its later, more restricted, meaning of an earldom, a county or those who constituted its court.[22] Symeon's usage echoes Bede's account of Wilfrid setting out for Rome with Benedict Biscop, a future bishop with a future abbot.[23] It suggests an extremely close association between Bishop Eadwulf and Abbot Eadred, while avoiding terminology only appropriate to a strictly monastic relationship.[24]

The norm of a monk-bishop and a fully monastic community was not recovered until 1083. When he came to describe the darkness before that dawn Symeon does admit shafts of light that he had omitted from the important passage associated with events of 875, in which Bishop Walcher (1071 – 80) is seen as embodying the most serious break in the strands of continuity.[25] Now, however, he can be portrayed as the forerunner of the new dawn. He welcomes the three Benedictines from the south, provides for the resumption of monastic life at Jarrow and Wearmouth, rejoices when it prospers, and augments its endowment. Assassination forestalls his decision to become a monk and to establish a monastic house at Cuthbert's shrine, but its foundations have been laid.[26]

The full return of the monastic theme is accomplished when William of St Calais, abbot of St Vincent in Maine, becomes bishop. With a grandiloquent dating-formula, Symeon presents the new bishop bringing the monks to Durham, binding them inseparably to Cuthbert's body. He divides their possessions from his, 'as ancient custom required', although death interrupts his plan of giving them a fully sufficient provision of lands. He never removes anything from the church. He acts as a model superior. He decrees that Prior Turgot and his successors shall be archdeacon in the diocese.[27]

---

[20] *The Durham Ritual*, ed. T. J. Brown (EEMF 16; 1969), 49 – 50; there are also additions written in a script associable with the reforms, see p. 41. For relations with Wessex, see above pp. 393 – 5, 413 – 24.

[21] Ibid., 87, 80.

[22] Latham and Howlett, *Dictionary of Medieval Latin*, pp. 389 – 90. Symeon uses it for earldom at *HDE* III, 23, p. 114 line 1; IV, 4, p. 124 line 23.

[23] *HE* V, 19.

[24] *HDE* III, 22, p. 111 lines 21 – 25 exactly exemplifies this in the case of Turgot before his monastic profession.

[25] *HDE* II, 6, pp. 57 – 8.

[26] *HDE* III, 21; III, 22, p. 113.

[27] *HDE* IV, 3 – 5; IV, 8, p. 129.

There is no coda. Symeon ends his work with Bishop William's death in 1096, closing with a dating-formula based on the year in which the monks were brought together in Durham. The long vacancy that followed finds no place, nor Bishop Ranulf Flambard, although he has figured earlier, as the tax-gatherer striken by Cuthbert for his intended exactions. Reference to the state of Cuthbert's body in 1104 is also neatly introduced much earlier, in the context of the saint's death in 687. It is with Bishop William, restorer of the pristine service of the cult, that Symeon rests his case, his *libellus*.[28]

Ground is not far to seek for anxieties to prompt the production of so skilful a piece of advocacy between 1104 and 1107. Ranulf Flambard had secured the see in 1099 in consequence of his effectiveness as the king's servant; his ruthlessness as an ecclesiastical sequestrator might well have made the monks apprehensive. As late as 1107 it is quite possible that the monastic community had little experience of him: the protracted resolution of the troubles that had broken over his head when William Rufus was killed in 1100 formed his principal pre-occupation and kept him in Normandy for extended periods.[29] He was present at the translation in 1104, cast in the monks' account as a doubting Thomas; perhaps his behaviour on that occasion made the monks aware of the need for the persuasive presentation of the ideal constitution of St Cuthbert's church that Symeon's *libellus* provided.[30]

It is doubtful whether the monks were entirely realistic if they feared that Bishop Flambard would risk the potential complications involved in ejecting them, and so it can hardly be said that Symeon equipped them with the arguments that saved the day; it was an exaggerated sense of crisis that pushed his work across the spectrum away from historiography towards polemic. On the other hand he did express a clear perception of the trend that Flambard's actions took: the bishop did not associate with the community in undivided company; he took the earliest opportunity to have an archdeacon other than the prior; he diverted funds away from the monks to advance the building of the cathedral; he was not quick to take up Bishop William's interrupted plans for their endowment.[31] But he was not unduly oppressive: when death approached, his restitution to the monks involved a few properties of modest value.[32] He did not, however, restore the prior's right to be archdeacon; had this become established, it would have given the community a diocese-wide franchise, an exceptional position certainly, but a potent cause for conflict

---

[28] *HDE* IV, 10, p. 135; III, 20; I, 10, pp. 34 – 5; IV, 2, pp. 121 lines 7 – 8; p. 11, lines 7 – 9.

[29] R. W. Southern, 'Ranulf Flambard', in his *Medieval Humanism and Other Studies* (Oxford, 1970), at pp. 183 – 205. H. S. Offler, 'Rannulf Flambard as Bishop of Durham', *Durham University Journal* 64 (1971), pp. 14 – 25; also separately as *Durham Cathedral Lecture 1971*.

[30] *Symeonis Dunelmensis Opera et collectanea*, ed J. H. Hinde (SS 51; Durham, 1868), 192.

[31] H. S. Offler, *Durham Episcopal Charters 1071 – 1152* (SS 179; Durham, 1968), nos. 14 – 18, 20 – 21.

[32] Ibid., nos. 24 – 25.

with subsequent bishops and a major objection to allowing it freedom to elect the prior.[33]

Symeon articulated several important features of Cuthbert's cult in the twelfth century. He records the terms of sanctuary and is the first to express the need to exclude women from Cuthbert's ground. This idiosyncratic attitude to women has been seen as a covert attack on the former community's wives, but this interpretation does not accord well with Symeon's restraint in his criticisms of that community; it may owe more to the local understanding of the ideals promoted by the Gregorian reform, possibly also to a heightened sensitivity to pollution in the vicinity of a saint whose incorruption attested his enduring chastity.[34]

At the start of his *libellus* Symeon set a triptych of saints: Oswald, Aidan and Cuthbert. This is not the only context in which the three are brought together in this way in the twelfth century. Among the fourteen twelfth-century copies of Bede's prose *Life of St Cuthbert* that belong to the textual group associated with the cathedral priory, there are five manuscripts, among them those most closely connected with the cathedral priory, that also contain passages drawn from the *Ecclesiastical History* to form lives of Oswald and Aidan.[35] The closeness of this parallel to Symeon's triptych is underlined in two ways. First, the supplementary material in the manuscript does not simply represent an attempt to create a compendium embracing all the saints whose relics were prized by the monks of Durham; that would have required the inclusion of Bede, to whom Symeon himself devoted considerable space.[36] Second, the monks generally gave Cuthbert their undivided attention. Their major material endowments were a portion of the lands that had formed the undivided Cuthbertine patrimony held by the former community with the bishop. The monks preserved the tradition of the saint's direct possession of their lands in the forms of their diplomatic: from an early date Cuthbert is the prime recipient of grants to the cathedral priory, even grants by the bishop, who enjoyed the other portion of the patrimony.[37] Their primary seal, quite possibly inherited from the former community to judge by the style of its lettering, bore the legend 'seal of Cuthbert bishop (*praesul*) saint'; subsequently they did take the relatively unusual step for a monastic community of

---

[33] Witness the disputes that arose from the monks' claims to much more limited franchises: F. Barlow, *Durham Jurisdictional Peculiars* (London, 1950).

[34] On sanctuary, see above pp. 425 – 36. V. Tudor, 'The Misogyny of St Cuthbert', *Archaeologia Aeliana* 5th series 12 (1984), pp. 157 – 67; also below pp. 456 – 8. I am indebted to Dr Meryl R. Foster and Ms Andrea Hodgson for discussion of this matter.

[35] *Two Lives*, pp. 20 – 39 (nos. 3, 4, 11, 21, 23), and p. 50 (group Bx).

[36] *HDE* I, 8; I, 11, p. 38; I, 13 – 14; III, 7, pp. 88 – 9.

[37] H. H. E. Craster, 'The Patrimony of St Cuthbert', *EHR* 70 (1954), pp. 177 – 99. W. Greenwell, *Feodarium prioratus Dunelmensis* (SS 58; Durham, 1872), pp. 98 – 206 nn. Offler, *Episcopal Charters*, nos. 14 – 18, 21, 24, 29 – 30, but cf. also nos. 20, 25 and 28 in which St Cuthbert is preceded by St Mary. Possessions associated with the dependency at Stamford in Lincolnshire were known as the fee of St Cuthbert down to the Dissolution: London, Public Record Office, SC 2/188/2.

adopting a design for the reverse, and chose an engraved gem of the head of Jupiter, adding the legend 'head of saint Oswald king', but that was not until the early thirteenth century.[38]

Symeon laid great emphasis on the role of seventh-century Lindisfarne as normative for the cathedral community's constitution. Not long after he wrote there is evidence of one of the most distinctive developments in Cuthbert's cult, the growth of a secondary centre at Lindisfarne. Apparently this was promoted at the direction of his superiors by Edward the monk, who was active there by about 1122; he arranged for hospitality at festival-time and supervised the building of a new church in Cuthbert's honour.[39] The focus of the cult is described as Cuthbert's tomb (*tumba*), and it appears to have been a cenotaph, not a shrine containing corporeal relics; it was hallowed by the fact that Cuthbert's body had once rested there, and Symeon presents this as the bishop's motive for replacing the timber church at Chester-le-Street with one of stone in the mid eleventh century.[40]

The monks seem to have given striking physical expression to Lindisfarne's normative relationship to Durham. The church of the later priory on Lindisfarne, presumably built to house Cuthbert's cenotaph, apparently in the earlier twelfth century, does not appear to have been a monastic church in its original design: the two doorways on the south side were in the south wall of the south transept and two-thirds of the way down the nave, not the normal monastic arrangement, while the stairs in the transept supposed to have been the monks' night-stairs are simply a product of the exact north-south symmetry of the plan.[41] What is very clear, both from the substantial standing remains and from eighteenth-century drawings of parts of the structure now collapsed, is that the building bore a marked resemblance to the coeval work at Durham, most obviously in the arrangement and incised decoration of the piers of the nave-arcade.[42] To see this simply as the result of an identical team of masons working on the two buildings discounts the capacity of the monks to

[38] W. Greenwell and C. H. Hunter Blair, 'Durham Seals', *Archaeologia Aeliana* 3rd series 15 (1918), no. 3427 and plate 64; nos. 3398 – 3594 provide a conspectus of English monastic seals. The reverse was introduced under Prior Bertram (d. 1213): Durham Dean & Chapter Muniments 2.4.Spec.4 and 5a.

[39] Offler, *Episcopal Charters*, pp. 93, 95 – 6. *Libellus* 21 – 22.

[40] *HDE* III, 9, p. 92 and above pp. 367 – 8.

[41] The earliest firm documentary evidence for a monastic community at Holy Island Priory may be as late as 1172: James Raine, *The History and Antiquities of North Durham* (London, 1852), App. no. DCCLXVI: one of the parties, Stephen de Bulmer, died between 1170 and 1172, see Pipe-Roll 17 Henry II (Pipe-Roll Soc. 16), p. 75 and 18 Henry II (*Eadem* 18), p. 67. Architectural evidence is perhaps found in the eastward extension of the eastern arm of the church, to accommodate a choir for the monks. I am indebted to Mr Eric Cambridge for invaluable discussion of the chronology of the monastic function of the building.

[42] Reproductions of important drawings showing the south internal elevation of the nave are in J. P. McAleer, 'The Upper Nave Elevation and High Vaults of Lindisfarne Priory', *Durham Archaeological Journal* 2 (1986), pp. 43 – 53; if McAleer is correct in concluding that the nave had groin vaults, with ribbed vaults throughout the rest of the building, the explanation for so eccentric an arrangement may perhaps be sought in a desire to create a 'primitive' impression.

calculate the effect thereby created, their awareness of the potential of architectural propaganda. An observant visitor coming to Durham from Lindisfarne would have seen the point: the larger offspring's likeness to its parent vouched for its legitimacy.

Close to Lindisfarne lay the island of Farne, where Cuthbert had spent his years as a hermit, so eloquently described by Symeon.[43] Here too the monks fostered the cult, taking their cue from the much wider eremitic movement of the period. The uncle of an early twelfth-century sacrist of Durham is the first imitator of Cuthbert on Farne to be mentioned.[44] In 1150 Bartholomew the monk, moved by visions of Cuthbert, was allowed by the prior to undertake the life of a solitary on Farne; another monk was already there then. Bartholomew continued on Farne until his death, forty-two years later, not invariably alone: a retired prior of Durham joined him for a period.[45] Other Durham monks pursued separate solitary lives there, some simultaneously. Pilgrims seeking Cuthbert's aid also came; there were brothers who cared for those in need, and a guest-house, with foundations said to be Cuthbert's handiwork.[46] Farne afforded a special opportunity for the cult to take on a form focused on the saint's life rather than his relics, an inspiration to direct imitation, which monks might readily undertake; this was not lost on the monks of Durham.

The centres on Lindisfarne and Farne came in due time to form permanent dependencies of Durham Cathedral Priory, while the cell at Lytham in Lancashire was a product of a local lord's devotion to Cuthbert.[47] Historical considerations doubtless played their part in the revival of monastic life at Jarrow and Wearmouth as cells of Durham.[48] These, with the other cells at Coldingham, Finchale and Stamford, formed significant, enduring, and sometimes troublesome, elements in the cathedral priory's pattern of life.

The historical perspective articulated by Symeon to justify the introduction of a Benedictine community as the cathedral chapter in 1083 was distinctively literary in its sources. The sweeping away of the old community in 1083 removed from the scene those whose historic identity involved the preservation of traditions from the more immediate past, for whom conservatism was a matter of living memory.[49] The new community was in a position to seek its own historic identity far further back, in the seventh-century community of Lindisfarne. For that to be possible required of course the historical knowledge for which Bede's writings were the primary source, and indeed the initial

---

[43] *HDE* I, 6 – 7.

[44] *Libellus* 27, 74, 29.

[45] *Vita Bartholomaei Farnensis* in *Sym. Op.* I, 299 – 300, 307, 322, and pp. xl – xli.

[46] *Libellus* 29, 117, 119 – 20, 62, 201. H. H. E. Craster, 'The Miracles of St. Cuthbert at Farne', *Analecta Bollandiana* 70 (1952), pp. 1 – 19.

[47] *Victoria History of the County of Lancaster*, ed. W. Farrer *et al.* (London, 1906 –   ), II, 107.

[48] A. J. Piper, *The Durham Monks at Jarrow* (Jarrow Lecture 1986), pp. 3 – 6.

[49] A telling contrast, where the old community remained, is provided by Christ Church Canterbury, see R. W. Southern, *Saint Anselm and his Biographer* (Cambridge, 1966), ch. 7.

inspiration for the Benedictine mission to the North in the 1070s was said by Symeon to have been drawn from Bede.[50] Thanks to Bede the first generations of Durham monks were able to make a sharp break with the immediate past and rapidly develop a distinctive sense of historic purpose. From this stemmed the shape and expression that they gave to St Cuthbert's cult. It would have been very different if Bede's writings had not been available to them, and so affords a fine example of historiography making history.[51]

---

[50] *HDE* III, 21, p. 108: 'historia Anglorum' presumably refers to *HE*. The copy given to the monks by Bishop William of St Calais is Durham Cathedral Library MS B.II.35.
[51] Citations in the notes above convey some measure of my debt to Professor Offler; I am also much indebted to Dr M. R. Foster for her comments.

The Cult of St Cuthbert in the Twelfth Century: The Evidence of Reginald of Durham

VICTORIA TUDOR

The twelfth century must surely rank as Durham's greatest age. The very beginning of the century, the year 1104, witnessed the triumphant passage of the relics of Durham's patron saint into the new cathedral church which was being constructed in his honour. At the same time inspection proved that God had not ceased to effect the chief miracle associated with the saint, the preservation of his remains from bodily decay. By 1133, furthermore, the present cathedral, demonstrating an unlooked-for capacity for innovation among its builders and still providing one of the greatest architectural experiences in Europe, was complete. More evidence of the vigour of the church is furnished by the literary achievements of its monks, particularly in the fields of hagiography and history: one writer, Maurice, was known to his fellows as a second Bede. By contrast, a set of events in the early 1140s demonstrated the pressure constantly applied to the northern border by the kings of Scotland. William Cumin, chancellor to King David I, made an attempt, ultimately unsuccessful, but with appalling short-term consequences, to foist himself upon the see. The years 1153 to 1195, more positively, were dominated by Bishop Hugh of le Puiset, one of the most masterful and flamboyant successors of St Cuthbert, who imparted to his see a splendour which seems to have marked it until the sixteenth century.[1]

Reginald of Durham was the foremost hagiographer to emerge from the

[1] I should like to thank Mr Alan Piper for help on various points of detail. For Maurice, see F. M. Powicke, 'Maurice of Rievaulx', *EHR* 36 (1921), pp. 17 – 29, and for Bishop Hugh, G. V. Scammell, *Hugh du Puiset, Bishop of Durham* (Cambridge, 1956). In this paper the following abbreviations have been used: *Memorials of St Edmund's Abbey*, ed. T. Arnold (RS 96, 3 vols.; London, 1890 – 6) (*Mem. Edm.*); Hermann, *Liber de miraculis sancti Eadmundi* in *Mem. Edm.* I, pp. 26 – 92 (Hermann, *Liber*); Samson, *Opus de miraculis sancti Eadmundi* in *Mem. Edm.* I, pp. 107 – 208 (Samson, *Opus*); *Liber Eliensis*, ed. E. O. Blake (Camden 3rd ser. 92; London, 1962) (*Lib. El.*); R. C. Finucane, *Miracles and Pilgrims, Popular Beliefs in Medieval England* (London, 1977) (Finucane, *Mir. and Pil.*); V. M. Tudor, 'Reginald of Durham and St Godric of Finchale: A Study of a Twelfth-century Hagiographer and his Major Subject' (unpublished Ph.D. thesis, University of Reading, 1979) (Tudor, 'Reg.'); B. Ward, *Miracles and the Medieval Mind, Theory, Record and Event 1000 – 1215* (revised edn., London, 1987) (Ward, *Mir.*).

monastery in this period and the author of works on Godric of Finchale, St
Oswald and, probably, Ebba of Coldingham. He was also responsible for *The
Little Book about the Wonderful Miracles of Blessed Cuthbert which were Performed in
Recent Times.*[2] Many of the wonders in the 'little book' or *Libellus* were effected
or recounted near the saint's tomb and it is thus to be seen primarily as a
collection of shrine miracles. The work begins with some preliminary
chapters, given in a confused form in the printed edition but almost certainly
consisting of the following: a letter to Reginald's friend, Ailred of Rievaulx;
an *Excusatio* in which Reginald protests his lack of literary skill; a preface,[3] and
finally the highly allegorical *Sermon on the Tabernacles of the Saints.*[4] Then come
the 129 miracle stories belonging to the period from 875 to the third quarter of
the twelfth century, though the vast majority appear to date from a time-span
beginning with the reign of Stephen, that is, the years 1135 to 1154, and
lasting to the 1170s.[5]

Reginald was led to begin his work after hearing Ailred recount examples of
Cuthbert's miracles on numerous occasions, and after inspecting the Durham
histories, which revealed that his friend's stories were not represented there.
The author's intention was to arrange his material chronologically,[6] but
examination shows that he was successful in this only up to a point. His stories
were based, he tells us, on the testimony of individuals who, for one reason or
another, were in possession of reliable information.[7] Thus his sources were
oral apparently and a comparison of his narratives with miraculous material
found in other Durham works to a very large extent confirms his statement.[8]

---

[2] *Libellus*, p. 16. For what we know of Reginald and his writings, see Tudor, 'Reg.', pp. 58 – 106.
[3] *Libellus*, pp. 1 – 8. On the confusion surrounding these first three sections in the printed edition,
see Tudor, 'Reg.', pp. 351 – 2.
[4] *Libellus* 4 – 11, pp. 8 – 16.
[5] Chapters 12 – 15 belong to the ninth century, chapters 16, 19, 26 and probably 20 also to the
eleventh. The translation of 1104 provides the substance of chapters 40 – 3 and chapter 74 should
be dated to 1113 or 1114 (see below p. 465). The events in chapters 17 and 18 occurred during the
pontificate of Bishop Geoffrey Rufus (1133 – 41), the beginning of which almost coincided with
Stephen's accession. We have no way of knowing if Reginald's concentration on these central
decades of the twelfth century indicates a particularly high incidence of miracles then or merely
reflects the period when he was gathering material, but the latter is possibly more likely.
[6] *Libellus* 3, p. 4; 1, p. 6. It was a commonplace of hagiography that some eminent person had
played a part in the inception of a work (cf. Ward, *Mir.*, p. 30), but the details of Ailred's
involvement given by Reginald sound convincing.
[7] *Libellus* 3, p. 5.
[8] Although he knew about events described in other Durham works, a comparison of such
materials reveals no evidence of direct borrowing. One example is furnished by the story of the
destruction of a Scottish army near Norham which is referred to in *Libellus* 73, p. 149 (cf. *HSC* 33,
and *De miraculis* 4). He may indeed have learned of such stories from oral tradition. He was aware
of the account of the 1104 translation of Cuthbert's body in the *De miraculis* (7, pp. 247 – 61) and
there are reminiscences of it, though nothing more, in the chapters which he devotes to the subject
(*Libellus* 40 – 3). Battiscombe ('Historical Introduction', in *Relics*, at p. 3, n. 1) has suggested that
he made use of written materials now lost in his description of the 1104 proceedings. From what
Reginald says of his sources (*Libellus* 40, p. 84), it seems more likely that this information was
being set down in writing for the first time in the *Libellus*.

The component of the *Libellus* derived from literary sources is virtually non-existent therefore.

The composition of the work probably occupied its author over a lengthy period. He witnessed two of Cuthbert's miracles in the early 1150s,[9] but 1165 is the first year to be mentioned in connection with the recording of events.[10] Towards the end of the work appear the troubles of 1173 – 4 when William the Lion of Scotland came to the aid of the eldest son of Henry II, in rebellion against his father. On two occasions the writer appears to refer to the invasions undertaken by William in support of his young ally as past history.[11] Thus the collection was probably completed in or after the second half of 1174.[12]

A terminal date in the 1170s poses a problem, however. In his letter Reginald declares his intention of sending the completed work to Ailred of Rievaulx.[13] Now the Cistercian abbot died on 12 January 1167. This apparent contradiction suggests the likelihood of at least two stages in the composition of the work: the first represented by a draft completed before January 1167; the second by the collection as we have it today. The first draft must have come to an end before chapter 112, which contains the earliest references to St Thomas of Canterbury, martyred in December 1170, and which mentions the year 1172. Indeed an inspection of the principal manuscript of the work — the arrangement of whose folios, it must be said, has undergone some modification — reveals that a new quire begins with this chapter. There is a distinct absence in the work, furthermore, of stories dating from 1167 to 1170, which would tend to support the idea of a hiatus in composition at this time. Thus the text of the *Libellus* as we have it today probably represents the following: the original collection, begun no later than 1165, completed before January 1167 and consisting of the first 111 chapters; combined with this a continuation, made up of the remaining thirty narratives, begun no earlier than 1172 and finished in or after the second half of 1174.

According to Reginald, his motive in gathering his material was to bring honour to his saint.[14] More broadly, collections of miracles such as this were witnesses to and also advertisements for the power of the saint and his shrine. They were usually kept at the tomb itself where they were open to the perusal of literate visitors.[15] The ultimate intention was to buttress and strengthen the

---

[9] *Libellus* 50, p. 104; 91, pp. 198, 201. The historical context of the first incident is the vacancy in the see between the death of Bishop William of Ste Barbe in 1152 and the consecration of Bishop Hugh in 1153. The second occurred not long after a visit of Archbishop William of York to Durham. He was entertained by Bishop Hugh who was enthroned on 2 May 1154 (*HDE, continuatio altera* in *Sym. Op.* I, p. 169), while Archbishop William died on 8 June the same year. Thus the second miracle must belong to 1154.

[10] *Libellus* 72, p. 148.

[11] *Libellus* 129, p. 275; 141, p. 290.

[12] That is, after 13 July 1174, when King William was captured by the English; see *Annals of the Reigns of Malcolm and William kings of Scotland*, ed. A. C. Lawrie (Glasgow, 1910), pp. 172 – 82.

[13] *Libellus* 1, pp. 5, 7.

[14] *Libellus* 3, pp. 4, 5.

[15] Finucane, *Mir. and Pil.*, p. 156.

economic, social and, in some cases, political position of the community who guarded the saint. Quite often his servants needed to maintain the position of their shrine against that of other saints and the continuation of Reginald's *Libellus* was probably designed to protect the cult against the threat posed by Thomas of Canterbury and Godric of Finchale.

The veracity of miracle stories is a vast and difficult question to which there will probably never be satisfactory answers and which cannot be tackled here. Contemporary shrine miracles have, however, been described by Sister Benedicta Ward as, 'generally speaking, a painstaking record of what people believed had happened to them by the power of the saint,'[16] while, as John Dickinson has pointed out, it was in the interest of the saint's community to produce an unimpeachable record of his wonders.[17] Our chief concern, furthermore, is not the precise events which lay behind each of Reginald's stories, so much as beliefs about and emotions directed towards Cuthbert in this period. Reginald's narrative cannot be relied on to provide an objective account of what happened but, as a source for what the people of the time thought had happened in certain instances, they are invaluable.

By the year 1100 the cult of St Cuthbert was already four centuries old. His capacity to survive profound political upheaval and to emerge from it with enhanced prestige had ensured his continued veneration in the north. Indeed he was without doubt the greatest saint of that part of England. In the revived monasteries of the south the high regard in which the works of Bede were held kept the memory of the saint fresh. Following the example of his predecessors, King Cnut had deemed it politic to visit the shrine and had outdone them in approaching bare-foot. Some decades later the new Norman rulers of England were forced to acknowledge Cuthbert's power, while the foundation of the Benedictine monastery of Durham in 1083 was in part an act of homage to him, one product of a movement which aimed to restore the monasticism of the greatest period of Northumbrian history. Cuthbert's monks faced the twelfth century with their patron already enjoying quite exceptional, nation-wide prestige and an unchallenged ascendancy in the north.[18]

Before looking at the main features of the cult in the years after 1100 it may be as well to introduce two other saints, comparison with whom might be instructive. Etheldreda of Ely and Edmund of Bury, who died in 679 and 870 respectively, were, like Cuthbert, Anglo-Saxon saints who emerged from the trials associated with the Norman Conquest with their reputations unimpaired. With both, also, was associated a claim to incorruption. Indeed, referring to the period before 1083, Reginald declares that Cuthbert, Edmund

[16] Ward, *Mir.*, p. 170; cf. p. 215.

[17] J. C. Dickinson, *An Ecclesiastical History of England: The Later Middle Ages* (London, 1979), pp. 379 – 80.

[18] On the cult in the eleventh century, see R. B. Dobson, *Durham Priory 1400 – 1450* (Cambridge, 1973), pp. 24 – 6 and D. Knowles, *The Monastic Order in England* (2nd edn., Cambridge, 1966), pp. 165 – 6, 169.

and Etheldreda were regarded as the greatest of English saints.[19] For all these reasons and because a significant number of miracles has survived for both from about this period their cults may profitably be compared with that of Cuthbert.[20]

If the eleventh century had seen veneration for Cuthbert reach new heights, the twelfth seems to have witnessed a further advance. The period must have represented the climax of Cuthbert's influence and glory. There are more miracles dating from the twelfth century than from any other period and Reginald's collection of the saint's wonders is the largest ever made. No doubt the prestige he had acquired before 1100 played a very large part here as did the events of 1104, with their reaffirmation of his incorruption, the chief proof that he enjoyed divine favour to a marked degree. Thus if there was an increased public interest in shrines — and the twelfth and thirteenth centuries have been called the 'heyday of pilgrimages'[21] — Durham was in a strong position to take advantage of it. Similar factors, however, encouraged the cults of Etheldreda and Edmund in this period and Cuthbert's miracles would seem to have outnumbered theirs.[22] Unlike them, the Durham saint enjoyed the advantage of an absence of serious rivals, in the early part of the period covered by the *Libellus* at least,[23] and his cult was diffused among a number of different centres.[24] For both these reasons, the total number of Cuthbert's miracles would have increased.

Needless to say, the image of the saint projected by the twelfth-century cult bore only a limited relation to the character of the living man. It conformed far more to the stereotyped personalities publicized by other shrines. At this time, just as at all other periods, Cuthbert was regarded as a being of immense, all-embracing and overwhelming power. From beyond the grave he could conjure up substance from nothing,[25] direct the elements — even to the extent of making the wind blow in two directions at once[26] — and indeed control the

---

[19] *Libellus* 19, p. 38; for the date, see p. 41.

[20] Naturally enough, I have concentrated mainly on the twelfth-century miracles of both saints, but, as their cults in the eleventh century also bore a strong resemblance to that of Cuthbert as described by Reginald, I have looked back to the wonders of the earlier century when that seemed useful. Etheldreda's miracles are found in *Lib. El.* (see index under Etheldreda). The principal source for Edmund's wonders has been Abbot Samson's *Opus de miraculis sancti Eadmundi*, but I have also made use of Abbo, *Passio sancti Eadmundi* (*Mem. Edm.* I, pp. 6 – 25), Hermann's *Liber de miraculis sancti Eadmundi* and narratives from Oxford, Bodleian Library MS 240 (given in *Mem. Edm.* I, Appendix E, pp. 358 – 77) where appropriate.

[21] J. Sumption, *Pilgrimage: An Image of Mediaeval Religion* (London, 1975), p. 160.

[22] As against the 118 miracles attributed to Cuthbert in the twelfth century by Reginald, thirty-one and thirty respectively were recorded by Edmund and Etheldreda within the approximate limits of the years 1100 to 1200.

[23] There appears to have been some rivalry between the other two saints themselves (cf. *Lib. El.* III, 32, p. 266; 130, p. 379), due no doubt partly to the proximity of their shrines (Ely and Bury are only about twenty-two miles apart).

[24] See below, pp. 461 – 4.

[25] *Libellus* 22, p. 49.

[26] *Libellus* 30, p. 69; cf. 23, p. 52; 28, p. 64.

whole of creation.[27] In fact, one might be forgiven for believing that some confusion existed in Reginald's mind between his patron and the Almighty. From time to time, Cuthbert is described in terms far more appropriate to God — 'father of the world to come, the prince of peace' form but one example[28] — and the author regularly attributes miracles to the saint alone without reference to the Deity.[29] Probably it would be unwise to read too much into Reginald's statements, but it is noticeable that the collectors of Etheldreda's and Edmund's miracles show no similar tendency to idolatry. One cannot help wondering, however, if any other devotees of the Durham saint fell into a similar error. That contemporaries thought of Cuthbert primarily in terms of power is suggested by the form he took in dreams. The saint usually appeared as a bishop, frequently of an unearthly and ideal kind,[30] and the stress laid on his episcopal office reflects his claim to authority and might.

If pressed, Reginald would no doubt have admitted that the true source of all power was God. The power of the saint was dependent on the favour of God and one indication that an individual possessed God's favour to a marked degree was the physical incorruption of his body. Thus Cuthbert's repeatedly confirmed incorruption was intimately bound up with his tremendous power. This characteristic had of course played a major role in establishing the saint's reputation and as early as the tenth century Archbishop Dunstan had quoted Cuthbert as a classic example of this phenomenon.[31]

Reginald devotes some space to this subject and it is a theme to which he returns repeatedly in the course of his work. Four of his chapters lovingly describe what was found when Cuthbert's tomb was opened in 1104 and constitute a detailed reaffirmation of the central miracle of the cult.[32] Incorruption was regarded as a sign of purity of life and Reginald explains that Cuthbert was thought especially to have earned the privilege by the self-mortification he practised on the Inner Farne.[33] He also makes plain that, in addition to being incorrupt, Cuthbert after death possessed a quality which made him unique. Not only was his body undecayed but it had retained the flexibility of its joints.[34] He also explains that Cuthbert was believed to breathe in some unaccountable manner. Suppleness of the limbs was dependent on the fluidity of the blood and this could only occur in an individual who was breathing.[35] This flexibility was evidence of great sanctity and was shared with

[27] *Libellus* 27, p. 60.

[28] *Libellus* 71, p. 145; cf. 70, p. 144.

[29] For example, *Libellus* 94, p. 210; 101, p. 225; 79, p. 164.

[30] For example, *Libellus* 23, p. 52; 30, p. 68; 112, p. 252.

[31] *Memorials of St Dunstan*, ed. W. Stubbs (RS 63; London, 1874), p. 379. On incorruption, see *Two Lives*, p. 338 and Finucane, *Mir. and Pil.*, pp. 22 – 3.

[32] *Libellus* 40 – 3, pp. 84 – 90.

[33] *Libellus* 102, p. 226.

[34] *Libellus* 3, pp. 3 – 4.

[35] *Libellus* 19, p. 39.

no other individual,[36] not even other saints who could claim incorruption. It meant that Cuthbert possessed greater power to work miracles than other saints.[37] Thus for Reginald the extraordinary phenomenon of his suppleness, added to that of his incorruption, evidently — though he usually hesitated to make the point explicitly — raised Cuthbert to the status of being the greatest of all saints. It would be interesting to know if this view of the importance of Cuthbert's flexibility represented the author's personal opinion or an idea current in the monastery at the time that he was writing. The *Capitula de miraculis*, a slightly earlier miracle collection, lays little stress on the saint's flexibility,[38] while I know of no other Durham source that refers to it. It is worth noting, however, that at both Ely and Bury the saint's claim to incorruption was supplemented by a further wonder: in Etheldreda's case an incision in the neck which had healed after burial and in Edmund's the fusion of his head with his decapitated body.[39]

Cuthbert's incorruption was so potent an idea that in this period subsidiary myths connected with it were current. Of these the most colourful were those associated with Alfred, son of Westou, who acted as guardian of the saint's body in the eleventh century. This individual was believed to have trimmed Cuthbert's hair and nails, and to have conversed with him from time to time.[40] Two similar figures appear in the miracles of St Edmund.[41] The *Libellus* also contains references to portions of 'the cloth of Blessed Cuthbert', one of the sheets removed from the tomb in 1104. These textile pieces demonstrated miraculous power because of the close contact they had enjoyed with the holy body.[42]

Here, then, was a being possessed, as his bodily incorruption indicated, of tremendous power. How was that power employed? In the *Historia de sancto Cuthberto* and Symeon's *History of the Church of Durham* Cuthbert is portrayed above all as a ruthless champion of his people and his rights. His supernatural might is generally used to punish and avenge, and its objects are those rash enough to threaten his servants and property, especially his lands.[43] The *Libellus* proves that in many ways the saint of the twelfth century had lost none of his earlier savagery. One of the later miracles in the collection describes how the former bishop appeared to the servant of Richard FitzRoger of Lytham when the servant had offended him in some way. The saint struck him in the

---

[36] In fact the Ely saint, Withburga, was also held to possess the gift of flexibility (*Lib. El.* II, 147, p. 232). Reginald may not have known this.

[37] *Libellus* 3, pp. 3 – 4.

[38] *De miraculis* 4 – 7, pp. 252, 253.

[39] *Lib. El.* I, 27, p. 45; Samson, *Opus* (*Mem. Edm.* I) I, 1, p. 111; I, 8, p. 134.

[40] *Libellus* 16, p. 29; 26, p. 57. On this individual, see *HDE* III, 7, pp. 87 – 90.

[41] Abbo, *Pass.* (*Mem. Edm.* I) 15, p. 20; Samson, *Opus* (*Mem. Edm.* I) I, 4, pp. 115 – 16; cf. I, 8, p. 132.

[42] For example, *Libellus* 54, pp. 111 – 12; 96, p. 214; 97, pp. 216 – 17. For the sheets taken from the coffin in 1104, see 42, p. 89.

[43] See for example *HDE* II, 13, 16, III, 9 and IV, 4. Cf. Ward, *Mir.*, p. 61.

face and pushed his lower jaw up into his head so that it became hideously swollen.[44] Even in this period, furthermore, Cuthbert was not averse to killing his enemies, like a certain Julian, responsible for the theft of cattle from the Durham estate at Normanton-on-Soar in Nottinghamshire.[45] This brutal and irascible figure was believed, in addition, to respond to harsh treatment himself, for example, the blackmail of Harpin of Thornley, one of his devotees.[46]

No doubt the severe side of Cuthbert as depicted by Reginald differed not at all from the saint of earlier centuries, but in the *Libellus* it reveals itself less often. In Reginald's collection only just under a fifth of the narratives are concerned with the theme of retribution[47] and none of these stories is concerned with the security of the Durham estates. In this respect at least, presumably, the monks felt secure by the twelfth century.

In the *Libellus* an attractive side of Cuthbert is demonstrated far more often. In many chapters Reginald stresses his patron's mercy and compassion and repeatedly declares that the saint will deny his assistance to no one invoking him in the right spirit.[48] Cuthbert is also depicted, paradoxically perhaps, as the 'mildest of saints'.[49] Naturally — and this is consistent with Cuthbert's earlier, harsher side — Reginald liked to believe that the saint's especial concern was reserved for his 'household',[50] that is, his monks. Their patron did not wish them to suffer sorrow and anxiety[51] and his comforting hand was stretched out more quickly to them than to others.[52] Reginald acknowledges nevertheless that the saint was not enclosed by geographical boundaries nor was he distant from those living a long way off.[53] Here we encounter a marked difference between the earlier Cuthbert and the saint of the *Libellus*: instead of restricting his ministrations to his own servants, Reginald's saint helps many individuals who are totally unconnected with him. Indeed such people constitute more than a third of all the beneficiaries mentioned in the *Libellus*[54] and this openness characterizes all parts — early and late — of the work.

Needless to say, the beneficent Cuthbert is not depicted as exerting himself in a vengeful manner. The vast majority of miracles in this collection reveal

---

[44] *Libellus* 132, pp. 280 – 1. For Richard FitzRoger, see below, p. 463.

[45] *Libellus* 67, p. 137; cf. 57.

[46] *Libellus* 75, pp. 156 – 7. This story dates from the time of Prior Roger of Durham, that is, perhaps, 1138 – 49.

[47] The *Libellus* contains a total of 118 twelfth-century miracles. Of the 141 chapters, eleven contain introductory matter, two (14 and 18) are not miracles of St Cuthbert at all, 47 and 54, together with 49 and 93 (less certainly) are duplicates, while eight narratives probably belong to the period before 1100. Twenty-two of the 118 are devoted to the theme of punishment.

[48] For example, *Libellus* 65, p. 130; 79, p. 164; 119, p. 264.

[49] *Libellus* 70, p. 143; 109, p. 246; 128, p. 274.

[50] *Libellus* 106, p. 238.

[51] *Libellus* 80, pp. 167, 168; 82, p. 174; 89, p. 193.

[52] *Libellus* 94, pp. 208 – 9.

[53] *Libellus* 84, p. 178.

[54] See below, pp. 455 – 6.

him assisting humanity and in a wide variety of ways.[55] Thus, for example, he is often portrayed as coming to the aid of seafarers by calming ferocious tempests or sending favourable winds.[56] Cuthbert was also responsible for the release of prisoners, some of whom, like the individual who carried away with him the bolts of Durham castle, proceeded to claim the right of sanctuary in the cathedral.[57] A number of stories, in addition, describe how the former bishop supplied his servants with food or drink at a time of shortage,[58] while in a significant number of narratives he concerns himself with birds or animals in some way.[59] No examples of stories belonging to the former category occur in the collections of Etheldreda's and Edmund's miracles, while of the latter only one instance occurs, among the wonders of the Bury saint.[60] Stories of both kinds appear in the early lives of Cuthbert, however, and their presence in the *Libellus* should probably be attributed to the continuing influence of these biographies.[61]

By far the most common of these miracles of assistance, however, are cures (which I take to include exorcisms) and with regard to these a change evidently came over the cult, in Durham at least, about the year 1170. About a quarter of all the wonders which Reginald describes as occurring before that date were examples of healing,[62] but of these a relatively small proportion happened in Durham itself,[63] and only two definitely took place in the cathedral.[64] Thus the saint was certainly credited with miracles of healing but these tended to occur in places other than Durham such as the Inner Farne. After about 1170 the situation changed radically. Of the miracles which appear to belong to the years after that date, over two-thirds are cures,[65] and of these over half took place in the environs of the cathedral.[66] One wonders if the shrine had become a centre for faith-healing in a way which it seems not to have been before. Perhaps the Durham monks were willing to encourage the sick in a way

---

[55] In over four-fifths of the stories Cuthbert is depicted as rendering help of some kind. There *are* chapters in the *Libellus* devoted to subjects other than punishment or assistance, for instance, visions; in many narratives the treatment of a number of different topics is combined, however, and either punishment or assistance, the themes which dominate the collection, figure in virtually every chapter.

[56] For example, *Libellus* 30, 52, 83.

[57] *Libellus* 95; see also 46, 50.

[58] For example, *Libellus* 21, 64, 106.

[59] For example, *Libellus* 68, 86, 133.

[60] *Mem. Edm.* I, Bodl. MS 240 8, pp. 365 – 6.

[61] For example, *VCP* 5, pp. 168 – 70; 11, pp. 192 – 4; 12, pp. 194 – 6 (the miraculous supplying of food) and 5, pp. 168 – 70; 10, pp. 188 – 90; 20, pp. 222 – 4 (narratives involving birds or animals in some way).

[62] Twenty-one out of eighty-eight narratives.

[63] Five.

[64] *Libellus* 44, 48; cf. 60.

[65] Twenty-three out of a total of thirty miracles from the period after 1170.

[66] Thirteen.

previously unknown in order to compete successfully with the new saints, Thomas Becket and Godric of Finchale.[67]

By the twelfth century the Cuthbert of an earlier age, the terrifying and overwhelmingly powerful champion of his people and his property, had mellowed somewhat. While still capable of exacting retribution he was portrayed more commonly as compassionately working for the benefit of individuals, often those who had no previous connection with him. This process of softening is frequently met with in the cults of long-established saints at this time and here Cuthbert was merely conforming to the developments of the age.[68] The one surprising element in this process is the lateness, or so it would appear, with which cures came to play a major role in the activity of the saint at Durham. Edmund and Etheldreda seem to have regularly performed cures long before such miracles were generally associated with Cuthbert,[69] and this cannot be explained by reference to any greater harshness in the Durham saint's image compared with theirs. All three were of a similar type, with the same mixture of severity, directed particularly against the enemies of their communities, and tender compassion. Moreover Cuthbert had shown no reluctance to assist in other ways those who invoked him. Perhaps the answer should be sought in the complacency of the Durham monks, who, confident of their saint's wide popularity and lack of serious rivals, until the 1170s had felt no need to make their shrine especially attractive to visitors. After 1170, with the rise of the cults of St Thomas of Canterbury and St Godric of Finchale, the need was felt and perhaps for this reason the idea of the shrine as a curative centre was given publicity.

A far more distinctive feature of the cult in this period was the famous misogyny of St Cuthbert. Foisted on their patron, most probably, by the first generations of Durham monks to discredit the married clergy whom they supplanted, it receives no corroboration in anything that is known of the bishop's life.[70] Reginald recounts only one story in connection with this trait of Cuthbert's, which suggests that his aversion to women was known and respected by the time the author was writing. The incident, belonging to 1113 or 1114, involved a woman called Helisend who was ejected from the cathedral having endured foul abuse from the saint and his sacrist. Reginald

---

[67] On the rivalry between Cuthbert and these individuals, see below, pp. 459 – 60.

[68] Cf. Ward, *Mir.*, p. 67.

[69] Edmund: for example, Samson, *Opus* (*Mem. Edm.* I) I, 5, p. 122; I, 14, pp. 145 – 6; Hermann, *Liber* 37, pp. 75 – 7. Etheldreda: for example, *Lib. El.* III, 29, pp. 264 – 5; III, 30, p. 265; III, 31, p. 265.

[70] On this subject in general, see V. Tudor, 'The Misogyny of Saint Cuthbert', *Archaeologia Aeliana* 5th ser. 12 (1984), pp. 157 – 67. Mr Piper has suggested that doubt is cast on this interpretation of Cuthbert's misogyny by the slight attention given to the ousted clerks by Symeon in his *History* (see above, p. 443). Having portrayed Cuthbert as a misogynist, however, the monks may well have felt that no further assaults on their predecessors were necessary.

concludes by describing the saint as an unbending persecutor of the female sex.[71]

It is obvious, nevertheless, that restrictions on women applied in only a few locations. In addition to the cathedral, its cemetery was subject to the ban and women may well have been excluded from the conventual church on Lindisfarne at this period. They were certainly not allowed in the chapel on the Inner Farne, though the churchyard there was open to them.[72] In none of the other churches dedicated to the saint and referred to by Reginald is there the slightest hint of a restriction on women. Thus, for example, the group of people celebrating the saint's feast in his chapel at Slitrig in Roxburghshire included Seigiva and Rosfritha, two women from Hawick.[73] One suspects that here and in other churches of which Cuthbert was patron the ban was not merely unobserved but unknown. His misogyny had come into being to serve a purpose associated with Durham and thus it was almost certainly limited to the monastery there and the two churches colonized by it in the twelfth century, Lindisfarne and the Inner Farne.

In the earlier decades surveyed by the *Libellus* the Durham monks may well have wanted the best of both worlds: a misogynist saint who, despite himself, possessed some attraction for women. Cuthbert, declares Reginald, writing at this time, would withhold his mercy from no one invoking him in a pious manner, irrespective of factors such as sex or rank.[74] He also tells us of a noble lady from Embleton in Northumberland who visited the Inner Farne, probably between 1150 and 1170, in search of a cure for some crippling ailment.[75] The saint restored the health of some other women at this time,[76] though not at Durham. Cuthbert's anti-feminism, however, could only have been a handicap in any attempt to encourage visitors to the shrine and here again the rise of the new cults in the 1170s seems to have found Durham vulnerable. That the threat was real is shown by a study of the posthumous miracles of St Godric: the majority of the pilgrims who visited Finchale were women.[77]

Some effort may have been made after 1170 to encourage female visitors. Just under a third of the cures recorded by Reginald as occurring at the cathedral after that year involved women.[78] There was obviously no question of admitting them to the building, but an attempt may have been made to publicize the area outside the west doors as a location for female cures. A local

---

[71] *Libellus* 74. For the date of the incident, see G. W. S. Barrow, 'Scottish rulers and the religious orders', *Transactions of the Royal Historical Society* 5th ser. 3 (1953), p. 85.
[72] Tudor, *Arch. Ael.* 12, pp. 160, 161.
[73] *Libellus* 137, pp. 285–6.
[74] *Libellus* 79, p. 164.
[75] *Libellus* 62. The incident happened when the monk Bartholomew was living on Farne, that is, from 1150 to 1193 (see *Sym. Op.* I, p. xli), while the position of the story in the collection suggests that the incident occurred before 1170 rather than after.
[76] *Libellus* 53, 99, 100, 108.
[77] Finucane, *Mir. and Pil.*, pp. 127, 142, 167, 169.
[78] Four out of thirteen incidents. The four relevant chapters of the *Libellus* are: 115, 121, 123 and 124.

blind woman received her sight there and, before she did so, experienced visions of Christ on the cross high up on the west wall of the church with Cuthbert interceding on her behalf.[79] Two other women are also described as regaining their health there.[80] Similar influences may have worked on Bishop Hugh of le Puiset when he decided to construct the Galilee Chapel. From this lady chapel women, to whom access was permitted, could even enjoy a distant view of Cuthbert's shrine.[81] But if the Galilee, apparently completed about 1175,[82] represented a softening in Cuthbert's attitude, it would seem that the monks could not afford to let his misogyny disappear from sight. In another work Reginald describes what happened when a little girl, who was playing nearby, strayed into the cathedral. She went out of her mind and her condition was interpreted as a punishment meted out by the saint. This incident almost certainly belongs to the 1170s.[83] The phenomenon of Cuthbert's anti-feminism appears to have been unique, at least as far as England is concerned. Needless to say, there is nothing comparable in the cults of Etheldreda and Edmund. Indeed one collector of Edmund's miracles referred to the crowds of both men and women who flocked to his church as the saint's 'special glory'.[84]

How did contemporaries view Cuthbert's relations with his fellow saints? At Ely Etheldreda was at times thought of as belonging to a group which included the other female saints whose relics the church possessed,[85] but there is nothing resembling this in the northern cult. On one occasion a monk keeping watch in the cathedral experienced a vision in which a number of early bishops of Lindisfarne, including Cuthbert, celebrated Mass.[86] Similarly, the monk Robert of St Martin once called upon Bede in addition to Cuthbert in his distress. Bede is made to appear very much the subsidiary figure in the story, however, and the miracle, when it occurs, is attributed to Cuthbert alone.[87] For the most part, therefore, there was little attempt, or presumably need, to associate any of the other Durham saints with Cuthbert. Not even St Oswald, whose head was the only relic, apart from the holy body, to be replaced in the coffin in 1104,[88] is allowed to share any of the glory of the church's principal saint.

[79] *Libellus* 121, pp. 267 – 8.

[80] *Libellus* 123, 124.

[81] Geoffrey of Coldingham, *Liber . . . de statu ecclesiae Dunhelmensis*, in *Historiae Dunelmensis scriptores tres*, ed. J. Raine (SS 9; Durham, 1839) 7, p. 11.

[82] A. W. Clapham, *English Romanesque Architecture* (2 vols., Oxford, 1930 – 4) II, pp. 92, 94.

[83] *Libellus de vita et miraculis S. Godrici, heremitae de Finchale*, ed. J. Stevenson (SS 20; Durham 1845), p. 403. The incident belongs to the period between Godric's death in 1170 (see below, p. 459) and some point after 1177 when Reginald's work seems to have been completed (Tudor, 'Reg.', p. 84).

[84] Hermann, *Liber* (*Mem. Edm.* I) 46, p. 87.

[85] *Lib. El.* II, 132, p. 212; II, 133, pp. 214 – 15. Their relics were translated with hers in 1106 (*Lib. El.* II, 148, p. 233).

[86] *Libellus* 38.

[87] *Libellus* 76, pp. 159 – 60.

[88] *Libellus* 42, p. 89.

It is often possible while reading the *Libellus* to observe the author indulging in a certain understandable pride in the status and achievements of his patron. Thus while some miracles are merely equated with those of, for example, St Nicholas[89] or St Peter,[90] elsewhere Reginald cannot resist pointing out the superiority of the wonder performed by the former bishop to some earlier model.[91] Before 1083 Cuthbert proves himself the most powerful in a trinity of major English saints,[92] while Brendan, patron saint of Brancepeth near Durham, is made to declare that Cuthbert is more famous than he, more powerful and much more effective in working miracles.[93] Not surprisingly, grateful beneficiaries of his intervention avow him the greatest of saints.[94]

To a large extent this lavish praise was but a way of upholding Cuthbert's honour and lacked practical implications. None of the saints mentioned in the earlier parts of the *Libellus* ever posed a genuine threat to the supremacy of the Durham cult in the north. But in a story which ends in 1172 the three most notable English saints have changed from Cuthbert, Edmund and Etheldreda, to Cuthbert, Edmund and Thomas of Canterbury.[95] After the archbishop's death in 1170 the Durham community was confronted by a major rival to their patron who was rapidly developing a national, and indeed international, following. Similtaneously, further competition, though on a smaller scale, appeared in the form of the cult of Godric of Finchale who died in the same year. The Durham monks had fostered this local cult but Godric appears to have developed into a rival to Cuthbert in a manner that they had not foreseen. In a number of Durham miracles dating from the 1170s therefore, the sick person had already applied to Thomas or Godric or both, before being restored to health in Durham. Out of thirteen cures which occurred there, six involved the martyred archbishop in some way,[96] while in four the sick person had either been to Finchale or had thought of going there.[97] Naturally all these stories prove Cuthbert's superiority to the wonder-workers of Canterbury and Finchale — he had performed the eventual miracle, after all — while in one narrative Reginald is quite explicit in stating the parity, indeed friendship, between the Durham saint and Thomas.[98] This merely gives the impression that the writer was trying to claim a share in the popularity of the Canterbury cult. The guardians of many shrines must have felt similarly insecure as Thomas began his rise to widespread popularity. The Bury monks certainly

---

[89] For example, *Libellus* 30, p. 69; 32, p. 74; 71, p. 146.

[90] *Libellus* 70, p. 145.

[91] *Libellus* 12, p. 19.

[92] *Libellus* 19, pp. 38 – 9.

[93] *Libellus* 46, p. 93.

[94] *Libellus* 75, p. 157; 79, p. 164.

[95] *Libellus* 112, pp. 251 – 2; cf. 115, p. 260.

[96] *Libellus* 112, 114, 115, 116, 125 and 126.

[97] *Libellus* 113, 121, 124 and 126.

[98] *Libellus* 116.

felt undermined and the new saint figures in three of Edmund's miracles, working in concert with him.[99]

Before moving away from Durham it is probably worth mentioning various objects which were in the care of the monks and which provided a tangible link with its patron saint. Of these the chief was of course the incorrupt body in its tomb. Reginald never provides a full verbal picture of the shrine, but we know that it stood in the 'inner church'[100] or choir on a thick slab of stone.[101] It was raised high above the floor,[102] at the top of some steps,[103] like the site of the shrine today. While the faithful could place themselves beneath it,[104] it was no taller than a kneeling man.[105] Coloured sheets, an outer one of silk and an inner one of linen, protected the shrine from dust.[106]

Of the other items belonging to the monastery perhaps the most famous was the 'banner of Blessed Cuthbert'.[107] Suspended on a lance with its corporal cloths[108] — from which it presumably derived its power — it was carried out, as indeed was the coffin itself,[109] to deal with particularly ungovernable fires. On the occasion that Reginald describes, perhaps in the 1150s,[110] it was thought to have been destroyed and its loss was widely mourned. This reaction suggests that it was already a well-established feature of Cuthbert's cult.[111]

The writer also mentions the 'little book of Blessed Cuthbert', almost certainly the Stonyhurst Gospel found in the coffin in 1104. It was kept lovingly in three bags of red leather within its reliquary and reverence demanded that anyone approaching it should fast and dress in an alb before touching it. The monk John who did neither and who held it with unwashed hands after eating was struck down with a chill. As a great honour it was hung by a cord from the necks of visiting dignitaries.[112]

---

[99] *Mem. Edm.* I, Bodl. MS 240 7, pp. 364 – 5; 9, pp. 366 – 7; 12, p. 368.

[100] *Libellus* 79, p. 164.

[101] *Libellus* 45, p. 92; 77, p. 161.

[102] *Libellus* 114, p. 257.

[103] *Libellus* 45, p. 92.

[104] *Libellus* 114, p. 259. Cf. op. cit. 60, p. 119.

[105] *Libellus* 130, p. 278.

[106] For example, *Libellus* 66, p. 134; 77, p. 161; 131, p. 279. In the cloister at Durham there was also a memorial indicating the spot from which Cuthbert's body was removed in 1104 (*Libellus* 48, p. 100). For a similar memorial on Lindisfarne, see below, p. 461.

[107] For the banner, see Battiscombe, 'Historical Introduction', in *Relics*, at pp. 68 – 72.

[108] According to Reginald, corporal cloths were found in Cuthbert's tomb in 1104 (*Libellus* 42, p. 89) and it is perhaps these that are referred to here.

[109] *Libellus* 39, p. 82.

[110] This fire may possibly be identified with one mentioned as occurring at the beginning of Bishop Hugh's pontificate by the historian Geoffrey of Coldingham (*Lib. . . . de stat.* (*Script. tres* (SS 9) 7, p. 12)).

[111] *Libellus* 39.

[112] *Libellus* 91, pp. 198 – 200. Reginald did not mention it in his account of the items found in the tomb in 1104. On this volume, cf. R. A. B. Mynors and R. Powell, 'The Stonyhurst Gospel', in *Relics*, at pp. 356 – 74 and plate XXIII.

Also associated with the saint was the *schylla* or bell of St Cuthbert, which hung above the prior's table in the monastic refectory. It was fairly small and according to tradition had belonged to the saint himself. Reginald describes it as being of ancient workmanship, made of tin and copper in unequal proportions. Prior Turgot had caused it to be covered in gold, thus giving it a surface like a clear mirror, and its pleasant tone summoned the brethren to meals.[113] Nor should the portions of the 'cloth of Blessed Cuthbert' be forgotten here.[114] At Bury and Ely similar cult objects were preserved ranging from the bloodstained undergarment in which Edmund had died[115] to the 'fetters of St Etheldreda' which had been donated by an escaped prisoner.[116]

One of the most striking features of the cult of St Cuthbert in this period is its diffusion among a number of different centres. Less than half of the twelfth-century miracles in the *Libellus* occurred or were recounted in Durham,[117] while almost the same number were associated with other locations for which there is evidence for devotion to the saint.[118] Two of these places had strong and obvious links with Cuthbert, and indeed with Durham, and it was under the tutelage of the monks that these sites developed into centres of the cult. Thus over a third of the miracles unconnected with Durham took place or were related on the island of Inner Farne.[119] This, the site of Cuthbert's own hermitage, became at this period the home of a number of Durham monks who had similarly chosen to lead the eremitic life.[120] Here visitors would be shown, in the lower part of the guesthouse wall, huge stones which, it was believed, the saint had put in place himself.[121]

Lindisfarne was another cult centre strongly associated with the saint's earthly life. Here, probably in the 1120s, the monk Edward was responsible for, amongst other things, the construction of a new church.[122] On the island the 'tomb' or memorial located on the site of Cuthbert's original burial place was the natural focus of devotion.[123] The settlement at Lindisfarne developed into a fully-fledged cell of Durham but even at the time of Edward crowds attended a service held on Cuthbert's feast day and then sat down to a meal held in his honour.[124] Despite this, however, it does not appear that the island was a general pilgrimage centre in this period: the individuals concerned in all

---

[113] *Libellus* 81, pp. 169 – 72. Cf. Battiscombe, 'Historical Introduction', in *Relics*, at p. 68.

[114] See above, p. 460

[115] Samson, *Opus* (*Mem. Edm.* I) I, 8, p. 133; I, 10, p. 137; II, 6, p. 174.

[116] *Lib. El.* III, 33, p. 269; III, 34, pp. 269 – 70.

[117] Fifty-four out of a total of 118 narratives.

[118] Fifty-one stories.

[119] Nineteen.

[120] For example, *Libellus* 27, p. 61; 29, p. 66; 58, p. 116.

[121] *Libellus* 102, p. 228; 117, p. 262.

[122] *Libellus* 21, p. 45. On Edward, see *Durham Episcopal Charters 1071 – 1152*, ed. H. S. Offler (SS 179, 1968), pp. 90 – 1, 92 – 3, 95 – 6.

[123] *Libellus* 21, p. 46; 22, p. 49.

[124] *Libellus* 22, p. 48.

the miracles recorded by Reginald belonged to the monastic community.[125] One oppressed serf from Middleton in Northumberland, however, fled there to live under the saint's protection.[126]

Also enjoying strong links with the cult, if not with the living bishop, was Norham, on the River Tweed. According to the *Historia de sancto Cuthberto*, the scene of an early translation of Cuthbert's body,[127] the village possessed a church dedicated to the saint to which both the bishop and the priory laid claim in this period.[128] The church was also believed to possess a relic of its patron himself. This took the form of a cross made from a table at which, so it was alleged, Cuthbert was accustomed to eat. With a hand touching the cross local people swore their judicial oaths.[129] The key of the church, in addition, having been miraculously recovered from the Tweed, immediately became the object of popular devotion.[130]

Reginald also provides us with glimpses of other churches dedicated to Cuthbert, for which there is evidence, in varying degrees, for veneration of the saint. One such building is that which Reginald describes as a 'mother church' *in Ardene*, not far from Nottingham,[131] but which Hamilton Thompson has shown to be located at Shustoke in Warwickshire.[132] Here, in the reign of Stephen, it was the custom of Robert the priest to mark the saint's feast day with exceptional acts of charity and generosity centring around a large-scale meal.[133] Shustoke was also the setting for two of Reginald's miracles.[134]

Two supernatural events, witnessed by Ailred of Rievaulx, likewise occurred at Kirkcudbright in Galloway on St Cuthbert's day, 1164. In the village, whose name was probably derived from a church dedicated to the saint, the abbot was present when the unusual offering of a bull was made to Cuthbert.[135] The same source provided Reginald with information about three miracles at or near another of the saint's churches. This was an unnamed building in 'Lothian', that is, south-eastern Scotland, not far from Melrose.[136] Here, in 1165, the 'peace of St Cuthbert', the ban on all crimes or unseemly

[125] *Libellus* 21, 22, 59.
[126] *Libellus* 105.
[127] *HSC* 9, p. 201.
[128] Scammell, *Hugh*, p. 198.
[129] *Libellus* 57.
[130] *Libellus* 73, pp. 150–1.
[131] *Libellus* 64, p. 127; 65, p. 130.
[132] A. H. Thompson, 'The MS list of churches dedicated to St Cuthbert, attributed to Prior Wessyngton', *Transactions of the Architectural and Archaeological Society of Durham and Northumberland* 1st ser. 7 (1934–6), p. 159.
[133] *Libellus* 64, p. 127.
[134] *Libellus* 64 and 65.
[135] *Libellus* 85. The animal should probably be seen as a valuable addition to the herd of the local priest, rather than the victim of some primitive sacrificial rite. Cf. A. L. Poole, *From Domesday Book to Magna Carta* (2nd edn., Oxford, 1966), p. 274, n. 2, and also *Libellus* 105, p. 236, where a man who had fled to Lindisfarne offered an ox in gratitude to the saint. The other Kirkcudbright miracle is described in *Libellus* 84, which supplies the date for both stories.
[136] *Libellus* 88, p. 188.

behaviour in or near his churches, was respected. The penalty for violating it, by attacking a stag which had taken refuge in the churchyard, was predictably severe.[137]

We have evidence for devotion to the saint at a further Scottish church, the chapel at Slitrig, dependent on a mother church at Cavers in Roxburghshire. Although the stone building was both roofless and remote from cultivated land, it was much visited by people from the surrounding area and miracles, according to Reginald, occurred there frequently.[138] One evening, on the saint's feast day, a large group of people gathered there, the older folk praying within, the younger dancing and amusing themselves outside.[139] Another year, a substantial number went to celebrate the feast by passing the night in prayer in the chapel.[140] A set of six miracles is recorded in connection with the chapel, the last of which belongs to 1173 or 1174.[141]

For four other churches the evidence is less substantial. Five miracles, which Reginald incorporated into his collection in 1165,[142] occurred at a chapel dedicated to the saint in Cheshire. Professor Barrow has identified this, rightly in my opinion, as located at Leighton in the Wirral.[143] As a result of miracles wrought there by the saint, he came to public attention and a building of wattle and thatch was replaced by an enlarged structure of stone.[144] Devotion to the saint in the village was evidently keen, for a time at least.[145]

At Bellingham in Northumberland an undated cure performed by the saint in his church may have been the stimulus leading to two further miracles.[146] Even at the time of the cure a spring, presumably near the church, was associated with the saint.[147]

Reginald also describes four supernatural incidents which happened at Lytham in Lancashire. Here the church of St Cuthbert was in the possession of the knight, Richard FitzRoger,[148] and by his gift it became about 1190 the

---

[137] *Libellus* 86, 87; see 88 for the other miracle which took place here. Although a number of churches were dedicated to Cuthbert in this area, it is not possible to identify the precise location of Reginald's stories.

[138] *Libellus* 136, p. 284; 137, p. 285.

[139] *Libellus* 136, p. 284.

[140] *Libellus* 137, p. 285.

[141] See *Libellus* 141, p. 290 and p. 449 above for the events of these years. The six stories are given in *Libellus* 136 – 41. On these narratives, cf. A. Campbell-Fraser, 'Glimpses of Teviotdale in the Twelfth Century, from the Latin of Reginald of Durham', *Hawick Archaeological Society Transactions* 56 (1924), pp. 24 – 8.

[142] *Libellus* 72, p. 148. The miracles are described in chapters 68 – 72.

[143] G. W. S. Barrow, 'Northern English Society in the Early Middle Ages', *Northern History* 4 (1969), p. 3.

[144] *Libellus* 69, pp. 141 – 2.

[145] *Libellus* 70, pp. 142 – 3.

[146] The cure is described in *Libellus* 108. The two additional miracles occur in *Libellus* 109 and 110.

[147] *Libellus* 108, p. 244.

[148] *Libellus* 132, p. 280. Reginald's narratives appear as chapters 132 – 5.

centre of the Durham cell of Lytham.[149] Plumbland in Cumbria, finally, was also favoured with miracles by the saint, according to the author. He furnishes only one example, however: the uncovering of an act of theft connected with his church. The incident resulted in the inhabitants of the region regarding his churches as uniquely safe depositories for valuables in 1173 – 4.[150]

For none of these locations is there anything to provide a link with Cuthbert other than his patronage of the church. None was connected with Durham, at least at the time of the miracles the writer describes, and none, so far as we know, claimed any relic of the saint. We do not know what prompted the original dedication, of course, and in some of these places there may possibly have been a long tradition of veneration for him. In some instances, for example Kirkcudbright, it is tempting to look back to the wanderings of the saint's body in the years after 875. Elsewhere, at Leighton and Bellingham, for instance, there appears to have been a spontaneous outburst of devotion to the saint, which may have been short-lived. There are no comparable stories among the miracles of St Edmund but a vision of Etheldreda, experienced apparently at her church in Hyssington in the Welsh borders — a great distance from Ely — may fall into the same category.[151] Thus these miracles are hard to account for, but perhaps show that parish churches played a larger part in the cults of their tutelary saints than has been realized.

There is, unfortunately, no space to investigate more superficial aspects of the cult such as the devotional habits of pilgrims or the votive offerings deposited by them at the shrine. Here, we may assume, the cult broadly resembled many others, both in this country and abroad. An examination of its beneficiaries themselves may be more instructive, however. As we have already seen, those with no known connections with the cult form more than a third of all beneficiaries in this period,[152] and miracles performed on their behalf are found even in the earlier parts of the *Libellus*. A similar pattern is discernible in the cults at Ely and Bury and in fact one is given the impression that Etheldreda and Edmund looked beyond their own communities even earlier than Cuthbert, isolated in the unstable conditions of the north. The remainder of the beneficiaries were associated with the saint in some way. A quarter of the total were Cuthbert's servants, that is, his monks and the clergy of his churches,[153] while the rest had some reason for regarding themselves as under his patronage. Inhabitants of Durham city and county, together with his staunch devotee, the sacrist of Norwich cathedral priory, would come into this category.[154]

---

[149] For the foundation of Lytham priory, see *Victoria County History, Lancashire*, ed. W. Farrer and J. Brownbill (8 vols., London, 1906 – 14) II, p. 107.

[150] *Libellus* 129.

[151] *Lib. El.* III, 43, pp. 281 – 3.

[152] Thirty-seven out of ninety-two identifiable beneficiaries.

[153] Twenty-three identifiable beneficiaries.

[154] Thirty-two beneficiaries. For the sacrist of Norwich, see *Libellus* 63. Cf. Ward, *Mir.*, p. 35.

The small role that women played in the cult,[155] in addition, should not be attributed solely to Cuthbert's reputed anti-feminism. They constituted only a slightly higher proportion of those who participated in the cult of Etheldreda, a female saint who might have been expected to attract women,[156] while those who resorted to St Edmund represented an even smaller element of the total.[157] This pattern reflects the situation at a number of different shrines which have been the subject of a recent study. At these churches, with only two exceptions, most of the pilgrims were men.[158]

In the case of all three cults the social status of a substantial proportion of the beneficiaries is unknown, so that it is difficult to draw conclusions in this respect. As far as Durham is concerned, we can only say that, according to Reginald's evidence, the number of those classed as poor seems to have been more or less matched by the noble, the wealthy and those of knightly status.[159] While visitors to the Inner Farne, furthermore, were in the main humble people, the more privileged did resort to the island, revealing that it was in no sense a poor man's Durham. More important members of the clergy, on the other hand, seem to have patronized Durham exclusively. The Scottish royal family continued to take an interest in the cult: David I, before his accession, stayed in Durham on his way northwards in 1113 or 1114,[160] while Ada, the mother of King Malcolm IV, twice experienced the saint's powers of healing.[161]

Over how wide a geographical area was the cult diffused? All those involved in miracles at the parish churches and chapels under Cuthbert's patronage apparently came from the immediate area. The visitors to the Inner Farne travelled for the most part from locations in Northumberland and Lothian, including one man from Dunbar, forty-one miles away,[162] and indeed it would seem that, north of the Tyne, the island was regarded as the chief centre of the cult. Conversely, most of Durham's pilgrims came from south of the Tyne, over half in fact from the city or county of Durham, Cleveland and North Yorkshire.[163] These visitors all came from within forty miles of the shrine, but about a fifth of the pilgrims had journeyed at least 140 miles.[164] Among these well-travelled devotees was the priest from Shustoke, over 150 miles away and the cult-centre furthest from Durham. A noble clerk from Bergen in

---

[155] They benefited from fifteen miracles and represent just over a sixth of the beneficiaries.

[156] They were beneficiaries in a fifth of the miracles.

[157] That is, one seventh.

[158] Finucane, *Mir. and Pil.*, p. 129.

[159] The samples are, however, very small: there are six examples of poor people and only five of the well-off.

[160] *Libellus* 74, pp. 151–2. For the date, see above, p. 448.

[161] *Libellus* 99, 100. The brother of King Edgar had been present at the opening of the tomb in 1104.

[162] *Libellus* 102, p. 226.

[163] Seventeen examples out of a total of thirty-three known places of origin.

[164] Seven instances.

Norway,[165] together with two penitents who had traversed the whole of Christendom,[166] had come a very long way indeed. The preaching tours, which were undertaken with some relics of the saint to raise money must, in addition, have played some part in diffusing the cult. On one of these trips Durham monks travelled as far as Perth[167] and Dunfermline,[168] both north of the Firth of Forth and over a hundred miles away. If the greatness of a saint is to be measured by the diffusion of his cult, we can perhaps use this evidence to compare the stature of Cuthbert with that of Etheldreda and Edmund in this period. It is obvious that Etheldreda was the least important of the three: her cult was predominantly local. The Bury cult was significantly less so, though fewer pilgrims had travelled more than 100 miles to visit Edmund's shrine than came to Durham. Cuthbert does appear to have been greater than his two fellows, judging by this criterion, but even he could not compete with the international cult of Thomas Becket.[169]

Turning, finally, to Cuthbert's acts of healing, we can see that these encompassed a wide range of ailments, from mental illness, dysentery, blindness and the effects of severe injuries, to a bad cold, a huge boil and toothache. Reginald explains at some length how a saint whose flesh was incorrupt was especially suited to cure the stain of 'leprosy', but there is only one example of this.[170] Neither Durham nor any of the other churches connected with the saint seem to have been associated with the cure of any particular ailment. Etheldreda was similarly catholic in her choice of suppliants, while the cup of St Edmund may have been associated with the cure of fevers.[171]

By rights, Durham's century of triumph should have been that of Cuthbert also. And so indeed it was, until about two-thirds of the way through. During the whole of the period for which we have evidence miracles were constantly observed — more than at any time before or subsequently — in Durham and at many other locations. Until about 1170 Cuthbert, more active than ever, reigned supreme in the north and made his mark elsewhere. The deaths of Thomas of Canterbury and Godric of Finchale in that year and the subsequent development of their cults seem to have put the Durham community on the defensive, however. By way of response, the monks tried apparently to alter the image of their saint in an effort to attract pilgrims. Certainly, in the short term, the miracles showed no sign of ceasing but we do not know if the cult ultimately succeeded in adapting to the changed environment. Another wonder collection of this period, the *Miracles of St Cuthbert at Farne*, which may be slightly later than the *Libellus*, suggests that

---

[165] *Libellus* 112.
[166] *Libellus* 79, 94. Their places of origin are unknown.
[167] *Libellus* 97, p. 216.
[168] *Libellus* 98, p. 217.
[169] Cf. Ward, *Mir.*, pp. 97 – 8.
[170] *Libellus* 19, p. 38.
[171] Samson, *Opus* (*Mem. Edm.* I) II, 19, pp. 203 – 4.

supernatural occurrences may have continued in that location at least.[172] Taking a longer view, it is quite possible that the rise of the Canterbury cult in particular spelt the end of the peak in Cuthbert's popularity. Becket rose to fame only to be superseded in his turn as newer saints and newer cults emerged to usurp his favoured position in popular esteem.

[172] See H. H. E. Craster, 'The Miracles of Farne', *Archaeologia Aeliana* 4 ser. 29 (1951), pp. 93 – 107 and *idem*, 'The Miracles of St Cuthbert at Farne', *Analecta Bollandiana* 70 (1952), pp. 5 – 19. The last narrative in the work seems to have been written in or after 1199.

INDEX

References to 'manuscripts' and 'silks' have been grouped under these headings. References to plates are preceded by the abbreviation 'pl.'.

Plates

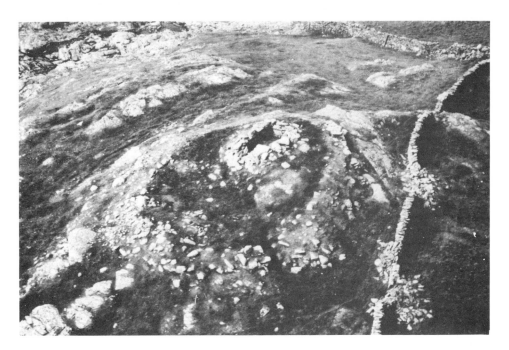

1. Inishark, county Galway, view of hermitage from north-east.

2. Caher Island, county Mayo, view of oratory enclosure from north-west showing
leachta *with cross-slabs within enclosure and at two stations to south; pond marked by*
growth of iris on right.

4. Cross-slab on station north of monastic enclosure, Caher Island.

3. Cross-slab above south landing-place, Ardoileán, county Galway.

5. Besançon, Bibliothèque municipale MS 186, fol. 9r. Bede's metrical Vita S. Cuthberti, Besançon recension.

6. The Vatican Paulinus (Rome, Biblioteca Apostolica Vaticana, MS pal. lat. 235), fol. 4r. Lindisfarne cursive minuscule script.

7. *The Barberini Gospels (Rome, Biblioteca Apostolica Vaticana, MS Barb. lat. 570), fol. 80v. Wigbald's half-uncial of 'Lindisfarne' type.*

8. *The Tullylease Slab, County Cork. Its half-uncial inscriptions and decoration resemble the Lindisfarne Gospels.*

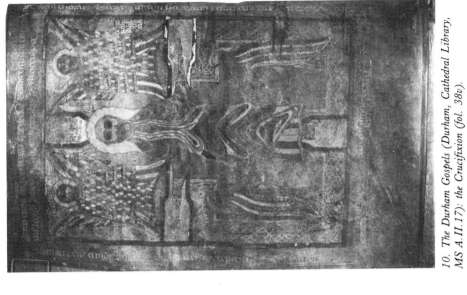

10. *The Durham Gospels (Durham, Cathedral Library, MS A.II.17): the Crucifixion (fol. 38v).*

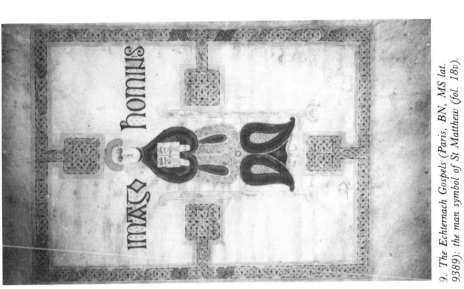

9. *The Echternach Gospels (Paris, BN, MS lat. 9389): the man symbol of St Matthew (fol. 18v).*

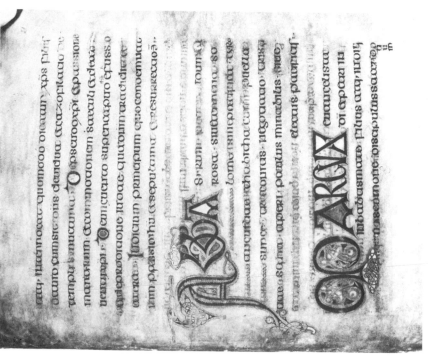

12. Initials and display capitals in the Durham Gospels. Durham Cathedral Library, MS A.II.17, fol. 39r.

11. Initial page to Luke in the Lindisfarne Gospels, showing typical bird decoration. A cat forms the right-hand margin. BL, Cotton MS Nero D.IV, fol. 139r.

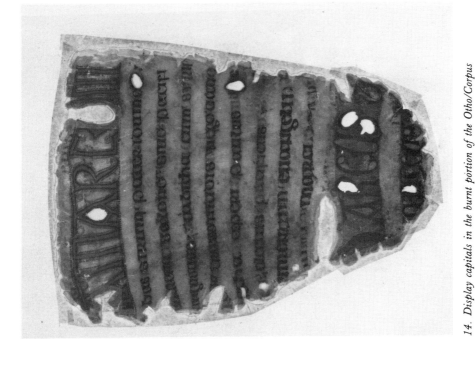

14. Display capitals in the burnt portion of the Otho/Corpus Gospels as they now appear. BL, Cotton MS Otho C.V., fol. 25v.

13. Handpainted facsimile of initials and display capitals in the burnt portion of the Otho/Corpus Gospels as they appeared before 1731. BL, Stowe MS 1061, fol. 36r.

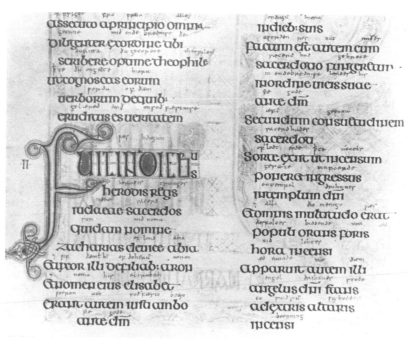

15. *The Lindisfarne Gospels (London, BL, Cotton MS Nero D.IV), fol. 139v. Eadfrith's half-uncial script, with Aldred's interlinear gloss.*

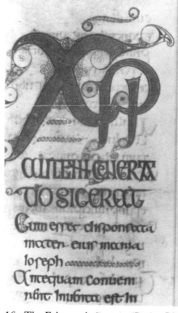

16. *The Echternach Gospels (Paris, BN, MS lat. 9389). Left, set minuscule script, fol. 19r; right, hybrid minuscule script, fol. 1v.*

17. *The Garland of Howth (Dublin, Trinity College Library, MS 56), fol. 74r. Irish half-uncial script. The change of hand in the centre represents a specimen teaching passage by a more experienced hand than that of the main scribe.*

18. *The Echternach Gospels (Paris, BN, MS lat. 9389), fol. 116r:* The Quoniam quidem *monograph.*

19. The Durham Gospels (Durham, Cathedral Library, MS A.
II. 17), fol. 2v: open interlace and terminal ornament.

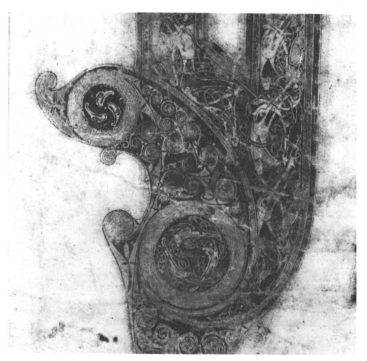

20. The Durham Gospels (Durham, Cathedral Library, MS A.
II. 17), fol. 2r: zoomorphic finials inside pen spirals.

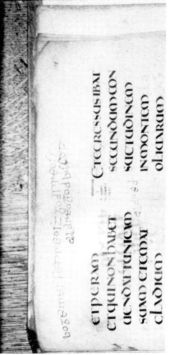

22. Small initial M from the Lindisfarne Gospels. BL, Cotton MS Nero D. IV, fol. 18v.

21. St Gregory. Initial to Book II of Bede's Ecclesiastical History (Leningrad, Public Library, Cod. Q.v.I.18, fol. 26v).

23. Durham, Cathedral Library, MS A.II.17, details showing Boge inscriptions: (a) fol. 80r, on the half-uncial Durham Gospels; (b) fol. 106r, on an uncial fragment of Luke.

24. Paris, Bibliothèque Nationale, MS lat. 10837 (Calendar of St Willibrord), fol. 44r: Easter table.

25. Augsburg Gospels (Augsburg, Universitätsbibliothek, cod. I. 2 4° 2), fol. 157v: verses with the Laurentius uiuat senio acrostic.

26. Vertical space fillers: (a) and (c), details from Calendar of St Willibrord (Paris, Bibliothèque Nationale, MS lat. 10837), fols. 38v and 34v; (b) Book of Durrow (Dublin, Trinity College, MS A. 4. 5 (57)), fol. 124r; (d) Augsburg Gospels (Augsburg, Universitätsbibliothek, cod. I. 2 4° 2), fol. 128v.

27. Trier Gospels (Trier, Domschatz Codex 61), Matthew Text, Liber generationis, fol. 20r.

28. Trier Gospels, Luke portrait, fol. 127v.

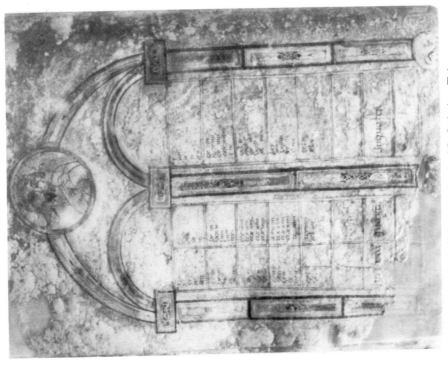

29. Freiburg Gospel Fragment (Freiburg-im-Breisgau, Universitätsbibliothek, Codex 702), Luke chapter summaries, fol. 2v.

30. Maeseyck Gospels (Maeseyck, church of St Catherine, Trésor, s.n.), Canon Table III, Bartholomew portrait, fol. 8v.

32. *Lindisfarne Gospels, fol. 259r. Aldred's colophon.*

31. *Durham Cathedral Library, MS A.II.10, fol. 2r.*

34. *Durham Cathedral Library, MS A.IV.19, fol. 84r. Aldred's additional prayers and colophon.*

33. *Oxford, Bodleian Library, MS Bodley 819, fol. 29r. A copy of Bede's Commentary on Proverbs probably written at Wearmouth/Jarrow, later glossed by Aldred.*

36. St Cuthbert's pectoral cross, Durham Cathedral Treasury (height 6 cm): back.

35. St Cuthbert's pectoral cross, Durham Cathedral Treasury (height 6 cm): front.

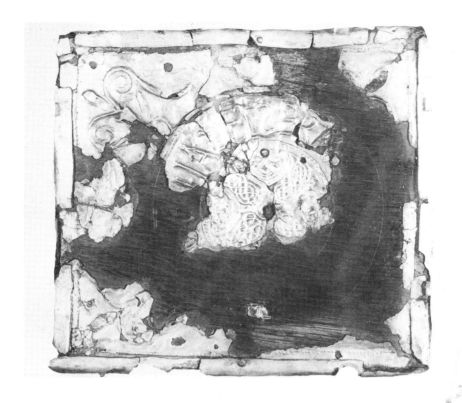

38. *Portable altar from St Cuthbert's tomb, wood covered with silver (back), Durham Cathedral Treasury (height 12.5 cm).*

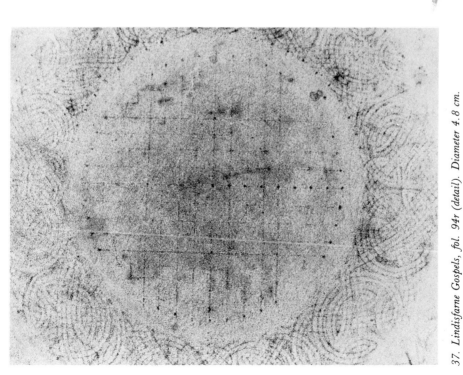

37. *Lindisfarne Gospels, fol. 94r (detail). Diameter 4.8 cm.*

a

b

c

d

e

39. *a) Mould with Luke evangelist symbol, from Hartlepool excavations, 1/1; b) mould with interlaced Hiberno-Saxon animal, 1/1; c) mould with interlace decorated cross, 1/ 1; d) name stone, from Lindisfarne, with feminine name Osgyth, not to scale; e) name stone from Hartlepool, with feminine name Hildithryth, not to scale.*

40. a) *Side panel of cross from Lindisfarne, with animal enmeshed in interlace; b)
broad face of same cross with interlaced animal; c) broad face of cross from Inner Farne,
with two panels of worn animal interlace; d) panel with interlaced birds, built into the
face of Billingham church tower; e) broad face of cross from St Oswald's church,
Durham, with panels with geometric interlace and animals; f) narrow face of the same
cross with panel of geometric interlace; g) broad face of the same cross with panels of
interlace and interlaced birds. All not to scale.*

41. Stone relief of St Peter (detail), Wentworth (Cambridgeshire).

42. Christ, the Virgin and St Peter. The New Minster Liber vitae *(BL, MS Stowe 944), fol. 6r.*

43. St Cuthbert's coffin, 1978 reconstruction: one of the long sides (Apostles' side).

44. St Cuthbert's coffin (detail of Apostles' side). Upper row: Sts Andrew and Peter. Lower row: unidentified apostle and St Paul.

46. a) Norham, cross-shaft (Corpus I, no. 5, face A); b) Norham, cross-shaft (Corpus I, no. 5, face B).

a

b

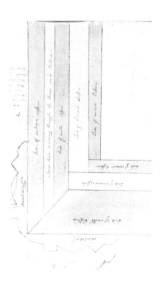

a

b

c

45. Coloured drawings from Durham Cathedral Additional MS 149 showing: a) outer coffin with mouldings, 'bandages', rings and (marked 'a' – 'd') points where iron rods passed through the sides and bottom of the coffin (see St Cuthbert, p. 185); b) plan showing relationship of sides and lids of coffins; c) St Cuthbert's skeleton with vestments and skulls.

a

b

c

d

47. *a) Chester-le-Street, cross-shaft fragment (Corpus I, no. 5, face D); b) Lindisfarne, cross-shaft fragment (Corpus I, no. 5, face A); c) Northallerton, cross-shaft fragment (after Collingwood); d) Lindisfarne, cross-shaft fragment (Corpus I, no. 5, face C).*

a

b

48. *a) Chester-le-Street, cross-shaft (Corpus I, no. 1, face A); b) Sockburn, cross-shaft (Corpus I, no. 3, face A).*

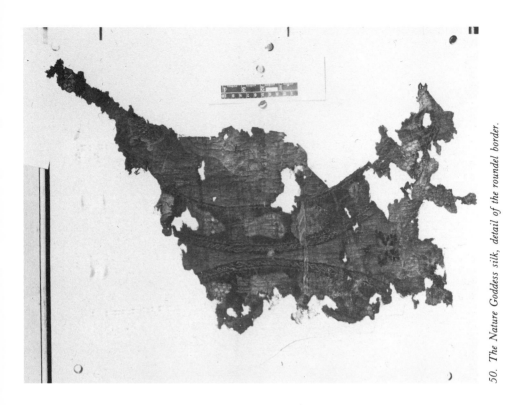

50. *The Nature Goddess silk, detail of the roundel border.*

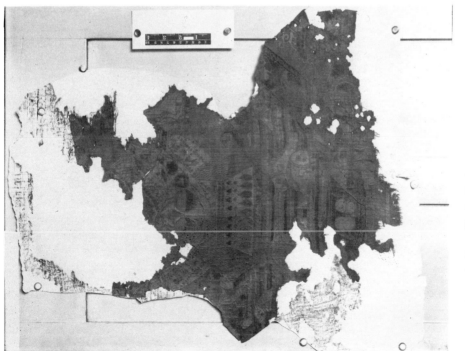

49. *The Nature Goddess silk, detail of the figure.*

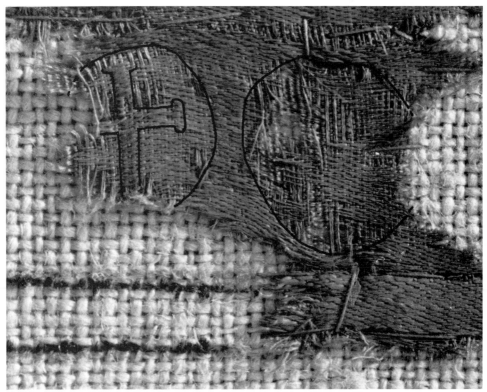

51. *The cross marking the beginning of the inscription on the Nature Goddess silk.*

52. *The remains of the inscription on the Nature Goddess silk. Each 'pearl' is c.2.4 cms wide; the decoupures have been indicated on the letters, but not on the outlines of the pearls.*

53. Egyptian tapestry of a nature goddess figure; roundel height c. *9 cm. British Museum EA 20430.*

54. Fragments 7 and 10 and 2 of the weft-patterned silks and the Soumak braid (see also fig. 23).

55. Fragment 4 of the Soumak braid, the remains of two lengths sewn together (total width, 6.7 cms). The guilloche plait is missing from the left and right sides. In the upper part of the fragment, the back of the purple and yellow compound twill silk is visible.

56. The tablet-woven braid with soumak brocading from Sant'Apollinare in Classe, width c.1.5 cms, Museo Arcivescovile, Ravenna: a) part of the back of the braid (the negative was reversed for printing); b) part of the front of another fragment.

57. *The Rider silk from the relics of St Cuthbert. Cf. fig. 27 on p. 349.*

58. *Detail of the Rider silk from the relics of St Cuthbert, showing the horse with seated Rider and bird of prey placed into a lobed octagon surround. Several silk pieces were stuck together to reconstruct this pattern. Cf. fig. 28 on p. 349.*

59. The Peacock silk from the relics of St Cuthbert.

60. Detail of the Peacock silk from the relics of St Cuthbert, showing in particular the pseudo-Kufic inscription across the body of the bird.

DATE DUE

PICTS

FIRTH OF FORTH

Aberlady

Tynir

Abercorn

Dumbarton

STRATHCLYDE

Clyde

Leader

Black

Melrose

Tweed

Jed

Teviot

Hoddom

Bewcastle

Ruthwell

Carlisle

SOLWAY FIRTH

Whithorn

Derwent

Workington

St. Herbert's
Island

Cartmel

Ribb

Land over 800 feet

------- Roman roads

0   30 miles

0   50 kilometres